Shakespeare from the Greenroom

SHAKESPEARE

from the Greenroom

Actors' Criticisms of Four Major Tragedies

by
CAROL JONES CARLISLE

The University of
North Carolina Press
Chapel Hill

Quoted passages from the following are used
by permission of the publisher, author, and editor:

Boswell's London Journal 1762-1763, *ed. Frederick Pottle,*
copyright 1950 by Yale University. McGraw-Hill Book
Company (New York) and William Heinemann Limited (London).

Shakespeare: Ten Great Plays. With an Introduction and
Commentaries by Sir Tyrone Guthrie, *copyright © 1962 by*
Western Publishing Company, Inc.

Sir Tyrone Guthrie, A Life in the Theatre, *copyright*
© 1959 by Tyrone Guthrie. McGraw-Hill Book Company.

Sir Tyrone Guthrie, "Why and How They Play Hamlet,"
© 1960 by The New York Times Company.

To My Mother and My Father

Although actors have not been entirely overlooked as critics of Shakespeare, no systematic survey of their writings has hitherto been conducted, and relatively few have been included in histories and anthologies of criticism. The present work, therefore, is intended to fill what seems to me to be an important gap.

My aim is to present a coherent and useful account of the best Shakespearean criticisms by English and American actors, past and present. (Because of the limitations of space and time I have not tried to include criticisms by the Shakespearean actors of other countries.) By "best" I mean both those that are most interesting *per se* and those that shed most light on the dramatic potentialities of the plays. Although I have collected criticisms dealing with all of Shakespeare's plays, I have chosen to concentrate on the four most popular tragedies, not only because they form a logical unit for discussion but also because they are the plays about which the actors have had the most to say—and the most interesting things to say.

The primary function of the work is to make available in convenient form a body of significant commentaries, hitherto widely scattered and in many instances inaccessible to the general reader. These commentaries occur in writings of diverse kinds: 1) books— theatrical histories, biographies and autobiographies, published diaries and collections of letters, book-length critical works; 2) periodical literature—essays, news releases, interviews, etc.; 3) manuscripts—primarily letters, journals, notebooks, and a few promptbook notations.

A second function is to provide for the student of Shakespear- ean criticism a clear, direct view of some of the actors' major ac- complishments as critics, accomplishments that I believe will stand the test of comparison with much of the criticism by writers who have devoted themselves entirely to scholarship or literature. I would not put too much emphasis on this last point, however. For one thing, it is impossible to draw a sharp line between the actors' interpretations and those of literary critics since I have included among the actor-critics some who have themselves been recognized primarily as literary men. And, for another thing, the actors' criticisms are too heterogeneous in form to allow for any meaningful comparison with other writers in the matter of literary quality—they vary from the most informal scrawl to the most care- fully constructed essay. Perhaps it would be better to speak of comparing ideas expressed by persons who have had professional theatrical experience with those expressed by persons who have not had such experience; but this is a cumbersome way of speak- ing.

A few words must be said about the selection and presentation of material.

For the purposes of this book, I am interested in Shakespear- ean criticism that deals with the plays as plays; with the char- acters as personalities to be projected in action on a stage; with the language as something to be spoken and to work its spell on a listening audience; with "themes," not as ends in themselves, but as guides in determining costume and setting, in deciding the tone of particular scenes, or in choosing one character interpretation over another that would be equally valid if that role itself were the only consideration. Obviously professional actors are not the only people who have approached Shakespeare's plays from the point of view that I have described. Many others could be named who, if they wrote about Shakespeare, would be likely to take this approach—indeed any experienced and enthusiastic playgoer might do so. It is equally obvious that one must draw the line somewhere. I have chosen to draw it at those who have had at least some experience as professional actors, for it has seemed to me that these would be likely to maintain more consistently than any other group the attitude and approach I have specified. The relatively broad criterion "at least some experience as professional actors" has been chosen over that of "exclusive or primary devotion to professional acting" because I feel that it is particularly valuable to have the opinions of dramatists and directors who have also had personal experience in the problem of trying to make an idea corporeal, to bring an imaginatively conceived character to life.

The criticisms discussed in this volume are limited to the direct expressions of opinion by actors in words, either written or oral (as in reported conversation). Implied criticisms of all kinds, no matter how interesting and significant, have generally been considered outside the bounds of this particular study. For example, I have left out of account, or largely so, the "criticism" implied in the stage interpretation of Shakespeare's characters. Although this is the actors' supreme contribution, not only has it been less neglected than their verbalized criticism but it is also much harder to render tangible and unambiguous. In the present work, at least, I have wished to be as accurate as possible in conveying the actors' own thoughts, rather than the diverse (and sometimes conflicting) impressions that their performances have made on the witnesses who have described them. One important exception has been made in the case of actors' critical descriptions of other actors' performances. The best of these are included because they offer valuable clues to the ideal held by the actor who writes, as well as to the stage interpretation of the actor who is written about. Descriptions of stage interpretations written by non-actors, for example biographers and critics, have been used only when the writer is known to have discussed the role with the actor or when the description is directly in line with something that the actor himself has said or written.

Another type of criticism—an important one—which I have not attempted to cover in this book is that implied in the cutting and arranging of Shakespeare's texts. A thorough study of the acting texts from the eighteenth century to the present would obviously require a separate undertaking. What I have done is to include discussions of text only when they furnish necessary background for the actors' own critical opinions.

As for presentation of material, each chapter (except the introduction and conclusion) is devoted to the actors' criticisms of a single tragedy, and each has the same major divisions—"The Play," "The Characters," and "From Criticism to Theatre"; but within those general classifications there is considerable variation. For example, the first section deals with such topics as structure, language, "meaning," theatrical effectiveness, setting, and costume —but not necessarily with all of these. Similarly, in the second section the characters chosen for discussion are those in which the actor-critics have shown the greatest interest. The "heroes" are always included, of course; minor characters like Osric in *Hamlet,* Oswald in *King Lear,* and Ross in *Macbeth* are always omitted, even though a few interesting comments can be found about them. It is in the characters of middle rank that inconsistencies occur. For example, actors have written a number of significant criticisms of Ophelia, Gertrude, Claudius, and Polonius in *Hamlet* but relatively few of Gloucester, Edgar, Edmund, or Kent in *King Lear.* Accordingly, Polonius is included but Gloucester is not. In the division "From Criticism to Theatre" an effort is made to illuminate the process by which an actor translates his critical ideas about Shakespeare into terms that can be realized on the stage. Actually, it is hoped that some light on this process will be diffused throughout the discussion of each play and its characters; but the final section of each chapter concentrates upon some aspect of the play that brings together thought and action, stage and study, in a striking and characteristic way. Since the problems involved in such relationships vary from one play to another, the kind of material treated in this section also varies; there is considerable difference, too, in length and complexity.

Obviously this book is neither a straightforward history of the actors' Shakespearean criticism nor a biographical and critical study of the individual actor-critics. (Very brief biographical sketches are provided in the appendix.) Its emphasis is upon Shakespeare's plays themselves as the actors have evaluated and interpreted them. Literary and theatrical history, though of secondary concern, is not completely neglected, however. The analytical method, with subheadings, is used for the sake of ready reference, but in the discussion of each separately headed topic the ideas of the various actors are presented in roughly chronological order, the chronology being determined principally by the dates of the actor's theatrical career. I have tried to keep firmly before the reader the relationship between a particular actor-critic and his age, to show how in his comments on *Hamlet,* for example, he reflects the critical opinion of his time or reacts against it.

One peculiarity of capitalization may need explaining. Since a great many names are mentioned in the course of a discussion—not only those of the actor-critics themselves but also those of scholars, literary critics, and actors whose stage interpretations (not criticisms) are at issue—I have felt it desirable to identify or emphasize the actor-critics in some way. Accordingly, in each subsection of a chapter, when an actor-critic is referred to for the first time, his name is given in capital letters.

In citing passages from Shakespeare I have used Hardin Craig's *The Complete Works of Shakespeare* (Scott-Foresman, 1961), which follows the popular Globe numbering. The reader should be alert to differences in line numbers in the *Furness Variorum,* for example in using Edwin Booth's notes on *Othello.*

In the interest of clarity I have sometimes found it desirable to discuss matters that are already well known to scholars. Since I hope this book will have other readers as well, I ask the indulgence of the specialist. If he finds himself nodding over a twice-told tale, I trust he will simply turn the page until he finds something fresh to ponder.

My thanks are due to a number of friends who have helped me. To the late George Coffin Taylor I owe, among other legacies of the mind and spirit, the original suggestion from which this book finally grew. To Dr. Arthur Colby Sprague, whose books alone would make me (and all others who study Shakespeare and the theatre) his debtor, I am doubly bound. He read most of my manuscript and gave me the benefit, not only of his factual knowledge, but also of his infallible sense of style and taste. If only his witty succinctness were contagious! I am particularly grateful to Professor Clifford Lyons of The University of North Carolina, who read the whole manuscript—in more than one version—and made numerous constructive suggestions. His interest and encouragement, as well as his wise counsel, have been invaluable.

I am grateful for the financial assistance that I have received. Two summers of profitable work in the manuscript collections of the Folger Shakespeare Library were made possible by research grants, one from the Folger Library itself, the other from the Research Committee of the University of South Carolina. The latter body also financed briefer periods of reading in other libraries, notably the Theatre Collection of the Houghton Library at Harvard, and provided funds for typing. As a fellow of the Cooperative Program in the Humanities, sponsored by The University of North Carolina and Duke University, I was freed from academic responsibilities in 1967-68 and thus was able to make necessary revisions in my manuscript. I am grateful to these universities for the opportunities provided by the program and to the University of South Carolina (especially to Dr. John C. Guilds, Head of the Department of English) for making it possible for me to participate.

I remember with gratitude the many courtesies that I have received from the staffs of the libraries where I have worked, most particularly from Miss Dorothy Mason of the Folger Shakespeare Library. Thanks are due, too, to Miss Helen Willard, Curator of the Harvard Theatre Collection, and to Mr. Arnold Wengrow for replying to my inquiries sent by mail, and to Mr. John P. Harthan, of the Victoria and Albert Museum, for supplying me with a photocopy of an unpublished letter in the Forster Collection.

To the staff of The University of North Carolina Press I express my warm appreciation, not only for their expert assistance but also for their graciousness and patience.

I acknowledge, with thanks, the permission I have received from the following libraries to publish extracts from the manuscripts in their collections: the Folger Shakespeare Library, for passages from some forty manuscripts specified in my notes; the Harvard College Library, for quotations from manuscripts by Benjamin Webster, Thomas Russell Sullivan, and Edwin Booth, also specified in my notes; and the Victoria and Albert Museum for generous portions of George Swan's letter to David Garrick (December 11, 1773).

It is a pleasure to make the following acknowledgments to authors and publishers for permission to quote from the books listed here: to Miss Rosamond Gilder, for several passages from Sir John Gielgud's "The Hamlet Tradition: Some Notes on

Costumes, Scenery and Stage Business," in her valuable book *John Gielgud's Hamlet* (Oxford University Press, 1937); to The Folio Society, London, for extracts from the introductory essays (by Sir Lewis Casson and Sir Donald Wolfit, respectively) to its editions of *Macbeth* (1951) and *King Lear* (1956), published for its members; to Robert Speaight and to The Bodley Head Limited, for quotations from *Nature in Shakespearian Tragedy* (published by Hollis & Carter, 1955); to The Hamlyn Group, for passages from Sir Donald Wolfit's *First Interval* (published by the Odhams Press Limited, 1954); to Random House, Inc. and to Heinemann Educational Books Limited for passages from Sir John Gielgud's *Stage Directions* (Copyright © 1963 by Sir John Gielgud); to Golden Press, Inc., for selected passages from *Shakespeare: Ten Great Plays*, with an introduction and commentaries by Sir Tyrone Guthrie (© 1962 by Western Publishing Co., Inc.); to *The New York Times* for quotations from Sir Tyrone Guthrie's "Why and How They Play Hamlet," published August 14, 1960; to McGraw-Hill Book Company for extracts from Sir Tyrone Guthrie's *A Life in the Theatre* (1959); to Sir Tyrone Guthrie for use of his works listed above and also for an extract from the program notes for his 1934 production of *Macbeth* at the Old Vic, reprinted in John C. Trewin's *Shakespeare on the English Stage 1900-1964* (published by Barrie and Rockliff, 1964); to the Yale Editorial Committee, to McGraw-Hill Book Company, and to William Heinemann Limited for passages from *Boswell's London Journal 1762-1763*, edited by Frederick Pottle (1950); to Hodder and Stoughton Limited for quotations from Sir Michael Redgrave's "Shakespeare and the Actors" in *Talking of Shakespeare*, edited by John Garrett (1954); to *Playboy* for an excerpt from Kenneth Tynan's interview with Richard Burton (published September, 1963); to Samuel French Limited of London for passages from George Skillan's commentaries and notes in French's Acting Editions of *Hamlet, Othello,* and *Macbeth;* to Dell Publishing Company for quotations from Maurice Evans' "Comments on Playing the Role of Hamlet" and from Dame Flora Robson's "Notes on Playing the Role of Lady Macbeth" in the *Laurel Shakespeare*, the *Hamlet* and *Macbeth* volumes (published in 1958 and 1959 respectively).

Finally, I must mention—though I cannot do it justice—the debt that I owe to the loyalty and forbearance of my husband and children.

CAROL J. CARLISLE

University of South Carolina
Columbia, South Carolina
February, 1969

CONTENTS

CHAPTER ONE · *Introduction*

I am contented with the spirit of the author you first taught me to admire . . . and often when I have taken the pen in my hand to try to illustrate a passage, I have thrown it down again with discontent when I remembered how able you were to clear that difficulty by a single look, or particular modulation of voice, which a long and laboured paraphrase was insufficient to explain half so well. . . .[1]

So wrote George Steevens, the Shakespearean editor, to David Garrick, the actor.

But scholars and critics have not always been so generous to men of the theatre, particularly where the interpretation of Shakespeare is concerned. The actor's understanding and taste, his critical judgment, his very right to represent Shakespeare's characters on the stage—all have been questioned at one time or another. As for his critical pronouncements on Shakespeare, these have been subject from the beginning to attacks by other critics. When JOHN HEMINGE and HENRY CONDELL praised Shakespeare for writing with such facility that there was scarcely "a blot in his papers,"[2] Ben Jonson (who chose to dissociate himself from "the players" despite his own earlier experience on the stage) countered with the wish that Shakespeare had blotted a thousand lines. "I had not told posterity this," Jonson wrote, "but for their ignorance who chose that circumstance to commend their friend by, wherein he most faulted."[3] Indications of disdain for the actors' critical judgment can be found in every age: for example, Pope's suggestion that many "trifling and bombast passages" in Shakespeare's text are interpolations by actors[4] and Lamb's expression of indignation when Garrick's name was linked with Shakespeare's.[5]

Actors, in their turn, have ardently defended their own interpretive abilities. HENRY IRVING, for example, maintained that a member of his "studious and enthusiastic profession" has several

1. *The Private Correspondence of David Garrick with the Most Celebrated Persons of His Time*, ed. James Boaden (London, 1831), I, 216-17. Letter of December 27, 1765.

2. *The Norton Facsimile. The First Folio of Shakespeare*. Prepared by Charlton Hinman (New York, 1968), p. 7.

3. "Timber: or Discoveries Made upon Men and Matter," *Ben Jonson*, ed. C. H. Herford and Percy Simpson (Oxford, 1925-52), VIII, 583.

4. *The Works of Shakespear. In Six Volumes. Collated and Corrected by the Former Editions. By Mr. Pope* (London, 1727), I, vii-xxi.

5. "On the Tragedies of Shakespeare," *The Complete Works and Letters of Charles Lamb*, ed. Bennet A. Cerf and Donald S. Klopfer (New York, 1935), pp. 289-90, 297.

advantages over the layman: the intensive study of his role and the knowledge of the stage traditions that have grown up around it are supplemented by a "natural dramatic fertility" which begins to operate as soon as he "feels at home in a part without being too familiar with it"—for "the mere automatic action of rehearsing and playing it at once begins . . . to give the personage being played an individuality partly independent of, and yet consistent with, and rendering more powerfully visible, the dramatist's conception."[6] Besides, the requirements of successful Shakespearean acting—"To touch the springs of motive, to seize all the shreds of expression, to feel yourself at the root and foundation of the being you are striving to represent"—presuppose intellectual and artistic gifts of a high order.[7] The same advantages that Irving ascribed to the stage interpreter as opposed to the armchair critic were claimed by HELEN FAUCIT for the actor as critical commentator. In the preface to her book on Shakespeare's heroines she writes:

I have had the great advantage of throwing my own nature into theirs, of becoming moved by their emotions: I have, as it were, thought their thoughts and spoken their words straight from my own living heart and mind. I know that this has been an exceptional privilege; and to those not so fortunate I have striven to communicate something of what I have learned in the exercise of my "so potent art."[8]

There is, as usual, something to be said on both sides. The habit of conceiving the plays in theatrical terms does result, sometimes, in the frittering away of important truths for the sake of a single brilliant characterization or even a flashy piece of business. (There is also, however, the opposite danger which confronts the scholar: the temptation of viewing the plays as static constructs of ideas.) But the notion that the best actors are impulsive creatures, incapable of analytical thought and therefore automatically disqualified as critics, is based on myth, not fact. My examination of the writings of English and American actors has convinced me that the critical views held by these men and women are often worthy of serious attention and that their value is not a matter of accident—that the most interesting ones usually reflect, not simply

6. Henry Irving, "The Stage as It Is," *The Drama* (New York, 1893), pp. 10-11.
7. "Shakespeare and Goethe," an address given before the Goethe Society of New York, March 15, 1888. Quoted by Austin Brereton in *The Life of Henry Irving* (New York, 1908), II, 120-21.
8. Helena Faucit, Lady Martin, *On Some of Shakespeare's Female Characters* (Edinburgh and London, 1887), p. viii.

the critical ability of a particular individual, but also some insight gained from the theatrical experience itself.

At the least, the actors' criticisms of Shakespeare complement in a fresh and attractive way those written by scholars and literary critics; they frequently help to redress the critical balance by subjecting extreme interpretations to pragmatic test; and in some cases they are even responsible for the development of new trends in formal Shakespearean criticism. These are large claims, and a full discussion of them must wait until the evidence of later chapters has been presented. For the present it will be enough to suggest, through a preliminary survey, the kinds of criticism the actors have to offer.

In many cases the actor-critics extol Shakespeare's plays for the same reasons that other writers do, but their praise is sometimes more zestful and convincing because it bears the stamp of practical experience. Take the matter of Shakespeare's universality—his appeal to simple and learned alike, his ability to transcend the boundaries of time and taste. Perhaps it was mere accident that John Heminge and Henry Condell (Shakespeare's fellow actors) were the first to call attention to the quality that has done most to insure Shakespeare's immortality in the theatre;[9] certainly a great variety of critics has continued to pay tribute to his universality from that day to this. But there is a special flavor to the actors' contributions on the subject. THOMAS DAVIES' comments (1780) grew out of his recollection of an unsuccessful attempt to revive an old play (Tomkis's *Albumazar*, revised by Garrick). Most dramas from the past, he concluded, "bear such marks of ancient and forgotten manners and customs that they cannot . . . please the present generation." Shakespeare's plays are an exception because they are "founded in that nature which will be eternally the same."[10] Helen Faucit, the nineteenth-century actress, also drew on personal experience when she contrasted Shakespeare's universality with Browning's limited appeal, for her outstanding popularity in Rosalind and Beatrice contrasted with the *succès d'estime* won as the original representative of Lady Carlisle, Mildred Tresham, and Colombe of Ravenstein. "The drama

9. *The Norton Facsimile*, p. 7.

10. Thomas Davies, *Memoirs of the Life of David Garrick* (Boston, 1818), I, 168-69. This book was first published in London in 1780. Davies also calls attention to Shakespeare's transcendence of national boundaries. See his *Dramatic Miscellanies* (London, 1783-84), II, 318-19.

should speak to all humanity," Miss Faucit observed, "and not to a few privileged poetic natures."[11] In the twentieth century a recurring theme in the actors' discussions of Shakespeare's universality has been the popularity of his plays among the British and American troops in wartime. LENA ASHWELL, SIR DONALD WOLFIT, MAURICE EVANS[12]—all have testified to this phenomenon. Evans, for example, when he produced his "G.I. *Hamlet*" for the soldiers in the Central Pacific Area (World War II, 1943), was eminently successful in drawing the parallel that he saw between the hero of the play and the members of the audience, each of them in his own way a Hamlet, "bewildered by the uninvited circumstances in which he found himself and groping for the moral justification and the physical courage demanded of him." So well did he accomplish his purpose that one soldier was heard to remark, "They must have done a lot of rewriting to bring this up to date."

Consider, too, Shakespeare's art of characterization, the theme of countless eulogies by critics. Because there *are* so many discussions of the subject, we are easily wearied even by very intelligent, well-phrased comments on the individuality, consistency, and naturalness of Shakespeare's characters. These truths have become familiar commonplaces—they skim over the top of our consciousness. But, just as a perceptive literary critic occasionally turns our attention to them anew by some particularly subtle or striking presentation, so the actor-critic can sometimes restore these same truths to us as fresh insights by showing us their relevancy for stage impersonation. For example: Shakespeare has frequently been praised for his ability to differentiate characters who are placed in superficially similar circumstances or who share a particular human emotion. MARY ANDERSON, the American actress who won fame as Juliet and who demonstrated her virtuosity by

11. Letter of February 2, 1857, to Miss Margaret Stokes; quoted by Sir Theodore Martin in *Helena Faucit* (*Lady Martin*) (2d ed.; Edinburgh and London, 1900), p. 250.

12. Lena Ashwell, *The Stage*. (London, [1929]), pp. 148-50; Donald Wolfit, *First Interval* (London, 1954), pp. 192-233; Maurice Evans, "Preface," *Maurice Evans' G.I. Production of Hamlet by William Shakespeare* (Garden City, New York, 1947), pp. 7-24. Miss Ashwell's experiences were with World War I; those of the others, with World War II. Among the twentieth-century actors who have emphasized Shakespeare's "modernity" without any context of wartime are Herbert Beerbohm Tree (*Thoughts and Afterthoughts* [London and New York, 1913], pp. 193-94) and Gordon Craig (*Henry Irving* [New York, 1930], pp. 139-40).

doubling the parts of Hermione and Perdita, saw in Shakespeare's individualizing tendency both a challenge and a means of meeting that challenge. In preparing to impersonate one of his heroines she found that her chief task, to become intimately acquainted with the personality she was to assume, was assisted by minute comparison of this character's behavior with that of Shakespeare's heroines in other plays.

Rosalind may be madly in love with Orlando, yet she can jest, be merry, and have a mock marriage; while gentle Imogen under the same conditions would droop and fade away. Desdemona may be separated from her love, yet she does not fret nor mourn for his absence. Absence to Juliet is death.

Thus comparative analysis (which had been a favorite critical pastime since the late eighteenth century) took on for Miss Anderson a direct practical value. By means of it she could answer such questions as "How would such a . . . woman weep under given circumstances? Would . . . she weep at all?" And so she could be sure of suiting the business of the part to the individual nature of the character.[13]

In some instances the actors' criticisms differ from those of other writers in substance and point of view as well as in application. For instance, actors have naturally taken a more pragmatic attitude toward Shakespeare's characters than other critics have done, for they have been concerned, not with abstract ideals, but with physical possibilities. Hence the flexibility of these characters is occasionally pointed to (particularly in our own century) as one of their greatest assets. In ELLEN TERRY's words: "Has there ever been a dramatist, I wonder, whose parts admit of as many different interpretations as do Shakespeare's? There lies his immortality as an acting force, for every ten years an actor can reconsider a Shakespeare part and find new life in it for his new purpose and new audience."[14] And SIR CEDRIC HARDWICKE suggested that Shakespeare's willingness to allow for the interpretations of individual actors accounts for his superiority to modern dramatists. Writers who "make their characterizations photographically accurate" saddle the actor with the dead weight of another's imagination, leaving him no scope for "leaven[ing] parts with his own personality."

13. Mary Anderson, *A Few Memories* (New York, 1896), pp. 193-94, 196-97.
14. Ellen Terry, *The Story of My Life* (London, 1908), p. 107.

It has been suggested that Shaw lacks the ability to create great characters such as Malvolio, Shylock, Iago, or Falstaff, but it must be remembered that Shakespeare's characters have passed through many generations of creative actors, who have all added something to the traditions which have grown up round them.[15]

Shakespeare's success in creating such flexible roles is traced by HARLEY GRANVILLE-BARKER (and by a number of other actor-critics) to his experience in the theatre, where he learned "the dramatist's master secret" of "intimate and fruitful collaboration" between author and actor.[16] His greatest virtues, as far as the actors are concerned, arose from his dramatic imagination—his ability to visualize a scene in action as he wrote, to project himself into the identity of whatever character was speaking at the moment without losing sight of the other characters and their probable feelings and reactions. (As SHERIDAN KNOWLES pointed out a century before Granville-Barker, Macduff "would never have pulled his hat over his brows to conceal the gush of . . . agony if when Shakespeare was setting down the speech of Ross, the bard had not seen him in the act of doing so."[17]) The self-forgetfulness that makes possible this union of intensity with objectivity might be called the theatrical side of Shakespeare's "negative capability."[18]

Sometimes the actors' comments on Shakespeare's merits as a dramatist interestingly supplement those of the literary critics; sometimes they reply to or even anticipate such criticisms. When the subject is one directly concerned with stage effect—for example, the adaptability of Shakespeare's plays to the creation of dramatic illusion—such relationships are hardly fortuitous. Mighty voices from the literary world were raised on the subject of illusion

15. Cedric Webster Hardwicke, *Let's Pretend* (London, [1932]), pp. 61-62, 218-19. *See also* John Gielgud's *Stage Directions* (New York, [1964]), pp. 106-7.

16. Harley Granville-Barker, *Prefaces to Shakespeare* (Princeton, 1946), I, 25-26. For other discussions of the ways in which theatrical experience contributed to Shakespeare's stagecraft see Henry Irving, "Shakespeare and Bacon," *The Complete Works of Shakespeare*. (Edina Edition; Edinburgh, [19-?]), pp. xl-xli; and Lena Ashwell, *Reflections from Shakespeare*, ed. Roger Pocock (London, [1926]), p. 44.

17. James Sheridan Knowles, *Lectures on Dramatic Literature Delivered . . . during the Years 1820-1850*, ed. Francis Harvey (London, 1873), p. 73. For an interesting discussion of Shakespeare's dramatic imagination see pp. 98-100.

18. This point is well discussed by Beerbohm Tree in *Thoughts and Afterthoughts*, pp. 106-11, and by Margaret Webster in *Shakespeare Without Tears* (Cleveland, 1955), pp. 62-63.

—Dr. Johnson's in the eighteenth century and Coleridge's early in the nineteenth—but some of their theatrical contemporaries had equally interesting (if less influential) things to say, and their remarks were sometimes more firmly anchored in actual plays. A particularly good example is FRANCIS GENTLEMAN, whose perceptiveness here is in pleasant contrast to the short-sightedness of much that he wrote. In 1770 he made some very "modern" comments on the opportunities that Shakespeare has provided in *Hamlet* for achieving the illusion of reality: The First Player's "Hecuba" speech and the whole play scene in the third act "are not only intended as preparatory means to convict the King of guilt, but are also meant to realize the characters of the main action; therefore the matter, manner, and action are evidently proposed as a contrast to fiction, to what is necessary the audience should think truth"; Hamlet's "O what a rogue," too, gains additional "force and reality" by its comparing the players' "fictitious feeling" with Hamlet's "substantial cause of grief."[19]

Even the more theoretical discussions of dramatic illusion by THOMAS HOLCROFT, Sheridan Knowles, and WILLIAM OXBERRY are interesting because of their reactions to and differences from those of the purely literary critics. (All three of these men had written for the stage, as well as acted on it, and Knowles with signal success.) It will be recalled that Johnson's argument against the "unities" as inflexible rules was based on a repudiation of the illusion of reality as an ideal capable of realization, whether or not the "unities" are preserved. Although Holcroft (1805-6) praised Johnson for his stand, he justified the rejection of the "unities" on very different grounds. Perfect illusion is impossible, he agreed, but the mind is capable of placing itself in an imaginative state in which time and place are only relative matters. "It cannot. . . distinguish the minuteness of the interval . . . in which it can suppose itself at Rome, hearing Marc Antony harangue over the dead body of Caesar, be called to recollection by the noise or elbow of a neighbouring spectator, and again be back at Rome . . . connecting the past and the present." When "unfettered" by preconceived notions, "it is led implicitly by the narrative, and

19. Francis Gentleman, *The Dramatic Censor* (London, 1770), I, 21-22. Years later Granville-Barker (*Prefaces to Shakespeare*, I, 85-86) and John Gielgud (*John Gielgud's Hamlet*, ed. Rosamond Gilder [New York and Toronto, 1937], p. 57) made similar points in discussing *Hamlet*.

even delights so to be led."[20] This statement, as I understand it, anticipates Coleridge's principle of the "willing suspension of disbelief." As Knowles later pointed out (1820-50), Johnson was "unquestionably right" as far as he went, but he was right only in the sense that "we never take the portraits for the originals." The awareness that you are looking at Kemble rather than at Coriolanus is "the business of your senses, and of your immediate perception" only; there is "another principle at work" which penetrates to the truth embodied in the fiction, summoning up reality "in all the palpability of a present existence" and calling "upon your sympathies as the tribute to real suffering."[21] Oxberry (1818), though in basic agreement with such reasoning (his language suggests the influence of Coleridge), added this qualification: although our acceptance of "reality" in a theatre does not depend upon unity, it does require an uninterrupted sequence of actions; thus in *The Winter's Tale* the imagination is not distracted by the multiplicity of events, but it is strained by the abrupt break in the time link, by having to suppose that years have passed when there have been no visible events to mark them.[22]

In dealing with other questions that arose from the artificial standards of neoclassicism—those of decorum and plot structure— the actors' comments are sometimes as interesting for their date of composition as for their content. For here, too, theatrical experience occasionally led to an appreciation of qualities that were either censured or ignored by many contemporary literary critics. In 1740, for example, when Shakespeare's mingling of comic and tragic elements was often deplored as "indecorous," COLLEY CIBBER —by no means a "dunce" where practical stagecraft was concerned —remarked that a "Laugh of Approbation" is sometimes aroused even by tragic heroes. He admired the "familiar Strokes" in the characterization of Macbeth, Hotspur, Richard III, and Henry VIII, "so highly natural to each particular Disposition, that it is impossible not to be transported into an honest Laughter at them"; and he added that such "happy Liberties," when "justly taken, may challenge a Place among [the] greatest Beauties" of

20. Thomas Holcroft, *The Theatrical Recorder* (London, 1805-6), I, 276-78. *See also* pp. 347 and 430.

21. *Lectures on Dramatic Literature*, pp. 129-31.

22. *The New English Drama*, ed. William Oxberry (London, 1818-24), III, *Hamlet*, xiv.

dramatic composition.[23] Similarly, when Shakespeare's structural proficiency was being questioned on the basis of his infraction of the "unities," SAMUEL FOOTE (1747) insisted that "Unity of Character" gave in itself sufficient order to a play and was worth more than the three classical "unities" put together.[24] (Actor-critics of that period, of course, did not always emancipate themselves from the dogma of the more pedantic literary critics. Even after Dr. Johnson had trampled upon the "unities" and defended tragicomic mixtures, such theatrical men as Francis Gentleman and CHARLES DIBDIN occasionally reverted to opinions of Shakespeare's "irregularities" that would have done credit to Rymer. It is notable, however, that they usually relaxed the standards in favor of scenes or characters which had proved particularly attractive in the theatre.)

Even more significant, perhaps, are the reverse examples from the nineteenth century. Several decades after Coleridge, with his principle of "organic structure," had discredited any standards imposed upon Shakespeare's plays from the outside, the actor-dramatist Sheridan Knowles, though surrounded by critics primarily concerned with character study, continued to devote serious attention to matters traditionally associated with structure. He even spoke out for unity of action, though he tossed aside the unities of time and place as clogs on dramatic artistry; but his reasoning was purely practical: an audience finds the interruption of one plot interest by another an annoying distraction. (Nor would he admit that this principle is invalidated by the success of plays in which one plot serves as a foil for the other, since even greater effectiveness might have been gained by another method—for example, if Shakespeare had omitted the casket plot from *The Merchant of Venice* he might have strengthened the Antonio-Shylock plot and built it to a "glorious climax.") But, since Knowles understood the dramatist's "great aim" in simple theatrical terms—"to excite expectation and to keep it up throughout" —unity of action was less important to him than a principle that

23. *An Apology for the Life of Mr. Colley Cibber,* ed. Robert W. Lowe (London, 1889), I, 122-24. (Cibber's book was first published in 1740.) Thomas Davies, in *Dramatic Miscellanies,* II, 21-24, praised Shakespeare for his "frequent and happy use" of low comedy characters and other characters of "levity, or oddity" in his most serious plays.

24. Samuel Foote, *The Roman and English Comedy Consider'd and Compar'd* (London, 1747), pp. 19-22.

he called "Climax of Action." Defined as the gradual heightening of interest until the final scene of the play, with each major division also climactically structured, it was well illustrated, Knowles thought, in *Macbeth, Othello, Coriolanus,* and *Measure for Measure.* He praised Shakespeare as a master of the techniques necessary to achieve this result: quick, effective exposition; constant forward motion; and the strategic introduction of new incidents to keep the attention of the audience.[25]

Henry Irving's tributes to Shakespeare's "consummate stagecraft"[26] and WILLIAM POEL's praise of his "constructive art"[27] (late nineteenth century and early twentieth) mention certain excellences that Knowles missed—such as Shakespeare's effectively contrived exits and entrances and the economy with which his transitions are made—but they supplement rather than contradict most of the older critic's discussion. Indeed the practical concerns of structure are never out of date for the actor, even though changes in the concept of the Shakespearean stage have in recent times shifted the emphasis somewhat. For example, whereas Knowles thought of Shakespeare's structural pattern in terms of separate but well-articulated units, Harley Granville-Barker and his followers have emphasized the fluidity of Shakespeare's action and the dramatic values that are gained by his juxtaposition, or even blending, of contrasting scenes. For this reason, among others, Granville-Barker is more consistently useful than Knowles, for all the former's relative sophistication and for all the latter's air of common sense. Yet Knowles's concept of gradual development, combined with his love of dramatic contrasts (inclinations he shared with his theatrical predecessors), overcame any tendency toward rigid compartmentalization. In the analysis of specific scenes his perceptions of irony and other subtle dramatic effects

25. *Lectures on Dramatic Literature,* pp. 123-26. *See also* James Sheridan Knowles, *Lectures on Dramatic Literature:* Macbeth (London, 1875), pp. 2-3, 38-39, 76-77. The latter volume presents a compact arrangement of part of the material found in the former.

26. Henry Irving, "Shakespeare as a Playwright," *The Works of William Shakespeare,* ed. Henry Irving and Frank A. Marshall (London, 1888-90), I, xviii-xix; also "Shakespeare and Bacon," pp. xl-xli. The latter contains the comment on Shakespeare's entrances and exits.

27. William Poel, *Shakespeare in the Theatre* (London and Toronto, 1913), pp. 39-40. Poel notes that in *Twelfth Night* Valentine's comment "If the Duke *continue these favours* towards you, Cesario. . . ." bridges with three words the gap in Viola's life from her appearance as a "castaway" after shipwreck to her reëntry as Orsino's favorite page.

are often very intelligent indeed (as we shall see in the chapters on *Hamlet, Othello,* and *Macbeth*) and are sometimes much like those of later critics. His preoccupation with "story" sometimes blunted his finer instincts, as in his criticism of *The Merchant of Venice;* but his best insights represent, I think, not a triumph over his basically practical theories of structure, but a transmutation of them.

Shakespeare's language and versification have drawn praise, of course, from critics of every kind (if we except the most stringent of neoclassicists). But, again, the actors' criticisms are frequently influenced, and sometimes illuminated, by the exigencies of the stage. Shakespeare's speeches, however beautiful or apposite, represent a task to be accomplished: they must be learned, spoken effectively, accompanied by appropriate action. And so the "rememberability" of the lines—a utilitarian virtue but, possibly, an index to merits of a higher order—is, for the actor, a significant part of their excellence. This quality has been frequently praised, especially by actors of the nineteenth and twentieth centuries. Some, like Mary Anderson, have found Shakespeare their "easiest study";[28] others—EDMUND KEAN, for example—have had difficulty memorizing the words but have found them, once mastered, more "stickable" (to use Kean's expression) than those of any other dramatist.[29] Several actors have attempted to account for the memorable quality of Shakespeare's speeches: LESTER WALLACK explained that "you cannot in Shakespeare find any words to improve the text" whereas in more commonplace dialogue you may stumble into substitutions without noticing the difference;[30] but Maurice Evans finds the "secret" in the fact that Shakespeare's lines are perfectly adapted to the human voice because, composing them with flesh-and-blood speakers in mind, the author "heard" the words as he wrote.[31] Another practical advantage of Shakespeare's lines, pointed out by FRANK BENSON and Mary Anderson[32]

28. *A Few Memories,* p. 172.

29. Kean's remarks are reported by John W. Francis in *Old New York; or Reminiscences of the Past Sixty Years* (New York, 1858), pp. 220-21. Gordon Craig recalls a similar experience with Shakespeare's lines. See his *Index to the Story of My Days* (New York, 1957), p. 16.

30. Lester Wallack, *Memories of Fifty Years* (New York, 1889), p. 130.

31. Maurice Evans, "Comments on Playing the Role of Hamlet," *Hamlet. The Laurel Shakespeare* (New York, 1958), p. 26.

32. Sir Frank Benson, *My Memoirs* (London, 1930), p. 177; Anderson, *A Few Memories,* p. 172.

among others, is that cues for movement and implications of stage business are often provided for the actor by the dialogue itself.

The attribute of "naturalness" so often claimed for Shakespeare's speeches has taken on a special meaning for actors, linked as it is with the problem of effective stage delivery. And here, I think, their comments are more interesting in relation to the contemporary drama than to the judgments of other critics. In the eighteenth century an actor of any sensitivity must have turned with relief from the stilted tragedies of that day, with their inflated rhetoric, to *Hamlet,* whose dialogue "approaches very near . . . the conversation of the present day" (to quote Thomas Davies), combining "wit as brilliant as Congreve with the ease and familiarity of Vanbrugh."[33] In the first half of the nineteenth century, too, the actor found refuge in Shakespeare's relative simplicity and earthiness from the excessive lyricism of plays only one step away from closet drama. As Sheridan Knowles remarked, the "most powerful" language in drama is generally "the most effortless and obvious; not that every man would have hit upon it, but that every man feels . . . at home with it the moment it is found out for him"—witness the effectiveness of the familiar word "knife" in Lady Macbeth's great soliloquy, the more terrible for its very homeliness.[34] (Knowles sought to imitate Shakespeare's methods in his own plays, and many of his contemporaries judged him successful. It would be interesting to know how many of his fellow-actors felt the distinction between Shakespeare's lines and the pseudo-Elizabethan poetry provided by such dramatists.)

Because of the obvious contrasts between Shakespearean dialogue and the close imitation of daily speech in modern realistic drama, some changes have occurred in the actors' assessments of Shakespeare's naturalness. William Poel declared (in the 1880's) that Shakespeare's characters spoke *"theatrically,* that is with exaggerated naturalness"; for example, in the "hurried lines" in which Othello repeatedly demands the handkerchief of Desdemona, "the questioning is unnaturally prolonged . . . for the purpose of giving the actor time to reach a climax of passion on the delivery of the word 'away!' "[35] A similar change in the actors' critical attitude is reflected in the phrase "naturally rhetorical"

33. *Dramatic Miscellanies,* II, 149.
34. *Lectures on Dramatic Literature,* pp. 140-42. See also pp. 105-7.
35. *New Shakspere Society Transactions,* Ser. I, No. 10 (1880-1886), Part III, p. 142.

with which Harley Granville-Barker described Shakespeare's lines (in 1929).[36] His concept was more subtle and more complex than Poel's, however, as the many readers of *Prefaces to Shakespeare* are well aware; for the analyses of Shakespeare's language in that valuable work are full of literary as well as theatrical insights. Many actors of the late nineteenth and early twentieth centuries lamented the increasingly naturalistic plays of this transition period ("filthy, sordid, realistic, ugly so-called problems," J. H. BARNES sputtered angrily[37]) and looked back nostalgically to the poetic and idealistic qualities of such plays as Shakespeare's. Others, though they accepted the new, realized that in training for this understated drama the actor might easily lose sight of qualities essential to the effective projection of Shakespeare's speeches.[38]

Most of the recent actor-critics, though grateful for the rich opportunities offered by Shakespeare's kind of "naturalness," have much to say of the problems that must be overcome in exploiting these opportunities. (Significantly, the writers who have dealt best with this subject have had experience in directing Shakespeare's plays.) One danger—loss of clarity and significance for the audience—arises from failure to cope effectively with the fanciful elaborations in Shakespeare's early verse or the complexities of syntax in his later. William Poel, conscious of this difficulty, emphasized the necessity for keeping the central idea of a passage clearly marked by stressing only key words and, "by modulation and deflection of voice," subordinating the qualifying

36. Harley Granville-Barker, "Tennyson, Swinburne, Meredith—and the Theatre," *The Eighteen-Seventies. Essays by Fellows of the Royal Society of Literature* (New York, 1929), pp. 169-75.

37. J. H. Barnes, *Forty Years on the Stage* (London, 1914), p. 308. Other actors who objected to the naturalistic drama and praised the ideal quality of Shakespeare's tragedies were Herbert Beerbohm Tree (*Thoughts and Afterthoughts*, pp. 182-83); Julia Marlowe (E. H. Sothern, *Julia Marlowe's Story*, ed. Fairfax Downey [New York, 1954], pp. 224-25); Lena Ashwell (*The Stage*, pp. 17-18); Oscar Asche (*Oscar Asche: His Life by Himself* [London, c. 1929], p. 232); Cedric Hardwicke (*The Drama Tomorrow* [Cambridge, 1936], pp. 17-19, and *Let's Pretend*, p. 250).

38. Barry Sullivan remarked that one of the new actors might "show to some advantage" in a modern drama. "But place the same player in a Shakespearean part, and the result is—surprise that an actor could look so little." Quoted by Robert M. Sillard, in *Barry Sullivan and His Contemporaries* (London, 1901), II, 203. James Murdoch, in *The Stage; or Recollections of Actors and Acting* (Philadelphia, 1880), pp. 154, 156, warns against the pitfalls awaiting the actor who attempts the wrong kind of naturalness in a Shakespearean part.

and ornamental ones.[39] MARGARET WEBSTER, however, warns that a meticulous annotation of each pause and each increased emphasis will get an actor "conscientiously nowhere"; if he makes the lines a part of himself and speaks them intelligently, they will reveal their own system of stress and relaxation. Another problem is the loss of effectiveness resulting from changes in the habits of stage speech. Actors accustomed to the relatively slight vocal demands of modern prose drama must work diligently to overcome the slovenly enunciation, shallow breath support, and spasmodic phrasing that sometimes mar their Shakespearean efforts.[40] Important for the meaning of Shakespeare's lines, as well as for their overall effect, is the problem which has been best discussed by SIR JOHN GIELGUD: that of reconciling their realistic with their musical and rhetorical elements. Just as the nineteenth-century actor was often tempted into oratorical excesses, so his modern counterpart may fall into the trap of realism "at all costs."

When Shakespeare wants to be naturalistic he writes: "Pray you, undo this button". . . . Such lines are extraordinarily simple, and every audience will find them moving. But they will only achieve their ultimate effect if they are supported by the rich scaffolding built so firmly round them in the speeches which precede and follow.

Because of this complexity of style the Shakespearean actor must be able to begin a speech in the heroic vein yet swiftly (and without awkwardness) make the transition to a tone of everyday simplicity.[41]

Criticism like that in the paragraph above, which deals with theatrical problems posed by Shakespeare's plays, has naturally been the peculiar province of the actor, though in some cases scholars and literary critics have complicated a particular problem

39. *Shakespeare in the Theatre*, pp. 57-59. See also Poel's *Monthly Letters* (London, 1929), pp. 14-18. Robert Speaight discusses Poel's ideas concerning the proper accenting of key words in *William Poel and the Elizabethan Revival* (Cambridge, Mass., 1954), p. 64.

40. For Miss Webster's sensible and very circumstantial discussion of such problems see *Shakespeare Without Tears*, pp. 21, 23, 87-92. Granville-Barker discusses the difficulties due to language changes, complexities of syntax, etc. in *Prefaces to Shakespeare*, I, 12-14.

41. *Stage Directions*, pp. 4-5; see also pp. 14, 25. Reconciling the ideal and the actual in the representation of Shakespeare's characters is a related, or overlapping, problem. In *Early Stages* (New York, 1939), p. 90, Gielgud expressed the opinion that, because of this problem, Shakespeare's roles are more of a strain on the actor than are those of a realistic dramatist like Chekhov; but he has evidently modified his views as his experience ripened. See *Stage Directions*, p. 13.

and in others they have furnished information leading to a solution.

Influences from the "outside"—from scholars, particularly, and from other actors—are often cited by actor-critics as one of the greatest problems in the interpretation of a Shakespearean role. Commentators are accused of the "obfuscation" (as one actor terms it) of Shakespeare's essential clarity either by masses of irrelevant detail or by needlessly subtle and complex interpretations.[42] Even if the actor, in building up his conception of a character, chooses only the best writings to study, he finds so many (and such conflicting) opinions that he is likely to be overwhelmed. He knows, too, that once he has worked out his own interpretation he must overcome the preconceptions of his spectators, many of whom will also have read the commentators; for, as MADGE KENDAL observed, if the audience is debating the correctness of an interpretation "the actor has not got hold of them."[43] Another danger—the worst of all, according to SIR MICHAEL REDGRAVE—is that too many critical theories, though interesting in themselves, are deduced from lines taken out of context; it is particularly important for the actor to see his part in its proper relation to the play as a whole.[44] The actor-critics complain, as well, of being handicapped by secondhand ideas forced upon them by past members of their own profession. Even today, when the emphasis is upon originality and freshness, there is still much borrowing of stage business, which in turn affects interpretation. Most outspoken against the stage "stereotypes" of Shakespeare's characters is SIR TYRONE GUTHRIE. In his opinion, reverence for any established interpretation is misplaced, even when it supposedly reflects the "author's intention"; for "the most im-

42. Some of the actors' complaints of Shakespearean scholars and commentators are found in the following: John Ireland's biographical sketch of Henderson, in *Letters and Poems by the Late Mr. John Henderson* (London, 1786), p. 7; *Macready's Reminiscences and Selections from His Diaries*, ed. Sir Frederick Pollock (New York, 1875), pp. 164, 655, 666; Martin, *Helena Faucit*, p. 208; Frederick Warde, *The Fools of Shakespeare* (New York, 1913), p. ii, and his *Fifty Years of Make-Believe* (New York, 1920), p. 293; Elizabeth Robins, *Both Sides of the Curtain* (London, [1940]), pp. 254-55; Margaret Webster, *Shakespeare Without Tears*, p. 17.

43. Mrs. [Madge Robertson] Kendal, *Dramatic Opinions* (Boston, 1890), pp. 57-60.

44. Redgrave also discusses ideas inherited from other actors. And he points out that an actor's approach to a Shakespearean role may be distorted somewhat by his effort to bring out some facet of the character that he thinks has been neglected. See his "Shakespeare and the Actors," in *Talking of Shakespeare*, ed. John Garrett (London, 1954), pp. 131-36.

portant part of an author's intention," since it is "implicit, not explicit in his text," can be but imperfectly realized at best.[45]

The problem we have just discussed is traceable in part to that quality of Shakespeare's characters most prized by actors, their flexibility. Nor is this the only coin of theatrical merit that has been tossed to reveal its other side. It is frequently remarked that Shakespeare's great roles have kept the stage because no performer can resist their stellar qualities—their mighty passions and their "gargantuan Falstaffian humours," which challenge and reward the actor's full powers.[46] Yet actor-critics from the eighteenth century to the present—among them, some of the finest artists of the English stage—have emphasized, as often as the rewards, the difficulties involved in meeting those challenges. Especially trying to the actor is the necessity of showing great emotion without the opportunity of "working it up." Thus Constance in *King John* seemed to SARAH SIDDONS the most difficult role "in the whole range of dramatic character" because she must come "before the audience in the plenitude of her afflictions . . . without any visible previous progress toward the climax of desperation." When she played the part, Mrs. Siddons kept the door of her dressing-room open so that, while offstage, she could hear the progress of the machinations against her son and thus prepare herself mentally for her passionate entrance in the third act.[47] A similar stumbling block for actors is the necessity of expressing sudden fluctuations in emotion or even apparent changes in character. For example, as Helen Faucit points out, Juliet's brief

45. Tyrone Guthrie, *A Life in the Theatre* (New York, 1959), pp. 19-20. See also Gielgud's *Stage Directions*, p. 16.

46. The quoted phrase is from Redgrave's "Shakespeare and the Actors," pp. 130-31. See also Lena Ashwell, *The Stage*, pp. 30-31; and Margaret Webster, *Shakespeare Without Tears*, pp. 84-85. Nineteenth century actors, like Joseph Jefferson and Dion Boucicault, conditioned by their own theatrical background, considered Shakespeare's "star" roles his greatest attraction. See *The Autobiography of Joseph Jefferson* (New York, [1890]), pp. 220-21; Francis Wilson, *Joseph Jefferson: Reminiscences of a Fellow Player* (New York, 1906), pp. 101-3; Dion Boucicault, "Shakespeare's Influence on the Drama," *North American Review*, CXLVII (December, 1888), 680-85.

47. Mrs. Siddons's essay on Constance, published in Thomas Campbell's *Life of Mrs. Siddons* (London, 1839), pp. 116-20. Yvonne Mitchell, when she played Cordelia to Redgrave's Lear (Stratford-on-Avon, 1953), tried a practice similar to Mrs. Siddons's. In "Playing in *Lear*," *Spectator*, CXCI (December 4, 1953), 665, she tells of sitting at the side of the stage during the great scene between mad Lear and blind Gloucester because its mood helped to prepare her for acting the reconciliation scene.

scene alone after the Nurse has advised her to forget Romeo and marry Paris is both crucial and difficult, for in it the actress must show Juliet's sudden maturity of character as the "child's trust in others falls from her" and she knows she must face the future alone.[48] Even when Shakespeare uses his more normal method of presenting emotion, with foreshadowing scenes early in the play, there are problems; for, as LOUIS CALVERT reminds us, the actor must keep the earlier evidences of passion at a lower pitch than he is tempted to do in order to build up to a climax later.[49] Shakespeare's passionate characters are not only difficult to perform; they are also physically exhausting. They "make elaborate demands on the breathing apparatus" and they necessitate the performance of athletic feats such as Hamlet's fencing match, to say nothing of the continual strain of moving about in armor or heavy robes. Accordingly, the actor must learn, as Sir Tyrone Guthrie advises, "where and how to rest, how to eke out limited resources of energy so that there will still be enough in reserve for the critical last lap."[50]

Some of the difficulties involved in staging the plays do not stem from any peculiarly Shakespearean quality; they exist for all plays that retain their theatrical value over a long period of time. For example, there is the problem of keeping the sympathy and understanding of the audience in spite of the changes in taste, thought, and experience that have occurred over the years. Some of Shakespeare's plays offer such excellent opportunities for acting that they have never been long absent from the stage; yet they also contain words, speeches, even whole scenes which have seemed at one period or another unnecessary, unintelligible, or offensive.

The barriers between Shakespeare and the modern audience which arise from loss of understanding have been interestingly

48. Helena Faucit, Lady Martin, *On Some of Shakespeare's Female Characters*, pp. 139-40. On p. 119 she discusses the difficult fluctuations of emotion in the balcony scene.

49. Louis Calvert, *Problems of an Actor* (New York, 1918), pp. 145-49.

50. *A Life in the Theatre*, p. 124. A number of actors have written of the physical strain of performing certain Shakespearean characters. For example, Sarah Siddons found Constance's "sublime and . . . intense" grief and her "rapid and astonishing eloquence" mentally overwhelming and physically exhausting (Campbell, *Life of Mrs. Siddons*, pp. 120-24), and Henry Irving had a similar experience with King Lear (see his essay, "My Four Favorite Parts," *The Forum*, XVI [September, 1893], 36-37).

discussed by two actor-critics of the present century, GEORGE FOSS[51] and Margaret Webster.[52] The latter is well known, but Foss deserves more readers than he has gained. Frequently sensible and sometimes original in his criticisms, he does a service in pointing out (like the "historical critics" of a more scholarly bent) the importance of Elizabethan attitudes and conventions to the interpretation of Shakespeare's plays; for example, he rightly argues that Bassanio is meant to be a thoroughly sympathetic character, his interest in Portia's fortune being both normal and honorable. Sometimes, however, like those same "historical critics," he goes too far in substituting "Elizabethan thought" for an equally important dramatic convention or a more universal human sympathy —for example in insisting too strongly upon Elizabethan disapproval of lovers who flouted their parents' wishes. (Sometimes, too, despite his avowed intention, his most interesting interpretations have little basis in Elizabethan thought.) Foss disclaims any rigid devotion to Shakespeare's original meaning as "the right and only way to produce the plays," but he suggests that in some cases this meaning is closer to our own understanding than is the sentimentalized interpretation inherited from the nineteenth century.

Actors of the earlier periods did not make much effort to recapture Elizabethan meanings[53] and Elizabethan values. Instead they substituted their own, editing and altering Shakespeare's texts to keep them in line with modern taste and modern stage methods. In the Restoration and the early eighteenth century, such radical adaptations as Tate's *King Lear* and Cibber's *Richard III* replaced the original Shakespearean versions, and some of them (including the two just named) continued to hold the stage throughout the eighteenth century and well into the nineteenth. Even plays that escaped such treatment (like *Othello* and, for many years, *Hamlet*) were cut so drastically and at such vital points as to modify character interpretation considerably. In the second half of the eighteenth century David Garrick restored

51. George R. Foss, *What the Author Meant* (London, 1932), pp. 3-4, 9, and *passim*.
52. *Shakespeare Without Tears, passim*. See especially pp. 29, 82-83.
53. Except in the case of individual word meanings. John Henderson compiled notes "illustrating" the meanings of Shakespeare's unusual and difficult words by references to passages in other Elizabethan writings. His notes were included in the Malone edition of Shakespeare in 1790 and again in the 1821 (Boswell-Malone) Variorum. Thomas Davies pays much attention to elucidating words and passages in his *Dramatic Miscellanies*. Examples of this sort could be multiplied.

many Shakespearean passages that had been omitted from earlier stage versions of the plays;[54] but, on the other hand, he took new liberties, such as adding a dying speech for Macbeth. An alteration of *Hamlet*, made late in his career, was his nearest approach to the radical methods of his predecessors. Obviously actors were largely responsible for the violence done to Shakespeare's text; in addition to participating in the alteration, they encouraged and utilized adapted versions of the plays. (Those literary critics, however, who measured Shakespeare's plays by classical standards and found them in need of "improvement" were also partly responsible.) But the eighteenth century actor-critics, though they accepted the practice of alteration in general, did not always approve specific alterations. (Their opinions of Garrick's *Hamlet*, Tate's *King Lear*, and Davenant's *Macbeth* will be discussed in the chapters ahead.)

A movement toward the "purity" of Shakespeare's text took place in the nineteenth century, with WILLIAM CHARLES MACREADY as one of the strongest leaders. During his brief but important periods as a theatrical manager he demonstrated his belief that Shakespeare's plays did not have to be doctored in order to be good theatre: in 1838, for example, he restored Shakespeare's *King Lear*, Fool and all (although Edmund Kean had earlier experimented with a restoration of Shakespeare's tragic ending, a thoroughly Shakespearean text had not been used for a century and a half). He was successful enough in inspiring imitation that when he retired from the stage in 1851 he was able to express gratification in the apparent "assurance that the corrupt editions and unworthy presentations of past days" would never return.[55] The "purity of text" for which Macready crusaded refers to an absence of non-Shakespearean speeches and scenes rather than to completeness of text or absolute fidelity to the original arrangement; for the most ardent restorer of that period usually did not question the desirability of cuts and minor transpositions. Even

54. See George Winchester Stone's articles on Garrick's handling of Shakespearean plays: e.g. "Garrick's Long-Lost Alteration of *Hamlet*," *PMLA*, XLIX (1934), 890–921; "Garrick's Handling of Macbeth," *Studies in Philology*, XXXVIII (1941), 627-28; "Garrick's Production of King Lear," *Studies in Philology*, XLV (1948), 89-103.

55. *The Diaries of William Charles Macready*, ed. William Toynbee (New York, 1912), II, 497. See pp. 18-19 for Macready's statement (in 1839) of his ambition to present Shakespeare's text "purified from the gross interpolations that disfigure it and distort his characters."

that concept of "purity" established itself but slowly: FANNY KEMBLE felt that she had been theatrically unwise when she replaced Garrick's conclusion of *Romeo and Juliet* with Shakespeare's, although she personally preferred the latter;[56] EDWIN BOOTH was persuaded to return to Cibber's *Richard III* after leaving it awhile for Shakespeare's text—and was rewarded by the "whistling stamping gallery gods' approval, and . . . the wild enthusiasm of the entire house."[57]

The skill of Shakespeare's dramaturgy became more apparent and the need for large-scale adaptations declined when Elizabethan staging was re-introduced in the late nineteenth century with the work of William Poel and his followers, but in the matter of cuts and alterations Poel himself was inconsistent. He scoffed at the practice of cutting the text in order to allow time for scene changes, and he had some hard words for certain traditional omissions which, in his opinion, had given rise to false interpretations; yet he defended his own retrenchment of *Coriolanus* on the principle that alteration of Shakespeare is legitimate when it is necessary for greater actability.[58] Some years later Harley Granville-Barker, more sensitive to the subtleties of Shakespeare's dramaturgy, declared that a Shakespearean play may be "delicately" though "robustly" organized and that we "carve it to our peril."[59] The idea that the plays should be acted uncut, or nearly so, is obviously a comparatively recent one. In the early years of the present century it was vigorously denounced by actor-critics like HERBERT BEERBOHM TREE and DAVID BELASCO,[60] but more recently a number of actors have spoken in its favor. For example, Sir John Gielgud, ROBERT SPEAIGHT, and Margaret Webster, all of whom have been connected with successful productions of the

56. Frances Anne Kemble, *Records of a Girlhood* (2d ed.; New York, 1883), p. 207.

57. Katherine [Molony] Goodale, *Behind the Scenes with Edwin Booth* (Boston, 1931), p. 57.

58. Poel's disapproval of cuts in the text for the sake of scene changes is expressed repeatedly in his writings; e.g. see *Shakespeare in the Theatre*, pp. 17-18. For comments on the damage caused to the interpretation of *Hamlet* by excisions see pp. 168-69; also Poel's letter to the *Era* (April 30, 1892), reprinted in Speaight's *William Poel and the Elizabethan Revival*, pp. 52-53. For Poel's cuts in *Coriolanus* and other plays, see Speaight, pp. 98-99, 151, 197, 259-62. His defense of cuts for the sake of actability is mentioned on p. 262.

59. *Prefaces to Shakespeare*, I, 21-23.

60. Tree, *Thoughts and Afterthoughts*, p. 53; *A Preface to the David Belasco Arrangement of Shakespeare's The Merchant of Venice* (New York, 1922), pp. 19-23.

uncut *Hamlet*,[61] have pointed out certain theatrical advantages offered by the complete text: less time must be wasted in explanatory business, a clearer conception of Hamlet's character emerges when it is seen in proper relation to the rest of the play, and the full version is actually "less tiring" than the others.[62] Although performances with no cuts at all are still rare, it is equally rare today to find such liberties taken with Shakespeare's text as were common a century ago.

Verbal emendations are another matter. Certainly there is no longer the neoclassical tendency to replace "low" words with "poetic" ones or the Victorian compulsion to whitewash off-color passages; but, as we have all noticed, substitutions for supposedly archaic or abstruse terms are rather frequent in contemporary theatrical performances. Other types of changes can be more serious. SIR LEWIS CASSON's suggested emendations in *Macbeth*, for example, are described as attempts to correct errors in the "corrupt" First Folio text; but his criteria of accuracy are his own tastes in meter and imagery and, in one instance, his personal interpretation of character. Casson explains that the producer and and actor "must decide firmly on their view of the author's intention at every moment, and expound it clearly to the audience. If they conscientiously believe that the existing text interferes with or misrepresents the author's intention . . . it is better service to the author to change the text than slavishly to follow it." His changes, however, are sometimes both unnecessary and decidedly un-Shakespearean.[63]

Problems arising from the text *per se* rather than from the accidents of the times have been of special concern to the actor-critics since the latter part of the nineteenth century; for William

61. Gielgud (1930) and Speaight (1932) as Hamlet, both in Old Vic productions directed by Harcourt Williams; Margaret Webster as director of the play in New York (1938) with Maurice Evans as Hamlet. Among the earlier performances of an uncut *Hamlet* were those of Frank Benson at Stratford-on-Avon in 1899 and again in London (at the Lyceum) in 1900. Lady Benson, in *Mainly Players* (London, [1926]), p. 178, recalls the nervous tension felt by the actors, who found it difficult to "sandwich in the unaccustomed speeches." The one advantage that she mentions was the improvement caused by the restoration of the dumb show in the play scene: it made "the whole story more understandable and more dramatic, leading up, as it did, to the 'King's' terror and 'Hamlet's' fury."

62. *John Gielgud's Hamlet*, ed. Gilder, p. 43; Speaight, *William Poel and the Elizabethan Revival*, p. 53; Webster, *Shakespeare Without Tears*, pp. 211-12.

63. William Shakespeare, *Macbeth*, intro. by Sir Lewis Casson (London: The Folio Society, 1951), pp. 6-9.

Poel was the first to point out the theatrical significance of the quartos published during Shakespeare's lifetime. He called attention particularly to some of their descriptive stage directions, not found in later texts, and to their continuity of story, unbroken by systematic act divisions; these characteristics, he was convinced, reflect the actual stage practice of Shakespeare's day. Although he did not advocate the exclusive use of the early quarto texts, Poel did feel that they should receive more attention than in the past and that they should be collated with First Folio texts (hitherto considered more authoritative) in an attempt to arrive at standardized stage versions of Shakespeare's most popular plays. The project should be the joint work of scholars and actors, he thought; for the scholars would need help in visualizing potential stage effects, and the actors must be prevented from losing sight of the play as a whole because of preoccupation with certain roles.[64]

Surely Poel was right about the desirability of closer collaboration between stage and study. The pragmatism that usually stands the actor-critic in good stead in other areas frequently betrays him where textual matters are concerned; yet it *can* be of assistance here if rightly applied. (The mistake is in too limited a view of what is theatrically practical.) Margaret Webster's comments on the First ("Bad") Quarto of *Hamlet* are an example of the way in which stage experience can serve as a check on scholarly theory: Miss Webster is skeptical of the hypothesis that the bad text is a memorial reconstruction by an actor who doubled as Marcellus and Voltimand; for, although the speeches of these two characters are exceptionally correct, the cue words, which their performer would have known in the lines of other characters, are inaccurate, and the speeches immediately preceding the entrances of Marcellus and Voltimand (to which the actor must have listened at each performance) are "wildly different" from those in the good texts.[65] On the other hand, the work of scholars is more essential to actors in the case of text than in any other field of study. Obviously the actor's editorial task cannot be precisely the same as the scholar's; for he cannot stop with the attempt to determine what Shakespeare actually wrote—he must remove the occasional stumbling blocks that exist, even for attentive, intelli-

64. *Shakespeare in the Theatre*, pp. 31-38.
65. *Shakespeare Without Tears*, pp. 117-18. Miss Webster's whole discussion of textual problems (pp. 112-33) is interesting.

gent, and reasonably sensitive members of a modern audience, because of changes in word meanings and connotations. But in general, I think, the theatrical editor needs more faith, not only in Shakespeare, but in his own contemporaries.

There are some discussions by actor-critics that are concerned, not with broadly dramatic subjects like characterization, structure, and language (and their attendant merits and difficulties), but with the more mechanical aspects of staging. Actors' attempts to determine the best types of scenery, costume, and stage for the production of Shakespeare's plays have rarely led to "criticism" in its fullest sense, though there are a few shining exceptions. But since these matters, technical as they seem, can influence the total effect of a play upon an audience and may even serve to enforce a particular interpretation, the discussions of them are interesting, I think, as tributaries to criticism, if not as contributions to the main stream.

Just how elaborately should Shakespeare's plays be dressed and mounted? Should historical "accuracy" be attempted in costumes and setting? These questions did not become important for actor-critics until the nineteenth century, for only then was there a sustained movement toward realistic settings and "appropriate" costumes. Throughout much of the preceding century Shakespearean roles had been dressed, as in Shakespeare's day, in contemporary fashion (or in some stylized costume associated with stage convention) ; but a few attempts had been made to suggest remoteness of period—beginning with the 1762-63 season in London, "old English habits" of a generalized nature were evidently used for all of Shakespeare's history plays—and an innovation in the direction of "historical accuracy" was made in 1773 when Charles Macklin used "old Scots dresses" in his production of *Macbeth*.[66] As for setting, stock scenery (wings, flats, drops) did

66. For comments on the use of "old English" dresses in Shakespeare's history plays as well as for the evaluation of Macklin's innovations in the costuming of *Macbeth*, see Muriel St. Clare Byrne's "The Stage Costuming of *Macbeth* in the Eighteenth Century," *Studies in English Theatre History in Memory of Gabrielle Enthoven, O.B.E.* (London, 1952), pp. 52-64. Two 1773 illustrations of Macklin as Macbeth are reproduced as Plate 4 (p. 49) of this publication. Miss Byrne points out that "Antient Scots" dresses had been used in Edinburgh in 1757 but that Macklin's production "introduced old Scots dresses to the *English* stage and 'old' dresses to *tragedy* for the first time." Macklin's MS notes giving plans for costume, setting, properties, and music for his *Macbeth* production are inserted in the extra-illustrated copy of Kirkman's *Memoirs of the Life of Charles Macklin*,

service for Shakespeare's plays along with many others. In the late eighteenth and early nineteenth centuries, when John Philip Kemble was managing Drury Lane and later Covent Garden, scene design had become more realistic than in Garrick's day, and some of Kemble's Shakespearean productions were rather elaborate. Although he was inconsistent in his ideas of appropriate dress (in Othello he wore "Moorish" dress on occasion but sometimes reverted to the uniform of a contemporary British officer), he produced some of the history plays, notably *Henry VIII*, with considerable emphasis upon "ancient habits and manners."[67] His brother Charles carried the new tendency further: for example, his influential production of *King John*, staged in 1823, featured costumes by Planché which were historically accurate in every detail.[68]

The attitude of most actors toward the Kembles' improvements probably did not differ much from that of their nontheatrical contemporaries. ELIZABETH INCHBALD, actress and dramatist, was perhaps a representative spokesman: her praise of the new Scottish decorations for *Macbeth* (published in 1808) suggests not only admiration for their accuracy and enjoyment of their spectacular qualities but a feeling of self-congratulation for living in an age superior to Garrick's.[69] This attitude was not unanimous, however; Charles Kemble's attempt at accuracy was foiled on at least one occasion by members of his own family. When he brought out his daughter Fanny in *Romeo and Juliet* (1829) the scenery and most of the costumes were designed to suggest medieval Verona, but, despite her father's plans and Mrs. Jameson's pleas, Juliet herself (on the advice of her mother) refused to give up her traditional white satin ball gown. No doubt feminine

Esq. in the Harvard Theatre Collection. Professor William W. Appleton in *Charles Macklin: An Actor's Life* (Cambridge, Mass., 1960), pp. 171-73, discusses these notes and quotes from them; as does Professor Arthur Colby Sprague in *Shakespeare and the Actors* (Cambridge, Mass., 1948), pp. 228, 235, 237. For a general discussion of scenery and costumes in the first three-quarters of the eighteenth century see G.C.D. Odell, *Shakespeare from Betterton to Irving* (New York, 1920), I, 179-81, 289-318, 415-46.

67. Odell, *Shakespeare from Betterton to Irving*, II, 85-109; William Winter, *Shakespeare on the Stage*, First Series (New York, 1911), pp. 249-50; Harold Child, *The Shakespearian Productions of John Philip Kemble* (London, 1935), *passim.*

68. Arthur Colby Sprague, *Shakespeare's Histories: Plays for the Stage* (London, 1964), p. 4.

69. *The British Theatre*, ed. Elizabeth Inchbald (London, 1808), IV, 3-4.

vanity had something to do with this conservatism (Macklin's Lady Macbeth had retained her contemporary finery too), but Miss Kemble explains it more impressively. It stemmed in part from the devotion of her mother (MARIE THÉRÈSE DE CAMP) to the principle of simplicity: "nothing was to be adopted on the stage that was in itself ugly, ungraceful, or even curiously antiquated or singular, however correct it might be. . . . The passions, sentiments, actions, and sufferings of human beings . . . were the main concern of a fine drama, not the clothes they wore."[70]

Simplicity was not, at that point, the wave of the future, however. William Charles Macready approved and furthered the effort to give Shakespeare's plays "the truth of illustration which they merit"; and during his experiments in management he successfully accomplished his announced aim "to make palpable to the senses of the audience" the things he had seen in imagination while reading Shakespeare's plays.[71] When he gave his famous production of *King Lear* in 1838, for example, his vision was realistically communicated through "heavy, sombre" castles, "druid circles ris[ing] in spectral loneliness out of the heath," and a storm that beggared all previous stage displays.[72] It was only after his retirement, when CHARLES KEAN (whom he disliked) was carrying "archaeology" to its extreme in the production of Shakespeare that Macready repented of having "set an example which is accompanied with great peril, for the public is willing to have the magnificence without the tragedy, and the poet is swallowed up in display."[73]

As for Kean himself, he evidently relished his chosen task of teaching the public delightfully through lavish and scrupulously accurate recreations of certain periods of history. In the program notes for his Shakespearean productions (later printed as introductions to the plays in his volume of acting texts) he explained, in each case, his reasons for adopting a particular setting and he carefully documented the authenticity of various details of the

70. Frances Anne Kemble, *Records of a Girlhood*, pp. 189-91.

71. *Diaries of Macready*, ed. Toynbee, II, 17-19. The quotation is from a speech that Macready gave on July 20, 1839, at a dinner in his honor. He had just completed his two-year management of Covent Garden.

72. *John Bull*, January 25, 1838. This review has been quoted by several writers, for example by Odell, *Shakespeare from Betterton to Irving*, II, 210-11.

73. Lady [Juliet Creed] Pollock, *Macready as I Knew Him* (London, 1884), pp. 83-84.

décor. The English history plays lent themselves well to this kind of treatment, and Kean's productions of *King John* and *Henry V* must have been, in their way, illuminating as well as beautiful. With plays like *The Winter's Tale,* however, choice of period became purely arbitrary, and there was danger that the period, once chosen, would become more important than the play itself. In his introduction to this play, after calling attention to its many chronological contradictions, Kean explains that he was guided in his choice of stage setting by references to the Delphic oracle—a natural choice since it plays an important part in the plot. But, of course, a winter's tale does not ask for factual precision. Kean had to change Bohemia to Bithynia (as Hanmer had suggested earlier) since no such country, with or without seacoast, had existed during the period he had chosen to "illustrate."[74] A love for spectacle without any Shakespearean basis whatever is revealed in a letter that Kean wrote to the architect and antiquarian George Godwin concerning the scenery and staging of this play:

I am very anxious about this said Palace of Polixines—I should like to make a grand display in this situation but cannot find a *cause*—a Banquet would not do as Leontes has one in the 1st act. . . . Can you think of any *reason* for an effect. . . .[75]

This typical showman's thought (which might have occurred as well to Garrick or to Kemble) is not cited to impugn Kean's basic sincerity; it is merely to illustrate how easily the means may become ends in themselves.

Although later actor-managers like Henry Irving and Herbert Beerbohm Tree were not so much concerned with archaeological detail as Kean had been, they did give attention to visual illusion, and they were sometimes accused of burying the plays beneath the scenery. A reaction against the "upholstering" of Shakespeare was bound to come; it was hastened and intensified in the late nineteenth and early twentieth centuries by increasing scholarly knowledge about the conditions and techniques of the Elizabethan stage. William Poel served as a bridge between stage and study. He maintained an active correspondence with W. J. Lawrence, one

74. *Selections from the Plays of Shakespeare. As Arranged for Representation at the Princess's Theatre,* ed. Charles Kean (London, 1860), I, 187-92.

75. MS letter in the Folger Shakespeare Library, dated only "Saturday." Kean's production of *The Winter's Tale* opened April 28, 1856.

of the foremost scholars of the Elizabethan stage, and he frequently expounded his own theories in papers and articles. Moreover he gave practical demonstrations of them in the performances of the Elizabethan Stage Society which he established, with subscriptions from men like Israel Gollancz, in 1894.[76] Poel maintained that Shakespeare's drama was composed for continuous performance, its variety serving instead of act pauses or musical interludes; proper fluidity of action could be gained only on an unlocalized, multiple-area stage like the one for which the plays were written. A sense of intimacy, important for Shakespearean drama, was easily effected in the Elizabethan theatre because of its jutting platform and its triple tier of galleries, accommodating large numbers of spectators in close proximity to the stage; in the vast nineteenth century theatres with their picture-frame stages it was impossible. Convinced that Shakespeare's plays should be presented according to the original methods, Poel advocated (and used) a platform stage, virtually bare, instead of realistic stage pictures; instead of costumes suggesting ancient Britain or medieval Scotland, Elizabethan dress for all the plays.[77]

Against ideas like these Beerbohm Tree defended his own conception of appropriate staging with the bravado proper to a beleaguered cause: the "scenic embellishment," he declared, should be as "beautiful and costly as the drama . . . seems to demand"—and, furthermore, "it should not be subordinate to, but rather harmonious with, the dramatic interest."[78] On the question of scenery no meeting of the minds was possible between the schools of thought represented by Poel and Tree. But, leaving aside Poel's insistence upon Elizabethan dress, the two men had

76. The Elizabethan Stage Society made its trial flight in 1893 with a performance of *Measure for Measure,* but it became formally established the following year. Robert Speaight, in Chapter III of his excellent *William Poel and the Elizabethan Revival* (pp. 90-131), discusses the organization and early performances of the Society.

77. These ideas are scattered throughout the two collections of Poel's essays, *Shakespeare in the Theatre* and *Monthly Letters,* and they are frequently repeated. A good discussion of continuous action is found in the former, pp. 11, 14-15, 40-42. The question of whether or not Shakespeare planned his plays to conform to the "classical" five-act structure has not yet been finally settled, by either actors or scholars. Divergent points of view are ably presented by T. W. Baldwin, *Shakespeare's Five-Act Structure* (Urbana, 1947); W. F. Jewkes, *Act Division in Elizabethan and Jacobean Plays* (Hamden, Conn., 1958); and Henry L. Snuggs, *Shakespeare and Five Acts* (New York, 1960).

78. *Thoughts and Afterthoughts,* pp. 56, 60-61.

much the same idea about the importance of costume. One of its major uses was to intensify dramatic effect, as in these examples: "Macbeth in his nightgown, Timon in his rags . . . and the very Ghost in *Hamlet* changing his mystical attire."[79] Another important function was to distinguish characters of different social and political stations: for example, Paris in *Romeo and Juliet* should be richly dressed and accompanied by servants wearing the Prince's livery; Capulet's rage at Juliet's refusal to marry the young man is made intelligible by a visual reminder that he is not only wealthy but a kinsman of royalty.[80]

Under Poel's influence, the problems of scenery which had concerned actor-critics for some time coalesced with the new problem of the type of stage best suited to Shakespearean production; and along with this came the question of continuous staging versus act and scene breaks. Harley Granville-Barker, who had once acted with Poel's company, was a more moderate spokesman for many of the older man's ideas. He considered an exact reproduction of the Elizabethan stage unnecessarily restrictive, but he believed, just as strongly as did Poel, in the necessity of an unlocalized stage (i.e. with no realistic scenery) and of continuous action. One product of these beliefs was his brilliant and influential criticism of the much-maligned structure of *Antony and Cleopatra*. As he pointed out, meticulous editorial place designations, stemming from a loss of Elizabethan conventions, had resulted in the impression of diffuseness bordering on chaos; for in the usual reading editions of this play Acts III and IV comprise twenty-eight distinct scenes, some only a few lines long. Yet, properly understood, this parade of short scenes, each dissolving into the next, represents Shakespeare's stagecraft at its best. What other convention could allow us, as Shakespeare's disregard for locality does, to be carried through the phases of a three-day battle in this panoramic fashion, "could so isolate the true drama of it"? Like Poel, Granville-Barker believed that Shakespeare composed his plays as organic wholes, that any interruption brings some loss of dramatic effect. Although he was willing to compromise with human frailty, he stipulated that any pause in the performance should conform to the natural structure of the play, not

79. *Ibid.,* pp. 63-64.
80. Poel, *Monthly Letters,* pp. 45-47.

to editorial act divisions.[81] Whereas Poel concentrated doggedly
upon the methods of Elizabethan staging and carried them out
(as he understood them) in literal fashion, Granville-Barker built
upon a few essential principles the critical analyses of structure that
constitute the most characteristic sections of his *Prefaces to
Shakespeare*. But the flowering would not have been possible
without the planting.

Recent actor-critics have generally agreed that the exact dupli-
cation of the Elizabethan stage can produce an antiquarian atmosphere destructive of audience involvement. Several have remained unconvinced that even an approximation to it is essential: Margaret Webster, for example, insists that a great actor
can achieve intimacy even on a picture-frame stage; and, though
she accepts continuity of action as desirable, she argues that
Shakespeare's "fluid manipulation of time" can take its course if
the conventional stage is made more flexible with rostra, steps,
and levels. In her opinion, "you can play Shakespeare anywhere
—in a gymnasium or a cathedral . . . if the director respects the
author and the actors have passion and truth."[82] Others—most
ardently and persuasively, Sir Tyrone Guthrie—insist that any
theatre which makes possible the most effective presentation of
Shakespeare's plays will be built on the basic Elizabethan pattern,
though modified and adapted to modern needs. The theatre at
Stratford, Ontario, designed for Guthrie by Tanya Moiseweitsch,
has triumphantly achieved its aim of bringing freshness and intimacy to the plays, substituting for realistic illusion an exuberant
though "ritualistic" sense of shared participation.[83] The modified

81. *Prefaces to Shakespeare*, I, 3-11, 37-38. *See also* the discussions of structure
in the preface to each play.

82. *Shakespeare Without Tears*, pp. 63-69. Miss Webster's disenchantment with
the Elizabethan stage grew out of her experience of both acting and directing on
a stage designed as a "miniature replica of the Globe." Arthur Colby Sprague
tells me, however, that when he saw the productions in question he felt that the
director had insufficient confidence in her stage to make the most effective use of it.
Other modern actors who have not been convinced that Elizabethan staging is
necessary for Shakespeare are Gordon Craig (*Index to the Story of My Days*, pp.
99-100) and Sir Michael Redgrave ("Shakespeare and the Actors," pp. 130, 140-42).
For an interesting, though not very detailed, account of a "practical attempt to
recreate the working conditions of an Elizabethan playhouse, and to test them
in the sphere of commercial entertainment," see Bernard Miles and Josephine
Wilson's "Three Festivals at the Mermaid Theatre," *Shakespeare Quarterly*, V
(Summer, 1954), 307-10.

83. The whole of Chapter 13 in Guthrie's *A Life in the Theatre* (pp. 195-214)
is devoted to the limitations of a picture-frame stage and to the desiderata of the

Elizabethan stage is certainly the trend at present, a trend welcome to scholars and critics and, as a result of the Shakespeare
festivals, familiar and often congenial to large numbers of spectators. (When a proscenium stage is still used, an apron often
carries the action out toward the audience, and continuity of
action is achieved by a revolving stage with simple sets, suggestive
rather than fully realistic.) It may even, as Robert Speaight suggested some years ago, combine with similar trends in non-Shakespearean staging, so that the "simple and ceremonious" theatre of
the Elizabethans will become the living theatre of tomorrow.[84]

One word more should be spoken about the question of costume, a new facet of which was exposed in the 1920's with Barry
Jackson's modern-dress productions of Shakespeare.[85] Although
the use of contemporary wear was actually a return to earlier
custom (including that of Shakespeare's own day), the effect was
naturally different—as was the critical reaction—because of the
changes in thought and practice that had occurred during the
intervening years. Granville-Barker's judgment was unfavorable:
the references to swords, doublets, etc. prevent us from experiencing the sense of identification that contemporary dress would
have given the original audiences. (His own feeling was that
half of Shakespeare's plays can appropriately be dressed in Elizabethan costumes but that the rest present too many individual
problems to admit of a general rule. The major criterion with
him was always dramatic effect.[86]) Several other actor-critics have
expressed reservations or outright disapproval.[87] Nevertheless,
as we all know, the modern-dress trend has flourished, putting

ideal stage for Shakespearean production. Other discussions favoring an Elizabethan-
type stage or staging methods are found in *John Gielgud's Hamlet*, ed. Gilder,
pp. 44-45, and in Speaight's *William Poel and the Elizabethan Revival, passim.*
(e.g. his sympathetic interpretation of Poel's ideas on pp. 77-81).

84. *William Poel and the Elizabethan Revival*, pp. 272-73.

85. Barry Jackson produced *Hamlet, Macbeth, The Taming of the Shrew, All's
Well*, and *Othello* in modern dress at the Birmingham Repertory Theatre. When
Maurice Evans referred, in 1945, to the "stunt" of using modern dress in his own
"G.I. *Hamlet*," Jackson wrote an article protesting this designation. He argued that
when Elizabethan costumes are used everything looks equally unfamiliar to a
modern audience, hence nothing seems particularly significant; modern dress, on
the other hand, instantly establishes the status of each character, after which the
audience can forget costumes and attend to the play. *See* "The Apparel Oft
Proclaims. . . ." *Theatre Arts*, XXX (1946), 734-37.

86. *Prefaces to Shakespeare*, I, 17-21.

87. For example, Lena Ashwell remarks that *Hamlet* belongs to neither time

forth, sometimes, strange offshoots—productions whose costumes represent a period neither ours nor Shakespeare's nor any suggested by the plot. Those like the American Civil War *Troilus and Cressida* (American Festival Theatre, 1961) and the nineteenth-century Sicilian *Much Ado about Nothing* (National Theatre Company, 1967) are usually justified by the director through an appeal to Shakespeare's universality or to some particular element in the play that is said to gain in relevance for us by this treatment. The dangers and the possibilities of "trick" productions have been touched upon—interestingly but too briefly—by several actor-critics. Robert Speaight, for example, takes a negative view: "Modernism on the stage can easily become an excuse for saying anything you like," he remarks wryly, ". . . by the simple expedient of pretending that Shakespeare said it first."[88] Sir Michael Redgrave is more tolerant: such productions, though they are usually more shocking than convincing, serve a purpose by giving a needed jolt to accepted ideas of character and style.[89]

The writings of actor-critics are not invariably distinguishable from the general mass of critical writings in their respective periods. Actors have had much to say, for example, about Shakespeare's "morality," his "genius," his historical accuracy (or lack of it) , his supremacy over "all other poets ancient and modern." Over such criticisms we thankfully pass. May they rest in peace.

This introductory sampling has been designed to present only the most characteristic of the actors' general criticisms of Shakespeare—to indicate the subjects that have attracted writings with

---

nor place but to the "ageless realm of pure thought," and adds: "One hardly gets that effect when it is shown in the costume of our time." (For this and other comments on costuming Shakespeare's plays, see her *Reflections from Shakespeare*, pp. 7, 70, 130-33.) Sir John Gielgud once called it "dangerous and confusing" to act the plays in costumes of a period later than Shakespeare's own, yet he himself used "rehearsal" costumes (modern dress, for the most part) in his 1964 production of *Hamlet*, with Richard Burton as *Hamlet*. For Gielgud's discussions of Shakespearean costume see his essay, "A Shakespearean Speaks His Mind," *Theatre Arts*, XLIII (January, 1959), 71; also *Stage Directions*, pp. 42-43, 69; and *John Gielgud's Hamlet*, ed. Gilder, p. 33. The last of these is especially interesting. Gielgud is particularly sensitive to the evocative qualities of costume, as his description of one of his productions of *Hamlet* (at the New Theatre, 1934) makes clear. (See *Early Stages*, p. 257.)

88. *William Poel and the Elizabethan Revival*, pp. 74-75. *See also* Margaret Webster's similar remarks in "Producing Mr. Shakespeare," *Theatre Arts*, XXVI (1942), 48.

89. "Shakespeare and the Actors," pp. 129-30.

a recognizable theatrical slant, to point out ways in which the actor-critics' approach may differ from that of other critics, and to illustrate some characteristic strengths and weaknesses of actors as critics. The necessarily sketchy histories of textual and staging problems should also serve as a kind of sidewalk artist's background for the criticisms in those kinds relating to *Hamlet, Othello, King Lear,* and *Macbeth.* One major type of actor-criticism—detailed character analysis—could hardly be "introduced." It must be encountered in its native environment, the actors' discussions of individual plays. To those we now turn.

CHAPTER TWO · *Actors' Criticisms of* Hamlet

I. THE PLAY

Criticisms of Plot

Although *Hamlet* was the most popular of Shakespeare's plays on the eighteenth century stage, and although it escaped tampering (except for extensive cuts and verbal substitutions) until the end of 1772, its plot caused much embarrassment for men of literary taste. The most damning criticism came from the French neoclassicists, particularly Voltaire, with his repeated gibes at *"Gilles Shakespeare"* and his notorious sneer that *Hamlet* seemed like the production of a drunken savage. Literary patriots were aroused to the defense of the national poet—among them the young ARTHUR MURPHY, with his "open letter" refuting the most egregious attack on *Hamlet*[1]—but being on the defensive made them unpleasantly aware that Shakespeare's "genius" had to cover a multitude of "faults." Samuel Johnson's intelligent reply to Voltaire as well as to the narrower neoclassicists at home (in the preface to his edition of Shakespeare) should have been sufficient to settle the qualms of English critics even if it could not convince the French. But some English writers were themselves concerned about Shakespeare's handling of the plot in *Hamlet:* not only his usual violation of the "unities" but his indecorous mingling of comic elements with tragedy (especially flagrant in this play), his offenses against poetic justice, and his assigning of inappropriate actions to some of the characters. George Steevens remarked in a letter to Garrick that, although Johnson had praised *Hamlet's* variety, he himself could never be "reconciled to tragicomedy" and that Shakespeare's play resembled a "looking glass exposed for sale, which reflects alternately the funeral and the puppet-show, the venerable beggar soliciting charity, and the blackguard rascal picking a pocket."[2]

1. *The Works of Arthur Murphy, Esq.* (London, 1786), V, 350-58. Murphy's "letter" to Voltaire was first published in the *Gray's Inn Journal* on July 28, 1753, a little over a year before the young writer was to try his talents on the stage; but it was among the papers that Murphy himself selected as having sufficient value to be included in his *Works.* For other "defenses" of Shakespeare against Voltaire, *see* Thomas R. Lounsbury, *Shakespeare and Voltaire* (New York, 1902), *passim.*

2. *The Private Correspondence of David Garrick with the Most Celebrated Persons of His Time,* ed. James Boaden (London, 1831), I, 451-52. For other critical fault-finding with the plot of *Hamlet* see Charles Gildon, "Remarks on the Plays of Shakespear," *Remarks upon Shakespear &c., By Mr Dryden, Mr Row & Mr Gildon*

Most of the eighteenth century actors who discussed the plot of *Hamlet* in their writings also found fault with it. But, although one or another of them repeated all of the charges made by the neoclassical critics, they were not always simply aping a literary fashion. For Shakespeare's conduct of the play not only violated the rules revered by the classical theorists; it went counter to the accepted notions of practical stagecraft as well.

Hamlet's sprawling structure, for example, was attacked on other grounds than infraction of the "unities": FRANCIS GENTLE-MAN pointed out the excessive length of the play, and in his phrase "rather irregularly carried on" he glanced at the lack of straightforward progression.[3] The concluding scenes, with the huddled, accidental *finale,* drew even more criticism—from Arthur Murphy and CHARLES DIBDIN as well as from Gentleman: the action becomes "tame" after the killing of Polonius;[4] the catastrophe is unnecessarily bloody, involving the indiscriminate slaughter of innocent and guilty;[5] and, in any case, a fencing match is a "wretched expedient."[6]

Another fault mentioned by the actor-critics—Shakespeare's failure to suit the action to the characters at certain crucial points —can obviously be tagged with the literary term "indecorum," but this theoretical sin probably does not fully account for the objections raised by Gentleman and Dibdin. Shakespeare's unconventional characterizations also posed a practical problem, since they sometimes cracked the mould of stock-company types. Accustomed to assign each role to a particular line of business, expecting it to yield to the appropriate member of the company an appropriate harvest of passion or humor (and ultimately applause), actors might be understandably chagrined to find the usurper Claudius—by all rights a haughty and ruthless tyrant— stooping to indirect and uncertain courses,[7] and the "amiable"

(London, 1709), pp. 352, 357; and Mrs. Charlotte Lennox, *Shakespeare Illustrated* (London, 1753-54), pp. 270-74.

3. *Bell's Edition of Shakespeare's Plays,* [ed. Francis Gentleman] (London, 1774), III, *Hamlet,* p. [3].

4. Charles Dibdin, *A Complete History of the Stage* (London, 1800), III, 64.

5. Arthur Murphy, "The Theatre," *London Chronicle,* February 15-17, 1757.

6. Murphy, *The Life of David Garrick, Esq.* (London, 1801), II, 84. Gentleman, in *Bell's Shakespeare,* III, *Hamlet,* p. [3], describes the "winding up" of *Hamlet* as "exceeding lame."

7. Francis Gentleman, *The Dramatic Censor* (London, 1770), I, 31-32. Gentleman finds it strange that a man who had been able to destroy his own brother

Laertes saddled by the author with a treacherous plot against Hamlet's life.[8] (Astonishly enough, however, Gentleman excused the latter indecorum with the reminder that Shakespeare drew men as they really are, not as they should be.[9]) As for Hamlet's soliloquy in the prayer scene, it was "more suitable to an assassin of the basest kind, than a virtuous prince and a feeling man."[10] THOMAS DAVIES, though he found less to censure in *Hamlet* than did his fellow actor-critics, concurred with Gentleman in this particular judgment: Hamlet's postponement of revenge until he could ensure Claudius' damnation seemed to Davies not only "shocking" in itself but "highly improbable" as well as "a poor contrivance to delay the catastrophe"; Garrick, he noted, was the first to omit this "horrid" speech.[11] (Garrick did omit it, but he restored it in his 1772 alteration.)

As most of these criticisms demonstrate, the judgment of the actor-critics was certainly restricted to some degree by theatrical conventions, even as that of some other writers was blinded by neoclassical prejudices. And yet the least defensible of their strictures—their objections to Shakespeare's violation of poetic justice—are also the ones least grounded in theatrical experience. Although the killing of Polonius in the closet scene is, and always has been, one of the most exciting moments of the play for the audience, both Gentleman and Dibdin described Polonius' death as unnecessary. And, despite his admiration for Ophelia's mad scenes, Dibdin regretfully pronounced them unsuitable, "poetically speaking" (i.e. by the standards of poetic justice). Gentleman indeed made a halfhearted attempt at giving some dramatic basis for his remarks: if Shakespeare had Polonius killed in order to cause Laertes' resentment and Ophelia's madness, "both might have been brought about on a better principle."[12] But Dibdin's reasoning on this subject is pure frivolity: a "little curiosity" was "not a crime of magnitude enough to deserve death."[13] In justice,

---

when the latter was "in the plenitude of power, and popular esteem should take such a roundabout way to dispose of a nephew he seems to fear."

8. Dibdin, *Complete History of the Stage*, III, 54-55.

9. *Bell Shakespeare*, ed. Gentleman, III, *Hamlet*, p. 205.

10. Gentleman, *Dramatic Censor*, I, 24.

11. Thomas Davies, *Dramatic Miscellanies* (London, 1783-84), III, 101.

12. *Dramatic Censor*, I, 25.

13. *Complete History of the Stage*, III, 54 and 65 (Ophelia's madness and death); 55 (death of Polonius).

it should be said that he probably stated the objection as ridiculously as possible in order to minimize its significance. For although Dibdin admitted the validity of the charges leveled against *Hamlet* by other critics (and agreed, one by one, on each of its "faults"), he spoke scornfully of the critics themselves for allowing a "mist of faults" to obscure the "splendour" of the play. Nevertheless his inability to emancipate himself from the narrower notions of his day (a day, too, that was waning fast), even when he recognized the dramatic excellence gained apart from them, demonstrates his limitations as a critic. Both he and Gentleman must be convicted occasionally of a pseudo-literary pose.

On the other hand, one of the characteristics most disturbing to some of the literary critics—Shakespeare's mingling of comic and tragic elements—was accepted, defended, even praised by most of the actor-critics. Murphy admitted that the original Hamlet story "abounds with Improbabilities; and is such altogether as would scarce have struck any Imagination but Shakespeare's."[14] Shakespeare wrote the play, too, in "his wildest manner, but, at the same time, with all the fire and energy of a superior genius": he developed his scenes with a "wonderful variety of serious, comic, and pathetic incidents, so artfully conducted, that they follow one another in regular series, with due subordination and the most perfect connection."[15] It is true that *Hamlet* contains some things that would normally be considered unsuitable to tragedy—for example, the graveyard scene—but they are justified by the use to which Shakespeare has put them.[16] Francis Gentleman agreed that, although the graveyard scene is "inconsistent with the dignity and decorum of tragedy," it is redeemed by its finely drawn characters, its "pointed satire and . . . instructive moral sentiments."[17] Davies, too, defended the scene on moral grounds: the sight of skulls "thrown wantonly about" in a freshly-opened grave and the words of Hamlet which grow out of the situation "excite reflections to abate our pride and strengthen our humanity."[18] These were literary arguments,

14. "The Theatre," February 15-17, 1757.
15. *Life of Garrick*, I, 42-43.
16. "Letter" to Voltaire, *Works*, V, 353. (*See* n.1, above.) Murphy also defends Ophelia's singing "in misery"; although this is "not usual in grave and serious tragedy," Shakespeare, by using what "occurs in nature," shows "the actings of the mind" and turns "the heart inside out."
17. *Dramatic Censor*, I, 27.
18. *Dramatic Miscellanies*, III, 130-32.

aimed at demolishing a literary objection. Behind them, no doubt, lay another, and more potent, argument: the delight taken by the general public in the Gravediggers and their drolleries.[19]

Some of the actor-critics were not content to point out the flaws in Shakespeare's plot; they also suggested ways of mending them. Gentleman's solution involved no halfway measures:

After the detection of the play, if his majesty, upon the principle of self-defence, had formed a design of taking the prince off by instruments at home; if that design had been made known to the Queen; had she, through maternal affection, put Hamlet on his guard; and had that prince taken measures worthy the motive of stimulation, a tyrant of some consequence and uniformity would have been shown in Claudius; a tender mother in the Queen, and a hero in Hamlet; the innocent characters, Polonius and Ophelia, might have been saved; and death prevented from stalking without limitation at the catastrophe.[20]

Murphy wondered why Shakespeare had not retained the catastrophe of the Hamlet story as it is found in Saxo Grammaticus: in this account, Hamlet gets the nobles intoxicated, sets fire to the palace, and in the confusion is able to reach the King's room without hindrance; proclaiming vengeance for his father, he kills the King, after which he secures the crown for himself. Despite his remark about the improbabilities in the original story, Murphy must have felt that it offered opportunities for the kind of "strong situations" that he relished; perhaps, since he admired Tate's version of *King Lear,* he also considered the "happy ending" an advantage. At any rate, he was sure that if Shakespeare had used this conclusion for his play he could have composed "the finest Scenes of Terror in the last Act that ever have been imagined: and then a Subject that opens so nobly would have been grand also in the Close."[21]

DAVID GARRICK, of course, did not stop with suggestions for improving the plot of *Hamlet.* In his famous alteration he attempted to remove the supposed blemishes by rewriting the conclusion of the play. The fact that this alteration was made late in his career, after repeated personal triumphs in Shakespeare's *Hamlet,* makes it likely that his motives were, to some degree,

19. Dibdin, however, conceded that Voltaire was right about the Gravediggers. (*Complete History of the Stage,* III, 55, 64-65.)

20. *Dramatic Censor,* I, 32.

21. "The Theatre," February 15-17, 1757.

unselfish. Garrick's Shakespeare-worship may have been partly histrionic, but he seems to have had a sincere desire to spread the Shakespeare gospel: his letters hint of spirited arguments with several of his French friends, people of literary taste who were convinced that Shakespeare's glories were mixed with barbarous absurdities; and when he received an invitation to visit Voltaire he even entertained the hope of "converting" that famous infidel.[22] In England, too, he was told of *Hamlet's* imperfections by influential friends like George Steevens and John Hoadly. (Both of these men encouraged Garrick in his "improvement" of *Hamlet,* and the latter even wrote, after reading a brief account of the alteration, that he was afraid the changes were not radical enough.[23]) Sensitive to such criticisms, Garrick probably made his adaptation not only to demonstrate his own good taste but also to redeem the reputation of Shakespeare by displaying his most famous drama in a form that even rigorous critics could admire.

In his revision Garrick eliminated the Gravediggers and Osric, thereby reducing the "indecorous" comic material. He also eliminated the Claudius-Laertes plot against Hamlet's life, perhaps to remove the stigma of low trickery from a king and a "very noble youth," as well as to provide a more dignified death for Claudius and a more direct, less accidental revenge for Hamlet. In Garrick's version Hamlet does not embark for England but somehow eludes his "keepers" and returns abruptly without explaining his escape (he is thus saved from the guilt of causing death for his school fellows) ; he rebukes Laertes' ranting grief over Ophelia's madness (there is no grave scene, no specific report of Ophelia's death), and Laertes prepares to attack him. The King calls the guards to carry Hamlet off to punishment. Hamlet

22. See the following letters in *The Letters of David Garrick,* ed. David M. Little and George M. Kahrl (Cambridge, Mass., 1963), II: to Voltaire (p. 428); to Jean Baptiste Antoine Suard (pp. 463, 523-24); and to the Abbé André Morellet (p. 730). The visit to Voltaire did not take place, but Garrick sent him a copy of his Jubilee Ode in praise of Shakespeare (see p. 669). Garrick was also among the "defenders" of Shakespeare against French criticism at home: for example, in his ironic "Attack on Shakespeare Worship," which he devised for the Shakespeare Jubilee of 1769. Descriptions of this act are given by Percy Fitzgerald in his *Life of David Garrick* (London, 1899), p. 334; by Martha Winburn England in *Garrick's Jubilee* (Columbus, Ohio, 1964), pp. 56-57; and by Christian Deelman, *The Great Shakespeare Jubilee* (New York, 1964), pp. 228-31. The MS text of the "Attack" is in the Folger Library.

23. *Private Correspondence of Garrick,* ed. Boaden, I, 451-52, 453 (Steevens); 515 (Hoadly).

turns on the King and stabs him to death. (Following a suggestion that Steevens had made,[24] Garrick evidently had Claudius defend himself manfully against Hamlet's attack and die fighting.[25]) Laertes then fatally wounds Hamlet, who does not retaliate but forgives him and asks him to join hands with his friend Horatio. The play ends with Hamlet's death and Horatio's "flights of angels" speech. Garrick's alteration, ridiculous as it is in its drastic changes, is not without some positive merits. For, as George Winchester Stone points out, the wholesale cutting of the last act is counterbalanced by the restoration of many lines and some whole speeches in the earlier portions of the play which had been customarily omitted in stage performance. Notable among these are the soliloquy "How all occasions do inform against me" (though the last line is eliminated in favor of this conclusion: "My thoughts be bloody all!—The hour is come—I'll fly my Keepers—sweep to my revenge) and Hamlet's soliloquy in the prayer scene (previously cut by Garrick himself). Restorations are made, too, in the speeches of other characters, particularly Polonius and Claudius.[26]

Although Garrick was elated by his success in the altered *Hamlet*—despite the Galleries' fondness for the Gravediggers, he reported to a French friend, he had won more applause than "at five & twenty"[27]—he evidently had serious misgivings. "It was the most imprudent thing I ever did in my life," he confided to Sir William Young, "but I had sworn I would not leave the stage till I had rescued that noble play from all the rubbish of the

24. *Ibid.*, I, 452.
25. In the MS there is no stage direction for the King's self-defense, but Davies' comments (among others) make it clear that this business was used on the stage. See *Dramatic Miscellanies*, III, 145-47.
26. George Winchester Stone, "Garrick's Long-Lost Alteration of *Hamlet*," *PMLA*, XLIX (1934), 897-900.
27. To the Abbé André Morellet, *Letters of Garrick*, ed. Little and Kahrl, II, 845-46. The MS letter is in the Folger Library. It is dated December 4, 1773, but Little and Kahrl have shown (p. 842, n. 1) that the correct date is January 4, 1773. Davies (*Dramatic Miscellanies*, III, 145) says that the public received the alteration out of respect for Garrick during his lifetime but "they did not approve what they barely endured" and "soon called for Hamlet as it had been acted from time immemorial." But Stone has shown that Garrick's version held the stage for eight years, was acted more times than the old version had been during the preceding eight-year period, and brought in more box office receipts than almost any other play. ("Garrick's Long-Lost Alteration of *Hamlet*," pp. 893-94.)

fifth act."[28] Was this mere effrontery, or was it a kind of whistling in the dark? The latter, probably, for Garrick, though an egotist, was no fool; nor was he unaware of the values to be derived from humorous or ironic touches in tragedy. Like Huck Finn, he was plagued by a double conscience, accepting as right and proper what his feelings and personal experience at once rejected. Garrick never published his alteration of *Hamlet*—very likely for the reason Stone suggests: that after Voltaire's renewed attack on Shakespeare (in his *Letter to the Academy*, 1776) such a publication would have made Garrick appear "recreant to the English and Shakespearian cause."[29]

In the theatre Garrick's alteration was such news that other actors were no doubt eager to get hold of it in order to capitalize on its notoriety. When Garrick refused to lend his copy, TATE WILKINSON composed his own version for the theatre at York; and there must have been other imitations as well.[30] But the long-range views of theatre-trained men were probably well represented by the comments of our old acquaintances Francis Gentleman, Arthur Murphy, and Thomas Davies. In the *Bell Shakespeare*, published while the alteration was still a fresh topic of discussion, Gentleman expressed concern because Garrick had "politely frenchified his alteration by endeavouring to annihilate what, though Mr. Voltaire could not like it, has indubitable merit." He objected to the omission of the Gravediggers (as Murphy was to do years later in his biography of Garrick), maintaining that their dialogue, though often "stigmatised as mere gallery stuff," is capable of pleasing "sensible boxes" as well.[31]

28. *Letters of Garrick,* ed. Little and Kahrl, II, 845-46. Letter dated January 10, 1773.

29. "Garrick's Long-Lost Alteration of *Hamlet,*" p. 902. Stone notes that Garrick admittedly bowed to French criticism in omitting the Gravediggers and Osric, that French critics, including Voltaire, were pleased by his alteration, but that after Voltaire's *Letter* of 1776 Garrick's personal letters show much anger and impatience with the French misunderstanding of Shakespeare. (See pp. 900-902.) Whatever the mutual influence between literary criticism and Garrick's alteration, Paul Conklin is undoubtedly correct in his assertion that Garrick's greatest influence on criticism came through his powerful acting of Hamlet. See his *History of Hamlet Criticism 1601-1821* (New York, 1947), pp. 42-43.

30. Tate Wilkinson, *The Wandering Patentee* (York, 1795), I, 166-73. G. C. D. Odell, in *Shakespeare from Betterton to Irving* (New York, 1920), I, 389-90, gives an account of radical German alterations of *Hamlet,* with "happy" endings and of Jean François Ducis' French adaptation, also with a victorious Hamlet.

31. *Bell Shakespeare,* III, *Hamlet,* p. 71.

Murphy, returning to his own earlier criticism of *Hamlet*'s conclusion, remarked that if Garrick had wished to do a real service
he would have confined his pruning to the fencing scene and
would have "added from his own invention something of real
importance to bring about a noble catastrophe."[32] Davies, less
impressed by neoclassical criticism of *Hamlet* than any of his
fellow actor-critics, was not impressed, either, by Garrick's alteration: Shakespeare's first act, which moves with "wonderful
rapidity," should not have been divided into two, Davies wrote;
the speech relating Ophelia's death should not have been omitted,
nor should the fate of the Queen have been left uncertain; Garrick was at fault, too, in allowing Claudius a dignified and manly
death, thus spoiling the characterization that Shakespeare intended.[33] Although none of these men objected to the idea of
alteration *per se*, perhaps, like Charles Dibdin, they believed that
in the case of *Hamlet* "the prodigious variety of characters and
incidents . . . produced in such rapid succession" makes it "difficult to lay a finger upon a fault without expunging a beauty."[34]

The actor-critics of the nineteenth century lived in a very
different critical environment from that of their predecessors.
By the time WILLIAM OXBERRY[35] was writing his introduction to
Hamlet for the *New English Drama* (1818) the romantic critics
like Coleridge and Hazlitt had replaced in popular esteem the

32. *Life of Garrick*, II, 83-84. Murphy wrote an amusing satire on Garrick's
alteration in the form of a parody of several scenes in the first act of *Hamlet*, which
he entitled "Hamlet, with Alterations; A Tragedy in Three Acts." It was not
published during his lifetime, but Jesse Foot included it in his *Life of Arthur
Murphy, Esq.* (London, 1811), pp. 256-74. In it the Ghost of Shakespeare appears
on the stage at Drury Lane and chides Garrick for his alteration of *Hamlet*, ad-
monishing him: "Attempt no more, nor let your soul conceive / Aught 'gainst my
other plays. . . ." After the Ghost leaves, however, Garrick reports that Shakespeare
is pleased with his alteration and wishes him to alter all the other plays. The
concluding lines are: "His plays are out of joint—*O cursed spite! /That ever I was
born to set them right!*" Murphy was frequently piqued with Garrick and the
parody probably reflects some personal spite. The tone of his criticism in his
Life of Garrick, however, seems judicious and objective.

33. *Dramatic Miscellanies*, III, 145-47.

34. *Complete History of the Stage*, III, 64-65. Dibdin's remarks make no specific
reference to Garrick's alteration—and they were published twenty years after
Garrick's death. But they are not without relevance, I think. Dibdin was at any
rate personally acquainted with Garrick's version of *Hamlet*, for he had been at
Drury Lane when it was first produced.

35. All comments by Oxberry in the next few paragraphs are from *The New
English Drama* (London, 1818-24), III, *Hamlet*, xxvi-xxviii.

once-venerated neoclassicists; and when SHERIDAN KNOWLES[36] was giving his lectures on the drama (at intervals between 1820 and 1850) Shakespeare worship was at high tide. Critics had ceased to speak of "judicious alterations," for purity of text was the professed ideal. The actor-critics could speak the language of their time: Oxberry, for example, lost no chance to condemn Samuel Johnson (whom he mistakenly considered a pedantic devotee of the "rules"), and he gave qualified praise to Hazlitt. Yet, whatever the attitude of their literary contemporaries, these men continued to point out some of the same flaws in *Hamlet* that had been mentioned in the earlier period. If their criticisms seem more original, it is not always because the basic ideas are different, but because the explanations are more concrete and detailed.

For example, in discussing the unusual length and fullness of the play, Oxberry explains that this is a problem mainly because of the unevenness of acting talent: since the actors available for the lesser roles cannot project their lines effectively, some of the secondary material must be cut to prevent the audience from becoming bored. Oxberry interestingly traces the relative slowness of the play's progression to the character of Hamlet himself; for, according to him, despite the "well-contrived and interesting incidents, which follow each other with wonderful celerity," Hamlet's "uncertainty and irresolution seem to make the story always beginning, and never ending." Knowles, too, graphically describes this peculiarity of *Hamlet*'s construction:

The power of this play is rather the effect of isolated parts than of a continuous whole. . . . From the last scene of the first act . . . the arm of . . . filial vengeance may be said to be raised and to be kept suspended, without making an attempt to strike the blow, until it accidentally descends in the closet scene. . . .

Oxberry does part company with earlier actor-critics in defending the much-discussed conclusion of *Hamlet*: Shakespeare knew, he says, that the most important events in real life are often effected by less-than-lofty means; the kind of conclusion called for by the critics would be too contrived. Knowles, however, reiterates the old objection to the "catastrophe," explaining that the death of the King "is perfectly accidental, and is rather an atonement for

36. All comments by Knowles in the next few paragraphs are from *Lectures on Dramatic Literature Delivered . . . during the Years 1820-1850*, ed. Francis Harvey (London, 1873), pp. 93-94.

the murder of Hamlet and the queen, than for that of Hamlet's father."

Such continued dissatisfaction with the conclusion of the play must have led to GEORGE VANDENHOFF's Garrick-like (but probably abortive) attempt at alteration. Vandenhoff's contemplated ending was a "happy" one: Garrick had saved the lives of Ophelia, Laertes, Rosencrantz and Guildenstern, but Vandenhoff went even further and saved Hamlet. Garrick had dispensed with Shakespeare's fifth act; Vandenhoff was prepared to sacrifice the fourth as well. The "Suggested Ter[mination]," handwritten in his promptbook of *Hamlet*, consists of one short scene designed to follow the closet scene. It begins at Hamlet's words about the Ghost: "Look where it goes, even now, out at the portal." At this point Gertrude shrieks aloud, and Claudius comes to see what the commotion is about. Hamlet stabs him. When the guard and the courtiers rush in with cries of "Treason!" Hamlet asks Horatio to justify his action to the crowd. Horatio does so, and the play ends with "Hail Hamlet!—Hail king of Denmark!"[37] I have not found any account of a performance in which this ending was used (the same promptbook includes manuscript directions for the fencing match) ; but the very existence of such a plan at the mid-century when purity of text was the watchword is testimony to the long-lived criticism of Shakespeare's plot.

Like most of Garrick's theatrical colleagues, however, the actor-critics of the nineteenth century were quick to justify the graveyard scene. EDMUND KEAN "declared himself unable to account" for Garrick's omission, "as he conceived Hamlet's recollections of Yorick, and indeed the whole scene, one of the most impressive, and one which, with all auditors, is the best recollected of the play."[38] William Oxberry admitted that the excessive clowning practiced by some Gravediggers is a burlesque on Shakespeare's intentions; but, correctly interpreted, he thought, the Gravediggers' callousness, Hamlet's "feverish sensitiveness," and

37. The promptbook is in the Folger Library. It is Vandenhoff's personal copy of *Shakespeare's Hamlet Prince of Denmark, A Tragedy; Revised by J. P. Kemble* (London, 1814). Vandenhoff has written in ink the 1853 cast of *Hamlet* at the Haymarket, with himself as Hamlet. He has made many manuscript annotations, including instructions for music, a plot (verbal, not diagram) of the fencing match, additions of lines from Shakespeare's text omitted by Kemble, etc.

38. William Wood, *Personal Recollections of the Stage* (Philadelphia, 1855), pp. 382-83.

Horatio's philosophic calm unite in a meaningful pattern of contrasts skillfully contrived and powerfully executed.[39] The most interesting justification—that of Sheridan Knowles—is also an interpretation of the scene. Although recognizably akin to the moralizing comments by eighteenth century critics, it goes beyond these in significance not only because it is more imaginatively expressed but also because it suggests a thematic relevance to the play as a whole. The humor of the scene, wrote Knowles, is far from the "downright farce" of which many have complained, for it is "chequer[ed] and chasten[ed]" with "glancing thoughts" of a more serious cast. This scene depicts the "insensibility and blindness of humanity to our most affecting predicament"—the gravedigger nonchalantly tossing earth out of the grave that may soon be his own. It speaks to us, too, of "the inevitable doom of mirth and wit themselves" and of the "fate of all that is exquisite," the lovely Ophelia "reduced by the all-leveling hand of death to the topic of an argument between two clowns." Thus the Gravedigger's "carol, and his dialogue with his man, and . . . with Hamlet" ironically prepare the "ear" of the audience for the tolling of Ophelia's knell.[40]

Actors' criticisms of *Hamlet*'s plot in recent years have revealed much less concern for structure in the conventional sense than did those of past centuries. Subtler elements in Shakespeare's design—parallels, ironies, imagery patterns—have occupied the writer's attention more often than dramatic progression, tragic decorum, or catastrophe. This trend is in line with criticism in general, of course, but it does not follow that the actors' discussions are purely imitative. SIR JOHN GIELGUD's comments on "double suggestion" in *Hamlet*, published in 1937, showed considerable originality at that time, and the insights they offer into Shakespeare's dramatic artistry are still valid and interesting. For example:

39. *The New English Drama*, III, *Hamlet*, xxv. Oxberry alludes to the farcical stage business, current at that time, of the First Gravedigger's shedding one waistcoat after another during the scene. *See* Arthur Colby Sprague, *Shakespeare and the Actors* (Cambridge, Mass., 1948), pp. 175-76. Sprague thinks that this business was of fairly late origin. The first reference to it that he has found is in a record of a provincial performance in 1780. He conjectures that it had reached the London theatres by 1800. This stage treatment, rather than any vestiges of devotion to the neoclassical principle of decorum, probably accounts for the continued protests against the graveyard scene to which the actor-critics refer in their "defenses."

40. *Lectures on Dramatic Literature*, pp. 137-40.

[Shakespeare] invites an audience to watch an actor pretending to be a Prince apparently weeping real tears for his father, and a few scenes later he shows them the same actor being impressed by the mimic tears of another actor weeping for Priam's slaughter. . . . He asks them to mock at the damnable faces of Lucianus and the next instant to be thrilled by the terror of the King; to grieve with Laertes at his sister's grave, and yet to sneer . . . at the violent ranting of the two young men. The effect of contrast is echoed in the characters them-selves—in the two sons avenging their fathers, the two princes waiting for their kingdoms. . . .

Gielgud also suggests ways in which Shakespeare's parallel effects may be pointed up in action: for example, the irony of Gertrude's death (by poison, the same agent that killed her husband) can be emphasized by having Claudius carry the poison in a ring and empty it into the cup in sight of the audience.[41]

But even the most modern of actor-critics have not been solely concerned with matters like these. Occasionally they have re-turned to questions of a more traditional kind. For example: What is the climactic scene in the play? The prayer scene is HARLEY GRANVILLE-BARKER's answer: the rest of the play depends upon it, for the result of inaction here is holocaust.[42] Gielgud disagrees: "The following scene, and the killing of Polonius is to me, as an actor, the climax of Hamlet's long inaction. The whole of the subsequent tragedy springs from this later moment. Besides, it is this physical act that seems to break the spell of doubt in Hamlet's mind and unloose his stream of repressed anguish and revenge."[43] ROBERT SPEAIGHT is halfway between these two opinions: the closet scene is the emotional, though not the theatrical, climax of *Hamlet.*[44]

Another point of a traditional kind—the irregularities in Shakespeare's design—is noticed by Granville-Barker but not in the old, mainly negative way. His question is always: How does each peculiarity serve Shakespeare's dramatic purpose? A good example of the criticism reflecting this attitude is his discussion of the purposeful variations of time in *Hamlet.* It is interesting to notice that he ties the irregularity of plot movement to the

41. *John Gielgud's Hamlet,* ed. Rosamond Gilder (New York and Toronto, 1937), pp. 57, 71. For additional discussions of verbal echoes and parallel stage effects see pp. 52, 59-60.

42. *Prefaces to Shakespeare,* I, 99.

43. *John Gielgud's Hamlet,* ed. Gilder, p. 62.

44. Robert Speaight, *Nature in Shakespearian Tragedy* (London, 1955), p. 36.

character of Hamlet, just as Oxberry did a century earlier.[45] His explanation is fuller than Oxberry's, however, and it carries no hint of theatrical inexpediency. Granville-Barker points out, for example, that the second scene of Act II (from the "fish-monger" encounter with Polonius through "O what a rogue"), though the longest in the play, does little to advance the main action. But its dramatic significance is its very irrelevance; for Shakespeare was faced here with the problem of dramatizing the lethargy and frustration that have overtaken Hamlet himself. The passionate soliloquy at the end of the scene "recharges the action to the full . . . and restores to us the Hamlet bent on his revenge."[46] Gielgud recalls that he had never noticed this significant truth until he read Granville-Barker's essay.

I was greatly helped by his remarks, forcing myself to decide on certain definite moments . . . in which Hamlet must remember his mission of vengeance and is shocked to find how easily he has been forgetting it. Yet, though I tried to make these moments clear in my by-play . . . there is so much else to watch and to listen to . . . that this point, so very important to the actor playing Hamlet, does not greatly matter to the spectator.[47]

The most surprising tie between past and present actor-critics of *Hamlet* is that which links Garrick's alteration of 1772 with MAURICE EVANS' "G.I." production of 1944. After rigorous cutting of the text, Evans found that the playing time was still fifteen minutes longer than the period available for the soldiers' entertainment. When he discovered that Garrick had omitted the graveyard scene, he was "emboldened to follow his example"; and, after adopting the omission for the sake of expediency, he decided that "the story-line is stronger and the climax more poignant without it." In his opinion the scene—probably inserted by Shakespeare as an afterthought for the sake of the low comedian—puts a blight on the character of Horatio (he must "heartlessly" allow Hamlet to joke with the Gravedigger, though he "knows full well for whom the grave is being prepared") and it presents acting

45. Granville-Barker considers the structure of *Hamlet* in three "movements" rather than in the conventional five acts. For his analysis of Shakespeare's treatment of time in each movement—precisely at some points, vaguely at others—and for his similar discussion of Shakespeare's special "unity of place" in this play, see *Prefaces to Shakespeare*, I, 38-43.

46. *Ibid.*, pp. 69-75.

47. *John Gielgud's Hamlet*, ed. Gilder, p. 52.

difficulties for Hamlet, who must make an abrupt transition from its "wild hysteria" to the "light banter" of the following scene.[48] Of Evans' concern for the character of Horatio one can only remark, "Consider it not so deeply." For the rest, perhaps we need not wonder at the cheerful sacrifice of the graveyard scene by a resolute opponent of the "Gloomy Dane" tradition. It is ironic that the cover of the *Laurel Shakespeare* edition of *Hamlet,* in which Evans' comments appear, is decorated with that favorite pose of the Gloomy Danes—Hamlet holding the skull of Yorick.

Discussions of Theatrical Effectiveness

Was it the B-26 which, theoretically, could not fly? If a pilot, after a number of successful missions in this aircraft, were to enumerate the characteristics that were supposed to make flight impossible, he would be a little like the actors who have conscientiously listed the flaws in the plot of *Hamlet;* for several of these actor-critics have gone on with the next stroke of the pen to testify to its effectiveness on the stage. For example, FRANCIS GENTLEMAN asserts paradoxically that "no play can afford more entertainment on the stage, or improvement in the closet, tho' abounding with superfluities and inconsistencies."[49] And SHERIDAN KNOWLES ends his discussion of the imperfections in the structure of *Hamlet* with these words: "Yet what is the effect of every scene in this play? Successively to arouse, to amaze, to appal, to melt, to awaken every chord of the human heart into thrilling, exquisite vibration."[50]

Actor-critics have suggested several reasons for *Hamlet*'s popularity in the theatre. The most frequently mentioned is the character of Hamlet himself—"not only the chief, but the sole support" of the play, in Gentleman's opinion, and "furnished with excellent materials for that purpose."[51] WILLIAM WOOD, an American actor-manager of the nineteenth century, came to the same conclusion: the other characters and their affairs are only "moderately" affecting, but the hero arouses such "deep and concentrated interest" that a larger number of bad actors have

48. *Maurice Evans' G.I. Production of* Hamlet *by William Shakespeare* (Garden City, New York, 1947), pp. 9-13; "Comments on Playing the Role of Hamlet," *Hamlet. The Laurel Shakespeare* (New York, 1958), p. 24.
49. *Dramatic Censor,* I, 37.
50. *Lectures on Dramatic Literature,* pp. 93-94.
51. *Bell Shakespeare,* III, *Hamlet,* p. 3.

been "patiently endured" in this play than in any other.[52] The foolproof qualities of this role have been repeatedly proclaimed by other actors—by WILLIAM CHARLES MACREADY,[53] for example, and, in recent times, by SIR JOHN GIELGUD.[54] And the universality of the character has been praised as often. BEERBOHM TREE's remark is typical: "It is because Hamlet is eternally human that the play retains its lasting hold on our sympathies."[55] Another reason suggested for *Hamlet*'s effectiveness is that Shakespeare gives in this drama an unusually dazzling display of theatrical technique. As OTIS SKINNER put it, "Scarcely a device of the theatre has been left out. . . . HAMLET was written by one who had as great command of the tricks of dramatic construction as David Belasco" (this in 1924 when Belasco's name was synonymous with show business).[56] And JULIA MARLOWE, elated by the attention that she and her husband had received from a "silent and enthralled" audience of five thousand school children, remembered that, after all, Shakespeare had written, in part, for the groundlings and that *Hamlet* is sufficiently exciting in its action alone to "engage the attention of a deaf man."[57] On the other hand, Beerbohm Tree attributed *Hamlet*'s appeal less to overt action than to its air of mystery and its rich suggestiveness, which allows both actor and spectator many "opportunities of weaving round the work of the poet the embroidery of [their] own imagination."[58] Finally, SIR TYRONE GUTHRIE surprises the layman by asserting that *Hamlet*, "for all its great length, complexity and profundity, is one of the most easily produced of Shakespeare's plays." He explains that most of its scenes involve only a few characters, that its big ensembles are short, and that the actor of Hamlet does not depend on his colleagues for effectiveness since his most revealing speeches are spoken directly to the audience.[59]

52. *Personal Recollections of the Stage*, p. 318.

53. *Macready's Reminiscences and Selections from His Diaries*, ed. Sir Frederick Pollock (New York, 1875), pp. 36, 164.

54. *John Gielgud's Hamlet*, ed. Gilder, pp. 50-51. See also *Stage Directions* (New York, [1964]), p. 57. According to Gielgud, *Hamlet*'s easy theatrical effectiveness is not always an advantage.

55. Herbert Beerbohm Tree, *Thoughts and Afterthoughts* (London and New York, 1913), p. 124.

56. Otis Skinner, *Footlights and Spotlights* (Indianapolis, 1924), p. 239.

57. E. H. Sothern, *Julia Marlowe's Story*, ed. Fairfax Downey (New York, 1954), pp. 195-96.

58. *Thoughts and Afterthoughts*, p. 107.

59. *Shakespeare: Ten Great Plays. With an Introduction and Commentaries*

Hamlet is obviously an excellent example of the discrepancy that may exist between theory and practice in the realm of theatrical effectiveness. This is true not only of the play as a whole but of individual scenes as well. And it is true in various ways.

One scene which has been singled out for praise by actors of all periods (the first scene in the play) is apparently difficult to stage so as to realize its potentialities. THOMAS DAVIES, who says that the whole first act of *Hamlet* "may challenge a preference" to that of "any tragedy, ancient or modern," explains the excellence of the first scene as any good manual for playwrights might do: Shakespeare artfully arouses the audience's expectation through the sentinels' talk of the apparition; he "fixes attention, and raises the admiration" through Horatio's "pathetic address" to the Ghost; and he judiciously keeps the Ghost silent in the first scene so that there will be no lessening of curiosity and terror before Hamlet's climactic interview with his father's spirit.[60] THOMAS HOLCROFT cannot remember any other drama except *Macbeth* "in which the grand subject of the play is so finely opened, or so deeply impressed, as in *Hamlet*."[61] And ROBERT SPEAIGHT agrees that Shakespeare never achieved a more masterly opening than in this play.[62] Yet Holcroft warns that actors are generally not careful enough to produce the atmosphere of awe and suspense necessary to the effectiveness of this scene and indeed of the supernatural element as a whole. Sir John Gielgud lists several hindrances to effective presentation besides inferior acting: the darkened stage, the unconvincing visual scene (usually a drop cloth to allow a hasty change or a permanent set in deep shadow), and the distraction created by late-comers in the audience. Only once in his experience, Gielgud wrote in 1937, had this scene been done as effectively as it should be—in a German production with Alexander Moissi (London, 1929).[63]

On the other hand, the scene of the fencing match, which has

by Sir Tyrone Guthrie (New York, [1962]), p. 288. See also *A Life in the Theatre* (New York, 1959), p. 65.

60. *Dramatic Miscellanies*, III, 23-24.
61. *Theatrical Recorder*, II, 135-36.
62. *Nature in Shakespearian Tragedy*, p. 11.
63. *John Gielgud's Hamlet*, ed. Gilder, pp. 34-35. George Skillan offers detailed suggestions aimed at making this scene effective. See his commentaries in *Hamlet . . . French's Acting Edition* (London, 1964), pp. 79-81.

been repeatedly described as "weak," has had dramatic possibilities discovered in it by at least one leading actor. According to SEYMOUR HICKS, the acting of this scene is usually much too perfunctory: the match is fought like "an academy contest presumably for no other purpose that that the victor might claim a silver-plated loving cup for the family side-board." But, as HENRY IRVING pointed out, the actors should remember that the real drama must lie in the tension generated by "the attitude of the conspirators, fearful that their plans would not materialize owing to the unexpected brilliance of the Royal adversary."[64]

Changes in social customs and modes of thought are reflected in the varying effectiveness of certain key speeches and at least one key scene. In 1937 Gielgud reported that neither Hamlet's soliloquy on the way to his mother's room (in which he must suppress thoughts of matricide) nor the following one in the prayer scene would "go" with a modern audience, perhaps because of being "too frankly Elizabethan in feeling."[65] Yet they seemed particularly appropriate to Richard Burton's sardonic Hamlet when Gielgud directed the play in 1964—perhaps because the "modern" audience had by then become accustomed to a literature of cruelty.

Hamlet has a succession of great scenes in which theory and practice have apparently gone hand in hand: expectation has been consistently high and consistently justified, regardless of acting styles and audience taste. Warm testimony to their effectiveness is found in actors' vivid descriptions of these scenes as interpreted by the giants among their colleagues—of the Ghost scene as acted by Betterton and Garrick, the nunnery scene by Kean, the Court scene by Booth and Irving. (Even here, there are shifts in emphasis, of course.) Yet in some cases these staples of public consumption have been prepared for years according to a recipe for effectiveness which—if Elizabethan principles of staging are accepted—was guaranteed to kill their distinctive flavor. The passionate soliloquy "O what a rogue" offers excellent opportunities for the actor; and its famous rhyme, "The play's the thing/ Wherein I'll catch the conscience of the King," makes an exciting conclusion for Act II—especially when accompanied, or followed, by some dramatic piece of business such as Irving's

64. Sir Edward Seymour Hicks, *Hail Fellow Well Met* (London, [1949]), pp. 58-59.
65. *John Gielgud's Hamlet*, ed. Gilder, p. 59.

seizing his tables and beginning "to write, hysterically . . . the speech . . . that was to convert 'The Murder of Gonzago' into 'The Mousetrap.' "[66] But what if continuous acting is used, and no curtain comes down? At the end of the soliloquy Hamlet rushes out, only to return after fifty lines or so, completely changed in mood, with "To be or not to be. . . ." GRANVILLE-BARKER calls attention to the effect of "surprise and contrast" which results when the emotion-torn Hamlet whom we saw so recently now appears "calm and self-contained." "These unmodulated changes from storm to calm smack a little—and are meant to—of 'madness.' " Yet Hamlet's "moral quality shows in the fact that he can thus escape from his suffering to this stoically detached contemplation of greater issues."[67] Sir John Gielgud and SIR ALEC GUINNESS have agreed that the effectiveness is increased when there is no act break between the two soliloquies. Gielgud comments: "the effect of despondency in 'To be, or not to be' is a natural and brilliant psychological reaction from the violent and hopeless rage of the earlier speech."[68] And Guinness writes that, in his opinion, the one real success that he achieved in his 1951 production of *Hamlet* resulted from his eliminating the act-break after "O what a rogue."

If the curtain is dropped at the end of that particular speech, the audience expects, and rightly, some startling theatrical effect. (When I played the part in 1938, I squatted on the stage like a gnome, tapping a drum. It didn't mean a thing, but it was an effect, and the curtain could safely come down.)

If the audience is deprived of this gaudy nonsense, what do they get in its place? They get "To be or not to be" within a minute and a half, followed by the "nunnery" scene, followed by the social ease of "Speak the speech"—in fact they get the greater part of Hamlet's character stripped bare before them—and all in the space of about fifteen minutes.[69]

66. Sprague, *Shakespeare and the Actors*, p. 150. Wood tells us (in *Personal Recollections*, p. 202) that J. P. Kemble omitted "O what a rogue" because his frequent attacks of asthma left him with insufficient breath for it and that other actors imitated him, even though they had no such disabilities, "till it became an almost universal practice, nay numerous acting editions were published wholly omitting this splendid and characteristic soliloquy." Kemble did not always omit it, however, at least not all of it. See *Shakespeare and the Actors*, p. 149, for a description of his "flourish" which accompanied the concluding couplet.

67. *Prefaces to Shakespeare*, I, 77-78.

68. *John Gielgud's Hamlet*, ed. Gilder, pp. 54-55.

69. Alec Guinness, "My Idea of Hamlet," *The Spectator*, CLXXXVII (July 6, 1951), 8.

Finally, there have been schisms between theory and practice in the realm of critical analysis. For occasionally an intellectually convincing theory regarding the meaning of a scene has proved incapable of being translated clearly and effectively into action. J. Dover Wilson's *What Happens in Hamlet*—one of the most interesting of the many studies of *Hamlet* to modern actors— provides examples of such theories as well as of some that have proved viable in the theatre. Particularly well known is Wilson's idea that Claudius does not see the dumb show because he is engaged in a whispered conversation with Polonius.[70] This suggestion has been rejected by several actor-critics: Granville-Barker, Gielgud, and Speaight (all three of whom, however, have accepted Wilson's Privy Council theory for the second scene of the first act).[71] Granville-Barker interprets the scene thus: When Claudius sees the pantomimic poisoning he is wary and alert but ostensibly unmoved; Hamlet, on the other hand, is quivering with excitement as by his mocking he tries to "pierce that admirable composure." Claudius' self-possession could not have been shaken by a single blow. "It is the long preliminary ordeal which is to wear him down." The moment when he breaks and everything goes into confusion is "simply the culmination of a long, tense, deliberate struggle" of the wills between the two men.[72] Speaight declares: "It is necessary for Hamlet, and supremely necessary for the audience, that all eyes—especially Claudius's—shall be fixed on the play. Unless Hamlet's eyes are on the King and the King's are on the performance, the electric current is interrupted."[73] Gielgud, though he finds Wilson's suggestions "fascinating," does not feel that "the scene itself would gain" if they were carried out "to the letter." He adds, however: "Well or badly played,

70. For an explanation of the theory *see* John Dover Wilson, *What Happens in Hamlet* (Cambridge, 1951), pp. 144-63.

71. Wilson's discussion of the "Privy Council" scene is on pp. 28-29 of *What Happens in Hamlet*. Gielgud, although he agrees with the interpretation, points out that the traditional staging—as a full Court scene, set in the throne room— gives a theatrical advantage that the Privy Council treatment does not. Granville-Barker's discussion is in *Prefaces to Shakespeare*, I, 49-52; and Speaight's comments are in *Nature in Shakespearian Tragedy*, p. 13.

72. *Prefaces to Shakespeare*, I, 85-88.

73. *Nature in Shakespearian Tragedy*, pp. 32-33. Speaight says that Michael Macowan told him that when he tried to produce this scene according to Wilson's theories it failed to function dramatically.

well or badly cut, this scene has been and always will be one of the most exciting ever invented."[74]

Obviously such gaps between the idea of stage effectiveness and the proved actuality can and do occur in connection with Shakespeare's other plays (and with those of other dramatists as well), but, judging by the actors' criticisms, they have been particularly noticeable in *Hamlet*.

Criticisms of Language

For the actor-critics, to mention the language of *Hamlet* has been to praise it—but not always for the same qualities.

Among the earlier writers, THOMAS DAVIES is the most emphatic and also the most circumstantial in his praise. He admires the dialogue of *Hamlet* for its brilliant wit, its idiomatic ease, its frequent profundity of thought, its "just and poignant satire." And he contemptuously dismisses Voltaire's objection to such "low" expressions as "Not a mouse stirring": "Men of solid judgment and true taste despise such refinement."[75] Davies' enthusiasm for the soliloquies (for their "warmth and energy" as well as their psychological and dramatic qualities)[76] is shared by CHARLES DIBDIN, who calls them the finest parts of all Shakespeare's writing,[77] and by ARTHUR MURPHY, who declares that they have never been equalled by any other writer.[78]

WILLIAM OXBERRY, of the romantic period, found in *Hamlet* a certain didacticism of language combined with lofty, flowing, and melodious verse; there is less compactness and energy than in *King Lear,* he thought, and more purely poetic expression.[79] It is interesting that Davies chose to emphasize energy of expression in *Hamlet* and that less than forty years later Oxberry was commenting on the relative lack of energy. Too much should not be made of this point, perhaps; even contemporaries might have differed in judgment, and, in any case, Davies was writing particularly of Hamlet's soliloquies whereas Oxberry was describing the language and verse of the play in general. Yet it is hard to get away from Hamlet himself in discussing any aspect of the play, and

74. *John Gielgud's Hamlet,* ed. Gilder, p. 57.
75. *Dramatic Miscellanies,* III, 6-7, 147-48.
76. *Memoirs of the Life of David Garrick* (Boston, 1818), I, 54.
77. *Complete History of the Stage,* III, 59.
78. *Life of Garrick,* I, 48.
79. *New English Drama,* III, *Hamlet,* xxviii.

the opposite conceptions of this character held by Davies and Oxberry are in harmony with their differing descriptions of the
speech.

Recent actor-critics have revealed almost as great a difference
from their predecessors in discussing the language of *Hamlet* as
in discussing the plot, and again there is some similarity to nontheatrical critics. For example, HARLEY GRANVILLE-BARKER analyzes the language minutely and extensively rather than (as earlier
actor-critics did) merely naming its most striking qualities; and
in his discussion of imagery he is obviously indebted to Caroline
Spurgeon (as who is not?). He points out three prominent series
of images: weeds, flowers, and forms of corruption such as garbage
and dead carcasses. Although he questions whether the related
images are noticeable to an audience since they are spaced throughout the play, he concludes that they probably produce a subconscious effect, if nothing more. The rest of Granville-Barker's discussion is more completely his own: for example, his analyses of
Shakespeare's word choices, focusing on the contributions to mood
and meaning made by certain vowel and consonant sounds, and
his consideration of the dramatic effects gained by the use of
prose or verse for particular passages. Perhaps his most interesting criticism of language is a detailed demonstration of the
way in which the sound of speech is suited to each character and
helps to reveal him.[80]

There is one actor, however—RICHARD BURTON—whose remarks
suggest no critical indebtedness at all. He is deliberately puckish
and irreverent: "I regard *Hamlet* as a play of the most primitive
and elementary ideas, clothed in the most massive language. It's
an elaborate, evocative, fabulous means of dressing up the obvious.
It appears to be an obscure play merely because its author happened to be a verbal genius." Allowing for the exaggeration
appropriate to Burton's colorful personality (as well as to the
occasion, an interview for *Playboy*), the main point here seems to
be the basic simplicity of the play—an idea that is not unique,
though it is expressed more often by actors (BEERBOHM TREE, for
example, and JOHN BARRYMORE)[81] than by literary critics. Burton

80. *Prefaces to Shakespeare*, I, 167-95. Needless to say, I have merely suggested
the kind of criticism found in these pages.

81. Tree, *Thoughts and Afterthoughts*, p. 124; John Barrymore, *Confessions of
an Actor* (Indianapolis, [1926]), Ch. IV (the pages are not numbered).

stands alone, though, in his insistence that the "convolved and curious" words are what make *Hamlet* not only "so fascinating to watch" but "so boring to perform." He explains that "there isn't a line in it that isn't infinitely, effortlessly speakable" and that it is "more fun" to attempt "something that isn't speakable," through subtlety and skill of speech to give an apparent distinction to originally undistinguished dialogue.[82] No doubt there is a certain truth in this statement, and therein lies a trap for the actor: the temptation to have "fun" histrionically in a Shakespearean role at the expense of both character and play by twisting the language into original readings or by deliberately "throwing away" important speeches simply because they are unbearably famous.

Interpretations of "Meaning"

Aside from a few moralizing passages and one or two keen interpretations of individual scenes, WILLIAM WOOD's observations (1855) are the earliest by an actor-critic that suggest an interest in "meaning" above and beyond plot or character per se. Wood notes that *Hamlet* is "marked by a recurrence of *advice* to a very curious degree," and he illustrates his point with numerous speeches and scenes, from simple passages like Polonius' advice to Laertes and Hamlet's advice to the players to more ambivalent ones like Hamlet's "wild counsels to Ophelia, in half madness." Wood reports that Edmund Kean found his discovery amusing and wondered how a busy actor-manager found time for such theorizing.[83] Probably Kean did not see how anything so abstract could be of use for stage interpretation. But if Wood had gone further and tried to find the significance of all this advice-giving, he might have arrived at something like the kind of criticism that Harry Levin was to write a century later in discussing the recurrence of doubt and questioning in *Hamlet*.

More comprehensive efforts at interpreting the play have all belonged to the modern period. None of the resulting explications can be completely separated from the character of Hamlet himself, a subject that we are shortly to consider, but a few which emphasize some central idea should be noticed here.

82. Kenneth Tynan, "Playboy Interview: Richard Burton," *Playboy* (September, 1963), p. 54.
83. *Personal Recollections of the Stage*, p. 383.

Several of these stress the importance of the political and social world depicted in the play. WILLIAM POEL's is the earliest of such criticisms, and the others—GRANVILLE-BARKER's interpretation and ROBERT SPEAIGHT's, as it appears in *Nature in Shakespearian Tragedy*—probably reflect its influence. Poel insisted that critics missed much of Shakespeare's intention because they put their emphasis too exclusively upon Hamlet himself and neglected his environment:

We have . . . a Danish court . . . over which an avenging angel is hovering with drawn sword . . . and, because the influence of good in this court is too weak to conquer the evil, the sword falls on the good as well as on the evil. . . . Something is rotten in the State of Denmark; no one there is worthy to rule; the kingdom must be taken away and given to a stranger. It is the play as an epitome of life which is interesting to Shakespeare, and not the career of one individual. . . .[84]

Granville-Barker also considers the political background important, but he does not make it central to his interpretation. As he points out, Shakespeare cannot devote much space to it but he impresses it on our minds at the outset in Horatio's explanation to the watch about Fortinbras. Speaight, however, believes, like Poel, that Denmark is even more important than the Prince of Denmark. Both of the later critics emphasize the corruption of the "brilliant and debased Court" (Granville-Barker's phrase) and the importance of Fortinbras as a symbol of restored purity and order. Granville-Barker also notes the effective contrast between the military tone of the passages in which Fortinbras is mentioned or appears and the laxity of the Court, where most of the action takes place; in particular, the stately ending "reminds us that this most introspective of plays has also been a tragedy of great events."[85] Speaight's interpretation is more complex and elaborate. Some of his ideas and terms (like "nature" and "grace") are derived from Renaissance thought but freely adapted to his own scheme, and his mode of presentation is near-allegorical. For example, he writes that Denmark is tainted with "social adultery" because the "unnatural society of Elsinore yields to the

---

84. *Shakespeare in the Theatre* (London and Toronto, 1913), p. 157. For Sir Cedric Hardwicke, however, as for earlier actors like Gentleman and Wood, the character of Hamlet is the whole play: "No matter what strenuous efforts are made to develop the rest of the play, it still remains the setting for the Prince of Denmark." (*Let's Pretend* [London, (1932)]).

85. *Prefaces to Shakespeare*, I, 48, 157-58.

political lust of the King, as the Queen yields to his carnal importunity." At the end of the play a whole corrupt society has perished, leaving, presumably, a phoenix-like replacement. Fortinbras is "the image of political virginity in a state of grace to espouse society; and when Georges Piteoff produced *Hamlet* in Paris, he had the inspiration to dress him in white."[86]

Of interest in connection with "Hamlet's world," though it cannot conclusively be called an interpretation, is SIR ALEC GUINNESS's brief explanation of his experiment with a "Spanish" *Hamlet*. Having previously acted Hamlet in modern dress at the Old Vic (1938), Guinness decided in 1951 to produce the play in Renaissance costumes at the New Theatre. Salvadore de Madariaga's *On Hamlet*, which had recently been published in an English edition (London, 1948) provided the inspiration for the Spanish aura that the world of Hamlet assumed in this production. In this little book Madariaga asserts that the sixteenth and seventeenth centuries were "the era of Spain" (just as the eighteenth century was "French" and the nineteenth "English") and that previous interpretations of *Hamlet* have erred by attempting to make the hero conform to some ideal of a later period (for example, the gentlemanly ideal of the Victorians) instead of seeing him as a man of the Renaissance. He describes the true Hamlet as vigorous, self-centered, rather sensual; one who views other people with detachment, who manipulates them in the callous "Borgian" manner, and who is moved to revenge only when his "own skin" is threatened. Guinness, who had read widely in *Hamlet* criticism without finding anything that "fired" him, was "thrilled and appalled for a week" after Madariaga's "bombshell" struck him. Although he finally decided that he "hardly agreed with a word" this writer said, there was one point on which he was "completely convinced"—"that the Elizabethan world was as much influenced by Spain as we are today by America." For his own production, then, "a fine Spanish designer was engaged and told not to be Spanish; but Andreu cannot help being Spanish, so the precise effect I was seeking was achieved."[87] Although Guinness does not say in so many words whether he accepted Madariaga's idea of the *nature* of the Spanish influence, the implication is that he did not. Perhaps it was only coincidence

86. *Nature in Shakespearian Tragedy*, pp. 11-12, 36-38, 42-43.
87. "My Idea of Hamlet," p. 8.

that his own portrayal of Hamlet was described by one critic in words that suggest Madariaga's interpretation: "intellectual rather than emotional," with a "charm too precisely fretted by brutalities and sardonic cruelties" to allow the gentle side of the character to show.[88]

Some of the actor-critics' interpretations have centered on a moral, ethical, or religious point. Among the most striking of these are three which have in common the idea that the vengeful murder of Claudius was not Hamlet's real, or chief, duty. They are by LENA ASHWELL,[89] GEORGE R. FOSS,[90] and Robert Speaight (in *The Christian Theatre*, which differs considerably from his earlier interpretation).[91] Although these three have a certain basic similarity, they differ in many important details.

According to Miss Ashwell, Shakespeare depicts in *Hamlet* the struggle of the "Modern Mind" to throw off the shackles of medieval thought. The ideals of Hamlet's day were brute courage and rash action; but Hamlet, representative of emerging rationality, seeks justice rather than the unthinking vengeance of the blood feud. Since the machinery of impartial justice is not yet available to him, he himself must be the executioner, but he cannot proceed against Claudius until investigation has proved his right to do so; and, in any case, he is more concerned with redeeming Gertrude than with punishing Claudius. Ultimately he becomes the instrument of Divine Justice; but his own death and the ascendancy of Fortinbras represent the momentary triumph of the Middle Ages—the time of the "Modern Mind" has not yet come.

Foss and Speaight reject not only the ideal of personal retaliation but also the idea that it was Hamlet's duty to kill Claudius at all. They differ, however, in their interpretations of the Ghost's command. In Foss's opinion, the exhortation to revenge does not imply the assassination of Claudius, for the Ghost describes even the "best" murder as "most foul." Hamlet could have carried out his father's bidding by denouncing Claudius openly and daring him to "ordeal by combat," or he could have

88. The London *Times* (May 18, 1951), p. 6. The critic did not notice anything Spanish in the production.
89. *Reflections from Shakespeare*, ed. Roger Pocock (London, [1926]), pp. 65-83.
90. *What the Author Meant* (London, 1932), p. 14.
91. Robert Speaight, *The Christian Theatre* (London, 1960), pp. 66-68. The "answer" to the "problem" raised in *Hamlet* is discussed on pp. 70-88.

fled the country and, after proclaiming the King's guilt, returned to head a rebellion as Laertes did; unfortunately he thinks of no solution but murder. Speaight simply considers the Ghost's mandate evil and declares that Hamlet's temptation was, not to elude it, but to obey it. Both critics are sensitive to the "divisions" that develop in Hamlet's nature as he struggles to determine his course of action. Foss explains them unsympathetically: Hamlet, a "perfectly moral, religious" young man at the beginning, allows his desire for perfection to ruin him "body and soul." Hating the thought of leaving Claudius unpunished, yet abhorring the idea of "staining his hands with blood," he hesitates between the "hateful" alternatives until his own dilemma becomes so "monstrous" to him that everything else seems insignificant. At the end his mind has become "acutely sensitive to one ethical point but morally dead to every other." Speaight, on the other hand, declares that the schism in Hamlet's personality arises from the struggle between his temptation toward vengeance and his inclination toward love. Hamlet's tragedy is "not that he fails, until the penultimate instant, to kill Claudius, but that a nature made for love should have turned itself to hatred." Like Foss, Speaight points to *Measure for Measure* and *The Tempest* as plays offering the real solution to Hamlet's problem. And like Lena Ashwell, though without the same implications, he declares that Hamlet stands at the transitional point "between the medieval and modern worlds." Speaight adds that the two-sided Hamlet thus "echoes the doubt which Montaigne had insinuated into the European mind" and that doubt, in the form of irony, permeates the play. Irony governs the plot (e.g. in Hamlet's mistaken killing of Polonius) and is implicit in the conclusion: "from what we know of Fortinbras' imperialism it may well be that Denmark will only exchange one Machiavellian ruler for another."

How seriously should these interpretations of *Hamlet* be taken? How deeply committed to them do the actor-critics appear to be, and to what extent would they probably allow these ideas to influence their own acting or producing of the play? Poel *did* put his interpretation into practice, particularly in one production which gave unusual prominence to Claudius. Granville-Barker's ideas about the political world of *Hamlet* seem to form a kind of general framework, lightly sketched in, for his more vivid and detailed studies of character, plot, and other subjects of dramatic importance. As he pointed out, Shakespeare's own references to the political world are slight but strategically placed. Lena Ashwell probably took her semi-allegorical interpretation very seriously, drawn to it by her interest in spiritualism and by her fascination with the idea of finding the same universal truths manifested—though sometimes imperfectly—in all of the great myths, philosophies, and religions of the world. She believed that mankind from the beginning struggled toward the understanding of these truths, the light becoming progressively brighter after the Renaissance, and that Shakespeare was ahead of his time in grasping them because he was willing to rely on intuition as well as on reason in its more restricted form.[92] Just how such ideas would be implemented in the acting of the play is not clear except that they would demand a completely sympathetic Hamlet. Of Speaight's two divergent interpretations, which "really" represents his thinking? Does the later one supersede the other just because it *is* later? It is not so long nor so fully worked out as the other. And since it is part of *The Christian Theatre* it might be suspected of being a bit of special pleading. It is as if the author were saying: "Let us look at *Hamlet* from a specifically Christian point of view. See how everything falls into place with the kaleidoscope set at this angle?"—not that he has abandoned other settings for all time. The prevalence of irony and ambiguity in the play itself—a point that Speaight (among others) has made well—permits, even perhaps encourages, two simultaneous views of Fortinbras and the restoration of order, if not of Hamlet and his task. For a stage production, I suppose, a single firm line would have to be taken, leaving the perception of ironies to the possibilities of after-vision.

There are obvious likenesses between the actors' interpretations of *Hamlet* and modern readings of the play by other critics. The ones emphasizing the social or political body and the necessity for purging it of corruption resemble, in this one point at least, recent interpretations by Maynard Mack and H. D. F. Kitto, to name only two. Obviously, similarities rather than influences

92. *Reflections from Shakespeare*, pp. 10-11, 50-51. Being a spiritualist, Lena Ashwell was also interested in Shakespeare's depiction of ghosts and other psychic phenomena. She was particularly impressed by his "accuracy": e.g. his emphasis on "bitter cold" in the ghost scenes properly suggests "the mechanism of materialization," for "the person manifesting must draw the material, called ectoplasm from the bodies of the witnesses, causing a sensation of intense cold."

are the point here. Speaight's interpretations do seem to reflect the influence of specific writers, however: John Danby in the earlier one, for instance, and John Vyvyan in the later.

Indeed, although actor-critics have occasionally been in the vanguard of critical movements (Poel, for instance, in decrying the concentration of interest on Hamlet's character), they have rarely been far out of line with literary tendencies in their basic ideas about the plot, language, or "meaning" of *Hamlet*. As we would expect, their most original criticisms of the play are related to its theatrical effectiveness, particularly to that of its individual scenes. And their best discussions of the other subjects— for example, Knowles's defense of the graveyard scene, Granville-Barker's analysis of time changes, and Gielgud's discussion of "double suggestion"—are those that combine a knowledge of theatrical effect with an appreciation of "literary" qualities.

II. THE CHARACTERS

HAMLET

A discussion of the actor-critics' interpretations of Hamlet can hardly escape the effect of "always beginning and never ending" which Oxberry ascribed to the plot of the play itself. And, like Oxberry, we can blame this diffuseness on the complex character of Hamlet. For the question of his energy versus his irresolution is hardly broached before the overlapping question of his moral flaws and dramatic inconsistencies must be mentioned—and these very characteristics contribute to the impression of humanity and universality for which he is praised by actor-critics of the later periods; they are essential ingredients, too, in any discussion of the histrionic rewards and challenges offered by the role. Is Hamlet frail or robust, callous or hypersensitive, a profound philosopher or an impulsive, undisciplined thinker, a dreamer or a doer? An attempt to disentangle these interwoven problems and to discuss them separately would result in the cutting of vital threads. For this reason, the criticisms relating to all of Hamlet's basic qualities—of personality, intellect, and moral character— will be included in a single, chronologically ordered section; separate sections will be devoted to the specific problems of his age, his madness, his attitude toward Gertrude and his attitude toward Ophelia. The last of these, however, will be postponed until later in the chapter because of its relevance to other matters.

Basic Interpretations of Hamlet's Character

During the eighteenth century and the early years of the nineteenth, the prevailing stage interpretation of Hamlet and the written interpretations by actor-critics generally went hand in hand; indeed, some of the most interesting of the latter took the form of theatrical critiques. Both in theory and in performance the emphasis was on a "heroic" conception of Hamlet—with one unequivocal exception and with a few signs of questioning or compromise. The conventional dramatic hero of the eighteenth century was courageous, resolute, energetic, passionate; ideally he was also characterized by moral rectitude, noble sentiments, and the gentlemanly manners that denote high breeding. The questioning of Hamlet's status as a hero came about on moral grounds and also on the ground of inconsistencies between his strong words and his weak deeds.

In the literature of the second half of the century there was an increasing emphasis on "sensibility"—a tenderness and refinement of the feelings which expressed itself in acute sensitivity to subtle shades of beauty and goodness (and their opposites), a sympathetic understanding of the feelings of others, and a ready perception of "the tears in things." This quality, which was noticed in Hamlet, was perfectly consistent with the character of a hero, if it was not overemphasized, since it set him apart from men of common mould. There was nothing effete about the gentlemanliness and sensibility attributed to Hamlet by the actor-critics of this time, as there was to be in the period of romantic criticism. These qualities were prized as signs of *noblesse oblige,* but they were secondary to the energy and passion that were most often emphasized in connection with Hamlet's character.

As far as I know, there are no written comments on Hamlet by an actor earlier than COLLEY CIBBER's critique of Thomas Betterton's performance (published in 1740). All clues to Betterton's interpretation are valuable, for not only was he a fine actor himself but he had the benefit of a stage tradition that went back, via Davenant's memory, to the period before the closing of the theatres.[93] As for that tradition itself, as Paul Conklin has shown, such indications as we have concerning the earliest interpretations point to a "bitterly eloquent and princely avenger" whose "mad" behavior was strongly represented.[94] (Burbage's leap into Ophelia's grave was remembered as a highlight of his performance.[95]) The actors of the Restoration period evidently resumed the concept of a dynamic Hamlet, somewhat less bitter perhaps but with great vitality and intensity of feeling. Indeed, judging by Cibber's remarks, they sometimes exaggerated these traits to the point of tearing a passion to tatters—a temptation avoided by Betterton.

In Cibber's opinion, the natural passion of Hamlet's speech beginning "Angels and ministers of grace" is confined to "an almost breathless Astonishment, or an Impatience limited by filial Reverence." Appropriately, Betterton's voice never rose "into that seeming Outrage, or wild Defiance of what he naturally rever'd."

. . . he opened with a Pause of mute Amazement! then rising slowly to a solemn, trembling Voice, he made the Ghost equally terrible to the Spectator, as to himself! and in the descriptive Part of the natural Emotions which the ghastly Vision gave him, the boldness of his Expostulations was still govern'd by Decency, manly, but not braving [i.e. blustering].[96]

According to this description, Betterton repudiated mindless rant in favor of effectively natural acting,[97] but he did not repudiate (nor did Cibber think he should) the virility and strong feeling that were evidently associated with Hamlet's character at that time.

Certainly the heroic conception of Hamlet continued to

93. Cf. John Downes' famous assertion: "Sir William [Davenant] (having seen Mr. *Taylor* of the *Black-Fryars* Company Act it, who being Instructed by the Author Mr. Shaksepeur) taught Mr. *Betterton* in every Particle of it; which, by his exact Performance of it, gain'd him Esteem and Reputation Superlative to all other Plays." (*Roscius Anglicanus*, ed. Montague Summers [London, 1927]), p. 21.)

94. *A History of Hamlet Criticism*, pp. 8-26, especially pp. 25-26.

95. *Shakespeare Allusion Book*, ed. J. J. Munro (London, 1932), I, 272.

96. *An Apology for the Life of Mr. Colley Cibber*, ed. Robert W. Lowe (London, 1889), I, 99-101.

97. Arthur Colby Sprague interestingly discusses the probabilities of Betterton's acting style as well as telling all that is known of his performance of Hamlet. See *Shakespearian Players and Performances* (Cambridge, Mass., 1953), pp. 13-20. Since Cibber himself adopted a chanting style of stage delivery, his idea of naturalness would hardly coincide with the modern actor's.

receive enthusiastic support in the age of Garrick—from Garrick himself in his stage portrayal and from the actor-critics FREDERICK PILON[98] and THOMAS DAVIES,[99] who wrote admiringly of that portrayal.

Pilon's own description of Hamlet might have served as a model for the ideal hero of his age:

Hamlet's understanding is sound, and his sensibility exquisite. He is moreover adorned with every liberal accomplishment, which can distinguish the gentleman and the scholar: his reasonings are deep, and his passions ardent; and as both are excited by great and adequate motives, his character affords the most ample field for the display of theatrical abilities.

The Hamlet of Pilon's conception was not by nature irresolute: "To be or not to be" shows him "weary of being *obliged* to procrastinate his revenge" (italics mine), but the King's confusion in the play scene removes all doubts and he resolves upon immediate revenge. Hamlet's soliloquy in the prayer scene, explaining why this determination is not carried out, is a vital speech; it should not be omitted, for without it Hamlet appears "weak and irresolute during the last two acts." (Davies found this speech intolerable, but Pilon, by recalling that Claudius had murdered Hamlet's father without allowing him an opportunity for repentance, implied that Hamlet's reasoning was just.) In his critique of John Henderson's stage interpretation, Pilon dwells more often on the "ardent passions" of the character than on the "exquisite sensibility," and he frequently refers to Garrick's spirited performance as a criterion of excellence.

Both Pilon and Davies emphasized Garrick's striking effectiveness in the ghost scene. The latter's description recalls Cibber's praise of Betterton: "his expostulations with the vision, though warm and importunate, were restrained by filial awe. The progress of his impassioned sensation . . . was accompanied with terrour and respect." Garrick's breaking from his companions to follow the Ghost was particularly impressive to these actor-critics. Pilon found Henderson too tame in this portion of the scene: since Hamlet's words show him to be "worked up to the most extravagant pitch of desperation . . . his look and gesture should

98. [Frederick Pilon], *An Essay on the Character of Hamlet as Performed by Mr. Henderson* (London, 1777), *passim*.

99. *Memoirs of the Life of Garrick*, I, 54-55.

be wild and his voice piercingly energetic." Garrick was superb here, for "he preserved Shakespeare's fire undiminished . . . and sent the animated shock of nature's flame home to the heart." Davies agreed that Garrick's "determination to obey . . . the ghost . . . was vehemently resolute; his following him awful and tremendous." In the soliloquies, too, "all the varieties of sentiment, impressed with passion, were delivered by Garrick with singular exertion. The strong intelligence of his eye, the animated expression of his whole countenance, the flexibility of his voice, and his spirited action, rivetted the attention." According to Davies, Garrick was particularly effective in "O what a wretch [rogue]," for this speech "afforded him the amplest room to display his varied excellencies." And Pilon, in attempting to describe those "excellencies," once again drew his simile from fire: in this soliloquy Garrick's every word "seems to rush from the burning mint of sensibility."

There is one actor-critic, however, ARTHUR MURPHY, whose description of Garrick's Hamlet differs from Davies' and Pilon's in both tone and emphasis. In the ghost scene, for example, Murphy dwells on the terror of the supernatural rather than on the "warm expostulations." Instead of singling out Hamlet's most passionate soliloquy, as Davies did, he praises Garrick's acting in "O that this too, too solid flesh would melt," where Hamlet's "grief, his anxiety, and irresolute temper are strongly marked." Indeed Murphy recalls with particular admiration Garrick's acting in the whole scene of Hamlet's first appearance: by "deep meditation" the actor "transformed himself into the very man," and while he remained "fixed in a pensive attitude . . . the sentiments that possessed his mind could be discovered" from his facial expressions.[100]

The fear, the grief, the occasional pensiveness suggested in these brief passages *were* among the elements in Garrick's portrayal of Hamlet, as other testimony indicates. The most active of Hamlet's representatives could hardly overlook these qualities in some portions of the play. That these portions impressed themselves most strongly upon Murphy's memory gives some insight into his own interpretation of Hamlet, but whether Garrick himself saw an "irresolute temper" in Hamlet's character is another matter. Garrick last acted Hamlet in 1776; Murphy's de-

100. *The Life of Garrick*, I, 46-47.

scription was published in 1801. Not only had twenty-five years elapsed, but during that period the romantic view of Hamlet had been gaining ground among literary critics. It may be that Murphy's memory was colored somewhat by afterthought.[101] If Pilon (1777) and Davies (1780) are correct in their emphasis, Garrick's vigorous and passionate Hamlet must have helped to counteract any inclination on the part of critics to describe the character as delicate, dreamy, and inactive—terms that were beginning to creep into print and would, in the next century, become commonplace.

Yet, while Garrick's career was still at its height, another actor, THOMAS SHERIDAN, was expounding a theory of Hamlet's character that clearly foreshadowed such conceptions as those of Goethe and Coleridge. Perhaps Sheridan's ideas—so far in advance of their time—would have been more immediately influential if he had published them in an essay rather than being content to discuss them with his companions. (Yet critics may have absorbed these ideas from Sheridan in the theatre. Davies reports that "in several situations of Hamlet's character" his stage portrayal was "original and different from all of his own time," and other evidence points to its unusual dignity and sentiment.[102]) We owe our knowledge of Sheridan's interpretation to an account in James Boswell's *London Journal* (unpublished, of course, until 1950). In the entry for April 6, 1763, we read:

[Sheridan] made it clear to us that Hamlet, notwithstanding of his seeming incongruities, is a perfectly consistent character. Shakespeare drew him as the portrait of a young man of a good heart and fine feelings who had led a studious contemplative life and so became delicate and irresolute. He shows him in very unfortunate circumstances, the author of which he knows he ought to punish, but wants strength of mind to execute what he thinks right and wishes to do. . . . His timidity being once admitted, all the strange fluctuations which we perceive in him may be easily traced to that source. . . . when the Ghost appears . . . we see Hamlet in all the agony of consternation. Yet we hear him uttering extravagant sallies of rash intrepidity, by which he endeavors to stir up his languid mind to a manly boldness, but in vain. For he still continues backward to revenge, hesitates

101. Cibber's description of Betterton was published thirty-one years after Betterton's last performance of Hamlet; however there was no significant critical change in Hamlet interpretation "in the air" during that time as there was during the latter part of the eighteenth century.

102. *Dramatic Miscellanies*, III, 115. For other evidence see article cited in n. 103.

about believing the Ghost to be the real spirit of his father, so much that the Ghost chides him for being tardy. When he has a fair opportunity of killing his uncle, he neglects it and says he will not take him off while at his devotions, but will wait till he is in the midst of some atrocious crime, that he may put him to death with his guilt upon his head. Now this, if really from the heart, would make Hamlet the most black, revengeful man. But it coincides better with his character to suppose him here endeavouring to make an excuse to himself for his delay.[103]

This valuable record not only gives a very early example of a fully developed romantic interpretation; it also testifies to the fact that Hamlet's "incongruities" were being discussed orally some years before they received any substantial treatment in print.[104] For, although earlier writers had occasionally noticed a certain cruelty, surprising in the traditionally sympathetic Hamlet, FRANCIS GENTLEMAN (1770) was apparently the first critic, theatrical or otherwise, to point out in detail the flaws and inconsistencies of this character—"impetuous, though philosophical . . . shrewd, yet void of policy . . . boastful in expression, undetermined in action." He conscientiously listed Hamlet's sins against both morality and dramatic decorum, making no distinction between the two—probably because in his mind there *was* no distinction when a hero was being discussed: for example, Hamlet's forging the death commission for Rosencrantz and Guildenstern was condemned, not simply on moral and humane grounds, but because it is a piece of "low chicanery" inappropriate to "a character of dignity." Some of Hamlet's other faults are his outrageous behavior at Ophelia's grave, his "mean prevarication" in the apology to Laertes (blaming a nonexistent madness for his past offenses), and his "unworthy" manner of killing Claudius, "urged by desperation, not just revenge." Despite Hamlet's failure to

103. *Boswell's London Journal 1762-1763*, ed. Frederick A. Pottle (New York and London, 1950), pp. 234-35. See also J. Yoklavich, "Hamlet in Shammy Shoes," *Shakespeare Quarterly*, III (1952), 209-18. This important article discusses Sheridan's significance as an interpreter of Hamlet both on and off the stage.

104. Even earlier evidence of romantic tendencies in oral discussions of Hamlet's character is found in an anonymous letter to Garrick written December 4, [1744]. The writer objects that in his performance Garrick "had not entered into the true character of Hamlet. . . . Instead of that lovely, unfortunate creature, in whose happiness the reader so warmly interests himself, and whose misfortunes he looks upon as his own, you exhibited a hot testy fellow, for ever flying into a passion. . . ." He tells of "mentioning this last Wednesday in a large company, where every one happened to be of our opinion." (*Private Correspondence of Garrick*, ed. Boaden, I, 26.)

conform to the requirements of a hero, however, he is—as Gentleman was forced to admit—"as agreeable and striking an object as any in the English drama," simply because of the "great variety" in his character and the theatrical opportunities it affords.[105] Apparently it did not occur to Gentleman that the variety which he praised might be another name for the inconsistencies he deplored. Nor did he make any effort, as Sheridan had done, to reconcile these inconsistencies. As Conklin justly remarks, such fault-finding criticisms led ultimately to romantic attempts at psychological justifications.[106] But Gentleman himself was content to point out Hamlet's flaws.

Literary critics were not far behind. It was only a few years later (1773) that George Steevens included in his edition of Shakespeare a long note listing Hamlet's shortcomings in much the same way that Gentleman had done, but without mentioning that actor-critic. Indeed Steevens asserted that Hamlet had always been regarded as a "hero," no writer having "taken the pains to point out the immoral tendency of the character." Steevens repeated the note in a later edition, adding to it Akenside's suggestion that the only excuse for the blemishes in the character would be the assumption that Hamlet's "intellects were in some degree impaired by his misfortunes."[107] Here was one possibility of psychological justification that would prove attractive to several actors of a later period.

At the moment, however, the chief reaction by an actor-critic was indignation at Steevens' "deformed" image of Hamlet. For

105. *Dramatic Censor*, I, 16-33.
106. Conkin writes (in *History of Hamlet Criticism*, pp. 64-65) that Gentleman opened the decade of a new kind of criticism in which emphasis began to be placed on Hamlet's inconsistencies: his cruelty, procrastination, etc. He comments that as soon as the "naive perspective" of the theatre "is abandoned, as Gentleman here gives evidence of abandoning it, the artistic unity evaporates . . . unless one does what critics were soon to do: remove Hamlet completely from his true sphere as a dramatic creation and give him a new life off the stage. . . . Gentleman does not seem to wish to do that. Thus he remains puzzled [by the fact that Hamlet's inconsistencies do not interfere with his theatrical effectiveness]." Gentleman, who had had considerable experience as an actor, would not think of removing any character completely from the dramatic sphere. Actually his concern for Hamlet's inconsistencies probably came as much from the habit of thinking in terms of stock characters as it did from any literary tendencies. Minute character analysis (often associated with the idea of "removing" a character from the dramatic sphere) was practiced by actors earlier, I believe, than by nontheatrical critics, as an aid to performance. Sheridan's analysis of Hamlet is a good example.
107. *The Plays of William Shakespeare* (London, 1778), X, 412-13.

Thomas Davies (1783-84), with his usual common sense regard for interpretations which had proved successful on the stage, could not be persuaded that a favorite like Hamlet was really unworthy of the audience's sympathy, even if he was not "a character for imitation." Among other things, he defended Hamlet for leaping into Ophelia's grave (he was "unexpectedly provoked") and for contriving the death of his old school fellows (they were unscrupulous spies who probably knew the contents of the original commission). He also exonerated Hamlet from blame for Ophelia's madness except insofar as it was the "unhappy consequence of a precipitant and mistaken action." As for Akenside's suggestion, though Davies said nothing to endorse it, he pointed out that it was not new: forty years earlier Aaron Hill had written in *The Prompter* that in addition to his assumed madness Hamlet showed "a melancholy which bordered on insanity, arising from his peculiar situation."[108]

If there were a straightforward chronological progression in the actors' criticism of Hamlet, THOMAS HOLCROFT (1805-6) might be considered a transitional figure, combining as he does the old interest in Hamlet's deviations from the conventional stage hero with something approaching the romantic attempt to account for his inconsistencies psychologically. He never goes as "far," however, as the 1763 interpretation by Sheridan. In fact, his concept of Hamlet's basic characteristics does not differ materially from Pilon's (and probably Garrick's), though he puts more emphasis on Hamlet's sensibility. In his *Theatrical Recorder*, Holcroft notes, while discussing dramatic roles by types for the benefit of young actors, that Hamlet is one of those characters "in which all the great qualities of the hero are seen; but their lustre is occasionally obscured by . . . strong passions." Since a hero must never lose his self-control, Hamlet cannot be considered a "pure hero" like Shakespeare's Henry V. He may be explained as the supreme genius portrayed in drama—sensitive, brilliant, judicious; erring from his natural rectitude only under the influence of "emotions which in their nature and cause are become irresistible." The lightning flash of Hamlet's thoughts, the rapid and forceful transitions of speech and action demand an actor capable

108. *Dramatic Miscellanies*, III, 143-44. A nontheatrical critic, Joseph Ritson, in his *Remarks on the Text and Notes of the Last Edition of Shakespeare* (London, 1783), replied to Steevens in much the same way.

of both suddenness and grace; on the other hand, his sensibility—an "essential quality"—requires an actor who will not speak the "playful" sallies so cynically as to enforce the worse of two possible meanings. For example, "I am too much i' the sun" should be spoken with a "solemnity of eye and deportment" which veils its real sarcasm. Gentlemanliness and nobility of demeanor must somehow be combined with ardor and resolution: in the ghost scene, for instance, Hamlet must not lose his dignity, even when breaking desperately from his companions, and his strange levity after the Ghost departs must be given a "wild sedateness." In short, the characteristics of several kinds of men must be manifested in this single complex character: "the strong, the impetuous, yet the generous passions of youth combined with the heroic qualities, and the perfect gentleman."[109]

Hamlet's high breeding is emphasized, too, in the personal letters of WILLIAM ("GENTLEMAN") SMITH (1814). A retired actor of Garrick's period, now in his eighties, Smith was much interested in news of the phenomenal Edmund Kean, who he hoped would "rescue the Drama from Pedantry, Bombast & false taste" (vices that Smith imputed to John Philip Kemble's lofty and sombre style) and "restore Nature & excellence to the Stage." But he was concerned by the report that in some passages "Mr. Kean is . . . too artificial, and in others almost *rude* both to the King & to Ophelia." This would not do; for "an elegant Figure, Deportment, Habit & Manners are *native* . . . in Hamlet as in Lord Townley—very great part of it shou'd not be *acted* but *be—Ease & simplicity* are absolutely necessary."[110] Perhaps an actor who had earned the nickname "Gentleman" and who had enacted in his time both Hamlet and Lord Townley (in Cibber and Vanbrugh's *The Provoked Husband*) might be tempted to overemphasize the

109. *The Theatrical Recorder* (London, 1805-6), II, 43-45 (general discussion of Hamlet's character), 138 (Court scene), 191-94 (ghost scene). Holcroft's similarity to Davies, Pilon (and, ultimately, Cibber) is shown in his advice about Hamlet's reaction to the appearance of the Ghost: there should be no hint of a coward's fears but, rather, "astonishment . . . intermingled with a wild and strange curiosity, and tempered only with profound filial respect." Holcroft also writes of the "burning indignation" with which "O what a rogue" should be spoken (pp. 271-73). He does not mention Hamlet's soliloquy in the prayer scene, which was customarily omitted in stage performances at that time; immediately after the play scene, in Holcroft's analysis of the play, we read that when next we see Hamlet he is in his mother's chamber (see p. 414).

110. A collection of Smith's MS letters to Thomas Coutts is in the Folger Library. My quotations are from letters dated February 28 and March 10, 1814.

qualities of princely courtesy and easy grace in Hamlet's character; but these qualities would be, in Smith's mind (as in Holcroft's), perfectly appropriate to the energetic and passionate acting of Kean as they would have been to that of Garrick.[111]

From Thomas Sheridan's interpretation of Hamlet (1763) to William Oxberry's (1818), there is no example of actor-criticism (as far as I know) that can be called fully "romantic," though a single comment of Murphy's suggests an inclination in that direction and though Gentleman's faultfinding may have encouraged other critics to explain away Hamlet's flaws by psychological interpretations.

Among the literary critics, however, the concept of a delicate, sensitive, overly-thoughtful Hamlet had begun to develop in the latter part of the eighteenth century, and, in the second decade of the nineteenth, it reached its full maturity. At the very period when the fiery Kean was taking London by storm, Coleridge was expressing his theory that Hamlet delays because the world of thought is more real to him than the world of action; Lamb was suggesting that Hamlet's acts are incapable of external illustration because nine-tenths of them are "transactions between himself and his moral sense"; and Hazlitt was interpreting Hamlet as a kind of Everyman, "as little of the hero as a man can well be." (Hazlitt considered the character unactable, by Kemble, Kean, or anyone else, since the ideal embodiment would be "as much of the gentleman and scholar as possible . . . and as little of the actor." Ironically this writer would be the most influential English critic of his period on the actor-critics to come.)[112] Goethe's novel, *Wilhelm Meister*, first published in 1796, would soon become more widely accessible through Carlyle's translation (1824)—and this book, of course, contains a description of Hamlet that epitomizes the romantic concept of lovely fragility. In a passage which

---

111. Davies, for all his admiration of Garrick's Hamlet, felt that he was too "boisterous" in the "nunnery" scene (*Dramatic Miscellanies*, III, 79-80).

112. *Coleridge's Shakespearean Criticism*, ed. T. M. Raysor (Cambridge, Mass., 1930), II, 192-98; "On the Tragedies of Shakespeare," *Complete Works and Letters of Charles Lamb* (Modern Library, 1935), p. 293; *Complete Works of Hazlitt*, ed. P. P. Howe (London and Toronto, 1930-34), IV, 232-37. *See also* Hazlitt's review of Young's Hamlet (*Ibid.*, XVIII, 244) in which he takes exception to the passionate delivery of the traditionally passionate "O what a rogue." Young did not convey "the idea of [Hamlet's] own melancholy and weakness as contrasted with the theatrical fury of the imaginary hero."

several actor-critics were to describe as the best analysis offered by
a literary commentator, the hero Wilhelm, an actor himself, imaginatively reconstructs Hamlet's personality as it was in happier
days: a "royal flower," gently nurtured—handsome, courteous,
idealistic, aesthetically refined, "without any prominent passion."
He then analyzes the character as we find him in the play: degraded in rank, robbed of trust in his mother and thus in all
women, burdened with a "heavy obligation" of "reflection and
sorrow" which is foreign to his nature. The one task which a
youth like Hamlet is incapable of accomplishing is the very duty
laid upon him in the ghost scene. "Pure" and "noble" but lacking the "strength of nerve which forms a hero," he "sinks beneath
a burden which [he] cannot bear and must not cast away." "There
is an oak tree planted in a costly jar, which should have borne
only pleasant flowers . . . the roots expand, the jar is shivered."[113]

During the greater part of the nineteenth century and the
early years of the twentieth, the actor-critics of Hamlet, with a
few notable exceptions, followed the tradition of the romantic
criticism represented by those writers who have just been mentioned: the details might vary considerably from one critic to
another; the basic conception was nonheroic but sympathetic.
Although several of the actor-critics denied the value of most
Shakespearean commentaries, there are more obvious literary
influences on the actors' criticisms of Hamlet in this period than
on their criticisms of any other character in any period.

Paradoxically, there is also a greater sense of personal understanding of this character. Macready wrote in his diary that he
could not find in the works of Goethe, Schlegel, or Coleridge
such appreciative understanding of Hamlet as had come to him
in his fifty-first year, "as long meditation, like long straining after
sight, presents the minutest portion of its excellence to my
view."[114] This is not simply an isolated case of egotism. Regardless how many hints they might have derived from specific writers
or from the general cultural environment, some of the actor-
critics felt strongly that their real knowledge came through a
direct relationship with Hamlet himself. Of no other character
are there such stories as the one of Booth's refusing to cover his

113. Wolfgang von Goethe, *Wilhelm Meister's Apprenticeship*, trans. Thomas
Carlyle (London and New York, 1937), I, 186-212.
114. *The Diaries of William Charles Macready*, ed. William Toynbee (New
York, 1912), II, 273. Entry for July 17, 1844.

gray hair with a wig when he played Hamlet because physical appearance did not matter since he was giving a "study of his own soul."[115] Or of Irving's lying awake at night thinking of "that poor young fellow . . . all alone with his misery in that abominable court."[116] Hazlitt's "It is we who are Hamlet" had a special meaning for the actors. Because he had had "the privilege . . . of experiencing personally . . . [Hamlet's] youthful aspirations, his scorn of the insolence of office, and . . . his love for the fair Ophelia," Beerbohm Tree felt peculiarly equipped for the "attempt to remove the seeming inconsistencies of Hamlet's character" for the reader of his essay.[117] More than one of the actor-critics seems to have been motivated by this missionary impulse.

One of the first things we notice about the new criticisms of Hamlet is a new attitude toward his inconsistencies. These were now accepted, not as evidences of Shakespeare's carelessness, but as examples of the complexity with which he endowed the most human of all his characters. As WILLIAM OXBERRY remarks, Hamlet's conduct is sometimes inconsistent with reason, but it is never inconsistent with his character; like all men in real life, he acts from mixed motives.[118] Some writers went so far as to consider Hamlet's shortcomings his most endearing traits. GEORGE VANDENHOFF, for example, becomes almost rhapsodic in describing "this wonderful incongruity, this harmonious discord, this paragon of imperfections adorned with every grace of person and mind." His emphasis upon the universally human rather than the heroic in Hamlet's character is much like Hazlitt's except for its ironic twist: "our vanity . . . [is] flattered by recognizing the reflection of our own imperfections . . . in so grand, so pure, so refined a mirror."[119]

115. Katherine [Molony] Goodale, *Behind the Scenes with Edwin Booth* (Boston, 1931), pp. 157–58.
116. Walter Herries Pollock, *Impressions of Henry Irving Gathered during a Friendship of Many Years* (London, 1908), p. 66. Irving's strong personal feeling for the character of Hamlet is commented on too by Sir John Martin-Harvey in his *Autobiography* (London, [1933]), pp. 180–81. Irving himself mentions it in a letter, dated November 27, 1884, to William Winter (MS in the Folger Library) and in his article, "My Four Favorite Parts," *The Forum*, XVI (September, 1893), p. 34.
117. *Thoughts and Afterthoughts*, pp. 124–25.
118. *New English Drama*, III, *Hamlet*, xv–xvi.
119. George Vandenhoff, *Leaves from an Actor's Note-Book* (New York, 1860), p. 273.

Several actor-critics agreed with literary critics that one of Hamlet's flaws is irresolution—or, as JAMES H. HACKETT saw it instead, "fickleness of purpose"—and, like them, a few attempted to explain this trait in terms of his intellect, imagination, or conscience. There was, perhaps, the most emphasis on imagination. William Oxberry, again, gives a typical evaluation: Hamlet has a beautiful mind, but his imagination is stronger than his understanding; "he is always busied in satisfying the cravings of a romantic fancy, picturing to himself what he will do, and thus losing the time for action."[120] And Hackett traces Hamlet's frequent changes of direction to a "morbid fertility" of imagination, which spawns ideas so fast that one cannot be fully expressed before another appears—a hectic, undisciplined energy of thought that is reflected, occasionally, in tangled and puzzling words. Hamlet is a creature of impulse; incapable of "mature and deliberate reflection" and steady execution of the resulting decision, he must form all "resolutions . . . out of some excitement of the blood." Thus he cannot kill Claudius at prayer because, although the deed would be just, its cold-bloodedness repels him. Both Hackett and JAMES MURDOCH deal with the idea of conscience as it relates to Hamlet's irresolution, but they reveal different understandings of the word. According to Hackett, "conscience makes a coward" of Hamlet because all contrasts to his own state of mind (the First Player's intensity, Horatio's equanimity), rather than whetting his purpose, merely "paralyze his own energies." Hamlet has the *"moral principle* of a hero," but he lacks the *"physical nerve"* necessary for cool and resolute revenge.[121] Murdoch, however, gives a specifically religious explanation: "In the flush of excitement [Hamlet] swears to perform a terrible deed, from which in his calmer moments his whole nature recoils. . . . The voice from the grave . . . cries 'Revenge! . . .' while echoed from the thunders of Sinai comes the sterner voice, 'Thou shalt not kill. . . .' " Unable to resolve this inner

120. *New English Drama*, III, *Hamlet*, xv-xvi.
121. James Henry Hackett, *Notes, Criticisms, and Correspondence upon Shakespeare's Plays and Actors* (New York, 1863), pp. 43-44. Also Hackett's letter of July 24, 1839, to John Quincy Adams. I have used the MS in the Folger Library, but the correspondence is printed on pp. 191-207 of *Notes, Criticisms, and Correspondence.* For the relevant passage see p. 206.

conflict, Hamlet "parleys too long with time and consequence, and purpose palls."[122]

Hackett's phrase "excitement of the blood" is unusual among the descriptions of Hamlet in this period; for a number of actor-critics, following the literary lead, considered Hamlet a passive dreamer: in FANNY KEMBLE's words, "a thoughtful, doubtful, questioning spirit . . . weary of existence upon its very threshold, and withheld alone from self-destruction by religious awe, and that pervading uncertainty of mind which stands on the brink, brooding over the unseen may-be of another world."[123] Oxberry explained that a "morbid melancholy seems to have unstrung his whole frame, and produced a mental lassitude which renders him incapable of exertion" so that he is happiest when "by some subtlety of excuse, he can deceive himself and escape from the reality of deeds."[124] CHARLES KEAN held a similar conception: he described the play as a "history of mind—a tragedy of thought," the story of "a gentle nature unstrung by passing events, and thus rendered 'out of tune and harsh.' "[125] In performance, he declared, such a character calls for "mental rather than physical illustration"; and when a critic found fault with Kean's tameness in the closet scene, the actor wrote indignantly: "Is it not enough to make a rational being mad . . .? The Thing supposes that because I am not in a devil of a passion . . . I cannot make . . . [my mother] feel."[126]

Under the influence of ideas like these, there was a tendency to soften Hamlet's sensibility into sentimentality. Often as his gentlemanliness and sensitivity had been stressed in the past, they had always been considered subsidiaries or companion traits to his energy and ardor. Never had an actor-critic proclaimed, as SHERIDAN KNOWLES now did, that the "master-feature" of Hamlet's character "is extreme sensibility." Nor would Pilon or Holcroft or "Gentleman" Smith have chosen to describe Hamlet's sorrow for

122. James Murdoch, "A Short Study of 'Hamlet,' " *Forum,* IX (July, 1890), 497-98.

123. Frances Anne (Kemble) Butler, *Journal* (Philadelphia, 1835), I, 73-74.

124. *New English Drama,* III, *Hamlet,* xv-xvi, xx.

125. *Selections from the Plays of Shakespeare. As Arranged for Representation at the Princess's Theatre* (London, 1860), II, 325-26.

126. See Kean's MS letters of July 15, 1851, and September 28, 1830, in the Folger Library. The first is to a critic whose account of his performance of Beverley in *The Gamester* had annoyed him; the second is to a Mr. Morris of New York (Kean was in Philadelphia at the time).

his dead father in such words as these: "No girl, bereft of a fond and idolized mother, could droop so piteously. . . ." Hamlet's friendship for Horatio, his tender memory of Yorick, his affection for the old actor—all these, according to Knowles, bear witness to his sensitive nature. And because of it "the wound, that has been done to the honour of his family by his mother and uncle's incestuous marriage, [is] insupportable." By his choice of words, even more than by his shift of emphasis, Knowles seems to herald the movement toward the feminizing of Hamlet's finer traits. As his other comments make clear, however, the Hamlet of his conception was not effeminate in the modern sense; he was, rather, a microcosm of ideal Victorian manhood: gentleman, scholar, friend, man of honor, lover, moralist, son—"and the prince in everything."[127]

It was later in the century that the finest of American Hamlets, EDWIN BOOTH, showed how far the "feminine" interpretation might be carried without giving, in that ladylike age, any hint of impropriety. His daughter, Edwina Grossmann, reports that, although Booth was "undoubtedly more in sympathy with the character of Hamlet" than with any of his other roles, he enjoyed escaping from its "monotone" occasionally to play "more robust parts."[128] Booth's conception of Hamlet as anything but robust (his mature conception, at least[129]) is confirmed by his own words, facetious but revealing, in a letter to his friend Adam Badeau: "The tragedy of Hamlet . . . is being 'done' in the paint-room, the wardrobe & the property-rooms of the Winter Garden for me—I shall be called upon to be genteel & gentle—or rather pale & polite, about the 27th of November. . . ."[130] The gentleness and pallor of Booth's ideal Hamlet were not just superficial traits; they were the essence of the character. This fact is evident from his interest in E. P. Vining's now notorious little book *The*

127. *Lectures on Dramatic Literature*, pp. 95, 100-101.
128. Edwina Booth Grossmann, *Edwin Booth: Recollections by His Daughter, and Letters to Her and Her Friends* (New York, 1894), pp. 8-9.
129. William Winter recalls that Booth in his early days was "brilliant and impetuous" in Hamlet as in his other roles. See his article, "Edwin Booth," *Harper's*, LXIII (June, 1881), 61-68; especially pp. 64-65.
130. MS letter in the Folger Library, addressed to Lt. Col. Adam Badeau of the Federal Army, dated only "New York Octr 14th." The emphasis on new scenery and the near-perfect coincidence of the opening November date which Booth mentions make it certain that he was preparing for the famous production that opened on November 26, 1864, and ran for one hundred nights.

Mystery of Hamlet (Philadelphia, 1881), whose thesis is that Shakespeare in his ultimate revision of the play intended Hamlet to be a woman. Vining argued that Hamlet has many "feminine" traits: gentleness, dependence upon others, shrewdness and subtlety rather than strength, a preference for winning by indirect means rather than driving straight ahead, an effective use of the power of speech as a weapon, a fear of death, impulsiveness, sensitiveness, a tendency to become hysterical. Booth shrugged off Vining's "theory" as "absurd" but agreed with "much that he urges in support of it."

I have always endeavored to make prominent the femininity of Hamlet's character and therein lies the secret of my success—I think. I doubt if ever a robust and masculine treatment of the character will be accepted as generally as the more womanly and refined interpretation. I know that frequently I fall into effeminacy, but we can't always hit the proper keynote.[131]

The idea of Hamlet that emerges from such passages as these seems—as Hamlet himself seemed to Hazlitt—essentially undramatic. Had the actor-critics been hypnotized by the literary men of their age into accepting an interpretation that could not be translated into theatrical terms? Or was Hazlitt wrong about the limitations of acting? It is difficult to imagine an effective impersonation of Booth's ideal—that gentle, poetic "study of his own soul." Yet descriptions of his performance, despite their Victorian sentimentality, still convey the impression of fascinating drama. Among the most graphic accounts by his theatrical colleagues is that of KITTY MOLONY, who particularly admired Booth's gift for dramatizing the mental and emotional life of a character without benefit of overt action. In Hamlet's first scene, Booth "sat in unaffected quiet—not a muscle contracted or relaxed—yet his audience read each separate thought of his mind; he did not even shift his eyes, but their color changed from flame to smoke and back again." Hamlet's suffering, his bitterness and suspicion were all expressed in Booth's reactions to his uncle's speech before his own voice was ever heard.

At the words, "Our sometime sister, now our queen," and again at "taken to wife," his audience saw his pain as if the skin were suddenly torn from his quivering nerves. Irony, even while listening, mastered

131. MS letter to William Winter, in the Folger Library. It is headed merely "At Nashville—10th," but a pencilled notation gives the date January 10, 1882.

his mind. . . . When later, he spoke his line to the Ghost, "Oh, my prophetic soul, my uncle!" it came not as surprise to the audience. They had already seen his prophetic soul.

This intense, quietly suffering Hamlet met his death not as a tragic hero but as a touching example of humanity. "For the most pitiful cry I have ever heard, 'Oh, I die, Horatio—' sobs echoed him from the front. Mr. Booth was not philosopher, here. It was youth robbed of life before it had lived. His pathos was unbearable. He was so cheated by death."[132]

HENRY IRVING was acutely conscious of Hazlitt's challenge. He replied to it in words as well as in his acting (his Hamlet of 1874-75, which ran for two hundred nights, was a deliberate attempt to dramatize a man's inner life). No actor can hope to "achieve . . . complete command" over all the elements that make Hamlet a universal figure, Irving admitted—his "striving," his "lovable weaknesses," his tenderness, his "groping" toward the unknown. "But . . . to disentangle . . . from traditions . . . one of the most vividly real of all the conceptions of art, to leave upon your generation the impression of Hamlet as a man . . . this is, perhaps, the highest aim which the English-speaking actor can cherish."[133] To "present the man thinking aloud" is the "most difficult achievement" of the player's art; yet "it is perfectly possible to express to an audience all the involutions of thought, the speculation, doubt, wavering, which reveal the meditative but irresolute mind."[134] Although he recognized Hamlet's universality, when he acted the part Irving stressed his personal idiosyncrasies; for he was interested in creating an individual, not a grand generalization. By combining tragedy and character acting he was able to make dramatic a seemingly undramatic trait which had been attributed to the character: an introverted habit of mind. As Edward R. Russell remarked in a review for the Liverpool *Daily News*: "[Irving] has noticed that Hamlet . . . has a trick—not at all uncommon in persons whose most real life is an inner one—of fostering and aggravating his own excitements."[135] Irving's own comments confirm and supplement this observation:

132. Goodale, *Behind the Scenes with Edwin Booth*, pp. 176-78, 181-82.
133. Henry Irving, "My Four Favorite Parts," *The Forum*, XVI (September, 1893), 34-35.
134. Henry Irving, *The Drama* (New York, 1893), pp. 60-61.
135. Quoted by Austin Brereton in *The Life of Henry Irving* (New York, 1908), I, 179.

In all Hamlet's assumptions of mental wandering he is greatly aided by the excitability of his temperament. His emotions are always ready to carry him away, and his wild imaginings easily lend themselves to the maddest disguises of speech. A flash of volition may often be the exponent of a chain of thought. . . .[136]

The histrionic strain that Irving evidently saw in Hamlet divided his mental conception of the character from Edwin Booth's, just as different acting styles divided their stage representations. But the two were alike in their general romantic tendency toward emphasizing the mind rather than the physical actions of Hamlet. They were alike, too, in a certain spiritual emphasis; for one of Irving's ideals in impersonating Hamlet was "to suggest that sense of the supernatural which holds the genius of romance like a veil, and that haunted look of one who is constantly with the spirit."[137]

As with Booth, there are admiring tributes from Irving's fellow actors which, by their descriptions, suggest the means whereby Hamlet's "mind" became interesting theatrical material. According to ELLEN TERRY, Hamlet's melancholy appearance was emphasized by Irving's very pale makeup, which "at a distance . . . gave him a haggard look." His first entrance was very much "worked up," for Irving never scorned theatrical effects. The scene began with a procession which, with the accompanying music, built up a feeling of anticipation.

At its tail, when the excitement was at fever heat, came the solitary figure of Hamlet, looking extraordinarily tall and thin. The lights were turned down—another stage trick—to help the effect that the figure was spirit rather than man. He was weary. His cloak trailed on the ground. . . . The hair was blue-black, like the plumage of a crow; the eyes burning—two fires veiled as yet by melancholy.

Miss Terry's most interesting description—one that Sir John Gielgud has used as a guide in his own acting—is of the scene in which Hamlet is told of the Ghost.

[Irving] began by being very absent and distant. He exchanged greetings sweetly and gently, but his head was towards the stars "where the eternal are." Years later he said to me of another actor. . . . "He would never have seen the ghost." Well, there was never any doubt

136. Sir Henry Irving, "An Actor's Notes on Shakespeare: II. Hamlet and Ophelia," *Nineteenth Century*, I (1877), 527.
137. "My Four Favorite Parts," pp. 34-35.

that Henry Irving saw it, and it was through his acting in this scene
. . . that he made us sure. . . . Bit by bit as Horatio talks, Hamlet
comes back into the world. He is still out of it when he says:
  My father! Methinks I see my father.
But the dreamer becomes attentive, sharp as a needle, with the words:
  For God's love, let me hear.

Obviously Ellen Terry saw no lack of theatrical appeal in Irving's
gentle, well-bred Hamlet—"touching . . . rather than defiant" in
his melancholy, and "never rude to Polonius"—for she declared
that Hamlet was Irving's greatest role "by far" and that Irving
was Hamlet's greatest representative.[138]

From 1818 to the end of the century, then, the romantic ideal
dominated the actor-critics' discussions of Hamlet, and it was
successfully embodied on the stage in some instances, particularly
in the acting of Booth and Irving. But this conception was not
universally held by actor-critics of the period; and still less was it
universally transmitted in the theatre. If the years that we have
scanned for evidences of romantic interpretation are surveyed
again for opposite tendencies, at least a few notable ones will be
found.

WILLIAM CHARLES MACREADY's conception, particularly, stands
out in contrast to the ultraromantic ones of his time. It is ironic,
and a little puzzling, that Macready nevertheless admired the
interpretation of Hamlet in *Wilhelm Meister*—the best idea of
the character that could be gained from reading a book, so he
remarked, and the nearest approach to what "a great actor and
critic would write if he could."[139] It is tempting to suppose that
he was attracted to this interpretation mainly because in the
novel it is expounded by an actor—and, moreover, by one who is
attempting to reconcile the apparent inconsistencies in the role
of Hamlet. For Macready himself was very much aware of those
inconsistencies: to render them "reconcilable and intelligible,"
he wrote, is "the artist's study"; although even mediocre actors
can win theatrical success in this character, they are "utterly in-
competent to investigate the springs of emotion which agitate and
perplex this amiable, reflective, and sensitive being."[140] Mac-

138. *Ellen Terry's Memoirs*, ed. Edith Craig and Christopher St. John [Christabel
Marshall] (New York, 1932), pp. 102-4, 106-7. For the influence on Gielgud, see
John Gielgud's Hamlet, ed. Gilder, pp. 39-41.
139. *Macready's Reminiscences*, ed. Pollock, p. 655.
140. *Ibid.*, pp. 36, 165.

ready's belief that the language of Hamlet is "often a disguise for the passion beneath it" must have helped him explain some of the seeming contradictions in the part, for by means of it he could discern in the speeches whose literal meaning did not fit his conception "a truth of feeling . . . in their opposition to truth of fact."[141] His ideas about Hamlet's progress through disillusionment to reconciliation would also have helped him to account for the disparate elements in the character. As he once remarked to a friend: "In the early acts of 'Hamlet' I seek to express . . . the impetuous rebellion of a generous nature when its trust has been cruelly deceived; in the last act, the resignation of a generous nature when the storm has spent itself;—in presenting the striking contrasts of this conception—its passion, its imagination, its irony, its colloquial realism."[142] Although Macready's occasional use of adjectives like "reflective" and "sensitive" suggests affinities between his conception and Wilhelm Meister's, Macready—as two of his diary entries make clear—endowed Hamlet with stronger passions and greater fixity of purpose that did Goethe's hero. On July 20, 1835, he wrote:

The ease and dignified familiarity, the apparent levity of manner, with the deep purpose that lies beneath, which should be marked distinctly in the representation of Hamlet—are so difficult of execution that I almost despair of moderately satisfying myself.

Several years later (February 7, 1844) he recorded his pleasure in a performance that did satisfy him: "Acted Hamlet . . . in a very Shakespearian style; most courteous and gentlemanly, with high bearing and yet with abandonment and . . . great energy."[143]

True to his conception of Hamlet, Macready made the character in performance "less the melancholy musing Dane than he is generally represented" (so Westland Marston recalled), with "more of passion than of sentiment in the rendering"—he was more bitter toward Ophelia in the nunnery scene than were his stage contemporaries, sterner toward his mother in the closet scene, more "keen, glittering, and venomous" toward Claudius

141. *Ibid.*, pp. 164, 661. An example is Hamlet's speech in the closet scene: "Almost as bad, good mother, / As kill a king and marry with his brother." The words are "inconsequent . . . unjustifiable, but they are what Hamlet would have said."

142. Westland Marston, *Our Recent Actors* (London, 1888), I, 81.

143. *Diaries of Macready*, ed. Toynbee, I, 242; II, 261.

in the play scene.[144] Yet Macready was sufficiently successful in portraying Hamlet's many-sided character that his friend Lady Pollock could remark: "after his highest flights of passion, his spirits fell back, subsiding into the attitude of gentleness which was the essence of his nature." (Lady Pollock's description of Macready's "flexible, impressionable" Hamlet brings his performance closer to Goethe's interpretation than do those of most other observers.) She tells us, too, how this Hamlet, because of the "towering state" of supernatural exaltation in the ghost scene, achieved the difficult task of giving "dignity to the wild and whirling words in the subsequent dialogue with Horatio, so long omitted on the stage before Macready restored them, knowing how he could use them."[145] In both theory and practice Macready's interpretation reminds us of the earlier tradition—of Burbage's, Betterton's, Garrick's bitterness, awe, and passion, tempered with the princely courtesy and the occasional gentleness prescribed by such actor-critics as Pilon and Holcroft.

One or two of Macready's contemporaries (in the first half of the century), though not so strongly influenced by the old tradition as Macready himself was, showed in their criticisms some lingering traces of it. As we noticed earlier, James H. Hackett differed from the more romantically inclined actor-critics in his idea of Hamlet's impetuosity, even though he was like them in other respects. It is interesting that he, like Macready, preferred Goethe's interpretation of Hamlet to that of most other writers. Hackett's critiques of other actors' performances reveal much about the extent to which he agreed, on the one hand, with the *Wilhelm Meister* conception and, on the other, with the traditional interpretation that had been continued, but more fully rationalized, by Macready. Although he ridiculed Edwin Forrest's impersonation of "an enraged and sinewy athlete" who, if given his way, would have ended the play in the first act, and

144. Marston, *Our Recent Actors*, I, 80-83. On pp. 82-83 Marston tells of a bit of Macready's interpretation at the end of the ghost scene: "About to depart, he turned to Horatio and Marcellus, and, saying, in a tone tender and hushed, 'Nay, come, let's go together,' led them off the stage." Marston remarked to Macready that "this act of fellowship . . . had greatly struck me, as indicating the sense of brotherhood . . . which the awe of a supernatural visitation would call forth." Macready, pleased, replied that this was "one of those minute touches . . . that an actor throws in only after long familiarity with a part."

145. Lady [Juliet Creed] Pollock, *Macready As I knew Him* (London, 1884), pp. 105-8.

although he wished for more quietness and refinement in Macready's Hamlet, Hackett also found fault with William Augustus Conway for his lack of "warmth" in the "spirited parts" of the role, and he praised Edmund Kean—most spirited of actors—for illustrating "the soul of Hamlet" more "ably" than any other performer he had seen. Since he admired Kean's pungent satire as well as his "intellectuality and sensitiveness," his "heart-stirring" passion as well as his plaintive melancholy, Hackett must have agreed with Macready that the character requires, not only gentleness and delicacy, but also "great energy."[146] His greatest difference from Macready (as far as theory was concerned)—and his greatest likeness to Goethe—was in the ideas of Hamlet's diffuseness of purpose and his lack of physical nerve.

Contemporary with Edwin Booth's "pale and polite" Hamlet was the startlingly heroic interpretation of Charles Fechter, the French actor (first given in England in 1861, in America in 1870). The detailed and sympathetic description of his performance written by KATE FIELD, an American actress and journalist, makes it clear that at least one actor-critic was emancipated from the romantic conception of Hamlet. Fechter's Hamlet, she writes, "was not the introspective student of tradition. He was a man of the world, in the noblest sense of the term, of joyous disposition, whose temper—and here he agrees with Goethe—assumed its mournful tinge upon the death of his father. . . ." This Hamlet showed frequent glimpses of his old self: in the humor that could not be stifled, even on the most tragic occasions; in the enjoyment of the actor's art; in the love of sports which made him "so sensitive of his prowess in fencing as to be somewhat jealous of Laertes' reputation." He was eager for revenge, and was withheld only by a "reasonable doubt" of the Ghost, "not vacillation of purpose." His self-accusations were those of an active man, restrained from his purposes by circumstances, who keeps himself "in training" by cursing a nonexistent cowardice. Fechter's Hamlet was not allowed to glimpse Claudius in the nunnery scene because if he had known that the King was spying on him he would not have

146. For his praise of Goethe see *Notes, Criticisms, Correspondence*, pp. 58-59. For his critiques of other actors' interpretations see pp. 123-24, 127, 143-44. I have greatly simplified Hackett's criticism of Macready, but I believe I have drawn a fair conclusion from the kinds of objections that he raised: e.g. to Macready's brisk and abrupt movements, unsuited to "one of princely education, leisurely habits, and a contemplative turn of mind."

needed *The Murder of Gonzago*. As soon as he caught the conscience of the King he was ready to drink hot blood; and the soliloquy in the prayer scene was meant quite literally. Claudius had Hamlet heavily guarded and dispatched to England immediately because he knew that Hamlet would kill him without hesitation. Miss Field remarks that Fechter's interpretation is "sympathetic" to her "in all things, except perhaps in this matter of vacillation; and even here one may make out a strong case." The only passage that seems to demand a vacillating Hamlet is the appearance of the Ghost in the closet scene. "Do you not come your tardy son to chide?" may be simply another unwarranted self-accusation. And the Ghost's desire to "whet thy almost blunted purpose" can be explained as an effort to restrain the infuriated Hamlet from killing his mother (whom he suspects of complicity in the murder) instead of the King.[147]

Fechter's Hamlet caused a furore among critics—Dickens said of it, "Perhaps no innovation in art was ever accepted with so much favor by so many intellectual persons, precommitted to . . . another system. . . ."[148] But there were other performers, less brilliant and less sensational, whose Hamlets also gave little impression of irresolution: for example, Daniel Bandmann. Of his interpretation CLARA MORRIS declared: "If *Hamlet* had had all that tremendous fund of energy, all that love of action, the Ghost need never have returned. . . ."[149] Indeed there was probably never a time when some of the stage Hamlets did not create an impression of greater robustness than the written descriptions would suggest. Some adherents of the romantic theory, though they considered Hamlet weak in determination, felt that he should occasionally give way to strong bursts of passion. (James Murdoch, for example, held this view. He tried to reconcile vehemence with indecisiveness by the statement that Hamlet's nature was "charged with the strong instincts of a northern race, but borne down by burdens too great for mortals to bear."[150]) On the stage such outbreaks might tend to suggest greater forcefulness of character than could be deduced from the theory behind them; for passion,

147. Kate Field, *Charles Albert Fechter* (Boston, 1882), pp. 87-117; especially pp. 89-96, 106, 110, 113.
148. *Ibid.*, p. 182.
149. Clara Morris, *Life on the Stage: My Personal Experiences and Recollections* (New York, 1901), pp. 158-59.
150. "A Short Study of 'Hamlet,' " p. 498.

if strongly expressed, sometimes creates the effect of action. Even those actor-critics who disliked the loud, physical manifestation of passion probably wanted Hamlet to give the impression of deep, inward feeling—particularly grief, or the agony of an unresolved mental conflict. Thus Miss Morris, despite her scorn for the active Hamlet, was equally dissatisfied with E. L. Davenport's "fair, high-browed, princely philosopher"; for, she complained, he had no conception of the "tender heart, the dread imaginings, the wounded pride and love, the fits and starts, the pain and passion that tortures *Hamlet* each in turn."[151] But an unusually fine actor is required to communicate such emotions quietly or to hold an audience's interest while attempting to make Hamlet's inner life more real than his outer one. (Charles Kean, for all his insistence on "mental rather than physical illustration," was sometimes accused of being melodramatic.[152]) It is not surprising, therefore, that Irving's deliberately Hazlitt-like interpretation was considered new in 1874 or that the unexpected quietness of the early scenes was, at first, disappointing.[153] Even after the combined influence of Booth in America and Irving in England had established more firmly the ideal of a romantic Hamlet on the stage as well as in the study, no doubt some of their less gifted colleagues, incapable of making "effects" with a Hamlet who is "little of an actor," fell back on the physical possibilities of the role.

Toward the end of the nineteenth century there were signs of increasing dissatisfaction with the romantic conception of Hamlet, even though it continued to dominate critical thought. DION BOUCICAULT, for example, accepted the interpretation (or much of it) but, in consequence, reacted against the character itself. Although his fulminations, vented during a convivial evening (a birthday celebration for Tommaso Salvini on January 1, 1883), probably carried more smoke than fire, they signaled the direction of his thoughts. When Hamlet's name was brought into the conversation he reacted with what must have been mock violence: "Don't talk to me about Hamlet! A man that ought to have been

151. *Life on the Stage*, p. 185.
152. Henry P. Phelps writes in *Hamlet from the Actor's Standpoint* (New York, 1890), p. 16, that Charles Kean's Hamlet was considered "too tearful for the best effect" and that "On the whole, it was thought that he was more melodramatic than Shakespearian."
153. Brereton, *Life of Irving*, I, 172-73.

a woman—that didn't know his own mind five minutes—an hysterical idiot—." When Salvini objected to this description, Boucicault retaliated with the eighteenth-century charge of cruelty: "Yes, he is, and *brutal* too! Always a brute when he is not a coward!" Salvini pointed out, reasonably enough, that Hamlet was reacting to the brutality of others, but Boucicault would not be persuaded.[154] No doubt his chief intention was to bait Salvini, who was himself a fine Hamlet; but, even allowing for exaggeration, his comments suggest that not all actors found the "feminine" Hamlet as appealing as Booth did.

Other evidence of dissatisfaction took more serious forms. WILSON BARRETT rejected certain elements in the now-conventional conception and made positive efforts to establish his own idea of Hamlet in public favor through his controversial stage interpretation in 1884 and through an essay, published in 1890, justifying his theories. And WILLIAM POEL, who shared some of Barrett's ideas,[155] expressed his opinions about Hamlet from time to time in essays and in letters to the newspapers over a period of several decades. Both of these men were convinced of Hamlet's youthfulness and sanity (points we will discuss later), and both thought that too much emphasis had been placed upon his indecisiveness and inaction.

In his essay Barrett summarized the plot of the play to demonstrate Hamlet's alertness and determination in most incidents. "Hamlet does not hesitate," he concluded; "he does pause and ponder at times, but at others the swiftness of his action is most marvelous; and surely both sides of his character should be considered."[156] (In acting, Barrett put most emphasis upon the energetic and resolute side: he was too "full-blooded and declam-

154. [Thomas Russell Sullivan], "Tommaso Salvini Amico ed Artista Ricordi d'Affelto." MS in The Harvard Theatre Collection. It is a Boswell-like account of the evening of Salvini's fifty-fourth birthday. Boucicault's off-the-cuff remarks recorded here are more interesting than the formal discussion of Hamlet in his lecture, *The Art of Acting* (Dramatic Museum of Columbia University, Papers on Acting No. I [New York, 1926]).

155. Not only his ideas about Hamlet's character but also about the production of the play. In a letter to Moy Thomas of the London *Daily News*, October 23, 1884, Poel called attention to the fact that the current production of *Hamlet* at the Princess's Theatre (Barrett's) was using several of the ideas that he himself had suggested in 1881 in a paper for the New Shakspere Society, later published in the *Era*. (MS in the Folger Library).

156. *Mr. Wilson Barrett on the Sanity and Age of Hamlet* (Reprinted from *Lippincott's Magazine*, April, 1890), p. 2.

atory" to be really Shakespearean, SEYMOUR HICKS decided, but was preferable to "some of the limp backboneless slayers of Polonius that we are so often treated to nowadays."[157])

Like Barrett, Poel accepted without question Hamlet's reasoning in the prayer scene, and he argued warmly that the omission of the soliloquy from stage versions not only distorts Shakespeare's portrayal of Hamlet's character but also ruins his carefully constructed chain of events. According to him, Hamlet is "a student, a controversialist, and a moralist"—the kind of person who "instinctively rebels" against the idea of murder; yet his devotion to filial duty is so strong that it triumphs over his natural temperament. Actors who omit the speeches that show Hamlet's real desire to kill the King are betraying Shakespeare's intentions by exploiting the sentiment of the character and glossing over its darker inclinations. Without the soliloquy in the prayer scene, plot as well as character is changed; for an important link is lost between the play scene and the closet scene, and the full consequences of Hamlet's "clemency" are not realized by the audience. Shakespeare shows Hamlet, at three different periods in the play, desiring to kill Claudius but being thwarted in some way:

. . . the Ghost's word must first be challenged; then the mother's wishes must be respected; while the King's prayers must not be interrupted; and when the next opportunity occurs the wrong man is killed. This is the sequence of the story, and it should not be broken.[158]

For Poel, as for Barrett, Hamlet had more than one side to his character—the active as well as the meditative, the bitter as well as the gentle, the colloquial as well as the lofty. He could not forgive actors for slighting any of these simply to make Hamlet a more sympathetic character (as by showing unwarranted tenderness to Gertrude in the closet scene) or to exploit the theatrical possibilities of individual scenes (as by railing at Ophelia in the nunnery scene). Nor could he repress a sneer at the tragic solem-

157. Seymour Hicks, *Twenty-four Years of an Actor's Life* (London, 1910), p. 207.

158. *Shakespeare in the Theatre*, pp. 168-69. *See also* Speaight, *William Poel and the Elizabethan Revival* (Cambridge, Mass., 1954), p. 56. Speaight remarks that Poel "rather cavalierly brushed aside the Ghost's 'thy almost blunted purpose' as evidence of chronic procrastination, and held that Hamlet's inaction was due to a genuine doubt . . . as to whether the King's death would be in accordance with Divine Will." Speaight considers this idea incongruous with Poel's acceptance of Hamlet's reasoning in the prayer scene.

nity with which some of them spoke the "tersest and raciest" dialogue in the English language.[159] It was because Salvini scorned
such staginess and because—as Poel thought—he was faithful to
Shakespeare's total conception of Hamlet (despite his badly-cut
version of the play, he gave evidence of having studied the character from the whole text) that the Italian actor seemed to Poel
the only perfect representative of Hamlet within living memory.[160]

But, regardless of such attempts to minimize Hamlet's irresolution and thus return to something more nearly approaching
the earlier tradition, the strongly-intrenched romantic tradition
retained its sway until well into the twentieth century. The influence of Booth and Irving was partly responsible, no doubt.
In 1900, seven years after Booth's death, ELIZABETH ROBINS was
still using the memory of his Hamlet as a criterion for other performances. In comparison with it, Sarah Bernhardt's interpretation seemed petty to her: instead of the gentle, melancholy prince,
it was "an amazingly good imitation of a high-spirited, somewhat
malicious boy." Miss Robins supposed that the Elizabethans had
held a similar conception, deriving from the pre-Shakespearean
Hamlet, and she admitted that "Hamlet in *action*" seems to justify
it; but she insisted that "the reflective Hamlet . . . is the essential
Shakespeare." Her own conception of the character is obviously
the one she identified with Booth's acting: Hamlet's "mental
isolation" is peculiar to his nature, not incidental to his position;
though his princeliness is essential, a peasant with the "same cast
of mind . . . would have walked lonely in plowed furrows." It is
this trait which makes the real tragedy: "not that he is foully
robbed of an earthly father, but that he is spiritually fatherless."[161]
Even as late as 1920 FREDERICK WARDE was looking back to Booth's
creation as his ideal Hamlet: "a light youthful figure . . . with
dark waving hair clustering around a pale, thoughtful face . . .
moving with a quiet dignity, his eyes indicating the deep sorrow
of his heart, and speaking in a sweetly modulated colloquial
tone."[162]

159. Speaight, *William Poel and the Elizabethan Revival,* pp. 52-53.
160. *Monthly Letters* (London, 1929), pp. 7-8. *See also* his letter to the *Era,*
April 26, 1884, quoted by Speaight (*William Poel,* pp. 26-27).
161. Elizabeth Robins, "On Seeing Madame Bernhardt's Hamlet," *North American Review,* CLXXI (December, 1900), 908-14. The quotations are from pp.
909-11, and Miss Robins's detailed comparison of Booth and Mme. Bernhardt is
on pp. 911-14.
162. Frederick Warde, *Fifty Years of Make-Believe* (New York, 1920), p. 118.

BEERBOHM TREE shows in his criticism of Hamlet the influence not only of Irving, whom he admired tremendously,[163] but also (directly or indirectly) of the romantic literary critics. For example, his description of the "young prince of lofty ideals" and "natural refinement" recalls Goethe's, except that it unnecessarily degrades the Danish Court by adding that the sensitive Hamlet is as much out of place there "as a jewelled ring in a hog's snout." His discussion of Hamlet's delay owes something, but not everything, to the Coleridge tradition. The original cause, according to Tree, is physical exhaustion after the ordeal of the ghost scene, but the continued postponement of revenge is due to an excess of thought, particularly to Hamlet's tendency to look at all sides of a question. His sense of humor, which enables him to laugh at himself, to joke and pun in the midst of the most tragic circumstances, is one manifestation of this tendency. Another is his skeptical questioning of conventional values. "There's nothing either good or bad, but thinking makes it so"—in this statement lies the key to Hamlet's character and to the whole tragedy. Unlike the practical Fortinbras, who looks straight ahead to his goal, Hamlet wanders into "the by-lanes of philosophical contemplation." Yet his attempt to determine what is right for him rather than accepting what is expedient is admirable, even though it leads to his downfall. Although Tree's basic conception of Hamlet is derivative, the limbs and outward flourishes are his own. Most individual of the branches is his idea of the "literary" nature of Hamlet's genius: when the drawn sword falls back into its scabbard, Hamlet seizes the pen instead (to record his uncle's smiling villainy in his "tables"); and in his feigned madness he "takes an intellectual and painful delight in exercising his ingenuity and wit upon the various dupes. . . . He is, in fact, always an artist—the literary man who makes copy out of his own emotions. . . ."[164] There is some likeness here to the self-dramatizing tendency that Irving discerned in the character, but there is also a rather unlovely difference.

Influences from the past were not the only nourishment for romantic criticism in the last years of the nineteenth century and

163. Maud Holt Tree, "Herbert and I," *Herbert Beerbohm Tree: Some Memories of Him and His Art*, ed. Max Beerbohm (New York, [1920]), p. 62.

164. *Thoughts and Afterthoughts*, pp. 125-35, 146, 152-56. Tree's discussion of Hamlet's sense of humor is found in his article in the *New York Times* (March 19, 1916), Sec. 4, p. 3.

ACTORS' CRITICISMS OF HAMLET · 93

the early years of the twentieth. Beerbohm Tree's stage interpretation was not greatly admired by his fellow players (except by his Ophelia, who was also his wife),[165] but another performance in the romantic tradition—that of JOHNSTON FORBES-ROBERTSON— must have been very influential. Actors joined the other critics in praising it: for example, J. H. BARNES described it as "the Hamlet of our time—graceful, feeling, pathetic, scholarly, lovable."[166] And Seymour Hicks, who saw it "three times in one week and paid on all occasions," wrote that this princely and gentlemanly Hamlet, though simple and untheatrical, held the audience "rivetted" from the moment he stepped upon the stage.[167] Forbes-Robertson's 1897 production of *Hamlet* was notable for its restoration of Fortinbras in the last act, made at the suggestion of George Bernard Shaw[168] (the acting editions of that time customarily ended with "The rest is silence"), and through the years this actor retained the innovation, convinced of its correctness. In 1913 he replied to a critic's objection that anything after Hamlet's dying speech is anticlimactic: "It seems to me important that Fortinbras the man of action should be contrasted with the dreamer Hamlet."[169] He assured another correspondent that he did not consider Hamlet a weakling: "No, my friend was neither wishy-washy nor namby-pamby, as I have always tried to impress upon my audiences, but, he was not a man of action."[170] Perhaps Ellen Terry was not simply telling Shaw what he wanted to hear when she wrote of Forbes-Robertson's conclusion: "I could never understand how Fortinbras could be left out, if the whole of what the play means is to be conveyed to the spectators. That

165. Lady Tree's enthusiastic description is found in "Herbert and I," p. 64. For a less sympathetic criticism see Mrs. Patrick Campbell, *My Life and Some Letters* (New York, 1922), p. 307. Constance Collier writes in *Harlequinade: The Story of My Life* (London, [1929]), p. 99, that Tree was physically unsuited to play Hamlet but that his conception of the character was the finest in her memory.

166. *Forty Years on the Stage* (London, 1914), p. 215.

167. Seymour Hicks, *Me and My Missus* (London, [1939]), p. 176.

168. Sir Johnston Forbes-Robertson acknowledges in his autobiography, *A Player under Three Reigns* (Boston, 1925), pp. 183-84, that his production of *Hamlet* owed much to a long letter of advice from Shaw but says that he has misplaced the letter. William A. Armstrong, in his article, "Bernard Shaw and Forbes-Robertson's *Hamlet*," *Shakespeare Quarterly*, XV (Winter, 1964), 27-31, reconstructs Shaw's suggestions.

169. Forbes-Robertson's letter, written October 20, 1913, was to Alonzo Church. Church quotes it in his own letter to William Winter, dated April 23, 1916. The latter, a MS in the Folger Library, is my source.

170. Letter to Hull Platt, dated February 1, 1910. MS in the Folger Library.

beastly *Do-er* coming in all swelling and victorious at the end of the play, makes me love more than ever the gentle dead prince."[171]

Although in the past half century or so the idea of an irresolute or largely inactive Hamlet has lost its dominant position in actors' criticisms, it has never completely died out. Let us begin our examination of modern interpretations by considering the romantic survivals—or, in some cases, mutations.

Occasionally a romantic view has been restated by a modern actor in unequivocal terms: for example, by JOHN BARRYMORE, who found Goethe's analysis the most satisfactory of all attempts to explain the character,[172] and, more recently, by SIR LAURENCE OLIVIER, who remarked that *Hamlet*, "the greatest of all plays . . . was the first to be created by an author with the courage to give his audience a hero with none of the usual excursions of heroism." Olivier recognized the many possibilities of interpretation, but the choice for his filmed production was clear-cut: "a nearly great man—damned by lack of resolution, as all but one in a hundred are."[173] In actual practice, however, neither of these actors adhered completely to the romantic interpretation that he espoused. Barrymore's performance was evidently more virile than might be suggested by his borrowed metaphor of the delicate vase shattered by the expanding oak tree: Poel, who rejected the idea of chronic irresolution, considered Barrymore's the best of contemporary English-speaking Hamlets.[174] As for Olivier, he opened his film with the words "This is the tragedy of a man who could not make up his mind"; but his omission of the soliloquy "How all occasions do inform against me" detracted somewhat from the interpretation, and, in Sir Tyrone Guthrie's opinion at least, Olivier's acting was robust enough to contradict the initial statement of theme.[175]

171. *Ellen Terry and Bernard Shaw: A Correspondence*, ed. Christopher St. John [Christabel Marshall] (New York, 1931), p. 182. The letter is dated September 4, 1897.

172. *Confessions of an Actor*, Ch. IV (the pages are not numbered).

173. Laurence Olivier, "An Essay in Hamlet," *The Film Hamlet*, ed. Brenda Cross (London, 1948), p. 13.

174. Speaight, *William Poel and the Elizabethan Revival*, pp. 27-28.

175. Tyrone Guthrie, "Why and How They Play Hamlet," *New York Times Magazine*, August 14, 1960, p. 42. Felix Barker says, in *The Oliviers: A Biography* (London, [1953]), p. 262, that Olivier considered "How all occasions. . . ." the "most illuminating" of all the speeches "in showing the development of Hamlet's character" but that he cut it from the final version of the film because it was

Certain other actor-critics of the modern period—HARLEY GRANVILLE-BARKER,[176] for example, and ROBERT SPEAIGHT[177]—have shown the influence of romantic criticism in a more subtle way. Granville-Barker's interpretation of Hamlet is certainly more complex and original than those mentioned above, yet it probably would not have been quite the same without his attraction to some aspects of the romantic conception. Speaight, though he shows his heritage even more plainly, does not exactly duplicate any of the earlier images of Hamlet. The older critic takes the more objective approach to Hamlet's inconsistencies: according to his reasoning, they were originally due to Shakespeare's inability to effect a complete fusion of his imaginative creation with the materials he inherited from the old story: yet this very imperfection became, through Shakespeare's genius, the "dramatic symbol of the true tragedy of Hamlet, which is the tragedy of a spiritual revolution." Speaight, on the other hand, is interested in Hamlet as a person in his own right rather than as a literary creation, seeing in his brilliant but contradictory endowments the evidence of a personality that "will never be . . . integrated."

Granville-Barker's discussion is the more sympathetic of the two: it shows a development in the character, and it assumes Hamlet's ultimate success, though at the price of suffering and death. At the beginning of the play Hamlet is inwardly divided and weakened by disillusionment in his mother; the supernatural shock divides him still further. Yet even without this schism he would have been unsuited to the task imposed upon him. In order to achieve his revenge, he must go through a "dire process of conversion" in which "his finer traits—gentleness, simplicity, generosity—must be blunted." He must learn to be callous, even cruel. We see him in the process of this change: the old Hamlet appears in his courtesy to the players, the new in his mockery of Polonius. When he returns from his brief but eventful voyage, we know from his attitude and manner (for example, his lack of remorse over the fate of his school fellows) that he is at last prepared to execute his task. Although much that was beautiful

nearly five minutes long and came at a moment when "it was unwise to be discursive."
176. *Prefaces to Shakespeare*, I, 231-32, 248-50.
177. *Nature in Shakespearian Tragedy*, pp. 11, 22-23, 26-28.

in his character has been sacrificed and although Hamlet has been ravaged, physically and mentally, his spirit has not been "debased." We feel that, once the terrible duty is accomplished, he will be at peace, will even be a better man because of his ordeal. "But that cannot be. The penalty of things done in that 'sore distraction' must be paid."

Speaight's Hamlet is a fascinating failure. His major trait—in fact, his tragic flaw—is his intense subjectivism. Since he has "made himself the measure of all things," seeing good and bad as merely relevant to his own thoughts, he has lost the spontaneous ability to translate right thoughts into right actions. One aspect of this subjectivism is his histrionic inclination—a characteristic that reflects his "divorce from reality." Hamlet's feigned madness is an escape into a "never-never land." His plan to have *The Murder of Gonzago* performed is equally irresponsible: the play could have been made to serve some practical purpose, but instead Hamlet "whips up a number of belated doubts" about the authenticity of the Ghost and plots to "catch the conscience of the King"—nothing more. In "O what a rogue" he does not reproach himself for doing nothing but for feeling nothing: rather than being crushed by his terrible knowledge, "he has been distracted, almost agreeably, by the game that he has been playing with the Court. His real emotions have grown numb." Because of his self-preoccupation and his lack of self-discipline, Hamlet's mission to cure a diseased society goes unfulfilled.

There is more than a glimpse of Wilhelm Meister's conception in Granville-Barker's description of Hamlet as he originally was. But the latter's delicate vase is not permanently shattered by adversity; it is remolded with a toughening alloy. Ideas associated with A. C. Bradley's exposition of Shakespearean tragedy—particularly "tragic waste," and, somehow coexisting with it, a feeling of regeneration—are implicit in Granville-Barker's interpretation as well. These elements, however, do not strike the reader as borrowings—except as one artist borrows inspiration from another. Speaight's echo of earlier ideas seems to me a little different. Mainly, he has restated them in terms of modern thought: thus the inconsistencies that once suggested universal humanity now suggest a fragmented personality; a self-dramatizing tendency, combined with a greater concern for the world of thought than the world of action, is easily translated into flight from reality; a man who is "little of a hero" becomes an antihero. The whole image is romantic, but it is reversed by the mirror in which it is reflected.

It is time now to look at some of the criticisms by actors of the present century that question or oppose the romantic interpretations. Some of them take the literary critics to task for misrepresenting Hamlet's character. LOUIS CALVERT[178] finds it "inconceivable that his conduct should be described by many commentators as consistently 'procrastinating,' 'hesitating,' 'delaying.' " And LENA ASHWELL[179] objects to such interpretations as those of Goethe and Coleridge. She is especially critical of the latter's suggestion that the words "O that this too, too solid flesh would melt" spring from "that craving after the indefinite—for that which is not—which most easily besets men of genius." This sort of idea is not at all helpful to the actor, she complains. She does praise A. C. Bradley, however: in her opinion, he comes closest of all the critics to expressing Hamlet's real tragedy when he speaks of the "moral shock of the sudden disclosure of his mother's true nature." Other actor-critics have taken exception to theatrical performances associated with the romantic tradition. SIR MICHAEL REDGRAVE, for example, made Hamlet all but heroic in the 1950 production in order to correct the "misconception" that had been "so heavily stressed" in Olivier's film. In his opinion, "Hamlet could make up his mind as well as anybody else, given those terrible circumstances, would be able to do."[180] Both MAURICE EVANS[181] and SIR TYRONE GUTHRIE[182] have vigorously attacked the stage tradition of the "Gloomy Dane"—a stereotyped character which the latter picturesquely describes as "a pale, irresolute, moon-struck, constipated weakling." Let us examine more closely the arguments against the romantic conception put forth by some of these actor-critics and the alternatives proposed by them.

In the first place, the idea of Hamlet's melancholy disposition

178. Charles Calvert, *An Actor's Hamlet* (London, 1912), pp. vi-vii, 15, 19, 21, 41, 43.

179. *Reflections from Shakespeare*, pp. 72-73, 77-79. *See also* pp. 76, 81-83.

180. "Shakespeare and the Actors," in *Talking of Shakespeare*, ed. John Garrett (London, 1954), p. 131.

181. *Maurice Evans' G.I. Production of "Hamlet,"* pp. 17-19.

182. *A Life in the Theatre*, pp. 20-22; "Why and How They Play Hamlet," pp. 44, 46. (The latter discussion is reprinted in Guthrie's book, *In Various Directions: A View of the Theatre* [New York, c. 1965], pp. 72-82.)

is rejected. Both Calvert (1912) and Guthrie (1959) point out that Gertrude's coaxing Hamlet to "cast his nighted colour off" implies that he is normally a cheerful person. Guthrie also cites as evidence of Hamlet's old self the bantering dialogue with Rosencrantz and Guildenstern when he first sees them. "It must be surprising, and potentially dangerous" that he refuses to throw off his mournful demeanor. But, although the depression in which we find him is unusual for one of his personality, it is sufficiently accounted for (Calvert says) by the grief and disillusionment that he has suffered; thoughts of suicide are humanly natural under such circumstances. Evans (1947) declares that Hamlet *is* the victim of melancholy, but in the Elizabethan, not the modern, sense of the word: that is (as Evans understands it), "a physical disorder proceeding from frustrated passion and having outward manifestation in the form of violent behaviour." This kind of melancholy did not "paralyze the will," as some romantic critics have thought, but "enforced inaction was often considered the *origin* of the malady." This is in line with Calvert's explanation of Hamlet's first soliloquy: that it reveals, not a weak man longing to escape painful reality, but "a strong man pinioned and bound" (Hamlet cannot strike at the "usurper" without wounding his mother, and, in his position, to denounce the evil would be "worse than futile").

These actor-critics do not consider Hamlet naturally weak-willed or irresolute. Calvert reminds us that, according to Ophelia's description (III, i, 158-68), he was a soldier as well as a scholar and that we have ample evidence of clear-minded determination in his early scenes: for example, when Horatio tells him of the Ghost Hamlet questions him with level-headed directness and immediately determines to confront the apparition himself; his behavior that night before the ghostly revelation is "resolute and firm," and the moment he learns of his father's murder he is ready to sweep to his revenge. Evans rejects the "whole theory of Hamlet's innate capacity to act"; and Guthrie declares that unless it is made clear that Hamlet is normally a "resolute and capable man" a "sharp psychological point is blunted" and the "dynastic" element in the play is undermined as well—for Shakespeare's tragedy concerns, not "a pathetic royal misfit, but . . . the jostling out of the succession of a potentially great King, and his destruction through the very greatness of his nature."

Despite these descriptions of Hamlet's normal temperament, however, most of the actor-critics whom we are discussing do not deny that within the bounds of the play he hesitates and delays. Maurice Evans is an exception: he describes Hamlet as simply "a normal man caught in the web of circumstances which denies him the *opportunity* to act." The others agree that Hamlet's peculiar circumstances are responsible for his delayed revenge, but they do not attribute the delay solely to external obstacles; rather, they admit that this normally strong and resolute man temporarily conducts himself in an irresolute manner. Their explanations are very divergent. According to Calvert, the shock that Hamlet receives in the ghost scene deranges him, and the resulting abnormality of mind accounts for the delay in revenge; when he recovers his sanity at the end of the play, he immediately executes Claudius.[183] Lena Ashwell (1926) also puts much emphasis upon the "blow" that he receives in the ghost scene (judging by her other comments, the knowledge of Gertrude's adultery and her probable complicity in the murder is even more important than that of the murder itself). It "sends him reeling, terrified lest he be gone lunatic"; then suddenly he realizes that, in his dangerous position, pretended lunacy may be his "one hope of being allowed to live." It is little wonder that he goes through a period of procrastination. With the arrival of the players he finds an opportunity to resolve all his doubts, and he "finds his worst fears realized, his mother guilty." Miss Ashwell does not blame Hamlet for refusing to "send his father's murderer to heaven" in the prayer scene; rather, she commends him for his brave attempt at a more urgent task, "to rescue his mother out of hell." At the risk of his own life he reveals his knowledge of her sin in order to touch her conscience and, if possible, make her repent. Judged by the violent standards of his day, Hamlet is irresolute; but he "shows no hesitation, delay, procrastination, in doing right. He is the Minister of Life, and not of Death." (Obviously, though she rejected the interpretation of Hamlet that we usually call "romantic," Miss Ashwell manufactured her own brand of romanticism.) Guthrie emphasizes that in one

183. For fuller discussion see the section of the present chapter devoted to Hamlet's madness, pp. 105-12.

matter only is Hamlet "rendered irresolute and incapable by self-conflict, by qualms of conscience": that of avenging his father's murder by murdering his uncle. Why is a normally resolute man affected in this way? Guthrie acknowledges more than one possibility (the Freudian theory is one[184]), but he is drawn toward Madariaga's suggestion that Hamlet does not so much fail to act as he postpones action. He develops this idea in his own way, however: "Hamlet regards himself as a passive instrument in the hands of divinity and refuses, despite agonies of self-reproach . . . to allow the vindictive Ghost to hustle him into a conscious decision."

The layman who reads these arguments and explanations can hardly avoid the question: Since we never see Hamlet under normal circumstances, what difference would it make to an actor preparing to impersonate this character whether he believed, with Oxberry, that Hamlet was naturally irresolute or, with Guthrie, that he was "rendered" irresolute only by one particular problem? In the latter case, I suppose, he would attempt to provide striking glimpses of Hamlet's old self whenever he found an opportunity in the text; or perhaps he would emphasize Hamlet's ingenuity and passion most of the time (as in his duel of wits with Claudius and his confrontations with Gertrude and Ophelia) but would lapse into quiet anguish or puzzled reverie in passages where the thought of his basic problem is uppermost. Whether the actor's particular belief about Hamlet's real nature, as opposed to his temporary aberration, carried across to the spectators would probably depend largely on their own individual notions. But one impression would surely be clear: that this Hamlet is a complex character.

It is Hamlet's complexity, rather than simple resolution or irresolution, dreaminess or robustness, that is most often emphasized in the interpretations by contemporary actor-critics; but vigor and passion are nearly always included in the list of his traits. For example, GEORGE SKILLAN's commentaries in *French's Acting Edition* suggest an unstable but lively and forceful character. Hamlet is referred to as "highstrung" and volatile," but his "virility" and "fierce determination" are also mentioned. His courtesy is noticed on occasion, but the idea of Victorian gentle-

184. See the section of the present chapter devoted to Hamlet's attitude toward Gertrude, pp. 112-17.

manliness is forestalled by the warning that Hamlet is not "just a nice boy."[185] SIR DONALD WOLFIT[186] balances active against passive traits in a list of Hamlet's paradoxical qualities: frenzy and tranquility, for example; irresolution and impulsiveness; timidity and courage. "Hamlet," he remarks, "is perpetually on the pounce, yet held in check by an acute sense of the vitality of all human actions." Although Wolfit seems to give equal value to both sides of Hamlet's character, there are one or two indications that he considers his delay the result of external pressures more than of personal shortcomings: for example, his particular pleasure in John Masefield's observation that Wolfit's Hamlet caught "in every line a vital point," missed by other actors, "that Hamlet was, and knew that he was, in deadly danger at every turn."

The complexity of Shakespeare's conception is sometimes used to justify the existence of widely different interpretations by different actors: RICHARD BURTON, for example, makes a case for his own robust Hamlet, yet considers Shakespeare's characterization sufficiently broad and inconsistent to accommodate Gielgud's more sensitive interpretation.[187] For most actor-critics, however, it is not enough to emphasize one aspect of this diversified character; a sense of his great diversity must itself be conveyed in the acting. As SIR JOHN GIELGUD[188] sees it, Hamlet has all the dazzling versatility with which the Renaissance endowed its ideal man: he is a great prince—which means he is both philosopher and soldier—and a great human being. In such a character there must be the reconciliation of many opposites.

The problem of dealing with Hamlet's complexity on the stage has drawn some interesting suggestions from both Wolfit and Gielgud. The former advises the actor not to attempt to "explain" the contradictory traits to the audience but to simply

185. *Hamlet. French's Acting Edition*, pp. 79-140, *passim. See* especially pp. 83, 91, 139.

186. *First Interval* (London, 1954), pp. 169-70.

187. William Shakespeare, *The Tragedy of Hamlet, Prince of Denmark*, intro. by Richard Burton (London: The Folio Society, 1954), pp. 3-5. See also the interview with Burton in Richard Sterne's *John Gielgud Directs Richard Burton in Hamlet* (New York, 1968), pp. 291-92.

188. Some of Gielgud's comments are taken from his description of Hamlet that precedes the reading of "What a piece of work is a man!" for "The Ages of Man," a record by Columbia Masterworks, No. OL 5390. Others are found in his book *Stage Directions*, pp. 56-60. See also Sterne, *Gielgud Directs Burton in Hamlet*, pp. 293-94.

establish these traits by a "variety of light quick indications," enabling the spectators to "feel *with* him." Gielgud lists formidable requirements for the ideal actor of Hamlet: "grace of person and princely bearing . . . energy . . . sensitivity"; the ability to display "gentleness" but also "power," "passionate violence" as well as "philosophical reflection," "a sense of the macabre" without being "morbid," to "impress us with his loneliness and agonies of soul without seeming portentous or self-pitying." Like Macready, Gielgud comments that it is easy enough to gain success in Hamlet by simply developing the histrionic possibilities in each scene but that the actor's duty is to find, amid the complexity of traits, "a complete basic character in which the part may progress in a simple convincing line."

The Question of Hamlet's Age

As early as the eighteenth century critics were noticing discrepancies between the suggestions of Hamlet's youthfulness at the beginning of the play and the Gravedigger's implication in Act IV that Hamlet is thirty years old. The question of Hamlet's age drew little comment from actors, however. If they were concerned at all by the problem, perhaps it was for the practical reason implied by TONY ASTON in the 1740's and firmly stated by WILLIAM CHARLES MACREADY a century later. Aston wished that Betterton, for all his superior ability, had in his later years resigned the role to a younger actor, for "when he threw himself at *Ophelia's* Feet, he appear'd a little too grave for a young Student, lately come from the University."[189] And Macready declared that no actor could hope to play Hamlet "with any approach to completeness until he was too old to look it."[190] The role was much too rewarding theatrically for Betterton to give it up; and, regardless of Aston's opinion, he won praise at seventy for the youthful vigor of his Hamlet.[191] Garrick kept Hamlet in his repertory until he retired. So did Macready. So did Edwin Booth. So did all the finest Shakespearean actors of the eighteenth and nine-

189. Anthony Aston, "A Brief Supplement to Colley Cibber, Esq.; His Lives of the Late Famous Actors and Actresses." Appended to Robert W. Lowe's edition of *An Apology for the Life of Colley Cibber* (London, 1889), II, 300-301.

190. Marston, *Our Recent Actors*, I, 83.

191. Cf. Steele's well-known description in No. 71 of *The Tatler*. This can be found in *The Tatler*, ed. Alexander Chalmers, Vol. II of *The British Essayists* (London, 1803), p. 242.

teenth centuries. Whatever the evidence of the text, the stage tradition certainly did not encourage the idea of an extremely youthful Hamlet. GEORGE VANDENHOFF in 1860, after considering the question in its more academic form, reached a conclusion which was probably typical at that time: that the Gravedigger's testimony must be accepted since Hamlet is too philosophical to be a very young man.[192]

WILSON BARRETT, however, was convinced that tradition was wrong; and in 1884 he challenged it with his performance of a "young" Hamlet, which he later defended in an essay. According to him, Hamlet was meant to be a youth of eighteen, or not more than twenty-one. Shakespeare's original intention is reflected, not in the Gravedigger's speech (which was probably inserted for the sake of a mature actor), but in Laertes' description of Hamlet's love for Ophelia as a "violet in the youth of primy nature, / Forward, not permanent." ("Forward," interpreted as *precocious,* would not fittingly describe the love of a thirty-year-old man.) An additional passage in Laertes' speech (I, iii, 11-14) can only mean that "Hamlet has not done growing either physically or mentally." A young Hamlet is necessary to make credible Claudius' passion for Gertrude. It also explains Claudius' election to the throne, since his supporters could rationalize their position by arguing that Hamlet was too young to assume the responsibility of ruling. There was precedent for this interpretation in the Saxo Grammaticus story, where, in Hamlet's address to the people there was a reference to his father's having been killed "before I had come to man's estate."[193] In addition to the reasons given in his essay (1890), Barrett mentions in a personal letter a psychological argument for Hamlet's youth: "Hamlet could not act as he does at thirty. The burthen would not have been too heavy to bear. . . . The mind would have been wide enough to grasp the situation. . . ."[194]

In the years since Barrett's controversial interpretation there have been more published comments by actor-critics concerning

192. *Leaves from an Actor's Note-Book,* pp. 274-78. Vandenhoff's reasoned conclusions agree with the bald statement made, in passing, by Thomas Davies three-quarters of a century earlier: "Hamlet is thirty years old. . . ." (*Dramatic Miscellanies,* III, 39.)

193. *Mr. Wilson Barrett on the Sanity and Age of Hamlet,* pp. 2-4.

194. Letter of October 23, 1884, to Moy Thomas, theatrical columnist for the London *Daily News.* MS in the Folger Library.

Hamlet's age than in preceding periods, but never so many on this subject as on other problems connected with the character. Although the criticisms are too few to justify any conclusive statement about trends, it is true that most of those which I have seen favor a youthful Hamlet. I have recorded only one—LOUIS CALVERT's (1912)—that specifically adheres to the Gravedigger's figure of thirty years. (Calvert points out that Ophelia's phrase "blown youth" suggests someone of this age.)[195] WILLIAM POEL emphasized the importance of Hamlet's youthfulness so much that at one time he suggested *The Revolt of Youth* as an appropriate title for the play. The "wild" words of the ghost scene were cited as evidence that Hamlet is "a young man, or, perhaps even a 'boy,' as his mother calls him in the first quarto, thrown into the intensest excitement."[196] Among the modern actors who have expressed opinions on the subject are EVA LE GALLIENNE, SIR JOHN GIELGUD, and GEORGE SKILLAN. Gielgud once described Hamlet as a young man but not an adolescent; his most recent comments, however, suggest very early youth: the part needs a "boyish discovery, not a mature thinker."[197] The other two actor-critics clearly consider Hamlet an adolescent. Miss LeGallienne argues persuasively: "His melancholy, his thoughts of suicide, his hero-worship of his father, his mercurial changes of mood, and above all his jealous resentment of his mother's second marriage, are touching and understandable in a boy of nineteen, whereas in a man of thirty they indicate a weak and vacillating nature in no way admirable or attractive."[198] Skillan goes even further: Hamlet's extreme youth is at the heart of the tragedy. It explains the last line of the first soliloquy, "But break, my heart, for I must hold my tongue": being a minor, he is helpless to assert himself against a situation that he knows to be evil. Later, for the same reason,

195. *An Actor's Hamlet*, p. 19.
196. *Shakespeare in the Theatre*, p. 161; also Speaight, *William Poel and the Elizabethan Revival*, pp. 222-23.
197. *Stage Directions*, p. 56; Sterne, *Gielgud Directs Burton in Hamlet*, p. 25.
198. Eva Le Gallienne, *With a Quiet Heart* (New York, 1953), pp. 105-6. Miss Le Gallienne suggests that an experienced actress can convey the necessary impression of youth as a mature actor cannot. She herself acted Hamlet in August, 1937, at the Cape Cod Playhouse, Dennis, Massachusetts. The tradition of women Hamlets goes back at least as far as Mrs. William Powell in the eighteenth century (C. B. Hogan, *Shakespeare in the Theatre, 1701-1800* (Oxford, 1952-57), II, 232, 234), but by far the largest number of actresses attempted the role in the nineteenth century. *See* Frank Wadsworth's interesting discussion, "Hamlet and Iago: Nineteenth Century Breeches Parts," *Shakespeare Quarterly*, XVII (1966), 129-39.

he must "accept the reversal of his hopes" in regard to Ophelia, even though he knows that their estrangement was forced by her father. And his lack of authority obviously hampers him in his proceedings against Claudius. As Skillan points out, however, the events of the play mature Hamlet "beyond his years" and, in the closet scene, he is able to rebuke his mother openly as he could not have done at the beginning.[199]

The Question of Hamlet's Madness

Not before the nineteenth century do we find in the actors' writings a definite argument for Hamlet's real madness. THOMAS SHERIDAN (in oral conversation, 1763) may have hinted at some kind of mental unbalance when he said that we "see Hamlet sometimes like a man really mad and sometimes like a man reasonable enough, though much hurt in mind."[200] In its context, the first part of this statement necessarily refers to the feigned madness; whether "much hurt in mind" was meant to indicate only mental agony or something more pathological is not clear. THOMAS DAVIES (1783-84) showed his awareness of the theory that in addition to the feigned madness Hamlet displays a "melancholy bordering on insanity," but he himself said nothing to endorse it.[201] The other actor-critics of the eighteenth century assumed that Hamlet is perfectly sane, but probably all of them would have agreed with FREDERICK PILON that madness is meant to be "counterfeited with great strength of imagination and masterly touches of nature."[202] Indeed FRANCIS GENTLEMAN felt that the theatrical possibilities of the "antic disposition," rather than any logical motivation, prompted Shakespeare to include it in his plot. Instead of serving, as it should, "some important secret purpose" related to Hamlet's revenge, it results only in "cajoling the King, distressing the Queen and Ophelia, bamming [i.e. fooling] Polonius and the courtiers, and giving great scope for capital acting."[203] The others, however, accepted the logic of Hamlet's plan: Sheridan, for example, said that Hamlet feigned madness in order to kill the King with less fear of the consequences, and Pilon thought that he did so to

199. Hamlet. French's Acting Edition, p. 84.
200. Boswell's London Journal, ed. Pottle, p. 235.
201. Dramatic Miscellanies, III, 143-44.
202. An Essay on the Character of Hamlet, pp. 13-15.
203. Dramatic Censor, I, 31.

"conceal his intentions." CHARLES DIBDIN's explanation is especially interesting since it is tied in with his conception of Hamlet's
character as a whole, including his reasons for delaying the promised revenge. According to Dibdin, Hamlet's "most beautiful
feature" is his "credulity on the side of virtue." Even before the
ghost scene Hamlet has a "secret admonition" that all is not well,
but he represses it because the suggested crime "seems too abominable for belief." When the Ghost reveals the truth, we realize
from Hamlet's exclamation, "O my prophetic soul!" that "from
the moment of his father's death, his suspicions, which . . . he had
unwillingly entertained, were influenced by feelings which human
nature could not controul." Even after the supernatural revelation, however, his "strong sense of moral duty" makes him "pant
for better proofs than he has already received." His feigned madness enables him to ask "odd questions," full of "shrewdness and
ambiguity," which, "by being satirically thrown in may obtain . . .
such answers as may corroborate the intelligence he has received
from the ghost." It is this desire to be doubly sure, combined with
the "milkiness of his disposition" (i.e. his humanitarian feelings),
that causes Hamlet to delay his vengeance.[204] Apparently, in
Dibdin's view, the "madness" was intended to be as much of a
"mousetrap" as the later presentation of *The Murder of Gonzago.*

In the period of romantic criticism the emphasis upon Hamlet's "morbid melancholy," as WILLIAM OXBERRY calls it,[205] and the
inclination to reject literal meanings in favor of psychological
interpretations increased the attractiveness of the idea that Hamlet's madness was not simply feigned (as he said) but real. Even
so, only a few actors accepted this view. FANNY KEMBLE was the
first, and one of the most insistent, of the actor-critics to offer a
written argument for Hamlet's insanity. Her father, CHARLES
KEMBLE, as she tells us, believed Hamlet to be actually mad, and
he portrayed him so on the stage (in the 1830's). She herself
agrees with this interpretation, which she expounds for the
reader: At the beginning of the play we find Hamlet depressed
by grief for his father, shame for his mother, disappointment in
his own ambitions, impatience at his dependent position.
"Gloomy" and "despondent," he is already a likely victim of
madness. The events that follow have a devastating effect: "A

204. *Complete History of the Stage,* III, 58, 61-62.
205. *New English Drama,* III, *Hamlet,* xv.

frightful . . . visitation from the dead; a . . . sudden revelation of the murder . . . thence burning hatred and thirst of vengeance . . . double loathing of his mother's frailty . . . an imperative duty calling for fulfillment, and a want of resolution and activity to meet the demand; thence an unceasing struggle between the sluggish nature and the upbraiding soul. . . ." The "bitter, dark, amazed, and uncertain" Hamlet that results is "as complete a madman as ever walked between earth and heaven."[206] Memories of Charles Kemble's mad acting in the nunnery scene are poignantly recalled: "The exquisite tenderness of his voice, the wild compassion and forlorn pity of his looks, bestowing that on others, which . . . he most needed, the melancholy restlessness, the bitter self-scorning" were so full of anguish that his Ophelia (Miss Kemble herself) was hardly able to speak for emotion.[207] Another, but less extreme, argument for Hamlet's madness was given by an American contemporary of Fanny Kemble's, JAMES H. HACKETT. He maintained that Hamlet at first feigns madness in order to "conceal his secret design" but that after the play scene he "actually becomes . . . the victim of temporary aberration of mind." His soliloquy "Now could I drink hot blood," his "violent excitement in the closet-scene . . . his rash slaughter of Polonius, there, and the conjuration of his father's spirit through the medium of his heated imagination, indicate a gradual tendency towards and reaching of a *climax of delirium.*" The ocean voyage, short as it is, proves salutary; for, in his graveyard moralizings he appears tranquil enough, until the sudden realization of Ophelia's death shocks him into another temporary outbreak, intensified by Laertes' own "frantic conduct." Hamlet's later apology, in which he blames his actions on "sore distraction," must be accepted as honest; otherwise he is guilty of incredible "meanness, cowardice, insincerity, and inconsistency."[208]

206. *Journal*, I, 73-75. See also *Records of a Girlhood* (2d ed.; New York, 1883), p. 327. A contemporary of Miss Kemble's, Samuel Laman Blanchard, who was an actor for awhile but was better known as a journalist, wrote an essay pointing out that Hamlet reveals the same traits as those described in Robert Burton's *Anatomy of Melancholy* and that melancholy, as the Elizabethans understood it, was a malady "not very distantly related to lunacy." See his *Sketches from Life* (London, 1846), III, 326-37.

207. *Journal*, I, 148.

208. *Notes, Criticisms, and Correspondence*, pp. 169-73. Hackett argues that the apparition in the closet scene differs significantly from the Ghost of the first act and that Shakespeare intended it to be a hallucination. To make this interpretation clear, when he acted Hamlet for the first time (October 21, 1840) Hackett used a

A number of actors of the nineteenth and early twentieth centuries specifically rejected the idea of Hamlet's madness. The most detailed arguments on this side of the question are presented in essays by JAMES MURDOCH[209] and WILSON BARRETT.[210] They both point out that no madness is revealed in Hamlet's soliloquies or in his scenes with characters like Horatio and the players; that a special point is made of his sanity in the closet scene (he admits that he is mad only "in craft," and Gertrude promises not to reveal this fact); that it would be an error in dramatic construction to make both Hamlet and Ophelia mad. In addition, Barrett reminds us that the Ghost is twice heard enjoining Marcellus and Horatio to swear that they will not reveal Hamlet's true sanity if he should later assume an "antic disposition." And Murdoch asserts that if Hamlet is only "a mindless involuntary agent" the play "loses all interest of plot-development." He explains Hamlet's assumption of the mad disguise as the ambiguous expedient of a character already "weakened by melancholy and loss of exercise" who is faced with a task involving insuperable difficulties. Too depleted in energy to assault the King directly, too sensitive of spirit to resort to assassination, denied legal remedy since the King is "above the law," Hamlet chose a "fantastic" form of madness which gave him "unrestricted liberty of observation and remark"; and he fixed upon it "as a means whereby he might do and yet not do the deed."

Other actor-critics of that period who accepted Hamlet's sanity as unquestionable were EDWIN BOOTH, HENRY IRVING, WILLIAM POEL, BEERBOHM TREE, and JOHNSTON FORBES-ROBERTSON.[211] Both Irving and Tree, however, called attention to an excitability

full-length portrait of Hamlet Senior and had the Ghost dress in clothes resembling those of the portrait. The Ghost stepped through a rent in the canvas, which closed immediately, and the picture then took on a blank but illuminated appearance because of a light behind it. When the Ghost disappeared, the light was extinguished and the portrait resumed its normal appearance (see pp. 54, 79-80). Sprague tells of Macready's also having the Ghost appear and disappear through a portrait, and he says that this became a popular custom. (*Shakespeare and the Actors*, p. 168 and p. 391, n. 158.)

209. "A Short Study of 'Hamlet,'" pp. 499-500, 502.
210. *Mr. Wilson Barrett on the Sanity and Age of Hamlet*, p. 2.
211. See Grossmann, *Edwin Booth*, pp. 19-20; *Ellen Terry's Memoirs*, ed. Craig and St. John, pp. 103-4 (Irving's emphasis on Hamlet's sanity); Speaight, *William Poel and the Elizabethan Revival*, p. 55; Tree, *Thoughts and Afterthoughts*, pp. 124-31; Johnston Forbes-Robertson, Introduction to George Macdonald's edition of *The Tragedie of Hamlet, Prince of Denmarke* (London, 1924).

and a self-dramatizing tendency in Hamlet's temperament which are compatible with his feigned madness and enhance its effect.[212] And Booth, the most interesting of actor-critics on this subject because he was the least academic, gave sympathetic thought to Hamlet's brilliant but erratic mentality which has led some critics to consider him mad. In his view, Hamlet typifies "uneven or unbalanced Genius," a "disease" that "isolates" the possessor—or, more properly, the possessed—in the midst of the masses he attracts, denying him "sympathetic communion with ordinary men"; and his unseasonably frivolous or hysterical speeches are really safety valves that preserve his reason. Booth had early learned to associate Hamlet's eccentricities with the notorious vagaries of his own father, Junius Brutus Booth.

At the moment of intense emotion, when the spectators were en-thralled by his magnetic influence, the tragedian's overwrought brain would take refuge from its own threatening storm beneath the jester's hood and, while turned from the audience, he would whisper some silliness or "make a face". . . . Only those who have known the torture of severe mental tension can appreciate the value of that one little step from the sublime to the ridiculous.[213]

Personal experience as well as intimate acquaintance with his father's "fantastic temperament," confirmed for Booth the verisimilitude of Hamlet's psychology. While he was acting Richard II at McVicker's Theatre in Chicago on April 23, 1879, he was fired at twice and narrowly missed by a madman named Mark Gray. Booth had a charm for his watch chain made of one of the bullets, mounted in a gold cartridge cap and engraved: "From Mark Gray to Edwin Booth." Four days after the shooting he wrote to E. C. Stedman:

My temporary self-control gave way after a day or two to a highly nervous excitement—a condition similar to that which I believe Shakespeare illustrates by Hamlet's frivolity after the ghost is gone, and the terrible tension of his brain is relaxed. I have a ghostly kind of disposition to joke about the affair which is hardly controllable.[214]

212. See the section of the present chapter devoted to Hamlet's basic temperament, pp. 81-82, 92.

213. See Booth's essay on his father in *Actors and Actresses of Great Britain and the United States*, ed. Brander Matthews and Lawrence Hutton (New York, 1886), III, 95-96; also his letter to William Winter, dated April 23, 1883 (MS in the Folger Library).

214. Quoted by Charles Copeland in *Edwin Booth* (Boston, 1901), p. 114. There

Except for Fanny Kemble, LOUIS CALVERT (1912) is the most determined advocate (among the actor-critics) of the theory that Hamlet is really insane during a large portion of the play.[215] As we have seen, however, Calvert's idea of Hamlet's basic temperament was entirely different from Miss Kemble's. No more depressed at the beginning of the play "than thousands of others would be under similar circumstances," Calvert's Hamlet reacts with his customary vigor and determination on all occasions, including his meeting with the Ghost, until he learns the identity of the murderer—his uncle, who was also his mother's lover! Hamlet's behavior after the Ghost vanishes betrays the severity of the shock that he has received. Although he vows to think of nothing but vengeance, he immediately "falls into hysterical railing against his uncle and his mother." And he even "takes out his tables to make notes"—a sure sign of awareness that "his brain has received a shock that may paralyze his memory." In the following scene with Marcellus and Horatio, when he hears the voice of his father issuing from underground (reminding him, I suppose, that his father is now a victim of fiendish torture), "the agony so overwhelms him, that he bursts into laughter and hysterically jokes at his father's ghost." His discovery that this "grotesque behavior acts as an antidote" to insanity determines him to use it in the future. But the shock he has received is too great; it transforms the normally active, clear-thinking Hamlet into a forgetful, abstracted, irresolute creature, capable of occasional outbursts of hysterical passion and brief flashes of his old vitality but always lapsing back into "bestial oblivion." At last, when he is wounded in the fencing match and when he realizes that his mother has been poisoned, the combined shock is sufficient to restore him to sanity. He "immediately becomes again

_____

is a similar passage in a letter written to William Winter on the same day (MS in the Folger Library).

215. Calvert became interested in the possibility of Hamlet's real madness when his mother, Mrs. Charles Calvert, of the Theatre Royal, Manchester, told him that "many clever people, including the late Tom Taylor [the dramatist and critic], believed that Hamlet was at times mad." His study of the character was also influenced by his reading of Charles Reade's *Put Yourself in His Place*, which impressed him so forcibly that he always used this maxim in acting his various roles. After imagining how he himself would react to the events that Hamlet experienced, he became convinced that madness would be the inevitable result. His book, *An Actor's Hamlet*, consists of an introductory essay arguing his case, then the text of the play, with notes on individual scenes.

the determined man of action" and successfully carries out the Ghost's command to kill the King. Calvert goes so far as to label *Hamlet* a "treatise on mental aberration," Hamlet's "partial derangement" being contrasted with Ophelia's "total derangement." Pedantic as this description sounds, he insists that the play is "much more interesting" if understood so, that the acting possibilities are strengthened, and that Horatio assumes more importance—becomes, in fact, "a kind of Greek chorus to Hamlet."[216]

Later writings by the actor-critics reflect mixed views, but none echo Calvert's uncompromising conviction of Hamlet's madness. SIR DONALD WOLFIT's confident assertion of Hamlet's sanity[217] probably represents the opinion of many of his contemporaries who have not specifically commented on the subject. But the fullest discussions of the question—those by GRANVILLE-BARKER and ROBERT SPEAIGHT—conclude without a categorical yes or no.

Granville-Barker considers the problem of Hamlet's madness the basic difficulty in the interpretation of the character. Shakespeare could hardly have eliminated the mock-madness, which was a distinctive feature of the inherited story; but, though it provided for some amusing and interesting passages, it also posed serious problems. It hindered character development, for example, since Hamlet must be shown continually behind a mask. And it created a dilemma for the dramatist: if "madness" were kept on the level of mere play-acting it would reduce the intensity of the drama, yet "sheer inconsequent lunacy" could hardly be allowed to dominate a tragedy. These problems explain "the alloy of sanity and insanity, pretense and reality, which we vainly try to resolve into its elements again." During the play Hamlet appears in three different guises, none of them his normal character: at first the "rebelliously singular" young man, "black-suited . . . amid the peacock brilliancy of the Court"; then the actor of the "antic disposition," who comes close to real distraction; and finally the Hamlet of the last act, the "fever in his brain . . . burned out." Shakespeare gives us occasional glimpses of the intrinsic Hamlet, however, in scenes with the players and Horatio. From his sincere and humble speech to the latter, for example, we learn that even under normal conditions he would always have been "passion's

216. *An Actor's Hamlet*, pp. v-xiv.
217. *First Interval*, pp. 169-70.

slave." Shakespeare "does marvels with this Hamlet who is neither mad nor sane," but, with all his skill, he "cannot . . . so assimilate character and story that no incongruities appear."[218]

Basically Speaight's conclusion is consistent with Granville-Barker's, but his reasoning is somewhat different. For instance, instead of treating the mock madness as a dramatic problem, he considers it an indication of Hamlet's histrionic nature. In putting on the "antic disposition," he says, Hamlet was taking the worst possible course for fulfilling his vow of vengeance. (Speaight is reminiscent of Francis Gentleman here, but, whereas the latter blamed Shakespeare for the illogical device, Speaight blames Hamlet himself.) It gave him a certain "freedom of insult and innuendo" at Court, but it also brought suspicion on him and intensified "the risk of his being silenced or sent away before he could carry out his mission." Not all of Hamlet's unbalanced behavior can be considered mere shamming, yet madness in the clinical sense is contradicted by his frequent displays of "intelligence, lucidity, foresight and even cunning." He cannot even be described as intermittently mad, for his "excessive conduct—sometimes ridiculous and sometimes ruthless"—is easily distinguished from the "ravings of Lear." Speaight concludes that Hamlet was "the victim of an inherent weakness" which was exposed and aggravated by his tragic experiences—he was, in short, not a lunatic but "the first neurotic."[219]

Hamlet's Attitude toward His Mother

Hamlet's disillusionment in his mother became especially important for actor-critics in the latter part of the nineteenth century. EDWIN BOOTH's emphasis on this idea is reflected in at least one textual reading and in several explanatory directions in his acting edition of the play (edited by William Winter). In the First Player's "Hecuba" speech Booth prefers "inobled queen" to the usual "mobled queen," and he directs Hamlet to speak his interruptive repetition of the phrase *"With momentary sad preoccupation. His thought is of his mother."*[220] In a letter to Winter,

218. *Prefaces to Shakespeare*, I, 31-32, 231-34, 244-47.
219. *Nature in Shakespearian Tragedy*, pp. 20-24.
220. *The Prompt-Book: Shakespeare's Tragedy of Hamlet as Presented by Edwin Booth*, ed. William Winter (4th ed.; New York, 1879), pp. 55-56. For the *Prompt-Book* series Booth made the textual cuts and furnished the stage directions, and Winter supplied the prefaces and appendices.

Booth explains: *"Ignobled* (or *Inobled*) expresses both the condition of *Hecuba* in her fallen state and the Queen of Denmark's degradation."[221] In the play scene, when Ophelia remarks that the prologue is brief and Hamlet replies, "As woman's love," Booth remarks: "This reference is to the Queen, and—mournfully —to the evanescence of all love."[222] The idea, implied in the last phrase, that Hamlet's disillusionment in Gertrude led to disillusionment in love itself became very important for other actor-critics in their interpretations of the Hamlet-Ophelia relationship. BEERBOHM TREE, for example, makes such an application in his essay on Hamlet and also at several points in his promptbook annotations.[223]

Both HARLEY GRANVILLE-BARKER[224] and LENA ASHWELL[225] stress Hamlet's previous idealization of his mother. The former speaks of the purity of the passion that he had cherished for her, and the latter declares that both Hamlet and his father had "reverenced this woman, worshipped her." According to Granville-Barker, Hamlet's tirade in the closet scene is consciously aimed at forcing Gertrude to repent of her sin, but beneath this motive is a deeper one that he may not recognize: "an embittered idealist's lust to be avenged upon this traitor to his ideal." Miss Ashwell puts this concept even more strongly: it is Hamlet's tragedy to find that his own mother—"the ideal on which he has built his life"—is "the Destroyer, that old serpent Lust"; it is the sudden destruction of his faith in her that "wrecks him."

As a result of the interest in psychiatry and, beginning early in the present century, the application of its principles to the analysis of literary characters,[226] a special interpretation of the Hamlet-Gertrude relationship made its appearance: that of the

221. MS letter in the Folger Library, dated July 27, 1879.

222. *The Prompt-Book: Hamlet,* ed. Winter, p. 71. According to Kate Field, Fechter gave similar interpretations both to this passage and to the "mobled queen" passage, though he retained the usual wording of the latter. See *Charles Albert Fechter,* p. 107.

223. See Tree's prompt-Book in the Folger Library (his personal copy of Wilson Barrett's acting edition, with Tree's own pencil-written annotations), pp. 47 ("mobled queen"), 52 (nunnery scene), and 58 (play scene). For relevant passages in Tree's essay, see *Thoughts and Afterthoughts,* pp. 237-39.

224. *Prefaces to Shakespeare,* I, 234-38.

225. *Reflections from Shakespeare,* pp. 78, 83.

226. An article, "The Alienist and Literature," in *The Nation,* XCV (October 17, 1912), 350-51, complains of the growing tendency to explain Shakespeare's characters in psychoanalytical terms.

Oedipus complex. Freud himself saw in Hamlet a victim of this complex, but the idea was popularized through the writings of Ernest Jones. The latter first expressed his theory in 1910 in an essay, "The Oedipus Complex as an Explanation of Hamlet's Mystery," published in the *American Journal of Psychology*. He later expanded his study and republished it several times in different forms, including a book, *Hamlet and Oedipus* (1949). To state his argument succinctly (and, of course, superficially), Hamlet's subconscious feelings of guilt because of his erotic attraction to Gertrude lead him to identify himself with Claudius, who has fulfilled Hamlet's own desires by killing his father and marrying his mother; he therefore finds it impossible to kill Claudius until his own death has become inevitable. In 1928 OTIS SKINNER found the idea that "Hamlet was in love with his own mother" preposterously alien to the play as he knew it, and he relegated "this lunatic German fellow Freud" to the "sour little group" of academicians whose interpretations Shakespeare himself would reject.[227] But several other actor-critics have been concerned, either positively or negatively, with the possible relationship between the Freudian theory and the stage interpretation of Hamlet.

In his biography of JOHN BARRYMORE, Gene Fowler notes that some critics (specifically Heywood Broun and Richard Watts, Jr.) saw Freudian implications in Barrymore's Hamlet (1922-23), and Fowler himself speaks of Barrymore's "incestuous Prince."[228] The only support that he gives for this idea, however, is the statement that Hamlet's scene with his mother was played "exactly as if it were a love scene." Evidently the closet scene was the high point of emotion in Barrymore's acting, but this is rather natural, whatever interpretation is used. (SIR JOHN GIELGUD, for example, considers this the climactic scene of the play,[229] but he does not advocate the Freudian theory.) As for its being a "love scene," actors of the past have often made Hamlet very affectionate toward Gertrude—unduly so, some of their colleagues have thought. Wrote TATE WILKINSON in 1790, long before the Freudian interpretation was conceived: "when I see Mr. Kemble kneel to his mother . . . and *kiss her hand* (*or neck*, if he can reach it,) with all the en-

227. Otis Skinner, *Mad Folk of the Theatre* (Indianapolis, [1928]), pp. 289-90.
228. Gene Fowler, *Good Night, Sweet Prince* (Philadelphia, c. 1943-44), pp. 213-14.
229. *John Gielgud's Hamlet*, ed. Gilder, p. 62.

thusiasm of filial love and duty, my idea of propriety is somewhat staggered."[230] A century later WILLIAM POEL was complaining that some modern actors caressed and embraced Gertrude in this scene, in flat contradiction to the fiercely satirical speeches which they had wrongly omitted from the acting text.[231] John Corbin, in a *New York Times* review (December 17, 1922), comments that the closet scene in Barrymore's performance was "perhaps the most tenderly impassioned and compelling passage of emotional acting in modern memory." He adds, however: "It will not do . . . to take this as the keynote of the drama, attributing to Hamlet the Oedipus complex. Throughout Mr. Barrymore's performance . . . chief emphasis is laid upon Hamlet's love and reverence for his father." Corbin's last statement seems to be corroborated by one that Barrymore himself made when he was asked why his Hamlet "seemed so calm, almost joyously serene, upon seeing his father's ghost." Barrymore replied that the elder Hamlet may have been a colossal bore to everybody else but that "Hamlet is fond of the old boy" and that the play "rather depends on this bond of sympathy."[232] As far as I know, he never said anything to indicate that he intended a Freudian interpretation.

It was inevitable, however, that sooner or later a Hamlet with an Oedipus complex would be attempted on the stage. And with the Old Vic production of 1937 this Hamlet materialized in the performance of LAURENCE OLIVIER. According to Felix Barker,

230. *The Wandering Patentee*, II, 6.

231. *Shakespeare in the Theatre*, p. 169. See also his letter to the *Era*, April 30, 1892, republished in Speaight's *William Poel and the Elizabethan Revival*, pp. 52-53.

232. Fowler, *Good Night, Sweet Prince*, pp. 210-11. Barrymore, however, did introduce in the closet scene an effect that calls for a psychological explanation of some sort. As Hamlet begins to describe in gross language his mother's relationship with his uncle, it becomes evident that his father's outraged spirit has taken possession of him. Lark Taylor writes in his promptbook for Barrymore's production of 1924: "Ham. becomes rigid—Hands stiff at side—white light envelopes him—He speaks in hoarse tone—In Cleveland, last wk. of 2d season—a picture was made of Pole as the Ghost—and thrown on Ham. to convey the effect of the Ghost taking possession of Hamlet." The Ghost does not actually appear. In Taylor's promptbook for Barrymore's 1922-23 production as well as in the one for 1924 (p. 104 in both) the printed direction "Enter Ghost" is struck through, but at this point "Light goes off Ham Ham gives loud gasp—collapses to knees—shrieking." He speaks "Save and hover o'er me" in a "Loud, Hyterical" voice. Obviously Barrymore, like Hackett, considered the apparition nonobjective. And obviously Hamlet somehow identified himself with his father in this "possession" scene. I do not see the suggestion of an Oedipus complex here, but perhaps there was meant to be. (Taylor's promptbooks are in the Folger Library.)

Tyrone Guthrie (director of the production) had become interested in the theory when he read a revised version of Ernest Jones's essay in a book called *Essays in Applied Psycho-Analysis* (Vienna, 1923). He persuaded Olivier that the Oedipus complex offered a much better justification for Hamlet's delay than the more conventional explanations. In his performance Olivier tried to "illuminate" this theory through "his tempestuously passionate playing of the closet scene, the gesture of wiping his mother's kiss from his face . . . on the line, 'O that this too too *sullied* flesh would melt,' and—like most Hamlets, but for a particular reason— in his constant revulsion at the petting between the King and Gertrude."[233] Many viewers of Olivier's film version of *Hamlet* felt that the Oedipus complex was strongly implied in this production also; but Olivier's own comments suggest that, although he accepted the *possibility* of the Freudian theory (along with that of Coleridge's overly-intellectual Hamlet), he did not intentionally use it as a basis of interpretation for his film.[234]

SIR TYRONE GUTHRIE has described Jones's theory as "by far the most interesting and convincing explanation of the crucial puzzle" in *Hamlet,* the procrastination of vengeance by a man who is normally resolute and capable. Against the argument that it is anachronistic he asserted that the "phenomena of the Oedipus complex were observable" long before Freud "isolated, analyzed and explained them" and that Shakespeare "recorded" them, not only in *Hamlet,* but also in *Coriolanus* and *All's Well.* On the other hand, Guthrie has come to believe that the idea of Hamlet's inhibition by a conflict of which he himself is unaware "offers little that can be expressed in the theatre"; for "an intelligent actor does not require a professional analyst" to tell him that Gertrude's remarriage is "a major emotional problem for Hamlet" nor that the closet scene is "violently ambivalent—love and hate mixed."[235]

At least two contemporary actor-critics have spoken out against the theory of the Oedipus complex as applied to Hamlet. MAURICE EVANS specifically dismisses the "Freudian portrait" of the char-

233. *The Oliviers,* pp. 118-20.
234. "A Essay in Hamlet," p. 13.
235. "Why and How They Play Hamlet," pp. 42, 44. Barker says (*The Oliviers,* pp. 120–21) that many people in the Old Vic audiences had no idea that Olivier was attempting a Freudian interpretation.

acter;[236] and SIR MICHAEL REDGRAVE says of his own 1950 performance: "I have always so strongly rejected the suggestion that Hamlet was in any way a victim of what we so lightly call an Oedipus complex that I used every possible opportunity to express Hamlet's love for his father."[237]

GERTRUDE

Although Gertrude is not usually considered a major Shakespearean role, a fine actress has always been able to discover excellent possibilities in it. THOMAS DAVIES tells us, for example, that Hannah Pritchard, chiefly remembered as Garrick's powerful Lady Macbeth, made the Queen in *Hamlet* the masterpiece of her acting.[238] The character has also received considerable attention from the actor-critics. The topics most often discussed are her physical charm, her age, and, particularly, the problem of her guilt.

HELEN FAUCIT (1880) seems to have been the first actor-critic to emphasize the "extraordinary attractions" that made this woman "another Helen of Troy . . . in the wonderful fascination which she exercises on all who come within her influence."[239] The fatal element in Gertrude's charm, suggested by Miss Faucit's use of the mythical parallel, was implied again in a description of the character by an ANONYMOUS ACTRESS (in 1914), and it was given a stronger and more sinister importance still later by LENA ASHWELL (1926). The former presents Gertrude as a very beautiful but passive woman, intensely loved by two men, and jealously so by her first husband, whose Ghost seems not at all perturbed by Claudius' usurpation of the throne but mainly resents his occupying the royal couch.[240] With Miss Ashwell's interpretation Gertrude becomes something more than the object of passion and the catalyst of violence. For this actress sees in the character one of the incarnations of the "dark lady"—a type of lustful woman, alluring but destructive, who appears in various forms in Shakespeare's dark comedies and tragedies as well as in his sonnets. In modern

236. *Maurice Evans' G.I. Production of "Hamlet,"* pp. 17-19.
237. "Shakespeare and the Actors," p. 131. *See also* p. 147.
238. *Dramatic Miscellanies,* III, 116-17.
239. *On Some of Shakespeare's Female Characters* (Edinburgh and London, 1887), pp. 10-12.
240. *The True Ophelia: and Other Studies of Shakespeare's Women. By an Actress* (New York, 1914), pp. 102-6.

life, says Miss Ashwell, we recognize this woman "in sensational divorce cases, or as instigator in an affair of murder, very amply reported by the press. She is extremely attractive, especially to the opposite sex, good-natured and charming, entirely and absolutely selfish, sensual, with the wit to camouflage her vice."[241]

The problem of Gertrude's age has invariably been connected with her sensual appeal. One of WILSON BARRETT's reasons for considering Hamlet a youth rather than a mature man was that his mother should be a "handsome, sensual, attractive woman of forty."[242] GRANVILLE-BARKER agrees that Gertrude should not be a "mature matron, the realistic mother of a man of thirty," an interpretation that post-Shakespearean stage tradition long encouraged. Shakespeare shows us in Gertrude "the woman who does not mature, who clings to her youth and all that belongs to it, whose charm will not change but at last fade and wither; a pretty creature . . . desperately refusing to grow old."[243] SIR JOHN GIELGUD declares that she "must be nearly fifty" but that the "modern custom of casting a younger woman . . . greatly enhances the effect of the part and the meaning of the story." He favors a Gertrude of "real fire and sensuality" such as Martita Hunt, Laura Cowie, and Judith Anderson made her.[244]

The most important evidence of Gertrude's sensual appeal—her relationship with Claudius—is bound up, of course, with the problem of her guilt. FRANCIS GENTLEMAN, with his eighteenth-century prejudices, was annoyed by the character of Gertrude; for instead of being the clear-cut object of either detestation or pity, she attracts an odd combination of both.[245] Later actor-critics have been less concerned with Shakespeare's failure to create a rigidly consistent character, but some of them have felt constrained to clarify the ambiguous position in which he placed her. Was she a direct accomplice in her husband's murder? Or did she, by reciprocating Claudius' passion, unwittingly inspire the crime? Was she, perhaps, innocent even of adultery and guilty

241. *Reflections from Shakespeare*, p. 74. Miss Ashwell's fullest discussion of the "dark lady" type of character is her treatment of Cressida, pp. 89-91.

242. *Mr. Wilson Barrett on the Sanity and Age of Hamlet*, p. 3.

243. *Prefaces to Shakespeare*, I, 226-27.

244. *John Gielgud's Hamlet*, ed. Gilder, pp. 60, 63; *Stage Directions*, p. 56; *Early Stages* (New York, 1939), pp. 258-59.

245. *Dramatic Censor*, I, 37.

only of a hasty and incestuous remarriage? Or can the stigma of incest itself be removed?

When the question of Gertrude's involvement in the murder has arisen, most of the actor-critics have acquitted her. A number of them have considered the possibilities of guilt implied in the closet scene, particularly in Hamlet's "Almost as bad, good mother, / As kill a king, and marry with his brother," and have decided against them. (Whether or not Hamlet really meant to accuse his mother is another matter. W. C. MACREADY was sure he did not: Hamlet's "random words," spoken in a moment of maddening excitement, are "inconsequent, they are unjustifiable, but they are what Hamlet would have said."[246] But, in LOUIS CALVERT's opinion, Hamlet believed—wrongly—that his mother was guilty.[247]) According to Helen Faucit, Hamlet's passionate words awaken "no echo" in Gertrude's "soul"; moreover the Ghost's tenderness toward her tends to absolve her of guilt.[248] Calvert describes Gertrude's reaction differently, but still innocently: she responds to Hamlet's implied accusation with indignation and astonishment.[249] And Gielgud, who considers it "obvious" that Shakespeare did not intend her to be a murderess, quotes a "feminine and shrewd" remark made by MRS. PATRICK CAMPBELL: "The point about Gertrude in the closet scene is not that she didn't know Claudius was a murderer, but that she doted on him so much that she wouldn't have minded if he had been."[250] Granville-Barker, with his usual gift for synthesis, relates Gertrude's experiences in the closet scene with those in the rest of the play: the Ghost's appearance spares her the knowledge that her second husband is the murderer of the first; only in her final moments will the truth flash upon her, when she is dying of poison as Hamlet's father did.[251] Emphasis on the importance of the quarto editions has simplified the problem for some modern actors: MARGARET WEBSTER[252] and SIR DONALD WOLFIT[253] accept the aid of the First Quarto,

246. *Macready's Reminiscences*, ed. Pollock, p. 661. Letter to Lady Pollock, February 19, 1852.
247. *An Actor's Hamlet*, p. 145.
248. *On Some of Shakespeare's Female Characters*, pp. 10-12.
249. *An Actor's Hamlet*, p. 145.
250. *John Gielgud's Hamlet*, ed. Gilder, p. 63. See also Sterne, *Gielgud Directs Burton in Hamlet*, pp. 13, 297.
251. *Prefaces to Shakespeare*, I, 228-29, 231.
252. *Shakespeare Without Tears* (Cleveland, 1955), pp. 124-25.
253. *First Interval*, pp. 153-54.

in which Gertrude plainly says in the closet scene, "I never knew of this most horrid murder." For ROBERT SPEAIGHT[254] and GEORGE SKILLAN,[255] however, the matter is not so easily solved. Both admit to uncertainty about Gertrude's complicity in the murder, but in their discussions of the play they seem to incline toward her innocence: Skillan presents the pros and cons but emphasizes the latter; and Speaight reveals his bias (perhaps unconsciously) when, in a passage not directly related to the subject, he mentions Gertrude's "stumbling upon the truth" about her husband's murder.

I have found only two actor-critics who consider Gertrude definitely implicated in the murder, the eighteenth-century Thomas Davies and the twentieth-century Lena Ashwell. Both of these use the play scene as evidence. Davies says that the Player Queen's speech, "None wed the second but who kill'd the first," was inserted by Hamlet in the script of the old play in order "to probe the mind of the Queen; and his immediate reflection on her behaviour plainly proves that [the words] stung her to the quick."[256] Miss Ashwell is less precise; she merely comments that the players help Hamlet "resolve all doubts" and that he finds "his worst fears realized, his mother guilty."[257] Although she does not explain the extent of the word "guilty," it is virtually certain that she means "guilty of involvement in the murder." Presumably she concurs in Davies' argument that "Wormwood, wormwood" implies Gertrude's guilty reaction to the speech of the Player Queen.

The question of Gertrude's adultery has not usually been debated as an issue in the same way as the question of her involvement in the murder, but most of the actor-critics who have discussed Gertrude's character have clearly implied their answers to this question. (Those of the eighteenth century are an exception.) And, on this charge, most of them have found her guilty. I have recorded only three charitable interpretations, though there may be others. Two of these are, predictably, from the nineteenth century: THOMAS HOLCROFT's and Helen Faucit's. (Although Holcroft's acting career went back to the 1770's, his relatively clement description of Gertrude's frailty may well have been influenced by the increasing delicacy of the age in which he was

254. *Nature in Shakespearian Tragedy*, p. 25. But see p. 20.
255. *Hamlet. French's Acting Edition*, p. 83.
256. *Dramatic Miscellanies*, III, 103-4.
257. *Reflections from Shakespeare*, p. 78.

writing.) The other, published by an Anonymous Actress in 1914, is, as far as I know, the only actor-criticism that specifically "disproves" the charge of adultery.

In describing the Queen's first scene, Holcroft emphasizes her uneasy demeanor, but he explains her feeling of guilt only in terms of "the wrong she has done her late husband by so quickly marrying his brother," and he balances her timidity in the presence of her son's accusing grief with her anxiety "to please her new husband and preserve her state, as a queen and mother."[258] Miss Faucit, Victorian though she was in her usual sentiments, was not quite so mild as Holcroft in imagining what Gertrude's moral lapses had been, but apparently her imagination stopped short of actual adultery: the "black and grained spots" which Gertrude saw in her own soul were emblems of remorse, not only for "her too speedy forgetfulness of her noble husband," but also for the "preference" that "she must have previously shown" for Claudius.[259] If these words are meant to imply adultery, they are an unusually genteel hint—even for Helen Faucit. As for the Anonymous Actress, she did not doubt that Gertrude found her virtuous husband dull and her suavely smiling brother-in-law attractive, but she was positive that the two were not "intriguing guiltily" before the elder Hamlet's death. Content with a kind of circular reasoning, she convinced herself of the Ghost's jealous disposition and, on the basis of this, argued that he would not have forbidden Hamlet to "contrive" anything against his mother if she had been guilty of adultery. This actress went so far as to suppose that Gertrude agreed to the hasty marriage with Claudius only because certain statesmen persuaded her that it was for the good of Denmark; it was after this that Claudius won her affections by his blandishments.[260]

The later actor-critics have overwhelmingly agreed on Gertrude's adultery. Most of them do not argue the point, but their assumption of it is basic to their interpretations of her character. Their attitudes toward her vary widely, however, from mild contempt to reluctant admiration to sympathetic compassion.

The conception of a weak and passive though charming wom-

258. *Theatrical Recorder*, II, 137.
259. *On Some of Shakespeare's Female Characters*, pp. 10-12.
260. *The True Ophelia*, pp. 106-7.

an, most fully set forth by Granville-Barker[261] but evidently concurred in by Gielgud[262] and Speaight,[263] is the one which resembles most closely that of literary critics (Bradley, for instance). This Gertrude is, in Granville-Barker's words, "shallow, amiable, lymphatic," yet "cunning enough to deceive her husband." She "hung on him" while he lived, using the obvious method to hide her infidelity, but her tears at his death may have been self-reproachful rather than hypocritical. She shows no remorse, however, now that she has made her relationship with Claudius decent, and she seems to think that if her "morose son would but come to his senses and take a more cheerful view of life" everything might turn out very well. In the closet scene her "bland immunity" to reproach stings Hamlet to ever greater fury, but it is only when he coarsens his attack to the point of intolerability that she finally pleads guilty. Her failure to see the Ghost implies a "blindness of soul . . . a sanity which Hamlet's 'madness' puts to shame." Speaight attempts to explain Gertrude's emotional shallowness concerning her first husband by adopting a suggestion made by the French actor Jean-Louis Barrault: that she had never "enjoyed erotic satisfaction" with King Hamlet. This would account, he thinks, for her utter lack of "reminiscent affection" and her unmoved acceptance of his death so soon after its occurrence, for "women rarely feel a deep pity for men who physically repel them." Difficult as it would be for an actress to convey such an idea, Speaight felt that Diana Wynyard had succeeded (in the National Theatre production, 1963): he describes her Gertrude as "morally indolent and physically beautiful, suggesting, as she should, a woman who has been satisfied by her second husband but not by her first."

A few actor-critics, for example Lena Ashwell[264] and George Skillan,[265] depict Gertrude as considerably more spirited and independent. Miss Ashwell's "dark lady" has admirable traits, even though they serve her in a wicked cause: She has not drifted helplessly into the affair with Claudius but has chosen her course, open-eyed, with enough "common sense" and "knowledge of the

261. *Prefaces to Shakespeare*, I, 226-29.

262. *John Gielgud's Hamlet*, ed. Gilder, p. 57.

263. *Nature in Shakespearian Tragedy*, p. 20; "Shakespeare in Britain," *Shakespeare Quarterly*, XV (1964), 377.

264. *Reflections from Shakespeare*, pp. 75, 78, 81.

265. *Hamlet. French's Acting Edition*, pp. 83, 115.

world" to realize what would be involved and enough "courage" to face the consequences. The Gertrude of Skillan's conception is, if anything, even stronger-willed and more selfish—until the closet scene: she is charming and "urbane," but she is also "hard" and "conscienceless," concerned only to please her own appetite and callous to the feelings of her young son. The two actor-critics disagree about Gertrude's reaction to the closet scene. According to Lena Ashwell, she is stirred by Hamlet's furious indictment, for she sincerely loves her son, but she rallies from the brief moment of penitence and persists to the end in her chosen role as Claudius' wife and queen. In Skillan's opinion, however, the scene brings about a complete reversal in Gertrude's character: it begins with an angry attack on her "unbearably aggressive" son, but it ends with humiliation, penitence, and readiness "to act in self-redemption."

Most sympathetic of all the interpretations is that of GEORGE R. FOSS. He imagines that Gertrude had been forced into a royal marriage while very young and that her husband, a proud and warlike king, had been too much occupied with affairs of state to show her much affection. Having hungered for love all her life, she "falls to the first man that makes love to her." The "sweet and wistful remorse she shows throughout the play is of a very loving woman who knows she has erred . . . but by no means in the gross and sensual way of which her son accuses her." (According to the official view of the Church, her marriage is not incestuous, for Claudius would have had to obtain a papal dispensation beforehand as Henry VIII did in marrying Katharine of Aragon.) Pathetically she hungers for Hamlet's love, as she had done for his father's, but only Claudius shows her any tenderness.[266] Obviously Foss, in his pursuit of "Elizabethan" meanings, was thinking more about the probabilities of real-life marriages of state than about the actualities of Shakespeare's text.

One problem in the interpretation of Gertrude's part has been mentioned in print only by modern actor-critics: After the closet scene does she take Hamlet's advice to abstain from his uncle's bed? The Anonymous Actress of 1914 wondered about this;[267]

---

266. *What the Author Meant*, p. 19; *see also* p. 16.

267. *The True Ophelia*, p. 101. The Actress decided that Gertrude did not take Hamlet's "ravings" seriously. (*See* p. 145.)

and Granville-Barker[268] and Skillan[269] have also raised the question. (Lena Ashwell would obviously have answered it negatively). Granville-Barker finds an implication—subtle and unclear though he admits it to be—that Gertrude did find excuses to put Claudius off. He discovers it in the latter's speech to Laertes beginning "Not that I think you did not love your father" (IV, vii, 111-27): when Claudius says that he can see "in passages of proof" that time "qualifies the spark and fire" of love, "Of what does that covertly speak . . . but of Gertrude's mute obedience to Hamlet's behest?" Skillan points out that, as far as the action of the play reveals it, there is no outward change in Gertrude's relationship with her husband; perhaps she realizes that "total abstinence" would arouse his suspicion that "something was radically wrong" and would lead to his finding out the truth. Amusing as it may seem to find the sex life of an imaginary character debated in this manner, the question is not, like some similar ones, totally irrelevant to the actor's task. For example, if Granville-Barker's interpretation is accepted, Claudius and Gertrude will show in their behavior that they are not as close as they once were, and Claudius will seem rather wistful, thinking his wife is tired of him. Although Skillan sensibly concludes that Gertrude's actions outside the bounds of the play should not be considered "too curiously," he also remarks, recognizing the implications for the demeanor of Gertrude, that each actress must decide the matter for herself.

CLAUDIUS

One point that has been discussed by actor-critics is the relative importance of Claudius, in regard to both his position in the play and his worth as a dramatic role. In the eighteenth century he was not regarded very highly in either respect, for the part of this character was much curtailed in the usual acting editions of *Hamlet*. It received substantial restorations in DAVID GARRICK's adaptation (1772), but this version held the stage only eight years, and, with the return of Shakespeare's fifth act, the King lost his temporary gains. The low estimation in which the role was held in the first part of the following century is illustrated by the attitude of EDMUND KEAN: in discussing the cast listed in a 1774 play-

---

268. *Prefaces to Shakespeare*, I, 224-25.
269. *Hamlet. French's Acting Edition*, p. 118.

bill of Garrick's *Hamlet* (one of Wood's prized mementos) he expressed surprise that the role of the King had been given to Jefferson, "an excellent actor then, and second only to Garrick," whereas the Ghost, "a part of great importance," had been assigned to Bransby, "an actor of no fame."[270] That the implied evaluation of Claudius was typical of the time is suggested by the fact that John Genest, in *Some Account of the English Stage* (1832), frequently omits this character from his records of the chief members of the cast, even when he includes the Ghost, Polonius, the Queen, and the First Gravedigger. When it is remembered, however, that the prayer scene was customarily omitted at this time, it is easy to understand not only why the role seemed less rewarding than we now realize it to be but why the character seemed a pettier conception. Although the low opinion of Claudius persisted in the second half of the nineteenth century, EDWIN BOOTH took a very different attitude. He wrote to Lawrence Barrett (in the 1880's) that "the neglected King is a part not to be despised." "I may be mistaken," he added, "but—with the exception of, perhaps, two scenes—I fancy that it is full of subtlety and affords scope for quiet but intense emotion: I consider it a very difficult part to portray properly." He himself had been studying it; for, as he remarked with a typical mixture of enthusiasm and self-amusement, "I must try [Claudius] some day or bust my regal belly-band!"[271]

In the present century, when fuller texts of *Hamlet* have be-

270. Wood, *Personal Recollections*, pp. 381-82. Evidently Kean himself was willing to give Claudius more of a hearing than usual; at least he contemplated restoring the prayer scene. There is an interesting letter in the Folger Library which Alfred Bunn wrote to Kean when the latter was planning to include this scene in a forthcoming production at Drury Lane. Bunn wrote that the whole scene could not be restored because it would be "impossible to get the King [Powell] to study that beautiful speech beginning 'Oh my offence is rank &c' " and suggesting that the only possibility would be to have "either a side-piece put in in the second entrance of this scene, & [or?] else have centre doors thrown open, with crucifix, &c & there let the King make his exit, previous to Hamlet's speech 'Now might I do it pat. . . .' " Not a very effective scene, and Kean evidently dropped the idea. (Note: Wood misread "Bransby" as "Bransley" in the Garrick playbill.)

271. The MS letter from Booth to Barrett, dated "Frisco—Mar: 14," is in the Harvard Theatre Collection. I am grateful to Arthur Colby Sprague for allowing me to use his transcription. Sprague supplies the year 1887, giving a reference to Edwina Grossmann's *Edwin Booth*, p. 269, and noting that John Malone, who is mentioned in the letter, first acted with Booth in 1885-86. A portion of the letter is published in Otis Skinner's *The Last Tragedian* (New York, 1939), p. 197.

come customary on the stage, discussions of Claudius' significance have been related to interpretation rather than simply to theatrical opportunities. WILLIAM POEL tailored the text to suit his own purposes, but not in the old manner of emphasizing the starring role. Sensing in the atmosphere of *Hamlet* (as he thought) a reflection of the "political intrigue and personal insecurity" at the Court of the ageing Elizabeth I, he overemphasized the character of Claudius in his 1914 production of the Second Quarto *Hamlet,* suggesting in the marriage with Gertrude something of an Elizabeth-Essex relationship. According to Speaight, he enforced this parallel by raising the curtain on "an elderly lady pompously enthroned and below her at a table Claudius [sitting] among the gallants," a " 'pale and neat young man,' still in his thirties." It was not Poel's sole purpose, however, to emphasize the political theme. The long-neglected character of Claudius was important to him as well for its central position in the plot: "Until we can trace back to the King the many tragic misfortunes of the play," he said, "commentators will fail to show us the true meaning of Shakespeare's *Hamlet.*"[272] This character has won attention from other actor-critics for itself as well as for its importance to the play as a whole. GRANVILLE-BARKER and ROBERT SPEAIGHT have even seen in it potentialities as a tragic hero. The first describes Claudius as a kind of preliminary sketch of Macbeth, "the man who does murder for his crown, cannot repent, and is drawn even further into ill." The touches of humanity in Shakespeare's portrait help us to envision not merely a "well-masked villain" but also "the man that he would be, could his crimes be left out of account." Yet, in Granville-Barker's opinion, the character does not come fully to life in reading the play; the material is there, but some of it is "incompletely developed . . . and the actor must use judgment in assembling it."[273] Speaight puts even more emphasis upon Claudius' potentialities, particularly as they are manifest in the prayer scene, saying that the Aristotelian concept of tragedy is "more clearly illustrated by Claudius" than by Hamlet himself.[274]

The usual underrating of the role in the eighteenth and nineteenth centuries explains the fact that most of the specific descrip-

272. Speaight, *William Poel and the Elizabethan Revival,* pp. 56, 222-23.
273. *Prefaces to Shakespeare,* I, 216, 222-23.
274. *Nature in Shakespearian Tragedy,* p. 39.

tions of Claudius' character are fairly recent (from the present century, primarily). It is probably significant, too, that, whereas the only eighteenth-century comment of any importance—THOMAS DAVIES'—is thoroughly unsympathetic, most of the modern criticisms put as much emphasis upon Claudius' admirable traits as upon his despicable ones. For, although his villainy is apparent no matter how the play is cut, the fuller the text of his part the more complex and human his character seems.

Davies, who disliked Garrick's adaptation, viewed Claudius with unmitigated contempt: this character was no Richard III, whom "we justly hate, but . . . cannot despise"; rather, he was "a coward as well as a villain and usurper." Davies particularly disapproved of Garrick's allowing Claudius a manly death, for in doing so he "lessened the meanness of his character, which the author takes pains to inculcate throughout the play."[275] Cowardice, however, is not mentioned by the later actor-critics. Those who paint Claudius in darkest hues emphasize, in addition to his crimes, such unpleasant characteristics as his unattractive appearance and "repellent" personality (both of which LOUIS CALVERT deduces from Hamlet's "mildewed ear" speech in the closet scene[276]) and his debauchery, especially his drunkenness (BEERBOHM TREE's "hiccoughing" and "reeling" demisavage is particularly bestial.[277]) Even these traits are denied more often than they are affirmed; for a number of actor-critics warn us against taking Claudius at Hamlet's valuation. GEORGE R. FOSS does give a certain amount of credence to Hamlet's speech: though he discounts its main tendency, he accepts the image of the "mildewed ear" as a kind of distorted clue to Claudius' physical appearance. As he points out, these words do not suggest "the ruddy, bloated drunkard some actors represent." He himself imagines a smallish figure, perhaps slightly deformed (lameness is suggested) and a "clever, eager face" with "haunted eyes."[278] Claudius' appearance is not described so minutely by the other actor-critics, but the reader finds himself forming a rather attractive mental picture because of the personality that they ascribe to the character: the wit, the charm, the urbanity, the ability to win friends and influence people. As for the excessive drinking with which Hamlet

275. *Dramatic Miscellanies*, III, 145-47.
276. *An Actor's Hamlet*, p. 15.
277. *Thoughts and Afterthoughts*, pp. 125-26.
278. *What the Author Meant*, p. 18.

charges his uncle, it is sometimes accepted as true but given a pathetic significance: Edwin Booth describes Claudius as "the conscience-striken Dane—soaked in Rhenish yet unable to become drunk in his agony of guilt";[279] and even Calvert, unsympathetic as he is toward Claudius, thinks of him as attempting to drown the memory of his crime. Sometimes the drunkenness is simply denied: Granville-Barker considers Claudius a "sensualist" but no more of a drunkard than "a clever man can afford to be"; and Foss conjectures that he cleverly established his popularity with the deep-drinking Danes by pretending to carouse with them but that he was "too diplomatic and had too much on his conscience to risk losing his wits."[280] Sometimes, too, Hamlet's picture of his uncle is seen in reverse, as H. B. IRVING views it, so that Claudius' "convivial habits" become the sign, not of swinishness, but of "genial goodfellowship."[281]

Admiration for Claudius—even, sometimes, for his evil traits—is evident in descriptions by several actor-critics. H. B. Irving, an amateur criminologist, arrived at his enthusiasm for the character by a strange route: Claudius is the "most successful, therefore perhaps the greatest criminal in Shakespeare"; but, despite its peculiar orientation, his essay on the character has interest for the ordinary reader of Shakespeare. For Irving's admiration is not limited to Claudius' skill in committing a near-perfect crime; it is also extended to his self-control, his efficiency, and his geniality—qualities that Granville-Barker notices too. Both of these actor-critics marvel at Claudius' ability to mask his real villainy and even his real remorse—the "consummate" hypocrisy, as Granville-Barker calls it, which explains why Hamlet sometimes wonders whether it is a "damned ghost" that he has seen. Some positive virtues, free from the taint of self-serving, are also attributed to Claudius. According to Granville-Barker, the character is rescued from any impression of conventional villainy by the prayer scene: "Here is a man who can face the truth, not only about his deed and its deserts, but about himself too." His genuine grief over Polonius' death and Ophelia's suffering are among the inconsistencies in his character that do most to make him seem like a person of flesh and blood.[282] Foss finds Claudius so sympathetic that he at-

279. Letter to Barrett, March 14, [1887]. See n. 271, above.
280. *Prefaces to Shakespeare*, I, 225; *What the Author Meant*, p. 18.
281. H. B. Irving, *A Book of Remarkable Criminals* (London, [1918]), pp. 13-14.
282. *Prefaces to Shakespeare*, I, 217, 221-22.

tempts to explain away much of his villainy, even to the extent of insisting that he is "no hypocrite." Claudius is "certainly no usurper," he declares, for election rather than direct succession is "harped on throughout the play" and no one "ever hints" that Hamlet rather than Claudius had the right to the throne. Moreover, Foss finds "altruistic" motives for the murder of King Hamlet: One is Claudius' remorse for his adultery with Gertrude and his "longing to quiet her conscience." The other is a patriotic desire to gain the throne in order to save Denmark from the threat of Fortinbras' "secret army" which had "come to his knowledge"; "the old King despised the danger, and had neglected to arm to meet the coming invasion," but Claudius, as soon as he had the power, started an intensive rearmament program and also sent a successful embassage to Norway.[283]

There is so much insistence upon Claudius' admirable qualities, in fact, that Hamlet's character is sometimes demeaned in comparison to his. For example, H. B. Irving contrasts "the bluff hearty man of action" with "his introspective nephew," who—if the Ghost had not intervened—"would in all probability have ended his days in the cloister, rewarded with amiable contempt by his bustling fellowmen." Foss praises the flawed but human Claudius, who acts promptly, then "suffers agonies of remorse," at the expense of the perfectionist Hamlet, who broods on one moral scruple until he becomes callous to everything else. And Speaight balances Claudius' composure and good judgment against Hamlet's helpless passion: "Claudius has controlled his purpose to an unscrupulous end; Hamlet has no purpose to control."[284]

POLONIUS

How much of a fool is Polonius? This question lies behind most of the discussions of the character by actors as well as by other critics. It goes back, of course, to Samuel Johnson's famous statement that in Polonius Shakespeare depicts, not folly, but "dotage encroaching upon wisdom." This pronouncement flatly contra-

283. *What the Author Meant*, pp. 15-17.
284. *A Book of Remarkable Criminals*, pp. 13-14; *What the Author Meant*, pp. 15-16; *Nature in Shakespearian Tragedy*, p. 36. H. B. Irving's contrast between Claudius and Hamlet may be slightly ironic, but it does not seem so in its context. Irving himself, like his illustrious father (and also his brother Laurence) acted Hamlet—and gave, according to Austin Brereton, a "lovable" interpretation. See the latter's *"H.B." and Laurence Irving* (London, 1922), pp. 138, 189-90.

dicted stage tradition, for not only had the role been played by a low comedian ever since the Restoration but the advice to Laertes (which gives Polonius his chief claim to wisdom) had long been omitted in performance.

The stage felt, briefly, the impact of the new theory some years before it was expressed in print; for Garrick, a friend of Johnson's, was evidently persuaded by him that the conception was valid. He had Woodward attempt to act Polonius with more dignity than was usually accorded the character, but, according to THOMAS DAVIES, Polonius, "divested of his ridiculous vivacity, appeared to the audience flat and insipid." At any rate, Woodward gave only two performances of the role, once in 1755 and once the following year; on other occasions he turned, perhaps gratefully, to the part of Osric. (Nearly twenty years later, in his famous alteration of *Hamlet*, Garrick restored the advice to Laertes. Was he still thinking of Johnson's theory, or was Polonius' gain only the casual result of Garrick's stretching the early part of the text to compensate for his sacrifice of the fifth act?) Davies himself considered Johnson's interpretation not only ineffective theatrically but unsupported by the text—and, judging by some of his remarks, he must have meant the text as a whole. Only one speech in the play—the lapse of memory in the scene with Reynaldo—favors the "supposed dereliction of the man's faculties"; all others show him "ready and furnished" with such substitutes for intelligence and eloquence as we may suppose he has always drawn upon. Hamlet's constant ridicule of Polonius, despite his love for the latter's daughter, is further evidence of the old man's folly. It is true that Polonius makes "some pertinent remarks," but these can be explained by recalling Mirabel's description of Witwou'd in *The Way of the World:* "He is a fool with a good memory; but, that failing, his folly is betrayed by not having recourse to his commonplace book." Davies' ideal Polonius was James Taswell, who made the character "a prating, pedantick, busy, obsequious statesman; a fool with a dash of the knave."[285]

But the actor-critics of Johnson's period were not uniformly opposed to the idea of a more serious Polonius. ELIZABETH GRIFFITH found the character entirely sympathetic and dignified. According to her, even when he sends Reynaldo to "inquire closely" into Laertes' conduct he "does it with . . . tenderness and

285. *Dramatic Miscellanies,* III, 37-42; *Memoirs of Garrick,* I, 37.

parental respect to the character of the young man." Mrs. Griffith insisted that Polonius "speaks very good sense, throughout, though with the natural and *respectable* mixture of the old man in it." His ridiculous description of Hamlet's madness (II, ii, 86-104) is not meant to reflect discredit on the character himself but to "ridicule . . . the old pedantic mode of definitions, or quaint distinctions, in logic and philosophy."[286] FRANCIS GENTLEMAN did not go as far as Mrs. Griffith in supporting the dignity of Polonius— he was ready to grant "some tint of the whimsical" in the character—but he did object to the buffoonery with which the "sly old statesman" was usually represented. Charles Macklin's interpretation—"oddity, grafted upon the man of sense"—was, in his opinion, the best the stage had offered.[287]

Samuel Johnson's explanation continued to influence a few actor-critics in the nineteenth century: WILLIAM OXBERRY,[288] for example, considered Polonius "on the very verge of dotage," and W. C. MACREADY[289] described him as "a well-intentioned man, with some knowledge of the world, but with waning faculties." These two actors differed widely in their attitudes toward the character, however. Oxberry had no sympathy for his "weakness" since, in his best days, Polonius had mistaken "cunning for wisdom." But Macready held a higher regard for Polonius' sincerity. He rejected the suggestion, sometimes made at that time, of "a plot to get his daughter married to the Prince," maintaining that the old man "honestly believed Ophelia to be the sole cause of Hamlet's lunacy."

Other actor-critics have recognized in Polonius a combination of shrewdness and ridiculousness but have not explained it by the theory of dotage encroaching upon wisdom. Although several explanations have been offered, they have not completely removed the impression, held by THOMAS HOLCROFT[290] in 1805 and by GRANVILLE-BARKER[291] more than a century later, that part of the difficulty lies in Shakespeare's inconsistent portrayal. Both of these

286. Mrs. [Elizabeth] Griffith, *The Morality of Shakespeare's Drama Illustrated* (London, 1775), pp. 508-10.

287. *Dramatic Censor*, I, 35.

288. *The New English Drama*, III, Hamlet, xxii-xxiii.

289. *Macready's Reminiscences*, ed. Pollock, p. 36; Lady Pollock, *Macready as I Knew Him*, pp. 10-11.

290. *Theatrical Recorder*, II, 191.

291. *Prefaces to Shakespeare*, I, 204-5.

men were concerned by the disparity between the wisdom and pithiness of Polonius' advice to Laertes and the tedious pomposity of his later speeches. Except for his first scene, wrote Holcroft, the character is "excellently preserved," and Granville-Barker went so far as to suppose that Shakespeare changed his mind about the characterization after writing the first part of the play. Both, however, noticed the dramatist's attempt (as they considered it) to smooth over the discrepancy. Holcroft actually implied that Shakespeare gave Polonius an unwonted wisdom in the early scene because a ridiculous father would have detracted from the sympathetic introduction of Ophelia and Laertes, which is the primary purpose of the scene. He also noted that Shakespeare blended this scene with the rest to some extent by increasing Polonius' verbosity in the otherwise intelligent advice to Ophelia after Laertes' departure. Granville-Barker believed that the scene with Reynaldo was inserted by Shakespeare as a kind of bridge between the old conception of Polonius and the new one. This critic's own analysis of the character, which we will discuss later, is based on the "new" Polonius.

Polonius' apparent folly has sometimes been reconciled with his worldly wisdom by the explanation that a politician and courtier must frequently mask his real thoughts. Two successful impersonators of the character, JOSEPH MUNDEN[292] and J. H. BARNES,[293] considered his "foolish" speeches mere diplomatic acquiescence in Hamlet's mad whims. Munden explained Polonius as "a pliant and supple courtier, and man of the world, ready to accord with any one's opinion whom he deemed it expedient to flatter" but capable of "sound sense and just reflection." Barnes emphasized his "keen eye for the main chance" and his constant solicitude for the welfare of his family. "Too . . . prudent to make an enemy" of Hamlet, whom he believed to be mad, Polonius was "ever ready, when meeting this prince, with what in modern slang is known as 'spoof.'" When Barnes used this interpretation on the stage the character was "as amusing as he had ever been, without losing a particle of his dignity."

It is interesting that in the modern period the sharpest argument against the "farcical" interpretation has also come from a

292. T. S. Munden, *Memoirs of Joseph Shepherd Munden, Comedian* (London, 1844), p. 48.
293. *Forty Years on the Stage*, p. 216.

successful stage representative of the character, ARTHUR BYRON, who performed Polonius to Gielgud's Hamlet in Guthrie Mc-Clintic's production (New York, 1937). Byron did not, however, like Munden and Barnes, explain Polonius' ridiculousness as tongue-in-cheek playacting; he simply denied its existence, except from Hamlet's prejudiced point of view. According to him, Polonius was "a statesman on whose advice the throne of Denmark had long depended," one whom "the new King held in high esteem" and to whom, in part, he probably "owed his throne." Although such a man might well be "tedious even to the point of boredom," he would not be a "buffoon." After years in a position of authority and respect, he would probably take on an air of self-assurance which would pique the young Hamlet, particularly since the latter was already irritated by the fact that this friend of his hated uncle was also the father of the girl he loved. This situation explains why Hamlet could not resist baiting the old gentleman.[294]

Although few actors' criticisms present Polonius as primarily a fool, obviously the old conception did not die out with the eighteenth century. Several of the commentaries that we have noticed are, in part, protests against this perennial stage interpretation or accounts of how the writers themselves transcended it in their own performances. At least two actor-critics of the early modern period (contemporaries of Barnes and predecessors of Byron) returned to a conception resembling Thomas Davies'. WILLIAM POEL considered the advice to Laertes a string of aphorisms (compare Davies' idea of the commonplace book), and when he played Polonius he "rattled them off" as if from memory.[295] LOUIS CALVERT described Polonius as "a kind of clown," "fond of the sound of his own voice" and absurdly vain of his own intellect, explaining his simplest thoughts over and over, for fear they will not be grasped by "meaner comprehensions." Yet Calvert did not deny his craftiness as a courtier or his skill as "an accomplished liar." The scene with Reynaldo is important because it gives us further insight into Polonius' spying, sneaking nature. Hamlet's behavior toward him is "easy to understand" after this:

294. "New Polonius Has Made His Escape from Tradition," *Boston Herald,* January 24, 1937.

295. Speaight, *William Poel and the Elizabethan Revival,* p. 224. *See also* p. 52 for Poel's letter to the *Era,* April 30, 1892, in which he describes Polonius as "the essence of genteel foppishness, ceaselessly chattering."

"He has taken the true measure of the man and treats him as he deserves."[296] (Compare Davies' "fool with a dash of the knave.")

The most recent actor-critics of Polonius, rather than arguing for a foolish interpretation or a serious one, have simply described the character, giving him elements of both. It seems to me, however, that, although all of these grant him a certain shrewdness as a politician and man of the world, his ultimate folly is even more important to them. Gielgud is perhaps an exception. In his interpretation knavishness seems to predominate, at least in Polonius' basic character—that of "an inquisitive, pompous, spying old fox, who had surely bought his position with the new king by tactfully forgetting his allegiance to the old." This real self is overlaid by the assumed roles of the elegant and diplomatic court official and the strict but loving parent. As for Polonius' mentality, Gielgud finds in him a difficult combination of real wisdom and mere sententiousness. In his opinion, the complexity of the character was not properly appreciated until the performance of A. Bromley Davenport in Barry Jackson's modern-dress *Hamlet* of 1925.[297] More folly and less deliberate knavery are implied in the discussions by Granville-Barker[298] and ROBERT SPEAIGHT:[299] for example, the former describes Polonius as "the complacent wiseacre, infatuate in opinion, precipitate in action—and usually wrong." Neither, however, considers the character a complete fool: according to Granville-Barker, "he can occupy his high place with dignity enough—only now and then calling pomposity to his aid"; and Speaight remarks that his "long-windedness" is merely the "idiom of his trade," that of professional politician. The descriptions by these two actor-critics are rather similar, but Granville-Barker's is more fully worked out. His Polonius is well-intentioned (like Macready's): even when he spies on Laertes and "looses" Ophelia to Hamlet he does not consider that he is acting ignobly or perhaps even cruelly. His manner is kindly and affable, his attitude toward other people a worldly mixture of cynicism and tolerance. Both Granville-Barker and Speaight convey a subtler idea of Polonius' folly than is expressed by earlier writers, but whereas Speaight chooses the advice to Laertes to illustrate his point the older critic evidently considered that speech

296. *An Actor's Hamlet*, pp. 33, 35, 37, 57, 139.
297. *John Gielgud's Hamlet*, ed. Gilder, p. 45.
298. *Prefaces to Shakespeare*, I, 205-7.
299. *Nature in Shakespearian Tragedy*, pp. 13, 16.

out of character for Polonius. According to Speaight, a "wealth of worldly wisdom" is contained here; what makes the sensible words seem comic is "the monumental complacency behind them; the implication that there is no wisdom beyond this worldliness." Granville-Barker applies a similar idea to the whole of Polonius' part—and in a more devastating fashion: If life were simply the "clever game" he thinks, then he would be, as he assumes he is, the wise "assistant to a state," whose advice has only to be followed to make all well. "But Shakespeare shows us, by a harsher light, a very different picture: of a silly old gentleman pettily maneuvering among passions and forces that are dark to him."

Looking back over the actors' descriptions of Polonius, we get the impression of several different kinds of personality: one Polonius is bustling, another suave; one is kindly and well-intentioned, another self-seeking and hypocritical. But when we compare the answers to the basic question "Is he a fool?" we find, I think, that the differences are mainly a matter of definition and emphasis (and sometimes of sympathy). Particularly if we were able to compare stage performances that deliberately attempted to convey these various interpretations, I suspect that in some passages at least all of them would seem comic. Those actor-critics who have argued most strongly for a wise and capable Polonius—Elizabeth Griffith, Munden, Barnes, and Byron—have nevertheless mentioned characteristics that would probably elicit laughter from the audience, no matter how they were explained by the performer himself. Mrs. Griffith, for example, might insist all she pleased that the speech "Your noble son is mad" is meant to ridicule old-fashioned rhetoric rather than the user of such rhetoric, but the audience makes no such distinction. Munden and Barnes probably did hit upon an interpretation that could be projected in the theatre: laughter would be aroused, but it would not necessarily be aimed at Polonius' folly. This would be true, at least, in the scenes with Hamlet—though even here some members of the audience might well laugh, sadly or sardonically, at the ultimate folly involved in attaining political and social goals at the expense of personal identity and self-respect. But what of "Your noble son is mad?" And what of the scene with Reynaldo? (In some cases the latter question would not arise, for the scene has frequently been omitted.) Byron's description of a serious and worthy Polonius gives an interesting insight into his own purpose and manner in acting the part, but it does not really explain away the laughable element in the character. Tediousness and self-assurance (traits which Byron admits in Polonius) may build patience or provoke disgust in real-life associates, but, if well acted, this combination normally produces laughter in a theatre. It is equally true that none of the actor-critics, even those who call Polonius a "fool" or "clown," consider him completely simple-minded. To speak in stock company terms, their conceptions would, in general, call for a character actor rather than either the Low Comedian or the First Old Man. The dramatic rationale for such a Polonius is well explained by GEORGE SKILLAN: The character "cannot be a straight part" or "he would be flat and purposeless." Since the other major roles are "strong and intense," a "singularly different" type is needed for relief. But, although eccentricity is appropriate to Polonius, buffoonery is not. Comedy is his *"mould,"* but *"tragedy comes out of his mistakes. This means that the element of his foolishness must not become absurd."*[300]

OPHELIA

"Tho the lady while in her senses said very little to affect us," wrote FRANCIS GENTLEMAN in 1770, her mad scenes provide a "pretty variation of action" and her death moves us if her life did not.[301] This was the typical eighteenth-century attitude toward Ophelia, for her part, like that of Claudius, was long considered negligible. (The reasons were not the same, of course. Ophelia's part, even without textual cuts, is very brief—less than a third as long as the King's in terms of lines and much shorter than that in terms of words, for her speech is very laconic.) Even in the first half of the nineteenth century, when Shakespeare's heroines as a group were receiving more attention from critics (led by the irrepressible Mrs. Jameson) and when a number of them were established as major roles on the stage, Ophelia was still comparatively ignored by actor-critics. As we might expect, when her importance did become a theme in their writings, it was because of the enthusiasm of the actresses who had represented her themselves.

Sir Theodore Martin credits his wife, HELEN FAUCIT, with

300. *Hamlet. French's Acting Edition*, pp. 86, 93.
301. *Dramatic Censor*, I, 26-27.

being the first actress to recognize Ophelia's real worth. According to him, at the time when she acted the part in Paris with Macready, 1844-45, no English manager would have "dreamed" of asking a leading actress to stoop so low, for Ophelia had long been considered "only good enough for the singing lady of the theatre." The character had a "peculiar fascination" for Miss Faucit, however, "because of the injustice which she thought had been done to it, not only on the stage, but also by commentators and critics." She gladly undertook it, and she won much acclaim from French critics for her portrayal.[302] Although she did not keep the part in her repertory after the Paris venture, probably because it was not considered substantial enough for star billing (she had recently left the London theatres for a career as a travelling star), she maintained a lifelong interest in it; and when, many years later, she wrote a series of essays on Shakespeare's heroines, it was of Ophelia that she thought first. "It hurts me," she declared, "to hear her spoken of . . . as a weak creature, wanting in truthfulness, in purpose, in force of character, and only interesting when she loses the little wits she had." Although the character is "delicately out-lined," its fine shadings are "so true to nature, and . . . so full of suggestion" that it offers strong proof

302. *Helena Faucit (Lady Martin)* (2d ed.; Edinburgh and London, 1900), p. 131. (*See* p. 137 for extracts from French critiques.) A study of the "Ophelia" entries in the indexes of Charles B. Hogan's *Shakespeare in the Theatre, 1701-1800* and of the casts of *Hamlet* listed by John Genest in *Some Account of the English Stage* (Bath, 1832) confirms in the main the statement that the role of Ophelia was not generally given to the leading actresses of London companies. Several outstanding actresses had performed the part, however. Some of them—e.g. Kitty Clive and Dora Jordan—were more often associated with comedy than with tragedy (Ophelia was considered an ingenue role, not one requiring great tragic power); others—like Susannah Cibber—were singers as well as fine actresses (Ophelia's madness, including the mad songs, was considered the chief attraction of the role). On one occasion, however (May 15, 1786), the great Sarah Siddons acted Ophelia to the Hamlet of her brother John Philip Kemble.

During the period when such actresses were occasionally acting Ophelia (the second half of the eighteenth century), the role was often assigned to minor actresses like Mrs. Morland, Miss Poole, Miss Kennedy (i.e. Elizabeth Griffith), Mrs. Billington, and Mrs. Davies. Genest's account of the first third of the nineteenth century would indicate that Frances Maria (Fanny) Kelly was the best known actress in the period nearer Miss Faucit's who undertook the role with any frequency. Miss Faucit herself made her London debut in 1836. During her first three seasons in London she acted a full dozen Shakespearean heroines (e.g. Juliet, Rosalind, Constance, Imogen); but she had never been asked to play Ophelia until the Paris venture with Macready.

of Shakespeare's faith in acting—in the ability to bring his subtle conceptions to "full and vivid life."[303]

Although several outstanding actresses in the latter part of the nineteenth century gave memorable performances of Ophelia— Ellen Terry, for example, and Helena Modjeska—the complaint that Ophelia was underrated continued to be made. In 1914 an ANONYMOUS ACTRESS wrote that she "never wanted to play Ophelia" because of its reputation as a nonentity but that when she was forced to study the part for herself she discovered, not "an insipid little creature" at all, but an interesting and tragic character.[304] At least two well-known actresses of the present century have held similar views. JULIA MARLOWE[305] recalls that she "astonished" her friends by playing Ophelia since the part was often assigned to "the second juvenile woman of the company," and ETHEL BARRY-MORE[306] sarcastically refers to the typical representatives of the part as "little flibbertigibbets, chosen apparently for both their youth and imbecility, so that when Ophelia does go mad, the shock which Shakespeare meant the audience to feel is no shock at all." Both actresses rated the role very highly: "one of Shakespeare's greatest female characters," Miss Marlowe called it; and Miss Barrymore described it as her favorite Shakespearean part, "very subtle, tragic, and beautifully poetic." I know of only one actress, LENA ASHWELL, who has ventured the opinion that Ophelia has been overemphasized, and this is because of Miss Ashwell's conviction that Gertrude is the central figure in Hamlet's tragedy.[307]

But the increased interest in Ophelia cannot be put down entirely to the actress's natural desire to find significance in her part. Some of it is due to the greater emphasis upon Hamlet's love for Ophelia (a point we shall discuss later), and some of it is obviously the outgrowth of modern concern for the psychology of sex. In our own time Ophelia's importance is upheld most strongly, not by actresses with a personal stake in the role, but by the actors GEORGE SKILLAN[308] and ROBERT SPEAIGHT.[309] The first

303. On Some of Shakespeare's Female Characters, pp. 3-4.
304. The True Ophelia, pp. 15-61, especially 15-17.
305. Julia Marlowe's Story, pp. 168-69.
306. Ethel Barrymore, Memories: An Autobiography (New York, [1955]), pp. 256-57.
307. Reflections from Shakespeare, p. 80.
308. Hamlet. French's Acting Edition, p. 85.
309. Nature in Shakespearian Tragedy, pp. 40-42.

of these stresses Ophelia's "vital concern" in the action of the
play, pointing out that her appearances, though comparatively
few, always occur at climactic moments and that during the long
intervals between these appearances she is kept in the memory
of the audience by important allusions. Skillan recommends for
Ophelia an actress with "a very marked personality that will
assert itself without effort," for, even though she has no opportunities for "lengthy or detailed development" of the character,
she must strongly impress the audience. Speaight, though he
does not discuss Ophelia as a dramatic role, is perhaps the most
emphatic of the actor-critics in asserting her importance, not only
to Hamlet personally, but to the meaning of the play as a whole:
"there is a striking parallel between the feigned madness of Hamlet and the real madness of Ophelia. Ophelia had been inadequate
to her situation as he is inadequate to his." In her death, too,
Ophelia's fate provides a significant parallel to Hamlet's, for her
suicide is "the sign of a personality divided against itself."

In specific analyses of Ophelia's character, the main considerations have been the question of her innocence or guilt (in matters
of both sex and probity) and the overlapping one of her weakness
or strength (intellectual and moral). The earliest actor-critics
apparently considered Ophelia innocent and sweet but little else.
COLLEY CIBBER's phrase "Innocence and Simplicity"[310] suggests a
kind of childlike naiveté, bordering on gullibility, which seems
to have been the main attribute associated with her character.
There is little change in attitude reflected in WILLIAM OXBERRY's
brief description published nearly eighty years later: Ophelia is
tender, simple, and affectionate, and her naturally sweet character shows through her beautiful and touching mad scenes.[311]
By the time Helen Faucit was developing her conception, however, although Ophelia was still considered an ingénue part in the
theatre, her innocence had been questioned by literary critics
(particularly the Germans) in two respects: her mad songs, being
highly improper for a virtuous young woman of gentle rearing,
seemed to cast some doubts on the spotlessness of her past experience; and her integrity was apparently blemished by her
duplicity toward Hamlet in the nunnery scene, both in playing
the part of a decoy and in answering Hamlet's question about her

310. *Apology*, I, 90.
311. *New English Drama*, III, *Hamlet*, xxi-xxii.

father with an outright lie.[312] Miss Faucit not only vindicated
Ophelia's innocence in both respects but described it as something
stronger and more positive than mere "simplicity." Her essay
on the character commands attention because of its pivotal position (originally published in 1880, it is the first detailed analysis
of Ophelia by a player) and because of its individualism.

To assist herself in filling the delicate "outline" of the character and to give unity to the glimpses which Shakespeare has
provided, Helen Faucit constructed in her imagination a predramatic life for Ophelia: The motherless child of an elderly
courtier, the "baby Ophelia was left . . . to the kindly but thoroughly unsympathetic tendings of country-folk." A lonely little
girl, she grew up among rougher natures with no one to understand her or share her thoughts. She developed a love of solitary
rambles among wild flowers and a knowledge of rural folkways.
(Later, in her madness, these childhood experiences would return
to her mind—the country burial customs, the "strewing the grave
with flowers," the singing of rude old songs. It is important to
remember "this part of her supposed life," wrote Miss Faucit,
"because it puts to flight all the coarse suggestions which un-
imaginative critics have often made, to explain how Ophelia came
to utter snatches of such ballads as never ought to issue from a
young cultured woman's lips.") When the play opens, Ophelia
has been at Court only a short time and does not yet know the
ways of the world, but she has found her ideal in "the one man

312. Helen Faucit's reconstruction of Ophelia's childhood is reminiscent of
Goethe's (or Wilhelm Meister's) reconstruction of Hamlet's youth, but the Victorian lady would have considered Wilhelm's explanation of Ophelia's songs indelicate. Tieck's interpretation would have been even less acceptable. (*Hamlet.*
Furness Variorum, IV [Philadelphia, 1877 (1905)], 286-87.) German critics were
also the most severe in condemning Ophelia's duplicity. An extreme example is
J. L. F. Flathe's theory of a conniving Ophelia, callous about Hamlet's feelings,
and interested only in cooperating with her father to force a royal marriage.
(*Furness Variorum,* IV, 314-15.) The English critics, though usually more sympathetic, were not all partisans of Ophelia. During the same decade when Miss
Faucit's study was published, Grace Latham presented a paper for the New
Shakspere Society in which she called Ophelia "one of the least interesting of
Shakspere's women," pure and sweet but somewhat cold and lacking in the
active virtues; ("O Poor Ophelia," *New Shakspere Society Transactions,* Ser. I, No. 9
[1880-84], 401-30). William Archer, in reviewing Miss Faucit's essays, took issue
with her for defending Ophelia against the charge of duplicity. Archer considered the essays helpful for actresses but too subjective and synthetic (rather
than analytical) for good criticism. See "Ophelia and Portia; A Fable for Critics,"
The Theatre, XV (June-December, 1885), 17-27.

about the court who was likely to reach it, both from his rare and attractive qualities, and a certain loneliness in his position not very unlike her own." Hamlet, too, finds in Ophelia "the subtle charm which the deep, philosophical intellect must ever find in the pure, unconscious innocence and wisdom of a guileless heart." This guilelessness remains untarnished even in the nunnery scene, for her intentions there are entirely honorable. It must have been "acutely painful to her sensitive nature" to "thrust herself upon her lover's notice" after repeatedly refusing to see him and to "become as it were, the partner in a trick." But she is thinking of Hamlet's mad behavior when last she saw him, and she hopes that the interview will determine whether her worldly-wise father is right in imputing the madness to love for her. "In this state of mind, surely she is not to be much blamed" for her half-willing, half-unwilling acquiescence in the scheme. Nor can she be blamed for lying about her father: since Hamlet has been speaking wildly and furiously, she fears that if he knows the truth he will kill Polonius; thus she lies, not weakly, but unselfishly and nobly as Desdemona does when she says, "Nobody. I myself." At the end of this scene, Ophelia's agony, too deep for tears, is first of all for Hamlet and his madness, and last of all for her own wretchedness. But the weight of her silently-borne grief eventually becomes unbearable, and her madness is caused as much by the "death of her love" as by the death of her father.[313]

Helen Faucit's noble, unselfish Ophelia, who combined "wisdom" with her "innocence," is not only different from earlier conceptions of the character but also, in some ways, from most later ones. Certainly strength of intellect has rarely been attributed to Ophelia (perhaps even Miss Faucit did not mean the word "wisdom" to suggest mental profundity but rather a kind of intuitive perception of values), and strength of character just

313. *On Some of Shakespeare's Female Characters*, pp. 3-21, especially 12-15, 19-20. Helen Faucit may have been influenced by Anna Brownell Jameson's essay on Ophelia in *Characteristics of Women* (Boston, 1853), pp. 109-22 (originally published in London, 1832). Among several "innocent" possibilities that Mrs. Jameson mentioned to explain Ophelia's mad songs was the suggestion that in infancy Ophelia may have had a nurse who sang her to sleep with such songs. By the time Miss Faucit wrote her essay, Mary Cowden Clarke's fanciful story "The Rose of Elsinore" had been published (in *The Girlhood of Shakespeare's Heroines* [London, 1850-52]). Mrs. Clarke gave Ophelia a country rearing, complete with a lovely foster sister who was "betrayed" by a courtier. But Miss Faucit's conception had no doubt been formed earlier, at the time she acted Ophelia.

as seldom so. But at least two actor-critics of later years—the Anonymous Actress[314] early in the present century and George Skillan[315] in our own period—have carried forward the idea of an Ophelia strong in both respects; indeed the first of these went beyond Helen Faucit in doing so. (The two actresses would not have agreed on what constitutes strength, however.) Both of the later critics describe her as "sensitive" and "intelligent." The Actress remarks that, although she is "utterly inexperienced in the ways of the world," she has "an unsuspected depth of nature which is revealed as the tragedy unfolds." And Skillan actually declares that her "complete absence of sophistication" is "the product of a strong character." Her deep respect for her father and her unquestioning obedience to his will are not signs of weakness; they are "characteristics of the social life of the times."

The Actress's analysis of Ophelia invites closer examination, for it offers an extreme example of a player's rationalization of the text to create a character of greater substance for herself. Given the idea of an Ophelia who is spirited and intelligent but inexperienced, it begins reasonably enough. Why would such a person give in so easily to her father's command that she stop seeing the man she loves? Because his cynical interpretation of their love, and particularly his revelation that her own behavior has been grossly misunderstood by other people, destroys the "exquisite joy of loving ideally" which has been hers and shocks her into a sad uncertainty about her situation. Is it possible that Hamlet himself has interpreted her obvious delight in his presence as a sign of cheap and unseemly aggressiveness? *Are* his intentions honorable? Rudely thrust into a world of mundane considerations previously unknown to her, she obeys her father because, in her own words, "I do not know . . . what I should think." Her subsequent behavior reflects the restraint and self-consciousness that have replaced her natural spontaneity. Ironically, just as pride is forcing her to assume a mask of indifference, her girlish idealism is ripening into an adult passion. But Hamlet, hurt by her apparent fickleness, wounds her in turn by retaliatory cruelty. She matures under suffering, however, and after the ordeal of the nunnery scene she determines to find out the cause of Hamlet's apparent madness, which, as she discerns, may be

314. *The True Ophelia*, pp. 18-61.
315. *Hamlet. French's Acting Edition*, p. 85.

only a deep bitterness. Here the Actress, ignoring the obvious meaning of Ophelia's "O what a noble mind is here o'erthrown," gives her the same sharp insight that Shakespeare reserved for Claudius. The most astonishing part of the interpretation follows: In the play scene Ophelia "never takes her eyes off Hamlet, praying passionately . . . that she may pierce his mystery." Her sensitive temperament responds to the feeling of tension in the air, as she perceives Hamlet's "fixed intention of provoking the King and Queen." Suddenly "the motive of Hamlet's behaviour breaks in on her, and she is in possession of his terrible secret." At the end of the scene she flies to her room, "whirled by horror, compassion for Hamlet, the desire to comfort him"; but just as she decides it may not yet be too late to help him someone brings her the news that Hamlet has killed her father. Madness ensues. The Actress gives a close analysis of the mad scenes, explaining each of Ophelia's allusions and suggesting stage business at certain points: for example, when she catches sight of the King she remembers the play scene and "shrinks back . . . exclaiming: 'It is the . . . false steward, who stole his master's . . .'—she points straight at the Queen, but cannot find the word she seeks—'daughter,' she utters finally, for want of the other word 'wife.' "

This Actress gets farther away from the text of the play than Helen Faucit does, even though she does not use the romantic device of a predramatic life for Ophelia. She frequently attributes to the character thoughts that never issue in any of Shakespeare's words and that cannot be deduced from any of them either. Much of her essay, in fact, may serve as a dreadful warning to other actresses. Yet the interpretation of the early scenes, including parts of the nunnery scene, offers some legitimate possibilities; and one or two suggestions in the mad scenes, far-fetched as they sound, might inspire some imaginative acting: the connection between Claudius and the "false steward," for example, might well seem the sudden intuition of madness rather than an indication that Ophelia had previously penetrated Hamlet's mystery.[316]

By far the most pervasive idea of Ophelia, in modern as in earlier times, has been that of a pathetically weak character rather than an admirably strong one. In a few instances her helplessness

316. Helen Faucit tells (in *Some of Shakespeare's Female Characters,* p. 20) of her own attempt to give Shakespeare's "deeper meaning" in Ophelia's mad scene by her changing attitude toward Laertes.

has even been represented as culpable or, at any rate, deplorable. Two actresses of the late nineteenth century, CLARA MORRIS[317] and ELLEN TERRY,[318] provide the most interesting examples of this kind of criticism. Miss Morris thought of Ophelia as a moral "weakling" who lost her pristine artlessness and candor by lack of resistance to her environment of intrigue. Though still comparatively innocent, this Ophelia had been exposed to the "training of court life, the warnings of a shrewd brother and . . . a tricky father"; she was "ductile in stronger hands and could play a part; could lead a lover on to speech, without giving the slightest hint of the hateful watching eyes she knew were upon him." Ellen Terry agreed that Ophelia was very weak, especially in courage.

She is scared of Hamlet when trouble changes him from . . . the "glass of fashion and the mould of form"—into a strange moody creature, careless of his appearance, bitter in his speech, scornful of society. She is scared of her father and dare not disobey him, even when he tells her to play the spy on Hamlet. She is scared of life itself when things go wrong.

Ophelia is, in fact, Shakespeare's only timid heroine. And she is weak in brain and body as well as in "soul." In the nunnery scene "it is not surprising that she should think Hamlet mad, for all he says . . . is completely beyond her." In Miss Terry's opinion, there should be, from the first, a suggestion of "something queer about her," for it is likely that the shock of her father's murder, rather than being the sole cause of her madness, "developed an incipient insanity." Neither Clara Morris nor Ellen Terry was without sympathy for the character, however; the former considered the very frailty of this "Rose of May" beautiful and touching, and the latter remarked that if the nunnery scene is properly acted "we feel a great compassion for the poor girl, whom Hamlet at once loves and hates."

But in most instances descriptions of the weak Ophelia have been brief and completely sympathetic; the traditional attributes of sweetness, simplicity, and fragility have been repeated, with no hint of depreciation—weakness is merely vulnerability. Among the actor-critics who have expressed this view are LOUIS CALVERT, OTIS SKINNER, JOHN BARRYMORE, and LENA ASHWELL.[319] GRANVILLE-

---

317. *Life on the Stage*, p. 357.

318. *Four Lectures on Shakespeare*, ed. with an introduction by Christopher St. John [Christabel Marshall] (London, [1932]), pp. 165-66.

319. Calvert, *An Actor's Hamlet*, pp. 31, 37; Skinner, *Footlights and Spotlights*,

BARKER also belongs with this group, but his conception has a little more individuality, partly because it is developed at greater length. He allows Ophelia a certain intelligence—the "touch of mischievous humor with which she counters Laertes' homily" in her first scene shows that she is no fool—but he does not go as far as Skillan and the Anonymous Actress with this idea. He presents her as a gentle, unsophisticated girl who feels that Hamlet's love is honorable but that she is duty-bound to obey her father. In the nunnery scene her attempt to return Hamlet's gifts is natural: "If he will not take them back things may then begin to mend between them. So simple are her tactics." After the blows that she receives in this scene her sanity is already wavering. When Hamlet cheapens her before the whole Court by "launching smutty jokes at her" in the play scene, she keeps up appearances bravely, but her fragile nature cannot sustain many more such "wrenchings at the root." The killing of her father by the man she loves is the "final and fatal wrench."[320]

Up to this point, none of the actors' criticisms give any hint of Ophelia's loss of innocence, as far as sex is concerned. And only one—that of the Anonymous Actress—even suggests any strong physical passion. With JOHN MARTIN-HARVEY's criticism, however, a certain change is descernible in the quality of the innocence attributed to Ophelia. Although he does not accuse her of immoral behavior, Martin-Harvey sees in Ophelia a sensual inclination which is "profoundly pitiful" as Shakespeare portrays it: Both brother and father recognize this element in her nature, as their warnings about Hamlet make clear (indeed they share it with her), and even the poor Queen, well qualified to sense such things, implies her understanding when she hopes that Ophelia's *"virtues"* will "bring [Hamlet] to his wonted way again,/ *To both your honours."* According to Martin-Harvey, Ellen Terry's stage portrayal of Ophelia emphasized her budding voluptuousness.

Her long, virginal limbs, her husky voice, her crown of short flaxen hair, her great red mouth, an inability to stand still for a moment, a mentality which could never have risen into her Prince's spiritual atmosphere, a poise so frail that one trembled for her sanity, a physical attractiveness which gave . . . ample excuse for Hamlet's

p. 203 (description of Helena Modjeska's Ophelia); Barrymore, *Confessions of an Actor*, Ch. V (praise of Fay Compton's interpretation); Ashwell, *Reflections from Shakespeare*, pp. 80-81.

320. *Prefaces to Shakespeare*, I, 212-16.

"Get thee to a Nunnery" . . . all these qualities prepared one's mind for the pitiful direction taken by her thoughts when she could no longer control them.

Ophelia's sensuality is only latent, however; she is as yet a sweet and innocent girl. Not only is she inexperienced sexually, but she is completely guileless in her dealings with Hamlet; indeed, she does not even know of the eavesdroppers' presence in the nunnery scene. It is true that she was onstage when her father and the King planned the spying, but, according to Elizabethan convention, she need not have heard what they said. She has been told only to walk there reading her prayer book, and she obviously supposes that she is to report Hamlet's conversation to her father afterwards (else why does Polonius later say, "You need not tell us what Lord Hamlet said"?). Since she thinks her father has really gone home, she is not consciously lying when she answers Hamlet's question.[321]

But is Ophelia's sensuality still latent indeed, or is it not, rather, full-blown? A few actors have tried to answer this question, which was raised in the first instance by other writers. The grounds for questioning Ophelia's sexual morality are Hamlet's indecent allusions in the fishmonger scene and his insulting language in the nunnery scene and the play scene, together with the "St. Valentine's" song which Ophelia sings in her madness. In the Saxo Grammaticus story, too, her nearest counterpart was Hamlet's mistress as well as a would-be spy for the King.

Some actor-critics—for example, Louis Calvert and George Skillan—have considered Ophelia's innocence obvious beyond question.[322] SIR JOHN GIELGUD rejects the idea of a previous affair, partly because there is no proof of it (the bawdiness of the mad songs can be explained in terms of "repression or wish fulfillment rather than reminiscence"), but chiefly because the play gains nothing by this interpretation. If Ophelia is lying to her father when she says that Hamlet "has importuned me with love in honorable fashion," the effect of her lying to Hamlet in the nunnery scene is lost, and "her innocence and purity as the thwarted ideal of his love" is ruined. Most important of all, the actress of Ophelia, who "has a difficult task in any case," would

321. *Autobiography*, pp. 29-30, 300-302, 306-7.
322. Calvert, *An Actor's Hamlet*, p. 31; Skillan, commentary on *Hamlet*. *French's Acting Edition*, p. 85.

find her difficulties compounded if she tried to suggest an Ophelia with a secret love affair on her conscience; and nothing in her words or actions would be clarified by such an interpretation.[323] At least two actor-critics, however (both contemporaries of ours), consider it highly probable that Hamlet and Ophelia have been lovers in every sense. SIR TYRONE GUTHRIE rejects the traditional concept of "childlike innocent," explaining that it originated in stock-company days when Ophelia was considered an ingénue part. "The ingénue is stereotyped as a pure virgin. But there is strong evidence that Ophelia is neither pure nor a virgin."[324] According to Robert Speaight, who goes into the matter more fully, it is likely that Ophelia has either become Hamlet's mistress already or is at the point of becoming so when the play begins: "it is at least clear that Hamlet is deeply and passionately in love with Ophelia, and that she, knowing as she must that marriage can hardly be in question, is nevertheless encouraging him." Polonius' command that she stop seeing Hamlet has a shattering effect on her as well as on her lover. When this "fragile, subtle, probably sensual girl" says "I shall obey, my lord," it is "for her the end of liberty and the end of life." Speaight particularly praises Rosemary Harris' interpretation in the National Theatre production (1963): "her mad scene showed the fury of sexual frustration working on a nature too delicate to sustain the double shock of her father's death and Hamlet's repudiation."[325]

Hamlet's Attitude toward Ophelia

The early actors seem to have assumed without question that Hamlet had loved Ophelia but that he found it necessary to give her up, along with all other interests, in order to fulfill his vow of single-minded vengeance. They saw little opportunity for acting the lover in the play, however: in the nunnery scene—the only one in which Hamlet and Ophelia speak together for any length of time—the main feature seemed to be Hamlet's feigned madness, which, as FRANCIS GENTLEMAN remarked, gave "much

323. *John Gielgud's Hamlet*, ed. Gilder, pp. 45-46. See also Sterne, *Gielgud Directs Burton in Hamlet*, p. 296. For Gielgud's interesting suggestions about Ophelia's mad scenes see pp. 16-17 in the latter book.

324. *A Life in the Theatre*, p. 21.

325. *Nature in Shakespearian Tragedy*, pp. 15-18; "Shakespeare in Britain," *Shakespeare Quarterly*, XV (1964), p. 378.

scope, particularly in this scene, for powerful acting."[326] Since
the character of Ophelia was secondary in importance to her
function as a sort of "feeder" for Hamlet's passion, the eighteenth-
century actors took virtually no part in the discussion of Hamlet's
mistreatment of her. CHARLES DIBDIN was typical: What better
way could Hamlet produce the impression of madness, he asked,
than by behaving outrageously to the one he loves best?[327] Even
Gentleman himself, one of Hamlet's harshest critics, had nothing
but praise for the speeches in the nunnery scene (they were "finely
imagined to puzzle the spies") or for the indecent comments to
Ophelia in the play scene, which he euphemistically termed "sport-
ive replies." In the long list of Hamlet's faults that Gentleman
compiled, only one suggests any disrespect for Ophelia—his wildly
indecorous behavior at her grave.[328] But the very effectiveness
of the nunnery scene, which probably accounts for the actor-
critics' sympathetic interpretation of it, evidently tempted some
stage Hamlets into excesses that had adverse effects on the criticism of Hamlet's character. Garrick's "boisterousness" in this
scene, for example, offended THOMAS DAVIES, even though the
latter was one of the major apologists for Hamlet's actions: "He
should have remembered, that he was reasoning with a young
lady to whom he had professed the tenderness of passion."[329] It
is easy to imagine that some of Garrick's followers, by imitating
his boisterousness without his talent for engaging the sympathy
of the audience, were partially responsible for the growing interest in such questions as these: Why is Hamlet so cruel to the
woman he is supposed to love? Did he ever love her, *really?*

By the early years of the nineteenth century these questions
had become more important because of the increasingly common
habit of analyzing dramatic characters as if they were real-life
people. THOMAS HOLCROFT did not consider Hamlet's behavior
cruel if correctly acted, but he objected that most actors, following

326. *Dramatic Censor,* I, 23.
327. *Complete History of the Stage,* III, 62-63.
328. *Dramatic Censor,* I, 16-33. Gentleman does blame Hamlet for Ophelia's
madness, brought on by the killing of her father, but this is not a form of personal
cruelty toward her. *See* pp. 28-29 for his comments on Hamlet's behavior at the
grave of "a Woman he pretends love for." I believe "pretends" means *professes*
here, not *feigns.* Gentleman's point is that Hamlet's actions are very unsuitable,
not that Hamlet does not love Ophelia. Admittedly, there is a short step from
one to the other.
329. *Dramatic Miscellanies,* III, 79-80.

Garrick in "strong feelings" but not in respect for the "intentions of the author," seemed "to persecute, nay to bully, Ophelia."[330] A few years later (1814) Edmund Kean showed how the sensitiveness and delicacy for which Holcroft pleaded could be suggested without any sacrifice of theatrical effectiveness. When he spoke the harsh words of the nunnery scene, he did so with trembling lip and tear-filled eye. And as Hamlet was leaving after the final "To a nunnery, go," he impulsively returned, caught Ophelia's hand and kissed it, then hurried off.[331] Kean's acting made it evident that Hamlet's frenzied speeches arose, not from wanton cruelty, but from his suffering over the necessity of renouncing Ophelia. This, at least, was the construction that SHERIDAN KNOWLES placed upon Kean's portrayal, an interpretation he warmly endorsed. The scene, he said, had never drawn tears before—only a fascinated admiration for "the height to which the storm of Hamlet's acted madness rose, with perhaps a shiver or two for the frail, helpless bark that reeled to and fro, the sport of its . . . relentless fury." But Kean had melted the hearts of the audience and had preserved "one of Shakespeare's noblest characters" from "the conduct of a coward and a savage."[332] The kiss that Kean introduced in the nunnery scene not only vindicated Hamlet's sensibility but also gave the play a "love interest" which had been largely lacking in earlier days. From this time on, no interpretation of Hamlet was complete that did not give some consideration to Hamlet's feeling for Ophelia.

Knowles himself and most of the actor-critics since his time have held that Hamlet's passion for Ophelia was, at the beginning, an ardent one. A small but insistent minority, however, has expressed the opposite point of view. Ironically, its three major spokesmen were all younger contemporaries or immediate successors of Kean—players whose careers coincided with the period of strong romantic influence. Let us examine the interpretations of these dissenters before noticing the variations in the opinions of the majority.

Although the depiction of Hamlet as a lover was congenial to the taste of the romantic period, too much emphasis upon strong passion would have been counter to the interpretation

330. *Theatrical Recorder*, II, 412-13.
331. Harold N. Hillebrand, *Edmund Kean* (New York, 1933), pp. 125-26.
332. *Lectures on Dramatic Literature*, pp. 94, 103-4.

of a gentle, sensitive, inactive Hamlet. Those who accepted Goethe's interpretation of the character, if they were consistent, would subscribe to his statement that Hamlet was "without any prominent passion," his love for Ophelia being "a still presentiment of sweet wants." This was exactly the view taken by both FANNY KEMBLE and HELEN FAUCIT. Hamlet is "sad and dreamy in his affection as in every other sentiment," wrote Miss Kemble; his love is "gentle, refined and tender, but without ardor or energy."[333] And Miss Faucit remarked that, being a contemplative rather than a passionate and sympathetic person, Hamlet was probably incapable of any deeper love than this imaginative sort. Helen Faucit's unusual interest in Ophelia made her more severe than other actor-critics in judging Hamlet: "He is so self-centred, so enwrapped in his own suffering, that he has no thought to waste on the delicate girl whom he had wooed. . . ." He actually behaves with more tenderness toward his mother, whom he thinks wanton and guilty, than toward Ophelia. The very language of his love letter came from the head, not the heart: "it is a string of euphuisms, which almost justifies Laertes' warning." And his declaration at Ophelia's grave ("I loved Ophelia: Forty thousand brothers/ Could not, with all their quantity of love,/ Make up my sum") is "of little worth" since it is not backed up by his actions. He cannot be judged by ordinary standards, however: caught in the toils of a fate from which he has not the strength of character to free himself, he unconsciously drags Ophelia down with him.[334] JAMES H. HACKETT differed somewhat from the two actresses. He shared their basic premise—that Hamlet's love for Ophelia was not a prominent passion—but he was less romantic than they in his explanation, and he extended the same idea to Ophelia's love for Hamlet (a point that Helen Faucit would have debated indignantly). According to Hackett, filial duty is of primary importance to both characters. Ophelia's docility in repelling Hamlet's visits and in acting as a decoy in the spying plot proves that she loves her father more than she loves Hamlet. Nor does Hamlet feel any serious disappointment on that account; indeed he willingly gives up his love in order to concentrate on revenge. The fact that Ophelia never mentions Hamlet in her madness proves that grief for her father was its sole cause. And

333. *Journal*, I, 73-75.
334. *On Some of Shakespeare's Female Characters*, pp. 17-19.

Hamlet's exclamatory speech at her grave is due, not to his great love, but to the shock of sudden discovery and the intemperate behavior of Laertes.[335]

Only one actor-critic of recent years—GRANVILLE-BARKER—came close to echoing Goethe's description: Hamlet's love for Ophelia was "still only in its imaginative phase," he wrote, when it was shaken by disillusionment.[336] Yet the bitterness that Granville-Barker attributed to that disillusionment suggests a love which was at least potentially strong; and his insistence that idealistic natures like Hamlet's, rather than lacking intensity, are capable of the greatest passions separates him from Goethe and his followers. Because of these and other ideas Granville-Barker seems more closely related to Ellen Terry and George Skillan than to Helen Faucit and James H. Hackett.

Those who argue that Hamlet's love for Ophelia is a strong emotion are not, like most of their opposite numbers, concentrated in a single period. If only the most interesting of them are chosen, and even if dates of published criticisms are the only chronological designations, they represent a wide span of years (their acting careers would cover an even longer period): in addition to Sheridan Knowles there are his contemporary w. c. MACREADY; KATE FIELD and JAMES MURDOCH, later in the nineteenth century; ELLEN TERRY, LOUIS CALVERT, BEERBOHM TREE, and the ANONYMOUS ACTRESS in the early years of the present century; and, in our own time, GEORGE SKILLAN and ROBERT SPEAIGHT.[337] Granville-Barker, as we have seen, has a foot in both camps. All of these except the last express the same opinion of Hamlet's original feeling for Ophelia, but they give varying reasons for this opinion and they differ considerably in explaining Hamlet's attitude during the course of the play.

It is interesting that some of the same "evidence" is used by these critics as was used by Fanny Kemble, Helen Faucit, and James H. Hackett, but with opposite conclusions. For example,

335. MS letter to John Quincy Adams, dated July 24, 1839 (Folger Library). Published in *Notes, Criticisms, and Correspondence*, pp. 200-201, 203-5.

336. *Prefaces to Shakespeare*, I, 235.

337. Irving and Martin-Harvey also considered Hamlet's love a strong passion. (See their interpretations of the nunnery scene in the section "From Criticism to Theatre" at the end of the present chapter.) Richard Burton is not sure that even Hamlet knew whether he really loved Ophelia, but suggests that he was attracted by her sweetness, her intelligence, and her "streak of moodiness." (*See* Sterne, *Gielgud Directs Burton in Hamlet*, p. 291.)

there is the evidence of Hamlet's temperament. Macready, for all his interest in Goethe's analysis of Hamlet, was himself convinced that Hamlet had a "passionate temperament" which "would not admit of a little love—he would love much or not at all."[338] And Kate Field argued that Hamlet's "intellect and depth of feeling" would necessarily make his love for Ophelia far stronger than her feeling for him. Passages from the play were, naturally, explained in opposite ways by the two schools of thought. Miss Field, who cited Hamlet's vows to Ophelia, his poem and letter, his distraught appearance in her chamber as she was sewing, and his declaration at her grave, declared that "the meaning of the text" was fulfilled by Charles Fechter as by few actors because he revealed Hamlet's ardor as a lover.[339] These passages were used repeatedly by later actor-critics for much the same interpretation. One of them, the letter, which seemed to Helen Faucit a mere "string of euphuisms," struck both the Anonymous Actress and George Skillan as a cry from the heart.[340] Hamlet's strange, silent invasion of Ophelia's chamber was dismissed by Hackett as a deliberate performance designed to start the rumor of love-madness; but both Calvert and Speaight have insisted that the anguish implied in Ophelia's description goes far beyond play-acting.[341] And the extravagance of Hamlet's outcry at Ophelia's grave, which, for Hackett, was evidence of recurring madness, has seemed to these others the natural hyperbole of strong emotion. Ellen Terry describes this speech as a "confession," wrung from Hamlet by Ophelia's tragic death, "of the truth which he may often have denied";[342] and Speaight finds in Hamlet's wild outcry, coupled with his "lunatic leap" into the grave, "incontrovertible evidence" of his love.[343] The greatest emphasis upon this passage, theatrically speaking, was Beerbohm Tree's. To make its message of love and grief inescapable in his own production of the play, Tree ended the graveyard scene with a pantomime, which he describes for the reader with maudlin relish:

Hamlet has departed, followed by the King, Queen, Laertes, and the courtiers. In the church close by, the organ peals out a funeral march.

338. Lady Pollock, *Macready as I Knew Him*, pp. 10-11.
339. *Charles Albert Fechter*, p. 91.
340. *The True Ophelia*, pp. 28-29; *Hamlet. French's Acting Edition*, p. 94.
341. *An Actor's Hamlet*, p. 61; *Nature in Shakespearian Tragedy*, pp. 24-25.
342. *Four Lectures on Shakespeare*, pp. 174-75.
343. *Nature in Shakespearian Tragedy*, p. 40.

Night is falling, the birds are at rest. Ophelia's grave is deserted. But through the shadows, Hamlet's returning form is seen gathering wild flowers. He is alone with his dead love, and on her he strews the flowers as he falls by her grave in a paroxysm of grief. And so the curtain falls.[344]

The most important passage involving Hamlet and Ophelia, the nunnery scene, is also the most complex and ambiguous for critics who are no longer content to admire its histrionic effects without questioning its meaning. Actor-critics have interpreted this scene in various ways (see the detailed analysis at the end of the present chapter), but the majority of them since the time of Kean have felt, even in Hamlet's bitterest words to Ophelia, a strong element of love. The same is true of the insulting implications of the fishmonger scene and the play scene. How, then, can the bitterness and the apparent repudiation be explained? The idea, formerly advanced, that Hamlet's love was among the "trivial fond records" which he had vowed to erase from memory hardly seemed consonant with that of a really strong passion. Nor could feigned madness alone serve any longer as a satisfactory reason for Hamlet's seeming cruelty; for, if closely considered, it suggested a certain callous exploitation of Ophelia which could not easily be reconciled with deep affection. Some of the actor-critics still clung to certain aspects of these traditional explanations but modified and softened them by additions of their own. For example, Macready accepted the idea that the supernatural revelation accounted for Hamlet's change toward Ophelia, but he interpreted the change itself, not as a product of deliberate choice (no matter how regretful), but as an irresistible consequence of a shock so overwhelming that it disturbed his "whole state of man."[345] The old explanation involving assumed madness was given a reverse interpretation by Sheridan Knowles and a sentimental disguise by James Murdoch. For Knowles, Hamlet's relationship with Ophelia was the main interest of the nunnery scene, not his game of wits with Claudius: Ophelia did not subserve the cause of Hamlet's pretended madness; rather the "madness" itself was donned for her benefit as a cloak of kindness over his painful but necessary purpose.

344. *Thoughts and Afterthoughts,* p. 149.
345. Lady Pollock, *Macready as I Knew Him,* pp. 10-11.

He feels that he is destined to become the shedder of blood, without the possibility of adducing any human warrant for the deed; and, consequently, doubtless anticipates his own destruction. He feels that the banquet of life . . . is spread in vain for him, with whom adultery and murder can claim kindred; and he bows to the stern necessity which compels him, indirectly and vaguely, to communicate this to her whose only interest in existence is the hope of partaking existence with him.

Hamlet has tried earlier, but "imperfectly," to make Ophelia understand the hopelessness of any future together (her speech in returning his presents indicates this). When he sees her on the present occasion, he summons up his courage to make the break complete, knowing "it is cruelty to spare." Since he cannot explain the real situation to her, he can best accomplish his purpose through his assumed madness.[346] Unlike Knowles, Murdoch retained the old idea that Hamlet's main intention in the "mad" renunciation of Ophelia is to confuse his enemies, but he stated it as sympathetically as possible: "Hamlet's manly spirit shrinks from the apparent sternness of this course, but he knows that nothing can so effectually veil his design." Murdoch's sentimentality shows itself mainly in his insistence that Hamlet has no real intention of breaking with Ophelia, that he trusts her to remain faithful during his supposed madness and he hopes, once his dreadful task is accomplished, to unite with her in a love even deeper than before.[347]

Some of the actor-critics have sensed in Hamlet's attitude real bitterness toward Ophelia herself rather than simply feigned madness or bitterness toward the fate that caused the lovers to part. Macready probably felt this; for it is likely that the disillusionment which he emphasized in his portrayal of Hamlet included disillusionment in Ophelia because of her duplicity.[348] This idea has never been discarded by actor-critics, but, like those discussed in the paragraph above, it has often been combined with other explanations.

Beginning in the latter part of the nineteenth century, Hamlet's bitterness has sometimes been traced to his loss of faith in Gertrude and thus in love itself. Representative variations of this idea are found in the interpretations of Ellen Terry and

346. *Lectures on Dramatic Literature,* pp. 102-3.
347. "A Short Study of 'Hamlet,'" p. 504.
348. Marston, *Our Recent Actors,* I, 83.

Granville-Barker. Miss Terry supposed that, although he originally loved Ophelia intensely, Hamlet had always been conscious of her limitations; he had been "subjugated" by her unusual beauty, "weak-witted" though she was. Now, with the revelation of his mother's frailty, he began to see the ugly side of passion, with the romance stripped away, and he hated himself for having succumbed to it. He tried to cast Ophelia out of his life, and the break was made easier by her weakness in failing to stand by him and in allowing herself to be made the tool of his enemies. Yet he could not help being attracted to her still—hence the mixture of brutality and tenderness in his treatment of her.[349] Granville-Barker also emphasized Hamlet's revulsion against his love, but, since he interpreted this love in less physical terms than Miss Terry did, he attributed the revulsion, not to the impurities that Hamlet recognized in himself, but to those wrongly imputed to him by others. The Hamlet of his interpretation is a chaste and chivalrous young man whose strong, pure passion for an idolized mother would have been transferred, little changed, to the woman he married. Now, just as he has learned of his mother's frailty, he also finds that his blameless love for Ophelia has been construed by Polonius as the same lustful passion with which Claudius had seduced Gertrude. Outraged idealism takes its revenge in the fishmonger scene, the nunnery scene, and the play scene, in all of which Hamlet ironically doubles the degradation of himself and Ophelia implied by her father's suspicions. Especially in the last of these scenes we are shown a romantically idealistic imagination "turned the wrong side out."[350]

Several actor-critics of the modern period have explained Hamlet's anger and bitterness as his hurt reaction to Ophelia's apparent rejection of his love. The Anonymous Actress, Robert Speaight, and George Skillan have all found Polonius' interference, rather than Hamlet's problems of revenge and disillusionment, at the root of the trouble between the lovers.[351] According to the first two, Hamlet, unaware of Polonius' warning to his daughter, supposes that Ophelia no longer loves him. Skillan believes that Hamlet realizes the truth but that he cannot help being pained

349. *Four Lectures on Shakespeare*, pp. 174-75.
350. *Prefaces to Shakespeare*, I, 238-44.
351. See their interpretations in *The True Ophelia*, pp. 19-46 (especially 19-20, 23-33); *Nature in Shakespearian Tragedy*, pp. 24-25, 40-42; *Hamlet. French's Acting Edition*, pp. 85, 93-96, 105-7, and n. 561 on p. 101.

by Ophelia's assumed indifference. All three emphasize the double shock that occurs when the frustration of his romance follows directly after the supernatural revelation. This last point is particularly important to the Actress and to Speaight. Both of them imagine an offstage scene following the ghost scene, in which Hamlet tries to pay his customary visit to Ophelia, only to have the door shut in his face. As Speaight points out, she and Horatio are the only two people to whom Hamlet could possibly have confided the Ghost's disclosures; we know that he told Horatio, and he probably meant to tell Ophelia. When she rejects him just as he needs her most, he has "a third ground for despair": his uncle is a murderer, his mother an adultress, and now "his mistress, or at any rate, the woman he loves, refuses to have anything more to do with him." The "ferocious blend of love and hatred" in his later treatment of her is traceable primarily, not to Gertrude's unfaithfulness to his father, but to "Ophelia's repudiation of himself." Skillan's idealistic young Hamlet, though he suffers much when his hope of love's fruition is abruptly cut off, is not merely selfish in his reaction. His main fear is that Polonius and the Court will succeed in turning Ophelia into something as dishonest and vicious as themselves. He tries to warn Polonius of this in cryptic language both in the fishmonger scene and in the "Jephtha" passage, for, being only a boy, Hamlet cannot speak plainly on such a subject; but his fears begin to be realized when he finds Ophelia acting a false part in the nunnery scene. His bitterness stems from his own disappointment but, even more, from the insidious destruction of the qualities he has loved in Ophelia.

III. FROM CRITICISM TO THEATRE

The best examples of the middle step between *Hamlet* as it is understood and *Hamlet* as it is realized in performance are found in the actors' analyses of the nunnery scene. For most of the actor-critics who have discussed Hamlet's general attitude toward Ophelia have also made suggestions concerning the expression of that attitude—in his thoughts, intonations, and actions—at precise points during this major encounter with her. Since this scene poses many problems involving both character interpretation and the details of stage business, it is not surprising that actors have written more about it than about any other in Shakespeare's plays.

One inspiration for the actors' discussions is their conviction that, in this scene particularly, light is shed upon Shakespeare's meaning by the necessity of turning it into action. BEERBOHM TREE, for example, remarks that, with the aid of imaginative stage treatment, the nunnery scene, which has "vexed the minds of the analytical" more than any other in *Hamlet,* takes on "all the clearness of a blue sky."[352] And HENRY IRVING challenges "the acute student to ponder over Hamlet's renunciation of Ophelia—one of the most complex scenes in all the drama—and say that he has learned more from his meditations than he could be taught by players whose intelligence is equal to his own." Both of these men wrote explications of the nunnery scene in order to share with the layman the understanding that they had acquired in acting Hamlet themselves.[353] Tree's is part of a lecture, later published as an essay, called "Hamlet from an Actor's Prompt Book."[354] Irving's is in the form of an essay, "Hamlet and Ophelia," written for *The Nineteenth Century.*[355] Irving gives most attention to the psychology that can be supposed to lie behind Hamlet's abrupt transitions from tenderness to cynicism to fury. Tree also explains these transitions, but more superficially, and he tells the stage business by which he attempted to illustrate Hamlet's thoughts or elucidate his words. From both we receive some insight into the process of interaction between criticism and theatre. Most of the other actors' discussions—those of KNOWLES, HELEN FAUCIT, HACKETT, CALVERT, the ANONYMOUS ACTRESS, GRANVILLE-BARKER, MARTIN-HARVEY, GIELGUD, and SPEAIGHT[356]—were also intended for

352. *Thoughts and Afterthoughts,* p. 136.
353. *The Drama,* pp. 60-61.
354. The portion on the nunnery scene is found in *Thoughts and Afterthoughts,* pp. 136-40.
355. Henry Irving, "Hamlet and Ophelia," *The Nineteenth Century,* I (March–July, 1877), 524-29.
356. Knowles, *Lectures on Dramatic Literature,* pp. 103-4; Faucit, *On Some of Shakespeare's Female Characters,* pp. 12-15; Hackett, MS letter to J. Q. Adams, July 24, 1839 (Folger Library) and *Notes, Criticisms, and Correspondence,* pp. 201-5; Calvert, *An Actor's Hamlet,* pp. 105-9; Anonymous Actress, *The True Ophelia,* pp. 34-45; Granville-Barker, *Prefaces to Shakespeare,* I, 78-79; Martin-Harvey, *Autobiography,* pp. 300-307; Gielgud, *John Gielgud's Hamlet,* ed. Gilder, p. 56, and Sterne, *Gielgud Directs Burton in Hamlet,* pp. 32, 33, 40; Speaight, *Nature in Shakespearian Tragedy,* pp. 29-30.

the general public as well as (in some cases) their theatrical colleagues. Two of them, however, were written exclusively for actors: HOLCROFT's analysis, with instructions, in *The Theatrical Recorder*[357] and SKILLAN's commentary in *French's Acting Edition* of *Hamlet*.[358]

In the following speech-by-speech analysis of the nunnery scene the point of view will be (except at the end) exclusively Hamlet's own. Ophelia's motivations and emotions, far less complex and important than his, have been sufficiently touched upon in the discussion of her character.[359] Obviously the detailed consideration of this single scene will be most meaningful as a bridge between conception and performance when it is read in conjunction with the more theoretical criticisms already presented, particularly those of Ophelia herself and Hamlet's attitude toward her.

Suspicions and Salutations

> *Hamlet.* . . . Soft you now!
> The fair Ophelia! Nymph, in thy orisons
> Be all my sins remember'd.
> *Ophelia.*   Good my lord,
> How does your honour for this many a day?
> *Hamlet.* I humbly thank you; well, well, well.
> *Ophelia.* My lord, I have remembrances of yours,
> That I have longed long to re-deliver;
> I pray you, now receive them.
> *Hamlet.*   No, not I;
> I never gave you aught.
> *Ophelia.* My honour'd lord, you know right well you did;
> And, with them, words of so sweet breath
>   composed
> As made the things more rich: their perfume lost,
> Take these again; for to the noble mind
> Rich gifts wax poor when givers prove unkind.
> There, my lord.

357. II, 412-13.
358. Pp. 105-8.
359. The most detailed analysis of Ophelia's thoughts and expressions in the nunnery scene is that of the Anonymous Actress.

When Hamlet first sees Ophelia, is he suspicious? According to the actor-critics, he may well be for several reasons: (1) Irving reminds us that in the early quartos (the "good" one of 1604 as well as the "bad" one of 1603) Hamlet enters just before the King and Polonius go out; Hamlet therefore is aware of their presence, but in his preoccupation with more important things he ignores it or forgets it for awhile. Speaight agrees: On the Elizabethan stage Hamlet, as he entered through one of the side doors, would see the other two characters disappear through the curtains of the inner recess. There is nothing suspicious about this at the moment; and, lost in thought, he does not notice Ophelia on the farther side of the room. (The presence of Ophelia on the stage during "To be or not to be" is debatable.[360]) Later, when he crosses to go out and sees her waiting for him, he remembers the two figures whom he has glimpsed and is immediately on his guard. (2) (Gielgud shows considerable interest in another reason for Hamlet's immediate suspicion: Dover Wilson's "clever theory" that in an earlier scene (II, ii) Hamlet had entered, unobserved, in time to overhear Polonius' plot to "loose" Ophelia to him.[361] But although Gielgud recognizes the advantages of this suggestion for the interpretation of both the fishmonger scene and the nunnery scene, after trying it out in two productions of the play he is not convinced of its practicability.[362] So much time has elapsed since Polonius' explanation of his plan that even if Hamlet has been shown overhearing it the average audience probably does not notice the connection. (3) Calvert mentions a further reason for Hamlet's suspicion: Even though he is engaged in philosophical contemplation ("To be or not to be") when we first see him, Hamlet has not wandered aimlessly into this part of the castle; for the King specifically tells Gertrude

360. See Sprague, *Shakespeare and the Actors*, pp. 151-52. Granville-Barker decides against her presence as too distracting during "To be or not to be." (*Prefaces to Shakespeare*, I, 77-78, n. 9.)

361. Wilson, *What Happens in Hamlet*, pp. 101-14. As Sprague points out (*Shakespeare and the Actors*, p. 147), at least one actor—Beerbohm Tree—anticipated Wilson's suggestion; Tree tried having Hamlet overhear Polonius' plan, but he saw the implications only for the fishmonger scene, not for the nunnery scene which comes later.

362. See *John Gielgud's Hamlet*, ed. Gilder, pp. 46, 51-52, 56. For the 1964 production of *Hamlet*, Gielgud, at Burton's suggestion, tried the overhearing in some of the rehearsals, but they both decided it should be abandoned. *See* Sterne, *Gielgud Directs Burton in Hamlet*, pp. 27, 55.

that he has "closely sent for Hamlet hither" (III, i, 29-31). Hence Hamlet's great surprise when he sees Ophelia. "Soft you now! The fair Ophelia!" is spoken in a tone that suggests the thought: "Why do I find Ophelia here? It was the King who sent for me." Still other reasons for mistrust have been given: (4) Helen Faucit says that Hamlet is wary because of Ophelia's sudden appearance after so many denials; and (5) Skillan comments that her presence, alone, in one of Hamlet's known haunts is at least "strange." Granville-Barker, however, rejects not only Wilson's theory but also the whole idea that Hamlet is suspicious from the beginning. "The meeting, for its first few moments," he writes, "passes as any such meeting may between two sensitive creatures sundered by no quarrel of their own; in reserve, in reproachful sorrow that they have let themselves be sundered, and a provoking of more misunderstanding by which to justify reproach."

Whatever his "lurking suspicion" of Ophelia's "unfair position" (to use Hackett's phraseology), it is generally agreed that Hamlet greets her "gently" (Helen Faucit). Skillan thinks that he is greatly moved by Ophelia's beauty, "enhanced" as it is "by her devotions." "Soft you now!" comes from "deep emotion," but Hamlet checks himself and assumes a certain reserve because of Ophelia's own air of "remoteness" and because of Polonius' "edict against his love's fulfillment."

Even if Hamlet does not suspect a trap when he first sees Ophelia, perhaps he senses the truth when she offers to return his remembrances. Some actors have thought so, at any rate. Helen Faucit, for example, writes that Hamlet sees in this gesture a "repetition of Rosencrantz and Guildenstern" and that the prospect of being "played with" again, this time by a girl he has supposed innocent, drives him to fury. Skillan's Hamlet is "instinctively on guard" when the gifts are mentioned, but for a different reason: he is determined to mask his hopeless love and to fight down the weakness of sentiment; his abrupt denial is prompted by resentment of the jilting he has received. But when Ophelia, "prayer-book in hand, deliberately revers[es] the truth" by implying that *he* has been unkind to *her,* Hamlet realizes with a shock that she is acting a false part (she who has always been "the pattern of uprightness and virtue"!)—and it can only be because there are witnesses present who have persuaded her to it.

Revolted by the evil that he has divined, Hamlet begins to attack Ophelia as the "outward evidence of the intrigue."

Some actors, however, have seen no cause for suspicion in Ophelia's attempt to return the gifts or in the reason that she gives. Knowles assumes a prior interview when Hamlet *had* appeared "unkind." The Anonymous Actress finds in Hamlet's reaction the bitterness of rejected passion rather than the suspicion of a plot: already hurt by Ophelia's refusal to see him or answer his letters, he would interpret her banal attempt at conversation ("How does your honour for this many a day?) as "an impudently heartless question" and her offer to return his gifts as a piece of gratuitous cruelty. His attempt at retaliatory cruelty, "I never gave you aught," prompts the indignant reply about unkind givers. For other actors, the bitterness in this part of the nunnery scene is not inspired by Ophelia herself but by the impossible situation in which Hamlet finds himself. According to Ellen Terry, Irving's hands "hovered" over Ophelia with "passionate longing" here.[363] In Tree's interpretation Hamlet looks tenderly at Ophelia and is about to embrace her when his hand falls by accident upon the medallion with his father's picture which he wears around his neck; suddenly remembering his oath to "wipe away all trivial fond records," he forces out the denial, "I never gave you aught."

Doubts and Denials

> *Hamlet.* Ha, ha! are you honest?
> *Ophelia.* My lord?
> *Hamlet.* Are you fair?
> *Ophelia.* What means your lordship?
> *Hamlet.* That if you be honest and fair, your honesty should admit no discourse to your beauty.
> *Ophelia.* Could beauty, my lord, have better commerce than with honesty?
> *Hamlet.* Ay, truly; for the power of beauty will sooner transform honesty from what it is to a bawd than the force of honesty can translate beauty into his likeness: this was sometime a paradox, but now the time gives it proof. I did love you once.

363. *Ellen Terry's Memoirs*, ed. Craig and St. John, p. 104.

> *Ophelia.* Indeed, my lord, you made me believe so.
> *Hamlet.* You should not have believed me; for virtue cannot so inoculate our old stock but we shall relish of it; I loved you not.
> *Ophelia.* I was the more deceived.

The "honesty" and "beauty" passage is usually given its simplest meaning by the actor-critics: Hackett explains that Ophelia is "allowing the effect of her *beauty* upon him, to be used by her father for a sinister purpose & at the expense of her *honesty.*" Calvert and Skillan give similar explications, but Skillan goes into some detail about Ophelia's misunderstanding of Hamlet's meaning.

"Our old stock" is explained with dogged literal-mindedness by Hackett: Hamlet loved Ophelia once but "upon consideration" found that he did not love her, after all, because she had inherited too much of her "old stock": i.e. "her father's courtier-like insincerity." Martin-Harvey's interpretation is more interesting:

"I did love you once, Ophelia, but with the same earthly taint that inoculates all our old stock. Look at my mother! Look at my uncle! That is the stuff of which 'our old stock' is made. Therefore I loved you not (that is, purely). . . . There is something in you which stirs base thoughts in me."

Skillan explains "I loved you not" in much the same way, but he says that Hamlet is deliberately lying here. Irving, who saw kindness in the apparent cruelty of these words (they were a "surgeon's knife" to effect a parting that had become inevitable), took the sting out of them by "affectionate by-play behind Ophelia's back" —an interpretation that Gielgud is not sure he can accept.

It is in this portion of the nunnery scene that some actors find the first evidence that Hamlet associates Ophelia with his degraded mother. Martin-Harvey's interpretation, already cited, is one example. Another—Henry Irving's—is the most interesting, as well as the most detailed, attempt to trace the train of thought behind Hamlet's words.

He feels the woe of Ophelia and his own. He writhes under the stigma of heartlessness which he cannot but incur. How remove it? How wipe away the stain? It is impossible. Cursed then be the cause. His whole nature surges up against it—the incestuousness of this King; the havoc of illicit passion, which has killed his noble father, wrecked his fairest hopes, stolen from him his mother's love—nay, robbed him even of the maternal ideal. . . . His mother was once fair and honest, honest as Ophelia is now. *Is* Ophelia honest? Impossible to think otherwise. But it were a mad quip to ask her, and let the after dialogue take its own course. Take what course it will, it must dwell on the one subject which will harden Hamlet's heart, and give rigour to his nature. . . . Hamlet's mother's beauty had been her snare, had tempted her adulterous lover. Let beauty and honesty therefore— here was a stroke of mad exaggeration—have no discourse.

Tree, who also makes an Ophelia-Gertrude connection at this point in the scene, would have Hamlet peer into Ophelia's face (like Diogenes with the lantern) and ask, "Are *you* honest?"— meaning "Is there one woman I can trust?" Calvert interprets the laugh that precedes this question as a signal that Hamlet is putting on the "antic disposition." According to him, the questions about "honesty" and "beauty" reveal Hamlet's suspicion of a plot: they are worded so as to mystify the eavesdroppers yet to provoke a guilty reaction from Ophelia if she is their confederate. (The thought that she may be "a party to such a mean action" is terrible to Hamlet, but he remembers that he was deceived in his own mother.) Ophelia, however, betrays no consciousness of guilt.

The First "Nunnery" Speech

> *Hamlet.* Get thee to a nunnery: why wouldst thou be a breeder of sinners? I am myself indifferent honest; but yet I could accuse me of such things that it were better my mother had not borne me: I am very proud, revengeful, ambitious, with more offences at my beck than I have thoughts to put them in, imagination to give them shape, or time to act them in. What should such fellows as I do crawling between earth and heaven? We are arrant knaves, all; believe none of us. Go thy ways to a nunnery.

Although many actors on the stage have appeared to "bully" Ophelia in the "nunnery" passages, most of the actor-critics have objected to such treatment, at least in the first of these speeches. They have given sympathetic interpretations of the repeated advice, "Get thee to a nunnery," and to the whole of the first tirade. According to Knowles, the very passages where actors have railed at Ophelia are really indicative of Hamlet's love for her: "is there not all the lover in the injunction, 'Go thy ways to a nunnery,' the lover writhing at the thought that his heart's jewel, which he must not wear himself, may go to grace another? . . ." Other actor-critics have given a less selfish interpretation to the "nunnery" admonitions. Some of them have emphasized Hamlet's desire to warn or protect Ophelia against the evils of the world. Holcroft makes this threatening world seem rather commonplace and Hamlet himself rather like a kind uncle cautioning a favorite niece about the "dangers of the marriage state." Others present Hamlet's view of the world as an abnormal one wrought by disgust and disillusionment. Irving, for example, suggests that a nunnery is the best "sanctuary" for escaping "the contamination on which . . . [Hamlet's] mind was still running." Martin-Harvey connects Hamlet's "exaggerated self-hatred" ("I could accuse myself. . . .") with his fears for Ophelia's purity; still thinking of the sensual element that he perceives in her, and loathing himself for responding to it, Hamlet advises Ophelia to remove herself from temptation before she makes more monsters of men (i.e. turns them to lustful thoughts). In the "unbalanced state of his soul" he is confusing "the perfectly normal promptings of nature" with the vice he has seen in his mother. Skillan's interpretation is less sexual in emphasis (he specifically repudiates the suggestion that "nunnery" should be thought of in the slang sense of "brothel"). He explains that Hamlet, seeing the perversion of Ophelia's honesty, fears that her whole moral nature will be undermined and that the only hope of salvation is to withdraw from the world, which in her case is the corrupt Court. Granville-Barker has made the most interesting attempt to tie in the first "nunnery" passage with the scene as a whole: "why wouldst thou be a breeder of sinners?" is, as he points out, a "pitiful" speech, the conclusion to the train of thought begun in "To be or not to be."

The self-condemning lines are most often explained, to borrow Holcroft's phrase, as Hamlet's effort to "persuade [Ophelia] that the loss of him is a benefit"; or, in Irving's words, "to snatch at and throw to the heart-pierced maiden some strange, morbid consolation." Calvert imagines that Hamlet's mind turns for a moment from the trap that has been laid for him and dwells on "the idea of how impossible it would be for Ophelia and himself to realize their happiness. He has the subconscious feeling that he is all wrong, and it would be a crime for him to deceive Ophelia as to his worth." Gielgud differs from the others in suggesting that Hamlet's self-accusation is most poignant when spoken as if pleading with Ophelia to admit that she is not being truthful: "He is giving her every chance to speak out by showing her that he has just the same weaknesses as she."

Although the "nunnery" speeches were traditionally considered Hamlet's best opportunity to display his feigned madness, this first one, as it is described by the actor-critics, does not sound particularly "mad." In Gielgud's opinion, Hamlet should be "soft and truthful" here, "so that . . . we get a recollection of Hamlet and Ophelia as they were before—both very much in love, though she more than he." A few actors, however, imply somewhat wilder behavior. Holcroft says that Hamlet "affects a kind of rational distraction" here, partly to "soften" the "repulse" of "I loved you not" and "partly to conceal the true feelings of his heart, while he justly suspects Ophelia is put upon him to wrest its secret from his lips." And Calvert probably intends the "antic disposition" which is put on (according to him) at "Ha, ha!" to continue in the present speech.

The Test

> *Hamlet.* Where's your father?
> *Ophelia.* At home, my lord.
> *Hamlet.* Let the doors be shut upon him, that he may play
> the fool no where but in's own house. Farewell.
> *Ophelia.* O, help him, you sweet heavens!

The stage business of having Polonius (or the King, or both) look out from behind the arras at some point in the nunnery scene, thus making Hamlet aware of their presence, dates back, as Sprague has found, to the 1820's (it was spoken of as "new" at that time).[364] One of the obvious points at which the business could be used is just before "Where's your father?" Judging by their descriptions of the scene, the actor-critics have been divided

364. *Shakespeare and the Actors,* pp. 152-54. Perhaps the business was introduced not so much to give a new interpretation as to make sure that no one in the audience missed the point of the old one. Holcroft in 1806 was already writing of Hamlet's suspicion in the nunnery scene, and Holcroft's acting career began in 1770.

in their opinions about the desirability of having Hamlet glimpse Polonius.

Irving, even though he points out that Hamlet was originally meant to see both Claudius and Polonius at the beginning of the scene, accepts a visual reminder of their presence at this later point. Granville-Barker (who does not allow any earlier suspicions) agrees that Hamlet should catch sight of Polonius here. Sometimes the audience has had its attention called to the eavesdroppers in very dramatic fashion—for example, in Beerbohm Tree's performance as he himself describes it: At the end of the first "nunnery" speech, "A great gust of pity and love surges up in Hamlet's nature. He takes Ophelia in his arms and is about to kiss her, when over her head he sees the forms of Polonius and the King, spying through the arras." Hamlet has trusted Ophelia, and now it seems that she too is false. "His soul full of loathing, he flings her from him."

Martin-Harvey is scornful of such "theatrically effective" interpretations. They are "easy" to act, he says, "and the groundlings will applaud. They will not stop to inquire the *meaning* of Hamlet's words to Ophelia after he has discovered the supposed trap." In his own opinion, Hamlet does not suspect the presence of the eavesdroppers at any point in the scene; if he had, he would not have "unburdened himself to Ophelia" as he does. Why, then, does Hamlet ask, "Where's your father?" Simply because he was "sent for" by the King and Polonius, and he wonders why they have not waited to see him.

As far as I know, none of the other actor-critics share Martin-Harvey's assumption. Some of them, however, consider Hamlet's suspicion (or his real knowledge) of the eavesdroppers' presence sufficiently clear without any actual glimpse of them. Calvert's Hamlet, who has suspected a plot from the beginning, has attempted—so far without success—to test Ophelia's part in it, but has been diverted from this purpose for a moment in the first "nunnery" speech. At the end of it,

The look on her face . . . betrays such innocent astonishment that he now puts a direct question to her, to prove whether she is innocent or not. . . . The obedient child cannot give her father away. . . . Being of an ingenuous and simple nature, she is covered with confusion, and Hamlet immediately grasps the fact that she is lying.

That is all. There is no mention of visual evidence except for
Ophelia's embarrassment. Speaight and Skillan are similar in
their comments. Hamlet "knows he's being watched," declares
the latter, "and he asks this deliberately, just to see what her
answer will be." When she lies, his rage reaches its full height.

Until recently Gielgud belonged in the same company: he
once rejected as unconvincing the traditional business of having
Hamlet glimpse the eavesdroppers; his own Hamlet knew from
the beginning that they were there. When he directed Richard
Burton in 1964, however, he agreed with the latter that it was
"more interesting" to let Hamlet discover their presence at a particular point in the scene.

The Second and Third "Nunnery" Speeches

> *Hamlet.* If thou dost marry, I'll give thee this plague for
> thy dowry: be thou as chaste as ice, as pure as
> snow, thou shalt not escape calumny. Get thee
> to a nunnery, go: farewell. Or, if thou wilt needs
> marry, marry a fool; for wise men know well
> enough what monsters you make of them. To a
> nunnery, go, and quickly too. Farewell.
>
> *Ophelia.* O heavenly powers, restore him!
>
> *Hamlet.* I have heard of your paintings too, well enough;
> God has given you one face, and you make your-
> selves another; you jig, you amble, and you lisp,
> and nickname God's creatures, and make your
> wantonness your ignorance. Go to, I'll no more
> on't; it hath made me mad. I say, we will have
> no more marriages: those that are married al-
> ready, all but one, shall live; the rest shall keep
> as they are. To a nunnery, go. [*Exit*]

Considerably more violence is suggested by the comments on
Hamlet's last two speeches. Tree remarks that his "torrent of
words" consists "partly of reproach to Ophelia . . . partly of *pretended madness*" (for the benefit of the eavesdroppers, obviously,
since in Tree's interpretation their presence has just been discovered). Calvert's Hamlet, already "deranged" by his experience
with the Ghost, is now driven to "distraction" by his conviction
of Ophelia's duplicity. Skillan, though he never considers Hamlet

mad, thinks that here his "emotions are wrought to the highest pitch of abnormality." And Speaight's description of Hamlet's histrionic behavior in the scene as a whole seems to apply best to the final speeches: "He can lash himself into frenzy with Ophelia. . . . The impression persists of energy feeding on emotion and of emotion feeding on itself." Hamlet's identification of Ophelia with the faithless Gertrude is particularly emphasized in these last two "nunnery" speeches, and always in language suggesting a kind of diseased vitality: Hamlet's "vision is distorted . . . he heaps together all womankind . . . he unpacks his sore and wounded soul before Ophelia—loving her still in spite of his scorn" (Martin-Harvey); his speech "boils with the heat of disgust . . . primed by the voluptuous nature of his mother's . . . marriage" (Skillan); Ophelia takes on "the guise of his mother the harlot," becoming "symbol and scapegoat of her kind" (Granville-Barker).

There are, however, a few mitigating comments about Hamlet's attitude, even in this part of the scene. Holcroft's interpretation, for example, is more restrained (but also less imaginative) than most of the others: Hamlet's "satire" is merely intended to excite Ophelia's disgust for the common failings of her sex so that she will avoid them herself; and the "advice to live single" should be spoken with "sympathetic friendship," not thundered forth as it generally is on the stage. Even Calvert, who considers these speeches the ravings of hysteria, insists that, however brutal the words, "underneath is the beautiful idea of Ophelia's welfare— she is not utterly lost, and might, within the shelter of a nunnery, save her soul. . . ."

The scarcely veiled threat to Claudius ("those that are married already, all but one, shall live") seems to Martin-Harvey convincing evidence that Hamlet has remained ignorant of the King's presence. According to both Calvert and Speaight, however (and presumably the others would concur), it is recklessly directed to the King behind the arras.

Conclusion

> *Ophelia.* O, what a noble mind is here o'erthrown!
>   The courtier's, soldier's, scholar's, eye, tongue, sword;
>   The expectancy and rose of the fair state,

The glass of fashion and the mould of form,
The observed of all observers, quite, quite down!
And I, of ladies most deject and wretched,
That suck'd the honey of his music vows,
Now see that noble and most sovereign reason,
Like sweet bells jangled, out of tune and harsh;
That unmatch'd form and feature of blown youth
Blasted with ecstasy: O, woe is me,
To have seen what I have seen, see what I see!
                    Re-enter King and Polonius.
King.   Love! his affections do not that way tend,
         Nor what he spake, though it lack'd form a little,
         Was not like madness. . . .

Ophelia's reaction to Hamlet's vituperations has been variously interpreted by the few actor-critics who have mentioned it. Hackett callously remarks that Ophelia will not feel wounded by anything that Hamlet says in this scene because she thinks that he is mad. Helen Faucit finds her noble heroine numb with grief for the tragedy of Hamlet's madness. Even after Hamlet has left the scene "no sob is heard . . . there is no time yet for self-pity." The Anonymous Actress imagines Ophelia physically exhausted but "mentally strung up," stabbed with a "presentiment of looming tragedy, as she utters her last speech very quietly, in dead tones, broken only here and there by a little dry sob of pain." Tree, however, pictures her kneeling at a couch, sobbing bitterly.

At this point Edmund Kean, in acting Hamlet, made the most influential of all "commentaries" on the nunnery scene: he returned and kissed Ophelia's hand. But, argues Tree, the tragedy of the situation lies in Ophelia's going to her grave without realizing Hamlet's love. Accordingly, his Hamlet returned and, unobserved by her, gently kissed one of her tresses. "Love! his affections do not that way tend"—so said Claudius. And Claudius, as Hackett reminds us, was a "keen observer." But perhaps one peep through the arras was not enough.

CHAPTER THREE · *Actors' Criticisms of* Othello

I. THE PLAY

General Evaluations

WILLIAM OXBERRY once remarked of *Othello:* "This Tragedy requires less peculiar comment than any of Shakespeare's Plays; it is indeed beautiful, but its beauties are of a kind the most obvious to the common reader."[1] The other actors seem to have agreed with him, for their criticism of the play itself (as distinguished from interpretation of its characters) forms a smaller body as a whole and is both simpler and sketchier in the individual contributions than that of the other three "great" Shakespearean tragedies. A good many actors have made general evaluations of *Othello,* however, rating it in comparison with Shakespeare's other plays and usually, though not always, explaining their reasons. In recent years the practice of "rating" Shakespeare's plays has declined, but the tendency to compare (and particularly to contrast) *Othello* with the other tragedies has continued.

In the eighteenth century *Othello* was believed by scholars to be the last of Shakespeare's tragedies, and it was often considered the ultimate in excellence as well. Actor-critics joined enthusiastically in the recognition of its greatness. Old GEORGE SWAN, who had long fancied himself an authority on the play, deliberately went beyond Samuel Johnson's praise (too tame for him), declaring that *Othello* "as it stands in the old Editions . . . is not to be amended by any Man whatever; . . . it is the best Tragedy, without any exception, that ever was wrote in our Language, or, perhaps, in any other."[2] Although his argument for textual integrity was very unusual, Swan was not alone in his claim for *Othello's* pre-eminence. ELIZABETH GRIFFITH, for one, described this play as the *"chef d'oeuvre* of dramatic composition."[3] And CHARLES DIBDIN challenged the critics to find any tragedy in the literature of the world that "appeals to the heart . . . satisfies the mind . . . [and] triumphs over all candid objection" as this one does.[4] Others, a little more restrained, were content to call it Shakespeare's masterpiece. THOMAS DAVIES, for example, confident-

1. *The New English Drama* (London, 1818-24), V, *Othello,* iii.
2. Letter of December 11, 1773, to David Garrick. MS in the Forster Collection, the Victoria and Albert Museum.
3. *The Morality of Shakespeare's Drama Illustrated* (London, 1775), p. 519.
4. *A Complete History of the Stage* (London, 1800), II, 398-400. *See also* III, 349.

ly listed the six best plays in the order of their excellence, with *Othello* at the head of the list. (Behind it, in a descending scale, were *Macbeth, King Lear, Hamlet, Julius Caesar,* and *King John.*)[5] Even those who backed different favorites for the prime position were usually ready with tributes to *Othello's* dramatic merits. DAVID GARRICK, if personal vanity were consulted, had little cause to love this play; yet, though he named *Macbeth* the greatest of Shakespeare's dramas, he added that Shakespeare's single finest scene was Iago's temptation of Othello.[6]

One reason for the admiration of *Othello* was its characterization: Dibdin valued the play for "truth of character" and "knowledge of human nature,"[7] and Davies regarded Othello himself as "the greatest character of the greatest poet."[8] Another reason was that the "lessons" taught by *Othello* fulfilled the current requirement of "morality." Mrs. Griffith, indefatigable collector of Shakespeare's moral truths, found a rich source in this play; nor did she stop with such negative morals as the warning against jealousy, for she was convinced that *Othello* contains "the compleatest system of oeconomical and moral duties of human nature . . . ever framed" without the aid of divine inspiration.[9] Still another excellence—unusual in Shakespeare's plays—was "regularity" of structure. Here the actors could express their admiration with a clear literary conscience, for Samuel Johnson himself had remarked that, if the events of the first act had been simply referred to rather than acted, the strictest critic would have been unable to find fault with the structure of *Othello.* Accordingly, as if on cue, the usually stringent FRANCIS GENTLEMAN, with only a passing regret for the shift from Venice to Cyprus, approved the plot design of this play as "sufficiently regular, pleasingly progressive, and well calculated to touch most sensibly the feelings of horror and pity"; he added that "the personages are well contrasted, and co-operate properly to the main action." As usual, however theoretical his language, Gentleman was obviously thinking, not only of literary standards, but of the requirements of a good theatre piece. Indeed, the theatrical potentialities of *Othello* must have been a major reason for the actors' fervent en-

5. *Dramatic Miscellanies* (London, 1783-84), I, 114.
6. Joseph Cradock, *Literary and Miscellaneous Memoirs* (London, 1828), IV, 247.
7. *Complete History of the Stage,* III, 350.
8. *Memoirs of the Life of David Garrick* (Boston, 1818), II, 176-77.
9. *The Morality of Shakespeare's Drama Illustrated,* p. 519.

dorsement of its critical reputation. Gentleman himself found only one flaw in dramatic effectiveness (and his opinion here is difficult to understand): although the play is "noble entertainment for the stage," it "wants business, and therefore in some places lies heavy on action."[10] Dibdin, however, found no such lags in the action; he particularly praised the plot, in fact, for "interest, gradually developed and greatly wrought up, that continually varies, occupies, and attracts."[11]

Nineteenth century actors continued to express enthusiasm for *Othello*, but their appreciation took a very different form. For example, when Oxberry attempted to describe the nature of this play's greatness (in 1819) he could not do so in specific terms: "though highly poetical, its excellence does not consist in its poetry; it is pure passion; its beauty is almost lost in its reality and grandeur." He could only resort to analogies with the most awesome of natural phenomena, equally "obvious" and equally indescribable—"the terrors of an earthquake, or the heights of the Andes."[12] Some of his contemporaries, though hardly less romantic, were more precise in naming the qualities which appealed to them in the play. ELIZABETH INCHBALD, for example (1808), was delighted with the element of romantic love, with the idea of "gradual passion taking possession of [Desdemona's] heart, through pity and admiration" and "rooted in [Othello's], from gratitude and tenderness." Unlike some of the literary critics, both in her own period and earlier, she found such a "rational apology" for this love and so much "natural eloquence" in Othello's account of its development that the exotic nature of it simply added to its interest for her. Her admiration was particularly excited, in fact, by Shakespeare's effective use of contrast—including the contrast between Othello and Desdemona. His power in delineating human emotions is so "vast," she wrote, "that a young and elegant female is here represented . . . as deeply in love with . . . a man different in complexion and features from her and her whole race,—and yet without the slightest imputation of indelicacy . . . whilst the Moor . . . dotes on her with all the transport of the most impassioned lover, yet without the smallest abatement of the rough, rigid cast of his nature." But Mrs. Inchbald's admira-

10. *The Dramatic Censor* (London, 1770), I, 149, 154.
11. *Complete History of the Stage*, III, 350-51.
12. *New English Drama*, V, *Othello*, iii.

tion was not limited to the love story. Even "more impressive" to her was the contrast between the "consummate art and malignant spirit of Iago" and "the generous mind and candid manners of Othello." Indeed she considered it "the highest point . . . of the poet's genius, to have conceived two such personages" and "to have brought them on the stage together in almost every scene."[13] The same praise was given later in the century (1860) by GEORGE VANDENHOFF, who described the opposition of the two antagonists, now in terms of a morality play—"this terrible duel between brain and heart"—and now in those of a bestiary—the magnanimous Othello "roused like a tiger to glut itself with carnage," the malicious Iago "tracking [his] victim with the patient . . . unwearied stanchness of a bloodhound."[14] Although the actor-critics of this period were less occupied with the plot structure of *Othello* than their predecessors had been, the pleasure that they took in Shakespeare's well-balanced contrasts indicates at least a general interest in design.

Most of the topics that caught the attention of the actor-critics in earlier periods have continued to be of some concern in the present century. For example, both HARLEY GRANVILLE-BARKER and ROBERT SPEAIGHT have discussed the structure of the play in terms reminiscent of former criticism. The latter, much like his eighteenth century forerunners, comments that *Othello* is the most carefully constructed of Shakespeare's tragedies, fulfilling in general design any classical definition of a well-made play.[15] The older critic, however, insisted that such unity as exists in *Othello* is the outcome, not of near-classical construction, but simply of "an economy of treatment peculiar to the needs of the play." There is certainly unity of theme, he argued, and unity of place is "vaguely established" for a succession of scenes, but "time is given no unity of treatment at all." In addition to the inconsistent relationships between the time of the imagined action and that of the actual performance (the two are equal in the first and last scenes, but the former is much compressed elsewhere), there are implications of two different time-schemes existing side by side: according to an obvious timetable of references to morning, dinner, supper, etc., Othello murders Desdemona only twenty-four

13. *The British Theatre* (London, 1808), V, *Othello*, 3-4.
14. *Leaves from an Actor's Note-book* (New York, 1860), pp. 223-24.
15. *Nature in Shakespearian Tragedy* (London, 1955), pp. 69-70.

hours after the consummation of his marriage; but a number of less conspicuously placed references suggest that weeks or even months have passed. In discussing this aspect of *Othello*'s structure, Granville-Barker adapted to his own purposes the well-known theory of "double time" first advanced in 1849 by "Christopher North" (John Wilson of Edinburgh) [16] and later echoed by a number of other writers. In his analysis the phenomenon noticed by literary critics is renamed "ambiguity of time," and its theatrical origin and purposes are explained: The two time-schemes are needed because, on the one hand, "If Othello were left time for reflection" the "whole flimsy fraud" would collapse, but, on the other hand, the events shown us are not convincing for the particular day following the consummation of Othello's marriage. Why not simply allow a likely lapse of time before Iago tried his poison? Because there has already been one break in the action (the trip from Venice to Cyprus), and Shakespeare does not want to risk another. In the Elizabethan theatre the whole burden of creating and sustaining illusion fell on the actor; if the "current" of rapport with the audience were broken by suspension of the action, it could not be automatically restored. In some plays character dictates structure; in this one, however, the story demanded a particular kind of structure, which in turn necessitated particular kinds of characters.[17]

Several twentieth century actors have, like their predecessors, praised *Othello* highly. In some instances the praise has been unclouded—for example, in MARGARET WEBSTER's description: "a document of the human race . . . not limited to any age or coun-

16. "Christopher North" first advanced the theory in connection with *Macbeth*, in the last section of his "Dies Borealis" paper for November, 1849, in *Blackwood's Magazine*. The "Dies Borealis" papers for April and May, 1850, deal with *Othello*, and large portions of them are devoted to the subject of double time. Immediately after the November, 1849, issue of *Blackwood's* came out, the Rev. N. J. Halpin of Dublin published a pamphlet, *The Dramatic Unities of Shakespeare*, in which he claimed to have discovered Shakespeare's time pattern twenty years earlier. Halpin's theory is similar to Wilson's but is more pedantically worked out; its chief difference is in comparing Shakespeare's dual time to an artist's method of creating perspective. I know of only one actor's reaction to the double time theory at the time it was first made public: Helen Faucit was impatient with Halpin's discussion and with all attempts to formalize Shakespeare's methods of constructing his plays. See her letter to Margaret Stokes, quoted by Sir Theodore Martin in *Helena Faucit*, (2d ed.; Edinburgh and London, 1900), pp. 207-8. Martin dates it February 20, 1849, but obviously this is incorrect. Probably it was February 20, 1850.

17. *Prefaces to Shakespeare* (Princeton, 1946), II, 10-12, 24-30. *See* pp. 96-98 for a discussion of the structural validity of the act and scene divisions in *Othello*.

try," a play that "stands alone," illustrating supremely Shakespeare's "genius," his "understanding" and "compassion."[18] Occasionally, however, the actors' enthusiasm for *Othello* has been mixed with an uneasy recognition of its problems: Robert Speaight, for example, has declared that it is better appreciated on the Continent than in Great Britain because it treats two problems that an Englishman finds it difficult to understand: "sexual jealousy excited to the point of paroxysm" and "a pure malignity which cannot be explained . . . except by a metaphysical conception of evil."[19]

Whatever their evaluation of *Othello,* some modern actors have recognized that this tragedy differs radically from Shakespeare's others. Speaight,[20] echoing A. C. Bradley, calls it the most natural of Shakespeare's great tragedies, and Margaret Webster[21] calls it the most human. Both note the absence of ghosts and other supernatural characters, and Miss Webster remarks as well that there are no "inexplicable convulsions of nature," that the play is, in fact, "an astounding extension of normal humanity to the level of high, poetic tragedy." But *Othello*'s uniqueness and the problems inherent in its special qualities have been most searchingly discussed by Granville-Barker. In this play, he points out, the evil impulse is externalized in Iago rather than originating in the hero as in Shakespeare's other tragedies, and the destructive force—Othello's jealousy, which "supplants" his love—is not "one of the nobler human ardors turned to evil" but, rather, an "ignoble aberration." For these reasons *Othello* is not a "spiritual tragedy" in the same sense as the other plays. "It is . . . an all but intolerable exhibition . . . of human wickedness and folly" which arouses "horror and anger" rather than pity and terror. Yet, "like all great tragedies, it is a tragedy of character." When Shakespeare adapted Cinthio's tale to his dramatic needs, he did not improve it as far as story value is concerned; but by charging the sordid matter with poetry and by showing us "the process of the spiritual self-destruction which can make . . . [Othello] capable" of murdering his wife, he created high tragedy.[22]

18. *Shakespeare Without Tears* (Cleveland, 1955), p. 237.
19. *Nature in Shakespearian Tragedy,* pp. 69-70.
20. *Ibid.*
21. *Shakespeare Without Tears,* p. 231.
22. *Prefaces to Shakespeare,* II, 3-9, 100.

Criticisms of the Text

Attitudes toward this play have not been complicated by the existence of an adaptation or alternate version, but, as Marvin Rosenberg has shown, the text suffered greatly from pruning as early as the eighteenth century in the interest of "decency." Significant scenes or portions of scenes (particularly scenes i and iii of Act IV) were omitted, and coarse expressions were cut or replaced with euphemisms. In the nineteenth century the language was refined still further,[23] and even in the early years of the present century severely bowdlerized texts were sometimes used.[24] Some cutting has continued in modern stage texts, but usually in the interest of time rather than delicacy. The long-omitted scenes in Act IV have been restored, and the language as a whole is faithful to the original.[25] The changing attitudes of the actor-critics can best be shown by typical comments on the scenes in question, for more has been written about these than about the language.[26]

Act IV, scene i / The custom of omitting from performances of *Othello* both the epileptic trance and the following episode of the eavesdropping became established early in the eighteenth century. The writer of a letter to the *Spectator,* protesting these omissions, stated that the trance had once given "great satisfaction";[27] but by

23. See Marvin Rosenberg, "The 'Refinement' of *Othello* in the Eighteenth Century British Theatre," *Studies in Philology,* LI (January, 1954), 75-94.

24. For example, see J. C. Trewin's discussion of Forbes-Robertson's Othello of 1902 in *Shakespeare on the English Stage, 1900-1964; a Survey of Productions Illustrated from the Raymond Mander and Joe Mitchenson Theatre Collection* (London, [1964]), pp. 22-25.

25. Marvin Rosenberg, *The Masks of Othello: the Search for the Identity of Othello, Iago, and Desdemona by Three Centuries of Actors and Critics* (Berkeley, 1961), pp. 143-44. The notes to the current *French's Acting Edition* (London, c. 1935), however, continue to suggest the possibility of euphemistic substitutions "if desired" or "if necessary." See p. 65, n. 9; p. 70, n. 11; p. 71, n. 23. George Skillan, the editor, occasionally brackets lines to suggest their omission. Although his proposed cuts are usually in the interest of brevity or directness, a few of them, such as Desdemona's pun on "whore" (p. 72) apparently stem from old-fashioned delicacy.

26. In regard to language, Francis Gentleman and Harley Granville-Barker are predictable opposites. Censure of indecent passages is sprinkled throughout Gentleman's discussion of *Othello* in the *Dramatic Censor,* I, 131-55. For Granville-Barker's suggestions about offensive passages see *Prefaces to Shakespeare,* I, 21-23. Most of his comments on language, however, are concerned with matters more pertinent to drama and poetry. See pp. 139-48.

27. The letter first appeared in a collection of hitherto unpublished letters,

the mid 1740's when DAVID GARRICK made the experiment of acting it, the episode was sufficiently unfamiliar for CHARLES MACKLIN to assert that "in the records of the Theatre" this "shameful" scene "had never been acted." Macklin indignantly rebuked Garrick for his "impudence . . . in offering such an absurd passage to a thinking and supposed judicious Public; . . . a passage, which . . . must be looked upon as an excrescence of the worst sort of the great genius that produced it."[28] Macklin's scornful repudiation can be explained by his adherence to the rule of decorum in characterization: a great general should never be represented as physically or mentally weak. The revival of the epileptic trance was short-lived, for Garrick, who made only three London appearances as Othello, did not attract imitators in this role. The *Bell Shakespeare* (1774) omitted the trance as well as the eavesdropping; and the editor, FRANCIS GENTLEMAN, described the discarded material as "tedious, confused, trifling, and often indecent" in addition to being unduly taxing for the already burdened actor of Othello.[29] Even in the nineteenth century, when many restorations were being made in the stage texts of Shakespeare, the episodes in question were usually omitted, probably because, neoclassical rules aside, it was felt that the sight of Othello grovelling at Iago's feet or lurking in the shadows to obtain evidence of his own shame would reduce his stature as a tragic hero.

The episode in which Othello strikes Desdemona, later in this same scene, has frequently been either omitted or underplayed by the actors (for example, a light blow with the folded letter has been substituted for the more brutal bare-handed slap).[30] EDWIN BOOTH omitted the whole of Act IV, scene i, in his acting edition, and he ignored it completely in his otherwise detailed notes on *Othello* in the *Furness Variorum*. He evidently could not reconcile the events of this scene with his concept of Othello as a noble, "simple-hearted gentleman."[31] Certain other actors, however, have

Original and Genuine Letters Sent to the Tatler and Spectator (London, 1725), but it had obviously been written more than ten years earlier. *See* Arthur Colby Sprague, *Shakespeare and the Actors* (Cambridge, Mass., 1948), p. 203 and p. 399, n. 69.

28. James Thomas Kirkman, *Memoirs of the Life of Charles Macklin, Esq.* (London, 1799), II, 260-61.

29. *Bell's Edition of Shakespeare's Plays*, [ed. Francis Gentleman] (London, 1774), I, *Othello*, 209.

30. Sprague, *Shakespeare and the Actors*, pp. 203-4.

31. *Othello, Furness Variorum*, VI (Philadelphia, 1886), 23-24.

deplored such omissions: for example, WILLIAM WOOD in the nine-teenth century and LENA ASHWELL in the twentieth. Wood, a practical actor-manager who held it no sin to cut and adapt Shakespeare for the sake of theatrical improvement, nevertheless objected to the "impudent innovations" made in the text by star actors intent merely upon building audience esteem. He par-ticularly objected to the omission of the episode that culminates in Othello's "personal violence against Desdemona; a scene of the utmost importance to the progress of his passion, and giving scope for the exercise of an actor's best talent."[32] Miss Ashwell suggested that "the library" was to blame for the custom of omitting this bit of action. Critics have found it

painful and incredible that a . . . General and a gentleman should so forget himself as to strike a woman. . . . But Shakespeare is rarely at fault in matters of this kind. In crimes of passion the poor wretch who is being torn to the point of losing self-control makes his first lapse, not in words, but usually in some small violent action.[33]

Miss Ashwell's attitude is typical of the modern tendency to accept rather than—as GRANVILLE-BARKER puts it—to "shirk" Shakespeare's unheroic, grotesque, or potentially debasing pas-sages. This same attitude toward the scene as a whole is amply illustrated both in Granville-Barker's own discussion of it[34] and in GEORGE SKILLAN's notes on it (in *French's Acting Edition*).[35] The best reason for the modern view is very well stated in the first of these: Salvini considered the eavesdropping out of char-acter for Othello, but "that is . . . the very point": "From the dignity of the play's beginning Othello sinks to this, to rise again to the tragic dignity of its end." Skillan emphasizes the emotional insights provided in this scene, pointing out that Othello here "passes through a remarkable series of changes," dramatic in themselves and vital for the play. (Both he and Granville-Barker provide detailed and imaginative analyses of Othello's reactions.) And he also notes the importance of the scene in the simple matter of plot, since Othello makes here "the major determination of the play . . . which resolves the direction of the succeeding action."

Act IV, scene iii / The obtuseness—almost willful, as it seems—

32. *Personal Recollections of the Stage* (Philadelphia, 1855), pp. 203-4.
33. *Reflections from Shakespeare*, ed. Roger Pocock (London, [1926]), p. 116.
34. *Prefaces to Shakespeare*, II, 52-56, 58-60.
35. Notes to *Othello. French's Acting Edition*, p. 61.

of some eighteenth century criticism is nowhere more apparent than in FRANCIS GENTLEMAN's comments on the willow scene between Desdemona and Emilia: "If Desdemona was to chaunt the lamentable ditty, and speak all that Shakespeare has allotted for her in this scene, an audience . . . would not know whether to laugh or cry, and Aemilia's quibbling dissertation on cuckold-making, is contemptible to the last degree."[36] Lest Gentleman be considered uniquely demented, however, we should remember that in this same period Murphy had to defend Ophelia's mad songs against neoclassical stricture, not simply because they were bawdy but because "sing[ing] in misery" was "not usual in . . . serious tragedy."[37] Perhaps a stronger reason than decorum was behind the omission or curtailment of the willow scene—namely, the low opinion of Desdemona's theatrical potentialities; since Othello and Iago were the whole show, why waste a scene, particularly if it was "unnecessary" to the plot, on Desdemona and Emilia? (Conversely, Desdemona's loss of her best scene helped to foster the idea that the role was negligible.) In any case, the willow scene was usually omitted or severely cut, not only in Gentleman's day but throughout the following century. EDWIN BOOTH, for example, sometimes omitted it entirely and at best used less than half of it.[38]

Not all actors were blind to its value, however, even during the time when it was lost to the stage. As early as 1819 WILLIAM OXBERRY expressed his appreciation of this "tender and touching" scene, this "song of death, but of such exquisite beauty as to make us in love with sorrow." He showed, too, an understanding of its mood and its contribution to the pattern of the play: the dialogue, with its pathos and repose, acquires from the dramatic situation a "deeper and more fearful colouring"; the scene has "all the calm horror of the pause which precedes the tempest."[39] GRANVILLE-BARKER's description, though written more than a century later, seems almost like a continuation or development of Oxberry's: "a scene of ordered calm; of ceremonial courtesy," after scenes of violence and distress, it prepares us "in its stillness, and in

36. *Dramatic Censor*, I, 146.
37. *The Works of Arthur Murphy, Esq.* (London, 1786), V, 353.
38. Sprague, *Shakespeare and the Actors*, p. 203 and p. 400, n. 70.
39. *New English Drama*, V, *Othello*, iv.

the gentle melody of the song, for the worse violence and the horror to come."[40]

Actresses of Desdemona must have wished for a restoration of the willow scene long before it came about. Certainly HELEN FAUCIT did so, for she remarked ironically: "How sad it is that the exigencies of our stage require the omission of the exquisite scene . . . so important for the development of . . . [Desdemona's] character, and affording such fine opportunities for the highest powers of pathos in the actress!" To illustrate her idea that much could be done in this scene with "silent acting," Miss Faucit pictured Desdemona's actions as they might suggest her train of thought:

[She is] seated, her sad thoughts wandering . . . while Emilia uncoils the pearls from her hair, untwists its long plaits. . . . Then, as Emilia kneels . . . to unfasten the embroidered shoes, Desdemona may put her hand admiringly on Emilia's head and smooth her fine hair. Meanwhile her thoughts are travelling back to her childhood—perhaps to that mother whose caresses she so early lost. . . . Then she remembers Barbara, her mother's maid. . . .[41]

It is interesting that in the modern period not actresses, but actors—Granville-Barker and GEORGE SKILLAN—have best discussed the importance of the willow scene to the character of Desdemona. Granville-Barker points out, for example, that the discussion with Emilia about unfaithful wives gives Shakespeare's finishing touch to Desdemona's character; its purpose is to remind us of her "too absolute goodness," which Iago has used as a tool to destroy her and Othello.[42] And Skillan, like Helen Faucit, considers the acting requirements as well as the significance of the scene. The actress must have a light touch, he writes, for the effects of the willow scene must be gained through skillful suggestion rather than through fully developed action. Properly presented, "the exposure of this fragile creature's own particular tragedy is as perfect as the thunders and lightnings of OTHELLO's dissolution."[43]

40. *Prefaces to Shakespeare*, II, 68.
41. *On Some of Shakespeare's Female Characters* (Edinburgh and London, 1887), pp. 75-76.
42. *Prefaces to Shakespeare*, II, 68-69.
43. *Othello. French's Acting Edition*, pp. 74-75.

II. THE CHARACTERS

OTHELLO

Theatrical Criticism

More than any other major Shakespearean hero, Othello has inspired the actors to write criticisms of a theatrical nature rather than pure character analysis. The matters discussed are more than mechanical, of course: The very question of makeup may have far-reaching implications; and the argument over the degree to which Othello should give way to physically expressed rage, though it may originate in response to a particular performance, is an argument over character interpretation rather than over simple stage effect. Nevertheless it seems safe to say that actors, like other critics, have traditionally considered Othello simple in character in comparison with Hamlet and Macbeth, just as they have considered the play magnificent drama that speaks for itself. Although theatrical considerations enter largely into all areas of Othello criticism by the actors and must, therefore, influence all our discussions of the character, one type of theatrical comment— the simplest and most technical—invites separate presentation. Criticisms of this kind constitute a set of variations on one consistent theme: the peculiar hazards confronting any adventurer for Othello's histrionic prizes.

Actor-critics in every age have recognized the potentialities of this role: it is a character "that a Master Actor would delight in," declared COLLEY CIBBER in 1740;[44] "to say . . . that a man plays Othello well . . . is to affirm that he . . . bodies forth the *chef d'oeuvre* of the English stage"—so wrote JOHN BERNARD in the early years of the following century;[45] "my favorite part," OSCAR ASCHE called it in 1929, and he added that it had always "proved a strong card" for him.[46] Yet the unusual difficulties of the role have also been recognized in every age—sometimes by the same actors who have extolled its greatness. Bernard remarked, for example, that it "requires greater abilities to do it justice, than any . . . of Shake-

44. *An Apology for the Life of Mr. Colley Cibber*, ed. Robert W. Lowe (London, 1889), II, 248.
45. John Bernard, *Retrospections of the Stage* (London, 1830), I, 27. Published posthumously; Bernard died in 1828.
46. *Oscar Asche: His Life by Himself* (London, c. 1929), p. 119.

speare's other conceptions."[47] And more recently (1930) FRANK BENSON, though he expressed a strong partiality to the role, reminded his readers that in the whole of the nineteenth century no one except Edmund Kean and Tommaso Salvini had "satisfied an audience in the part."[48]

What are the reasons for Othello's greatness? And, more important from a practical point of view, what are the difficulties that must be overcome in order to do justice to that greatness? There is little disagreement about the answer to the first question: The role offers incredible opportunities for the actor to use his characteristic stock-in-trade, the expression of human emotion—to use all varieties of it, and always in their most intense forms. According to Colley Cibber, Barton Booth showed himself "thrice the Actor" in this part that he could in Addison's "declaiming Patriot," the much-admired Cato, for the actor of Othello "is carried through the different Accidents of domestick Happiness, and Misery, . . . torn, and tortur'd by the most distracting Passion, that can raise Terror, or Compassion, in the Spectator."[49] As John Bernard pointed out, however, the very qualities that make Othello a great role—particularly the expression of "the highest and most opposite elements of tragic character"—are those that make it a difficult one.[50]

Of the stumbling blocks mentioned by actor-critics, only one is unrelated to the emotional requirements of the role: namely, the problem posed for the hero by the unusual prominence of his antagonist. Thus SAMUEL FOOTE remarked in 1747 that he could recall no other character which "so absolutely depends on . . . the Returning of the Ball," for "the greatest Othello that ever was born, unless he be well provided with an Ancient, [cannot] properly . . . express either the Hero or the jealous Lover."[51] And in our own age (1964) SIR LAURENCE OLIVIER has called attention to a different aspect of the same problem: the strong competition for Othello posed by Shakespeare's interest in Iago and the resulting view of the play as a duelling ground for actors.[52]

As for the main difficulty, that of effectively expressing Othel-

47. *Retrospections of the Stage*, I, 27.
48. *My Memoirs* (London, 1930), p. 217.
49. *Apology for the Life of Mr. Colley Cibber*, II, 248.
50. *Retrospections of the Stage*, I, 27.
51. Samuel Foote, *A Treatise on the Passions* (London, [1747]), p. 36.
52. "The Great Sir Laurence," *Life*, LVI, No. 18 (May 1, 1964), 80-A.

lo's passion, several aspects of this problem have been discussed by the actor-critics. They are all related, however, and there is little difference between the basic ideas that have been held in the various periods. For example, a number of actor-critics—from FRANCIS GENTLEMAN in the eighteenth century to LOUIS CALVERT and Sir Laurence Olivier in the twentieth—have emphasized the unusual physical strain of the role. As Gentleman puts it, the "length of periods" and the "extravagance of passion" in Othello's part cannot be "found in any other, for so many successive scenes."[53] Calvert analyzes the problem more systematically than the others: he points out that, although the major climax comes in the third act, the fourth and fifth acts require of the actor "a power of endurance, an intensity and rage" that he will not be able to supply unless he has husbanded his force in the early scenes; for an actor must not only work up to a crescendo but, after the climax has passed, he must follow through, sustaining the sense of emotional reality by showing the effect the crisis has had upon the character.[54] Olivier remarks more bluntly that the role is poorly planned, too full of big moments for Othello. He himself has triumphantly met its challenges (his interpretation, though controversial, was tremendously successful), yet his "theory" about the inception of *Othello* is perhaps only half jesting: It seems that Shakespeare and Burbage got drunk one night and Burbage boasted that he could act any role Shakespeare could invent. Shakespeare accepted the challenge—and that's when he wrote *Othello*.[55]

There is a corollary to the difficulty we have been discussing, for in addition to imposing a strain upon the actor's resources, Othello's continual bursts of passion can exhaust the audience's power of sympathetic response. TATE WILKINSON suggested (in 1790) that Othello would arouse "more pity and less fatigue" if he were not so "incessantly in sight."[56] And Olivier remarks that when a character is too constantly enraged the audience begins to fidget with embarrassment.[57]

Another aspect of the difficulty—less technical and more basic—is mentioned by Frank Benson. The problem posed by Othello,

53. *Dramatic Censor,* I, 150-51.
54. *Problems of an Actor* (New York, 1918), pp. 145-49.
55. "The Great Sir Laurence," p. 80-A.
56. *Memoirs of His Own Life, By Tate Wilkinson* . . . (York, 1790), III, 151.
57. "The Great Sir Laurence," p. 80-A.

he writes, is the opposite of the one involved in playing Hamlet: "Just as, in Irving's words, the difficulty of Hamlet is to express emotion in terms of intellect . . . it is still more difficult to express the deepest feelings of our nature in terms of pure emotion."[58] The requirement noticed by Benson becomes an impediment to theatrical success, not simply because of a lack of histrionic resources, but because of a certain habitual restraint in the feelings and expressions of English-speaking people. Thus SIR MICHAEL REDGRAVE once gave as a reason for his not undertaking the role of Othello the fact that he himself was "too rational" to "understand all that jealousy."[59] And ROBERT SPEAIGHT, among other actor-critics, has noticed that men of the uninhibited Latin temperament have most often excelled in the part.[60] Not that English-speaking actors are incapable of expressing emotions—even violent ones— but, to amplify Benson's idea that "pure passion" is difficult to convey, perhaps they are (in recent times at least) more at home in parts that keep strong emotion in balance with other elements in the character. Othello is built on large and simple lines; it offers for the actor's solution none of the puzzling complexities in which Hamlet is so rich, and, within its limits, the role is so fully realized in the text that it provides few opportunities for building up the character through personal idiosyncrasies or subtle implications. Perhaps that is one reason why SIR JOHN GIELGUD, synonymous in many minds with Hamlet himself, was disappointed when he undertook Othello. Having achieved notable successes in jealous characters of a lesser sort, Leontes in *The Winter's Tale* and Cassius in *Julius Caesar*, Gielgud expected that the "marvellous" character of Othello, "being more basically sympathetic and more fully drawn . . . would be easier to bring to life." But, as he ruefully recalls, "I was soon to discover that I was mistaken."[61] Perhaps actors as well as audiences have lost a certain zestful spontaneity enjoyed in earlier days, before psychology and naturalism choked the frank delight in passion for passion's sake. But if this particular difficulty is greater than it once was, the problems—and the rewards—involved in playing Othello have changed, on the whole, very little from the eigh-

58. *My Memoirs*, p. 217.
59. Richard Findlater [Kenneth Findlater Bain]) *Michael Redgrave, Actor* (London, [1956]), pp. 140-41.
60. *Nature in Shakespearian Tragedy*, p. 79.
61. *Stage Directions* (New York, [1964]), p. 46.

teenth century to the present. Judging by the remarkable similarity of the actors' evaluations, Othello has always been the alexandrite among Shakespeare's theatrical gems.

In actors' tributes to successful interpreters of the role, the same names recur time after time. Such tributes would indicate that the greatest Othellos of the English-speaking stage have been, in the post-Betterton era at least, Spranger Barry in the eighteenth century and Edmund Kean in the nineteenth, and that they were both eclipsed by the Italian Tommaso Salvini. All three of these actors could create the effect of intense passion, and two of them—Barry and Salvini—attained an apparently effortless mastery of the demand for sustained physical and emotional power. (Kean's passionate outbursts were set off by intervals of deliberate underplaying—for artistic shading, as he said,[62] but also, perhaps, to stretch his physical resources.) According to Francis Gentleman, Barry "rode through all the passions to the utmost height of critical imagination, yet still appeared to leave an unexhausted fund of expression behind."[63] And FRANK ARCHER praised Salvini for the same excellence. In the latter case an additional point was made: there was nothing "stilted or unnatural in the performance," wrote Archer, no attempt to force "points" in order to win applause. "When they were made—and how they impressed one!—they rose naturally and truthfully from the situations."[64] Because he expressed Othello's passion without restraint yet without any hint of ranting, Salvini moved the most decorous of audiences to strong emotional responses. E. L. DAVENPORT, himself a respectable American Othello, had never been "made to weep" in witnessing the play until he saw Salvini in it. "I have never been so carried away," he wrote to William Winter, "as by some of his exquisitely powerful and thrilling effects."[65] On one occasion when Salvini gave a special performance of Othello for the "leading representatives of the English stage," SQUIRE BANCROFT was a member of this select and critical audience. "No ovation that I have taken part in," he recalls, "equalled in enthusiasm the reception from [Salvini's] up-standing comrades at the close

62. See Carol J. Carlisle, "Edmund Kean on the Art of Acting," *Theatre Notebook*, XXII (Spring, 1968), 119-20.
63. *Dramatic Censor*, I, 150-51.
64. Frank Archer, *An Actor's Notebooks* (London, [190-]), p. 164.
65. MS letter of November 2, 1873, in the Folger Library.

of the third act."[66] Something of that same enthusiasm communicates itself in critiques of Salvini's performance—and, to a lesser degree, of Barry's and Kean's—written by other "comrades" in the profession. No doubt Sir Laurence Olivier's Othello, the most spectacular of recent times, will inspire some vivid writing in the pages of future theatrical memoirs—and, again, the expression of intense and prolonged emotion (pushed, in this case, to almost unendurable limits) will inevitably become a major point.

It is not really a paradox that the Shakespearean role with the greatest histrionic potentialities should also be the one in which the fewest actors have been really great. But some of the failures are surprising—David Garrick in particular. This versatile actor, brilliantly successful in Hamlet, Macbeth, and Lear, certainly had the requisite fire and passion for Othello. It is hard to believe that his short stature was alone capable of thwarting Garrick's genius; Kean rose above the same handicap. One reason for his failure may have been his lack of tenderness, a characteristic in which his contemporary Barry abounded. (Barry surpassed him in Romeo as well). To discuss this point, however, would be to leave the mechanical considerations of Othello as a theatre role for the more subjective questions of character interpretation. Let us turn now to some problems of the latter type.

Problems in the Interpretation of Othello

The Question of Color / When the critic André Morellet was visiting England in 1772 he questioned DAVID GARRICK about Shakespeare's reason for making Othello black, explaining that, for the French people, "that Moorish face greatly diminished . . . interest" in the hero and "made Desdemona's virtue almost incredible." Garrick answered that "Shakespeare had shown us white men jealous in other pieces, but that their jealousy had limits, and was not so terrible; that, in the part of Othello, he had wished to paint that passion in all its violence, and that is why he chose an African in whose veins circulated fire instead of blood."[67] Whatever the questions about Shakespeare's reasoning and taste, there was evidently no question at that time of his intention to make Othello black. Certainly stage tradition suggested no doubts on

---

66. Squire Bancroft, *Empty Chairs* (London, 1925), p. 157.

67. Quoted and translated by F. A. Hedgcock, in *A Cosmopolitan Actor: David Garrick and His French Friends* (London, 1912), p. 341.

the matter. Garrick acted the part in black makeup, as did Barry and the others, but he added an oriental touch in the form of a turban. (This costume, together with Garrick's short stature, gave James Quin, a rival Othello, the opportunity for his famous jest that Garrick looked like a little Negro footboy who ought to be carrying a teakettle.[68])

But the question of Othello's color, so confidently answered by Garrick, soon became a stumbling block for actors. Literary critics were already uneasy about it, for Morellet's point of view was not confined to France. As early as 1692 Thomas Rymer had expressed disgust at Shakespeare's providing a blackamoor with the daughter of a "great Lord" instead of "some little drab" and making him a general of the Venetian Army instead of a mere trumpeter;[69] and a few years later Charles Gildon had declared that it was shocking to find a Negro the hero of the play and that Desdemona's love for a man of "so opposite a Colour . . . takes away our Pity from her, and only raises our indignation against him."[70] By the nineteenth century even some of the most intelligent English critics were finding unsavory implications in the idea of a black Othello. Neither Coleridge[71] nor Lamb,[72] for example, could sympathize with Desdemona's love for a Negro. The latter indeed found nobility in the *idea* of her giving up all because of Othello's inner worth, but when he saw the play on the stage he was repelled by her romance with a *"coal-black Moor."* Lamb simply concluded that the play should be read, not acted. Coleridge, however, argued against the blackamoor interpretation

68. John Hill, *The Actor: or, A Treatise on the Art of Playing* (London, 1755), pp. 152-53.

69. Thomas Rymer, *Critical Works*, ed. Curt A. Zimansky (New Haven, 1956), p. 184.

70. "Remarks on the Plays of Shakespear," *Remarks upon Shakespear &c., By Mr Dryden, Mr Row & Mr Gildon* (London, 1709), pp. 362-63.

71. *Coleridge's Shakespearean Criticism*, ed. T. M. Raysor (Cambridge, Mass., 1930), I, 46-47. Raysor suspects the authenticity of the following strongly-worded passage about Desdemona: "It would be something monstrous to conceive this beautiful Venetian girl falling in love with a veritable negro. It would argue a disproportionateness . . . in Desdemona." He points out that this passage, interpolated from the *Literary Remains*, is in a style "utterly unlike Coleridge" and that H. N. Coleridge in similar cases sought in his own words to make his uncle's meaning clear. There is no doubt, however, that the general idea of the impropriety of Othello's being a Negro is Coleridge's.

72. *The Complete Works and Letters of Charles Lamb*, ed. Bennet A. Cerf and Donald S. Klopfer (New York, 1935), p. 299.

itself; he questioned whether Shakespeare was "so utterly ignorant as to make a barbarous *negro* plead royal birth," and he discounted the expression "thick lips" as a just epithet for Othello since it was used by a rival. Not all writers were of this mind, of course; the question of Othello's color was to be debated by scholars and critics for many years to come. Still, the critical climate was amply prepared in the second decade of the nineteenth century for the stage innovation—attributed to EDMUND KEAN—of using brown, or tawny, makup for Othello.

It may be that Kean himself was convinced, as his biographer Hawkins says he was, that it was a "gross error" to make Othello a Negro, but it seems likely that in using a lighter makeup he was motivated primarily by theatrical considerations. (Hawkins acknowledges that it facilitated his task as an actor.[73]) Leman Rede, writing in 1827, little more than a decade after Kean's first London performance of the part, noted that "Othello . . . in former days . . . wore the same sables as Mungo in *The Padlock*" but that "this, as being destructive of the face, and preventing the possibility of the expression being noted, has become an obsolete custom. A tawny tinge is now the colour used for the gallant Moor . . . Spanish brown [a red brown] is the best preparation."[74] And in 1831 a theatrical biographer speculated that the reason for Garrick's failure in Othello was that the black makeup had obscured the play of his countenance.[75] (Garrick, like Kean, was famous for his facial acting.) Since practical stagecraft was, in this matter, consonant with the social attitudes of the times, it is not surprising that the innovation soon became the accepted custom.

It is possible, however, that Kean was not consistent in the degree of "blackness" he gave to his Othello. Two well-known pictures of him in the character differ considerably in this respect: one of them (by J. W. Gear) depicts an Othello of relatively light

73. Frederick Hawkins, *The Life of Edmund Kean* (London, 1869), I, 221-22.

74. Leman Thomas Rede, *The Road to the Stage* (London, 1827), pp. 38-39. I am grateful to Miss Muriel St. Clare Byrne for calling my attention to this reference. For an excellent short history of stage makeup see her article on the subject in the *Oxford Companion to the Theatre*, ed. Phyllis Hartnoll (London, New York and Toronto, 1951), pp. 498-509.

75. John Galt, *Lives of the Players* (London, 1831), I, 268. It is notable that when Kean performed Zanga in *The Revenge* the London *Times* critic remarked (May 27, 1815) that the part was not "judiciously chosen for his powers. The play of his countenance is necessarily lost under the sable covering of the Moor."

complexion, but the other (by E. F. Lambert) shows him as dark-skinned as many real-life Negroes. It is interesting that in both of them the hair appears tightly curled. This feature, together with the dusky skin, gives the second picture the look of a Negro rather than an Arab or a Spanish Moor.[76]

Whatever the change in makeup, it did not imply a change in conception. In Lambert's striking portrayal, the combination of fierceness and horror depicted on Kean's face suggests unleashed savagery, in keeping with Garrick's explanation to Morellet. We remember, too, Hazlitt's strictures on Kean's Othello (which he nevertheless considered "the finest piece of acting in the world"): "Othello was tall, but that is nothing: he was black, but that is nothing. But he was not fierce, and that is every-thing."[77] Hazlitt could not quite approve the change in Othello's appearance because, despite his own reservations about Desde-mona's taste, he was convinced that Shakespeare had intended his hero to be black. It seems ironic that at the same time he refused to recognize in Othello's temperament the fierceness fre-quently associated with a black Othello. It is obvious that Kean's substitution of tawny for black makeup did not carry with it any such connotations of gentlemanliness and glamour (in opposition to elemental passion and force) as the lighter makeup of some later

76. See the plates opposite p. 116 in Giles Playfair's *Kean* (New York, 1939) and opposite p. 128 in H. N. Hillebrand's *Edmund Kean* (New York, 1933). The latter, a black and white reproduction of a lithograph in the Harvard Theatre Collection, is much the more interesting of the two. In it the skin appears to be very nearly black. I have seen a colored lithograph in the Folger Library, also from Lambert's picture, which shows the skin as a dusky brown. It bears the printed legend: "Drawn by E. F. Lambert" (the lithographer was W. Sheldrick), which would indicate that the original was a drawing rather than (as Hillebrand's notation says) a painting. (Lambert also made a drawing of Kean as Richard III in the latter's dressing room, 1829. See *Catalogue of Dramatic Portraits in the Theatre Collection of the Harvard College Library*, ed. Lillian A. Hall [Cambridge, Mass., 1931], II, 340, item # 25.) I have tried without success to find out the present location of the original picture, if it is extant. I am grateful to those who have replied to my inquiries and have attempted to help me in my search: Miss Helen Willard of the Harvard Theatre Collection; Mr. Edward Di Roma of the New York Public Library; Mrs. Henry W. Howell, Jr., of the Frick Art Reference Library, New York; Mr. G. W. Nash of the Victoria and Albert Museum, London; Mr. John Sunderland of the Courtauld Institute of Art, University of London; Mr. Levi Fox, Director of the Shakespeare Centre, Stratford-on-Avon; Mrs. M. Hill of the National Portrait Gallery, London; and Miss Dorothy Mason of the Folger Shakespeare Library.

77. From a review in *The Examiner*, January 7, 1816. See *Complete Works of Hazlitt*, ed. P. P. Howe (London and Toronto, 1930-34), V, 271.

Othellos was to do. Perhaps this was why one writer—George Henry Lewes, who saw and admired Kean's Othello in its latter days—evidently associated the performance in memory with the "black" conception. Some years later Lewes objected to Charles Fechter's "loud" but "not fierce" Othello, partly because he was made up as a "half caste, whose mere appearance would excite no repulsion in any woman outside America." "Othello is black," Lewes insisted—"the very tragedy lies there; the whole force of the contrast, the whole pathos and extenuation of his doubts of Desdemona, depend on this blackness." In the next paragraph of the same essay he remarked, "We, who remember Kean in *Othello* . . . believe we have seen Othello *acted*, and so acted as there is little chance of our seeing it acted again. . . ."[78] Although this statement is not directly connected with his discussion of Othello's color, there seems to be an implied connection in the fact that the same critic who considered blackness the essence of Othello's tragedy also found in Kean his ideal Othello of the stage.

In America the question of Othello's color had become particularly acute. Thus Henry Wallack was considered ill-advised when he selected Othello for his first appearance in this country (during the 1818-19 season in Philadelphia)—"and more so," writes WILLIAM WOOD, "from his persisting to make him a black, in a place where the general practice prevailed of showing him a tawny man."[79] The presence of Negro slaves in the United States made the idea of Desdemona's marriage to a black man seem to many people not only shocking but incomprehensible, and Garrick's conception of violent passions unrestrained by the time-ingrained habits of civilization would have suggested to Wallack's American audience an immediate threat to society.

Actors of the later nineteenth and early twentieth centuries, British as well as American, generally used tawny, or bronze, makeup, though with varying degrees of darkness or lightness. (More or less burnt cork mixed with the brown pigment would make the difference.[80]) The suggestion of the orient which Gar-

78. George Henry Lewes, *On Actors and the Art of Acting* (New York, c. 1957), pp. 128-29. *See* pp. 116-19, 128-42 for the whole discussion of Fechter's Othello. The book, a collection of essays that had previously appeared in periodicals, was first published in 1875.

79. *Personal Recollections of the Stage*, p. 227.

80. According to Miss Byrne, a handbook of stage makeup copyrighted in 1877 by Samuel French advises that "a little of the Prepared Burnt Cork should be mixed

rick had attempted now dominated the whole dress of the character, and actors looked to Arab or Indian models for the physical appearance of Othello. DANIEL BANDMANN found his ideal in Babu Keshub Chunder Sen, a "learned and enlightened native" of India, whom the actor met while on an extended tour with his dramatic company.

With a grand, imposing, athletic figure, a noble bearing, he combined an expressive dignity which reminded one of the patrician Roman. He was fully six feet high, broad shouldered, deep chested, of slightly olive complexion, mild, eloquent eyes, firm, set lips, genial chin, black moustache, and long black hair, which hung carelessly over a well-developed forehead. The stamp of nobility was upon him.

The next time he played Othello, Bandmann made up to look as much as possible like this *"beau ideal"* of the character.[81] EDWIN BOOTH's tastefully bronzed Othello, his robes glittering with barbaric splendor[82] and his carefully-planned gestures eloquent of his oriental heritage (e.g. holding a scimitar aloft to form the crescent[83]) was just exotic enough to intrigue the imag-

with the Mongolian [the principal ingredient in the makeup for Red Indians]" for Othello. (See *The Oxford Companion to the Theatre*, p. 504.) It is easy to imagine the possible variations in shade. Such sophisticated makeup was perhaps not available to many provincial actors, however. In an interesting letter to me, dated April 19, 1966, Sir Donald Wolfit recalled that in old dressing rooms in his youth he saw bricks which had been hollowed by former actors who had used them for rouge; lampblack, or even soot from the chimney, was used for blackening the face.

81. Daniel Bandmann, *An Actor's Tour* (New York, 1886), p. 136.

82. William Winter writes that Booth intended his costumes "to depict a gorgeous barbaric taste, modified by partial conformance to Christian and Venetian custom." One of those used in 1881, when Booth and Irving alternated the role, was "a long gown of cashmere, wrought with gold . . . looped up on the hip . . . with a jewelled fastening. A Moorish burnoose, striped with purple and gold. Purple velvet shoes, embroidered with gold and pearl. A sash of green and gold. A jewelled chain." Winter also describes Irving's costume for the same occasion (*Shakespeare on the Stage*, First Series [New York, 1911], pp. 277-78). Irving varied in the kind of costume and makeup he used for Othello. When he first produced the play (1876) he used a light bronze makeup and wore the dress and armor of a Venetian general. He told Walter Pollock that his lack of success was due to "the fact that they expect to see Othello as something entirely eastern and mysterious." When he alternated the role with Booth in 1881, however, he was "gorgeously apparalled" in the oriental manner and used makeup that was "blacker than was the custom." (*See* Laurence Irving, *Henry Irving: The Actor and His World*, by *His Grandson* [London, (1951)], pp. 272, 377.) George Foss's sketch of Irving as Othello in 1881 may be seen on p. 77 of his book *What the Author Meant* (London, 1932).

83. Booth's suggestions for "oriental" gestures may be found in the *Furness Variorum*, VI, 23-24, 54, 141.

ination of a romantic girl. The young actress Kitty Molony described him as "beautiful," and Booth remarked that she was much like Desdemona in her reaction.[84]

Othello must be set apart from Desdemona and her countrymen, if not by a pronounced color difference, then in some other way. The idea that he is meant to be, not a "blackamoor," but a true Moor—a person of mixed Berber and Arab ancestry, with Mauritania as his people's native home and with the conquest of Granada as one of their exploits—met this requirement in a particularly satisfying way since it made him an exotic figure without offending the taste or prejudices of the audience. Booth's younger contemporaries, and the actors of the following generation as well, usually imagined Othello as Bandmann and Booth described him —that is, as a highly civilized demi-oriental. HERBERT BEERBOHM TREE, for example, considered him a "stately Arab of the best caste."[85] LENA ASHWELL, preferring to think of the Spanish Moors rather than of their African forebears, described Othello's people as belonging to "that Mediterranean stock which includes the French, Spaniards, Italians, and our own Celts," and she expatiated on the contributions—mathematical, scientific, architectural—that they had made to civilization. As late as 1926 she was expressing sarcastic disapproval of stage productions that might lead the audience to suppose that Shakespeare's descendant of royalty is a "nigger."[86]

In the decades that have followed, however, there has been an increasing tendency for actors to return to the "blackamoor" conception of Othello—a conception that was never completely abandoned by scholars and critics, even in the periods of greatest squeamishness. Arguments over the Elizabethan meanings of "Moor" and "black," over the literal or dramatic interpretation of "thick lips" and "sooty bosom," over the demands of Shakespeare's thematic design and his psychological portrayal of Othello —these had flourished during the "Bronze Age",[87] but they had left the stage largely untouched. (The "African Roscius," Ira Aldridge, was, in his rare appearances, a novelty in the role.) Now

84. Katherine [Molony] Goodale, *Behind the Scenes with Edwin Booth* (Boston, 1931), p. 208.

85. Maud Holt Tree, "Herbert and I," in *Herbert Beerbohm Tree: Some Memories of Him and His Art,* ed. Max Beerbohm (New York, [1920]), p. 148.

86. *Reflections from Shakespeare,* pp. 98-100.

87. For some examples see the *Furness Variorum,* VI, 389-96.

the more scholarly of the actor-critics—men like HARLEY GRANVILLE-BARKER[88] and, a little later, ROBERT SPEAIGHT[89]—showed their concern for Shakespeare's intentions in the matter of Othello's color and especially for the problem of carrying out such intentions in the theatre. Both of these men expressed the conviction that Shakespeare had meant Othello to be black, but they also declared that the indications of Negroid features, such as "thick lips," are not to be taken literally and that, to use Granville-Barker's words, no actor of the part "is called upon to make himself repulsive to his audience." Speaight prefers an unrealistically black Moor to an actual Negro; Granville-Barker simply advises the actor that, since audience tastes vary widely according to time and place, the main thing to remember is that Othello's looks should reflect the quality that Desdemona found in his mind. Despite the latitude allowed in Othello's stage appearance, however, his separateness from the other characters is important to both actor-critics: Speaight considers him "clearly an exotic," and Granville-Barker mentions his blackness as an important element in his vulnerability.

But there have been other reasons, less academic, for the return of a black Othello to the theatre, and there have been other actor-critics less inclined to compromise, not only on the subject of Othello's color but also on that of his Negroid features. Outstanding among the reasons is the influence of great actors, past and present. The influence of Kean, originally responsible for the tawny oriental of romantic tradition, was turned, with a kind of poetic justice, toward a Negro Othello in the modern period. This was true, at any rate, in the case of SIR DONALD WOLFIT. "The light chocolate colour of Forbes Robertson was not for me," writes Wolfit of his first essay at the character (in 1938). "The Kean portrait was in my mind"—that is, the dusky, ferocious-looking Othello of the Lambert picture already referred to.[90] The Othello

88. *Prefaces to Shakespeare*, II, 116-18, 148-49.

89. *Nature in Shakespearian Tragedy*, pp. 71-72. See also "Shakespeare in Britain," *Shakespeare Quarterly*, XV (1964), 379.

90. *First Interval* (London, 1954), p. 193. In a letter dated April 19, 1966, Sir Donald graciously replied to my inquiries about his own concept of Othello's complexion and of Kean's interpretation. He confirmed my guess that the "Kean portrait" which he had mentioned in his book was the one reproduced in Hillebrand's biography, and he reiterated his conviction that his own conception of Othello was in the Kean tradition.

of Wolfit's conception was not a "smooth courtier" or a "handsome lover" (except to Desdemona of the inward eye) but a "somewhat uncouth curly haired North African," "the noble savage who when taunted and goaded into jealousy by Iago becomes the tortured bull."[91] Capable Negro actors of the present century, like Paul Robeson and Earle Hyman, have, no doubt, contributed tremendously to the re-establishment of a black Othello tradition. MARGARET WEBSTER, who directed one of the Robeson productions (New York, 1943-44), has set forth the rationale for a Negro Othello. In her opinion, blackness is vital to an understanding of the character and, particularly, to a credible performance. It explains at a glance Othello's supposed gullibility: For he and Desdemona, "once their first concord is broken," are separated not only by a difference in color but by "a gulf between two races, one old and soft in the ways of civilization, the other close to the jungle." Othello's alienation from the "whole society by which he is surrounded, its religion, morals, conventions," is "the vital point of weakness on which Iago fastens." Again, a black Othello makes the later violence understandable: For "in the tribal world to which he belongs" a betrayed husband "is himself tainted and dishonored"; and shedding the blood of the guilty wife is not "revenge or murder. It is a terrible sacrifice offered by the Priest-King to the primal gods. . . ."[92] The value that Miss Webster claims for a Negro interpreter of the role has been recognized by critics outside the theatre as well. Dover Wilson, for example, found the play so illuminated by Robeson's first performance of the character (London, 1930) that he gave this experience as his chief reason for believing Othello was meant to be a black man.[93]

In very recent years the widespread interest in the "emerging nations" of Africa and in the "Negro revolution" in the United States has strengthened the attraction of a black Othello. Thus when a white actor, SIR LAURENCE OLIVIER, performed the role in 1964 he made up, not simply in the blackface used by Barry, Garrick, and Kemble, but also with careful attention to the details of Negro physiognomy.[94] Never one for caution or restraint,

91. *First Interval*, pp. 193-94.
92. *Shakespeare Without Tears*, pp. 233-37.
93. See his introduction to the "New Cambridge Edition" of *Othello*, ed. J. Dover Wilson and Alice Walker (1957), pp. ix-x.
94. See the pictures in *Life*, May 1, 1964, pp. 80-B-85.

he even risked laughter in some places by the grotesquerie of his Negro imitation (more caricature than idealization)—yet who can forget the tragic mask of that black face distorted with agony? According to Olivier, the play is heavily saturated with the emphasis upon Othello's blackness. Although the race question today is not quite the same as it was in Shakespeare's time, nevertheless it was considered scandalous to marry a black person— witness Brabantio's horrified incredulity. On this last point Granville-Barker, Speaight, Margaret Webster, and others have agreed. They have not been quite so ready as Olivier, however, to focus upon the sensational element in the love of Othello and Desdemona: he insists upon a potent sexuality, more highly charged because of Othello's blackness, and deliberately meant to be shocking.[95]

The Question of Othello's Basic Character / In the eighteenth century critics frequently remarked that the character of Othello is a combination of the "hero" and the "lover," two of the major stage types. Most actor-critics agreed that both aspects of the character are important, but it is obvious that emphasis upon one or the other would lead to somewhat different interpretations. The greatest potential source of differences, however, was in imagining (and in projecting on the stage) the changes wrought in the "hero" and the "lover" by the passion of jealousy.

Although self-control was a hero's trait (and Othello demonstrates this at the outset in "Put up your bright swords. . . ."), rage on a grand scale was also considered a kind of Olympian quality if it had an adequate cause, such as an affront to the hero's honor. As JOHN HILL put it, a hero is "naturally mild, tho' when provoked, terrible." A hero's revenge, however, was usually taken openly upon his adversary; Othello's was upon a defenseless woman. This fact, which had provoked Rymer's censure, apparently did not offend the actor-critics (the murder scene was too effective), but the problem inherent in it did not escape their notice. Hill explained that although we see in Othello "a kind of savage . . . this is not from nature, Iago works him to it slowly, difficultly, and with the deepest cunning. His fury would be too horrible without these circumstances; but as it is, when Iago is

95. "The Great Sir Laurence," p. 88.

well acted, we hardly blame him for the crime. . . . Shakespeare has reconciled it with the character of a hero."[96]

But Othello's violence, being, as Hill admitted, "savage" as well as awesome, was in danger of being reduced to mere brutality if it were not softened by the pity and rendered sympathetic by the anguish of Othello the lover. It was the gentler side of the character that needed the greater emphasis, so SAMUEL FOOTE believed. According to him, the actor's most essential task in Othello was to excite in the audience a "Compassion for himself" even greater, if possible, than they would naturally feel for Desdemona; "and, for this Purpose, the Strugglings and Convulsions that torture and distract his Mind, upon his resolving to murder her, cannot be too strongly painted, nor can the Act itself be accomplished with too much Grief and Tenderness." Not only was it expedient to arouse pity for the hero in this way but Shakespeare had so depicted Othello as to make this the natural reaction. No character, Foote declared, had ever been "more generally misunderstood by both Audience and Actor," for "the most tender-hearted, compassionate, humane Man" had been too often mistaken for a "cruel, bloody, and obdurate Savage." Othello's expressions of love and pity, even after he no longer doubts his wife's infidelity, his dwelling on "her most minute excellence, even to her Skill with the Needle," his pathetic concern for her soul during the murder scene itself—all these clearly indicate his true nature. If the actor rightly interprets Othello, the killing of Desdemona will "appear as a Sacrifice to the Hero's injur'd Honour, and not the Gratification of a diabolic Passion."[97]

In order to reconcile the two aspects of Othello's character and to show the effect of passion working through them, it would seem that the ideal performance of Othello, according to eighteenth-century standards, would achieve the difficult combination of tenderness, turning to pathos but avoiding weakness, and grandeur, losing itself in fury without sinking to brutality. According to THEOPHILUS CIBBER, Barton Booth successfully effected such a union: "the heart-breaking Anguish of his Jealousy would have drawn tears from the most obdurate;—yet all his Grief, though

96. *The Actor*, p. 216.

97. *A Treatise on the Passions*, pp. 33-35. Foote's detailed discussion of Othello's character is among the earliest such discussions of a Shakespearean character by an actor-critic.

feelingly expressed, was never beneath the Hero: When he wept, his Tears broke from him perforce:—he never whindled, whined, or blubbered:—In his Rage,—he never mouthed or ranted."[98] Spranger Barry's Othello was also famous for giving due value to both sides of Othello's character. Foote preferred it to James Quin's interpretation because it was gentler and more humane.[99] Hill, on the other hand, admired its heroic fury, particularly in that "great and soldier-like" passage, "Had all his hairs been lives, / My great revenge had stomach for them all!"

> We see Mr. Barry redden thro' the very black of his face; his whole visage becomes inflamed, his eyes sparkle with successful vengeance, and he seems to raise himself above the ground. . . . As this actor pronounces the words, accompanying the delivery with that exalted and magnificent deportment we feel with the character . . . the hero and husband betray'd, injur'd, and glorying in his insatiable revenge. . . . Nay, so perfectly does the delusion possess us, that we . . . forget for the time . . . that Desdemona was innocent. . . .[100]

CHARLES MACKLIN brought together both aspects of the performance in his tribute: Barry, he said, "described the contrasted passions of *love* and *jealous rage* in a manner much superior" to Booth's, and indeed "to all the Othellos he had ever seen."[101] It is easy to understand, after reading these descriptions, why Barry is considered one of the finest Othellos of the English stage. (COLLEY CIBBER, we are told, preferred him to Betterton.[102]) In realizing the emotions proper to hero and lover, he was also arousing the pity and terror prescribed by the classical definition of tragedy.

One actor-critic of that period, however—THOMAS SHERIDAN—seems to have emphasized the "hero" in Othello almost exclusively.

98. Theophilus Cibber, "The Life and Character . . . of Barton Booth, Esq.," in *The Lives and Characters of the Most Eminent Actors and Actresses* (London, 1753), p. 50.

99. *A Treatise on the Passions*, p. 35.

100. *The Actor*, pp. 9-10.

101. [William Cooke], *Memoirs of Charles Macklin, Comedian* (London, 1804), p. 16. There are interesting relationships among Macklin, Hill, Foote, and Barry. Both Hill and Foote had been members of a group of amateurs whom Macklin trained for the stage and brought out in 1744, *Othello* being the first play that he produced with them. Foote, in fact, made his debut in Othello, with his instructor as Iago. Although Barry was not Macklin's "product" in this way, Davies tells us (*Dramatic Miscellanies*, III, 441) that Barry's Othello owed "many admirable strokes of passion" to Macklin's suggestions.

102. [Cooke], *Memoirs of Macklin*, p. 183.

He could not join in the all-but-universal admiration for Barry's interpretation because "Mr Barry acted the distress of Othello, the Moorish warrior whose stubborn soul was hard to bend, and that of Castalio [In Otway's *The Orphan*], the gentle lover who was all tenderness, in the self-same way."[103] Insofar as this brief statement can tell us, Sheridan's conception differed somewhat from the others of his period: his stern, inflexible warrior seems less human than the Othello described by Cibber and Foote and less fiery than the one described by Hill. (Sheridan's own Othello was hardly a moving performance. FRANCIS GENTLEMAN remarked that if "meaning alone" could satisfy an audience, this actor might have been highly esteemed in the part, "but execution being as necessary as conception, we can only afford him the praise of barren propriety."[104])

In one respect at least, these Othellos—Sheridan's included—are all alike: they are men of stature; there is no hint of pettiness in any of them, no taint of baseness. Their pathos is not marred by sentimentality; their fury, savage as it may be, speaks of anguish or exaltation, never of natural barbarity. GARRICK's description of "an African in whose veins circulated fire instead of blood" does suggest a rather primitive Othello, but the emphasis (as far as we can tell from Morellet's account) seems to be upon the terrible rather than upon the brutal or the sordid. Othello might have been, in Garrick's view, a savage, but if so he was a noble savage. Indeed there is no interpretation of Othello advanced by an actor-critic of that period that might not bear the stamp of nobility upon it.

The conception of Othello's character expressed by most nineteenth century actor-critics is much like that of the preceding century: Othello is basically a noble character, capable of great fire but also capable of great tenderness. Again, actors' descriptions of Othello's character are frequently related to their critiques of other actors' performances—to Edmund Kean's or Tommaso Salvini's or Edwin Booth's, just as in the earlier period they were related to Barton Booth's or Spranger Barry's.

Kean's Othello, like Barry's, was praised for its combination of passion and pathos. JUNIUS BRUTUS BOOTH once told his son

103. *Boswell's London Journal, 1762-1763*, ed. Frederick A. Pottle (New York and London, 1950), pp. 135-36.
104. *Dramatic Censor*, I, 152.

Edwin that "in his opinion no mortal man could equal Kean in the rendering of *Othello*'s despair and rage; and that above all, his not very melodious voice in many passages, notably that ending with 'Farewell, *Othello*'s occupation's gone,' sounded like the moan of ocean or the soughing of wind through cedars." EDWIN BOOTH himself, though he had never seen Kean, believed from what he had heard that this actor, because of his ability to "express Othello's tenderness, as well as his sombre and fiercer passions, must have been capable of portraying the sublimest, subtlest, and profoundest emotions."[105] And WILLIAM WOOD named Othello, along with Hamlet, Lear, and Richard II as parts in which Kean showed his highest talent because they "mingle the tender with the severe."[106]

Some actor-critics, however, found fault with Kean's fiery Othello. JOHN PHILIP KEMBLE granted that the execution was brilliant but regarded the whole conception as "a mistake, the fact being that the Moor was a slow man." THOMAS COOPER, who agreed, particularly condemned Kean for his "snarling, snappish speech and his gusty flights of vehement passion," which, he said, "are directly opposed to the physical and intellectual forces of Othello." That Othello is meant to be a massive rather than a frenetic force seemed evident to Cooper "by the conscious deliberation and dignity of language in which Shakespeare has presented the character" and by Othello's past life as a soldier, which would have taught him "the force of unyielding discipline." Such a man, when he lets "the curb once snap," is more terrible than one who is more easily moved. According to Cooper, Kean was "not susceptible to the full force of the . . . tumultuous passions" which "seethed" in Othello's heart and which finally burst forth in "the majestic passion of the roused lion conscious of power."[107]

Such objections to Kean's Othello, though they differed in substance from Sheridan's protest against Barry's impersonation,

105. Edwin Booth, "A Few Words about Edmund Kean," in *Actors and Actresses of Great Britain and the United States,* ed. Brander Matthews and Lawrence Hutton (New York, 1886), III, 7.

106. *Personal Recollections of the Stage,* p. 379.

107. James Murdoch, *The Stage: or Recollections of Actors and Acting, from an Experience of Fifty Years. A Series of Dramatic Sketches* (Philadelphia, 1880), pp. 143-45. Murdoch reports a discussion which Cooper held with "a company of gentlemen" at his home "on the banks of the Delaware, Pennsylvania."

were probably based on the same kind of reasoning: i.e. anything that reduced the stature of the great general, whether tenderness or fits of rage, did violence to Shakespeare's conception. What these critics wanted was a naturally majestic, unyielding figure who gave the impression of controlled fury until the breaking point was finally reached and a tidal wave of emotion inundated the scene. This conception is particularly hard to express in action, however. Neither Kemble nor Cooper could match Kean in dramatic effectiveness. The former, according to ELIZABETH INCHBALD, sustained the "grandeur" of the character very well but was deficient in Othello's "wonderful *simplicity.*" An Othello with Kemble's "penetrating eye," she decided, would have obliged Iago to abandon any attempt at deception.[108] Cooper, a hand-some, well-built man with an eloquent voice, might have expected to present an imposing Othello. But his "slow" Moor held his "native fires" in check until the last act and, to quote one critic, disappointed the audience by his "tameness and equanimity."[109] Ironically the little Kean, with his petty conception—as Cooper considered it—inspired critics to such epithets as "lion-like" and such images of grandeur as "the marble aspect of Dante's Count Ugolino."[110] Actually those actor-critics who admired Kean's interpretation were no less firmly convinced of Othello's nobility than the others; they simply held different ideas about the characteristics that convey this effect on the stage and those that detract from it.

Another protest against pettiness was made by WILLIAM CHARLES MACREADY in his criticism of Charles Fechter—pettiness that took the form of literal-mindedness on the one hand and melodramatic showmanship on the other. Fechter could not perceive, said Macready, that Shakespeare "in his profound knowl-

108. *See* Elizabeth Inchbald's manuscript of her introduction to *Othello,* written for *The British Theatre,* Vol. V. The printed version of the introduction contains the statement about Kemble's "penetrating eye" but omits the two sentences commenting on his failure to convey the impression of Othello's simplicity. Mrs. Inchbald's friendship with the Kembles probably caused her to lighten her criticism of Kemble's Othello by deleting this passage. The manuscript is in the Folger Library.

109. *See* Isaac Harby, *A Selection from the Miscellaneous Writings* (Charleston, South Carolina, 1829), pp. 260-71.

110. Lewes, *On Actors and the Art of Acting,* p. 133; *Complete Works of Hazlitt,* ed. Howe, XVIII, 263 (from "Mr. Kean's Othello," originally published in the London *Times,* October 27, 1817).

edge of the human heart" sometimes gives his characters "language
. . . in direct contradiction of the feelings that oppress them." De-
servedly censured was a particularly vulgar piece of business just
before Othello's suicide: Fechter dragged Iago to Desdemona's
bedside and forced him to kneel; at the words "circumcised dog"
he seemed ready to stab Iago but stabbed himself instead. For
Macready, the French actor demonstrated his "complete blindness
as to the emotions of the character" by this "demission of [Othel-
lo's] lofty nature to bestow a thought upon that miserable thing,
Iago, when his great mind had made itself up to die!"[111]

In the latter part of the nineteenth century appeared the
Othello frequently described as the greatest interpretation of all
time, that of Tommaso Salvini. As we saw earlier, Salvini's fellow actors in England and America lavishly praised his performance. Most of them, however, also pointed out instances of
what they considered poor taste. E. L. DAVENPORT was willing to
grant that, in the context of Salvini's interpretation, such apparent offenses seemed "all right and to the purpose,"[112] but
some of his colleagues were less broad-minded. CLARA MORRIS, for
example, was reminded of "a tiger's spring upon a lamb" when,
in the greeting at Cyprus, Salvini's Othello "fiercely swept into
his swarthy arms the pale loveliness of Desdemona . . . . Passion
choked, his gloating eyes burned with the mere lust of the 'sooty
Moor' for that white creature of Venice. It was revolting, and with
a shiver I exclaimed aloud, 'Ugh, you splendid brute!' "[113] FRANK
ARCHER objected to Salvini's "seizing Desdemona by the hair of her
head" in the murder scene and "half dragging her across the
stage." Most offensive of all was the shockingly realistic manner
of the suicide: "With a short scimitar he literally cut or hacked
at his throat, and fell to the ground gasping and gurgling."[114]
SQUIRE BANCROFT agreed that this was "too like an animal dying

111. *Macready's Reminiscences and Selections from His Diaries,* ed. Sir Frederick Pollock (New York, 1875), p. 693. Macready based his criticism on a study
of Fechter's acting edition, sent to him by Lady Pollock. He had not seen the
actual performance. For a description of Fechter's stage business preceding
Othello's suicide see Sprague, *Shakespeare and the Actors,* p. 221.

112. *See* Davenport's letter to William Winter, dated November 2, 1873. MS
in the Folger Library.

113. Clara Morris, *Stage Confidences: Talks about Players and Play Acting*
(Boston, 1902), p. 240.

114. *An Actor's Notebooks,* p. 168.

in the shambles."[115] But most of the English-speaking actors, though shocked and disgusted (sometimes fascinated as well) by Salvini's occasional effects of animalism or vulgarity, would have agreed with Archer that these were but "spots on the sun," that the performance as a whole was "beyond praise."[116]

Whatever its momentary deviations from the Victorian ideal (and even a modern reader can agree that an "appeal to the morbid" was ill-advised at the ultimate moment of Shakespeare's overwhelming tragedy), Salvini's performance was undeniably based on the concept of Othello's nobility. This is clear, both from his own description of the character[117] and from Archer's account of the performance, the longest and most detailed one provided by an English-speaking actor.[118] The latter is full of such adjectives as "magnificent," "superb," "splendid," and "noble." It presents Salvini's interpretation as "a magnanimous one," "that of a simple but grand nature that finds the statements of Iago utterly incomprehensible" but, when forced to believe them, is swept by an "anger and grief [which bears] everything before it." Nobility is suggested, too, in other actors' critiques of Salvini's performance, notably in their descriptions of the Senate scene: Bancroft was impressed by Salvini's calm, motionless dignity here,[119] and Clara Morris was full of admiration for the "splendid presence, the bluff, soldierly manner, the open, honest look" which "made one understand, partly at least, how . . . [Desdemona] had come at last to see Othello's visage in his mind."[120]

Archer's praise of Salvini recalls earlier tributes to Barton Booth, Barry, and Kean, particularly in the statement that Salvini combined "in an extraordinary degree, two great qualities—tenderness and power." His descriptions of memorable scenes in the performance provide many illustrations of both characteristics. The softer virtue is noted, for example, in the Senate scene, when Salvini's "eyes and features" expressed, during Desdemona's speeches, a "fond and loving exultation," and in the "beautifully

115. *Empty Chairs*, p. 157.
116. *An Actor's Notebooks*, p. 168.
117. *See* Tommaso Salvini, "My Interpretation of Othello," *Putnam's Magazine*, III (October, 1907), 23-28.
118. *An Actor's Notebooks*, pp. 164-68.
119. *Empty Chairs*, p. 157.
120. *Stage Confidences*, p. 240.

rendered" reunion at Cyprus (obviously Miss Morris' objection was not universal) ; even in the brothel scene, as Archer recalls it, the "bitter sarcasm" was countered by moments of "exquisite pathos." Greater still, however, is the emphasis given to the tempestuous power of Salvini's Othello. From his leonine force in stopping the Cassio-Montano fight to the savage fury of the fifth act, Salvini moved his admirer to praise which, the latter admits, can only sound "extravagant." But it is in Act III, with its crescendo of passion, that the "unequalled display of tragic power" is best recalled in terms of specific action. Strikingly memorable, for example, is the description of the "marvellous effect" that Salvini produced "when he seized Iago by the throat and threw him down as if to trample the life out of him: then suddenly remembering himself, he gave him his hand and helped him to his feet." Even Clara Morris remembered with admiration —though no doubt with another shiver—the picture presented in that climactic moment by "the perfect animal man, in his splendid prime, . . . in a very frenzy of conscious strength."[121]

Very different in both conception and performance was the Othello of Edwin Booth, American contemporary of Salvini. Booth's idea of the character has already been lightly and somewhat obliquely suggested through his comment on Edmund Kean, but it deserves fuller consideration. For Booth's portrayal of Othello, though usually regarded as inferior to his Iago, was among the best that the English-speaking theatre had to offer in his time; and his notes on the play, preserved in the *Furness Variorum,* provided much insight into his interpretation of both characters.

In one single matter—the central one—was Booth's conception like Salvini's: a conviction of Othello's nobility. In his criticism, indeed, we find almost unremitting insistence upon this point. But this nobility was of too refined and gentle a type to produce the awe-inspiring avalanche of power that overwhelmed the audience when Salvini (or Barry or Kean) performed the role. Booth was particularly repelled by any suggestion of primitivism or brutality, and he was saddened when those who saw his performance failed to understand his attempted idealization. In a letter to William Winter he complained:

121. *Ibid.*

A Shakespearian (?) friend—who gloats over my Iago—fails to discover in Othello—either read or acted (by me or any one)—anything but a "beast"—as Shakespeare intended him to be! Did you ever?! ! ! I cannot possibly see the least animalism in him—to my mind he is pure & noble; even in his rage . . . I perceive no beastiality.[122]

Booth's ideal Othello, revealed in his detailed *Variorum* notes, was a "modest, simple-hearted gentleman," a man of quiet dignity, "not a braggart as Iago would make him out." His speech before the Senate should be spoken without "a breath of bluster" or declamatory flourish; his anger, aroused by Cassio's drunken brawl, should be "restrained . . . not loud."[123] Othello's feeling for Desdemona seemed to Booth a vital but also an ideal love, touched with delicacy and gentleness. Several times in his directions to the actor he points up the tender, almost spiritual quality of this love. For example, when husband and wife meet in Cyprus he warns them to "embrace, with delicacy," and he even prefers to omit the customary kisses. In the very midst of his later suspicions of Desdemona, Othello's tenderness continues to be evident. When she offers to bind his head with her handkerchief, Booth advises the actor: "gently push the handkerchief from her hand. . . . Pass her . . . with forced indifference, but turn lovingly, and holding your arms for her to enter them, say, 'Come, I'll go in with thee.' Then with a long soulful look into her eyes, fold her tenderly to your heart and go slowly off."[124] Booth thought that most actors showed Othello becoming jealous too quickly and remaining too constantly infuriated. By correcting these faults he evidently sought to give the impression of a man "not easily jealous."[125] Throughout, his comments reveal an Othello of more grief than rage. At "I'll tear her all to pieces!" (III, iii, 432) even Booth allows the "*savage* [to] have vent,"—"but," he cautions, "for the moment only; when Othello next speaks he is tame again and speaks sadly."[126] Booth's murder scene was a quiet one compared with the usual stage interpretation, and particularly com-

122. MS letter in the Folger Library, written from London, February 15, 1881.
123. *Furness Variorum*, VI, 23-24, 54, 141.
124. *Ibid.*, pp. 112, 194.
125. See Booth's comments on the first temptation scene, Act III, scene iii, *Furness Variorum*, VI, 181. See also his MS letter to William Winter, dated June 4 [1878?], in the Folger Library.
126. *Furness Variorum*, VI, 208. See also his directions (p. 190) for speaking "If I do prove her haggard. . . ." (III, iii, 260-63).

pared with Salvini's.[127] When he acted Othello in Vienna, the critics felt that his quiet fifth act spoiled the effect of his third and fourth, which they praised highly. Wrote Booth in annoyance: "They want the *howler* here. . . . I don't care! They can't make me *yank* Desdemona about the floor like a clothes bag."[128]

Booth's Othello drew a mixed response from his fellow actors. OTIS SKINNER describes it as "infinitely human and at the same time infinitely poetic and lovely," showing, like his Macbeth, "flashes . . . of alternating spirit and depression; sweeps of passion and depths of sorrow; levels of splendid dignity, and moments of uncontrolled weakness."[129] JOHN MARTIN-HARVEY praises the "large and simple style" that made Booth's Othello a "very dignified figure" in contrast to Henry Irving's "grotesque" one (this apropos of the famous series of performances in London, 1881, when Booth and Irving alternated the roles of Othello and Iago).[130] FREDERICK WARDE, however, did not appreciate Booth's "poetic" Othello. In his memoirs he states bluntly: "Mr. Booth was not suited to the character of Othello, either by physique or temperament. He lacked the virility of John McCullough and the ferocity of Salvini."[131]

Throughout the nineteenth century there was, as far as I know, only one actor-critic who specifically questioned Othello's nobility. This was HELEN FAUCIT. As in her remarks on Hamlet, her partiality for the heroine and her sense of personal identification with this character were probably responsible for her harsh judgment of the hero. Othello's description of himself as "not easily jealous" struck Miss Faucit as extremely ironic and indicative of self-ignorance. "It seems to me," she wrote, "that the spark scarcely touches the tinder before it is aflame." Marveling, too, at Othello's belief in Iago's honesty, she asserted that, even if such credulity is granted, Othello cannot be excused for listening to his slanders of Desdemona. He should have realized that some men, though "manly" and "fairly decorous . . . in their conduct," are "quite incapable of conceiving the noblest qualities of

127. *Ibid.*, pp. 297-303.
128. MS letter in the Folger Library, written to William Winter and dated April 5, 1883.
129. *Footlights and Spotlights* (Indianapolis, 1924), p. 99.
130. *Autobiography* (London, [1933]), p. 42.
131. *Fifty Years of Make-Believe* (New York, 1920), p. 120.

womanhood"; Iago, therefore, "might be in a sense 'honest,' yet totally unfit to speak . . . on such a subject."

Had Othello been really the "noble Moor," as "true of mind" as Desdemona thought him, he would, at the lightest aspersion of his wife, have recoiled from Iago as from a serpent. He would have crushed the insolent traducer and his vile suggestions beneath his heel in bitterest contempt.[132]

The essay in which Miss Faucit made these remarks—the first negative criticism of Othello's character by an actor—was originally published in 1881, but her ideas were probably formed when she was acting Desdemona some forty-five years earlier. Yet, even though her reasoning and her phraseology are those of a Victorian lady, her accusation of self-ignorance has a very modern ring.

A generation after the publication of Helen Faucit's essay came another hint—this time an ambiguous one, from LOUIS CALVERT—that there might be cracks in Othello's armor of nobility. Calvert interpreted Othello as a tragedy of *hybris;* and, although this interpretation need not have involved any diminution of nobility, the wording does suggest that possibility. Certainly the vainglorious egoist of his description is in strong contrast to Booth's "modest, simple-hearted gentleman."

[Othello's] manner is grandiose, and it would be overbearing and offensive were it not for his great dignity. Forbes-Robertson and Lewis Waller both played Othello and failed to make any noteworthy success. . . . They made Othello a lover; and consequently the real tragedy of the story, indeed the point of it, was lost. Othello, Lear, Macbeth, and Coriolanus are all tragedies of overconceit, tragedies of the downfall of men who had an exaggerated belief in their power. They believe themselves super-men, and the tragedy of each play comes when, because of this, they are hurled from their high place.[133]

Calvert's objection to the "lover" interpretation and his comparison of Othello to Coriolanus and Macbeth suggest that this actor-critic belongs in the tradition of Thomas Sheridan and John Philip Kemble (Sheridan's phrase "stubborn soul" would fit appropriately into Calvert's description) but that Calvert saw the very grandeur of Othello as a manifestation of moral weakness. Since the same thing might be said of many noble heroes, Calvert's view of Othello could be termed "noble" or not, depending upon

132. *On Some of Shakespeare's Female Characters,* pp. 61-63.
133. *Problems of an Actor,* pp. 234-35.

the manner in which it might be translated into action on the stage. But the concept of Othello as a victim of his own arrogance rather than as the wholly innocent and admirable victim of a conniving villain is in itself unusual for an actor of Calvert's time. Whatever the implications of Calvert's discussion, they were not followed up by other actor-critics. Although the present century has seen a complete about-face in Othello criticism by scholars and literary men, most actors, on and off the stage, have deviated very little from the traditional sympathetic view.

This does not mean that the modern interpretations are all alike. Actually they offer a number of variations in details, some of them significant ones. Although most of the actor-critics accept the idea of a noble character, at least in the beginning of the play, they differ somewhat in describing Othello's intellect and personality. The major differences appear, however, in discussions of his fall—its implications and effects. A comparison of interpretations by HARLEY GRANVILLE-BARKER,[134] ROBERT SPEAIGHT,[135] and GEORGE SKILLAN[136] will reveal the variety of ideas held by actor-critics who begin with more or less traditional assumptions.

What is Othello like, according to these men, when we first see him? Granville-Barker depicts him as "a quite exceptional man; in high repute and conscious of his worth, yet not self-conscious; of a dignity which simplicity does not jeopardize; generous in praise of those who serve him; commanding respect without fear." Salvini and his devotees would have accepted this description without question; so would Booth and his. Speaight, in his analysis, comes close to the noble savage conception that Garrick evidently held: Othello is "primitive and *naif*," but he has "the habit of command." Skillan, most extravagant of actor-critics in his claims for Othello's greatness, endows him with higher intellectual gifts than are generally attributed to the character and thus reduces his simplicity (any element of primitivism disappears); but, if possible, he increases the effect of nobility. According to him, Othello is shown throughout the first

134. *Prefaces to Shakespeare*, II, 32-33, 107, 112-20.

135. *Nature in Shakespearian Tragedy*, pp. 75-80. The same discussion of *Othello* as that found on pp. 70-81 was published in French two years before it appeared in the book just cited ("Reflexions sur Othello," *Mercure de France*, CCCXVIII [1953], 478-93).

136. Notes in *French's Acting Edition of Othello*, pp. 12, 14, 26, 33, 38, 39, 42, 43, 45, 47, 48, 51, 60, 67, 81, 82, 86, 93.

two acts to be calm, firm, and self-disciplined, "a character based on certainties." Toward others he is "trusting, generous and wholesome" in his attitudes, absolutely impartial in his justice. He is the kind of man who refuses to act upon mere suspicion or rumor but investigates the facts and arrives at reasonable conclusions. Particularly striking in his character is the pull toward greatness, "his high ideals and determined effort to reach those ideals."

For the reader of these descriptions one question is inevitable: How could such a man have been successfully fooled, tortured, and wrought upon to murder his loving and virtuous wife? Here is the crux for modern actors of Othello (and here, of course, is the reason that some modern literary critics reject the traditional image of the character) : the problem of credibility stemming from Othello's gullibility and from the resulting upheaval and reversal in his character. Although they realize that an actor of Iago can do much to make Othello's belief in him seem credible, some of the actor-critics feel compelled to search Othello's own psychology and experience for further explanation.

In his analysis Granville-Barker brings out a number of points which help the reader to reconcile Othello's nobility with his vulnerability to Iago's temptation. A particularly interesting one is the interrelationship of Othello's view of himself and his view of other people—a potentially dangerous tie since the undermining of one makes it easier to assault the other. Being "no egoist," Othello spontaneously translates his serene and justifiable self-confidence into faith in others. But faith given without question is hardest of all to restore once it is lost: thus Othello may forgive Cassio for the drunken brawl, but he can never feel quite the same toward him again. And disillusionment in one he has trusted results in "some latent loss of self-confidence too." Another vulnerable point in Othello's character is his powerful imagination, the kind that can make for either greatness or disaster. Since he "has exercised it in spiritual solitude . . . it is the less sophisticated and the more easily to be victimized by alien suggestion." Othello's limited use of his analytical and speculative abilities during an active, nonintellectual life has not prepared him to combat Iago's suggestions or to probe for concealed motives. He is further vulnerable because of his lack of experience with jealousy: being free of envy and distrust himself, he does not notice these qualities in others; and he has never before cared enough for a woman to be jealous of her. The newness of his experience with love, which has come to him later than to most men, puts him at a disadvantage in spite of the joy that it has brought him. Finally, there is the matter of Othello's black skin, which, along with the rootlessness of his past life, has contributed to his isolation from the other characters. Granville-Barker sees in the character, admirable and sympathetic though it is, all these potential weaknesses for Iago to work upon. Yet the final step from jealousy to murder is one that, apparently, he cannot explain; for he finds the "descent to catastrophe" shockingly "sudden and swift." The Othello whom we saw at the outset, he insists, could not have murdered Desdemona; "an ignorant brute in him" performs the deed. Othello's tragedy is "to have proved that from the seemingly securest heights of his 'soul's content' there is no depth of savagery to which man cannot fall."

For Speaight, Othello's jealousy seems so sudden and the change in the quality of his love so complete that the transformation can be accounted for only by Freudian speculations about the couple's extra-dramatic life. Perhaps the "experience of consummation was so strong and . . . so startling" that the hitherto "chivalrous" Othello could never regard the "gentle" Desdemona in "quite the same way" again; there must have been "something in their mutual delectation . . . which added fuel to his jealousy." Thus the man whose greeting at Cyprus suggests "the sublimity, not the sensuality of love," behaves a short time later like any other suspicious lover; and as he yields more and more to jealousy "his language becomes charged with physical and sexual allusions." The subsequent descent to savagery proves that "the primitive instincts of his race were always strong in him; . . . the veneer of civilized man, acquired by the discipline of military service and the . . . [acceptance of Christianity], were only superficially grafted on them; . . . an animality, of whose force and fury he was probably unconscious, lurked behind an habitual control."

Skillan is the only one of these actor-critics who is satisfied to attribute Othello's fall solely to Iago's persistence and craft. The reader receives the impression that, in his opinion, no human being, whatever his character, could have resisted the unremitting mental and emotional pressure that Othello undergoes. Once convinced of Desdemona's perfidy, Skillan writes, Othello becomes the victim of his own greatness, for "force of any kind if obstructed in one direction will break out in another." The power of his love manifests itself in his suffering; "it holds him on the rack where something of less selfless quality would snap its tie." He embraces hatred as a relief, for "agony seeks to destroy what it cannot endure. But . . . the essence is indestructible." He goes through a brief period of madness, but emerges into a "highly wrought sanity exalted to the pitch of intense moral power." Now able to love the offender while condemning the offense, he is nevertheless convinced that her sacrifice is necessary. It is in this state that he kills her.

But the greatest differences among these interpretations occur in their final views of Othello's character. Granville-Barker's is totally pessimistic: "Harrowing" as it is to witness the destruction of "such beauty and nobility and happiness," the experience effects no catharsis "since Othello's own soul stays unpurged . . . what alchemy can now bring the noble Moor and the savage murderer into unity again? . . . Othello wakes as from a nightmare only to kill himself, his prospect hell." Speaight, however, sees a certain restoration of nobility at the end of the play: Othello's repentance and self-execution stop short of "perfect contrition" since "his thought is too exclusively centred upon himself. But he does recover a measure of stoical self respect. . . . Like Cleopatra, he will make death proud to take him." At the opposite extreme from Granville-Barker is Skillan. He has no doubt that Othello's grandeur is completely restored at the end of the play, that in his last speech and his suicide he returns to "repose," to an ordered union of "nobility, courage and love" as great as before if not greater.

Of these three actor-critics, then, only Granville-Barker sees an ultimate and irreparable loss of nobility. And, since he insists as strongly as anyone upon the true nobility of Othello's character at the beginning, he can hardly be forced into the tiny group of actor-critics who have reversed the telescope of tradition before making their observations.

There is one modern actor, however, who has offered us a reduced view of Othello and—to change the figure—impudently forced a pigmy to carry a giant's load. This, of course, is SIR LAURENCE OLIVIER. Although it is doubtful that Olivier's study of Othello owed anything to the discussions of other actor-critics, his published comments on the character, setting forth the interpretation that he used in his 1964 performance, interestingly combine Helen Faucit's idea of self-delusion and Louis Calvert's idea of excessive pride. He and his director, John Dexter, had rejected the traditional interpretation of a noble but naive Othello and had adopted, instead, the idea of a man only moderately good but marked somehow with the self-affixed label of nobility. Olivier argued that Othello's complacent egotism in the Senate scene amply demonstrates a false conception of his own lofty nature. But the Othello described by Olivier, though he lacks self-knowledge, is more canny than the traditional hero in his dealings with other people. At the beginning of the temptation scene he actually suspects Iago's real motive, and he gives play to his insinuations in order to probe for the truth. In doing so, however, he unexpectedly falls under the spell of suspicion and becomes jealous without understanding what has happened. (In Olivier's opinion, this interpretation gives Othello a needed ascendancy over Iago and, by diminishing his gullibility, makes him more credible and more tragic to a modern audience.) Why does an Othello, aware of possible treachery, fall into the trap in spite of himself? The chief reason is the false "self-image": believing himself impervious to irrational emotion, he overconfidently exposes himself to Iago's suggestions. Another reason is his savage and pagan background which reasserts itself once the unsuspected emotion is aroused. He is a prey as well to the irrational but all too human desire to find the loved one guilty. And his temptation to murder is a universal one.[137]

Olivier's comments are more in line with the views of certain nontheatrical critics of recent years than with either traditional stage interpretations or—with the two exceptions already mentioned—the views openly expressed by actors. (Olivier seems to have been influenced primarily by F. R. Leavis, but there are several other critics and scholars with similar interpretations: among them, Robert Heilman, Leo Kirschbaum, and George R. Elliott.[138]) Marvin Rosenberg, in preparing his book *The Masks*

137. "The Great Sir Laurence," p. 88.
138. See F. R. Leavis, "Diabolic Intellect and the Noble Hero: A Note on Othello," *Scrutiny*, VI (1937), 259-83; Leo Kirschbaum, "The Modern Othello," *ELH*, II (December, 1944), 283-96; G. R. Elliott, *Flaming Minister* (Durham, North Carolina, 1953), *passim*; Robert Heilman, *Magic in the Web* (Lexington, Kentucky, 1956), pp. 137-68.

of Othello, asked six leading representatives of Othello on the British and American stage—Earle Hyman, Anthony Quayle, Paul Robeson, Abraham Sofaer, Wilfred Walter, and Sir Donald Wolfit —to express their opinions about the idea that Othello speaks in flamboyant language to cover an immature need for assurance and the idea that Othello is self-deceived into an opinion of his own nobility. With one voice the actors responded negatively to both suggestions. Rosenberg himself stated that "the weight of acting intuition rejects any interpretation centering on self-deception or pretended nobility. So does the weight of critical intuition."[139] That was in 1961. Did the climate of opinion change in so short a time? Or did Olivier by his powerful depiction of Othello's suffering create a sympathy that the audience might not be expected to feel for an egotistical, self-deceived character such as he described?

The "volcanic passions" so often mentioned by *Othello* critics are forcefully realized by anyone who merely listens to the recording of Olivier's performance. The arrogance is discernible, but it is more like the *hybris* of an Agamemnon than the overcompensation of an insecure braggart. Viewers of the film version may get an impression nearer to Olivier's declared intention, for such mannerisms as the self-congratulatory grin and the ungainly prance (hardly the prowl of Olivier's imaginary "soft black leopard," though the camera may have distorted the original effect) seem to reduce visually the size of a character that is audially tremendous.

Although most of the early criticisms of Othello by actors may seem rather mechanical and naive in comparison with some recent ones, it is well for us to listen again to the old simplicities, the old certainties they represent: Othello is a hero—a *real* hero, not an arrogant fraud; Othello is a lover—a lover of Desdemona, not himself. Of the recent criticisms Skillan's is most like an elaboration of the earlier ones, and this is good—up to a point. Some of his elaborations, however, seem to be inspired by his own idea of nobility rather than by anything in the text. Speaight's suggestion about Othello's nuptial night is rather like Keats's concern for the nonexistent little town, "emptied of its folk this pious morn." The only person who could possibly benefit by it would be an actor who is trying to convince himself that Othello could *really*

139. Rosenberg, *The Masks of Othello,* pp. 189-91.

be as jealous as Shakespeare makes him. Perhaps such an actor should simply forget about playing Othello.

For me, at least, Granville-Barker's analysis is the most interesting and helpful of all, as long as it is dealing with Othello's basic character and particularly with its points of vulnerability. Granville-Barker gave up, however, before the end: because he detected in the noble Othello no early signs of a potential murderer, he found Shakespeare's conclusion unsatisfactory as either "life"or art. The fact that the hero's fall is engineered by outside agency prevents catharsis, as he thought, for no meaningful self-recognition can take place. But this is to demand a rigid "tragic flaw" formula which may not be essential to produce tragic effects. Logical analysis may carry the critic a significant distance, but there is a point at which poetry and passion must be allowed to take over. Had Granville-Barker yielded at that point, he might have believed, even if he could not have demonstrated, that the man he had described was, under such circumstances, capable of committing murder. We need not suppose that Othello is an egoist in order to enter into his feeling that Desdemona's perfidy is a blow to his very selfhood: "there where I have garnered up my heart, / Where either I must live or bear no life." Nor, in our receptive state, can we escape the horror of her self-desecration as he imagines it: the rottenness and filth beneath the alabaster perfection. To imagine that this demon-driven man should murder the supposed betrayer is not hard to do, once we have allowed ourselves to enter the emotions suggested by his words. To insist that a brave, generous, and loving man could not have felt this way smacks of the "bookish theoric." It is actually unrealistic; and, even if it were not, it would not apply here: for everything points to the fact that in this play a brave, generous, and loving man *does* feel in this way. Unless we are busy demonstrating our own perceptiveness, our own knowledge of psychology, we cannot fail to retain our sympathy for a man whom we have seen tortured—as it seems—beyond the limit of his endurance. Yet we cannot say that Iago was totally responsible for Othello's fall. A great and good man *may* allow the "ignorant brute in him" to take charge when he is so beset, but we must feel that he *should* not. Everything may be against him, yet he should resist with that last ounce of strength that he does not know he possesses; should endure that last moment more. Granville-Barker's pessimism at the end is unjustified, for it is contradicted by the sound and meaning of Othello's words. Othello is plunged, at first, into a fury of agony by the recognition of his criminal folly. He comes out of it, however, not cheering himself up, as T. S. Eliot said, but accepting himself—not simply the hideous self that he has come to see but all of himself: a murderer, yet an honorable soldier; a fool, but one capable of great love; a base Indian who threw a pearl away, but who knows at last the value of that pearl. Watching and listening, having glimpsed the "ignorant brute" in ourselves, we see now the broader, more uplifting vision. Granville-Barker is like a man who has crossed the ocean in a boat of his own building; when the boat sinks within sight of the shore, instead of swimming he goes down with his vessel. With a little faith he could have walked the rest of the way.

Olivier's view of Othello, though borrowed from literary sources, is also consonant with his own attitude toward tragedy in general: "to ennoble was not the original purpose of tragedy, at least not through ennobling qualities of its subjects. Its usefulness lay in its power as a cathartic, a jolly good blow in the stomach, purification of the soul through shock treatment, literally." There is surely some truth in the "shock treatment" definition of catharsis. It is not by chance that the world's greatest tragedies are rocked by murder, incest, or madness. But are not these things the more shocking because they are performed or suffered by persons of stature—persons admirable for strength or courage or will power or aspiration? It is largeness of soul, not moral perfection, that we mean when we demand nobility of our tragic heroes. Sometimes an enormous capacity for suffering is enough to give this effect. But the finer and more admirable the hero is in the first place, the more appalling the view of potential human folly or depravity when the barely suspected fissure opens up and the chasm is revealed. We can agree with Olivier that the main concern of the theatre, whether in tragedy or comedy, is "the teaching of the human heart the knowledge of itself." In tragedy the enlightenment that the audience receives is of slower development and longer duration than the moment of recognition that comes to the hero himself, but in that moment it is focused and intensified because of identification with the character. And, however black the light that is shed, the wisdom won through suffering seems at that moment precious. If the hero, in spite of his sin and his fall, retains some semblance of his nobility, it is enhanced and glorified for us in this epiphany. And this accounts for the ennobling effect of tragedy that Olivier denies. Let him deny it as much as he will. Many a spectator who has seen his film of *Othello* must have felt in the last scene, along with the pain and the trancelike repose which follows its final release, a sense of ineffable beauty and inestimable worth. "Anything ennobling about . . . the end of *Lear*? *Othello*?" asks Olivier.[140] He has answered that question himself—and answered it most effectively.

IAGO

Theatrical Opportunities

The idea that the role of Iago offers the actor an opportunity at least comparable to that offered by Othello is usually tacitly assumed if not specifically expressed. Actors as far apart as SAMUEL FOOTE (1747)[141] and SIR LAURENCE OLIVIER (1964)[142] have noted Iago's importance. GEORGE FOSS (1932) went so far as to say that "there is a great danger of his being more interesting than Othello and playing the star off the stage."[143] And, if actions speak louder than words, testimony to Iago's histrionic reputation is offered by such "fencing matches" as those of 1817, when Edmund Kean's new rival, Junius Brutus Booth, gladly (though mistakenly) accepted the challenge of playing Iago to Kean's Othello, and 1881, when Henry Irving and Edwin Booth alternated the two roles, providing for the critics two excellent Iagos and two less satisfactory Othellos.

Yet a few actors have complained that the role of Iago has serious disadvantages. One of these, shortly to be discussed, is the difficulty of making Shakespeare's conception credible on the stage; but this is more of a problem for the interpretation of the play as a whole than a practical hazard for the individual actor, since Iago himself may be theatrically effective even if Shake-

140. Sir Laurence Olivier, "The Tragic Theme," *Plays and Players & Theatre World* (January, 1966), p. 28. I am indebted to David Dreiman for this reference.
141. *Treatise on the Passions*, p. 36.
142. "The Great Sir Laurence," p. 80-A.
143. *What the Author Meant*, p. 79.

speare's overall design is ignored. The disadvantage most often mentioned as a threat to the actor is that Iago's villainy is so flagrant as to alienate his stage representative from the good graces of the audience. COLLEY CIBBER (1740) was apparently unaware of his own deficiencies in acting Iago,[144] but he was conscious of being disliked in the role. When he acted villains like Richard III and Iago, he declared, half of his auditors were convinced that "a great share of the wickedness of them must have been in my own nature." He considered such "Aversion . . . an involuntary commendation" of his acting, but he added that few actors can endure this type of praise.[145] JAMES H. HACKETT decided, after his own attempt at the role (New York, 1828), that it is "one of the most uncertain and least profitable of *great* parts . . . within the whole range of Shakespeare's dramas."[146] Not only did he find it difficult to translate his interpretation into action, but he also agreed with Cibber that the presence of Iago was so "hideous and repulsive" to the audience that the actor's career might be jeopardized in consequence.[147] Even the great EDMUND KEAN, successful in Iago as in Othello, insisted that he had acted the part merely to show that he had carefully studied both characters but that he could not imagine anyone's seriously entertaining the notion of their equality, even if Shakespeare had carried them out side by side to the end of the play. As it is, he said, "Othello holds all the interest . . . while Iago becomes an offensive cypher after the third act." Although Kean had built up much of his reputation on "repulsive" roles, he was, according to William Wood, "deeply sensible to the advantage of being seen occasionally in amiable characters" and he frequently warned young actors against "the passion of distinguishing themselves in the terrible and the guilty."[148] OTIS SKINNER, however, writing in the present century, took the opposite point of view: "An audience loves . . .

144. Davies, *Dramatic Miscellanies*, III, 440-41. According to Davies, Cibber's passion for acting tragic characters "exposed him to severe censure," but he persisted in it to the last. "The truth is, Cibber was endured in . . . [Iago] and other tragic parts, on account of his general merit in comedy."

145. *Apology*, I, 282-84. Cibber himself professes a preference for villains over "characters of admiration" because "they are generally better written . . . and . . . nearer to common life and nature."

146. *Notes, Criticisms, and Correspondence upon Shakespeare's Plays and Actors* (New York, 1863), pp. 309-10.

147. *Ibid.*, p. 306.

148. Wood, *Personal Recollections of the Stage*, pp. 379-80.

to be bullied. Witness how it always responds to the brutal woman-taming of *Petruchio,* the triumphant villainy of *Iago.* . . . The accomplished liar hoodwinking perfectly innocent people. . . . I think it is one reason I have loved to play rascals."[149]

Leaving aside the actor's concern for his public image (which now seems more appropriate to the average Hollywood star than to the serious Shakespearean performer), the role of Iago has usually been much safer to undertake than has that of Othello. For, being less demanding physically and more flexible to interpretation, it is easier to convert into theatrical success. EDWIN BOOTH summed up more than his own experience when he said that "Othello taxed him strenuously, while Iago sat upon him as a thistledown."[150]

The Problem of Credibility

Actor-critics of every period have emphasized the importance of acting Iago in a convincing manner (the character of Othello suffers otherwise, and the whole play becomes incredible); and they have warned particularly against the temptation of overacting his villainy. According to THOMAS DAVIES, the eighteenth century stage had "no proper outline" of Iago until 1744, when Charles Macklin drew a "faithful picture" of the character, with Foote as his Othello. Colley Cibber, an earlier Iago, had been "so drawling and hypocritical, wearing the mask of honesty so loosely, that Othello who is not drawn a fool, must have seen the villain through his thin disguises."[151] We are reminded of Cibber's mistake again in reading a nineteenth-century protest— that of JAMES H. HACKETT—against the conventional Iago of his time who betrayed in his whole appearance and facial expression the "characteristics of a barefaced ruffian."[152] WILLIAM CHARLES MACREADY reproached himself more than once for "scowling" instead of maintaining the "clear expression" necessary to Iago's hypocrisy, and he also reminded himself to strive for greater "abstraction" in the soliloquies (i.e. to convey the impression of really thinking). His attention to these matters paid handsome dividends, for—as he himself wrote (and there was ample confirma-

149. *Footlights and Spotlights,* pp. 67-68.
150. Goodale, *Behind the Scenes with Edwin Booth,* p. 132.
151. *Dramatic Miscellanies,* III, 440-41.
152. *Notes, Criticisms, and Correspondence,* pp. 308-9.

tion from others) —Iago became one of his most "finished person-
ations."[153] Later in the century two other remarkably successful
Iagos—EDWIN BOOTH and HENRY IRVING—reiterated the need for
preserving Iago's apparent guilelessness,[154] and the warning has
been repeated by several modern writers. Since Booth was frequently praised by critics for the plausibility of his Iago,[155] his
advice to other actors is particularly noteworthy: "You must seem
to be what all the characters think and say you are, not what the
spectators know you to be; try to win even *them* by your sincerity. Don't *act* the villain, don't *look* it or *speak* it (by scowling
and growling, I mean) but *think* it all the time."

Attitudes of the actor-critics vary concerning the difficulty of
portraying Iago convincingly. For the actor who is more conscientious than inspired, the problem of Iago's credibility can be
particularly acute. As Hackett remarked, the role is a skillful
blend of "subtlety and hypocrisy," of "direct and sinister motives."
Since the real motives are artfully concealed in varying degrees
according to the particular situation or associate of the moment,
the character took on for Hackett the quality of a kaleidoscopic
design, which he painstakingly sought to analyze, reassemble, and
display intelligently to his audience. At least one critic appreciated his attempt: John Inman, writing in the *New York Evening
Post* (April, 1828), observed that the actor had made Iago "assume
three distinct characters" (to Othello, to Roderigo, and to Cassio)
and had revealed the fourth, or real, character in the soliloquies.
Hackett himself, however, felt that the role had been too difficult
for him and he gave it up, concluding that only an experienced
actor of "great talent in portraying dissimulation" could hope to
produce the proper effect.[156] Perhaps Hackett worked too hard
at distinguishing Iago's several assumed personalities and thus

153. *Macready's Reminiscences,* ed. Pollock, pp. 94, 262, 296. The diary entries
in which Macready criticizes his own performances are those of February 21, 1833,
and January 16, 1834.

154. Throughout his notes on Iago's part Booth stresses sincerity of manner.
See *Furness Variorum,* VI, especially pp. 146 and 214. My quotation is from the
latter page. For Irving's comments, see "My Four Favorite Parts," *The Forum,*
XVI [September, 1893], pp. 35-36.

155. *See* Arthur Colby Sprague, *Shakespearian Players and Performances* (Cambridge, Mass., 1953), p. 126. Sprague's valuable description of Booth's Iago is
found on pp. 121-35.

156. Hackett, *Notes, Criticisms, and Correspondence,* pp. 296-305 (Inman's
critique); pp. 309-10 (Hackett's own opinion).

magnified his task beyond reason. On the other hand, MARGARET WEBSTER, whose involvement with the role has been less personal, probably oversimplifies the problem. In fact, the problem of Iago's credibility does not exist for her "so long as the actor does not interfere." All the characters believe in his honesty, she reminds us; even Emilia, who comes close to guessing the truth, fails to identify her husband as the source of the villainy she suspects. Iago's self-assurance is so great and Shakespeare's writing of the part so "dazzling" that if the actor is careful to preserve a façade of honesty the audience, too, will "accept Iago hook, line, and sinker."[157]

It is easy to issue warnings against making Iago's villainy too obvious, but there is no general agreement as to the characteristics that contribute to an impression of obvious villainy. Nor, to put the matter another way, is there any consensus about the kind of man most likely to deceive.

For some actors, like Edwin Booth, a "sinuous" charmer, hiding his hatred under a smooth, genial exterior, is exactly the character to seduce Othello's mind.[158] LENA ASHWELL is one of this group: for the Iago of her conception, though "fiendishly malignant," wins the trust of his victims by his "frank and lovable ways."[159] And Henry Irving is another: he points out that, although Iago is "a simple soldier and no politician," he has the traits of Machiavelli's "Italian adventurer" as Macaulay described him—a man who masks hatred and revenge with a cordial smile and stabs his rival in a friendly embrace.[160] To him, and to the others of this persuasion, a costume and manner suggestive of Machiavelli seemed appropriate. Even though Irving, in acting the part, did not abstain from the "devices of the stage" as completely as his theory demanded, he evidently did draw a sharp distinction between Iago's outward geniality and his real villainy. ELLEN TERRY, who acted Desdemona with him, considered his Iago convincingly "honest" except when he deliberately revealed his true nature in the soliloquies and with Emilia;[161] and GEORGE FOSS testifies, "His marvellously expressive face enabled him to keep up the

157. *Shakespeare Without Tears*, pp. 232-33.
158. *Furness Variorum*, VI, 214.
159. *Reflections from Shakespeare*, pp. 104-5.
160. "My Four Favorite Parts," pp. 35-36.
161. *The Story of My Life* (London, 1908), p. 206.

appearance of blunt honesty and yet to show his devilish enjoyment of the torture he is inflicting on Othello."[162]

For other actor-critics, however, a stocky figure and a rude, downright manner are essential to "honest Iago." A graceful Italianate look and a smooth style of expression are enough to arouse instant suspicion. There have even been protests against a dark-haired Iago. James H. Hackett objected to the black wig and heavy eyebrows used by the conventional Iago of his stage, not only because they were tasteless attempts to proclaim his villainy on sight, but also because—as Hackett assured his readers —there have been more blonds than brunets in actual criminal records.[163] FRANK MAYO was even more exacting in his requirements, though he was hardly so earnest in his convictions: Iago should be "a blond," yes, but he should also be "fat . . . almost lazy; even perspiring!" Booth's famous Iago was, in Mayo's opinion, "inartistic," too attractive to be convincing; for "no good-looking, graceful man is ever spoken of as honest. . . . When there is no adjective people can think of to apply to a man except honest —they mean he is close to being a fool. . . . That's why every one trusts Iago."[164]

As for personality, any suggestion of the traditional Machiavel (clever, sardonic, occasionally melodramatic) strikes some actor-critics as destructive of the "honest Iago" image, even when the more flagrant manifestations of villainy are confined to the soliloquies—and this despite the fact that successful deception is an invariable characteristic of the Machiavellian villain. Irving's Iago is a case in point: although praised by some critics for its credibility, it was considered by others more exciting than convincing. According to JOHN MARTIN-HARVEY, the two most memorable moments of the performance were marked, respectively, by "sardonic, Italianate . . . irony" and "triumphant malignity." Although he admired Irving's portrayal for its theatrical effectiveness, he questioned "whether so subtle a villainy could ever have earned him the title of 'honest.' "[165] Viewed by modern standards, Irving's love of bravura touches was in conflict with his

162. *What the Author Meant*, p. 80.

163. *Notes, Criticisms, and Correspondence*, pp. 308-9.

164. Goodale, *Behind the Scenes with Edwin Booth*, pp. 279-80. Mayo may have been teasing young Kitty Molony by speaking disrespectfully of her hero Booth.

165. *Autobiography*, p. 42.

desire for realism and credibility, even though he himself (and some of his spectators) saw no such conflict. A striking bit of business that Irving recalls from his own performance provides a good example: during the brawl between Cassio and Montano he "used to enjoy a mischievous sense of mastery by flicking at them with a red cloak, as though they were bulls in the arena."[166] Since this action was analogous to an "aside" in speaking, theoretically it would not interfere with the credibility of Iago's reputation for honesty. But since the audience does not stop to think through such matters, the very flamboyance of the gesture might increase the feeling that Iago's villainy is too obvious to escape detection. Modern notions of credibility apparently demand an Iago who would, we think, have a fair chance of fooling *us*. "Machiavellian villains" are automatically disqualified because we know all about them and are imaginatively on guard against them. (The very word "villain" carries the stigma of melodrama for some of us, and the literary associations of "Machiavellian" give it connotations of artificiality.) Thus HENRY CHANCE NEWTON rejected the image of Mephistopheles which he associated with such villains and welcomed the "commonsensible . . . view" of Iago offered by Henry Forrester (and, in an earlier day, by Samuel Phelps and Hermann Vezin) —the "secretly sinister revengeful, but outwardly bluff soldier."[167] Since that time the "bluff" Iago has been frequently in evidence in successful performances. And it was this conception that SIR LAURENCE OLIVIER agreed upon in 1964 for Frank Finlay's Iago, considering it the practical complement to his own Othello.[168]

Specific Problems of Character Interpretation

Although it is true, as Olivier says, that most conceptions of Iago can be classified under two general types, the choice of one type or the other does not necessarily solve all the actor's problems. It is probable that the "Renaissance villains" will be higher in the social scale than the "NCO's," more lively and intellectual, more satanic—but these relationships are by no means automatic. Each Iago must decide for himself (or the director must decide for him) whether he is to be coarse or refined, brilliant or petty-

166. "My Four Favorite Parts," pp. 35-36.
167. Henry Chance Newton, *Cues and Curtain Calls* (London, 1927), p. 28.
168. "The Great Sir Laurence," p. 88.

minded, consumed with jealousy or coldly malignant. On matters like these the actors' criticisms generally reflect the influence of the outstanding stage interpretations of their respective periods, just as those of Othello's character do.

In the eighteenth century Charles Macklin seems to have realized for most of his colleagues the ideal Iago. Accordingly, SAMUEL FOOTE,[169] in discussing Iago's social position, specifically refers to Macklin's interpretation; and FRANCIS GENTLEMAN[170] and CHARLES DIBDIN,[171] whose descriptions of the character are so similar as to be almost interchangeable, probably saw the well-known performance in the mind's eye as they wrote. Foote, who conceived of Iago as not only Othello's inferior officer but also a dependent of the general—"nay, perhaps a Domestick, from the Imployment assign'd to *Emilia*"—commended Macklin's "distant, obsequious" behavior toward Othello. He pointed out that Othello sometimes sends Iago on errands that bear no relation to his command; for example, "Go to the port and disembark my coffers" and "Fetch Desdemona hither." (Foote misunderstood Emilia's position, of course—a waiting woman is not a servant girl; but if he, and Macklin, overemphasized Iago's servility, some of his successors were to wander even farther afield in the opposite direction.) In describing Iago's personality the eighteenth century actors emphasized his deliberateness (Gentleman called him "slow," Dibdin, "studied"); his grim, morose disposition (Gentleman's term is "irascible," Dibdin's is "sullen"); and his lack of human sensibilities (the one pronounced him "dead to every good, or tender feeling," the other, "cold-blooded," "insensitive to honour, friendship, or gratitude"). As for his mental endowments, both Gentleman and Dibdin used the word "subtle," which, though it refers mainly to his deceit, also suggests intelligence of a shrewd, conniving kind. There was no hint of admiration for his intellectual ability, however: the character was too "underhand," too "mean" and "base" to inspire any such feeling. Nor was there any questioning of Iago's motives: jealousy and disappointment were clearly the springs of his hatred if the text were literally read, and revenge was a frequent dramatic *motif*—these things were too evident to need discussion.

169. *Treatise on the Passions*, pp. 37-38.
170. *Dramatic Censor*, I, 152.
171. *Complete History of the Stage*, III, 350.

Early in the nineteenth century a new Iago emerged—an Iago with a light touch, a light step, a sprightly wit, who reveled in his own ingenuity and sometimes charmed the audience into reveling with him. Edmund Kean was a masterly Iago of this type; and, although Hazlitt took him to task for "abstract[ing] the wit of the character and mak[ing] Iago an excellent good fellow," his interpretation gained instant popularity.[172] Kean's contemporary Charles Mayne Young conceived the character in somewhat the same way but played him less subtly: a jolly rogue, this Iago drew "much laughter" and "frequent applause" from the audience.[173] And William Charles Macready, though he probably gave his Iago less gaiety, did make him play a game of wits with his victims as pawns.[174] Iagos like these differed from the old conception in several ways but chiefly in two: their intellectual gifts were of a higher order, and their temperaments were more sanguine, less saturnine. Both of these new characteristics had potentialities beyond the obvious changes in Iago's manner of speaking and acting. His intellectual superiority, for example, tied in with Coleridge's interpretation, new in that period, and with the whole question of Iago's motivation which was opened up with the phrase "motiveless malignity"; the unprincipled adventurer who took his pleasure in manipulating the lives of others no longer needed motives of jealousy and revenge to set him off—but if he caused as much havoc as Iago finally did, well, the satanic implications were obvious. Then, too, as Iago took on the characteristics of a wit and a *bon vivant*, he was likely to rise in the social scale. The results of this last possibility became particularly evident later in the century: Henry Irving, for example, though he recognized that Iago was a "simple soldier," chose nevertheless to model him on Machiavelli's politician and to dress him in "raiment distinctly unsuitable because of its opulence."[175] In the criticisms of Iago by nineteenth century actors, there are responses, both positive and negative, to the new conceptions of his personality and intellect; but the positive ones predominate.

Iago's temperament is less frequently mentioned in these

172. "On Mr. Kean's Iago," *Complete Works of Hazlitt*, ed. Howe, IV, 14-17. *See also* Hillebrand, *Edmund Kean*, p. 129.

173. Hackett, *Notes, Criticisms, and Correspondence*, pp. 134-35.

174. *See* Lady Pollock's description in *Macready as I Knew Him* (London, 1884), pp. 111-12.

175. Winter, *Shakespeare on the Stage*, First Series, p. 278.

actors' remarks than his mental endowments, but several of the descriptions that emphasize the latter also imply a certain high-spirited self-assurance. Of the two actor-critics who were most specific in expressing their views of this subject, one—EDWIN BOOTH—stressed Iago's liveliness and ostensible good humor, but the other—JAMES H. HACKETT—warned against an overemphasis of these very traits. The latter's comments were in reaction to Charles Mayne Young's performance. Despite Hackett's dislike of the heavy villain interpretation of Iago, he could not approve this "gay, bold faced, broadly conceived" characterization either. "*Iago* should indeed assume a blunt but *cynical* humor," he observed, but the man who feels hatred gnawing his inwards like a poisonous mineral cannot be sincerely joyous. By neglecting to "display in strong colors" Iago's "rancor at heart," Young made his humor "too easy and spontaneous instead of forced and un-natural."[176] Booth, while recognizing Iago's inner bitterness, felt that it should normally be disguised under a "genial, sometimes jovial" pose and a humorous manner of delivering his barbed remarks. Only occasionally should Iago's real feelings be revealed in his features. (The moments when hatred and malignity became visibly manifest were the more striking in Booth's performance because of the shock with which the audience remembered that the usual attitude of friendliness and good humor was only as-sumed. As Booth himself remarked, "The more sincere your manner, the more devilish your deceit.") It is Booth, too, whose comments most suggest an Iago of breeding and polish. He directs the actor to be "always gentlemanly," and he consoles him-self for the lack of military bluffness in his own performance (a desirable trait, he admits) by the argument that "we know [Iago] more as a courtier than as a soldier."[177] (How did he rationalize that passage from the play which his wording ironically calls to mind: "You may relish him more in the soldier than in the scholar"?)

Most of the actor-critics of this period regarded Iago as in-tellectually superior. WILLIAM CHARLES MACREADY described him as a "consummate deceiver," one who is "indeed 'all things to all men,' whose perfect accomplishment in craft might 'send the learned Machiavel to school.'" After a particularly successful per-

176. *Notes, Criticisms, and Correspondence*, pp. 134-36.
177. *Furness Variorum*, VI, 214. *See also* pp. 107, 146.

formance of Iago (January 22, 1851), Macready, in congratulating himself for an unprecedented "elucidation" of the "inward feeling of the part," mentioned, as one of the major traits that he had demonstrated, a "delight in the exercise of his own intellectual power" (the other traits were "selfishness" and "sensuality").[178] JOHN COLEMAN obviously accepted Macready's interpretation, even as he admired his ability to transmit it to the audience. "What a revelation," he exclaimed, "of subtle, poetic, vigorous, manly, many-minded deviltry!"[179] Edwin Booth, in his notes as in his own performance, emphasized Iago's mental agility by a corresponding litheness of motion, which he described as snake-like;[180] and FREDERICK WARDE paid tribute to these same qualities in Booth's Iago: "fascinating in its intellectual villainy," he called it, "sinuous and graceful in movement."[181] But there was one actor-critic of the nineteenth century who differed from all the others on the subject of Iago's intelligence. The Iago of HELEN FAUCIT's conception is as far as possible from that of Macready, with whom Miss Faucit in her younger days played Desdemona: He can hardly delight in his intellectual superiority, since his "artifices" are not only "vile" but "shallow" and vulnerable to "the merest casualty." He trembles in "hourly terror that the net he has woven to ensnare others may enmesh himself," yet he persists in his sordid game because "he has not wit enough" to realize that eventual defeat is inevitable. This Iago is totally irreconcilable, too, with the conception of Booth, whose stage career was contemporary with Helen Faucit's essay: No graceful courtier, this one, but "brutish in mind as, when he dare be, he is in manners." He has a petty, revengeful spirit and a low form of cunning, but that is all; he is "a poor trickster at the best."[182]

The use of such words as "deviltry" in some of the actors' descriptions of Iago, and such analogies as the snake, suggest a compatibility with the idea that a satanic spirit rather than understandable human motive is responsible for Iago's villainy. Actually I recall only one comment by an actor that sounds like a direct echo of Coleridge: WILLIAM OXBERRY's statement that Iago "loves

178. *The Diaries of William Charles Macready*, ed. William Toynbee (New York, 1912), II, 488.
179. John Coleman, *Fifty Years of an Actor's Life* (London, 1904), II, 504-5.
180. *Furness Variorum*, VI, 214.
181. *Fifty Years of Make-Believe*, p. 120.
182. *On Some of Shakespeare's Female Characters*, pp. 64-65.

evil as others love good; he has a natural delight in the pain of others."[183] But Macready's emphasis upon Iago's "delight in the exercise of his own intellectual power" may be easily stretched into something like the same thing. Indeed it was so interpreted by his friend Lady Pollock, who may or may not have reflected Macready's own opinion: "When Macready planned and plotted and weaved his web," she recalled, "we saw him gloat over the ignorance and the imagined pangs of his victims. He revelled as he felt himself the master of their passions. . . ." His audience had no need to seek for "concealed causes of hatred. . . . Iago's motive was found in his own nature; he contrived mischief with satanic ecstasy." Even Lady Pollock, however, did not use "satanic" in a purely metaphysical sense, for she went on to argue that Macready's conception was actually true to life since the records of great poisoning cases reveal that such men have existed.[184] As for Coleman's term "deviltry," perhaps his use of "manly" in the same sentence should give us pause. Again, some of Booth's phrases can be construed to support the idea of satanism—and indeed OTIS SKINNER described Booth's performance as "radiant with devilish beauty"[185]—but if all of his notes are read it is clear that he accepted human jealousy as one motive of Iago's hatred, whether or not he considered it a sufficient one. (His stage directions for the first Cyprus scene—e.g. when Cassio kisses Emilia—are proof that he did not regard Iago's suspicions of his own cuckoldry as mere "motive-hunting."[186]) But the one actor-critic of that century who rejected unequivocally the idea of "motiveless malignity" was James H. Hackett. According to the friendly critic John Inman, this actor made it clear in his own performances that Iago's true motives are those unmistakably set forth at the beginning of the play—jealousy and disappointed ambition—not mere love of wickedness. Hackett himself explained that Iago must reveal in his soliloquies his *"real and absolute*

183. *New English Drama*, V, *Othello*, iii-iv.
184. *Macready as I Knew Him*, pp. 111-12.
185. *Footlights and Spotlights*, p. 93.
186. *Furness Variorum*, VI, 105, 107. Junius Brutus Booth, in acting Iago, had also emphasized jealousy of Emilia. At the end of the play, "he looked at *Othello* with a significant gaze, then pointed to his own wife, as if to express that her violation by the *Moor* was the cause of all his perfidy" (Sprague, *Shakespeare and the Actors*, p. 223). The younger Booth was more subtle than that. In his later performances, however, Edwin Booth apparently used the satanic interpretation. (*See* Sprague, *Shakespearian Players and Performances*, p. 128.)

misery and sufferings," for these feelings "constitute the key which unlocks . . . the secret motives of his envious, jealous . . . revengeful nature."[187] I suspect that most actors, even at the height of the romantic influence, gave some weight to Iago's human characteristics and human motives but that those like Kean and Macready, Booth and Irving also gave to the character more than a touch of the spirit that inspired his revenge to outgrow those motives. Hence the charm of a Mephistopheles or the grandeur of a Lucifer. Hackett might protest the charm and Helen Faucit deny the grandeur,[188] but the one did not succeed in his performance of Iago, and the other never acted him at all.

On the whole, the actor-critics of the present century have moved away from the conception of a brilliant and fascinating Iago. It is true that one of them, LENA ASHWELL, described Iago in a manner that, if anything, was more romantic than her predecessors'. But Miss Ashwell's experience in the play was as early as 1902, when she acted Emilia to Forbes-Robertson's Othello and Herbert Waring's Iago;[189] and her book on Shakespeare was published in the 1920's. There is no criticism more recent than hers that corresponds so closely to the interpretation associated with the great actors of the nineteenth century. Indeed several of the modern actor-critics may be called "debunkers" of Iago's reputation for glamour, especially GEORGE R. FOSS (1932) and HARLEY GRANVILLE-BARKER (1946). Others, like GEORGE SKILLAN and ROBERT SPEAIGHT, have seen in the character a complex, sometimes a paradoxical, combination of traits: the charming and the despicable, for example, or the petty and the grand. Occasionally the phrases used in modern criticism remind us of Gentleman and Dibdin, but none of the actor-critics have returned completely to the simple villain of the eighteenth century—mainly because a concern for credibility (or something deeper in their cultural

187. *Notes, Criticisms, and Correspondence*, pp. 296-99 (Inman's relevant remarks); p. 136 (Hackett's own statements).

188. "I see no grandeur in a 'demi-devil' of this type," wrote Helen Faucit. She considered him an "inhuman villain" for whom even the worst circle of the Inferno would be "too good," but she accepted hatred as his driving motive: hatred of Othello for keeping him out of the lieutenancy, of Cassio for supplanting him in office, of Emilia for "outliv[ing] his liking," of Desdemona for being "impervious to his arts." His suspicions of cuckoldry, however, are explained as mere "juggles with his conscience" (*On Some of Shakespeare's Female Characters*, pp. 64-65).

189. Waring's Iago was hardly congruent with Lena Ashwell's conception of the character, however. See Trewin, *Shakespeare on the English Stage, 1900-1964*, p. 22.

environment) has forced them to ponder Iago's motivation rather than to accept it on faith. (MARGARET WEBSTER declares for faith, but she also gives an interesting description of Iago's mental makeup.) It is this subject of motivation, in fact, that has dominated the discussions of Iago in the present period. Only a few actor-critics have bothered to specify Iago's social standing; several have remained silent about his intellect and personality; but every one who has had anything substantial to say about Iago has attempted to answer the question of motive.

What discussion there has been of Iago's social position is sharply divided between the aristocratic identification and the plebeian; there is no middle ground. Lena Ashwell was even more insistent upon Iago's courtliness than Booth had been, and considerably more fanciful in describing the character: He is, according to her, "a patrician, exquisitely bred, widely traveled, brilliantly accomplished, tremendously alive." He can be "fathered" on Machiavelli's *The Prince,* or, better still, on Machiavelli's model, Cesare Borgia; for Iago has all the "silken grace" of the Italian prototype, "but don't forget the steel."[190] It is difficult to believe that the same character that inspired this romantic tribute is also the subject of the merciless analyses by Granville-Barker and Robert Speaight. "A foul-mouthed and coarse-tongued . . . braggart," Granville-Barker called him, "decrying in others the qualities he himself lacks, bitterly envious, pettily spiteful, morbidly vain."[191] And Speaight not only emphasizes his personal uncouthness but also suggests that "the itch of social inferiority is behind a good deal of his mischief." The Iago of his interpretation has been deluded by his ambition into expecting the lieutenancy, for he is actually "the last man Othello would have taken as an aide-de-camp." Contrary to Miss Ashwell's idea that Iago is the "confidant and bosom friend" of the other characters is Speaight's contention that Othello never talks to Iago as one friend to another, that the latter "only gains his confidence by a reputation, cunningly built up, for honesty and plain speaking."[192] It seems that Speaight, in his turn, protests too much. His interpretation does not satisfactorily account for the "three great ones of the city" (there is no reason to think Iago is lying in this particu-

190. *Reflections from Shakespeare,* p. 101.
191. *Prefaces to Shakespeare,* II, 99.
192. *Nature in Shakespearian Tragedy,* pp. 82-84.

lar) or for the charm that Iago seems to hold for Roderigo, who, though "silly," is in birth and fortune a "gentleman." But, if one must choose between his idea and Miss Ashwell's, surely his does less violence to the text.

In regard to Iago's intellect and personality, Lena Ashwell's interpretation[193] is, again, the most traditional one of the modern period; but on these points, at least, her view is not unique. George Skillan's description of Iago, in the current *French's Acting Edition*,[194] is recognizably similar if expressed with more restraint. Miss Ashwell is particularly lavish in her praise of Iago's intellectual accomplishments: he "thinks with lightning swiftness, sees with an amazing clarity of vision, speaks with delightful precision, and mordant wit in glittering epigram." Skillan contents himself with the adjective "super-subtle." Both of these writers depict Iago's assumed personality much as Edwin Booth did earlier: Miss Ashwell speaks of the "humorous and kindly" manner that masks his villainy, and Skillan advises the actor to preserve a "lightness" of deportment that will make the character "both companionable and plausible."

There was one actor-critic, contemporary with Miss Ashwell, who testified to the danger of overemphasizing Iago's geniality. MAUD HOLT TREE recalled that her husband had fallen into this trap, misled by his admiration for Maurel's "easy, jocose" performance in Verdi's *Otello*. Maurel was a perfect "braggadochio, instinct with the bouncing lissomness of *embonpoint*," and Beerbohm Tree attempted to follow his lead. Perhaps Lady Tree did not object to the idea of such an Iago as much as she considered it inappropriate to her husband's talents. Tree, who was very successful as the sinister Italian villain Macari in the melodrama *Called Back*, would have been "the greatest of all Iagos" if he had made the character a "Shakespearean Macari" instead of a "Ralph Royster Doyster."[195]

Later actor-critics, however, with the exception of Skillan, have departed more radically from tradition in their estimates of Iago's mental and personal endowments. The completely derogatory view, of which Helen Faucit was the sole advocate in the preceding century, has been presented with considerable per-

193. *Reflections from Shakespeare*, p. 101.
194. *Othello. French's Acting Edition*, pp. 18, 49.
195. "Herbert and I," p. 23.

suasiveness by Harley Granville-Barker and George R. Foss. According to Granville-Barker, Iago is "the clever but essentially stupid fellow, the common man of common mind," whose "radical stupidity" is shown by his failure to understand Emilia's attachment to Desdemona and the threat this poses for him. Iago does not even have self-knowledge: in such speeches as "Virtue! a fig!" he "vaunts his doctrine of reason," but "it is not reason that serves him"; his ability lies, not in logical planning, but in spur-of-the-moment inspiration.[196] Foss agrees, and he credits Iago with even less art in using his "inspiration" than Granville-Barker does. For him, this villain is only "a somewhat shallow, mischievous imp, with a restless brain" who "says anything that comes into his head that he knows will hurt his victims."[197]

There are other actor-critics whose interpretations have elements congenial with both Miss Ashwell's and Granville-Barker's but which, though closer to the latter, differ significantly from both. They also differ from each other. Margaret Webster, for example, is aware of the "brilliant speed" of Iago's thinking, but she is also aware of its pettiness; she sees both the "dash of recklessness" and the "complete worldly armory of his mind, the plenitude of his will and the absolute lack of imagination." Iago's intellectual gifts and deficiencies, contradictory though some of them may be, pose no problem for Miss Webster; rather, they cohere into an unmistakable and convincing mental personality—one that is "contrasted unerringly with Othello's alien temperament."[198] For Robert Speaight, however, Iago is more complex and more difficult to understand. This actor-critic, stirring a memory of Hackett, writes that four Iagos speak during the course of the play: the three personalities assumed, respectively, for Othello, Roderigo, and the other characters, and the fourth Iago, revealed in the soliloquies. All but the last have "the same character of *faux-bonhomme*. . . . This Iago is boastfully of the world; he knows its ways and despises them. With his ready smile and his slap on the back he is a jocose parody of the 'natural man' " like Faulconbridge and Mercutio. The fourth Iago is not described in the same neat, concentrated fashion, but Speaight's image of this more complex personality may be built

196. *Prefaces to Shakespeare*, II, 102-3, 110.
197. *What the Author Meant*, pp. 81-82.
198. *Shakespeare Without Tears*, pp. 231-33.

up from his remarks on motivation, a subject that will be discussed shortly. The chief problem the character poses for Speaight lies in Shakespeare's paradoxical presentation of him: from the first moment of the play Iago exercises "an intellectual and personal dominance, a compulsive energy and fascination, which go some way towards explaining the rapidity of Othello's fall. There is nothing great in him—there is everything petty—yet he remains immense."[199]

As we have remarked, the question of Iago's motivation has been of more concern than anything else to the modern actor-critics. And always in reading their answers to this question we are conscious of a legacy, literary and theatrical, from the past century: the theory of "motiveless malignity" and its connotations of satanism. Sometimes these ideas are brought to mind because they are being attacked; occasionally because they are being restated, with alterations. Even new theories of Iago's motivation often seek to resolve, by different methods, the same problem that the romantics saw in the character—an outrageous disproportion between Iago's stated motives and the unlimited wickedness of his behavior. Given the modern interest in psychoanalysis, it was probably inevitable that Iago's own words, soliloquies included, would have ceased to be taken at face value by many modern thinkers, even if Coleridge and his followers had never lived. But, as things are, the idea of "motiveless malignity" not only prepared the way; it remains, whether we consciously accept it or not, as part of our imaginative equipment, subtly influencing our reactions to all new treatments of the subject. This is particularly true if our imaginations have been enriched by descriptions of Iago's great moments on the stage: of Macready's "demoniacal smile" as he looked upon the murdered Desdemona,[200] of Irving's lazily eating grapes and venomously spitting out the seeds as if they were so many virtues,[201] of Booth's "quick, fiendish smile of triumph" and "rapid clutch of the fingers" in the temptation scene, "as though squeezing [Othello's] very heart."[202]

Let us consider first the discussions of motivation that bear the most direct resemblance to those from the past century. Not

199. *Nature in Shakespearian Tragedy*, pp. 82, 87-88.
200. Sprague, *Shakespeare and the Actors*, p. 223.
201. Ellen Terry, *The Story of My Life*, p. 206.
202. *Furness Variorum*, VI, 188.

surprisingly, these are also the earliest chronologically. They are, first, H. B. IRVING's forthright acceptance of "motiveless malignity" —but for his own purposes—and, second, Lena Ashwell's Booth-like comments, combining a respect for the truth of Iago's expressed motives with an interest in the fiendlike aspects of the character. Although both of these interpretations have recognizable affinities with those of the nineteenth century, they also show the old conceptions in the process of adaptation or questioning.

H. B. Irving (son of the greater Irving) was drawn toward the "motiveless malignity" theory, not because he was convinced of Iago's satanism in any supernatural sense but because the pursuit of his hobby, criminology, had led him to believe that such malignity is typical of the criminal nature. According to him, Iago shares the distinctive traits of several real-life villains— Robert Butler, Lacenaire, Ruloff—"their envy and dislike of their fellowmen, their contempt for humanity in general, their callousness to the ordinary sympathies of human nature." Only one thing interfered with Irving's interpretation—Iago's suspicion of an affair between Othello and Emilia—and this, he felt, was a "weakness in the consistency of the play." If there is any ground for Iago's jealousy—and "Emilia's conversation with Desdemona in the last act [sic.] lends colour" to this belief—Iago's "character as a purely wanton and mischievous criminal" is greatly weakened, and Othello's character "as an honorable and high-minded man" is correspondingly lowered. On the other hand, if Iago's fear is only a "morbid suspicion . . . a mental obsession," then the villain "becomes abnormal and consequently more or less irresponsible."[203] In this last sentence we see the sign of things to come: psychology would be replacing theology, and Iago would become abnormal rather than supernatural.

But the aura of satanic splendor would never completely fade from the actors' image of Iago, though there would be efforts to dispel it. And when Lena Ashwell was collecting her thoughts on Iago the magic was still strong. Miss Ashwell's attraction to the

203. *A Book of Remarkable Criminals* (London, [1918]), pp. 12-13. According to Gordon Crosse (*Shakespearean Playgoing 1890-1952* [London, 1953], p. 42), there was an "interesting contrast" between H. B. Irving's "sharp, sardonic" Iago, "with its Mephistophelean humour and its grim intensity," and his brother Laurence's "plain and homely young soldier" with only an occasional hint of his real "diabolical wickedness peeping out." Crosse named Laurence Irving "the best Iago of my time."

satanic theory is evident in her statement that "the Snake in Eden might well be the prototype and ancestor to Iago." Yet she refrained from embracing the idea of "motiveless malignity"; in fact, she endowed the character with considerable humanity. "Evil he is, yet give the devil his due. Twice he says outright and possibly believes that Othello seduced his wife. The preferment of Michael Cassio has wrecked his professional prospects, giving the lie to Othello's apparent friendship." Up to this point Miss Ashwell is hardly original. Her further suggestions, however, are unlike anything written about Iago by other actor-critics, either contemporaries or predecessors. What seems to be cold inhumanity in his nature, she points out, may be the result of actual passion: i.e. the pains of jealousy may be so intense as to corrode all other emotions. Thus, "unconscious of the ruin within himself, callous to the sufferings inflicted upon others," when he "has accomplished his own destruction, and the deaths of the friends who trusted him, he cannot explain his conduct, even to himself." Judging by her comment on Iago's end, Miss Ashwell even saw the character as a tragic figure: "He has put his soul to death by torture, and all the torments doomed upon his body will hurt him less than that."[204] Lena Ashwell was just the person to be fascinated by a Lucifer-like conception; yet, of all modern actor-critics, she took most seriously the human motives that Iago himself professed, and she entered most sympathetically into the analysis of his character and fate.

Among the later actor-critics there are several who have rejected all belief in acceptable human motives for Iago's actions, but at least two of them have rejected even more scornfully all tendencies to make him a Lucifer figure. Granville-Barker is an uncompromising spokesman for this point of view: "the actor who tries . . . to present Iago as a sort of half-brother to Milton's Satan only falsifies both character and play," for Iago is merely "a shoddy creature . . . possessed by his mountebank egoism, his envy and spite." The love of evil for its own sake, which strikes some critics as satanic, is contemptuously reduced to "innate malignity, crass appetite, and mere itch to do evil." Granville-Barker does speak of Iago's need to "reduce the nobility confronting him to baseness," but, for him, such depravity requires no supernatural explanation. Yet the Iago of this conception, man

204. *Reflections from Shakespeare*, pp. 100-101, 104-5.

though he is, not devil, has little human feeling: "neither love nor lust. . . . Even his hate is cold." He is stimulated only by the excitement of pulling the strings that make the puppet Othello dance; this provides "meat and drink to thwarted, perverted vanity." Although Granville-Barker permits the character his petty motive for revenge (injured vanity is a weak substitute for sexual jealousy or ruined ambition), he puts just as much emphasis upon the exhilaration that Iago finds in using his "chameleon-like ability" as an "actor." For this Iago, though he lacks "genuine capacities," has "the power of counterfeiting them," and the "intuition of an artist" enables him to extemporize adroitly. His success in getting Cassio dismissed stimulates him to further ingenuity. Forgetting the profit he has achieved by this coup, he is obsessed now with the profitless scheme to ruin Othello. "Here is the artist who will do the thing for its own sake, and out of sheer delight in the doing let himself be carried beyond all bounds of 'reason' and prudence."[205] Some of the same ideas about Iago's motivation have been expressed by George R. Foss[206] and George Skillan.[207] Both of these actor-critics deny that jealousy of Emilia is an important factor in Iago's behavior: Skillan, in fact, cautions the actor against "vehemence" when Iago first mentions his suspicion, declaring that it is "only a growing tendency of his mood, an excuse to execute some form of assault." Foss merely attributes Iago's villainy to a cruel streak in his nature and a restless urge for action. "If the wars had gone on and he had found something to keep him employed he would probably . . . have . . . been a capable but not brilliant soldier, played cruel tricks on his comrades, and snarled enviously at any one who had a bit of luck"; the tragedy of Othello would never have happened. According to Foss, the true nature of Iago was "well illustrated" by Laurence Irving's "lazily catching flies," at the end of the first act, "and burning them in the candle." It is obvious that Foss, like Granville-Barker, was bent on reducing the size of the character. This is less true of Skillan, whose conception of Iago's personality is closer to the earlier tradition. But, in context, there is no real hint of satanism in his statement that Iago's "particular pleasure in life" is "to bring creation's nobility into

205. *Prefaces to Shakespeare*, II, 7-9, 100-110.
206. *What the Author Meant*, pp. 81-82.
207. *Othello. French's Acting Edition*, pp. 20, 26.

contempt and destruction." His phraseology is, in fact, close to Granville-Barker's.

The relationship between the satanists and their deadliest opponents is interesting. They are alike in denying the importance of jealousy as a motive and in emphasizing Iago's pleasure in manipulating or destroying others. The difference is in their attitudes toward the character himself: one group feels awe, the other contempt. The satanists speak of Iago's delight in the exercise of a superlative intellect; the "debunkers" speak of the fun of playing cruel tricks. Both see an inclination toward evil for its own sake. But for one group this implies demonic possession; for the other, simple human meanness will do. H. B. Irving, though similar to these later critics in some respects, found human depravity fascinating in its purest forms; he could therefore speak of Iago as a "supreme villain"—a phrase that Granville-Barker would have found both annoying and naive. But is there not something naive, as well, in vehement protests against Iago's fascination?

The explanations that we have been discussing are in a sense "psychological" since they account for Iago's behavior by describing the kind of warped personality from which it would realistically emanate. For critics deeply committed to the idea of psychological analysis, however, the destructive elements in Iago's nature—his perverted egoism, his love of cruelty, his need to debase—require, in their turn, some explanation. And to search beyond these, of course, is to explore the realm of the subconscious. A few actors (but only a few) have been attracted to a Freudian interpretation of Iago. The possibility of such an interpretation first occurred to TYRONE GUTHRIE, director, and LAURENCE OLIVIER, actor of Iago, when they were preparing for a production of *Othello* at the Old Vic (February, 1938). They had attempted a Freudian Hamlet the year before, using Ernest Jones's theory; and now—to quote Guthrie—they were "full of theories about the psychological relation of Iago and Othello." They spent two evenings of great excitement with Dr. Jones,[208] discussing his idea that Iago was motivated, not by hatred, but by an abnormal attraction to Othello which he himself did not understand and which he repeatedly denied by protesting "I hate the Moor." They were particularly interested because (as

208. Tyrone Guthrie, *A Life in the Theatre* (New York, 1959), p. 193.

Olivier's biographer points out) this unexpressed, unrealized relationship would explain "why Othello was so irrationally influenced by Iago" and it would give new significance to the "great climax in Act III, when Iago and Othello kneel together with Othello's 'Now art thou my lieutenant' and Iago's 'I am your own forever.'" Olivier was willing to try the new interpretation, but his audiences did not, in general, realize what meaning was intended to lie beneath the lively and (in some places) comic behavior of his Iago.[209] He has since stated that he would no longer subscribe to the Freudian reading of the character, adding that, even though such an interpretation may be acceptable, there is no point in touching on a purely unconscious emotion "in any detail of performance."[210] Other psychological theories have been tentatively endorsed by Robert Speaight. Noticing that Iago's references to sex are always couched in bestial terms, he accepts the possibility that Iago is impotent or that he is incapable of enjoying a normal sexual relationship because it requires a "certain abdication of the self" that is beyond his comprehension.[211] Possible sexual frustration is suggested, however, not as a complete explanation of Iago's behavior, but only as a contributing factor.

For Speaight, as for the romantics before him, the ultimate solution to the problem of Iago's wickedness is metaphysical. And it is in his interpretation that we find the most fully developed modern version of the satanic theory. The key to his reading of the character is nihilism, an idea related to satanism since "our contemporary experience of evil has taught us to know it by the signs of absence and absurdity." Even the degrading references to sex can be interpreted as "the nihilist's blasphemy of Being, the voice of a purely destructive instinct, which cannot rest until it has attacked every manifestation of normal life." Nihilism would account, too, for the effect of motiveless malignity: Iago believes in nothing, and therefore his motives are inadequate. Perhaps he did once covet the lieutenancy, but this motive quickly drops from the dialogue. "As the play proceeds, he reasons less and less; becomes the master technician of evil, who does not stop to think." His nature is cankered with a diabolical cynicism, the result of a "need to destroy in [himself] and in other people all truth and

209. Felix Barker, *The Oliviers: A Biography* (London, [1953]), pp. 135-36.
210. Rosenberg, *The Masks of Othello*, p. 182.
211. *Nature in Shakespearian Tragedy*, pp. 84-85.

beauty and goodness." Significantly, he refuses to explain his villainy at the end; his silence typifies the absence of meaning and belief. Although Speaight insists that Iago is neither monster nor abstraction but man, he explains that the powerful effect created by this essentially petty character is due to Iago's being a satanist without knowing it. The "spirit of evil, pure and undivided," is at work in him, but the real source of his malignity is hidden from his own eyes and is only rarely implied in words (as in the "Divinity of hell" speech, II, iii, 356 ff.).[212]

The modern love of subtlety and complexity is well illustrated by the psychological and metaphysical interpretations of Iago which we have discussed. In these the actors have responded to the same influences that have been at work on other critics of their time. But the practical demands of the theatre—for simplicity and, in our own day, for some degree of realism—have also had their effect. SIR JOHN GIELGUD, for example, seems to be theoretically but not pragmatically satisfied by a satanic view of the character. He describes Iago as "a monster," "without moral sense," but he adds that "he must . . . if an actor is to play him convincingly, justify his wickedness to himself."[213] And, as we have seen, Olivier abandoned the Freudian view of Iago because it has no potentialities for the theatre. It is perhaps not surprising that Olivier afterwards adopted one of the simplest and most "normal" of all interpretations: i.e. that Iago's motivation originated in an army man's natural antagonism toward an overbearing superior, building up, with daily irritation, to obsessive proportions. And, significantly, this conception was based, not on theoretical speculation, but on personal experience.[214] Simplest of all the answers to the question of Iago's motivation is Margaret Webster's, for she considers the critics' probing unnecessary. If Iago is well acted, we in the audience "do not stop to fuss for the reasons." When he says "I hate the Moor," the "pure venom" of his speech "chills the blood; it also compels us to belief."[215] Perhaps Miss Webster's answer is *too* simple, since, in concentrating upon audience effect, it takes no account of the actor's own understanding. But it serves as a timely reminder that, ultimately, Iago must be judged by the

212. *Ibid.,* pp. 81, 85-88.
213. *Stage Directions,* pp. 44-45.
214. "The Great Sir Laurence," p. 88.
215. *Shakespeare Without Tears,* p. 232.

theatre's standards of reality, not by those of the library or the clinic.

DESDEMONA

Like most of Shakespeare's other heroines, Desdemona rarely attracted the attention of eighteenth century critics, theatrical or literary. COLLEY CIBBER (1740), who seems to have been typical, actually mentioned her, together with Ophelia, as an example of the limitations that the boy actress imposed upon Shakespeare's characterization of women.[216] And FRANCIS GENTLEMAN (1770) remarked disparagingly that Desdemona, a part of "unvarying gentleness," has "no shining qualifications" and that Emilia "has much more life than her mistress."[217] ELIZABETH GRIFFITH, however, protested that the character was "much mistaken and slighted," a fact that had often surprised her. "It is simple, indeed," she granted, "but that is one of its merits: for the simplicity of it is that of *innocence,* not of *folly.*"[218] Desdemona's moral and intellectual worthiness, not her dramatic importance, was Mrs. Griffith's main concern, but her recognition that innocence need not be equated with simple-mindedness is worth remarking.

Theatrically, Desdemona was far more attractive to leading tragic actresses than Ophelia was; yet the character was "slighted" on the stage, as in criticism, if contrasted with the more forceful and colorful roles like Lady Macbeth. There were numerous occasions when the Desdemona of the evening was an actress who normally rose no higher in the Shakespearean scale than Celia, Hero, Virgilia, or Lady Macduff.[219] Performances like theirs

216. *Apology,* I, 90.
217. *Dramatic Censor,* I, 154.
218. *The Morality of Shakespeare's Drama Illustrated,* p. 523.
219. Among the outstanding tragic actresses who sometimes acted Desdemona but never (or almost never) acted Ophelia were Mrs. Pritchard, Mrs. Yates, and Mrs. Pope (neé Younge). Mrs. Siddons performed Desdemona about seventeen times in the first fifteen years of her London career but Ophelia only once during that same period. On the other hand, Mrs. Pritchard took the role of Emilia as often as she did Desdemona, and she and the other actresses mentioned acted Lady Macbeth from four to six times as often as they did Desdemona. (*Macbeth* was performed more frequently than *Othello,* but, even allowing for this fact, the role of Lady Macbeth was much more attractive to the great actresses.) A few well-known actresses who were more gifted with pathos than with grandeur acted Desdemona more frequently than Lady Macbeth: the beautiful George Anne Bellamy, for example, who was Garrick's Juliet in the famous contest between Drury Lane and Covent Garden; and Mrs. Barry, who was a popular Desdemona to her hus-

probably helped to perpetuate the idea—for it obviously *was* perpetuated—that Desdemona is sufficiently characterized by terms like "fond" and "simple." What a change must have come over the character when Sarah Siddons acted it! Rosenberg states, with good support from Boaden, that "audiences were amazed at the transition from her erstwhile tragic majesty [in characters like Constance, Queen Katherine, and Lady Macbeth] to sweet tenderness."[220] But, according to ELIZABETH INCHBALD, too much tragic majesty remained. Although Mrs. Siddons' "judgment dictates to her how Desdemona should be acted," she wrote, ". . . her face can never express artless innocence, such as the true representative of the part requires: her features are too bold, her person too important for the gentle Desdemona." Another comment by Mrs. Inchbald—"Desdemona is the last part in the world where *acting* is requisite, and yet Mrs. Siddons can only convey an idea of the character by casting off *herself*"[221]—reveals to us in one stroke the average Desdemona with which she was familiar: a pretty girl with a sweet manner who is expected to do nothing more than "be herself." Mrs. Siddons must have given the part the stature and the intensity that later actresses like Helen Faucit and Ellen Terry were to insist upon in their criticisms as well as in their acting.

Whatever her personality and dramatic importance, the Desdemona envisioned by the earliest actor-critics was morally impeccable: Cibber called her "virtuous," and Mrs. Griffith considered her a "perfect . . . model of a wife."[222] In essence this attitude continued to be held by later writers—CHARLES DIBDIN (1800) described Desdemona as "sweetly innocent" and WILLIAM OXBERRY (1819) as "pure and tender"—but it was sometimes mod-

band's great Othello. Mrs. Cibber would also belong in this category. Of these three only Mrs. Cibber acted Ophelia. Among the actresses of second rank who performed Desdemona rather often were Mrs. Thurmond, Miss Younger, Mrs. Buchanan, and Mrs. Ridout. Numerous others of this rank (or lower), like Mrs. Davies, Mrs. Ward, Miss Miller, and Mrs. Elmy, occasionally acted Desdemona. *See* Charles B. Hogan, *Shakespeare in the Theatre, 1701-1800* (Oxford, 1952-57), Vols. I and II, *passim*.

220. *The Masks of Othello*, p. 51.

221. MS version of Elizabeth Inchbald's introduction to *Othello*, written for *The British Theatre* (Folger Library). The printed version omits this criticism of Sarah Siddons's Desdemona.

222. Cibber, *Apology*, I, 90; Griffith, *The Morality of Shakespeare's Drama Illustrated*, p. 523.

ified by the mention of a culpable irregularity in her actions. According to Dibdin, her conduct betrays a "degree of capriciousness" which contributes to her tragedy. Iago considers her love for Othello unnatural, Dibdin reminds us, and "the disparity must often occur to Othello" himself. Shakespeare, by showing the consequences of Desdemona's imprudence, has warned human nature against such foibles.[223] Oxberry points out that Desdemona's "hypocrisy to her father and subsequent flight are scarcely consistent with her general character," but he adds that "perhaps a sufficient reason for this may be found in her unbounded passion for the Moor, which almost approaches adoration."[224] Apparently he saw nothing unnatural in this passion; perhaps, like Mrs. Inchbald, he even considered the contrast between the lovers a dramatic merit. But his own charge of hypocrisy (even hypocrisy that was "all for love") was like Dibdin's charge of imprudence: they suggested the possibility of flaws in Desdemona's innocence at the same time that the innocence itself was being reaffirmed.

With such mild reproaches, however, the actor-critics were content. (We must go all the way to the twentieth century to reach the only actor-criticisms that present Desdemona as a seriously flawed character.) When a former president of the United States, John Quincy Adams, attacked Desdemona's character, the American actor JAMES H. HACKETT came to her defense. Adams considered her coarse and unnatural in her tastes, bold and undutiful in her elopement, and obviously destined to come to grief through her marriage. He admitted that Othello had everything to make him a desirable husband except his color, but he insisted that this should have been the one insuperable barrier to a delicate, pure nature such as critics have attributed to Desdemona. Hackett replied that he "must differ materially with Mr. Adams in his estimate of the character of *Desdemona*," and he emphasized the fact that she "saw *Othello's* visage only in his mind." He did not reject the idea of a "moral" in the play, but the one that he suggested was aimed at Brabantio rather than at Desdemona: that fathers should not introduce into their homes any man who

223. *Complete History of the Stage*, III, 350, 352-54.
224. *New English Drama*, V, *Othello*, iv.

might "prove an unsuitable husband" for a young, impressionable, warm-hearted daughter.[225]

President Adams's censure of the character was extreme, but his basic disapproval of her actions was certainly not unique in that period. Several literary critics raised questions about Desdemona's delicacy. One writer went so far as to assert that if Desdemona "really 'saw her husband's visage in his mind' . . . she was the only woman on record . . . who ever did so"; he himself was inclined to agree with Iago that the disparity between Othello and herself had helped to instigate Desdemona's love, not that more intellectual and spiritual feelings had risen above that disparity.[226] Even Hazlitt confessed to being "a little of Iago's council in this matter"; he gave Desdemona "infinite credit for purity and delicacy of sentiment," but he added that "purity and grossness sometimes 'nearly are allied,/ And thin partitions do their bounds divide.' "[227] Leigh Hunt went some distance toward adopting Iago's view, though he later reversed himself and attacked the "gross commentators" who had misconstrued "one of the loveliest [characters] ever conceived."[228] In an age when Juliet's "Gallop apace, you fiery-footed steeds" was sometimes considered too immodest to be quite womanly, Desdemona aroused in some minds the uneasy suspicion that, even if there was nothing abnormal in Othello's attractions for her, she was more sensuously inclined than an ideal heroine ought to be. (In his later and more en-

225. *Notes, Criticisms, and Correspondence*, p. 226 (footnote). For Adams's comments see pp. 223-26, 234-49.

226. These statements were made in an unsigned note appended to the concluding portion of an essay by Hazlitt on Edmund Kean's Iago, published in the *Examiner*, August 7, 1814. The note is probably not by Hazlitt (it is not reprinted in the collected editions of Hazlitt's works), but Leigh Hunt, in replying to it, assumed that it was. See *Leigh Hunt's Dramatic Criticism 1808-1831*, ed. Lawrence H. and Carolyn W. Houtchens (New York, 1949), p. 305. The editors conjecture that the note was written by Thomas Barnes, then the theatrical critic for the *Examiner* and later editor of the *Times*.

227. Hazlitt made these comments in his essay on Kean's Iago mentioned in n. 226, above. See *Complete Works of Hazlitt*, ed. Howe, V, 217.

228. Hunt's reply to the note mentioned in n. 226, above, was published in the *Examiner* on August 14, 1814. Hunt wrote that his opinion about Desdemona had always been much the same as the author's: "Not that we go quite to his extreme . . . but *Iago's* observations, as far as a connexion like hers is concerned, have had their weight with us. . . ." See *Leigh Hunt's Dramatic Criticism*, ed. Houtchens, pp. 78-83. Hunt's later change of heart is reflected in the sympathetic criticism of Desdemona found in *Dramatic Essays, Leigh Hunt*, ed. William Archer and Robert W. Lowe (London, 1894), pp. 208-9.

lightened days, however, Hunt argued against this idea, boldly insisting that, with a "good and warm-hearted" woman, physical pleasure was a perfectly natural accompaniment to love originating in intellectual and spiritual inspiration.)

But, despite occasional misgivings on the part of some critics, the usual image of Desdemona throughout the Victorian period continued to be that of a pure, innocent, and very unworldly character. It was, if anything, more ethereal than before, for literary critics like Mrs. Jameson were now at work upon it. The stage, too, nourishing tradition even while adapting it to new ideas and customs, had an important part in maintaining the image of an "innocent" Desdemona. Hackett, though he defended Desdemona's character, did not deny that her marriage was "unsuitable"; nor, presumably, would any of his colleagues have done so. Indeed the "unsuitability" of this marriage, by conventional standards, is important to the play. But on the stage the unconventionality and individualism of Desdemona's behavior were evidently ignored, as far as the average actress was concerned. Even that ardor which, as Oxberry noticed, "almost approaches adoration," was softened to gentle affection—happily so, one actor-critic thought. ROBERT DYER (1833) praised Miss Phillips for avoiding "voluptuousness" in her portrayal of the role—the "common error of actresses," as he termed it (though, as far as I know, without much basis); her "passion," he wrote, was "the most delicate emanation of feeling imaginable."[229] It required a greater actress, who was at the same time in tune with her period's notions of "delicacy," to restore Desdemona's fervor without any loss of her ideality.

The "artless innocence" which had seemed to Mrs. Inchbald the essence of the character was probably the chief impression conveyed by most stage Desdemonas of the nineteenth century; sweetness and gentleness abounded, but little strength of mind or character. A mid-century dramatic magazine contained this description of Charlotte Vandenhoff's Desdemona: "It is an unalloyed delight . . . to see her sad, fearful, yet gentle as a bruised dove bend meekly to the implacable jealousy of the swart Othello, and receive her death, while kissing the hand which gives it."[230] Literary critics offered the same interpretation: Hazlitt recognized

229. Robert Dyer, *Nine Years of an Actor's Life* (London, 1833), p. 139.
230. *Tallis's Dramatic Magazine*, April, 1851, p. 168.

Desdemona's "angelic sweetness," but he remarked that, if the "commencement of her passion" is disregarded, "her whole character consists in having no will of her own"—and that even the exception, "fantastical and headstrong" as it seems, may simply reflect her "inability to resist a rising inclination."[231] Mrs. Jameson declared that, despite some "transient energy, arising from the power of affection," the "prevailing tone of the character" is "gentleness verging on passiveness—gentleness, which not only cannot resent—but cannot resist."[232] Even Leigh Hunt, who gave Desdemona credit for stronger passions, reconciled them with her purity by the idea that she "has the heart of a child with all the feelings of a woman."[233] Writers for the popular periodicals echoed the praise of her gentleness and tenderness, the regret for her excessive passivity.[234] Such criticisms as these suggest a kinship between Desdemona and Ophelia similar to that which Colley Cibber saw earlier. Both characters had gained in literary reputation since Cibber's time because of the new emphasis on Shakespeare's heroines, but the demands of the theatre did not allow much practical capitalization on these gains. The star system was in its heyday. No ambitious actress would attempt to build her reputation on the drooping, wavering creature the critics described —especially when she is flanked in the same play by the passionate Othello and the devilishly fascinating Iago. It is little wonder that when FANNY KEMBLE offered to play Desdemona to his Othello, MACREADY expressed surprise at her willingness to undertake a part in which "nobody can produce any effect"[235]—just as Helen Faucit's friends were shocked when she agreed to play Ophelia to Macready's Hamlet.

But there were several actor-critics of the nineteenth century who protested against the idea of a passive Desdemona. Fanny

231. "The Characters of Shakespeare's Plays," *Complete Works of Hazlitt*, ed. Howe, IV, 205.

232. *Characteristics of Women* (Boston, 1853), p. 157. Both Hazlitt and Mrs. Jameson used a quotation from the play—Iago's "Ay, too gentle," followed by Othello's "Nay, that's certain"—to support their notions of Desdemona's passive, yielding disposition. These romantic critics were incredibly vulnerable to Iago's spell.

233. *Dramatic Essays, Leigh Hunt*, ed. Archer and Lowe, p. 208.

234. For example, an author who signed himself "H.T." wrote in the *Othello* number of *Tallis's Shakspere Gallery of Engravings* (London and New York, 1850): "Poor Desdemona is the perfection of womanly gentleness and tenderness. . . . If she has a fault, it is that she is too passive."

235. Frances Anne Kemble, *Records of Later Life* (New York, 1882), p. 638.

Kemble was one of them (see the analysis of the murder scene at the end of the present chapter); but those who discussed the character most fully were HELEN FAUCIT, EDWIN BOOTH, and ELLEN TERRY.

All three of these deplored the usual interpretation, which they considered weak and unworthy. Miss Faucit recalled that Desdemona had been one of her girlhood heroines. "How could it be otherwise? A being so bright, so pure, so unselfish, generous, courageous—so devoted in her love, so unconquerable in her allegiance. . . ."

I did not know in those days that Desdemona is usually considered a merely amiable, simple, yielding creature, and that she is generally so represented on the stage. This is the last idea that would have entered my mind. To me she was in all things worthy to be a hero's bride. . . . "Gentle" she was, no doubt. . . . But . . . in the Italian and old English sense, implying that union of nobility of person and of disposition which shows itself in an unconscious grace of movement and of outward appearance.

The firm, courageous poise that Desdemona shows in the Senate scene, the request to follow her husband to Cyprus (not the plea of a timid girl, surely), Othello's appropriate greeting, "O my fair warrior"—all these pointed, in Helen Faucit's opinion, to a character of strength and substance.[236] Booth was slightly more traditional in some of his remarks, but he too declared that Desdemona is not "the darling 'daisy' we see on the stage . . . but a true woman, with a mind of her own, a deathly devotion to the man of her choice."[237] And Ellen Terry insisted that a "great tragic actress, with a strong personality and a strong method, is far better suited to the role" than the usual "actress of the dolly type," for Desdemona is no "ninny"—she is "strong, not weak." Her pertinacity in pleading for Cassio does not show lack of intelligence. "Let the actress give a charming 'I'm not really asking much of you' tone to Desdemona's suit . . . and a very different impression will be produced."

Her purity of heart and her charity . . . are sufficient explanation of her being slow to grasp the situation. It is not until she has been grossly insulted and brutally assaulted that she understands. Her

236. *On Some of Shakespeare's Female Characters*, pp. 47-48, 59-60.

237. Letter to Howard H. Furness, quoted in Edwina Booth Grossmann's *Edwin Booth: Recollections by His Daughter, and Letters to Her and Her Friends* (New York, 1894), p. 257.

behaviour from that dreadful moment should surely convince us that she is not a simpleton, but a saint.[238]

In explaining Desdemona's love for Othello, Helen Faucit and Edwin Booth had rather similar ideas. As in the case of Ophelia, the actress imagined a predramatic life for Desdemona: her mother must have died early, and her father was probably rather cold and unsympathetic, blind to the heroic dreams of his daughter which caused her to be fascinated by Othello and his stories of adventure. (Brabantio's lack of understanding, not Desdemona's hypocrisy, would thus account for her father's shocked surprise over the choice made by his "maiden never bold.")[239] Booth drew on his own experience—as a famous actor he had been a hero-figure for many young girls—and came to much the same conclusion to which Miss Faucit's imagination led her. When KITTY MOLONY, a novice in his company, saw Booth in his bronze make-up, she exclaimed impulsively, "You are the most beautiful creature I have ever seen!" and added that he was the first Othello who had not made her shudder at the idea of Desdemona's marriage. Booth replied: "You are a young girl. Desdemona's psychology is not unlike your own. I contend Othello should be attractive enough for Desdemona to fall in love with. Othello is not a tragedy of abnormal passions."[240] Booth pointed out on another occasion, however, that Desdemona was intellectually superior to the average girl who is smitten by hero-worship. "She saw *Othello*'s visage in his mind; had she not been similarly endowed she might have been fascinated . . . asked for his autograph, giggled, and said 'Yes'—to repent at leisure. She never repented her love and marriage . . . even in her own death. . . ."[241]

A new and individual point of view was revealed in the explanation of Desdemona's love given by Ellen Terry. On the basis of Brabantio's description ("So opposite to marriage. . . ."), Miss Terry decided that "there is something of the potential nun" in Desdemona.

She is more fitted to be the bride of Christ than of any man. . . . Her virginal heart is profoundly moved by the meeting with Othello. . . .

238. *Four Lectures on Shakespeare*, ed. with an introduction by Christopher St. John [Christabel Marshall] (London, [1932]), pp. 128, 130-31. See also *The Story of My Life*, p. 207.

239. *On Some of Shakespeare's Female Characters*, pp. 53-55, 57-59.

240. Goodale, *Behind the Scenes with Edwin Booth*, p. 208.

241. Letter to Furness, quoted in Grossmann's *Edwin Booth*, pp. 256-57.

The story of his life rouses her compassionate interest. . . . Whereas the handsome faces of the curled darlings had seemed ugly . . . because their minds were ugly, Othello's face seemed fair to her because his mind was fair.

This woman does not use the word "consecrate" lightly. "Love to her is a sacrament," and consecration of herself to Othello makes her capable of violating "all the conventions for his sake." Even by nature, however, she is unconventional.

Othello's doubts that she is chaste are usually made to seem absolutely monstrous in the theatre, because Desdemona's unconventionality is ignored. She is not at all prim or demure; on the contrary, she is genially expressive, the kind of woman who being devoid of coquetry behaves as she feels. Her manner to Cassio might easily fertilize the poisonous seed of suspicion Iago has sown in Othello's mind.[242]

Ellen Terry's point about unconventionality is well taken. It should be reinforced by the reminder (which would not have been necessary when she was giving her readings) that Desdemona is also a great lady, like Portia, who is thoroughly at ease with the outward conventions of her world, who graciously performs the accepted duties of household and court, and who joyfully participates in the accepted pleasures. Because of this her unconventionality is the more striking, and the more dangerous to her. It proceeds, not from a conscious rebellion against her society and its codes, but from a natural superiority to them bred of an unusual frankness and generosity, an independence of spirit united with a great capacity for devotion.

Miss Terry's Desdemona was very much her own creation, yet it was also very much in harmony with Miss Faucit's: there is a certain Joan-of-Arc quality in both, a union of courage and idealism; a highborn girl who spends the lonely hours of her youth in heroic daydreams might well have developed the qualities of a potential nun; the whole-hearted devotion to the man who has realized her ideal accounts for Desdemona's ardor in both interpretations, an ardor that transcends the sentimental as it does the merely physical. Of all the actor-critics, whether in their own period or in others, Helen Faucit and Ellen Terry demonstrated the finest understanding of Desdemona.

Both of these actresses, too, were eminently fitted to play the part as they conceived it: both had the presence for it—they were

242. *Four Lectures on Shakespeare*, pp. 129-30.

tall, graceful, and extremely attractive in the literal sense of the word (not merely pretty) ; both had the gift of combining womanly charm with deep emotion; both were able to suggest qualities of intellect and nobility—Miss Faucit's Antigone became one of her finest performances, Miss Terry was an admirable Portia. Their acting styles were different, but they had much the same effect on the audiences of their respective days. Helen Faucit acted Desdemona at intervals during her London period, 1836-43, often with Macready as Othello, and again late in 1844 during a brief engagement in Paris. Although she was a novice of nineteen when she first undertook the role, she must have matured sufficiently in her art after a few years to embody effectively the conception that she later expressed in writing. EDWARD WILLIAM ELTON, who played Brabantio in a number of the performances, warmly approved her spirited interpretation, saying that "it restored the balance of the play by giving [Desdemona's] character its due weight in the action, so that . . . he had then seen the tragedy for the first time in its true *chiaro-oscuro.*" Even Macready, who was not easy to please, told Miss Faucit, as she recalls, "that my brightness and gaiety in the early happy scenes at Cyprus helped him greatly, and that, when sadder, I was not lachrymose, and, above all, that I added intensity to the last act by 'being so difficult to kill.' "243 Not all Desdemonas "bent meekly" to their deaths! Unfortunately Miss Faucit's interest in Desdemona—apparently a sincere one—fell as a victim to the star system, for she rarely acted the role during her touring days, the longer and much the finer part of her career. Rosalind, Juliet, Beatrice, sometimes Lady Macbeth—Shakespearean parts like these composed her repertory then, along with modern heroines like Pauline in *The Lady of Lyons.* A star, whether woman or man, had to shine as the dominant light in a play, not merely contribute to the effect of chiaroscuro. Some forty-odd years after Helen Faucit's London performances, Ellen Terry acted Desdemona, with Irving and Booth as alternating Othellos. At the height of her powers, she gave a memorable interpretation, spirited as well as pathetic. But when that series of performances (four times a week, from May 2 to June 17, 1881) came to an end, Irving determined never to stage *Othello* again. Since Miss

243. *On Some of Shakespeare's Female Characters,* p. 50.

Terry's theatrical fortunes were bound up with his, her Desdemona was lost to the stage from that time. There were other effective Desdemonas in the nineteenth century, of course, but it is ironic that the two actresses who should have been most identified with the role actually performed it for relatively brief periods.

Desdemona's boldness and unconventionality need to be recognized. If they are exaggerated or misinterpreted, however, the character suffers. This kind of reaction has occurred occasionally in the present century, particularly in LENA ASHWELL's[244] and GEORGE R. FOSS's[245] criticisms and, to a lesser extent, in ROBERT SPEAIGHT's.[246] Miss Ashwell, for example, overstated the case against the golden-haired "angel" of traditional interpretations when she wrote that the Othello who suspects such a woman is "a fool . . . when he smothers her he is a coward. The audience is bored, and feels that she ought to be smothered, but that the man who does it is beneath contempt." Colorful language aside, she was echoing Ellen Terry's point that an overly decorous Desdemona undercuts the credibility of Othello's jealousy. The trouble was that exaggeration was used not only in stating the problem but also in solving it. Apparently Miss Terry's rather moderate (and intelligent) description of Desdemona's unconventionality seemed by Miss Ashwell's time too mild to stem the tide of skepticism. Only by finding serious faults in Desdemona's character could Miss Ashwell convince herself that Iago would dare his accusation and Othello would believe it. Actually her interpretation of Desdemona is a mixture of admiration and blame, and in one passage she stresses the fact that the faults are "all on the surface, the virtue deep and true." Yet, in her eagerness to convince the reader that the faults do exist, she creates in other passages the impression that they predominate: for example, when she insists that Desdemona is not an "innocent and joyous heroine" but "an angel of the red variety," "the spark which kindles soul-destroying passions."

The more or less derogatory tendency in recent Desdemona criticism, represented by the actor-critics whom I have mentioned, reflects two modern preoccupations: the demand that the passions of Shakespeare's characters be rationalized (the basis of

244. *Reflections from Shakespeare*, pp. 107, 110, 112-13.
245. *What the Author Meant*, pp. 75-76.
246. *Nature in Shakespearian Tragedy*, pp. 73-76 (especially p. 74); p. 83.

Speaight's criticism as well as Miss Ashwell's) and the attempt to explain Shakespeare's plays in terms of Elizabethan attitudes and customs (the basis of Foss's interpretation).

Foss gives the darkest picture of the character—at least, as far as her initial behavior is concerned. By Elizabethan standards he finds her guilty of two "reprehensible crimes": her disobedience and deception of her father, and her marriage with a black man. (In his opinion, Shakespeare's contemporaries were so horrified by this type of union that they would have considered Tamora's love for Aaron in *Titus Andronicus* the "most degrading" of her "many crimes.") Modern tolerance of filial disobedience and (in some countries) of mixed marriages should not blind us to the fact that the virtuous Desdemona has conducted a "vulgar underhand intrigue with a man whom she knows her father, her friends, and her countrymen regard as of an inferior race." Similarly, Othello, though basically noble, has behaved "dishonorably to his patron and host." Their punishment is deserved, yet "we who have seen that punishment, pity, forgive, and usually forget all about the follies . . . that brought it about." Foss suggests that in *Othello* Shakespeare deliberately "set himself the task" of gaining sympathy for a woman whose conduct has been utterly deplorable, just as in *Julius Caesar* he had won sympathy for a man who had "committed the most despicable crime possible."

Desdemona's unconventionality wins a certain admiration from both Lena Ashwell and Robert Speaight. The latter describes her as "ardent and courageous"; and the former remarks more effusively: "Only an unconventional woman would have seen through the dark skin of the Moor into the deep grandeur of his manhood, and married him in the teeth of all conventions. . . ." But for both of these actor-critics deceptiveness is a weakness in Desdemona's character that cannot be overlooked. "Only a hussy would fool and betray her father," Miss Ashwell declares uncompromisingly. Desdemona's elopement cannot be excused, as can Jessica's in *The Merchant of Venice,* on the grounds of an unhappy home life: her father has not only surrounded her with luxuries but has given her "considerable freedom" and his "entire confidence." Her betrayal of that confidence, and its possible implications for her future behavior toward her husband— this is the "key to the whole action." Important as the color difference seems to the audience, it is not that so much as Brabantio's warning, "vigorously thrust aside at the time" but remembered later, which makes possible the success of Iago's treachery. Miss Ashwell points out, too, that at a time when Desdemona's "probity" is crucial to her husband's peace of mind, it is tested and found wanting (in the lie about the handkerchief). Speaight, who describes Desdemona as "obstinate and cunning," goes so far as to compare her character with Iago's in the respect that it presents "a contrast between appearance and reality." Although he quickly adds, "Not, of course, Iago's monstrous lie, but a quite innocent deceptiveness," the fact that any comparison has been made at all sticks in the reader's mind.

In other points the discussions of Desdemona by Miss Ashwell and Speaight differ considerably, and each reflects the particular bias of the critic. For example, Desdemona's pleas for Cassio's reinstatement probably seem to most readers (or members of an audience) an untimely but gracious attempt to reconcile two worthy friends. To Miss Ashwell, however, daughter of Commander Pocock of the Royal Navy, they mark Desdemona as a type of officious wife, well known in service families, who "interferes with appointments and promotions to the ruin of her husband's efficiency in command and reputation." As for Speaight, his interest in Freudian psychology is reflected in his suggestion that Desdemona, in consummating her marriage, revealed a hitherto unsuspected inclination toward sensual enjoyment which, though it casts no shadow on her purity, helps to explain Othello's jealousy.

Neither Miss Ashwell nor Speaight (nor, for that matter, Foss) has offered any really revolutionary theories about Desdemona, as far as criticism in general is concerned. (For example, although Speaight's notion of "sexual precocity" is unique, as far as I know, the basic idea of Desdemona's sensuous nature is not new; as we have seen, some literary critics of the nineteenth century advanced it.) But these writers do represent a new phenomenon among *actor*-critics. The predominant influence of the stage, in acting and in criticism, has been on the side of a thoroughly wholesome as well as innocent and sympathetic Desdemona.

Not all modern actor-critics have gone to extremes in reacting against the sweet but spineless heroine of traditional interpretations. HARLEY GRANVILLE-BARKER's analysis of Desdemona is not only more sympathetic than the ones we have just discussed but more traditional than Helen Faucit's or Ellen Terry's. As his criticism usually does, however, it modifies and enriches tradition and, at some points, contradicts it.

The Desdemona of his conception is far from being a "ninny" (her "gently obstinate incredulity of evil" is ascribed, not to obtuseness, but to her innate goodness combined with her strict, isolated upbringing) ; but her personality is less positive than the one described by Miss Faucit or Miss Terry. She is not exactly an "angel," but she certainly differs from Miss Ashwell's conception in being "selfless, high-minded, reasonable of heart"; and her "too absolute goodness" is recognized, rightly, as the "fiber of which Iago's enmeshing net is made." Her courage and self-confidence, particularly in the Senate scene, are duly appreciated. But the courage that Granville-Barker describes is neither self-assertive nor obviously unconventional; its gentle, unobtrusive nature, indeed, probably accounts for her father's failure to suspect "what ardor and resolve might lie beneath her accustomed quiet." One point supporting a quiet Desdemona is particularly interesting: her reticence in times of emotion—which, as Granville-Barker remarks, is a source of "mortal peril" to her. "Moments of great joy leave her at a loss" (compare the expressiveness of Othello's greeting at Cyprus with the restrained brevity of her reply) , and "moments of misery leave her dumbfounded too" (she is "half-asleep" after the gross insults of the brothel scene) . She habitually hides her true feelings under stress (e.g. in the first Cyprus scene she cloaks her anxiety for Othello's safety by pretending to joke) , but not from a wish to deceive. Her basic truthfulness outshines her occasional "ingenuous streaks of self-deception, or the scared fib about the handkerchief, even as it transfigures the incredible lie of her dying . . . [speech] into a shaming of the mere truth."[247]

Granville-Barker's interpretation is surely the most satisfactory of the modern group. There is nothing in it that contradicts either the letter or the spirit of the text. And at one or two points it suggests thought-provoking possibilities for the reader to contemplate and for the actress, perhaps, to develop. It presents Desdemona as rather too mild and self-effacing, perhaps, but it does allow for sterner stuff beneath the gentleness and restraint of her surface. The resulting character cannot quite be identified with Helen Faucit's "fair warrior," but she is a shy young cousin.

247. *Prefaces to Shakespeare*, II, 51, 65, 69, 79 (footnote), 122-26.

III. FROM CRITICISM TO THEATRE

The union of interpretive analysis with practical suggestions for the theatre is well illustrated in some of the actors' criticisms of *Othello* that have already been discussed—for example, in Helen Faucit's description of Desdemona's actions and mood in the willow scene. But the largest number of interesting examples can be found in their commentaries on the murder scene.

The earliest relevant document, and in many ways the most interesting, is a manuscript letter, now in the Victoria and Albert Museum, from the quondam actor-manager GEORGE SWAN to David Garrick (December 11, 1773). In it Swan describes a set of notes, or "minutes," as he calls them, that he has compiled on *Othello* and that he offers to Garrick in the hope that the great actor will not only use them in a production of his own but will give them some literary finish and have them published (a vain hope, evidently). He indicates that the major difference between his conception of the play and that found in traditional performances is in the murder scene, and he proceeds to give a detailed analysis of it, including the rationale for each bit of action that he suggests. The analysis reflects a careful, if sometimes literal-minded, reading of individual lines and an attempt to suit the action to the words. It also indicates an interest in the psychology of Othello's character—not psychology of a very subtle or complex sort, but at least an attempt to explain the thoughts that lie behind Othello's actions. The result suggests an exciting sequence of action (provided the acting is good enough to rise above the awkward off-again-on-again effect that one gets in reading), with a Desdemona rather more athletic than usual and an Othello rather less efficient at murdering. Since Swan's letter is relatively inaccessible, I shall quote from it at more length than it would, perhaps, deserve otherwise.

The other commentaries upon which I have drawn most heavily in this section were also written by actors for actors (though Granville-Barker has a wider audience as well). They are EDWIN BOOTH's notes to *Othello* in the *Furness Variorum*, HARLEY GRANVILLE-BARKER's *Prefaces to Shakespeare*, and GEORGE SKILLAN's notes in *French's Acting Edition* of the play.[248] Since these are readily available to most readers, selections from them will be

248. Booth, VI, 297-326; Granville-Barker, II, 76-96; Skillan, pp. 81-94.

restricted to those that seem to me particularly interesting for purposes of comparison. There will also be brief extracts from the writings of FRANCIS GENTLEMAN, FANNY KEMBLE, and HELEN FAUCIT relevant to particular points made by the others. Although relatively few works are drawn upon here, they are representative of several different time periods: Swan and Gentleman are from the eighteenth century; Miss Kemble, Miss Faucit, and Booth from the nineteenth; Granville-Barker and Skillan from the twentieth.

Othello's Entrance and Opening Soliloquy

SWAN's Othello enters with poniard ready to strike, for he intends to stab Desdemona immediately. In contrast, SKILLAN's Othello is unarmed and very quiet; he "enters with bowed head, deliberately not looking at DESDEMONA." Whether he does so or not, the Othello of the usual conception could enter without a weapon, or with his weapon undrawn, for he intends to stifle or strangle Desdemona, not stab her.[249] Whatever one may think of Swan's reasoning, however, his dagger-bearing actor would present a *picture* more in keeping with the attitude usually attributed to Othello than would one who approached with empty hands. For there is one point on which there is general agreement, from Swan to Skillan: that Othello at the beginning of this scene shows the awful deliberation of a priest, or a minister of justice, about to perform a necessary sacrifice.

Ironically, if Swan's logic is rigidly applied, this emphasis upon justice rather than vengeance is not really consonant with the dagger-bearing Othello that (in his opinion) the text demands; for Swan consistently connects actual bloodshed with a mood of rage or impulsive violence and considers strangling a "milder" or more merciful form of killing. The incongruity arises from a close and literal reading of the text, including a portion of the preceding scene (V, i, 28-36), when Othello makes a brief appearance at a "Balcony, or Window," hearing from a distance the cries from the Roderigo-Cassio fight. (This scene was customarily

249. Othello has sometimes entered with a drawn sword, but without using it in the murder. A note in Oxberry's edition (1819) objects to this "modern practice" in view of Othello's determination to strangle Desdemona in bed. Professor Sprague points out, however, that the words "Yet I'll not shed her blood . . ." are "not . . . inappropriately accompanied by his laying down his sword—as Theobald had perceived back in the eighteenth century" (*Shakespeare and the Actors*, p. 210). Swan has Othello pocket his dagger at these same words.

omitted at the time of Swan's letter, but he considered it very important.[250]) Swan overcomes his difficulty by reconstructing Othello's state of mind as it must have been between scenes, even providing him with an offstage soliloquy. In the "balcony" scene, the sounds that seemingly arise from Iago's fulfillment of his promise to murder Cassio excite in Othello a determination to kill Desdemona immediately. He plans to use a dagger, for he says, "Thy bed, lust-stained, shall with lust's blood be spotted." (This speech reflects a later decision than that made in IV, i, 217-222, when he had considered poison and had accepted Iago's suggestion of strangling instead.) He goes into another room to "fetch an Instrument proper for executing this resolve," but as he takes the poniard in hand and approaches the bedchamber, he begins to ask himself:

"What is the use I am going to make of this weapon? To murther a defenseless, a sleeping woman? I who have so often dared the greatest dangers of the bloody Field, 'tis base! it is dreadful!—but it must be done—my Honour is at stake. My Friend Iago has already executed his part, I must not fail in mine: besides! the Cause will justify me to God, & Man."

The words, "It is the Cause," with which Othello enters the murder scene are "the close of this reflection, or soliloquy, which he has been making without." Thus Swan's Othello finds himself with an instrument of violence, but by the time he is prepared to use it he is no longer in a violent frame of mind. As he approaches the bed, he is deterred from his resolution by the sight of Desdemona's "body and beauty," as he had previously feared that he would be. The actor should "stop short, &, turning from her, put up the Poniard into his pocket," before he goes on to say, "Yet I'll not shed her blood. . . ." With his eyes turning away

250. Professor Sprague comments that Rowe's direction to Othello to enter "*above at a window*" apparently implies that Rowe had seen him do so in a theatre but that, beginning with Bell's edition of 1774, the acting texts regularly omit Othello's appearance in this scene. Swan, who was writing in 1773 but whose memory went back, no doubt, to his own acting of Othello thirty years earlier, uses the phrase "the Balcony, or Window, Scene" in a casual way which certainly suggests familiar stage practice. According to Tate Wilkinson (*Memoirs*, II, 151-52), Swan, while living at York (his home when he wrote to Garrick), "taught Mr. Jackson, now the Edinburgh manager, how to undraw the curtain in his favorite balcony scene [in *Othello*] never acted but by his direction. . . ." This would indicate that the York theatre continued to use the scene—perhaps at Swan's insistence.

from that beauty which has "unprovided his mind," Othello realizes "That She must dye; else she'll betray more Men." Justice, not rage, dictates this thought, and Othello "now again resolves upon the milder method of dispatching her."

Later interpreters put more emphasis upon the religious element in Othello's attitude. Skillan, for example, remarks of his opening words: "He is now appealing to his soul, to the spiritual representative of Heaven in himself"; he is "resolved upon . . . the greatest sacrifice he could make for the sake of what he fervently believes to be the demands" not only of "justice" but also of "the salvation of the one he loves." In Skillan's interpretation Othello has somehow arrived at the idea that he can purge Desdemona's soul by making her atone physically for her sin and he therefore hopes to be reunited with an innocent Desdemona in a better world. Throughout the scene this Othello reveals "a mind tuned to high spiritual reception." GRANVILLE-BARKER also describes Othello's attitude as that of "a priest come to do sacrifice," but, as he uses it, this image is more pagan than Christian (or Hebraic), and it certainly does not imply a concern for Desdemona's soul. Like Skillan, however, Granville-Barker believes that Othello is in a state of controlled exaltation: "Exalted in his persuasion that it is justice that he deals and not vengeance, he regains a satanic semblance of the nobility that was."

The passage "Put out the light. . . ." is interpreted by Swan as further evidence of Othello's enslavement to Desdemona's physical beauty. Othello turns back toward the bed and "makes a motion as with design to strangle" Desdemona, but once more he "finds it impossible to execute his purpose, whilst those Charms are visible. He therefore determines to 'Put out the light. . . .'" Skillan focuses his attention, not on the reason Othello thinks of extinguishing the light, but on the emotional effect that this thought creates.[251] He imagines Othello giving "a furtive look towards the candle on the table," saying, "Put out the light and then—," pausing as he is moved to awe by "the tremendous significance of the death he is about to usher in." Skillan's idea of the effect exercised by Desdemona's beauty is more spiritual than

251. Madge Kendal writes, "I have heard the most clever and intelligent and gifted men in my profession argue—I had almost said for hours—over the reading of these few words. . . ." (*Dramatic Opinions* [Boston, 1890], pp. 61-63). For some of the ways in which actors have tried to illuminate this passage through action, see Professor Sprague's discussion in *Shakespeare and the Actors*, pp. 210-11.

Swan's. When Othello says, "Be thus when thou art dead," it is "her look of lovely innocence which he is addressing," and "I will kill thee/ And love thee after" means that "once she has atoned for her sin he will love her perfectly."

Desdemona's Fight for Life

Several actors have expressed the feeling that Desdemona should be much more spirited in the murder scene that she is usually represented. Most of them refer to action involving the murder itself, but SKILLAN's remarks apply also to Desdemona's earlier reactions. He reminds us that she was not "aware of the depth or nature" of Othello's feeling until the latter part of the play; now, when he awakens her and talks of killing, a woman of her "quality and strong spirit" naturally reacts with abhorrence to the sudden threat of violent death and fights for self-preservation. When Othello accuses her of having given the handkerchief to Cassio, "There is just a moment's pause while she realizes this hitherto unthought of notion. Then she springs to her feet and gives her denial with tremendous emphasis." "Ay, but not to die" is spoken spiritedly as "firmly on her feet . . . she [challenges] her fate." Although at the line "And have you mercy too!" she falls to her knees and clings to Othello's clothes, she never weeps until she learns of Cassio's death and realizes that she has lost the means of proving her innocence. Then she "collapses on the bed and her tears burst forth."

SWAN's remarks apply to the actual murder. Here, he was convinced, Desdemona should so effectually resist Othello's efforts to smother her that he would be forced to use the dagger after all. Swan interpreted the text to imply that Desdemona twice struggles free from Othello's grasp—a fact indicated by her speaking "so as to be heard by the Audience" on two separate occasions. (Evidently he reasoned that her voice would have been too muffled for distinct speech if Shakespeare had not intended this action.) This is what happens: Othello, excited to "rage little short of madness" by her weeping at Cassio's death, attempts to smother her. She breaks away and pleads, "O banish me, my lord, but kill me not." Othello's "Down, strumpet!" indicates that "his rage is still violent" and also "implys a great resistance on her part." She frees herself again and says, "Kill me tomorrow, let me live to-night."

Here he, exasperated at her having twice broken from his grip . . . resolves instantaneously, in the heat of the action, to take some other course. The obvious, and, indeed, the only meaning of his next sentence "Nay, if you strive." Thus resolved, what course so ready as an Application to the Poniard. . . .

Desdemona, seeing the weapon, begs, "But half an hour." But, "fearful that if he hesitates longer, her body & beauty may again get the better," he says, half aside . . . 'Being done, there is no pause.' "

He therefore lifts his hand to strike the blow, upon which she intreats a still shorter time—"But while I say one prayer."—he immediately stabs her, and looking, with horrour, on the bloody ponyard, says—"It is too late"—which . . . he would not with any sort of propriety, have said, if he was still endeavouring to strangle her.

The typical stage Desdemona in the eighteenth century probably did not put up the vigorous struggle that Swan imagined for her. Nor did she in the nineteenth century, if Charlotte Vandenhoff's death scene (already described) was the ideal that her reviewer represented it to be. When FANNY KEMBLE was preparing to act Desdemona for the first time, she determined to "make a desperate fight" of the murder scene. Although she felt that there is nothing in Shakespeare's text to justify Othello's chasing Desdemona around the bedroom as on the Italian stage, where actresses "run for their lives," she could not resign herself to the behavior of the English Desdemonas, who "acquiesce with wonderful equanimity in their assassination." Miss Kemble decided to get up on her knees in bed and "throw her arms tight around Othello's neck in a last appeal for mercy."[252] A Desdemona who struggles instead of meekly surrendering would point up the difficulty the warrior Othello has in killing a woman, obviously much weaker than he.

Did it ever occur to you what a witness to Othello's agony in murdering his wretched wife his inefficient clumsiness in the process was—his half smothering, his half stabbing her? *That* man not to be able to kill *that* woman outright . . . how tortured he must have been. . . .[253]

252. *Records of Later Life*, pp. 630-31. From a letter to Harriet St. Leger, dated February 18, 1848.

253. *Ibid.*, p. 643. From a letter dated "Wednesday 23d, 1848."

HELEN FAUCIT, too, felt that Desdemona should resist with all her strength Othello's efforts to kill her, not only because this would be natural in any case, but also because she could not bear to die before proving her innocence. When she acted the death scene, Miss Faucit said, "I felt for *him* as well as myself, and therefore I threw into my remonstrances all the power of passionate appeal I could command." In her identity as Desdemona, "I thought of all his after-suffering, when he should come to know how he had mistaken me! The agony for him which filled my heart, as well as the mortal agony of death which I felt in imagination, made my cries and struggles no doubt very vehement and very real."[254]

The Coup de Grace

There has been considerable question about Othello's action at the lines

> Not dead! not yet quite dead?
> I that am cruel, am yet merciful;
> I would not have thee linger in thy pain—
> So, so.
>
> (V, ii, 84-88)

According to Sprague, a pillow was employed to murder Desdemona "from quite early times," but the tradition of giving her the *coup de grace* with a dagger dates from some time in the eighteenth century—how early is uncertain, but one writer reported the story that Powell (who died in 1769) had used it.[255] As far as I know, the first actor who referred in print to the propriety of having Othello stab Desdemona was FRANCIS GENTLE-MAN (1770): "The revival of Desdemona from a state of suffocation and her expiring without any fresh violence, we apprehend to be rather absurd, therefore highly approve Othello's stabbing her with a dagger,—drawing blood accounts naturally for gaining power of speech, and yet may be mortal."[256] It is possible that SWAN had used a dagger nearly thirty years earlier when he acted Othello in 1742 (at the Theatre Royal, Dublin) but not at this point in the action. (It is not clear whether his notes reflect the business that he himself had used or whether they were the result

254. *On Some of Shakespeare's Female Characters*, pp. 77-78.
255. *Shakespeare and the Actors*, p. 215.
256. *Dramatic Censor*, I, 148.

of his ruminations after his retirement from the stage.) As we have seen, Swan felt that a dagger should be used in the murder scene, but earlier, while Othello is under the influence of "rage and horror." He scornfully rejected the suggestion that it should be used for the *coup de grace*: "A strange idea, sure, of mercy, to imbrue his hands in the blood of a dying woman."[257] Rather, Othello "mercyfully (according to his Idea of Mercy) presses his hand against her throat, until She ceased to move."

But, Swan to the contrary, stifling or "strangling" continued to be used for the first part of the murder and, frequently, a dagger at "So, so." EDWIN BOOTH was a particularly merciful Othello who used a dagger for the *coup de grace*. He expressed Othello's anguish in the direction: "Hide your face in trembling hand while you stab and groan 'so, so'; the steel is piercing your own heart."

SKILLAN, however, thinks that no bloodshed is necessary at any point in the scene. His Othello stifles Desdemona with a pillow during the first part of the murder; at "So, so," he "presses his thumbs into her throat." According to Skillan, these two methods, taken together, would "leave her face pale and free from discoloration as well as allow for a short recovery a little later on."

The Aftermath of Murder

BOOTH and GRANVILLE-BARKER offer some interesting contrasts in their interpretations of the murder scene. "Remember how often he is moved to tears," Booth says of his anguished murderer. But, according to Granville-Barker, Othello kills Desdemona "in cold, deliberate anger." Booth's Othello feels the dagger in his own heart; the *coup de grace* is, in Granville-Barker's phrase, mere "hangman humanity." "She's like a liar gone to burning hell" should be spoken, according to Booth, "with deep emotion, not

257. This objection is stated in a letter to Garrick published by Boaden, a later one than the MS letter containing the analysis of the murder scene. Garrick in the meantime had sent Swan's analysis to George Steevens, who, in his 1773 edition of Shakespeare, had noted the effectiveness of having Othello stab Desdemona, for the same reason that Gentleman had given, and had suggested that an original stage direction to this effect had been lost. Steevens, however, like other adherents to the dagger theory, felt that the stabbing should take place at "So, so." He wrote Garrick that he and Swan were agreed "in the main point, that a dagger is necessary" but that they disagreed on the "period" in the action at which it should be used. Steevens' letter, as well as Swan's comment on it, is found in *The Private Correspondence of David Garrick with the Most Celebrated Persons of His Time*, ed. James Boaden (London, 1831), I, 592-93, 598-99.

harshly." But for Granville-Barker, Othello in this speech is "frenetically, exultantly invoking an eternal vengeance . . . upon the gentle dead."

For SKILLAN, the "burning hell" speech is the point at which Othello's artificial restraint in Emilia's presence breaks down and he bursts into "fierce hysteria." The effort to accomplish his "immense sacrifice" has been "too exhausting"; now that mind and will are no longer "harnessed to a supreme . . . purpose," they become "paralyzed." Skillan feels, incidentally, that Emilia should not run from the scene when she calls for help but should stand doggedly rooted to her mistress's side,[258] expecting each moment to be her last, yet defying Othello with "supernatural" courage. Thus she becomes a kind of Nemesis figure for Othello, who is limp and helpless in the presence of "something stronger than himself."

There are striking similarities as well as differences among the comments by Booth, Granville-Barker, and Skillan: for instance, their descriptions of Othello's trancelike condition immediately after the murder, when, during Emilia's knocking, he fears that she will speak to his wife—"My wife, my wife: what wife? I have no wife." Booth describes him as pausing after the first use of *wife* "as if stunned, or, rather puzzled by so strange a word"; he "mutters it twice inquiringly, then, under the full force of horror, he almost *screams,* 'I have no wife!' and falls prostrate. . . ." Granville-Barker writes that Othello is "still benumbed," hardly aware of what he has done, until he speaks the "intimate" word *wife;* then he "stumbles . . . into the light of irrevocable fact" and cries out "in amazed agony." Skillan's conception of Othello's mood is similar, but not the manner of expressing his final enlightenment: Othello looks "straight in front as he repeats himself," then, after turning to look down at Desdemona, "announces the revelation to himself in that cold and stunned way when fact confirms some deadly rumor."

Toward the end of this final scene of *Othello* both Booth and Granville-Barker discover echoes of the memorable passage in Act II when Othello and Desdemona were reunited after the storm. In Othello's speech to Iago, "I'd have thee live,/ For in my sense 'tis happiness to die," is heard—says Booth—the "same sad refrain" as in the speech that marks the height of his happiness, "If it

258. Cf. *Shakespeare and the Actors,* pp. 216-17.

were now to die,/ 'Twere now to be most happy." And Granville-
Barker notices that "Here is my journey's end, here is my butt/
And very sea-mark of my utmost sail" is reminiscent of "O my
soul's joy! If after every tempest come such calms. . . ." Skillan
chooses the same early speech as a kind of compendious expression
of the whole tragedy. At the very end of his notes on the play, he
writes: "The labouring bark has climbed hills of seas Olympus
high and ducked again as low as Hell's from Heaven. The winds
have blown till they have wakened death and after the tempest
has come such calm."

These words are indicative of the mood of reconciliation that
Skillan feels at the end of *Othello*. Othello's nobility is recovered,
and his last speech focuses anew on the heroic qualities of the
man. We can be reconciled to his tragedy because we are aware
that the greatness of his love was at the root of all his actions.
And, although Granville-Barker remarks elsewhere that there is
no catharsis in this play, that "Othello wakes as from a nightmare
only to kill himself, his prospect hell," even he describes Othello's
last moments in words that suggest reconciliation as the effect to
be conveyed: Othello at the last knows better than "Venice can
decide what is due to an Othello, traitor to his Christian self, from
him who is now that self again"; he dies with Desdemona in his
arms, and the "simple rhythm and the simple sentiment" of his
last speech "harbors peace in oblivion."

CHAPTER FOUR · *Actors' Criticisms of* King Lear

I. THE PLAY

Attitudes toward Textual Alteration

Any critic who wrote about *King Lear* during the years 1681-1838—and especially any critic intimately connected with the stage—was obliged to consider, not simply Shakespeare's text, but one or more revised versions of the play. For during that period, of course, Nahum Tate's adaptation, together with such modifications as George Colman's and David Garrick's, held the stage in preference to the original play. Tate's omission of the Fool, his addition of a love story linking Cordelia and Edgar, his happy ending in which Lear is restored to the throne, and his alterations of Shakespeare's language in the interest of regular meter and polished diction are well known.[1] Even if the actor-critics had given no thought to the question of alteration per se, they would necessarily have been influenced in their conceptions of the play by the stage texts with which they were most familiar. But a number of them did specifically discuss the desirability of alteration as a principle and the merits (or weaknesses) of the individual adaptations, especially Tate's.

There is a paradoxical quality in the attitude toward *King Lear* expressed by the eighteenth century actor-critics, much as there is in their attitude toward *Hamlet*. Several of them agreed on the greatness of Shakespeare's play: FRANCIS GENTLEMAN spoke of its "genius" and of the scope for good acting provided by the title role;[2] ARTHUR MURPHY rated it as Shakespeare's masterpiece;[3] and THOMAS DAVIES asserted that in none of Shakespeare's tragedies are the "passions . . . extended with more genuine force, the incidents more numerous and more dramatically conducted, nor the moral more profitable, than in Lear."[4] Yet all three of these

1. Tate's *King Lear* has recently been republished in Christopher Spencer's *Five Restoration Adaptations of Shakespeare* (Urbana, 1965), pp. 203-74. Hazelton Spencer's discussion, in *Shakespeare Improved* (Cambridge, Mass., 1927), pp. 241-52, is, of course, well known. George Branam comments on Colman's and Garrick's revisions in *Eighteenth-Century Adaptations of Shakespearean Tragedy* (Berkeley and Los Angeles, 1956). See also G. W. Stone, "Garrick's Production of King Lear," *Studies in Philology*, XLV (1948), 93-94, 96-100.

2. *Bell's Edition of Shakespeare's Plays*, [ed. Francis Gentleman] (London, 1774), II, *King Lear*, [3].

3. *The Works of Arthur Murphy, Esq.* (London, 1786), VI, 237-38. Originally published in *Gray's Inn Journal*.

4. *Dramatic Miscellanies* (London, 1783-84), II, 329.

men agreed on the need for alteration; and, in general, they accepted Tate's revision as an improvement. Some of the reasons which they gave were recognizably "literary" in inspiration, but they usually included an element of theatrical expediency; others were dramatic in a purely practical sense.

Structurally, *King Lear* offended neoclassical taste by its double plot, a violation of unity of action; but "diffuseness" of plot, to use Gentleman's terminology,[5] was also of practical concern. Murphy seems to have had both aesthetic and practical considerations in mind when he wrote that if *King Lear* had been "planned with more art, and without that multiplicity of incidents, which draw off our affections from the principal object," it would have been "a piece for the united efforts of *Greece* to envy." He softened his criticism somewhat by adding that the Gloucester plot is not "entirely detached from the main subject" since Edmund "acts the same unnatural part as *Lear*'s daughters."[6] Tate, of course, retained the double plot in his alteration, but, in Davies' opinion, his introduction of the love story strengthened the connection between the two plots.[7]

Offenses against "decorum" in *King Lear* were pointed out by actors as well as by other eighteenth century critics. The presence of the Fool in a tragedy, for example, was described by Gentleman as Shakespeare's concession to the barbarous taste of his age.[8] Perhaps Tate himself omitted the Fool out of respect for the rule against mixed *genres*, but—regardless of Gentleman's "literary" comment—the continued absence of this character from the stage cannot be explained by such deference on the part of actors. Davies reflected their attitude better when he remarked that Garrick feared to restore the Fool in his version of the play lest his "buffooneries" should "counter-act the agonies of Lear."[9]

Another example of "indecorum" was the blinding of Gloucester in the sight of the audience. The scene was retained in all of the adaptations, but Tate saved Cornwall from performing the deed with his own hands (the servants were ordered to do it), and Garrick had the actual blinding occur just offstage—within sound

5. *Bell Shakespeare*, II, *King Lear*, [3].
6. *Works*, VI, 270-71.
7. *Dramatic Miscellanies*, II, 262.
8. *Bell Shakespeare*, I, prefatory remarks, 5-6.
9. *Dramatic Miscellanies*, II, 266-67.

but not sight of the audience.[10] Gentleman, however, wished that it could have been merely reported,[11] and Davies found the whole incident abhorrent. The latter admitted that even classical drama affords some parallels (e.g. Sophocles' Oedipus appears onstage immediately after blinding himself), but he maintained that "no authority . . . will justify the exhibition of a spectacle which affrighted nature shrinks from."[12] Gentleman objected to the scene not only because of the horror of the blinding but also because of the "ludicrous" indecorum of having the Duke of Cornwall scuffle with his domestic servant. (Even the adapters knew better than this, however, for the noble servant continued to defy his wicked master.) Yet this same actor-critic, who here and elsewhere exasperates us with his literal-minded rigidity, was also capable of brief flights above such earthbound thinking. For example, he disagreed with Colman's opinion that the "Dover Cliff" scene is too improbable for representation.[13]

Tate's happy ending could be justified by an appeal to "poetic justice," which Shakespeare had offended by making Lear suffer more than he deserved and by meting out a tragic fate to the innocent Cordelia. Typical of eighteenth century sentimentality is Murphy's comment that *"Lear*'s restoration [to the throne] and the virtuous *Edgar*'s alliance with the amiable *Cordelia,* can never fail to produce those gushing tears, which are swelled and ennobled by a virtuous joy." But something more than abstract principle lies behind this delight in "virtue rewarded." Murphy professed a desire to see someone experiment with the tragic ending on the stage, but he added that, in his opinion, Tate's version would "always be more agreeable to an audience" since, "after the heart-piercing sensations which we have endured through the whole piece," it would probably be "too much" to see Shake-

10. See *Five Restoration Adaptations of Shakespeare,* ed. Spencer, p. 244. In Tate's text there is no indication that Gloucester is led offstage to be blinded; and Professor Branam considers Garrick's handling an innovation (see *Eighteenth-Century Adaptations,* p. 151). According to Charles B. Hogan, however, "The blinding of Gloucester occurs off stage" in Tate's version as well (*Shakespeare in the Theatre, 1701-1800* [Oxford, 1952-57], I, 244). Perhaps Garrick only made clear in the dialogue what was already being done on the stage. Acting texts of the early nineteenth century, for example Elizabeth Inchbald's, followed Garrick's plan.

11. *The Dramatic Censor* (London, 1770), I, 362; Bell *Shakespeare,* II, *King Lear,* 50.

12. *Dramatic Miscellanies,* II, 301-4.

13. *Dramatic Censor,* I, 362-63.

speare's conclusion actually performed.[14] Davies, who agreed that the tragic ending is too "shocking and terrible" for human nature to bear, exclaimed that if Samuel Johnson could scarcely endure to read it, "what exquisite grief and unutterable horror would such a painter as Garrick have raised in the breast of a spectator?"[15]

In addition to such arguments as these, combining literary and dramatic considerations, the same actor-critics gave some purely theatrical justifications for the altering of Shakespeare's play. Gentleman remarked, for example, that the character of Cordelia is underdeveloped in the original text.[16] (Tate provided a better part for the actress.) And Davies applauded Tate's addition of the love story because it provided "relief to the harassed and distressed minds of the audience" and it lifted some of the burden from the actor of Lear, upon whom the action of the play would otherwise "fall too heavily."[17]

Although they agreed that Tate had done a service by revising *King Lear* for the stage, these writers were conscious of imperfections in the "improver" and his work. Davies credited him with rescuing the play from the oblivion to which the actors had consigned it, but he also derided the man for his ostentatious vanity.[18] Gentleman commented that in some passages Tate had "enervated the versification by endeavouring to give it a smoother flow," and he commended Colman for showing more restraint in altering Shakespeare's language. In general, however, he considered Tate's version more successful than Colman's. (Colman omitted the love story.) When Gentleman wrote the introduction to the play in the *Bell Shakespeare* (1774), he expressed the opinion that the text published in that work (i.e. Garrick's version, which restored a number of Shakespearean passages) "by judiciously blending of Tate and Shakespeare, is made more nervous than Tate's alteration itself."[19]

Gentleman, Murphy, and Davies were typical. Sensitive to contemporary taste, the actor-critics of their century were nearly unanimous in agreeing upon the desirability of an altered version of *King Lear* for the stage and upon the general suitability of

14. *Works*, VI, 270-71.
15. *Dramatic Miscellanies*, II, 265-66.
16. *Dramatic Censor*, I, 360.
17. *Dramatic Miscellanies*, II, 262-63.
18. *Ibid.*, pp. 258-64.
19. *Dramatic Censor*, I, 352-53; *Bell Shakespeare*, II, *King Lear*, 3.

Tate's adaptation, or something like it. Nearly unanimous, but not quite. There was some faint questioning of these premises by ELIZABETH GRIFFITH (1775), who wavered in preference between Shakespeare and Tate. Chief spokesman for Shakespeare's morality, she was forced to admit that Tate's version surpassed the original play in fulfilling the dramatic duty "to recommend virtue and discourage vice"; yet she could see beyond the subject of her book enough to add that, "if *pity* and *terror,* as the Critics say, are the principal objects of Tragedy, surely no Play that ever was written can possibly answer both these ends better than . . . [Shakespeare's own] text."[20] But it was not until the final year of the century that an actor-critic spoke out unequivocally for the supremacy of Shakespeare's play in its original form.

The champion was, surprisingly enough, CHARLES DIBDIN. In defending the plot of *Hamlet* this critic largely defeated his own purpose, for the many faults that he conceded, one by one, are likely to remain in the reader's mind despite his insistence upon their relative unimportance. In writing of *King Lear,* however, he expressed his appreciation warmly and whole-heartedly. In Shakespeare's play, he declared, "the three grand ends of tragedy are completely effected. Pity, terror, and delight . . . are excited, in a manner masterly even to astonishment." The emotions are represented with "vehemence" but also with "judgment"; the conduct of the action is both correct and spirited, and the interest never sinks for a moment. The language, especially in the storm scenes, is "poignant, noble, and profound," combining grandeur with simplicity and truth. Even the Fool, scorned by neoclassicists, received a good word from Dibdin: "though he retards the action, [this character] is full of exquisite wit." The play is "certainly injured" by Tate's alteration, Dibdin argued, "because it takes away from the grandeur of the original plot and the justice of the catastrophe." The death of Lear, "in mind an angel, in temper a man," is, in fact, not only just but "inevitable." He and the other honorable characters "live to behold the discomfiture of their enemies, but it is then too late to repair the ruin of which their imprudence had been the cause. On the other hand the infamous set who had dared put nature, honour, and decency at defiance, fall execrated even by one another." The public prefers Tate because of a desire to see the play end happily, but this idea is

20. *The Morality of Shakespeare's Drama Illustrated* (London, 1775), p. 351.

far "from the purpose of tragedy." In short, Dibdin considered Shakespeare's play not only unsurpassed for "the closet" but also, "with a very few judicious alterations [i.e. such cuts and transpositions as were common to the acting texts of other plays], . . . a most complete tragedy for the stage."[21] Published nearly forty years before Macready finally restored Shakespeare's text, Dibdin's avowals were a remarkable testament of faith for a theatre-bred critic.

The early decades of the nineteenth century were a period of transition in the actors' attitudes toward *King Lear*. The influence of romantic critics like Hazlitt and Lamb would soon begin to show its effect, but in the meantime Tate's version of the play, or the derivatives of that version, continued to hold the stage. (Kemble, for example, though he restored some Shakespearean passages, retained Tate's love story and happy ending, continued to omit the Fool, used the offstage blinding of Gloucester, and, like Colman, prevented the imaginary leap from Dover Cliff.[22]) There is an interesting contrast in the opinions expressed by two actor-critics of this period, each of them writing as the editor of *King Lear* for a collection of plays popular on the contemporary stage: ELIZABETH INCHBALD for *The British Theatre* (1808) and WILLIAM OXBERRY for *The New English Drama* (1820). Current practice is reflected in the texts that are used: being acting editions, both are adaptations, not the original play. But the dichotomy in the thinking of the actor-critics is shown in the introductory essays. Mrs. Inchbald, who preferred Tate to Shakespeare, repeated, parrot-like, the old ideas and the old phrases, including Tate's own description of the original play as "a heap of jewels; unstrung and unpolished, yet . . . dazzling in their disorder."[23] Oxberry, on the other hand, devoted much of his essay to a discussion of Shakespeare's superiority to Tate. "This tragedy alone," he wrote, "is a sufficient proof that Shakespeare was not [a] rude uncultivated genius" whose plays need polishing to please the taste of a more refined age. Oxberry was interested in dramatic values, but, unlike Gentleman and Davies, he did not think the play needed alteration in order to meet the requirements of good theatre. His comments were less concerned than theirs with

21. *A Complete History of the Stage* (London, 1800), III, 320-26.
22. See G. C. D. Odell, *Shakespeare from Betterton to Irving* (New York, 1920), II, 55.
23. *The British Theatre* (London, 1808), IV, *King Lear*, 4-5.

purely practical considerations, like providing an attractive part
for a leading actress, and more concerned with dramatic artistry;
for in this respect, he felt, *King Lear* was unsurpassed "in the
whole circle of the drama." He precisely reversed Murphy's complaint of superfluous characters and incidents by pointing out the
unity of emphasis gained in this play through a pattern of contrasts. Shakespeare's supreme achievement, he said, was not in
individual characterizations, fine as those are, but "in the mutual
action and re-action of the characters on each other";

> in the whole numerous groupe there is not a single figure, whether
> it stand in light or in shadow, which does not tend to heighten the
> effect of the principal character. The assumed idiotism of Edgar,
> the satire of the fool, the cruelty of Regan and Goneril, and even the
> folly of Oswald, are made essential to this point.

Oxberry rejected Samuel Johnson's reasoning that the tragic
ending is too terrible to bear, and he cited Addison and Schlegel
in support of his own conviction that Shakespeare's conclusion
is the only right one. (He might have cited Lamb as well, for
his argument was much like the one in Lamb's essay "On the
Tragedies of Shakespeare," 1811.) "Is not the restoration of Lear
to felicity, after so much suffering, an anticlimax?" he asked.
"Is not death the only thing that could be superadded without
untuning the mind of the spectator, wrought up to the highest
pitch of sensation?"[24] Writing twenty years after Dibdin, Oxberry
was the second actor-critic to argue for the supremacy of the play
as Shakespeare wrote it.

To speak literally of a "first" or "second" such actor is, of
course, misleading. We can use these terms only loosely to
refer to available written records of actors' preferences. There
must have been considerable oral debate on the subject in the
greenroom and other theatrical haunts. A tiny fragment of one
such conversation—between BENJAMIN WEBSTER and FANNY KELLY
—has been preserved in the form of a diary note of February 14,
1827, which Webster jotted down in his memorandum book:
"Miss Kelly said she should like, with necessary omissions, to see
King Lear acted as Shakespeare wrote it for she thought it very

24. *The New English Drama* (London, 1818-24), X, *King Lear*, iii-vii. According to Odell (*Shakespeare from Betterton to Irving*, II, 126), Oxberry's text generally follows that of the later Kemble as Elizabeth Inchbald's follows the early one
but it restores some of Shakespeare's lines and omits many of Tate's that Kemble
retained.

absurd to see Cordelia running about after Edgar instead of her father—."[25] It is possible that this comment reflects the influence of Charles Lamb, for he was Miss Kelly's friend and admirer (she was the "Barbara S—" of his unfulfilled dreams); but, then, the actress was also a woman of independent mind.

In the meantime another of Miss Kelly's old friends, EDMUND KEAN, had made his famous—though short-lived—experiment of partially restoring Shakespeare's text to the stage. Kean had already acted Lear successfully in a version that was basically Tate's, but he was not satisfied. Apparently he wished to gratify the romantic critics and at the same time to move his audiences as never before by the pathos and horror of his acting. "No one, he declared, could know what he was capable of until they had seen him over the dead body of Cordelia." Accordingly R. W. Elliston, the actor-manager of Drury Lane, produced *King Lear* for him (February, 1823) in a new version, which, though it retained Tate's love story and continued to omit the Fool, returned to Shakespeare's tragic conclusion. The audience failed to respond as Kean had hoped, however (perhaps it was true that they laughed to see the little man stagger under the weight of Mrs. W. West's Cordelia), and the "restored" text was abandoned after three performances.[26] Three years later the American actor JAMES H. HACKETT saw Kean's performance of Lear in New York and expressed "surprise at his choice of Nahum Tate's alteration to the *great Original*'s conclusion."

Mr. Kean observed: "I do not prefer it, but . . . when I had ascertained that a large majority of the public—whom we live to please, and must please to be popular—liked Tate better than Shakespeare, I fell back upon his corruption; though in my soul I was ashamed of the prevailing taste, and of my professional condition that required me to minister unto it."[27]

25. Handwritten memorandum book in the Harvard Theatre Collection.

26. H. N. Hillebrand, *Edmund Kean* (New York, 1933), pp. 233-34. The text that Kean and Elliston used is discussed by Odell, *Shakespeare from Betterton to Irving*, II, 155-56.

27. *Notes, Criticisms, and Correspondence upon Shakespeare's Plays and Actors* (New York, 1863), p. 227, footnote. When Hackett himself acted Lear (at the Park Theatre, New York, 1840), he announced it as "terminating according to the great dramatist's text and original catastrophe." He retained at least some of the Tate material, however, for the character of Aranthe was listed in his cast (*see* G. C. D. Odell, *Annals of the New York Stage* [New York, 1927], IV, 444). Hackett's interest in the theatrical possibilities of Shakespeare's own text continued, for when Macready was acting Lear at the Astor Place in 1847, Hackett

Shakespeare's *King Lear* was finally restored to the stage, of course, by WILLIAM CHARLES MACREADY in 1838—including the Fool, who had not made his appearance for nearly a century and a half. This very successful production pleased audiences and critics alike, thereby encouraging other actors to follow suit. Naturally, performances of Tate's version did not automatically cease. The Shakespearean text was not introduced on the New York stage, for example, until September, 1844, when Macready himself acted there.[28] (He had seen Edwin Forrest perform Lear in New York a year earlier and had written, rather self-righteously, that for "an actor to speak the words of Tate with Shakespeare's before him . . . criticizes his own performance."[29]) The best American Lears, in fact, were slow to abandon Tate: Junius Brutus Booth never did;[30] Forrest used the tragic ending but retained some Tate material, and on one occasion (1860) he tried the strange expedient of letting several members of the cast, himself included, speak Shakespeare's words and the rest speak Tate.[31] But, as far as the actor-critics were concerned, the question of alteration was settled in 1838.

Answers to the Question of Actability

It is obvious that, if the more theoretical of neoclassical arguments are disregarded, the question of textual alteration was also a question of the actability of Shakespeare's play as written. Thus what might be called the preliminary phase of the debate which we are about to discuss ended with the re-establishment of Shakespeare's text on the stage and the discovery that it was possible to

---

paid his own prompter "to make a perfect copy of Macready's Prompt Book of *King Lear*" (*see The Shakespeare Promptbooks; a Descriptive Catalogue* [by] *Charles H. Shattuck* (Urbana, 1965), p. 214, item #38).

28. Odell, *Annals of the New York Stage*, V, 87.

29. *The Diaries of William Charles Macready*, ed. William Toynbee (New York, 1912), II, 229.

30. After Booth's death, Thomas R. Gould, in his tribute, *The Tragedian; an Essay on the Histrionic Genius of Junius Brutus Booth* (New York, 1868), pp. 149-50, deplored the fact that Booth had used the Tate version, thereby foregoing Shakespeare's great concluding scene. Edwin Booth originally used the Kemble version, a Tate derivative, but later gave this up and used his own acting version of Shakespeare's text. *See* Charles T. Copeland, *Edwin Booth* (New York, 1901), p. 108. Booth's version was published in *Shakespeare's Tragedy of King Lear, as Presented by Edwin Booth*, ed. William Winter (New York, 1878).

31. Odell, *Annals of the New York Stage*, V, 323; VII, 323.

give a successful production of *King Lear* without offering such sops to the audience as a love story and a happy ending.

Actually, whether in altered form or not, *King Lear* was never as much of a popular success as any of the other three "great" Shakespearean tragedies, except in Garrick's period; it slightly outdistanced *Othello* at that time—obviously because Garrick himself was a superlative Lear and a disappointing Othello. Nineteenth century audiences found the play exciting when a favorite like Edmund Kean or Edwin Forrest, particularly identified with the role, struck lightning from Lear's passion or thundered forth the mighty rhetoric of the storm scenes; but, other things being equal, they much preferred *Hamlet, Macbeth,* or *Othello*.[32] Still, most of the great actors attempted the role of Lear, and usually with enough success to give it a place in their repertories.

It was not the actors but the literary critics who initiated the second phase of the debate over *King Lear*'s actability. This time the question was divorced from any thought of "improving" the play in an artistic sense; indeed some of the characteristics that were recognized as elements in its greatness were also named as reasons for its lack of suitability for the stage. The irony of the situation is evident. Macready's decision to restore Shakespeare's play was undoubtedly influenced by romantic criticism and by his own literary training. And one of the critics who had insisted most warmly upon Shakespeare's immense superiority to Tate— Charles Lamb—had made in the same essay his famous assertion that *King Lear* is incapable of being acted at all. Lamb's scornful references to "an old man tottering about the stage with a walking-stick" and to the "contemptible machinery by which they mimic the storm" are well known. In his opinion, "the greatness of Lear

32. Charles B. Hogan's tabulations show that on the London stage in the first half of the eighteenth century *King Lear* was eighth in the order of popularity of Shakespeare's play's (*Hamlet, Macbeth,* and *Othello* were first, second, and third respectively), but in the second half of the century it was in the seventh position, with *Othello* in the ninth (*Hamlet* and *Macbeth* were still ahead) (see *Shakespeare in the Theatre 1701-1800,* I, 460-61; II, 716-17). Odell's *Annals of the New York Stage* reveals that in that city *King Lear* was performed less frequently than *Hamlet, Macbeth,* or *Othello* throughout the nineteenth century except for an occasional brief period. As I have indicated, however, audiences would sometimes flock to see particular performers in Lear. This character seems to have been Edmund Kean's most successful part during his first visit to America, in 1820; and Edwin Forrest had a noteworthy success in Lear when he went to London in 1836 (see Odell, *Annals of the New York Stage,* II, 589, 591, 592; also Richard Moody, *Edwin Forrest* [New York, 1960], p. 154).

is not in corporal dimension, but in intellectual" and an actor "might more easily propose to personate the Satan of Milton" than to convey an adequate impression of Lear's volcanic grandeur. Lamb had never seen the original play on the stage, of course, but he explained that Tate had "put his hook in the nostrils of this Leviathan" so that the actors could "draw the mighty beast about more easily."[33] It is doubtful that any production of the play, no matter how pure the text, would have satisfied him, for his conception was more epic than dramatic. A. C. Bradley, nearly a century later, felt much the same way, even though he had the advantage of being able to see the original play. Like Lamb he pointed out the ludicrous ineffectiveness of the storm when it is artificially simulated rather than imaginatively experienced as in reading, and, like Lamb, he felt that Shakespeare's vastness of conception could at best be only inadequately realized in performance. To these difficulties he added others: that many of the characters are more like abstractions than individuals, that place and time designations are unusually vague, and that symbolic meanings which suggest themselves in reading must either lose their impressiveness in the theatre or harden into unacceptable allegory.[34]

By the time that HARLEY GRANVILLE-BARKER wrote his "Preface" to *King Lear* (first published in 1927) some actors had probably become convinced of the cogency of the critics' remarks. For *King Lear* as a stage play had suffered reverses in the late nineteenth and early twentieth centuries. In New York, for example, after Forrest's farewell performances of 1870, no one acted it for several years (there had not been so noticeable a gap in the records of this play since early in the century). Edwin Booth, who became the most frequent representative of Lear after Forrest, did not have his predecessor's drawing power in the character; audiences preferred to see him in Hamlet, Iago, and other parts. And after his last New York performance of Lear in 1888 the play again vanished from the theatres for a period of years.[35] In

33. "On the Tragedies of Shakespeare," *Complete Works and Letters of Charles Lamb*, ed. Bennet A. Cerf and Charles S. Klopfer (New York, 1935), pp. 298-99.

34. A. C. Bradley, *Shakespearean Tragedy* (London, 1941), pp. 243-70. The book was first published in 1904.

35. *See* Odell, *Annals of the New York Stage*, Vols. IX-XV. See X, 15, for an interesting list of the receipts from Booth's performances in an engagement at Daly's Theatre in 1875. He played Lear three times with average receipts of

London the most famous actor of the day, Henry Irving, failed miserably in the role (1892), perhaps because his vocal instrument could not stand the strain of the assumed voice which was part of his characterization.[36] As for the present century, during its first three decades Londoners could have seen eight productions of *King Lear* to twenty-eight of *Hamlet* and thirteen of *Othello*. The records of the Shakespeare Festival at Stratford-on-Avon tell an even sadder story: in the first twenty-two years (beginning in 1879) there were only two productions of *King Lear*; then Frank Benson produced it three times in four seasons, after which it was absent from the bills for another seventeen years.[37]

Nevertheless, Granville-Barker gave no quarter to the critics who preferred reading the play to seeing it staged. Shakespeare meant *King Lear* to be acted, he pointed out, and Shakespeare was a very practical playwright. Before stating that the storm scenes (or any others) would lose their "very essence" on the stage, Bradley should have considered Shakespeare's stagecraft. The theatre for which the play was written was severely limited in its storm effects, and even the music of that day did not lend itself to the creation of a tempestuous mood. Human rather than mechanical means were relied upon. "The storm is not in itself . . . dramatically important, only in its effect upon Lear. How, then, to give it enough magnificence to impress him, yet keep it from rivalling him? Why, by identifying the storm with him, setting the actor to impersonate both Lear and—reflected in Lear —the storm." Answering the criticism that *King Lear* in performance fails to convey the significance felt in reading, Granville-Barker cautioned that a play need not make "its full effect, point by point, clearly and completely . . . as the performance goes along." For a drama like *King Lear* one might need several hearings, just as the "alertest critic" would need for a comparable piece of music. To keep his story "currently clear and at least provisionally significant," Shakespeare uses the *raisonneur* in the

$1436, but he played Iago three times with an average of $1696, and Hamlet nine times with an an average of $1855.

36. Laurence Irving suggests this reason for Irving's disappointing performance, particularly on the first night when his voice was barely audible (see *Henry Irving: The Actor and His World, by His Grandson* [London, (1951)], pp. 550-52).

37. See the appendices to J. C. Trewin's *Shakespeare on the English Stage, 1900-1964; a Survey of Productions Illustrated from the Raymond Mander and Joe Mitchenson Theatre Collection* (London, [1964]), pp. 257-307.

form of the Fool and of Edgar as Poor Tom, but these characters are so blended into the action that they "never . . . lower its emotional temperature by didactics." If we become so identified with Lear in his agony that its significance escapes us at the moment, memory may still make it clear later; this same process takes place in the emotional experiences of real life. We cannot be detached and critically observant or Lear will seem an "intolerable tyrant." To enable us to share his ordeal, Shakespeare uses "all those things of which Bradley complains, the confusion of pathos, humor and sublime imagination, the vastness of the convulsion, the vagueness of the scene . . . the strange atmosphere and half-realized suggestions. . . ." The "reconciliation of grandeur and simplicity" in the language of the play typifies the union of concrete story and universal meaning; even when the passion becomes inarticulate, "the seeming failure of expression [gives] us a sense of the helplessness of humanity pitted against higher powers."

There was one point at which Granville-Barker did agree with past critics, including those of the eighteenth century: that the play "suffers somewhat under the burden" of the subplot. Like Murphy, however, he noted that the character of Edmund achieves a partial blending of the two plots, and he added that Edgar too is "drawn into Lear's orbit" for awhile, though at the expense of his own character development. But the imperfect solution to this problem gave him no qualms about the actability of the play as a whole.[38]

Despite Granville-Barker's eloquent arguments, however, at least two modern actor-critics have sided with Bradley on this matter. MARGARET WEBSTER[39] readily concedes the greatness of *King Lear*, "probably the most hypnotic" of all Shakespeare's works, as far as the reader is concerned; but she "cannot believe" that it "ever was or ever will be a good play in the sense of 'a theater piece.'" SIR TYRONE GUTHRIE[40] goes further and asserts that in addition to the "difficulties, some of them apparently insurmountable, in staging the play," there are "difficulties and imperfections which mar the play's greatness even for a reader."

For Miss Webster the first stumbling block to effective dramatic presentation is the unsympathetic character of Lear himself. She

38. *Prefaces to Shakespeare* (Princeton, 1946), I, 261-71, 283.
39. *Shakespeare Without Tears* (Cleveland, 1955), pp. 214-23.
40. Sir Tyrone Guthrie, "'King Lear," in *Shakespeare: Ten Great Plays* (New York, c. 1962), pp. 350-51.

cannot accept the improbabilities of the first scene, even for the sake of granting the dramatist his starting point; for, in her opinion, Lear's intolerable behavior here makes it impossible for an average audience to pity his later (and seemingly deserved) sufferings. Despite this major difficulty, however, she admits that an audience may be held fascinated by the "sheer size of the play" —up to the storm scenes, which, as Lamb and Bradley saw, are the crux of theatrical difficulty. Thunder-sheets, wind machines, and other storm effects "succeed only in drowning out the actor's voice without arousing either pity or terror." Yet it is almost impossible for the actor to "show us the convulsion in Lear's soul" when "no wind stirs his beard and the accompanying storm sounds barely reach voice level." In reading the play, the "surging, battering words, the enormous images full of doom and fury" overcome logic and "unseal the springs of terror." Theoretically this should happen in the theatre as well—but "in my experience it does not." Guthrie agrees on this point.

Like Bradley, Miss Webster describes the characters (all except Lear, Gloucester, and the "sparsely but subtly developed" Albany) as "pure white or dead black," and, like Bradley, she considers the play undramatic in its attempt to portray giant abstractions. She explains that if the dramatist overloads the actors "with more than flesh and blood can convey" he overloads in turn "the capacity of the audience to absorb or ultimately to believe."

Both Margaret Webster and Tyrone Guthrie join with other actors in finding the double plot a drawback. The parallel patterns of the two stories "may indeed enforce with savage fury the picture of a dark, relentless world," says Miss Webster, but the subplot keeps the structure from standing "clean and firm, around its central character" and the compression necessitated by the handling of so much material "adds to the many conflicting perplexities of the play." Guthrie points out in addition that the "dissimilarity of style" in the treatment of the two stories leads to many difficulties. The Lear plot has the simplicity and symmetry of a fairy tale, and its majestic style is suggestive of allegory; but the Gloucester material is "complicated and sensational" in plot, "prosaic" in style, full of imperfect craftsmanship. Perhaps Shakespeare intended the "monumentality and high style" of the Lear portions "to be offset and increased by contrast with the

melodramatic goings-on amongst the characters of lower stature";
if so, the effect is not achieved, for the contrast "is at once jarring
and insufficient."

In Guthrie's opinion, the play loses its force whenever it attempts to be realistic. "Regan and Goneril . . . are marvelous
when they are simply embodiments of Evil; so is Edmund. But
on a human, realistic level, none of the three is credible or interesting. . . ." Indeed, even the occasional touches of common
humanity in Lear's own speeches, though effective in themselves,
are destructive of larger purposes. For example, when Lear, in
lamenting over Cordelia's body, says, "Pray you undo this button,"
a fine actor can always draw tears from an audience. But since
the scene as a whole is "concerned with the ironic end of a tragic
figure," the much-admired passage actually "reduces both scene
and character from tragedy to pathos."

Guthrie concludes that in *King Lear,* the "untidiest" of Shakespeare's tragedies, the "sprawling fecundity" and "fiery humanity"
of the author's genius are "at odds with a theme which demanded a
more formal, austere and removed approach." (In other words,
Shakespeare *should* have written, not a tragedy arousing pity and
terror, but a modern drama of irony and alienation.) I suppose
Guthrie cannot be accused of a secret admiration for Nahum
Tate's version of *King Lear* since it increased the melodramatic
element and reduced the possibility of allegorical interpretation,
but he would no doubt remark that Tate did achieve a certain
kind of consistency. At any rate, Guthrie's evaluation of Shakespeare's play as "a flawed masterpiece, a great jewel of which the
surface has been scratched" is so reminiscent of Tate's as to raise
the suspicion that, like Elizabeth Inchbald's, it is a deliberate
echo.

Other modern actors have agreed with Granville-Barker rather
than with Guthrie and Margaret Webster about the actability of
King Lear. ROBERT SPEAIGHT, for example, points out that the
"contemporary English theatre has seen several magnificent Lears,"
including particularly fine ones by Sir John Gielgud and Sir
Michael Redgrave. (According to him, the tide in the play's
fortunes turned with Gielgud's performance at the Old Vic in
1931.) Speaight, however, does suggest that "these great sym-
phonies of suffering . . . have not always helped us to understand the play." For, "abstracted from their context they have

fortified the suspicion that . . . what we admire in the play are spurts and jets, gusts and ground-swells of genius—not the rounded artefact of the conscious, shaping mind." Actually, "none of Shakespeare's plays is better constructed than this; none reveals a more sophisticated range of feeling."[41] SIR DONALD WOLFIT, the other major defender of the play's actability, has no reservations concerning the recent theatrical successes of "the greatest of Shakespeare's tragedies." And there is good reason for his elation: for Wolfit himself was responsible for almost half of the London productions of *King Lear* in the 1940's and 50's, a period when as many productions were given as in the four prior decades. Writing in 1956, he estimated that in the preceding twenty-five years a virtually complete text had been more consistently used than at any time since the Puritan closing of the theatres, and he noted the increasing popularity of the play during the same period. He attributed the current interest in *King Lear* to its relevance for modern experience as epitomized by "two world-wide and gigantic wars . . . comparable to the titanic struggle that went on in the mind and soul of Lear, conflicts based on greed, ingratitude, jealousy and self-aggrandizement." Reviewing the attitudes of past critics, Wolfit dismissed Tate as "an astonishingly impertinent idiot," imputed Lamb's heresy to the effect of the "truncated, deformed imitation" of Shakespeare's play which his theatre offered, and praised Granville-Barker not only for his "unanswerable" replies to Lamb and Bradley but also for his encouragement (along with William Poel's) that led modern producers to rediscover the "superb stagecraft" of the play.[42]

The tremendous success of Peter Brook's recent production of *King Lear* with Paul Scofield in the title role (first performed at Stratford-on-Avon in November, 1962) has been a living demonstration of the actability of the play. For this internationally acclaimed production not only made Lear a believable human character but also dealt superbly with the symbolic element which seemed a theatrical stumbling block to both Bradley and Margaret Webster. Even the storm was mainly concentrated in the actors, as Granville-Barker thought it should be, rather than in

41. Robert Speaight, "The Actability of King Lear," *Drama Survey*, II, No. 1, (Spring, 1962), 49. See also *Nature in Shakespearian Tragedy* (London, 1955), pp. 90-105.

42. Sir Donald Wolfit, Introduction to the Folio Society Edition of *King Lear* (London, 1956), pp. 3-5.

the "effects."[43] Yet in his recent book, *King Lear in Our Time* (Berkeley, 1965), Maynard Mack adds Brook's production to the long list of unsatisfactory attempts to stage Shakespeare's play, stretching from the Restoration to the present time. Professor Mack feels that the "siren's rock on which efforts to bring *King Lear* to the stage . . . oftenest split is the desire to motivate the bizarre actions . . . in some 'reasonable' way." Actually, the characters often act in a dreamlike, irrational manner whose real significance is best understood by reference to parallels in folklore, morality play, and homily. There is, however, a dualism in the play and its characters: on the one hand, human vitality; on the other, archetypal abstraction. Edmund, for example, is a debonair young opportunist, but he is also "a force of Appetite." The actor should "convey to us something of both his modes of being, and the assignment will not be easy."[44]

In an interesting review of Mack's book, PAUL SCOFIELD takes issue with the assertion that the "psychological processes that ordinarily precede or determine human action" have little part in *King Lear*: "it is surely, to quote one instance only, a psychological consequence of Lear's long absorption with personal power that causes him to become emotionally out of touch with his daughters, and causes them to turn on him when he relinquishes that power." To insist that actors represent "the emblematic nature of the characters" in morality-play fashion is to impose too severe a limitation upon their art; for an actor "must honour the specific mortal nature of the man he represents. An archetype cannot be acted, just as a performance cannot be written."

If we are to be convinced by the heavy tide of tragic human experience in "King Lear," then the irrational and insane twistings and leapings of those creatures who are swept along by it must be seen to be natural and inevitable. A. B. Walkley asks "How are these primitive and absurd folks going to excite in you the proper tragic emotions?"

43. For a French critic's recognition of Brook's achievement in meeting Bradley's objections see René Kerf, "King Lear, Peter Brook et Bradley," *Revue des Langues Vivantes*, XIX, 362-69.

44. Actually Maynard Mack's thesis that the real and the symbolic exist side by side in *King Lear* is compatible with Peter Brook's statement (successfully demonstrated by the production itself) that this play requires the use of several styles of acting. *See* Stephen Watts, "New Approach to an Old Drama," *New York Times*, May 17, 1964, Sec. 2, p. 3. Professor Mack objects, however, as some other critics have done, to the particular meaning which Brook tried to project, as well as to his use of psychological rationalization.

The answer is that they do; perhaps because they *are* primitive and absurd, which most of us are at some time or other. If we are to be impatient of paradoxes in the behaviour of Shakespeare's characters, or frustrated by their often enigmatic personalities, then the heart of his plays is lost to us. In the major roles of all the great plays there is a seeming contradiction of purpose or ambiguity of character; it is only by the acceptance of paradox as being intrinsic to human behaviour that Lear or Hamlet, Othello or Macbeth can be more than objects of intellectual interest.[45]

The Question of Appropriate Setting

It is very important, as Scofield has demonstrated in acting as well as in words, to recognize the human reality that informs the most fantastic moments of *King Lear*. WILLIAM OXBERRY realized this as long ago as 1820 when he wrote that the basic realism of *King Lear* contrasts with the fantasy of *The Tempest*, for the tragedy gives a "faithful picture of the human mind in its ordinary habits," even though the manners of Lear's barbarous period, which color the action, tend to blind us to this fact.[46] The unusual pattern of opposing elements in this play—not only the rational and the irrational, but the familiar and the remote, the realistic and the legendary—has posed a problem in the matter of physical production. Which setting best translates the essential *King Lear* into visual terms? A scene of primitive and pagan life harmonious with our ideas of ancient Britain (the location of the Leir legend)? This would be true to one element in the play. But would it not be destructive of another, and more important, element? Would not a heavy emphasis on antiquity in the visual world of *King Lear* tend to blur the effect of reality, of universal significance? The question is, perhaps, largely academic—certainly most productions of the play set the story in ancient times—but it has been interestingly argued by several modern actor-critics.

The choice of a "period" for costumes and setting actually became a problem in the early nineteenth century, when the change from contemporary to historical dress took place in the staging of Shakespeare's plays. But for many years the question was primarily a matter of mechanical "accuracy." For example, EDMUND KEAN, in preparing for the 1820 production of *King Lear* at Drury Lane, attempted to choose between the precedents set

45. Paul Scofield, "The Mortal Nature," *The Sunday Times*, April 24, 1966, p. 33.
46. *New English Drama*, X, *King Lear*, iii.

by other actors but was unable to reconcile any of them with references in the text: John Philip Kemble should not have worn silk hose, for they had not been "seen in this country till the end of the 15th century"; but, on the other hand, actors who wore the "Saxon *Hosa*" were "equally incorrect" since, according to Holinshed, Leir reigned "nearly 800 years before the first conquest by Caesar." His solution, finally, was to ignore precise periods and "to blend Dramatic effect with Traditional Simplicity."[47] His son, CHARLES KEAN, was, of course, unwilling to approve such generalized and merely suggestive costuming. Priding himself on the carefully researched archaeological details of his productions, he found it essential to fix upon a specific historical period for his setting. In the introduction to his acting edition of *King Lear* (1858) he wrote that the play belongs to the prehistoric age, "when the land was peopled by rude Heathens, and the minds and hearts of men, as yet unreclaimed by the softening influences of Christianity, were barbarous and cruel." Since he could find no reliable information about the costumes and properties appropriate to that day, however, he chose for his production an Anglo-Saxon setting of A.D. 800.[48] The details of the production could thus be consistent, even if not textually accurate, and—Kean must have reasoned—the chosen period was remote enough to create the atmosphere he had described.

But it was not until early in the present century (1909) that an actor-critic broached the more important question. (Oxberry's comment, to which we referred earlier, was not aimed specifically at the problem of setting, though it had a kind of prophetic relevance for it.) This was when WILLIAM POEL attacked a current production of the play, whose setting had been described much in Charles Kean's manner. What he objected to was the implied divorce between the evil and cruel actions of the play on the one hand and the amenities of modern civilization on the other. Shakespeare's story, he wrote, "is one that may happen to-day in any kingdom and any home!" Scenes and costumes that leave the opposite impression do not truly "illustrate" the play. Poel, how-

47. MS letter from Edmund Kean to Robert William Elliston, dated "31st May." The letter is in the Folger Library. On the back of it is a note, signed by Elliston, dated April 3, 1820.

48. *Selections from the Plays of Shakespeare. As Arranged for Representation at the Princess's Theatre* (London, 1860), II, 5-6.

ever, did not advocate modern dress; for him, the costume of Elizabethan England was contemporary enough.[49]

Other modern actor-critics have not agreed with one another concerning the most effective setting for *King Lear*. GRANVILLE-BARKER decided, despite his recognition of some Elizabethan elements, that the "prevailing atmosphere" of the play is primitive and remote. The costumes, accordingly, should reflect a "splendid barbaric temper" but without sacrificing the degree of sophistication that Shakespeare himself chose to retain.[50] ROBERT SPEAIGHT, however, believes that *King Lear* is "not a play about ancient Britons in a setting of Stonehenge. It is a play about Elizabethans in a setting of Hampton Court and Hardwicke." This does not mean that savage cruelty is out of place in its world: it means that Shakespeare exposed the "fathomless corruption" beneath the "sophisticated façade." Like Poel, Speaight attempts to relate Elizabethan costume and setting to an impression of universality. Shakespeare is modern, or immortal, he affirms paradoxically, because he is inseparable from his moment.[51]

Obviously the question of setting can never be finally determined. For one thing, there is no general agreement as to what kind of setting best conveys the impression of universality. Charles Kean's description was misleading, not because it placed the scene in primitive times, but because it implied that the "hearts of men . . . were barbarous and cruel" only in some era of the long-forgotten past. At the other extreme, to claim modernity and universality for an Elizabethan setting, and to declare that the "mists of antiquity" tend to obscure the meaning of Shakespeare's play is merely to attribute one's personal set of connotations to the majority of the play's potential spectators. There must be many people for whom "barbaric" or "primitive" costumes serve to emphasize the barbaric and primitive elements in the play—not only in the behavior of a fabulous Goneril, a mythical Lear, but in that of the humanity they represent, bestial and foolish at times in every age. (Even if the matter of period could somehow be settled, there would still be the question of whether to make the costumes and décor suggest the realities of life in that period or to treat them in the simplified, stylized manner that some of

49. *Shakespeare in the Theatre* (London, and Toronto, 1913), pp. 176-89.
50. *Prefaces to Shakespeare*, I, 326-27.
51. *William Poel and the Elizabethan Revival* (Cambridge, Mass., 1954), p. 228.

us associate with the symbolic element of the play.) But the chief reason why the question of setting must remain an open one is implicit in the play itself: namely, the unusual mixture of divergent elements that we noticed at the beginning of this discussion. In 1960 when Robert Speaight directed *King Lear* at Immaculate Heart College in Los Angeles, he found it convenient to set aside his own declared conviction and lay the scene in antiquity, using the simpler, less expensive costumes traditionally associated with the play. Even though he still expressed the wish to employ the "alternative solution" one day—"Renaissance men and women moving against a background as bare as the universe itself"—he evidently did not feel that the meaning of the play had been obscured on the occasion in question. He excused his departure from principle by the fact that "the spiritual ambience of the play is pagan, even if . . . a Christian meaning can be distilled from it."[52] This statement need not be read as mere rationalization: it is a recognition, I think, that the Shakespearean moment is something more than a point in time.

Interpretations of "Meaning"

Although a number of eighteenth and nineteenth century actors wrote analyses of Lear's character, those few who attempted to interpret the play as a whole were content with general statements about the evils of filial ingratitude, the sufferings consequent upon imprudence, etc. Several actors of the present century, however, have written more detailed interpretations. These actor-critics differ widely in their readings, but they have some common concerns. For example: What is the relationship between man and the gods in *King Lear*? And another: Is the overall effect of the play pessimistic, or not? These, of course, are matters that have occupied the attention of nontheatrical critics during the same period; indeed, a close consideration of them would seem to have more bearing on *King Lear* as a literary work than as a stage play. It is obvious, however, that it would make a great deal of difference whether the director (or the individual actor of Lear) viewed the play as a drama of redemption, an indictment of society, or a bitter statement of the meaninglessness of existence.

52. "The Actability of *King Lear*," pp. 53-54.

King Lear as a drama of social protest has evidently appealed to the actors less than other readings of the play. WILLIAM POEL adopted this interpretation, however. Endowing Shakespeare with a twentieth century social conscience as well as a modern scorn for astrology, he found the key to the play in Edmund's speech denying the influence of the stars (I, ii, 128 ff.). "All through the play," he wrote, "Shakespeare denies omnipotence to man's self-made gods." For in *King Lear* society has left to the gods what it should have assumed as its own responsibility, the care of its individual members. Because he is illegitimate, Edmund is refused the right to use his considerable talents "for the good of the State or for the benefit of the individual." He "therefore becomes embittered, and revenges himself" upon his society. The "vicious and self-seeking" Goneril, Regan, and Cornwall "make use of Edmund's abilities to serve their own ends," thereby bringing about the catastrophe. Poel pointed out that, although Shakespeare is often blamed for being intolerant of democracy, in *King Lear* he "abundantly proves his sympathy with the hard lot of the poor." The play "preaches no pessimism," for the troubles endured by Lear, Gloucester, and Edgar "are brought upon themselves by their own short-comings" and "are mitigated by the gain to their moral natures of a fellow-sympathy for the sufferings of those who have done no wrong."[53]

Interpretations of *King Lear* with a spiritual emphasis have been offered by LENA ASHWELL[54] and ROBERT SPEAIGHT.[55] As usual, there is a semiallegorical approach by both writers. This is particularly noticeable in Miss Ashwell's vision of Lear's world: a Divine Comedy in which the characters occupy different planes according to the degrees of good and evil they represent. At the topmost level are the Fool and Edgar—wise, brave, loving, and self-sacrificing, "the two best men in Shakespeare's gallery." Both of them suffer "a month of torture," and the Fool is finally hanged; but for ideal characters of this sort death is nothing less than a "translation . . . into beings of radiant light." On the next plane, but "much lower," are Cordelia, Gloucester, and Lear himself; they are not saintly like the others, but their selfishness is "burned

53. *Shakespeare in the Theatre*, pp. 181-84.
54. *Reflections from Shakespeare*, ed. Roger Pocock (London, [1926]), pp. 149-50, 153, 162.
55. *Nature in Shakespearian Tragedy*, pp. 91-121.

out by suffering," and they meet their fate with dignity. On a somewhat lower level is Albany, who is still in the process of reformation at the end of the play. Finally, "in the nether depths" are Goneril, Regan, Cornwall, and Edmund, "irreclaimable creatures of perdition," with Regan the worst of all.

Both Lena Ashwell and Speaight picture the operation of an inexorable moral order in the world of Lear. The first describes it as the law of cause and effect: "we have to face the consequences of our deeds . . . and a more dreadful Nemesis waits upon our stupidities than on our overt crimes." The other points out that most of the characters engender evil and suffering by disobeying the rules of nature and right reason (as the Renaissance humanists would call it). Lear himself, for example, gives up his crown to satisfy a caprice; Edmund denies the demands of ordered nature and chooses the free-for-all of the jungle. Only Cordelia remains true to nature: she loves her father according to her "bond," a word that signifies the "right ordering of things." The world of Lear, like that of Hamlet, is "out of joint . . . desperately needing redemption."

The lowest point in the play, Gloucester's anguished cry, "As flies to wanton boys are we to the gods," is of concern to both critics. Miss Ashwell admits that there is a note of pessimism here reminiscent of Greek tragedy, but she adds that "Character, not Fate" determines the damnation of some characters and the redemption of others. Speaight describes Gloucester's words as among the most terrible in Shakespeare, but he warns that a philosophy of nihilism must not be deduced from them. In his view, the world of *King Lear* actually receives the redemption it needs—redemption that comes actively with Cordelia's army and passively with Lear's endurance of his purgatory.

Obviously neither Speaight nor Miss Ashwell finds the play intolerably pessimistic. The latter, in fact, justifies an optimistic interpretation by invoking the principle of "Compensation." "Only through suffering and sorrow comes that wisdom, which in the drama of Lear is notably typified by the love of Cordelia for the King, and of the gentle Edgar for blinded Gloucester." Thus the darkness and pain in this play are not ends in themselves; they are necessary to show us "the contrast," and their "issue" is "incomparable in the whole literature of the world for sheer intensity of beauty." Speaight's view is sterner, yet there is for him no question of the rightness of Shakespeare's tragic conclusion. In "another" play Cordelia would have been materially as well as spiritually triumphant, but the world of *Lear* is "too monstrous for the reign of innocence." In a sense, however, she lives on in the person of Edgar; for, metaphysically, Cordelia and Edgar are one—"the active and the passive counterparts of a single redemptive process. They answer . . . the tragic agnosticism of the play. . . ."

Other actor-critics have interpreted *King Lear* as a work of deep pessimism or despair. MARGARET WEBSTER, for example, rejects the idea that the play is a drama of redemption and suggests instead that it is a "gigantic attack upon humanity itself" which we are "too squeamish" to accept. It is also, she feels, a "bitter and terrible cry against the overwhelming power of the gods." In his later tragedies Shakespeare was moving toward a "terrible confrontation between his tragic 'heroes' and the cosmic forces beyond human knowledge." There is in these plays "an ever-present sense of some terrible force which can be unleashed by man's weakness or his capacity for evil. Once set in motion, he is powerless to control its direction. . . ."[56] And MORRIS CARNOVSKY, a popular and effective American Lear (Stratford, Connecticut, 1963), discussed the play with reporters in terms that suggest an existentialist interpretation:

Lear, [Carnovsky] contends, is everyman: his disasters are everyman's and the tragedy, in Shakespeare's eye, "is not in Lear himself but in life." . . . Lear is a man stripped of everything except the strength to protest. His final act . . . "is to accuse the gods, to say if you can do this, then life is not worth living. Lear then consents to die."[57]

The pessimistic interpretation which has received the greatest publicity, however, is not one associated with any particular actor and his ideas. It is that attributed to Peter Brook's production of the play as a whole, which was influenced in turn by the Polish critic Jan Kott. For Kott considers *King Lear* a symbolic presentation of two old men who at the outset believe passionately in absolutes like gods and justice but who are forced through cruelty, despair, and madness to accept the Clown's philosophy that the universe is irrational. The play, as he reads it, is grotesque drama rather than classical tragedy, and is thus related to modern The-

56. *Shakespeare Without Tears*, pp. 221-23.
57. "Show Business," *Time* (August 16, 1963), p. 44.

atre of the Absurd.[58] Since Brook's interest in Kott's ideas was widely known, critics were prepared to see a production of a Shakespearean *Endgame,* and a number of them—Robert Speaight among them—did see and review the performance as such. Holding a contrary view of the play, Speaight was naturally unsympathetic with Brook's intentions, and he was displeased with much that he saw. Brook "had a perfect right" to his beliefs, he wrote, but "he pushed his advocacy beyond legitimate means."

The scene following the blinding of Gloucester, where Cornwall's "good servant" shows the mettle of his charity, was cut altogether; and so were Edmund's vital words in the last act: "some good I mean to do in spite of mine own nature." These are among the great redemptive moments of the tragedy.

(Such passages were indeed deliberately omitted, as Charles Marowitz, Brook's assistant director, has told us, in the attempt to counteract the play's natural tendency to produce a catharsis.[59]) It is dangerous to ask "What can Shakespeare mean to us?"— Speaight observed—before asking the more important question, "What did Shakespeare himself intend?"[60]

I cannot resist a personal comment at this point, for I saw the Brook production in New York on June 1, 1964. The abstract look of the setting and the simplicity of the costumes did suggest symbolic overtones, and the technique of pantomine instead of realistic acting was effectively used at certain points in the play, notably the "Dover Cliff" scene. But, for me at least, these technical aspects of the production did not by any means impart the impression of meaninglessness. The Lear of the final scenes, though gaunt and drained, seemed an affirmation, not a denial, of man's inner majesty. Whatever Brook's intentions, the play, as I experienced it, was a great humanistic tragedy—largely because of Paul Scofield's magnificent Lear, but also because of the intrinsic humanism of Shakespeare's *King Lear* which can hardly be expunged without drastic rewriting.

58. Jan Kott, "King Lear and Endgame," *Shakespeare Our Contemporary,* trans. by Boleslaw Taborski (Garden City, New York, 1964), pp. 87-124. For the influence of Kott on Brook see Martin Esslin's introduction, pp. xix-xx. Brook read Kott's essay on *King Lear* in French in 1962.

59. Charles Marowitz, "Lear Log," *Tulane Drama Review,* Winter, 1963, pp. 113-14.

60. Robert Speaight, "Shakespeare in Britain," *Shakespeare Quarterly,* XIV (1963), 419-21.

Feeling as I did, I wrote PAUL SCOFIELD to ask whether he agreed with the Kott interpretation. He replied, in part:

I think in preparation for the production of "King Lear" it occurred to few of us in the company—actors that is—to use the possibilities of comparison with Beckett. It was discussed, & interest was certainly stimulated by the fact that the Dover scene for instance (Between Lear & Gloucester) had much in common with the exchanges of Beckett characters, but it was clear to me that if one scene by Shakespeare can be equated to an entire Beckett play then the whole of "King Lear," of which this isolated scene is simply one facet, must be approached with the help of a wider vision than Beckett's—& whose wider than Shakespeare's?

As an actor who attempts to interpret Shakespeare I think it is not possible to interpret an interpreter—like Kott. One can only use one's *own* responses—& this is what I did. The Beckett analogy was fun, & influenced the production visually—but I think that under different visual circumstances, i.e. costumes & scenery, my response to the role would have been the same. The humanistic tragedy that you found is certainly what I would like you to find.[61]

This statement might serve, I think, as an answer to other questions than the one that prompted it. For a "wide vision" is the one essential in solving the problem of *King Lear*'s actability as well as in reaching out for the meaning, or meanings, that the play may hold for its audience. *King Lear* is not a "diffuse" or "sprawling" play, as actor-critics as far apart as Gentleman and Guthrie have called it; as Speaight has noticed, it is actually well articulated. But it *is* a big play, and it *does* employ an unusual complexity of styles. We are fortunate to live in a period when theatrical experimentation has prepared us to accept a mixture of symbolic and realistic techniques which can cope effectively with its diversity. We are equally fortunate, in an age of director-controlled theatre, that there are still great actors who, though stimulated by the suggestions of other thinkers and disciplined by the needs of the production as a whole, know that, in the final analysis, they must mold their characters out of the Shakespearean clay and animate them with their own human spirits.

61. Personal letter from Paul Scofield, dated April 3, 1965.

II. THE CHARACTERS

KING LEAR

Theatrical Criticism

Several actors have considered King Lear Shakespeare's most remarkable creation: DAVID GARRICK wrote, in 1769, that there is "Nothing like it in ye whole Circle of ye Drama";[62] his contemporary ARTHUR MURPHY put Lear first in a list of the four greatest characters in all drama;[63] and FREDERICK WARDE, many years later (1920), called him Shakespeare's "greatest character."[64] Others, from FRANCIS GENTLEMAN[65] in the eighteenth century to HARLEY GRANVILLE-BARKER[66] in the twentieth, have recognized the potentialities of the role but have also noted certain difficulties for the actor. HENRY IRVING,[67] for example (1893), named King Lear as one of his four favorite parts, yet he doubted "whether a complete embodiment is within any actor's resources."

As with Othello, the very characteristics that make Lear a great dramatic character may be seen as sources of difficulty for the average performer. For example, both Garrick and Murphy traced Lear's greatness to his expression of powerful, sometimes conflicting passions and to his ability to arouse a corresponding emotional turmoil in the audience. But the paradoxical character from which such conflicting passions must emanate seemed to Gentleman an unusual challenge to the actor's powers. To undertake the role of the "odd and violent old monarch," he wrote, is a "daring flight of theatrical resolution." The successful actor of King Lear needs "a wide and various complication of requisites," chief of which is "an imagination possessed of the same fine frenzy which first drew him into light." Irving's experience in acting King Lear confirmed him in the same view. Not only did he discover that the physical demands were unusually exhausting, but he decided that "to represent the struggles of an enfeebled

62. *See* Garrick's letter to Charles Macklin [? October, 1769], *The Letters of David Garrick*, ed. David M. Little and George M. Kahrl (Cambridge, Mass., 1963), II, 673.
63. *The Life of David Garrick, Esq.* (London, 1801), I, 99.
64. *Fifty Years of Make-Believe* (New York, 1920), pp. 253-54.
65. *Dramatic Censor*, I, 368-69.
66. *Prefaces to Shakespeare*, I, 283-84, 293.
67. "My Four Favorite Parts," *The Forum*, XVI, September, 1893, pp. 36-37.

mind with violent self-will," as one must do in this character, is "without doubt the most difficult undertaking in the whole range of the drama."

Interpretive Criticism

Several subjects connected with King Lear have been of recurrent interest to actor-critics: for example, his moral character and the degree to which he is responsible for his own sufferings; also the question of his physical weakness or strength, and the related question of majesty *versus* pathos in the representation of the character. Actually, all of these subjects are interrelated, as a moment's thought will show. King Lear is, by his own statement, "fourscore and upward." Do we think of him, then, as shrunken and feeble with age? Does sympathy for his weakness soften for us the culpable and irrational behavior of the early scenes? (Why should this tired old man struggle any longer under the cares of office? Who cannot understand an aged father's longing for affectionate reassurance from his family—and his helpless anger when it is withheld?) Or do we, on the contrary, picture him as a colossal figure, matching in physical power the grandeur of his speeches? Do we find his behavior, then, more appalling than pathetic? Shocked or awed by his assumption of godlike authority (at the moment, too, when he has renounced the responsibility that should accompany power), do we not foresee as inevitable the fate reserved for the victims of *hybris*? In his later sufferings, does he move us most with the poignance of his grief or with the glory of his cosmic rages? Such reasoning from physical characteristics to moral and emotional ones is not always followed, of course, by actor-critics or anyone else. I have suggested it only to show the possibilities of intricate relationships. But, more often than not, an answer to one question regarding King Lear has implications for the others.

In the eighteenth century there was general agreement among actor-critics that Lear is a basically sympathetic character whose suffering can be traced to the flaw of uncontrolled rashness or choler. SAMUEL FOOTE, for example, described him as "a good hearted Man, easily provoked, impatient of Contradiction, and hasty in Resolution."[68] THOMAS DAVIES noted his mixture of

68. *A Treatise on the Passions* (London, [1747]), pp. 16-17.

"amiable" and reprehensible qualities: Lear, he wrote, is "brave, generous, frank and benevolent; but, at the same time, wilful, rash, violent, and headstrong." Davies felt that Shakespeare's purpose in the play was "to hold forth to mankind the unhappy consequences of yielding to the sudden and impetuous impressions of anger."

> One unhappy resolution . . . precipitates [Lear] and his dearest friends into inextricable ruin: from the short fury of anger he is provoked . . . into unlimited resentment, furious indignation, and the most violent rage. Consequent agony and distress lead him to the door of madness.

Thus, although he did not minimize the evil of Goneril and Regan, Davies considered Lear ultimately responsible for his own fate.[69] ELIZABETH GRIFFITH particularly praised Shakespeare for his excellence in portraying such "mixed characters" as Lear: "Most other authors . . . present us either with a *flowery mead* or a *savage desart*," but Shakespeare depicts "the demesne of human nature, which includes both the fruitful field and the barren waste, within one inclosure." Mrs. Griffith did not excuse Lear's rashness and folly, but she put much greater emphasis upon his sympathetic qualities. His decision to confer his responsibilities on "younger strengths" struck her as a "rational, a manly, and a virtuous purpose," and his curses on his unnatural daughters as "justly provoked." The latter, though "very horrid and shocking to humanity," she wrote, were intended by Shakespeare "merely to raise an abhorrence in his audience" against the black sins of "ingratitude and undutifulness"—not, we infer, to reflect discredit upon the character of Lear himself. She cited several "beautiful" and "tender" passages in Lear's speeches—for example, his "Poor naked wretches" (III, iv, 28 ff.)—that help to "render this unhappy man a real object both of commiseration and esteem, notwithstanding the weakness, passion, and injustice he has so fully exposed in the beginning of the Play."[70]

But the actor-critics of that period did not always agree on the way in which this "mixed" character should be represented on the stage. The acting of the curse on Goneril, for example, was naturally considered crucial in winning or losing audience sympathy—but which way of acting it gave the best impression of Lear's moral character? The arguments over this scene were also

69. *Dramatic Miscellanies*, II, 315-16.
70. *The Morality of Shakespeare's Drama Illustrated*, pp. 353, 358, 359-60.

related to the question of majesty *versus* pathos, which was related, in turn, to the proper acting of the mad scenes. And discussions of all these subjects had implications for Lear's physique, personality, and motivation.

We do not know how Lear was represented in Shakespeare's day, but from the Restoration until the time of Garrick the major actors evidently conceived him as a character of tremendous vitality and power. This was true, at least, in the scenes that they and their colleagues chose to emphasize in their writings. According to Gildon's report, THOMAS BETTERTON said that the curse on Goneril should be "spoke with an elevated Tone and enraged Voice, and the Accents of a Man all on Fire, and in a Fury next to Madness." This speech, he thought, required much the same delivery as Othello's furious threat to Iago, "Villain, be sure thou prove my love a whore. . . ."[71] Barton Booth's interpretation was similar. THEOPHILUS CIBBER, who found his ideal in Booth's representation, named as Lear's chief characteristics "a Kingly Pride . . . and an impetuous Temper, as soon susceptible of . . . Fury; as Flax is ready to catch Fire." In the mad scenes, Booth's Lear seemed to swell "with an Enthusiasm of Passion which elated him . . . and expanded his whole Frame"; "when crowned with Poppies, &c. the Monarch, jealous of his Power, seemed to rise above himself . . . assumed the God, and grasped his Sceptre of Straw like the Thunderbolt of a Jupiter Tonans."[72] The tradition was varied somewhat by Anthony Boheme, for, as Davies had heard, his "manner of acting Lear was very different from that of Booth." CHARLES MACKLIN reported, approvingly, that Boheme gave the character "a trait . . . of the antique." Yet, judging by Davies' description (based, presumably, on what Macklin told him), there was nothing weak in this actor's portrayal of old age: "In his person he was tall, his features were expressive, with something of the venerable cast, which gave force and authority to the various situations and passions of the character; the tones of his voice were equally powerful and harmonious.

71. [Charles Gildon], *The Life of Mr. Thomas Betterton* (London, 1710), pp. 115-16.

72. Theophilus Cibber, *Two Dissertations on the Theatres* (London, [1756]), "Second Dissertation," pp. 31-32; also "The Life and Character of That Excellent Actor, Barton Booth, Esq.," in *The Lives and Characters of the Most Eminent Actors and Actresses of Great Britain and Ireland* (London, 1753), pp. 52-53.

. . ."[73] The reader gets the impression that this Lear was probably less fiery than Betterton's and Booth's but that he was nevertheless an imposing figure.

The idea that Lear should be represented as physically infirm seems to have originated with DAVID GARRICK, who greatly emphasized the pity aroused in the audience by the "*distresses at his years.*"[74] Being smaller than his most famous predecessors in the role, Garrick was well suited to his own conception of the character; and the pathetic dignity that he gave to the battered old king is graphically suggested by Benjamin Wilson's well-known painting of him in the storm scene. Since the physical appearance of this Lear was an innovation, however, traditionalists must have found it, at first glance, ludicrously inappropriate. According to JOHN HILL, it took powerful acting to overcome this impression:

When we see the little, old, white-haired man enter, with spindle-shanks, a tottering gait, and great shoes upon the little feet, we fancy a Gomez or a Fondlewife: but when he speaks, and enters into the business of the character, we find him every inch a king. . . .[75]

Hill's reference to Gomez (in Dryden's *The Spanish Fryar*) and Fondlewife (in Congreve's *The Old Bachelor*), two characters of the "pantaloon" type, is significant, for on the eighteenth century stage the weaknesses of old age were likely to be associated with comedy rather than with tragedy. Another difficulty that Garrick had to overcome in his interpretation was the possibility that physical feebleness would bring to mind senility as well. When Edward Tighe observed that Lear's weakness and folly detract from the tragic effect of the play, Garrick replied:

Lear is certainly a *Weak* man, it is part of his Character—violent, old & *weakly* fond of his Daughters . . . but I cannot possibly agree . . . that the Effect of his distress is diminished by his being an *Old Fool*— his Weakness proceeds from his Age . . . & such an Old Man full of Affection, Generosity, Passion . . . meeting with what he thought an ungrateful return from his best beloved Cordelia, & afterward, real ingratitude from his other Daughters, an Audience must feel his distresses & Madness which is ye Consequence of them—nay . . . had

73. *Dramatic Miscellanies*, II, 277.

74. MS letter in the Folger Library, dated merely February 23. Published in *Letters of Garrick*, ed. Little and Kahrl, II, 682-83. The editors suggest 1770 as the year.

75. *The Actor: or, A Treatise on the Art of Playing* (London, 1755), pp. 128-30, 151-52. *See* pp. 112-13 and p. 234 for additional comments on Garrick's Lear.

not ye source of his unhappiness proceeded from good qualities carry'd
to excess of folly, but from vices, I really think that ye bad part of
him would be forgotten in ye space of an Act. . . .[76]

It was one of Garrick's triumphs that he was able to portray
Lear's violence as well as his weakness, his majesty as well as his
pathos. For him, these qualities were not irreconcilable. In
the famous curse on Goneril, for example, he gave a masterly
exhibition of conflicting emotions. He daringly departed from
the Betterton-Barton Booth tradition, and, instead of rush-
ing headlong into the furious speech, he threw aside his crutch,
sank to his knees, and spoke the curse as an invocation. There
was no loss of power in this performance—indeed the audience
found it "so terribly affecting . . . that . . . they seemed to
shrink from it as from a blast of lightning."[77] But there was
also pathos: grief strove with anger, and at the end the prayer for
vengeance melted into tears. (This business was warranted by
Shakespeare's text—"these hot tears, which break from me perforce," I, iv, 320—but not by Tate's. In Garrick's period it was an
innovation.) The scene was a tremendous theatrical success. Even
so, adherents of the Barton Booth tradition, like Samuel Foote and
Theophilus Cibber, objected to the awesome preliminaries of
Garrick's curse and the unaccustomed pauses that occasionally
interrupted the fiery words. Foote thought the whole speech
should have been given "with a Rage almost equal to Phrenzy";
not only the "Premeditation" and "Solemnity" but even the
tears seemed out of place to him.[78] And Cibber insisted that
Garrick's "deliberation" cast a shadow on Lear's morality and
jeopardized the audience's sympathy for him.

So dire is the Curse, Nature can scarce endure it, unless delivered in
the rapid Manner, the wild Transport [that] the choleric King . . .
would surely give it:—when it appears premeditated,—it speaks Ran-
cour, Spleen, and Malice . . . not a Burst of Passion, from an o'ercharged
Heart.[79]

Thomas Davies, however, preferred Garrick's interpretation to
Booth's. If Lear were "agitated by one passion only," he wrote,

76. See n. 74, above.
77. *Dramatic Miscellanies,* II, 280. An earlier Lear had been chided by Aaron
Hill for kneeling and speaking the curse with "calmness and reverence." See *The
Prompter,* ed. W. W. Appleton and K. A. Burnim (New York, 1966), p. 104.
78. *A Treatise on the Passions,* pp. 16-17.
79. *Two Dissertations on the Theatres,* "Second Dissertation," pp. 31-32.

then the latter's "remarkably energetic" performance, with its unrelieved "impetuosity," would have been superior. But Shakespeare wrote the curse "for a father as well as a monarch, in whom the most bitter execrations are accompanied with extreme anguish." Lear, then, is moved by a "tumultuous combination" of passions—rage, grief, and indignation—"where all claim to be heard at once, and where one naturally interrupts the progress of the others."[80]

Davies' reminder that Lear is a "father as well as a monarch" reflects another critical controversy which was no doubt inspired by the conflicting stage interpretations: Which of Lear's roles was the more important? What was the true source of his madness—loss of royal power or grief over the treatment he received from his daughters? Cibber's description of the mad scenes, as acted by Booth, clearly indicates his commitment (and, in his opinion, Booth's) to awe-inspiring majesty rather than fatherly grief. Samuel Foote, in his *Treatise on the Passions* (1747), formulated a theory to support such an interpretation. Lear's mind, he explained, is "at first entirely possessed with the Thoughts of his Daughters' Ingratitude, which was the immediate Cause of his Distress," but these thoughts do not overturn his reason. It is when he "looks back to the remote Cause, which was a voluntary Resignation of the Regal Power," that his mind begins to turn. For "the Idea of his former Grandeur" possesses his imagination; he contrasts it with his "present Misery," and, knowing the "Impossibility of remounting the Throne," is driven to madness. "The Desire of Royalty then is the Point that distracts *Lear*'s Judgment; and the Belief that he possesses that Royalty, the State of Madness; all his Expressions are full of the Royal Prerogative." For this reason he should be portrayed as extravagantly majestic, not idly playing with straws or indulging in other forms of childish behavior.[81] ARTHUR MURPHY, however, took issue with this interpretation. Foote's theory had in the meantime been reiterated by the nontheatrical critic Joseph Warton in *The Adventurer*, 1754. When Murphy first expressed his opposition to it, in his *Gray's Inn Journal*, 1754, he himself was a "nontheatrical critic" in the narrowest sense; but he was following the stage closely at this time, he had friends among the actors, and his two-year career in the

80. *Dramatic Miscellanies*, II, 279-80, 315-16.
81. *A Treatise on the Passions*, p. 20.

theatre, which began shortly afterward, did not change his mind
on the subject. According to him, the behavior of Goneril and
Regan is always uppermost in Lear's mind and their treatment
of him is the cause of his insanity. Thus his feelings as a father
are more important than kingly pride.[82] This interpretation is
in line with Garrick's remark that an audience, seeing Lear's
reaction to the ingratitude of his daughters, "must feel his distresses & Madness which is ye Consequence of them." Being an
admirer of Garrick's Lear but also a personal friend of Foote,
Murphy probably debated the matter in private as well as in
print.

Actor-critics of the nineteenth century evidently found nothing
questionable in Lear's moral nature; for they gave little consideration to this subject per se, and their discussions of other
matters usually reflected the tacit assumption that Lear is a basically "good" and sympathetic character. The problem that chiefly
concerned them was the antithetical possibilities in interpreting
his physical and emotional personality: weakness and pathos on
the one hand, strength and grandeur on the other. Although
Garrick had managed to combine these traits, his emphasis upon
the more sentimental aspects of Lear's character and situation had
been very influential. Edmund Kean, whose acting was much like
Garrick's, undoubtedly gave fire as well as pathos to his characterization, but there may well have been other inheritors of the
Garrick tradition who justified Lamb's mocking reference to "an
old man tottering about the stage with a walking-stick." By
w. c. MACREADY's time, the older interpretation, once associated
with Betterton and Booth, was apparently considered unusual—
at least by English actors and their audiences. Macready himself
revived it, however, or worked out an interpretation bearing some
resemblance to it; and in America it lived on in the acting of
Edwin Forrest, whose physique and talents were particularly
suited to it.

Macready, who once remarked that *King Lear* is "not a very
pathetic play,"[83] was conscious of differing from "most actors,"
including Garrick, Kemble, and Kean, in his interpretation of
Lear's character. They "represented the feebleness . . . of old age,"
he wrote; but actually Lear's was "a 'lusty winter': his language

---

82. *Works*, VI, 233-44.
83. MS letter to T. J. Serle, dated August 10, 1832. In the Folger Library.

never betrays imbecility of mind or body." Although he does confer his kingdom on "younger strengths," he is still sufficiently vigorous "to ride, to hunt, to run wildly through the fury of the storm, to slay the ruffian who murdered his Cordelia, and to bear about her dead body in his arms."

There is, moreover, a heartiness and even jollity in his blither moments, no way akin to the helplessness of senility. Indeed the towering rage of thought with which his mind dilates . . . and the power of conceiving such vast imaginings, would seem incompatible with a tottering, trembling frame, and betoken rather one of "mighty bone and bold emprise," in the outward bearing of the grand old man.[84]

Physical vigor, however, could not give an adequate impression of Lear on the stage without some further suggestion of the intellectual grandeur that "betokened" it. It was the lack of this quality that Macready deplored most in Edwin Forrest's performance. "In the storm," he declared, ". . . there was nothing *on* his mind, fastened *on* and tearing and convulsing him with agony. . . . There was much to praise in Forrest's execution . . . but he has not enriched, refined, elevated, and enlarged his *mind*."[85] Macready's criticism may have been influenced by jealousy, but it was written too early to have been biased by his now-famous feud with the American actor. Actually he was not alone in detecting a lack of imagination in Forrest's acting; and it was this, I think—Forrest's failure to *attempt* Lear's intellectual sublimity, rather than his failure to convey it adequately—that disturbed Macready. For Macready knew from personal experience how difficult such an attempt could be. On one occasion (in 1833) he despaired of making "an effective character" of Lear on this account. "I am oppressed," he wrote in his diary, "by the magnitude of the thoughts he has to utter, and shrink before the picture of the character which my imagination presents to me."[86] Happily, he did feel sometimes that he had risen to Lear's chal-

84. *Macready's Reminiscences and Selections from His Diaries*, ed. Sir Frederick Pollock (New York, 1875), pp. 149-50. Although Edmund Kean was among those who emphasized the infirmities of age, he remarked to John Wakefield Francis that "none but a young man could perform old Lear" (see *Old New York; or Reminiscences of the Past Sixty Years* [New York, 1858], p. 227). Similarly Sir Donald Wolfit commented in a letter to me (April 19, 1966) that he himself acted Lear best when he was in his forties.

85. *Diaries of Macready*, ed. Toynbee, II, 229. Entry for October 21, 1843.

86. *Ibid.*, I, 68-69. Entry for October 11, 1833.

lenge. When he last acted the role, for example (in 1851), he re-corded exultantly that "Power, passion, discrimination, tender-ness, [were] constantly kept in mind."[87]

The then-traditional conception of Lear against which Mac-ready rebelled was upheld in the writings of his American con-temporary JAMES H. HACKETT. And, not surprisingly, Hackett's ideas on the subject were expressed in his reviews of performances by Macready and Forrest. His own ideal of the character looked backward to the influential interpretation of Garrick as it had been described by Murphy: "a feeble old man, still, however, retaining an air of royalty." Naturally, then, he found fault with Macready for forgetting (as he thought) "in the carriage of his body, and by the quickness and the vigor of his lungs, that Lear was 'four-score and upwards and *a weak and infirm old man.'*" Actually, however, Hackett's interpretation seems to have been an exaggera-tion of Garrick's rather than a faithful echo of it. Garrick, though he thought of Lear as weakening in judgment, had stoutly denied that he was "an *Old Fool*"; but Hackett described him as a "doting and imbecile Octogenarian"—and this in the first scene of the play. Apparently, too, despite Hackett's use of the word "despot" at one point, kingliness and rage were even less important for him than they had been for Garrick (if we can judge by Davies' de-scription of the latter), and the paternal tenderness and pathos that Garrick had lifted into prominence took on for Hackett a halo of "benevolence" which blinded him to darker elements in the character. Since Macready had tempered Lear's grandeur with tenderness, Hackett found much to admire in his performance despite their disagreement about the physical and mental strength of the character. He was more censorious of Forrest. This actor's nature, he thought, was "too rough . . . to cherish such delicate impulses" as Lear's "gushes of tenderness." Even Forrest's makeup (especially the shaggy eyebrows, which obscured the expression of the eyes, and the long beard, which covered some important facial muscles) was too "inflexible . . . and forbidding" to allow the effective depiction of fluctuating emotions. Forrest tried "to make sternness and the mortified pride of the pagan despot *Lear*'s strongest characteristic," but, in Hackett's opinion, these are "only . . . sudden and transient flashes of a consuming heart . . . clearly alternate and *secondary* to the philanthropy which pervades

87. *Ibid.*, II, 491. Entry for February 3, 1851.

the nature of the sensitive old father." Forrest omitted the "bit of pathos" that Shakespeare introduced into the curse on Goneril (the "hot tears," which Tate did not include in his text) ; but Hackett himself, on the few occasions when he acted Lear, restored this passage. It "breaks the continuity of cursing," he explained, it softens the "abhorrent quality" of Lear's bitterness, and it reveals that "malevolence, though provokable, is neither uppermost, nor wanton . . . nor unremitted in *Lear*'s nature." Since Hackett considered uncontrolled anger a reversion to "barbarism," he hardly appreciated the "startling paroxysms of rage" for which Forrest was famous. He agreed that Lear's "outraged sensibilities" require "earnest and forcible expression," but he placed more emphasis upon his "innate benevolence" since it affords opportunities for "those tender strokes of art" which leave the "most enduring impression" upon the hearts of thoughtful spectators.[88]

In deploring Forrest's thundering tirades Hackett was hardly speaking for the average member of the audience, and he was smugly aware that he was not. In that age of melodrama, of spellbinding oratory, Forrest was by far the most popular of American Lears. (Indeed he would probably have been impressive in any period.) Yet Hackett was himself a man of his time as far as his critical tastes were concerned. The refinement and sentimentality that beset Victorian criticism are almost as obvious in his interpretation of Lear as in the "feminine" conception of Hamlet, a phenomenon of the same period. The extent to which the refinement was sometimes carried is suggested by the fact that, a little later in the century, some critics complained of the "absurd violence" of EDWIN BOOTH's King Lear in the first two acts. Booth (chief advocate and representative of the feminine Hamlet) was surely no melodramatic actor. Indeed his lack of physical strength prevented his reaching "the height of Lear's passion"—or so FREDERICK WARDE reports; he was at his best in the "suffering of the poor distracted king," which he depicted with "extreme" pathos, and in the reconciliation with Cordelia, which was "beautifully tender."[89] Booth's performance may have fallen short of his intentions, but it seems clear that he conceived Lear in Garrick's manner: as a "mixed" character, capable of great rage as well as

88. *Notes, Criticisms, and Correspondence*, pp. 96-99, 112-13, 228.
89. *Fifty Years of Make-Believe*, p. 121.

great tenderness. As Booth himself remarked, the violence to which some of his critics objected was "Shakespeare's design (whether right or wrong), and not the actor's fault."[90]

A return to something like Macready's conception can be seen in the comments of Booth's younger contemporary HENRY IRVING. Although, in acting the character, Irving originally attempted "to combine the weakness of senility with the tempest of passion," he found this to be "a perfectly impossible task." "Lear cannot be played," he decided, "except with the plenitude of the actor's physical powers, and the idea of representing extreme old age is futile." As far as written criticism is concerned, Irving's greatest difference from Macready was in regard to Lear's intellect; it has begun to "decay," he felt, before the opening of the play, and during the course of the ordeal it is reduced to a "ruin." Yet, even here, Irving saw nothing petty in the character: for "some of the original grandeur can still be traced" in the ruin, and the pity that the actor is asked to arouse is not simply for Lear himself but "for human frailty which is the most universal of social bonds." Irving's experience convinced him that in Lear, more than in any other Shakespearean part, the performer is "overshadowed by the supreme majesty of Shakespeare's genius" and that the actor truest to the poet is the one "who portrays with the grandest power the Titanic force and energy of Lear."[91]

Actor-critics of the present century have agreed that Lear is meant to be vital and impressive rather than merely pathetic. Several of them have described the character in terms reminiscent of Macready's criticism and suggestive, ultimately, of the stage tradition that goes back to Thomas Betterton and Barton Booth. WILLIAM POEL, for example, rejected the interpretation of "a decrepit, commonplace old man" which a contemporary production had presented. The Lear of his own vision was "as hale and active at eighty as he was at forty; a large-hearted, good-natured giant, with a face as red as a lobster." "One of the spoilt children of nature," he had come to think of himself as omnipotent because his position had placed him above responsibility. "No one but Lear must be 'fiery,' no one but him unreasonable or contrary.

90. MS letter to A. I. Fish, December 24, 1870. In the Folger Library.
91. "My Four Favorite Parts," pp. 36-37; also *Papers on Acting: The Art of Acting, A Discussion by Constant Coquelin, Henry Irving and Dion Boucicault* (New York, 1926), p. 52.

In the crushing of this strong, unyielding, but lovable personality lies the drama of the play."[92] Both HARLEY GRANVILLE-BARKER[93] and ROBERT SPEAIGHT[94] have noticed the combination of abstract grandeur and personal vigor in the character, the former being uppermost in the first scene (where, according to Granville-Barker, Lear is "more a magnificent portent than a man") and the latter in Lear's second appearance (I, iv). Speaight graphically pictures "the man, wilful, impetuous, and companionable" as he springs to life on this latter occasion: "ruddy from the chase," strong of appetite, vigorous of body. "Nothing of Father Christmas here." In his comments on various stage performances Speaight's chief criterion of excellence is the actor's success in communicating a sense of grandeur. His greatest admiration is accorded Sir Michael Redgrave's Lear (1953), which conveyed "an impression of . . . a crumbling Colossus bringing down all his world about him," and Sir John Gielgud's performances of 1931 and 1950, in which "the full diapason of his wonderful voice" was employed, with the effect of "more power than pathos."

The most successful of modern Lears in the Garrick-Kean tradition was SIR DONALD WOLFIT. In performance he greatly emphasized the characteristics of old age—the shaking hands, the waggling head—especially at the beginning of the play.[95] Yet the impression received from his written comments on King Lear can be epitomized in the word "grandeur." During his first performance of the role (at Cardiff, 1942), Wolfit recalls: "The magnitude of the task and the unnerving cosmic quality of the tragedy became apparent to me. . . . I seemed to myself to resemble a small boy who, wading into a rough sea, sees the big waves coming, jumps in the air to avoid being overwhelmed, and is flung on to the shore." With the second performance, he suddenly felt "inside" his part.

But half-way through the play my mind refused to grasp any more of the suffering king. I could not encompass the task and fell back on sheer technique. . . . I found the long rest after the Hovel Scene when Lear loses his wits to be absolutely essential to the actor to

92. *Shakespeare in the Theatre*, pp. 186-87.
93. *Prefaces to Shakespeare*, I, 285-86.
94. *Nature in Shakespearian Tragedy*, p. 98; "The Actability of King Lear," p. 50.
95. Professor Arthur Colby Sprague gave me these details of Wolfit's performance.

recover his own before he plays the tragic encounter with the blinded Gloucester and the awakening scene with Cordelia.[96]

But if, like Macready, Wolfit was awed by his conception of Lear's inexpressible sublimity, he was able, when he had matured his performance, to move his audiences powerfully. James Agate declared that Wolfit's Lear was "the greatest piece of Shakespearean acting" he had seen.[97]

There has been little concern in the modern period over the relative importance of Lear's political and domestic roles. Instead there has been an increased emphasis upon his role as a representative of universal humanity. If we glance backward for a moment, however, to the late nineteenth century, we can find these two subjects brought together in BARRY SULLIVAN's analysis of the the character. According to his biographer, Robert Sillard, Sullivan traced Lear's development toward universality in three movements: in the first, "Lear, although generous, is always the autocratic king, great, majestic, passionate, and violent"; in the second, "feeling keenly his daughters' ingratitude, he becomes more father than king"; and, finally, weighed down by suffering, "he forgets for a little his mortal pain, and, rather than father or king, shows himself a man reacting against rebel nature."[98]

But, in the actor-criticisms of the present century, the interest in Lear's universality has been most often linked with interest in his moral flaws—a subject that has received new emphasis in this period. As in the eighteenth century, Lear is usually thought of as a "mixed" character, both culpable and sympathetic. LENA ASHWELL stressed his humanity, pointing out that his mistakes at the beginning proceed from common weaknesses: the desire to shift the burden of responsibility onto someone else and the "incapacity for giving freely." Once he has committed these errors, she wrote, he must endure his consequent destiny, and the self-pity that overwhelms him throughout much of the drama— another very human trait—does not help him to endure. "When in the end Cordelia comes with healing in her great love, at last he forgets self in his sorrow for her. . . ."[99] Granville-Barker recognized even greater flaws in the character: Shakespeare does

96. *First Interval* (London, 1954), pp. 212-13.
97. *Ibid.*, p. 219. *See also* Speaight, "The Actability of King Lear," p. 50.
98. Robert M. Sillard, *Barry Sullivan and His Contemporaries; a Histrionic Record by Robert M. Sillard* . . . (London, 1901), I, 274.
99. *Reflections from Shakespeare*, pp. 152-53.

not minimize Lear's "stiff-necked perversities," he pointed out, nor does he ask our sympathy "on easy terms." Granville-Barker did not even attempt to mitigate the outrageousness of the famous curse; he emphasized it, rather, for he suggested that the terrible words be spoken, not with ungovernable rage but with deadly quiet. The theatrical effectiveness of this interpretation is obvious, since the curse is "lodged between two whirlwinds of Lear's fury," but, in his opinion, the dramatic purpose is far more important. "Not indifferently did Shakespeare make this a pagan play, and deprive its argument of comfortable faith in virtue rewarded, here or hereafter. And it is upon this deliberate invocation of ill that we pass into spiritual darkness." Shakespeare set himself a difficult task with Lear, yet it was necessary to begin with the unreasonableness and the evil in order to show us "the way of . . . [his] soul's agony and salvation." Throughout the rest of the play Lear makes the progress "from personal grievance to the taking upon him, as great natures may, the imagined burden of the whole world's sorrow."[100] Robert Speaight's basic concept is similar, but he has expressed it in more abstract terms: for example, he describes Lear's giving up the crown as "a sort of suicide," explaining that the king could not separate himself from his lawfully inherited power without allowing the natural order to collapse, thus bringing disaster; and he ascribes the love-test and its consequences to the fact that Lear dislikes to face the truth, preferring (in common with Goneril and Regan) a "game" of "macabre illusion." Lear brings his sufferings upon himself, but he gains our sympathy as he becomes "the mouthpiece of a universal accusation. It is not Goneril and Regan alone, but all society which stands at the bar."[101]

At least two modern actors, however, have described Lear in simple, "unmixed" terms—MARGARET WEBSTER as almost entirely unsympathetic, and Sir Donald Wolfit as almost entirely sympathetic. According to Miss Webster, Lear's improbable abdication and his rejection of "the one daughter whose love is immediately patent to the dullest of us" are enough to convince the ordinary playgoer that he is a "pigheaded old tyrant who will deserve whatever he gets." In the ensuing scenes "Lear behaves like a choleric, self-willed megalomaniac, whose presence in the home would be

100. *Prefaces to Shakespeare*, II, 283-89.
101. *Nature in Shakespearian Tragedy*, pp. 93-95, 107-8.

intolerable even to the most dutiful of children." A reader may be moved, in the storm scenes, by his "senseless, pitiful arrogance . . . his challenge of the unchallengeable," but a theatre audience finds its sympathetic impulses stifled by his own self-pity. As for the repentance and regeneration that critics have found in these scenes, they simply do not make themselves felt in the theatre—so Miss Webster believes: "the change is more likely to seem a gigantic swing of the pendulum of wrath, so that . . . the despot who has had no thought for the poor and wretched . . . now rails with equally insensate fury against every representative of riches, authority or power. We are aghast at the glorious frenzy of his speeches; but do we, truly, care?"[102] Wolfit naturally saw the character in a different light, for his own experience had demonstrated, again and again, that an audience might "care" very much about Lear. Though one of the most successful Lears of the present century, he was probably the least "modern" of them all in his basic interpretation. For Wolfit was convinced that "the tragedy rests firmly on the opposition between parental love and filial ingratitude" and that nothing is to be gained by sophisticated attempts to rationalize the behavior of the characters. He rejected, for example, the idea that Lear is in his dotage, as well as the explanation that Goneril and Regan react to their father as they do because of some mistreatment they have received in the past. This type of criticism, he argued, only "blurs the contrast" that Shakespeare intended, and "bestows . . . on the villains" much of the "admiration and sympathy" that belongs to the "heroes and heroines." Not only did Wolfit accept Lear's goodness without question, but he had no doubt of the "sublime end" that crowns his tragic ordeal: "the ascension of Lear's spirit to the empyrean to rejoin Cordelia there after their earthly reconciliation."[103]

CORDELIA

Cordelia has received less comment from the actor-critics than any of the heroines in Shakespeare's other major tragedies—obviously because of the relative slightness of the role. Indeed, several of the criticisms that do exist are concerned with the minimal development of this character. Considering theatrical

102. *Shakespeare Without Tears*, pp. 216-19.
103. Introduction to the Folio Society edition of *King Lear*, pp. 3, 5-6.

conditions in the eighteenth century, it is easy to understand
FRANCIS GENTLEMAN's complaint that Cordelia "makes too incon-
siderable a figure; is too seldom in view, and has not matter enough
for a capital actress to display extensive talents in." For it is true
that Cordelia has fewer lines to speak than Ophelia, even; that
she is absent from the stage after the first scene of the play until
the middle of the fourth act; and that she shares importance with
her evil sisters, each of whom has a role as substantial as hers.
Gentleman approved Tate's additions to Cordelia's part, including
the romance with Edgar, but he felt that even further development was needed.[104] Despite Tate's padding of the part, the actor-
critics of that period virtually ignored Cordelia, as far as character
analysis was concerned. THOMAS DAVIES, for example, merely
described her as a "pious Daughter." Reports of stage history
were equally slight: according to Davies, "Mrs. Cibber, the most
pathetic of all actresses, was the only Cordelia of excellence."[105]
In the nineteenth century Cordelia began at attract somewhat
more attention from actors (and considerably more from literary
critics), even though, with the disappearance of Tate's version,
she lost her spurious love interest. There was no champion among
the actresses, however, to insist—as did Helen Faucit for both
Ophelia and Desdemona—that the importance of the character had
been underestimated. ELLEN TERRY, rarely at a loss for words,
found little to say about Cordelia in her lecture on "Shakespeare's
Pathetic Women" (first given in 1910-11) and fell back on quotations from the play. "Cordelia is a most difficult part," she remarked. "So little to say, so much to feel! Rarely does an actress
fathom the depths of those still waters."[106]

In the modern period, the emphasis upon the ensemble rather
than upon leading performers in acting Shakespeare tends to
make Gentleman's concern for the "capital actress" seem rather
old-fashioned. Consideration for the play as a whole leads to
the recognition that some of its significance, its careful balance,
would be lost if Cordelia were allowed to occupy our attention
more fully. HARLEY GRANVILLE-BARKER, always conscious of matters
like these, yet aware too of the player's task, took a more positive

104. Dramatic Censor, I, 360.
105. Dramatic Miscellanies, II, 316, 320.
106. Four Lectures on Shakespeare, ed. with an introduction by Christopher
St. John [Christabel Marshall] (London, [1932]), pp. 153-56.

approach than earlier actors to the subject of Cordelia's development as a character: what others have called sketchiness he described as economy. According to him, Shakespeare both demands
and makes possible an unusual technical achievement in the acting
of Cordelia—producing a maximum effect by minimum means.
"The character itself has . . . that vitality which positive virtues
give. Cordelia is never in doubt about herself; she has no vagaries"; hence our impression of her is "clear cut."

Add to this her calm and steadfast isolation among the contending
or subservient figures of that first scene—and the fact . . . that from this
very thrift of herself the broadcast violence of the play's whole action
springs—then we see how with but a reminder of her here and there,
Shakespeare could trust to her reappearance after long delay, no jot
of her importance nor of our interest in her abated.[107]

Despite the logical sound of this argument, however, one suspects
that the actress, no matter how modern and enlightened, will
always find herself closer to Ellen Terry's wistfulness than to
Granville-Barker's optimism in assessing the effectiveness of
Cordelia's reticence.

As for character interpretation, Cordelia is hardly complex
enough to offer many points of disagreement for critics. There
is just one, in fact, that has had any importance for actors: Is
Cordelia a representative of ideal goodness—a sort of morality-play
incarnation of Virtue? Or is she a more human, individualized
character, basically admirable but with unmistakable flaws? On
the one hand, she forfeits a kingdom for the sake of truth, and
for the sake of love she loses her life in trying to save the father
who has disowned her. These actions, admirable enough in
themselves, gain additional lustre by contrast with the cruel and
hypocritical behavior of her two sisters. And so some writers,
especially literary critics of the nineteenth century, have idealized
Cordelia: Anna Brownell Jameson, for example, described her
as "a saint ready prepared for heaven," "governed by the purest
and holiest impulses and motives, the most refined from all dross
of selfishness and passion"; and Dowden considered her an example of "redeeming ardour," one of the "beautiful heroic souls"
whose very existence counterbalances evil and suffering. On the
other hand, Cordelia's behavior—especially in the first scene—
admits of a different, and less creditable, interpretation; her

107. *Prefaces to Shakespeare*, I, 303-5.

rigidly uncompromising answer to her father may reflect stubbornness and lack of sympathy rather than a saintly devotion to truth. Thus even some of the romantically-inclined critics found a certain imperfection in Cordelia's character: Coleridge, for instance, noted "some little faulty admixture of pride and sullenness"; and Gervinus, though he called her "martyr and saviour—the precursor of a better time," granted that her fall was partly due to her own nature. Modern literary critics, like Robert Heilman, have generally seen both admirable and faulty elements in her character.[108] But what of the actor-critics?

Those whose comments on Cordelia are more than casual have generally emphasized her flaws rather than, or in addition to, her virtues. In the eighteenth century, for example, Francis Gentleman was not content with the sympathetic phrase about filial piety with which Cordelia, when she was mentioned at all, was usually tagged; he called attention to her less lovely aspect, deploring the "unjustifiable cynical roughness" of her "barren, churlish answer" to her father.[109] And in the following century JAMES H. HACKETT was apparently uninfluenced by the sentimental interpretation of the character that was then at its height. When John Quincy Adams asserted that Lear's distresses win audience sympathy largely because of their effect on Cordelia, Hackett reminded him that Cordelia herself was partly responsible for those distresses. For, he wrote, "instead of gently and innocently humoring her weak but loving and *partial* father," she showed "obstinacy and reserve"—a "slight . . . fault" but tragic in its consequences. "To her truth and coldness, and her father's rashness and folly, then, may be traced the primary causes of the sad catastrophe."[110]

Actors have sometimes worried about the possibility that Shakespeare's heroine would lose the sympathy of the audience by her behavior in the first scene. Gentleman credited Tate with softening its effect by making Cordelia's reply spring from her affection for Edgar, but he felt that further softening was needed. And

108. Anna Brownell Jameson, *Characteristics of Woman* (Boston, 1853), pp. 189-205 (especially pp. 189 and 200); Edward Dowden, *Shakespeare: A Critical Study of His Mind and Art* (London, 1897), pp. 227-28; *Coleridge's Shakespearean Criticism*, ed. T. M. Raysor (Cambridge, Mass., 1930), I, 60; G. G. Gervinus, *Shakespeare Commentaries* (London, 1892), pp. 637-42 (especially p. 641); Robert Heilman, *This Great Stage* (Seattle, 1963), pp. 35-36.

109. *Dramatic Censor*, I, 353.

110. *Notes, Criticisms, and Correspondence*, p. 228.

as recently as the early 1900's WILLIAM POEL suggested that the actress attempt to overcome the adverse effect of Cordelia's severity by speaking "in tones choking with emotion, not in the least defiant."[111]

But all such efforts to mitigate the harshness of Cordelia's words met with disapproval from two modern actor-critics, LENA ASHWELL[112] and Harley Granville-Barker.[113] Writing in the 1920's, Miss Ashwell recalled sarcastically that in her youth actresses were taught to say "Nothing, my lord" in saccharine tones which were meant to suggest her "perfection." (At least Poel's way was better than *that!*) And Granville-Barker evidently considered this practice common enough, still, to require a warning against it. Both felt that, in the latter's words, to portray Cordelia as a "meek saint" is to misrepresent her character, for she "has more than a touch of her father in her": she is as "hot-headed and peppery as he is," Miss Ashwell wrote, "and as lovable"; and Granville-Barker added that, "for all her sweetness and youth," she shares Lear's obstinacy and pride. The actress describes Cordelia's behavior in the first scene like this: affronted by her sisters' insincerity, disgusted by her father's credulity, determined not to sacrifice her own integrity for a third of the kingdom, she strikes out at her father in a "direct, uncompromising" and rather cruel way; "then comes hot-headed explanation." This Cordelia is not peculiarly self-centered or unreasonable; she is typical of idealistic youth— "intolerant," always, of its "foolish elders," "quick and fierce in [its] judgments." There is even something fine about such single-minded devotion to truth; but the sympathetic understanding which could have saved Lear at this point is lacking. For Granville-Barker, the correct representation of Cordelia in the first scene has an importance beyond that of the character itself; it is necessary for the capturing of "Shakespeare's first important dramatic effect: the mighty old man and the frail child, confronted and each unyielding."

In discussing Cordelia's later behavior Lena Ashwell becomes a victim of her own semiallegorical interpretation of the play. She hardly thinks of an individual character any more, but only of one who has learned to follow her "heart" rather than make

111. *Monthly Letters* (London, 1929), pp. 51-52.
112. *Reflections from Shakespeare*, pp. 155-56.
113. *Prefaces to Shakespeare*, I, 303-5.

narrow intellectual judgments and has thus become an agent of redemptive love. But Granville-Barker offers a more consistent view of Cordelia. He points out that in the reunion with her father she is characteristically terse in her language, as if speech were not "simple or genuine enough" to express her deepest emotions. Her "No cause, no cause" is "the complement" of her earlier "Nothing." Ironically, her great virtue is "no gain" to her father. "Her wisdom of heart showed her Regan and Goneril as they were; yet it was an inarticulate wisdom and provoked evil in Lear. . . ." Her self-sufficiency is such that "neither good fortune nor ill can touch Cordelia herself; this is her strength and her weakness both."

There is rarely an actor-critic who sees no imperfections in Cordelia. But ROBERT SPEAIGHT is such a critic, and a very articulate one. Her answer to her father's love-test may be "tactless and inopportune," he grants, but the truth is frequently both. "Nothing, my lord" is not spoken simply because the plot requires it, nor does it indicate that Cordelia shares her father's willfulness; it signifies her refusal to take part in the game of pretense which the other characters are playing. With his penchant for symbolism, Speaight finds Cordelia representative not only of Truth but, even more, of Love. "She is Nature redeemed and remade; she is mercy and reconciliation. . . ." Moreover, she is the "point of transition" between Shakespeare's tragedies and his final plays, like *The Tempest,* in which "so many contradictions would be resolved in the light of religious intuition."[114]

THE FOOL

Except for comments on the propriety or impropriety of the Fool's presence in the tragedy, there was little discussion of the character by actors before 1838, when WILLIAM CHARLES MACREADY restored him to the stage after an absence of a century and a half. Even Macready did some soul-searching before he finally decided to take this step. On January 4, 1838, he confided to his diary the fear that, "like many such terrible contrasts in poetry and painting," the Fool's presence in actual performance would "fail of effect," would "either weary and annoy or distract the spectator." The next day, however, he met with a suggestion from another

114. *Nature in Shakespearian Tragedy,* pp. 93-94, 100, 104, 121.

actor that solved the problem of greatest concern to him: namely, the inability to visualize a performance by his comedian, Meadows, which would realize his own conception of the role. When he had described "the sort of fragile, hectic, beautiful-faced, half-idiot-looking boy" that he believed the Fool should be, "Bartley observed that a woman should play it." "I caught at the idea," Macready records, "and instantly exclaimed: 'Miss P[riscilla] Horton is the very person.' "[115] This charming actress and singer, who also played Ariel in Macready's production of *The Tempest,* gave a very successful performance of Lear's Fool. Macready himself was delighted; and later, when he was travelling as a star rather than managing his own company, he continued to stipulate that the Fool be acted by "a clever woman who sings and is a *lively* actress."[116] The innovation was very influential, and for years the part was frequently assigned to an actress.

There was at least one of Macready's contemporaries, however, who did not share his interpretation of the Fool. JAMES H. HACKETT, after discussing the matter with Macready, decided that the latter's idea was "pretty" and "ingenious" but not really convincing. One of Macready's arguments in favor of a woman in the role was that she could "*look like a boy of eighteen,*" but Hackett imagined the Fool to be a mature man. He described the character as "a sort of *practical* cynic" who, out of "acute observation . . . and much *experience* of the *world,*" utters "scraps of moral caustic" designed to "*extract* and *point the moral* of the passing scene to the *understanding* of the *audiences* of Shakespeare's day."[117] Hackett seems to have been impatient, too, with what he considered overemphasis on the Fool's importance. At least he objected to Forrest's construing Lear's speech, "And my poor fool is hanged" (V, iii, 305) , as a reference to the Fool's death, "as though Lear could abstract his thoughts then from *Cordelia* to inquire about the fate of his professional 'fool' or jester."[118]

Oversimplifying somewhat, we may say that Macready introduced the "sentimental" view of the Fool which was to be

115. *Diaries of Macready,* ed. Toynbee, I, 437-38.

116. Letter of January 24, 1848, from Macready to E. D. Davis, manager of the Manchester Theatre. MS in the Folger Library.

117. *Notes, Criticisms, and Correspondence,* pp. 111-12. Edwin Booth, like Hackett, disapproved of a woman's being cast as the Fool. *See* his letter of September 6, 1875, to Augustin Daly. MS in the Folger Library.

118. *Notes, Criticisms, and Correspondence,* p. 109.

supported and sometimes exaggerated by several later actor-critics and that Hackett maintained a "commonsense" view based upon the function of the historical court jester.

The sentimental interpretation has been predominant in actors' criticisms of the Fool, certainly through the early decades of the present century. Even WILLIAM POEL was not influenced by Elizabethan customs in interpreting this character. His description of a "gentle, frail lad who perishes from exposure to the storm, a child with the wisdom of a child, which is often the profoundest wisdom" sounds like an echo of Macready's. (Note the assumption that the Fool dies in the storm—he is never seen after Act III, scene vi—rather than, as some have thought, by hanging after being captured with his master.) Poel's ideal Fool was, in fact, even more pathetic than Macready's and less lively: his face was "infinitely sad"; his bits of song were "improvised at the moment," not really sung but "intoned in a light musical cadence" and "moan[ed] . . . as if to himself"; his witty replies to Lear were accompanied with a laugh, "good-natured but sad." An integral part of the play's pattern, this Fool was a foil to the King: in contrast to the aged but powerful Lear, he was young and helpless, perhaps even a cripple or a dwarf; he countered the King's obtuseness with his own keen wit. But his most important function was to win sympathy for Lear by bringing out the latter's capacity for "deep affection." Poel was so convinced of the Fool's significance that he placed this character with Lear and Cordelia when he wrote: "There is no other play of Shakespeare's which contains three tragic figures drawn with such masterly skill and deep pathos."[119] The sentimental view was carried to even greater extremes by FREDERICK WARDE, author of the longest and most detailed study of the Fool by an actor (in The Fools of Shakespeare, 1913). Physically he pictured the Fool in much the same way as Macready and Poel except that he made him a "young-old man" instead of a lad and he gave him a "homely" rather than a beautiful face. But, if possible, he increased his pathos: not content with a plaintive moaning of the songs, he imagined that "tears force themselves through the fragments of melody and almost choke the utterance." Most of all, he emphasized the moral beauty of the character—the "unswerving loyalty" and selfless love. In his own production of King Lear, Warde in-

119. *Monthly Letters*, p. 52.

creased the Fool's importance by bringing him on in the first scene as a silent observer of Lear's folly, one who revealed in pantomime his "surprise . . . awe . . . consternation . . . horror" and, when the courtiers had gone out, crept over to Cordelia with "doglike devotion" and furtively kissed the hem of her robe. Warde rejected the theory held by "some recent commentators" that the Fool and Cordelia are "one and the same person," but he did accept the interpretation that these two characters suffer the same fate. "And my poor fool is hanged" might refer to Cordelia, he conceded, with "fool" as a term of endearment, but it was more satisfying to think of the Fool's "unselfish devotion" fittingly climaxed by death and his "gentle spirit" waiting patiently above "for the poor tortured soul of his loved master to share the peace which he has found."[120] After this assurance of the Fool's heavenly translation, we can hardly be surprised even by LENA ASHWELL's mystical vision of the character: a saintly being, cheerful even in martyrdom, inhabiting the topmost plane of Paradise.[121]

It was GRANVILLE-BARKER who called a halt, at last, to such "etherealized" conceptions of the Fool. As he pointed out, they only add to the difficulties faced by a modern director who wishes to achieve a genuine Shakespearean effect—a formidable task at best, since changes in social and dramatic conventions have necessarily wrought changes in audience reaction. The Fool, familiar to Elizabethan audiences as both traditional Court figure and stock stage character, was Shakespeare's answer to a recurring problem in the writing and acting of tragedy: the necessity for "the alternate creating and relaxing of emotional strain." In order to give its characteristic enjoyment, tragedy must take us "out of ourselves"; yet "the tenser the strain, the less long can an audience appreciatively endure it." To restore the balance with a dash of comedy, yet without resorting to anything so crude as the usual comic relief, Shakespeare found the Fool invaluable; for "this

120. Frederick Warde, *The Fools of Shakespeare* (New York, 1913), pp. 187-214. The theory to which Warde refers (that Cordelia and the Fool are "one and the same person") had been advanced by Arthur J. Stringer in an article, "Was Cordelia the King's Fool?," *The Shakespeare Magazine*, III (January, 1897), 1-11. Stringer suggested that Cordelia disguised herself as the Fool in order to accompany her father. *See* Thomas B. Stroup, "Cordelia and the Fool," *Studies in Philology*, XII (Spring, 1961), 127-32. For a less extreme idea about the relationship between the two characters, see n. 123, below.

121. *Reflections from Shakespeare*, pp. 149-50.

familiar figure, even though turned to tragic purpose, kept for that audience, if insensibly, its traditional hail-fellow quality." Since the professional fool is no longer part of our everyday lives, much of this value is irrecoverably lost for modern audiences. Nevertheless the effort must be made to restore as much as possible of the "aboriginal strength" of the role. The Fool who comes closest to Shakespeare's intentions will "sing like a lark, juggle his words so that the mere skill delights us, and tumble around with all the grace in the world." He will be represented, not as a "half-wit," but as a "natural":

he does not . . . draw all our practical distinction between sense and nonsense. . . . But he lives in a logical world of his own. Lear has petted him as one pets a dog; he shows a dog's fidelity. It is foolish of him, no doubt, to follow his master into such a storm—but, then, he *is* a fool.

After Shakespeare has gained the necessary dramatic use of this character, he drops him. The line "And I'll go to bed at noon" (III, vi, 92) is "a very short and bitter jest" in which the Fool tells us that he is "pretty well done for." Nobody knows or cares what happens to him after that.[122] Granville-Barker's analysis of the role mainly in terms of dramatic technique lacks the human warmth that he usually brings to his discussions of Shakespeare's characters; and his last-mentioned statement ignores the demands of human curiosity as well. But, on the whole, his chilly common-sense is a welcome relief after the fogs of sentiment in which the Fool was shrouded for many years.

One interpretation remains to be considered. ROBERT SPEAIGHT invests the Fool with considerably more meaning than Granville-Barker did, but his discussion of the character is somewhat less romantic than Poel's or Warde's. (Speaight's most sentimental remark—about the "unbearable pathos" of Lear's line "And my poor fool is hanged"—is based on his acceptance of the unlikely theory that Cordelia and the Fool were originally played by the same actor.[123]) It is "etherealized," but in a different way from

122. *Prefaces to Shakespeare,* I, 309-12.
123. "The Actability of *King Lear*," pp. 49-50. The suggestion that the roles of Cordelia and the Fool were originally doubled had been made as early as 1894 by Alois Brandl and had been discussed a number of times over the years by scholars and critics. A brief survey may be found in Professor Stroup's "Cordelia and the Fool" (see n. 120, above). Arthur Colby Sprague makes a convincing case against

the more sentimental interpretations: the Fool becomes an abstraction ("Reason itself") rather than a saint, and his choric function is greatly emphasized ("He is there to announce in riddles the things that Lear knows already") .[124] In a way, Speaight's discussion is less interesting than any of the others, for his Fool is annoyingly nebulous as a person. Yet some of his remarks seem more applicable to the theatre of the present moment, when a fairly large number of the audience appreciates the ironic and symbolic connotations of the clown figure, than do those of either the Victorian sentimentalists or the neo-Elizabethans. This is particularly true of Speaight's second thoughts about the character, published in an article discussing modern productions of *King Lear* (1962). Intriguing, if rather enigmatic, is his comment on the Fool's mentality and fate:

There is a widening crack running down the skull of Shakespeare's later clowns, as if they were at last the victims of their own folly. Feste is a neurotic where Touchstone was sanity itself. The Fool in *Lear* is rather more than neurotic, and perhaps that is why he so inexplicably disappears.

The most interesting aspect of Speaight's interpretation, however, is his insistence upon the Fool's ambiguous, paradoxical nature: for example, in his comment that the role is "a mixture of sympathy and self-pity, of near lunacy and prophetic vision," and in his brief but suggestive critiques of Goeffrey Wilkinson's Fool (Stratford-on-Avon, 1936), who "guarded incommunicable secrets," and Marius Goring's (the Fool to Redgrave's Lear, 1953), who "was a mask moving us to a hundred guesses."[125]

III. FROM CRITICISM TO THEATRE

Among the problems involved in translating interpretation into action perhaps the one most characteristic of *King Lear* is that of endowing persons and objects with abstract significance. Remember, Margaret Webster, like A. C. Bradley, considers this play

it, however, in a recent Society for Theatre Research pamphlet, *The Doubling of Parts in Shakespeare's Plays* (London, 1966), pp. 33-34.

124. *Nature in Shakespearian Tragedy*, pp. 99-100.

125. "The Actability of *King Lear*," pp. 49-50, 51-52, 55.

unsuited to the stage partly because of its incommunicable symbolic overtones. The most pertinent actor-criticisms in this connection are comments on three different scenes—the mock trial (III, vi), the reconciliation of Lear and Cordelia (IV, vii), and the final scene of the play—all by GRANVILLE-BARKER. For these comments emphasize meaningful "pictures" rather than specific business for the individual actors.

Granville-Barker thought of all three scenes as parallels to the Court scene at the beginning of the play. In the "trial" scene, one kind of "court" suggests the other:

Where Lear, such a short while since, sat in his majesty, there sit the Fool and the outcast, with Kent, whom he had banished beside them; and he, witless, musters his failing strength to beg justice upon a joint-stool. Was better justice done, the picture ironically asks, when he presided in majesty and sanity and power?[126]

In the reconciliation scene, the symbolism hinges on an original stage direction for bringing in the sleeping Lear in a chair. The implications are lost in some reading editions of the play, which have Lear, sleeping on the bed, present from the beginning of the scene. "For when he comes to himself it is to find that he is royally attired and as if seated on his throne again. It is from this throne that he totters to kneel at Cordelia's feet."[127]

Ironic appropriateness is found, once again, in the concluding scene of the play. There is a Court setting just as there was at the beginning; the same people are present (though some are now lifeless). At the outset Cordelia had angered and shamed Lear by her silence. Now she is dead, and therefore dumb, in his arms, and again he "reproaches her silence" before his heart breaks.[128]

Imaginative use of stage properties and deliberate grouping of characters to correspond with the pictorial pattern of the opening scene would probably serve to communicate the effects that Granville-Barker perceived in these scenes.

126. Prefaces to Shakespeare, I, 294.
127. Ibid., p. 298.
128. Ibid., pp. 277-78, 299.

CHAPTER FIVE · *Actors' Criticisms of* Macbeth

I. THE PLAY

Stage Versions and Textual Problems

Macbeth underwent alteration even earlier than *King Lear*—some time before 1668, at the hands of Sir William Davenant (his adaptation was first published in 1674). Actually it may have been altered to some extent long before Davenant got hold of it, perhaps even in Shakespeare's lifetime. The First Folio text of *Macbeth* (the only one that has come down to us from Shakespeare's period) has been conjectured to represent, not the original play, but a shortened stage version with some non-Shakespearean embellishments. These decorative additions must be briefly considered in connection with Davenant's adaptation, for there is a direct relationship, but the problem of textual authenticity per se will be reserved for later discussion since actors became aware of its importance mainly in the modern period.

There was not so long a stage history for Davenant's *Macbeth* as for Tate's *King Lear*; or, to speak more exactly, later acting versions of Macbeth owed much less to the radical adaptation of Davenant than later versions of *King Lear* owed to Tate. Still, some Davenant elements were preserved in these later versions, and through them the altered *Macbeth* continued to exert a certain influence throughout the eighteenth and nineteenth centuries. This influence must be taken into account, I think, in reading some of the actors' interpretations of the play and its characters.

Davenant's most lasting alterations were the additions of music and spectacle, which brought *Macbeth* into kinship with the new and popular mode of English opera. Matthew Locke composed the music,[1] which remained for two centuries a standard adjunct to the play. Not only did the Weird Sisters sing several songs (including two in a freshly-composed scene, placed at the end of Act II), but they were joined by a large chorus of singing witches and dancing spirits. In performance the spectacular element was very striking: the witches flew about the stage with the aid of mechanical contrivances; and, when Davies saw a production

---

1. John Downes, in *Roscius Anglicanus* (London, 1708), attributed the music to Locke, and this attribution has generally been accepted. Two other musicians, however—Purcell and Leveridge—have also been suggested as the composer of the music used in the Davenant *Macbeth*.

of Davenant's *Macbeth* in the 1730's, the best dancers of that day "were employed in the exhibition of infernal spirits."[2]

Although Davenant certainly made his alterations to please the taste of his own time, he may have considered the operatic additions true to the spirit of the play as he found it. For in the First Folio text of *Macbeth* both songs and dancing are mentioned. Indeed two of the four songs that Davenant used had already become associated with the play: they are named by their first lines in stage directions of the Folio—in the Hecate scene and the cauldron scene, respectively. And in the latter scene a dance is called for as well. It was not until many years after Davenant's period that scholars were to reject the Hecate passages (III, v and IV, i, 39-43) as non-Shakespearean intrusions; Davenant would hardly have suspected their authenticity. Perhaps he did not know, either, that the songs in question had been "lifted" from Middleton's *The Witch*, for which they were originally composed. For the manuscript of that play, then still unpublished, was probably not accessible to him, and the texts of the songs may well have come to him by another route.[3] As for Davenant's original songs, one of them at least was more Shakespearean in style and more pertinent to the play than those already associated with it.[4] Therein lay its attractiveness for later "restorers" of Shakespeare, like Garrick and Macready, and therein lay its danger, as far as interpretation was concerned.

One other change of Davenant's received partial warrant from the Folio text. The Folio has two stage directions regarding the combat between Macbeth and Macduff: "*Exeunt fighting. Alar-*

2. *Dramatic Miscellanies* (London, 1783-84), II, 116. The text of Davenant's adaptation has been edited, with a scholarly introduction, by Christopher Spencer: *Davenant's Macbeth from the Yale Manuscript* (New Haven, 1961). The adaptation is also discussed by Hazelton Spencer in *Shakespeare Improved* (Cambridge, Mass., 1927), pp. 152-74.

3. *See* John P. Cutts, "The Original Music to Middleton's *The Witch*," *Shakespeare Quarterly*, VII (Spring, 1956), 203-7. The songs fit the context of Middleton's play exactly, and it is virtually certain that they were originally composed for it. *The Witch* was not published until 1778 (the only known manuscript apparently remained in private hands from the beginning), and its relevance to *Macbeth* was first pointed out by the Shakespearean editor George Steevens.

4. Christopher Spencer was so struck by its style and appositeness that he even suggested that its first ten lines were composed by Shakespeare himself (*see Davenant's Macbeth from the Yale Manuscript*, pp. 67-71). But to accept this attribution we must also accept his theory that Davenant had access to a manuscript of Shakespeare's *Macbeth*, now lost.

ums" is one; and, immediately after it, *"Enter fighting, and Macbeth slaine."* The second has usually been considered incompatible with the rest of the action, for if Macbeth were killed in sight of the audience, how could his severed head be brought on later? Most editors, from the eighteenth century on, disregarded this direction, and some still believe it is evidence of a reviser's tampering. But several modern scholars are convinced that both stage directions are valid, and indeed the two can be reconciled in terms of Elizabethan staging.[5] Davenant, of course, had no interest in recapturing the methods of an earlier day. He staged the whole combat in sight of the audience, and he eliminated the severed head. But at least Shakespeare's text (free, as yet, from editorial emendation) provided him with an apparent alternative in the manner of Macbeth's death.

There was no possible appeal to tradition, however, for Davenant's other changes. With an eye to decorum he omitted the Drunken Porter and also the slaughter of Macduff's family in the sight of the audience. He altered the language on every page, making numerous cuts and verbal substitutions in the interest of simplicity and clarity. Rhyming iambic couplets, which were at that time considered appropriate to tragedy, were introduced in some passages, particularly in the more sententious of the original additions. Following his own convictions about good dramaturgy, Davenant achieved greater balance among the characters (and incidentally provided more substantial parts for two players) by developing the roles of the Macduffs: Macbeth's ultimate antagonist was introduced early in the play (he was substituted for Ross in I, ii and iii) and he and his wife were given several new scenes, in one of which they received prophecies from the Weird Sisters; Lady Macduff's importance was greatly enlarged, so that she became a foil to Lady Macbeth. Further balance was effected (and theatrical excitement gained) by a scene in which Lady Macbeth was plagued by the Ghost of Duncan. Many of these changes were made in the interest of "morality" as well as style and theatrical effect. Lady Macduff had an edifying lecture at hand for every occasion: against the hollowness of glory gained in

5. *See* the new Cambridge edition of *Macbeth,* ed. J. Dover Wilson (1947), p. 171, and the new Arden edition, ed. Kenneth Muir (London, 1965), p. 167. *See also* Richard Flatter, "Who Wrote the Hecate-Scene?" *Shakespeare Jahrbuch,* XCIII (1957), 196-97.

war, against the folly of believing in the Witches, against the evils of regicide and ambition. Macbeth's great soliloquy lost not only its mixed imagery (a favorite target of neoclassical criticism) but much of its meaning as well: "If it were done when 'tis done" became "If it were well when done"; Macbeth's impious willingness to "jump the life to come" was omitted; and no feared retribution for murder was mentioned except the loss of "Nature" in himself and the destruction of his peace of mind. Macbeth could not even die without the moral-pointing line: "Farewell vain world, and what's most vain in it Ambition."

The only actor-criticisms of Davenant's *Macbeth* that I know of, a comment or two by FRANCIS GENTLEMAN and a longer discussion by THOMAS DAVIES, were published many years after Garrick's version had supplanted Davenant's on the stage. They are hardly unbiased, then. But since the same two actor-critics also commented on Garrick's version, their reactions may help to explain why some of Davenant's alterations survived and some did not.

Both Gentleman and Davies were favorably disposed toward the musical additions to the play. The former found their effect "just and pleasing,"[6] and the latter approved the "solemn adaption" of the songs "for the beings for whom they were composed." "Had Davenant stopped there," Davies wrote ominously, "it would have been well for his reputation. . . ."[7]

Although these actor-critics held divergent views about Shakespeare's language in *Macbeth*, neither was impressed by Davenant's attempts to reform it. Gentleman was, as usual, concerned about lack of decorum: Lady Macbeth's "Was the hope drunk, . . ." was a "vulgar and nauseous allusion" for a "lady of rank," and her use of the word "blanket" was "low." (Davenant changed the latter to "Curtaines" but, strangely, left the former intact.) Again as usual, his comments were partly theatrical in basis: he thought, for example, that in the much-discussed soliloquy Shakespeare, "pursuing energy . . . border'd upon obscurity, especially if we consider those passages as only repeated on the stage, where the ear must inevitably be too quick for conception." Theoretically, then, Gentleman should have been in sympathy with Davenant's purpose of simplifying and refining Shakespeare's language. Yet

6. *The Dramatic Censor* (London, 1770), I, 96.
7. *Dramatic Miscellanies*, II, 115-16.

he specifically declared that the alteration of the soliloquy only succeeded, "like most other paraphrases," in destroying "the essential spirit."[8] Davies obviously saw no need to alter this speech; for he admired the image of "Pity, like a naked new-born babe" and "the more sublime idea of an angel mounted on the wings of the wind"[9]—both of which had been omitted by Davenant, and both of which were singled out by Gentleman as "strained figures at least." As for Davenant's couplets, they were out of fashion by the time Davies was writing, and he could afford to sneer at the Frenchified taste that had once made the "jingle of rhyme" delightful to "our court critics."

It was Davenant's "ridiculous and foreign additions" to the plot that most disgusted Davies, however: "this ill-instructed admirer of Shakespeare," he wrote, "altered the plan of the author's design, and destroyed that peculiarity which distinguishes Macbeth." Davies waxed particularly sarcastic about the addition of Duncan's Ghost, which he described as an attempt "to supply the deficiency" in Shakespeare's "quantity of spectres." Indeed, he charged, Davenant "disfigured the whole piece" with his "added deformities" and "sad mutilations."[10]

Even so, the adaptation had held the stage completely until 1744, when Garrick discarded it for a stage version much closer to Shakespeare's text. (Davenant's *Macbeth* continued to be performed at Covent Garden until 1751.) Garrick omitted all the extraneous material regarding the Macduffs, and he restored most of Shakespeare's language. He retained some of the operatic additions, however, including the Davenant witch scene at the end of Act II.[11] Perhaps he reasoned, as Francis Gentleman did, that it "is a very seasonable relief to a feeling mind, from the painful weight of horror which some preceding scenes must have laid upon

8. *Dramatic Censor*, I, 85-87.
9. *Dramatic Miscellanies*, II, 128.
10. *Ibid.*, pp. 116-17; *Memoirs of the Life of David Garrick* (Boston, 1818), I, 115-16.
11. Garrick, however, reserved Shakespeare's II, iv for the beginning of Act III. Garrick's version of *Macbeth* is published in Vol. I of *Bell's Edition of Shakespeare's Plays*, [ed. Francis Gentleman] (London, 1774). It is discussed by George W. Stone in "Garrick's Handling of Macbeth," *Studies in Philology*, XXXVIII (1941), 610-28, and by George Branam in *Eighteenth-Century Adaptations of Shakespearean Tragedy*. University of California Publications. English Studies, 14. (Berkeley and Los Angeles, 1956). Kalman A. Burnim interestingly discusses Garrick's production of *Macbeth* in *David Garrick, Director* (Pittsburgh, [1961]), pp. 103-26.

it" and that the Weird Sisters "continue the story predictively as a kind of chorus." Garrick also followed Davenant in omitting both the Drunken Porter and the onstage butchery of the Macduffs. Again Gentleman approved. He understood Shakespeare's reason for the Porter—to gain time for Macbeth—but considered him a poor expedient since, "at such an interesting period," his quibbling speeches destroyed the mood that had been built up. As for the other scene, he described it as "farcically horrid," a "disgraceful oddity . . . with great justice omitted in representation." (Gentleman disliked the scene of Banquo's murder, too, as "partly trifling, partly shocking," and usually laugh-provoking; but it was retained in all the adaptations.) [12] Garrick made one important omission that Davenant had not but in this he seems to have been simply following stage custom: in his version Lady Macbeth did not appear in the scene in which Duncan's murder was discovered. Davies approved this change for practical, though not for interpretive, reasons. The London audiences, being less attuned to critical subtleties than "such an one as Oxford or Cambridge could supply," was likely to laugh at Lady Macbeth's "surprize and fainting . . . however characteristical such behaviour might be."

> Mr. Garrick thought, that even so favourite an actress as Mrs. Pritchard would not, in that situation, escape derision from the gentlemen in the upper regions. Mr. Macklin is of opinion, that Mrs. Porter alone could have credit with an audience to induce them to endure the hypocrisy of Lady Macbeth.[13]

In the concluding scene Garrick not only followed Davenant but improved upon his improvement: his Macbeth died onstage, speaking not one line but eight. The new death speech—full of the vanity of ambition's "delusive dreams" and the torment of "darkness, guilt and horror" which awaited him—seemed to Davies "unlike Shakespeare's manner" though "suitable perhaps to the character." Davies added, rather cynically: "But Garrick excelled in the expression of convulsive throes and dying agonies, and would not lose any opportunity that offered to shew his skill. . . ."[14] Gentleman, however, was more enthusiastic. He could not "imagine" why Shakespeare "chose to execute so great a culprit behind

12. *Dramatic Censor,* I, 90, 92, 94, 97.
13. *Dramatic Miscellanies,* II, 152-53.
14. *Ibid.,* p. 118.

the scenes, thereby depriving the audience of a most satisfactory circumstance." "The present mode of representation" seemed "much better" to him; and, since Macbeth was to die before the audience, "dramatic custom" decreed that he speak "some conclusive lines." Gentleman could conceive "nothing . . . more suitable or striking" than the dying villain's consciousness of guilt and "horrid visions" of hell as Garrick had expressed them. And he paid tribute to Garrick's acting without reservation: "who has heard his speech . . . uttered with the utmost agony of body and mind, but trembles at the idea of future punishment, and almost pities the expiring wretch, though stained with crimes of the deepest die?"[15]

John Philip Kemble's productions represented no new departures: there was considerable emphasis upon music and spectacle (we all know the story that Edmund Kean in childhood danced as a spirit in one of them) ; the extra witch scene was retained; Macduff was spotlighted early in the play by speaking Ross's lines in the second and third scenes; the Drunken Porter was omitted, and Lady Macduff was now left out of the cast entirely; Lady Macbeth did not faint; Macbeth gave his death speech.[16]

As I suggested before, there are several aspects of the Davenant, Garrick, and Kemble versions of *Macbeth* that should be remembered when we consider, later in this chapter, the interpretations of the play and its characters. Did Mrs. Siddons know, for example, that Mrs. Betterton's Lady Macbeth (she acted the Davenant version) was haunted by Duncan's Ghost? If so, her own idea that both Macbeths see the Ghost of Banquo is not very startling, after all. There are obvious implications for Lady Macbeth's character, too, in the customary omission of the fainting fit. Several of the alterations probably helped to give Macbeth a more sympathetic image than he would have had otherwise: for example, Davenant's rewriting of the crucial soliloquy so as to emphasize only the most acceptable ideas (Garrick restored Shakespeare's words, but who can tell how many of his contemporaries continued to impose the old thought pattern upon them?) and

15. *Dramatic Censor*, I, 104, 108.
16. G. C. D. Odell discusses Kemble's production of *Macbeth* in *Shakespeare from Betterton to Irving* (New York, 1920), II, 54, 87, 92, 103. *See also* Harold Child, *The Shakespearian Productions of John Philip Kemble* (London, 1935), pp. 9-10, 20. Elizabeth Inchbald's edition of *Macbeth* in *The British Theatre* (London, 1808), Vol. IV, is based on Kemble's text.

Garrick's death speech, which, as Gentleman observed, tended to win some pity for Macbeth. More important than all these, I suppose, was the ultra-Shakespearean emphasis upon the supernatural element, with its probable influence upon the interpretation of Macbeth's character and also of the play as a whole. No firm assertions can be made about this, for the witch scenes, with their music and spectacle, were perhaps more entertaining than impressive. But since witches and demons, however presented, received a heavy emphasis at key points in the action, it would have been natural for the spectator to assume that the "instruments of darkness" exerted a powerful influence on the events. The witch scene added by Davenant, and preserved by Garrick and Kemble, has a particularly deterministic tone. In it the Weird Sisters gleefully celebrate Duncan's murder and predict (or even, as it seems, decree) Macbeth's continuation in his evil course:

> Many more murders must this one ensue
> As if in Death were propogation too
> He will
> He shall
> He must spill much more blood. . . .[17]

Kemble's nineteenth century successors continued many of the old practices in their productions of *Macbeth*, but there were also some signs of changes to come. The Drunken Porter, for example, was usually omitted still, but Charlotte Cushman restored the character, to good effect, in her readings of the play,[18] and Edwin Booth made partial use of him in his acting version.[19] Although no less a critic than Coleridge expressed his belief that the Porter scene was spurious, SHERIDAN KNOWLES spoke up for it, noting, as Gentleman had done earlier, the Porter's usefulness in gaining time for Macbeth; he apologized for the more indelicate passages but justified them to some extent on the basis of realistic character portrayal. Knowles also argued for a restoration of Lady Macbeth to the scene in which Duncan's murder is discovered: it is only natural, he pointed out, that the hostess should be on hand to determine the cause of the disturbance; besides, Lady Macbeth

17. *Davenant's Macbeth from the Yale Manuscript*, ed. Spencer, pp. 104-5.

18. Emma Stebbins, *Charlotte Cushman: Her Letters and Memories of Her Life* (Boston, 1878), pp. 213-14.

19. Arthur Colby Sprague, *Shakespeare and the Actors* (Cambridge, Mass., 1948), p. 245.

would not have left to Macbeth alone the carrying off of this important part of their plan; and her fainting, though it is only pretense, is in keeping with her true emotional state—"that sudden revulsion of the spirits which attends the transition from the extreme of danger to escape and comparative security."[20] Both HELEN FAUCIT[21] and ELLEN TERRY[22] restored the fainting fit, and even insisted that it was genuine. But EDWIN BOOTH omitted it from his acting edition, over the protest of William Winter. "A *great* actress, of course, could make much of this little bit of nature," he explained, "but the *stick* (I beg her parding, I mean the *stock-*) actress would 'knock it galleywest,' as we say i' the classics."[23]   Garrick's death speech was eventually abandoned, but Macbeth continued to die onstage, often with much emphasis on his desperate fight to the last, in the manner associated with Kean's Richard III.[24]   As for the operatic element, even the purist Macready made use of the Locke music, with its chorus of singing witches—and, more shocking still, he retained Davenant's witch scene at the end of Act II.[25] Samuel Phelps banished all signs of Davenant influence from his 1847 production (he even had Macbeth's head brought in on a pole), but he later relapsed into use of the conventional materials.[26] Charles Kean, of course, could not resist the music and spectacle.[27] Finally, HENRY IRVING compromised with tradition: he retained only the two songs mentioned in the First Folio—since they *were* so mentioned, he argued, Shakespeare must have sanctioned their use—and he had new music composed by Sir Arthur Sullivan.[28]

In the modern period the theatrical traditions stemming ulti-

20. *Lectures on Dramatic Literature: Macbeth* (London, 1875), pp. 57-61.

21. *On Some of Shakespeare's Female Characters* (Edinburgh and London, 1887), pp. 234-35.

22. *Four Lectures on Shakespeare,* ed. with an introduction by Christopher St. John [Christabel Marshall] (London, [1932]), p. 161.

23. MS letter to Winter, dated May 30, 1878, in the Folger Library.

24. Sprague, *Shakespeare and the Actors,* pp. 278-79.

25. Alan S. Downer, *The Eminent Tragedian William Charles Macready* (Cambridge, Mass., 1966), pp. 328-29. Downer provides a fascinating and detailed description of Macready's *Macbeth* on pp. 318-38. Macready's version was much like Kemble's except that he restored Lady Macbeth to the scene in which Duncan's murder is discovered.

26. Odell, *Shakespeare from Betterton to Irving,* II, 274-75; Sprague, *Shakespeare and the Actors,* p. 279; Charles H. Shattuck, *The Shakespeare Promptbooks; a Descriptive Catalog* (Urbana, 1965), p. 250, item #63.

27. Odell, *Shakespeare from Betterton to Irving,* II, 275.

28. *Ibid.,* p. 409.

mately from altered versions of *Macbeth* have had relatively little influence on productions of the play. Instead there has been a tendency to return to what is in the Shakespearean text. The Drunken Porter, for example, has come into his own now. Lady Macbeth always has her faint—or feint, whichever the actress decides to make it. Lady Macduff and her little son are regularly killed in sight of the audience. It is in the actors' criticisms of this last scene that we find the most striking differences between the attitudes of the eighteenth and twentieth centuries. HARLEY GRANVILLE-BARKER found the scene "abhorrent," just as Francis Gentleman had found it "horrid"; yet he not only had no thought of omitting it but even warned against a natural tendency "to try to gloss it over in action." Indeed he prescribed that "the killing of the child should be done very deliberately." When the boy is "mettlesomely played," he explained, the "dramatic enormity is belittled by the open-eyed, heroic readiness with which the child faces death. This heroism strikes the note upon which the scene must end."[29]

Occasional reminders of the past are found, however, in modern productions. *Macbeth* is no longer an opera, but the present century has not been without some reversions to gratuitous spectacle. According to LARK TAYLOR's promptbook, the first few performances of E. H. Sothern and Julia Marlowe's *Macbeth* (1911) featured at the conclusion of the cauldron scene a "Witches dance" in which "crowds" of "Witches . . . fairies and goblins" participated, "whirling—dancing—singing." Taylor remarks, however, "The scene was cut—and I think the play was better without it."[30] The amount, and kind, of emphasis given to the Weird Sisters has varied from one producer to another. Though deprived of Davenant's extra scene, they have sometimes made other appearances uncalled for by Shakespeare's text: in one production they came on, cackling, after some ceremonial pageantry in which Duncan had been conducted to bed; in another they appeared in silhouette at the end of the play, as if their influence still hung

29. Harley Granville-Barker, Preface to *The Players' Shakespeare: The Tragedie of Macbeth* (London, 1923), p. l.

30. The promptbook is in the Folger Library. It is a looseleaf notebook with printed text pasted in and detailed directions and descriptions in the margins. (A notation opposite p. [58] indicates that the promptbook was finished in April, 1911.) The description of the spectacle in the cauldron scene is given opposite p. 38. See the flyleaf opposite p. 1 for Taylor's critical comment.

over Scotland—or the world.[31] On the other hand, in some productions they have lost whole scenes that do appear in Shakespeare's text (as we shall see in a moment) and have had their influence reduced in others.

In the staging of Macbeth's death scene apparently the traditional method (though without any dying speech) has generally been considered the simplest and most dramatic. There have been some attempts, however, to return to the "Shakespearean" method. In this case a decision must be made about the authenticity of the stage direction *"Enter fighting, and Macbeth slaine."* GEORGE SKILLAN, editor of *French's Acting Edition*, omits it in the manner of most Shakespearean editors; he therefore has Macbeth killed offstage and the head brought in on a pole.[32] Granville-Barker, however, reconciles all the stage directions of the Folio in his suggested plan of action: the major portion of the duel is fought on the lower stage, near the audience, but the final phase takes place on the gallery; Macbeth is killed on the "inner upper stage" so that the curtains can be closed to hide the body; and the head is brought in later, according to the text.[33] His method, set forth in 1923, has been followed (or a similar one has been suggested) as the probable Shakespearean staging by several recent scholars.[34]

Modern actors' criticisms of *Macbeth* have been significantly influenced by scholarly theories concerning retrenchment and corruption in the First Folio text. As we saw earlier, this text is usually considered a revision (slight or radical, depending on the individual scholar) of Shakespeare's original play. The theory that it is an abridgment was prompted by the observation of two characteristics: its unusual brevity (*Macbeth* is shorter than any other Shakespearean tragedy) and its occasional ambiguities (attributable, perhaps, to awkward cutting). Examples of the latter are the references to the Thane of Cawdor in I, ii and iii, which have long given trouble. In the first of these scenes Ross states

31. J. C. Trewin, *Shakespeare on the English Stage, 1900-1964; a Survey of Productions Illustrated from the Raymond Mander and Joe Mitchenson Theatre Collection* (London, [1964]), p. 44; G. Wilson Knight, *Shakespearian Production* (London, 1964), p. 47. The first of these productions was Beerbohm Tree's (1911).

32. *Macbeth. French's Acting Edition*, [commentaries by George Skillan] (London, c. 1959), p. 57.

33. *The Players' Shakespeare: The Tragedie of Macbeth*, pp. xxxi-xxxii, lvii.

34. See n. 5 of the present chapter.

unequivocally that the King of Norway, "Assisted by that most disloyal traitor / The thane of Cawdor," has been valiantly opposed by "Bellona's bridegroom" (logically deduced from the context to be Macbeth) with resulting victory for Duncan's forces. Yet Macbeth in scene iii cannot believe that he himself is to receive Cawdor's title because "the thane of Cawdor lives, / A prosperous gentleman." How can he be ignorant of Cawdor's condemnation as a traitor after defeating him in battle? True, Angus later implies that Cawdor's treacherous assistance was secretly given, but it is then rather late for Shakespeare to be mending dramatic fences. There must have been, at one time, a fuller explanation in the earlier scene, which was cut out when the play was revised.[35] Once the idea was accepted that the Folio text is incomplete, a number of theories were advanced about scenes that had once existed. For example, a "lost" scene has been postulated in which Macbeth "breaks the enterprise" of murder to his wife "when neither time nor place did then adhere" (this, of course, to explain Lady Macbeth's allusion in I, vii, 47-52).[36] In addition to conjectures about possible omissions scholars have also dealt with the question of additions, substitutions, or revisions in the Folio text made by some writer other than Shakespeare. We have already had occasion to mention the Middleton songs, the lines introducing the witch dance in the cauldron scene, and the Hecate passages. Because there is evidence that these small portions of the play are non-Shakespearean, some scholars and critics have assumed that other portions are also spurious. Their arguments are almost entirely subjective. Coleridge's rejection of the Porter scene has been noted earlier. A number of other scenes have been questioned at one time or another: for example, the first witch scene (I, i) and the Bleeding Sergeant scene (I, ii). The "dis-

35. Dr. Johnson had a long note in his edition of Shakespeare on the "incongruity of all the passages in which the Thane of Cawdor is mentioned" (see the *Furness Variorum* [Revised ed.; Philadelphia, 1903], II, 29-30). Francis Gentleman also remarked upon the difficulty (*Dramatic Censor,* I, 82). Davenant softened the discrepancy somewhat by omitting the word "prosperous" from Macbeth's description of the Thane of Cawdor. Dover Wilson discusses the problem in his edition of *Macbeth*, pp. xxv-xxvi. He believes that Shakespeare originally included at least a short explanation of Cawdor's secret treachery in I, ii.

36. Both J. Q. Adams and Dover Wilson have argued in their editions of *Macbeth* for such a scene. But the arguments against this possibility are more convincing. See Alwin Thaler, "The 'Lost Scenes' of *Macbeth,*" *Shakespeare and Democracy* (Knoxville, 1941), 88-105; also Kenneth Muir, the Arden *Macbeth,* pp. xxiii and lxi.

integrators" were particularly busy during the first part of the present century, but much of their work has been canceled out in recent years. The present tendency is to accept the Folio text as almost entirely Shakespeare's (the witch songs and the Hecate portions are the exceptions—and Richard Flatter has even argued for the legitimacy of the latter[37]) but to suggest that there may have been some cuts and transpositions, notably in I, ii. Kenneth Muir asserts, with good reason, that we need not "suppose that cuts and alterations have greatly damaged the unity and power of the play."[38] But the many textual arguments of earlier years have left their mark on some of the criticisms of *Macbeth* by actors.

There have been changes, for example, in attitudes toward the first scene of the play. In the nineteenth century THOMAS HOLCROFT considered it the only scene in all drama that could compare to the opening of *Hamlet*,[39] and Sheridan Knowles asserted that there was in no other play "an instance where so much is effected in so narrow a compass."[40] In the present century, however, Granville-Barker—blind to the kind of artistry he usually understood so well—accepted the theory that the scene was spurious.[41] How could he have been convinced by the arguments used to support that theory? That the scene was unnecessary to the plot, for example, and that the Witches' line "Fair is foul, and foul is fair" was suggested to the reviser by Macbeth's "So fair and foul a day I have not seen" (in scene iii)? The same critic has commented very sensitively on the thematic importance of equally "unnecessary" scenes in other plays, and on the significance of verbal echoes. But his "Preface" to *Macbeth* was published very early, and he did not live to publish a revision of it, as he did of other plays. Had he done so, surely he would have had second thoughts about this scene.

Several of the actor-critics—Granville-Barker, GEORGE R. FOSS, and DOUGLAS CAMPBELL—have discussed problems posed by the second scene of the play. They seem to have been impressed by

37. "Who Wrote the Hecate-Scene?" pp. 198-210.
38. The new Arden *Macbeth*, p. lxx.
39. *The Theatrical Recorder* (London, 1805-6), II, 135.
40. *Lectures on Dramatic Literature: Macbeth*, pp. 2-3. The same discussion is found on p. 146 of the more inclusive publication *Lectures on Dramatic Literature Delivered . . . during the Years 1820-1850*, ed. Francis Harvey (London, 1873).
41. *The Players' Shakespeare: The Tragedie of Macbeth*, pp. xxv-xxvi.

the observations that commentators have made about the discrepancies in the accounts of the two battles, for some of their own remarks read like echoes or modifications of these. The basic problem is, of course, that the first battle (with Macdonwald) apparently took place somewhere in the vicinity of Forres and the second (with Norway), at Fife—about a hundred miles away. Since the second followed hard upon the first, how could Macbeth have fought in both? The easiest answer is that Shakespeare, who was telescoping three different battles from chronicle accounts, treated Scottish geography in an equally cavalier manner. But more difficult, and more impressive, solutions have been offered: for example, that the scene, or a portion of it, is spurious; and that "Bellona's bridegroom," in Ross's account, does not refer to Macbeth. Foss regarded the Bleeding Sergeant passage as unnecessary, illogical, and probably non-Shakespearean—thus reducing the two battles to one.[42] Granville-Barker was convinced that the scene had been "mauled" by someone—the stage manager, or Middleton (at that time blamed for all the "revisions" of *Macbeth*), or the compositor—but he also suggested that "Bellona's bridegroom" was not Macbeth but "some other general." If this theory were correct, not only would it overcome the geographical difficulty but it would explain why Macbeth is ignorant of the Thane of Cawdor's complicity with Norway. But there is no reason whatever for accepting it. Granville-Barker's explanation that there are two different battles with "Norweyan" forces, one in which Macbeth and Banquo defeat a "Norweyan lord" and another in which Norway himself and the Thane of Cawdor are defeated by General X, makes as great a problem as it solves.[43]

42. *What the Author Meant* (London, 1932), pp. 52-53. The authenticity of the scene has been defended by J. M. Nosworthy, in "The Bleeding Captain Scene in *Macbeth*," *Review of English Studies*, XXII (1946), 126-30. Kenneth Muir, in the new Arden *Macbeth*, p. 5, accepts the scene as Shakespeare's but grants that it may have been badly cut.

43. *The Players' Shakespeare: The Tragedie of Macbeth*, p. xxvii. "Bellona's bridegroom," in Ross's account of the second battle, surely refers to Macbeth: it parallels "valour's minion" in the Bleeding Sergeant's account of the first battle; Macbeth is properly rewarded with the Thane of Cawdor's title after defeating the enemy whom Cawdor had assisted; and the new Thane of Cawdor becomes, in his turn, a traitor—as more than one critic has pointed out. However the epithet has given trouble ever since the eighteenth century, when some strict classicists, interpreting it to mean Mars, took Shakespeare to task for his ignorance. John Philip Kemble was among the critics who explained that Shakespeare meant Macbeth. (Davenant in his version of *Macbeth*, left no room for doubt: he sub-

The Bleeding Sergeant reports the death of Macdonwald by the hand of Macbeth and the flight of the rebel army but tells of a fresh battle that ensued because of a Norwegian attack—a fierce one that was still raging, its issue "doubtful," when he left. If Ross's later account refers to a different "Norweyan" battle, then Shakespeare leaves the conclusion of the other one unreported— a very strange lapse. No, there was a single battle against Norway, and Macbeth was its hero just as he was hero of the preceding fight with Macdonwald. (See Ross's speech, in delivering Duncan's message to Macbeth, I, iii, 90–100.) Flimsy as Granville-Barker's theory is, however, Douglas Campbell seems to have built his own interpretation upon it. He has even given General X a name: it is none other than Macduff.[44] (As we shall see, this identification is particularly convenient for Campbell's reading of the play as a whole.) The fact that a battle took place at Fife probably suggested the idea to him, just as it may have inspired Davenant— and a succession of followers—to make the Thane of Fife, rather than Ross, the bearer of the victory news.

The Porter scene is another matter. Its authenticity was accepted without hesitation by Granville-Barker,[45] and its artistic purpose confirmed by ROBERT SPEAIGHT. The latter suggests that the scene originated in the practical necessity of providing a part for the principal comedian but that Shakespeare "knew how to give the fooling an ironic edge." Through his unconscious emphasis upon the themes of equivocation, hell, and sleep, the Porter helps us to see what has happened in a new light: "Hitherto we have been inside Macbeth; now we are outside him, ready at any moment, to share the general shock and condemnation."[46]

As for "lost" scenes, SIR LEWIS CASSON seized eagerly upon the idea of a scene in which Macbeth specifically broached the subject of murder to his wife. For Casson could not believe that Macbeth

stituted "brave Macbeth" for "Bellona's bridegroom.") Apparently the geographical problem was not noticed until years later. E. Litchfield pointed out this problem in 1892 and suggested anew that the epithet referred, not to Macbeth, but to Mars, or the fortunes of war (see *Furness Variorum*, II, 27). Ross's description, however, strongly suggests a flesh-and-blood hero—as Granville-Barker no doubt realized.

44. Douglas Campbell, "A Director's Interpretation: The Politics of Power," *Encyclopaedia Britannica Films*. The pertinent discussion is in Part I of this filmed lecture.

45. *The Players' Shakespeare: The Tragedie of Macbeth*, p. xxviii.

46. *Nature in Shakespearian Tragedy* (London, 1955), pp. 56-57.

had thought of killing Duncan before the beginning of the play, as some critics have inferred from Lady Macbeth's famous speech in scene vii. Indeed he contended that Macbeth did not entertain the idea until after Duncan had dashed his hopes to the ground by naming Malcolm Prince of Cumberland. To maintain this latter point, Casson had to change the word "murder" to "matter" in Macbeth's first sololiquy (following the Weird Sisters' prophetic greetings) —but he boldly used the supposed corruption of the text as his excuse for doing so.[47]

The loss of other scenes has been suggested by Campbell—scenes building up the importance of Macduff, who, as he points out, is underdeveloped as Macbeth's chief antagonist.[48] With this suggestion we have completed a kind of circle: for Davenant's addition of scenes involving the Macduffs could be looked upon as an intuitive replacement of such "lost" scenes as Campbell imagines to have once existed.

Actor-critics have been confronted by a greater variety of textual problems in connection with *Macbeth* than with any of the other "great" tragedies. The influence of altered stage versions upon their interpretations is difficult to calculate, but it is certainly reflected to some extent in the eighteenth and nineteenth century criticisms. The influence of textual scholarship, confined mainly to the present century, is more directly seen. Although, as I remarked in my introductory chapter, actors are in much need of the scholars' help in the area of textual study, it is obvious that in the case of *Macbeth* such "help" has frequently been detrimental. The distortions of the play by its alterers were hardly greater than those suggested by some of its disintegrators and emenders. At best incapable of proof and at worst wildly fanciful, some of their notes and commentaries[49] have seemingly encouraged actor-critics to ignore the text of the play as we have it and to depend for interpretation on the inspiration of their own private oracles. (Luckily there are correctives available: for example, the

47. Introduction to the Folio Society edition of *Macbeth* (London, 1951), pp. 6-7.

48. *Encyclopaedia Britannica Film* on *Macbeth*, Part I.

49. *The Furness Variorum*, for example, is a fascinating but undiscriminating repository of commentaries. Consider the amount of space given to excerpts from F. A. Libby's "ingenious and carefully worked out hypothesis" that Ross is the real villain of the play (II, 24, 26, 30-31). It is worthy of a place in Thurber's "The Macbeth Murder Mystery." More misleading, perhaps, because less blatantly fanciful are outdated scholarly works like the original Arden edition of *Macbeth* (1912), with its "disintegrating" notes by Henry Cunningham.

sane and easily digested introduction to the new Arden edition.) The wonder is that, travelling between the Scylla of theatrical alteration and the Charybdis of textual theories, so many actor-critics of *Macbeth* have managed to steer a comparatively even course.

Interpretations: The Supernatural Element

Hints of the supernatural are everywhere in *Macbeth:* Lady Macbeth's invocation to the spirits of evil, Macbeth's vision of the dagger, the Ghost of Banquo, the apparitions in the cauldron scene, Hecate (if she is genuine) —not to mention the non-Shakespearean demons which were an integral part of the stage play for more than two centuries. But the most substantial dramatic reminders of the influences at work in Macbeth's story are the Weird Sisters—and they themselves are not supernatural. Or are they? A number of actors have tried to answer such questions as these: Did Shakespeare intend these figures to be grotesque old women like those accused of witchcraft in Jacobean times? Or did he mean them to represent supernatural forces: are they incarnations of Evil, perhaps, or of some other lofty power like Fate or Nemesis? How can his intention best be carried out on the stage?

During the eighteenth century it was customary to give the parts of the Weird Sisters to the low comedians (nearly always men, of course). There were some objections from critics that the players thus distorted Shakespeare's meaning; but, as far as I know, none of the actors agreed. THOMAS DAVIES specifically defended the practice on both practical and artistic grounds. Even if theatrical tradition, from the Restoration and possibly earlier, were wrong, he reasoned, it would be difficult to change since the comedians of the company were the only actors not required for the other roles of the play. But the critics' charges were ill-founded, in any case: "There is, in the witches, something odd and peculiar, and approaching to what we call humour" that is "more suitable to our notions of comic than tragic action." Since the kind of comic distortion that Davies meant by "humour" might well provoke a wry smile and a painful twinge in the vitals rather than a hearty laugh, his whole discussion indicates an eccentric interpretation of the Weird Sisters but not necessarily a hilarious one. This fact is confirmed by his assertion that the "present comedians . . . have too much understanding" to sacrifice meaning to "grimace" and "buffoonery."[50] FRANCIS GENTLEMAN evidently held a similar conception. Shakespeare intended the Witches "as beings out of the course of nature," he argued, and therefore "furnished them with a peculiarity of style, why should we not suppose he meant a peculiarity of deportment and utterance? He certainly did, as much as for Caliban."[51] ARTHUR MURPHY's remark that the French writers would have considered these characters beneath the dignity of tragedy suggests that the traditional assignment of the roles did not strike him as inappropriate; yet nothing that he said about the Witches would specifically connect them with laughter—quite the reverse.[52]

On the matter of costume the actor-critics were a little less inclined to accept stage tradition. Davies, for example, spoke disparagingly of the comic dress that he associated with the Davenant *Macbeth*.[53] His remarks would have been more significant, however, if they had been applied, either positively or negatively, to contemporary productions. According to Kalman Burnim, GARRICK's Witches "usually wore blue-checked aprons, torn mobs . . . topped with high crowned black hats" and looked "more like basket women and trulls than creatures of enchantment." Garrick is said to have approved at one time the plan of dressing the Witches as magicians "with long beards and black gowns" in order "to produce awe and horror" but to have abandoned it "for fear of offending the Gallery."[54] Gentleman would probably have welcomed some change in the Drury Lane costumes—toward the grotesque, however, rather than the awesome. He considered the epithet "filthy hags" an obvious clue to their appearance, and he suggested that they be made as "outré . . . hagged and squalid" as decorum would allow. In writing (1770) of a "supposed amendment" that had taken place at Covent Garden in the Witches' "speaking and dressing," Gentleman described the changes as inappropriate: costumes "in the Sybillic taste" transformed Scottish figures to Roman, and "a languid propriety of natural ex-

50. *Dramatic Miscellanies*, II, 118-20.
51. *Dramatic Censor*, I, 112-13.
52. *The Life of David Garrick, Esq.* (London, 1801), I, 74-78.
53. *Memoirs of Garrick*, I, 91-92.
54. *David Garrick: Director*, p. 109.

pression" destroyed their "pleasing and characteristic oddity."[55]

Covent Garden made one innovation in 1769 that Gentleman did not mention: in that year a woman, Mrs. Ann Pitt, took the part of one of the Witches, a role that she continued to act at intervals for a period of nearly twenty years. (She was the only female Witch on the eighteenth century London stage.) But, whatever the changes in dress, voice, deportment, and sex of the Covent Garden Witches, there were no changes, as far as I can tell, in the assignment of the roles to comic actors. Mrs. Pitt, for example, though she had once acted the vengefully prophetic Margaret in *Richard III* and even the Duchess of York in that same play, more frequently took such roles as the Hostess in the *Henry IV* plays and the Nurse in *Romeo and Juliet*. And one of her "sisters," the comedian John Quick, had also acted a Witch the previous year. No doubt the degree of ludicrousness in the interpretation of the Weird Sisters varied with the different impersonators. Comments by the actor-critics of the eighteenth century imply, however, that these roles were considered character parts. Certainly a number of the actors who portrayed them (Charles Macklin, for example) were accustomed to roles like Shylock, Polonius, Fluellen, and Menenius as well as Dogberry and the First Gravedigger.

The actor-critics of that period differed with one another regarding the nature and powers of the Weird Sisters. Because of the derivation of "weird," Davies realized that some kind of association with the Fates was implied; he compared Shakespeare's creations with the Eumenides, "prototypes of the northern Parcae"[56]—perhaps because the snaky-haired Furies, grotesque though terrible, were a closer approximation to his own semicomic ideal than were the more majestic Norns of Holinshed's depiction. Gentleman, on the other hand, considered them nothing more nor less than witches. *Macbeth,* he wrote, with an attempt at stern disapproval, "strongly inculcates power of prediction, even in the worst and most contemptible agents; inculcates a supernatural influence of one mortal being over another." Although obviously intrigued (even delighted) by the Weird Sisters and all the scenes in which they appear, Gentleman in his capacity of moralist felt obliged to deplore the unfortunate in-

55. *Dramatic Censor,* I, 112-13.
56. *Dramatic Miscellanies,* II, 121-22.

fluence that Shakespeare's "fatalism" might exert upon weak and superstitious minds.[57] Murphy's attitude was somewhat ambiguous: on the one hand, he pronounced the Weird Sisters "vile impostors, who pretend to have praeternatural communications"; on the other, he admitted that they "make so deep an impression" by the "solemnity" of their "language and incantations" that "from the beginning to the end, we believe them to be supernatural agents." One thing he was sure of: they were not imaginary beings: "they existed in the world"—that ancient world of "darkness and barbarism" which Shakespeare portrayed in *Macbeth*.[58] In their ambivalent attitudes toward these characters (wavering between classical mythology and Scottish folklore, balancing disgust with awe) these actor-critics were typical of their own time—and they would have been at home in ours as well.

The "amendment" which Covent Garden attempted in portraying the Weird Sisters presaged a number of more thoroughgoing reformations, beginning with John Philip Kemble's 1794 production of *Macbeth*. Kemble is said to have eliminated all comic element and to have made the Witches appear as "praeternatural beings, distinguished only by the fellness of their purposes, and the fatality of their delusions." Edmund Kean, in the following century, seems to have gone even further in the direction of making these characters "the engines of terror rather than of laughter." And William Charles Macready took pains to make the supernatural element impressive in his productions.[59]

Ironically, there were distinct protests from the actor-critics of the nineteenth century against the misplaced comedy that they found in the witch scenes of contemporary productions. Typical were the criticisms by FANNY KEMBLE[60] and JAMES MURDOCH.[61] The one English, the other American, they described the average stage trio of their day in such similar terms that a composite picture may be formed, as follows: "three jolly-faced fellows" in peaked hats, their "faces bedaubed . . . as a juvenile's with a jam pot, their beefy bodies in the petticoats of fishwives," carrying

57. *Dramatic Censor,* I, 104-5. See also pp. 79-80.
58. *Life of Garrick,* I, 74-78, 87.
59. Odell, *Shakespeare from Betterton to Irving,* II, 92; Frederick Hawkins, *The Life of Edmund Kean* (London, 1869), I, 280-81; Downer, *The Eminent Tragedian,* pp. 328-29, 333.
60. *Journal* (Philadelphia, 1835), II, 115-16.
61. James Murdoch, "A Short Study of 'Macbeth,'" *Forum,* X (September, 1890), 73-75.

broomsticks and "speaking with the cracked and querulous voices of very broad comedy." If the language of exaggeration is discounted, the costumes do not sound very different from those worn in Garrick's day. Were the actors themselves much more ridiculous than those of the past, who, Davies assured us, would never stoop to buffoonery? Perhaps the "reforms" that had been made in a few cases caused the unreformed impersonations to seem more glaringly incongruous with tragedy. Or perhaps the actor-critics of this period, most of them romantically inclined, simply took a more elevated view of the supernatural and all its approaches than their predecessors in the Age of Reason had done.

In giving their own ideas of the Witches the actor-critics emphasized the bizarre, the ominous, and, in one or two instances, the sublime. SHERIDAN KNOWLES[62] objected to the "grotesque effect" which he said was generally created by the actors; but by "grotesque" he must have meant simply "incongruous with Shakespeare's purpose," for the same word in the sense of fantastically strange or unnatural, might well be applied to his ideal description of the Weird Sisters:

unearthly, wild, blasted things to cower and feel troubled at; less welcome than the storm that brings them; creatures accurst, whose looks bespeak their errand; the traffickers in things forbid; abominable and unutterable.

The words read like an incantation. Miss Kemble, who seems to have had much the same view of these characters, wrote that if the casting of *Macbeth* were her responsibility, she would

give the witches to the first melodramatic actors on the stage . . . who understand all that belongs to picturesque devilry . . . and give them such dresses, as without ceasing to be grotesque, should be a little more fanciful, and . . . would accord a little better with the blasted heath, the dark, fungus-grown wood, the desolate, misty hill-side, and the flickering light of the cauldron cave.

Murdoch was even more romantic—and more demanding: the Witches ought to be dimly seen, "hovering through 'the fog and filthy air' of a vague and hazy distance," and "their language, so chillingly weird," should be spoken with "grandeur, dignity, and solemnity." HENRY IRVING approved of the effort "to divest Shakespeare's Witches of that semi-comic element which at one time

62. *Lectures on Dramatic Literature: Macbeth*, pp. 4-5.

threatened to obscure . . . their supernatural significance." As he explained, his own contributions to this effort were the innovation of assigning the parts to women (in his 1889 production) and the introductory spectacle of the Witches "coming out of a thunder cloud, suggesting that their home is among the dark and tempestuous elements of nature."[63]

It is perhaps natural that most of those who preferred "terrible" to semicomic Witches were inclined to view these characters as supernatural powers in their own right. Irving evidently took this view, though his phrase "supernatural significance" is ambiguous. Certainly his predecessors Knowles and Murdoch did so. Knowles, like Davies before him, called the Weird Sisters "the furies of Aeschylus" (he seems to have pictured the Furies more grandly than Davies did), but he also called them the "presiding, directing spirits of tragedy." And Murdoch would have gladly appropriated this last phrase, for it precisely describes his conception of their purpose: "In each step of [Macbeth's] bloody course . . . they are with him, nerving his arm, steeling his heart, and inspiring his soul with words of most fair foulness . . . until at last they break in upon his life in awful mockery." According to him, they are "as essential to the play as Macbeth himself"; in fact, the character of Macbeth would have no dramatic existence without them. Deprived of its supernatural element, the play would be reduced to the level of "cheap sensationalism." For this reason no "modernization" should be attempted. If the current audience proved too skeptical to accept *Macbeth* as written, the players should leave it unacted until the advent of "some more imaginative time."[64]

Although few later actors have emphasized the supernatural to the extent that Murdoch did, there was one—GORDON CRAIG—whose conception of the Weird Sisters was, if anything, even more exalted. In his mystical interpretation, they are spiritual presences: representing the God of Force, who crushes those human souls "not hard enough to resist," they are sternly beautiful like "the militant Christ scourging the money-changers"; but, in their roles of clinging, insinuating tempters of those souls they would crush, they are horrible. Their ambivalent appearance is not

63. *Macbeth, A Tragedy by William Shakespeare, As Arranged for the Stage by Henry Irving* (London, 1888), pp. 6-7.
64. "A Short Study of 'Macbeth,'" pp. 73-75.

strange, for "the spirit may take as many forms . . . as thought." Although Craig was not specific about staging, presumably he conceived the visible characters, representing the spirit in its tempting mode, as grotesque in appearance; he mentioned no overt symbol of the godlike presence, but would evidently trust for that to psychological suggestion through acting and particularly through the visual part of the production. If *Macbeth* were produced as it should be, he wrote, we should feel the presence of the spirit as Lady Macbeth is tempted; we should sense the spirit's desire for her to resist, to allow herself to be annihilated rather than submit to the influence that is testing her; we should feel the spirit's horror when she surrenders. The supernatural itself is not outdated ("the reality of the presence of spirits around us [is] a thing which all ordinary intelligences should be reminded of") ; but as it is handled on the stage—with ineptness, embarrassment, mechanical trickery—it is ineffective.[65] When Craig wrote this, in his essay "On the Ghosts in Shakespeare's Tragedies," he was no longer an actor but a stage designer and revolutionary theorist of the art of the theatre. Although he had acted Shakespearean roles and was continuing to work with productions of Shakespeare's plays, he had embraced the heresy that these plays should be read, not seen. Despite this attitude, and despite the fact that his interpretation of *Macbeth* is too abstract to be fully realized in the theatre, he directed that interpretation specifically at those engaged in the actual staging of the play; he even gave them a "practical word or two" about implementing his ideas. Craig published his essay in 1911, the same year that Beerhohm Tree staged his *Macbeth*—the production for which Craig had drawn designs, only to have them destroyed by Tree as impractical. In his own way—hardly the impressionistic way that Craig recommended—Tree's emphasis on the supernatural was as great as anyone's. His crashing tempest, his flying Witches carried forward the Irving tradition into the twentieth century.[66] But, as SIR JOHN GIELGUD wrote in 1942, Tree's "melodramatic" effects would hardly move an audience today as they might once have done.[67]

65. Edward Gordon Craig, *On the Art of the Theatre* (London, 1911), pp. 264-80, especially pp. 270-79.

66. *See* Mr J. C. Trewin's account in *Shakespeare on the English Stage 1900-1964*, pp. 42-44.

67. John Gielgud, "Before Macbeth," *Theatre Arts,* XXVI (February, 1942), 116.

Most of the modern actor-critics have agreed that the Weird Sisters are correctly described, not as supernatural beings, but as witches—strange, depraved old women who have sold their souls in return for magic powers. This interpretation seems to suit Banquo's description of the Sisters, as well as their own language and activities; it is also in line with Jacobean interests and beliefs. Yet some of those who accept it as reasonable also find it inadequate. They remember that Shakespeare would have read in Holinshed about the "three weird women in strange and wild apparel, resembling creatures of the elder world," who prophesied, "like goddesses of destiny . . . nymphs, or fairies"; and they feel that some of the sublimity of this conception haloes the characters of Shakespeare's fantasy, grotesque though they are. Or they sense in the play the presence of some vast unseen power which seems to find embodiment from time to time in the Weird Sisters—the power of Satan himself, presumably, if they *are* witches. The problem is not so much the ambiguity of the conception (after all, witches cannot be other than ambiguous) but the difficulty of making apparent on the stage both the literal and the symbolic nature of Shakespeare's creations.

GRANVILLE-BARKER felt that Shakespeare had "deliberately blended the two types"—i.e. the Norn-like sybils of Holinshed's account and the witches of common superstition—but that it would be a mistake to emphasize the latter too heavily. In his opinion, if the Middleton material, with its "comic opera" effect, is cut away (and, as we have seen, he unfortunately included the first witch scene in that category), "the part of their witchcraft that is essential to the play is given dignity and mystery."[68] Other actors have not balked at presenting the Weird Sisters as grotesque hags, but they have sought some way of suggesting the presence of the powers that they serve. WILLIAM POEL modeled the Witches of his production on Reginald Scot's description in the *Discoverie of Witchcraft:* "An old weather-beaten crone, having her chin and her knees meeting for age, walking like a bow, leaning on a staff, hollow-eyed, untoothed, furrowed, having her lips trembling with the palsy, going mumbling in the streets." But in the cauldron scene he "surrounded Hecate with three attendants, all four being in masque costumes." In Robert Speaight's words, "These attendants were a kind of superior Fates and they spoke for the

68. *The Players' Shakespeare: The Tragedie of Macbeth,* pp. lii-liii.

silent apparitions, thus giving to their utterance an effect of sinister ventriloquy." A somewhat similar expedient was used by SIR MICHAEL REDGRAVE in his production at the Aldwych Theatre (1947): "his three crones of the blasted heath were shadowed, from the beginning, by three stately counterparts," which Speaight interpreted as "the metaphysical *figurae* . . . of their prophecy and equivocation."[69] LENA ASHWELL differed from most of the others in believing that the Weird Sisters were immaterial presences, "the embodiment of Macbeth's desire, seeming to him the noblest aspirations of the great; but to us, only the diseased impulse goading to ghastly crime." Shakespeare, she explained, gave these appearances the guise of witches rather than Norns in order to convey a sense of horror to the audience. Although the once-impressive rituals have lost their effect for modern sophisticates and the grotesque runs the danger of becoming "funny," the significance of the Weird Sisters could be suggested, even today, with the aid of lighting effects: "As the figures move round the cauldron, they might seem at one angle of vision the beautiful, terrible Fates, revealing the future to Macbeth, but from another angle the repulsive hags practising filthy rites of their black magic."[70]

For several modern actor-critics, however, the "beautiful, terrible" element is non-existent, as far as the Witches are concerned: they are not supernatural in any respect but subnatural; never awe-inspiring, only disgusting. These "hideous, bearded females," writes ROBERT SPEAIGHT, "who lend their raucous voices to the desires that Macbeth has not yet dared to formulate," are very different from such supernatural characters as the Ghost in *Hamlet*. They are "instruments not of Providence but fatality"; and they "make use of nature only to defile and abuse it." Apparently, fatality is, for Speaight, only a delusive shadow of Providence, just as the Black Mass is not a ritual in its own right but merely a "sinister charade" and "superstition is the false coin of faith." For this reason, although he emphasizes the ambivalence of the Witches as much as any other actor-critic—"Everything they say and do is counterfeit and equivocal"—he refuses to grant them even a fleeting and illusory grandeur.[71] Two other actor-

69. Robert Speaight, *William Poel and the Elizabethan Revival* (Cambridge, Mass., 1954), pp. 188-89.
70. *Reflections from Shakespeare*, ed. Roger Pocock (London, [1926]), pp. 124-25.
71. *Nature in Shakespearian Tragedy*, pp. 45-47.

critics of our time, though they have not specifically argued for the subnormal interpretation, have discussed the Witches of their own productions in a manner that strongly implied it. Sir John Gielgud emphasized the bizarre appearance of these characters in his 1942 production: "costumes in strange shades of lemon-yellow, white and pale blue, with antlers on their heads, and their arms and legs veined and monstrous like creatures from the pictures of Hieronymos Bosch."[72] And DOROTHY ROSE GRIBBLE unmistakably characterized the Witches in the performances given by a touring company called Plantagenet Productions (1954) : "Satanists of the ugliest, most obscene kind, cold joyless creatures, each partaking of the nature of her own familiar spirit"—an idea conveyed by the use of "animal half-masks of flesh-colored hues, giving a rather horrible effect of degraded humanity."[73]

Sometimes actors who have felt a strong supernatural element in the play but not in the Weird Sisters themselves (or not adequately expressed there) have found Hecate—authentic Shakespeare or not—a useful symbol of this element. Poel's use of her in the cauldron scene has already been mentioned. He also retained her earlier appearance (III, v), immediately following the banquet scene, in order to make an interpretive comment by dramatic means. Bringing Hecate on "sharp on top of Macbeth's last line 'We are yet but young in deed'" created, according to Speaight, a powerful effect. As Poel himself explained, "It was as if the Fates . . . had taken fright at the thought of their own mischief and the awful tragic developments that were threatening in consequence."[74] For ELEANOR CALHOUN, too, the character was particularly significant. The scene just mentioned holds, as she thought, one of the key ironies of the play, in Hecate's lines:

> And you all know, security
> Is mortal's chiefest enemy.

In addition Hecate's appearance is important as the visual image of the demon that has possessed Lady Macbeth; to make this point clear, Miss Calhoun suggested, the two parts should be represented

72. "Before Macbeth," pp. 115-16.

73. Dorothy Rose Gribble, "Our Hope's 'Bove Wisdom, Grace and Fear," *Shakespeare Quarterly*, V (Autumn, 1954), 404.

74. Speaight, *William Poel and the Elizabethan Revival*, pp. 188-89.

by the same actress.[75] Although Hecate is no longer as much in favor with actors as she was in the early part of the century, Miss Gribble has described what she considered an effective use of the character in the 1954 production by her company: the bestial Witches of this performance were balanced by their supernatural Circe: "a beautiful, frosty she-devil, whose sole delight lay in the spiritual wickedness of her victims. . . . She was . . . the prologue to the second part of the play, and was represented . . . wearing a flame-colored robe with sleeves and head-dress also resembling flame."[76]

On the other hand, there have been several actor-critics in the past few decades who have minimized the supernatural element in *Macbeth*. GEORGE R. FOSS (1932), for example, rejected the Hecate scene not only because he considered it intrusive but because he refused to accept its implication that "the powers of evil are leagued against Macbeth." (Hecate's speech in that scene is the only one in the play that overtly expresses this idea.) According to Foss, the Weird Sisters "have the Scotch gift of second sight" and can do various things traditionally associated with witches such as "flying away on their brooms," but that is all; and "they are certainly not especially antagonistic to Macbeth."

The presence of Hecate and the custom of making the Witches uncanny spirits . . . have made Macbeth into a kind of weird, fate-haunted figure far removed from our everyday existence and have therefore detracted from the human moral. . . .[77]

SIR TYRONE GUTHRIE is another such actor-critic. In his 1934 production of *Macbeth* at the Old Vic, he omitted the first scene and all the supernatural material except what was essential to the plot. "By making the Weird Sisters open the play," he explained, "one cannot avoid the implication that they are a governing influence."

But surely the grandeur of the tragedy lies in the fact that Macbeth and Lady Macbeth are ruined by precisely those qualities which make them great; he by the imagination and intellectual honesty which enable him to perceive his own loss of integrity and to realise the fullest implications of the loss; she by the relentless driving-force and iron self-control that would in different circumstances have made her so great a queen; both by their genuine love for one another. All this

75. Princess Lazarovich-Hrebelianovich (Eleanor Calhoun), *Pleasures and Palaces* (New York, 1915), pp. 300-301.
76. "Our Hope's 'Bove Wisdom," p. 404.
77. *What the Author Meant*, p. 51.

is undermined by any suggestion that the weird Sisters are in control of events.[78]

This kind of argument has been carried even further by DOUGLAS CAMPBELL; for, although he recognizes various possibilities for interpreting the Witches, he himself inclines toward a completely rationalistic view. These characters are only poor, deluded women, spiteful of nature, outcasts from society. They believe themselves to be witches, and Macbeth accepts them as such because their prophecies are in harmony with his own dreams of power. Perhaps they have been skulking about military camps and have picked up the rumor that Macbeth is to be made Thane of Cawdor. Since the monarchy is elective, they reason, why not King as well? As for the cauldron scene, it is the product of Macbeth's own fantasy: he knows that Macduff is powerful, and he may even have heard of his unusual birth; imagination, working on this subconscious knowledge, produces the "prophecies."[79]

The theatrical treatment of *Macbeth*'s supernatural element has had a history of extremes—from inflation and embellishment to retrenchment and depreciation. Yet this element is too important to be exploited or ignored without serious consequences to the characters of the protagonists and to the play as a whole. Excessive emphasis on the supernatural, particularly upon its deterministic power, must have made it easy, from Davenant's time through Macready's, to consider Macbeth a victim of forces so great that, no matter how he might struggle, he could hardly hope to overcome them. (The tendency toward a fatalistic interpretation was counteracted to some extent, however, by a heavy moralistic emphasis.) Thus we can follow with some sympathy Sir Tyrone Guthrie's reasoning, and George R. Foss's: we do not wish to see Macbeth reduced to a marionette with the Weird Sisters pulling the strings. On the other hand, there is a danger that belittling the supernatural will result, not in increasing the stature of the human characters, as Guthrie hoped, but in diminishing it. I shall have more to say about this later in discussing the character of Macbeth.

Even if we assume the desirability of eliminating the supernatural, as Douglas Campbell advocates, can the relevant scenes be effectively "naturalized" in the theatre? A well-known pro-

78. Quoted by J. C. Trewin in *Shakespeare on the English Stage 1900-1964*, p. 161.
79. *Encyclopaedia Britannica* Film on *Macbeth*, Parts I and III.

duction that attempted to translate the supernatural into realistic terms was Komisarjevsky's *Macbeth* at Stratford-on-Avon,
1933: "the witches, with strong Scottish accents . . . were fortune-
telling drabs found plundering the dead, and Banquo's ghost was
Macbeth's own shadow"; the cauldron scene was "a long tossing
nightmare in which Macbeth dreamt his visit to the Weird Sisters
. . . and spoke much of the dialogue himself." Mr. J. C. Trewin,
always a perceptive critic, remarks: "Some of this had a sombre,
menacing terror; some of it was entirely insignificant."[80] It seems
to me that even the most imaginative attempt at "naturalization"
would always be under the threat of being commonplace.

What can we say, then, of a constructive nature about the interpretation and handling of the supernatural element? And, specifically, what can we say about the Weird Sisters, since they have
been the chief concern of the actor-critics? It seems to me that the
effect aimed at, though not always achieved, in the Witches of the
average modern *Macbeth* (and I include the most amateurish
productions of schools and community theatres) is the proper one.
In other words, the vague popular notion of "witches" that still
exists in an unbelieving age, is closer to the mark than the suggestions of some scholars and the experiments of some sophisticated producers. Although Shakespeare took the incident of the
three weird women from Holinshed, I do not think that Holinshed
can interpret Shakespeare's creations for us. The Weird Sisters
are not Norns. There is nothing in the text to suggest the august
or the sublime—that is, nothing directly connected with the Weird
Sisters themselves. Everything about them *does* suggest the
popular conception of witches, freely and imaginatively interpreted: not confined to the literal aspect of old village women but
translated into the fantastic forms that witches may be supposed
to take when they are about their hellish business. They are
ugly, deformed, grotesque—the gargoyles of humanity. (The idea
of the monstrous, or the subnatural, though not strictly "Shakespearean," is not inappropriate.) I do not think a semicomic
element can be avoided: there is a grisly kind of humor even
in naming over the ingredients of the cauldron. (It is difficult

80. *Shakespeare on the English Stage 1900-1964*, p. 167. At least two critics—
Wilson Knight and Gordon Crosse—did not understand the significance of the
shadow when they first saw the performance. *See* the latter's *Shakespearean
Playgoing 1890-1952. Illustrated from the Raymond Mander and Joe Mitchenson
Theatre Collection* (London, 1953), p. 136.

not to think of Burns's lines in a similar situation: "Wi' mair o' horribu' and awfu' / Which e'en to name wad be unlawfu'.") Vices and devils were both comic and terrifying in medieval drama. The Witches in *Macbeth* are like this. Since even the most sophisticated of us sometimes make jokes of things that horrify us, perhaps we can still respond to these "filthy hags" with at least some of the feeling that the audience was intended to have.

There *is*, however, a sense of evil sublimity in the play, and the Witches, far from sublime themselves, are sometimes conductors of it: Macbeth becomes "rapt" after their prophecies, and Lady Macbeth, in reading about them, is "transported . . . beyond / This ignorant present" and feels "The future in the instant." Thus I see the value of attempts, as in Poel's and Redgrave's productions, to suggest the power that stands behind the Witches. Unfortunately, such attempts are sometimes merely baffling and distracting to the audience. One critic, for example, found the three shadowing figures in Redgrave's production a "meaningless addition."[81] The usefulness of Hecate as a visual symbol of the supernatural has declined: her name is no longer one to conjure with, notwithstanding the newly-revived interest in the occult. A truly awe-inspiring Queen of Darkness might justify the use of this character despite the fairly strong evidence against her genuineness (though the deterministic tone of her scene is still to be considered), but an elder sister of Titania cannot do much for *Macbeth*. If something like Lena Ashwell's suggestion about dual effects through lighting could be effectively carried out, perhaps it would be helpful. Otherwise I suppose that imaginative acting by Macbeth and Lady Macbeth would suggest the power of the supernatural better than any specific symbolic device.

Interpretations: The "Meaning" of the Play

Statements of *Macbeth*'s theme or purpose and discussions of its "meaning" are distributed over a considerable period of time, rather than being concentrated in the twentieth century, as in the case of Shakespeare's other tragedies. The recent interpretations tend to be more diversified than the earlier ones, however, and they are sometimes presented in more detail.

Writers of the eighteenth and early nineteenth centuries

81. Crosse, *Shakespearean Playgoing 1890-1952*, p. 151.

tended to describe *Macbeth* in terms of a sermon; and the actor-critics were no exception. ARTHUR MURPHY, for example called it a lesson in "the fatality that attends wild ambition";[82] and ELIZABETH INCHBALD declared that everything in the play illustrates "one great precept"—"*Thou shalt not murder.*"[83] No doubt the overtly moralizing tone of Garrick's death speech influenced these actor-critics to some degree (and perhaps some traditional ideas inherited from the days when Davenant's version of *Macbeth* had held the stage). But, even if the play had remained undoctored, its obvious elements of crime and punishment, temptation and conscience, would have lent themselves to the neoclassical doctrine that moral instruction is an important purpose of drama—an idea that continued to be maintained by some defenders of the drama throughout the nineteenth century. Yet the approach taken by the critics we have mentioned—and by their contemporaries, like CHARLES DIBDIN and SHERIDAN KNOWLES —was hardly so simple-minded as their didactic language suggests to the modern reader. FANNY KEMBLE, writing some years later, may have had no more subtle understanding of the play than Murphy did, but her terminology pleases us more because it reminds us of symbolic drama rather than homiletics: *Macbeth,* she wrote, is not simply a dramatization of the hero's fall but also a great morality play telling to "every human soul . . . the story of its own experience."[84]

Actually some of the early interpreters of *Macbeth* seem to have had a rather sophisticated appreciation of its organic nature and of the artistry with which its themes are carried out in terms of imagery and structure. Murphy, for example, wrote in quite a modern spirit, "The Language takes a Tincture from the Subject, which being dark and gloomy . . . the Poets Choice of Words, and their Arrangement, are calculated to fill the Mind with Imagery of the most solemn and awful Aspect."[85] Mrs. Inchbald's appreciation was more superficial, but when she remarked, "Spirits are called from the bottomless pit, to give additional horror to

82. *Life of Garrick,* I, 87.

83. *The British Theatre,* IV, *Macbeth,* pp. 3-4. Thomas Davies also considered *Macbeth* a "powerful . . . dissuasive or dehortation" from murder. See *Dramatic Miscellanies,* II, 148.

84. Frances Anne Kemble, *Notes upon Some of Shakespeare's Plays* (London, 1882), pp. 21-22.

85. "The Theatre," *London Chronicle,* February 24-26, 1757.

the crimes," she was interpreting the spectacular element of the play, not as pure decoration, but as a visual extension of the moral theme.[86] The fact that she chose to emphasize a part of the spectacle that did not originate with Shakespeare himself cannot be overlooked, yet it does not negate the value of the critical attitude—the attempt at wholeness of conception—that her comment implies. But the didactic critics of the eighteenth and nineteenth centuries came closest to speaking the universal language of critical perception when they implied, as they repeatedly did, the essential oneness of plot and theme in *Macbeth*. For it was not ambition itself (or, as we would say, lust for power) that they emphasized, but ambition-in-action: the process through which this demon drives a man once it is allowed to take control. Charles Dibdin, who praised Shakespeare's vivid depiction of ambition's "destructive consequences, and its . . . headlong downfall," must have imagined, as he described the play, a kind of Raphaelite counterpart of "The Rake's Progress": "the principal character in the picture is constantly held up to you, always in a different attitude, and each attitude more terrible than that which went before it."[87] And Sheridan Knowles, though he also used the pictorial image, gave, even more, the impression of an action sequence: *Macbeth*, he wrote, is a "magnificent and instructive portrait . . . of guilty ambition in all its fearful stages—its portentous infancy, its appalling maturity, the gradual hardening of the usurper's heart from flesh to steel!"[88] The announced theme was ambition, but what these men were really describing was the theme of moral deterioration. Fanny Kemble, who recognized the importance of the latter, extended its universal implications by giving a more general name to the agent of that deterioration. According to her, *Macbeth* dramatizes the insidious nature of temptation:

its imperceptible advances, its gradual progress, its clinging pertinacity, its recurring importunity, its prevailing fascination, its bewildering sophistry, its pitiless tenacity, its imperious tyranny, and its final hideous triumph over the moral sense.[89]

86. *The British Theatre*, IV, *Macbeth*, pp. 3-4.
87. *A Complete History of the Stage* (London, 1800), III, 327.
88. *Lectures on Dramatic Literature: Macbeth*, pp. 79-80.
89. *Notes upon Some of Shakespeare's plays*, pp. 21-22.

In general actor-critics of the present century have avoided the idea that *Macbeth* is a simple object-lesson in ambition or crime. But, whatever their own predispositions and whatever the critical tendencies of their age, they could hardly have disregarded entirely the moral themes with which their predecessors were mainly concerned. What some of them have done is to emphasize the element of irony in these themes themselves or in some larger theme that they subserve. ELEANOR CALHOUN (1915), for example, saw within the tragedy of *Macbeth* a "kind of grim, exalted comedy" built upon the basic irony that "crime slays the assassin."[90] Another ironic theme—moral without being moralistic—has been suggested more recently by SIR TYRONE GUTHRIE. Deriving the ideas of mystery and secretness from recurring images of darkness and the ideas of guilt and violence from recurring images of blood, Guthrie decided that the basic theme of the play is "the violence which is secretly concealed beneath the outward appearance of civilized, social Man, even of kingly, heroic Man, so that his very kingship is used to procure a license for his essential barbarity." (He recognized the presence of such ideas as "vaulting ambition o'erleaping itself" and "Thou shalt not kill" but felt that it would be "too simple and naive" to consider either as the primary theme.)[91] DOUGLAS CAMPBELL, who expresses a similar idea, adds, however—as no earlier critic would have needed to do—that Shakespeare, in revealing the lust for blood hidden in every man, does not create the effect of despair and meaninglessness; that his emphasis is on the capacity for both good and evil in the human soul.[92]

Other actor-critics have gone behind the moralizing approach into metaphysical issues implied but not always discussed by earlier writers. Macbeth's damnation, particularly, was assumed from the beginning, and it was potential in all the moral interpretations of the play; but it has been discussed more fully and with more originality in the modern period. The approaches to this subject have varied widely, from GORDON CRAIG's strange spiritualism with its Nietzschean overtones[93] to ROBERT SPEAIGHT's more

90. *Pleasures and Palaces*, pp. 300-301.

91. *Shakespeare: Ten Great Plays* (New York, c. 1962), p. 406.

92. "A Director's Interpretation: The Politics of Power." The pertinent discussion is in Part III.

93. *On the Art of the Theatre*, pp. 269-70.

traditional conception of a Faustian "contract";[94] from GRANVILLE-BARKER's interpretation of "self-damnation" to a hell that is "here" rather than "hereafter"[95] to GEORGE R. FOSS's idea of damnation as a tragic delusion.[96]

The political as well as the moral or religious elements in *Macbeth* have been emphasized by a few modern actor-critics. Both Robert Speaight and Douglas Campbell are examples, but their interests and methods are very different. Speaight, the more theoretical and "Elizabethan," emphasizes (as in his other Shakespearean interpretations) the idea of world order—its shattering when nature is violated, its restoration when nature is redeemed by grace. Campbell is more interested in the game of power politics as it has been played by unscrupulous men in any age. According to Speaight, Macbeth's unnatural act, which breaks the bond of blood and the laws of hospitality, brings chaos to his world: the moral anarchy is reflected in the physical confusion of the strange night when chimneys topple and horses turn cannibal. Because of the king's position in the political microcosm, Macbeth's crimes transform Scotland into the "kingdom of sin"; but England, ruled by the saintly Edward and harboring the innocent Malcolm, becomes the "kingdom of grace." As the play draws to a close, "avenging grace" has done its work, harmony is being re-established in the universe, and "a new Scotland is just perceptible through the mist."[97] Campbell names as *Macbeth*'s central problem the conflict for power, but says that its prominence is somewhat obscured by the corrupt condition of the text (i.e. the loss of scenes that, he theorizes, once bolstered Macduff's importance in the action). He boldly traces this conflict, anyhow, as follows: There are three men, all generals, who are at first in potentially powerful positions: Macbeth, Banquo, and Macduff (identified by Campbell as hero of the battle against Norway). Any one of them would have made a worthy successor to the throne, but Duncan—not a wise and noble king at all, but a "man of wayward arrogance, corrupted by power"—appoints the inexperienced lad Malcolm. Macbeth, whose imagination becomes diseased through the effect of the weird womens' rumor-monger-

94. *Nature in Shakespearian Tragedy*, pp. 52-55, 60.
95. *The Players' Shakespeare: The Tragedie of Macbeth*, p. xxv.
96. *What the Author Meant*, p. 56.
97. *Nature in Shakespearian Tragedy*, pp. 52-68. There is a briefer discussion in Robert Speaight, *The Christian Theatre* (London, 1960), pp. 68-69.

ing "prophecies," makes the first move and secures the throne; he must then eliminate Banquo, who is cautiously but just as ambitiously seeking the aggrandizement of his family; and finally he faces the showdown with Macduff, the leader who values personal integrity and legitimate government more than his own ambition. Banquo loses his life through compromising his scruples. Macduff pays a heavy price but retains his integrity. At the end his iron determination contrasts with Macbeth's feeling of futility and hopelessness. When the two men fight, two forces symbolically meet.[98]

The Question of Appropriate Setting

If the spectacle associated with the supernatural is left out of account, the most important question concerning the physical mounting of *Macbeth* is much the same as that of *King Lear*. Although the quality of legendary remoteness is not as great here (the story is medieval rather than prehistoric), the problem remains: the events take place in an early period, and much of the action is savage in its violence; should the costumes and setting be "barbaric" as well? This question has been discussed chiefly by actor-critics of the present century.

GRANVILLE-BARKER brought up an interesting point: Shakespeare must have intended the Scots to wear a distinctive costume of some type—else why does he have Malcolm say as Ross approaches (IV, iii, 160), "My countryman; but yet I know him not"? Although he considered Elizabethan costumes appropriate to many other plays, Granville-Barker prescribed for *Macbeth* (as for *Lear*) something suggestive of an earlier age and also, in this case, of "the barbaric grandeur with which we may suppose Macbeth would emphasize his regality."[99] Thus his idea did not differ materially from that implicit in the practice of his predecessors except for those who emphasized "period" for its own sake or who allowed the decoration to "clog the action." Judging by stage practice, most of his successors have continued to feel that *Macbeth* demands a certain untamed, primeval quality in its costumes and setting. Several of the most articulate actor-critics, however, have either rejected this idea or heavily qualified it.

98. *Encyclopaedia Britannica* Film on *Macbeth*, Parts I and II.
99. *The Players' Shakespeare: The Tragedie of Macbeth*, pp. xxxii-xxxiii, xxxv-xxxvi.

Both SIR JOHN GIELGUD and SIR MICHAEL REDGRAVE evidently agreed with Granville-Barker's principle, but differing conceptions of "barbaric" are apparent in their descriptions of Macbeth's world as it was conjured up for their respective productions (1942 and 1947–48). Gielgud's suggests a kind of fantastic beauty: there is much emphasis on colors, apparently with symbolic associations: pastels for the scenery with "stronger tones" like "steelblue" and "dried blood" for "many of the cloaks and draperies"; and the anticipated effect is described as "rich and romantic, though also macabre and wild."[100] A starker primitivism is pictured in Redgrave's statement: "We are aiming . . . to reach back into the world of semi-barbarism. . . . Down to the mud spattered on their boots, our Scotsmen we hope will look like they were, a wild, violent, strange race."[101]

There is no denying a certain barbarism in *Macbeth*. But, as MARGARET WEBSTER has pointed out, it is related not simply to historical antiquity but to universal tendencies, "to primitive impulse and savage imagination." Shakespeare's story, in which "the forces of evil . . . take possession of two people of high ability and authority and through them almost wreck a nation," has been repeated in "even more terrible" form in our own time.[102] Some actor-critics feel that if the barbaric quality is too heavily emphasized in the costumes and scenery there is a tendency to ignore its deeper and wider significance. ROBERT SPEAIGHT suggests, in fact, that one reason why the play is rarely satisfactory in the theatre is that the usual costuming "evokes irresistibly a time which is too remote to touch us." Predictably, he recommends the dress of Shakespeare's own day. None of the plays is more Elizabethan than this one, he declares: its barbarism is that of "Bothwell, not of Boadicea," and Macbeth's soliloquy, "If it were done when 'tis done" might have served John Donne as a nucleus for a sermon.[103] SIR TYRONE GUTHRIE also objects to the usual staging of

100. "Before Macbeth," pp. 115-17.

101. Michael Redgrave, "A Medieval 'Macbeth' Made for Moderns," *New York Times*, March 28, 1948, Sec. II, pp. 1, 3. When this article was published, Redgrave was preparing for his United States debut in *Macbeth*. He had performed the play in London in 1947.

102. Margaret Webster, "Shakespeare for the Millions," *The Daily Tar Heel* (Student Newspaper of The University of North Carolina), Chapel Hill, January 15, 1949. This article was published when Miss Webster's Shakespeare on Wheels Company was touring the United States (1948-50).

103. *William Poel and the Elizabethan Revival*, p. 184.

Macbeth, with its "orgy of horn and hair"; but in recommending a change he stresses effect—a "dignified regality of aspect"—rather than a particular period.

> Neither Macbeth nor his Lady . . . think or speak in a primitive, unsophisticated manner. Moreover, the violence of their conduct is only shocking if it is at odds with their appearance . . . and the decay of the kingdom, which is one of the tragic consequences of Macbeth's regicide and usurpation, has no meaning if, even at the start of the play, Scotland is presented as an epitome of barbarity and poverty.[104]

It seems obvious to me that Speaight has a stronger case for Elizabethan costumes in *Macbeth* than in *King Lear:* not only are there no deliberate allusions to pagan antiquity here (there is no occasion for them) but the legendary element is less noticeable since the prophecies are worked out in terms of Jacobean belief, and the materials of the story—intrigue, assassination, lust for power, the Faust theme—are all associated with the Renaissance period. Although I cannot see that the costumes of an earlier period are necessarily destructive of the play's meaning, it seems to me that to depict the Scots in general as a "wild, violent, strange race" (as Redgrave described them) does endanger that meaning. For Macbeth's atrocious deeds are not meant to be understood as typical of his people: they are the terrible results of evil in one man's life, and, through him, spreading to infect his country—a man keenly aware of the claims of civilization and Christianity, even though he betrays them. Whatever the period chosen, Guthrie's main point is surely well taken: a richness of dress (in the Court scenes at least) and a gracious ceremoniousness of demeanor should contrast with the bloody thoughts and the increasingly violent deeds.

Criticisms of Dramatic Structure

Until the present century actor-critics praised the structure of *Macbeth* more enthusiastically than that of any other Shakespearean play except *Othello.* For ARTHUR MURPHY and FRANCIS GENTLEMAN (in the eighteenth century), Shakespeare's expert handling of dramatic progression in this tragedy compensated for his ignoring the "unities" of time and place. Gentleman remarked that in performance the play "does not strike . . . with any offensive

104. *Shakespeare: Ten Great Plays,* p. 407.

ideas of improbability, but rises by very just degrees to a catastrophe, which is well wrought up."[105] And Murphy elaborated: "Through the whole piece, the incidents grow out of one another . . . seeming to retard, but at the same time hurrying forward, to the catastrophe." Because of the "connected train of events" the action "appears to be one and entire."[106] SHERIDAN KNOWLES (in the nineteenth century) found in Macbeth proof that the classical "unities" are not only unnecessary but "absolutely hostile to the excellence of the drama" since only by violating them could Shakespeare have shown us the various stages in Macbeth's fall. In his lectures Knowles devoted considerable attention to the structural analysis of this play. According to him, the excellence of Shakespeare's plan is evidenced in the economy of exposition, the successful sustaining of tension, and the unerring use of striking situations at the moment of greatest theatrical effect.[107] In the modern period, however, as we have noted in discussing the influence of textual scholarship, several actor-critics have seen gaps or intrusions in the sequence of Macbeth's events which, for Knowles and the others, did not exist. It is pleasant to find MARGARET WEBSTER faithful to the earlier view. Trusting her theatrical sense, she writes that if the Folio text is a substantially cut version it is hard to see what could be added to improve it; for "its design is exact, its pattern as precisely balanced as a Bach fugue, its action taut and muscular, its language many times magnificent."[108]

Considerable attention has been devoted to the purpose and effect of specific scenes or sequences of scenes as they fit into the dramatic pattern of Macbeth. In some instances the actor-critics have differed with one another very markedly in their ideas about these matters: for example, in discussing the purpose of the scene in which Duncan and Banquo arrive at Macbeth's castle (I, vi), noticing its "pleasant seat" and the "temple-haunting martlet" which nests there; and in suggesting the proper stage treatment of the long interview between Malcolm and Macduff in England before the arrival of Ross (IV, iii, 1-139). In other instances

105. Dramatic Censor, I, 106.
106. Life of Garrick, I, 72.
107. Lectures on Dramatic Literature: Macbeth, pp. 79-82. See also pp. 76-77. Other passages praising Macbeth's structural excellence are found on pp. 2-3 and pp. 37-39. In Lectures on Dramatic Literature, see pp. 146-47, 179-81.
108. Shakespeare Without Tears (Cleveland, 1955), p. 226.

there has been close agreement: for example, in discussing the denouement of the play.

The "martlet" passage has frequently been noticed for its gracious and tranquil atmosphere as compared with the gloom and strife typical of the play as a whole. But Sheridan Knowles, receptive always to Shakespeare's ironic undercurrents, found this idea rather superficial. In particular, he replied to Sir Joshua Reynolds' remark that the scene is "an example of relief, analogous to what is technically called repose in painting." The audience cannot join in the innocent and pleasant admiration of the castle, Knowles pointed out. "The unconsciousness of the destined victim to the fate that awaited it . . . must have served, not to assuage, but to aggravate in the beholder the feeling of its predicament." The scene, therefore, is actually "another and a higher step in the climax of action."[109] This is a true evaluation, I think, if one must plot a structural graph, as Knowles was constantly doing in his dramatic criticism. Yet irony by definition cuts two ways; and in this case the "higher step" is a vantage point from which the audience may see Macbeth's gracious past as well as his bloody future. So it is not surprising that other actor-critics have differed from Knowles in their interpretations. ROBERT SPEAIGHT takes the more usual view: that the atmosphere of the play, "sultry with conspiracy," clears with the arrival of Duncan.[110] And GEORGE SKILLAN suggests that the scene has more than one purpose: "a pleasant lightening of the action . . . and . . . the creation at the same time of a contrast against which the forthcoming tragedy is to be set."[111] These comments, though they differ from one another, can all be reconciled, perhaps, with A. C. Bradley's well-known remarks about the "beautiful but ironical passage where Duncan sees the swallows flitting round the castle of death."[112]

The scene in which Malcolm tests Macduff's integrity by deliberately blackening his own character has often been drastically cut in the theatre on the theory that much of it is unnecessary and boring. Both HARLEY GRANVILLE- BARKER and SIR LEWIS CASSON argue against this practice, but for different reasons, and they give

109. *Lectures on Dramatic Literature: Macbeth*, pp. 23-24. *Lectures on Dramatic Literature*, p. 169.

110. *Nature in Shakespearian Tragedy*, pp. 51-52.

111. *Macbeth. French's Acting Edition*, p. 66.

112. *Shakespearean Tragedy* (London, 1941), p. 334.

very different recommendations for playing the scene. Granville-Barker urges not only that the whole interview be retained but that everything possible be done to enhance its importance as "the starting-point of the play's counteraction." Its purpose is to provide a "breathing-space in which to recover from the shaking effects of the tragedy" as it has been developed so far and "to prepare for the final rush of events." The "formalism in the writing" underlines Malcolm's level-headedness, but, despite this surface tone, the scene is charged with unexpressed emotion. "Given an actor of the right authority for Malcolm, the scene can be made interesting enough." The contrast between the natures of the two men should be stressed: "Macduff outspoken; Malcolm reserved, over-cautious at first, though never cold."[113] Casson, on the other hand, considers the scene dull; he cautions against cutting simply because of the danger of unintelligibility, which would make for still greater dullness. His recipe for stage effectiveness is for Malcolm to play the scene as "fairly broad comedy, taking the audience boldly into his confidence as he pulls the leg of the simple honest Macduff."[114] Of the two methods suggested here Casson's would probably be more effective in terms of immediate audience reaction, but at this point in the action (very accurately pinpointed, I think, by Granville-Barker) it would hardly serve the purpose of the play as a whole to turn the saviors of Scotland into a practical joker and his stooge.

In reading the actors' discussions of *Macbeth*'s last two acts we are struck by the similarities between the criticisms by Sheridan Knowles[115] of the nineteenth century and Granville-Barker[116] of the twentieth. Both men had been dramatists as well as actors, however, and so were keenly sensitive to such problems of dramatic construction as Shakespeare faced in "keeping up the interest . . . from the banquet scene to the catastrophe." Knowles explained the difficulty in this way: "No one is left that we care much about . . . whose jeopardy preserves the tension of that horror which has

113. *The Players' Shakespeare: The Tragedie of Macbeth*, pp. xlvii-xlviii.

114. Folio Society edition of *Macbeth*, p. 11.

115. *Lectures on Dramatic Literature*, pp. 37-41. Knowles points out (pp. 41-42) that Sophocles' conduct of the action in *Oedipus Tyrannus* is "so similar to that of Shakespeare in constructing the last two acts of 'Macbeth' that the one cannot fail to remind you of the other, although . . . the Englishman is here decidedly superior to the Greek." On pp. 42-60 he gives a critical analysis of *Oedipus*.

116. *The Players' Shakespeare: The Tragedie of Macbeth*, pp. liv-lvii, especially pp. liv-lv.

hitherto been kept upon the strain." And Granville-Barker added the more important point: "In character development Shakespeare has perhaps done all he can do—for his protagonists at least—even before the end of Act III. The rest is catastrophe, skilfully retarded." Both actor-critics wrote interesting analyses of Shakespeare's concluding pattern of action. Only one major question is left to be answered, Knowles pointed out: the manner in which Macbeth is to meet his end. The subject is introduced in the first scene of Act IV and is kept "constantly in view" until the end of the play "without ever . . . allowing . . . expectation to flag."

Macbeth is threatened with his doom—he is assured against it. It approaches him—he defies it. One ground of confidence having vanished, he clings to the other; that also fails him. He has nothing but his despair to confide in; he trusts in it and falls!

Shakespeare's careful construction is illustrated by the fact that each of the predictions in the cauldron scene is the impulse for some later action: for example, the first prediction "prompts Macbeth to an act which whets, as it were, the weapon by which he is destined to fall." Granville-Barker expressed equal enthusiasm for the "mastery" with which Shakespeare "marshal[s] . . . the play's action to its end." In terse and vivid sentences he sums up the purpose, effect, tempo, and atmosphere of one scene after another. Here are some examples: "We have in the scene with the weird sisters the whipping up of evil in Macbeth to the top of its fury, immediately followed by its most savage outbreak —sudden & short—upon Lady Macduff and the child." The "gathering of the Scottish lords" is compared to "men escaping from prison and despair. The 'drum and colours' here strike a new note; lifted spirits are marked by such means as the rising inflection of Angus's second speech with its 'Now . . . Now . . . Now . . .'; and the repeated 'March we on' and 'Make we our march' begins the movement to the play's end." Macbeth's "I 'gin to be aweary of the sun" may be "designed to emphasize by contrast the rush to the end." At the point when Macbeth receives news of the moving wood, "if one were charting the scene as a fever is charted, one would show a perpendicular leap in energy." Thus in a few bold strokes Granville-Barker graphically traces the movement—its steady rush, its pauses, its bursts of fury—toward the "catastrophe, skilfully retarded."

Discussions of Theatrical Effectiveness

If any of Shakespeare's plays can be called "theatrical," surely it is *Macbeth,* with its witches, its ghost, its multiple murders, its hand-to-hand combat. And indeed it has been praised repeatedly for its quality of excitement. SHERIDAN KNOWLES went so far as to declare that " 'Macbeth' is the most melodramatic tragedy in the whole range of the drama, and it is to the credit of Shakespeare that it is so."[117] And actors of our own period, like MARGARET WEBSTER[118] and GORDON CRAIG,[119] have also used the term "melodramatic" unabashedly, and favorably, in describing *Macbeth.* Craig, who rated "melodrama at its best very highly," explained that it "is not afraid of the spectacular or the heroic, of *bravura,* or of the impossible. It shuns one thing purposely— the matter-of-fact." He called *Othello, Richard III,* and *Hamlet* "big and noble melodramas," and even insisted that there is much melodrama in the *Divine Comedy.*

Among the scenes most often admired for their impact in the theatre is the murder scene in this play. FRANCIS GENTLEMAN wrote that it is "calculated to awake the drowsiest feelings, and to alarm the most resolute heart."[120] It is hardly necessary to search for the reasons. The whole scene, as we read, calls out for acting. In its highly-charged fragments of dialogue, Shakespeare provided, as THOMAS DAVIES remarked, "only an outline to the consummate actor.—*I have done the deed!—Didst thou not hear a noise?— When?—Did you not speak?*—The dark colouring, given by the actor to these abrupt speeches makes the scene awful and tremendous to the audience."[121] And JOSEPH JEFFERSON found in this scene an example of the "hidden treasure" that is disclosed only in acting, not reading.

Macbeth, standing with his wife in a dark and gloomy hall, looks at his bloody hands and apostrophizes them in . . . terrible words. . . . Now there is a silence, and when he is alone there echoes through the castle a knocking at the gate. The friends of the murdered guest . . . thunder at the portals, while the blood-stained host stands as if stricken down with terror and remorse. It is not the dialogue, as

117. *Lectures on Dramatic Literature: Macbeth,* pp. 76-78; *Lectures on Dramatic Literature,* pp. 37-41.
118. "Shakespeare for the Millions."
119. Gordon Craig, *Henry Irving* (New York, 1930), pp. 91, 143.
120. *Dramatic Censor,* I, 89-90.
121. *Dramatic Miscellanies,* II, 149.

powerful as it is, which strikes the audience with awe; it is simply a stage direction of the great dramatic master—"a knocking at the gate."[122]

Theoretically, then, *Macbeth* is one of Shakespeare's most effective plays for the theatre; in practice, however, it has often proved disappointing. On the eighteenth century stage it was indeed one of the most popular Shakespearean plays;[123] Macbeth was a great role for Garrick, and the Lady Macbeth of Hannah Pritchard was much admired. Later came the ever-memorable Sarah Siddons, whose Lady Macbeth was the most famous of all her impersonations. And Macbeth was the Shakespearean character that Macready acted most often and with greatest acclaim. (His farewell to the stage, February 26, 1851, was in a performance of Macbeth.)[124] But for the later actors the play has had a checkered career. Comments on the theatrical worth of *Macbeth* and its characters are, accordingly, very mixed.

As early as the eighteenth century there are hints that, for some reason, the potentialities of this play frequently remain unrealized in performance. Although the play as a whole (in Davenant's version) was very popular in the pre-Garrick period, the reputation of the title part among actors was, according to Thomas Davies, rather low: "Macbeth, they constantly exclaimed, was not a character of the first rate; all the pith of it was exhausted . . . in the first and second acts of the play." GARRICK, however, "smiled" when he heard this "and said he should be very unhappy if he were not able to keep alive the attention of the spectators to the last syllable of so animated a character." He was very successful, of course, partly because his mastery of the "terrible graces of action" produced unexpected "effects" in the scene with Banquo's Ghost.[125] Even Lady Macbeth, though a great role in the hands of Mrs. Betterton, Mrs. Porter, and Mrs. Pritchard, was not always a successful vehicle for the actress. Francis Gentleman

122. *The Autobiography of Joseph Jefferson* (New York, [1890]), pp. 185-87.

123. Charles B. Hogan, *Shakespeare in the Theatre, 1701-1800* (Oxford, 1952-57), II, 716-17. *Macbeth* was fourth in popularity among the twenty-nine plays of Shakespeare acted in the period 1751-1800 (*Romeo and Juliet, Hamlet,* and *Richard III* surpassed it). If the century as a whole is considered, only *Hamlet* was performed more often than *Macbeth.*

124. For a description of Macready's Macbeth, *see* Arthur Colby Sprague, *Shakespearian Players and Performances* (Cambridge, Mass., 1953), pp. 87-103. Macready's success in this role is discussed on pp. 91-93.

125. *Dramatic Miscellanies,* II, 166.

remarked that, although this is not a difficult role, "several first-rate actresses" had made only mediocre Lady Macbeths. He added, interestingly, that "few female spectators" like this play.[126]

Most of the other comments of this nature are from actor-critics of the late nineteenth or the twentieth century. Both MARY ANDERSON (1896)[127] and J. H. BARNES (1914)[128] expressed great admiration for *Macbeth* as a work of art—the former maintained that no play appealed to her more in reading, and the latter called it "perhaps the greatest play in our language, as well as the nearest model of the great Greek tragedies"; but each had discouraging words about the theatrical possibilities. According to Miss Anderson, "Lady Macbeth is not only the most difficult of all Shakespeare's women to impersonate naturally, but the most unsympathetic to the public." And Barnes felt similarly about the role of Macbeth. "It is only when you get on the stage in it," he testified ruefully, ". . . that you find out what a wilderness of words it is, and every line right 'in the teeth of the audience.' Not a moment when the audience is not antagonistic. . . . It is like rolling a barrel up a hill. . . ." SIR MICHAEL REDGRAVE (1954) pointed out another difficulty: the public, nourished on romantic criticism, could hardly fail to be disappointed by Macbeth's character in the theatre; for the actor who asks, as he studies, *"What does the text mean?"* is "appalled" to discover how little is said in Macbeth's own part to enable him to build up the "great terrifying figure" of popular imagination.[129]

Other actor-critics of the modern period have been more sanguine about *Macbeth*'s potentialities as an acting play. CONSTANCE BENSON recalled, in her memoirs (published in 1926 but concerned, of course, with earlier years) that *Macbeth* never failed to draw large houses when the Bensonians were on tour and that the part of Lady Macbeth was always a favorite with actresses.[130] And GEORGE R. FOSS (1932), though he recognized the problems mentioned by other actors, suggested that solutions were not impossible. He traced the poor showing of Macbeth's character to the overemphasis on the "fascinating and comparatively easy

126. *Dramatic Censor,* I, 112.

127. *A Few Memories* (New York, 1896), pp. 82-83.

128. *Forty Years on the Stage* (London, 1914), pp. 136, 141.

129. "Shakespeare and the Actors," in *Talking of Shakespeare,* ed. John Garrett (London, 1954), pp. 138-40.

130. *Mainly Players* (London, [1926]), p. 269.

part of Lady Macbeth," and the relative lack of popular appeal in the play as a whole to Shakespeare's failure to weave "humour into the fabric" as he did in the other tragedies. But he felt that if the actor could arouse pity for the murderer and show the audience his basic nobility, and if Lady Macbeth were subordinated so as not to "distract us from the very human tragedy of Macbeth," this play might still have "a chance of . . . being as popular and as understandable as the others on the stage."[131]

Actually, there has been an unwarranted emphasis by some writers on the unpopularity of *Macbeth* and its major roles in the theatre. It is somewhat misleading, for example, to write, as one modern scholar has done, "No actor since Shakespeare's time seems to have made a name for himself playing the part of Macbeth. . . ."[132] The popularity of the play did suffer some reverses in the latter half of the nineteenth century (the decline on the New York stage was particularly sharp[133]), and some fine modern actors have been frustrated—and frustrating—as Macbeth. But of the four "great" tragedies *Macbeth* has been second only to *Hamlet* in the number of productions at Stratford-on-Avon since 1879, and either second or third (with *Othello* in the alternate position) in the major London theatres during the present century (to 1964).[134] Even so, there is something more than its reputation for being "unlucky" that makes the play loom ominously before those who are about to try their mettle in it.

A part of the difficulty may be that there is no longer, since the pruning of the operatic embellishments, much of a sop to the

131. *What the Author Meant*, pp. 53, 58-59. *See also* p. 56.

132. Elizabeth Nielsen, "*Macbeth:* The Nemesis of the Post-Shakespearian Actor," *Shakespeare Quarterly*, XVI (Spring, 1965), 193-99. Miss Nielsen's sentence "Famous men have played the role, but they have gained their fame elsewhere first" saves her, perhaps, from outright inaccuracy; but she strongly implies just before that statement that there have "rarely, if at all" been any famous stage interpretations of Macbeth since Shakespeare's time. This is incorrect.

133. *See* G. C. D. Odell's *Annals of the New York Stage* (New York, 1927), *passim.* Although Odell does not provide complete statistics, his records do furnish a general guide to the relative popularity of the plays. Apparently *Macbeth, Hamlet,* and *Othello* were about equal in popularity during the first two decades, with *Othello* perhaps slightly below the other two, and *Lear* considerably below all three. For the next fifty-odd years *Macbeth* was either second or third in popularity among the four "great" tragedies. But in the period 1875-79 it dropped even below *Lear,* and after this it alternated with *Lear* in third and fourth position, both plays significantly lower than the other two.

134. *See* the appendices in Trewin's *Shakespeare on the English Stage 1900-1964,* pp. 257-307.

spectators who demand simple "entertainment." As Foss noticed, there is not even Shakespeare's usual change of pace through the use of comic material—at least there is very little. Another difficulty may be that *Macbeth* has been oversold as "melodrama." The defiant claims made for it by Sheridan Knowles and Gordon Craig have much truth in them, but these men understood, as the rest of their criticism indicates, that the violent actions are not interesting for themselves alone but for their origins in and effects upon the minds and souls of the perpetrators. *Macbeth* may be, as Margaret Webster once called it, a "thriller." But if there are no metaphysical thrills, the excitement declines (as the eighteenth century actors noticed) after the first two acts. The cruxes, then, are the treatment of the supernatural and the interpretation of the two Macbeths. The first has already been discussed, but we shall return to it in the section "From Criticism to Theatre." The other subject claims our attention now.

II. THE CHARACTERS

MACBETH

Actor-critics have been particularly interested in Macbeth. Not only have a large number of them written and published their ideas about this character, but, on the average, their discussions are longer and more detailed than those concerned with any other Shakespearean hero except Hamlet. As a body, however, this Macbeth criticism is relatively simple, for the actor-critics have dealt again and again with the same few subjects.

Differences of opinion are usually related to two broad questions. The first is perhaps two questions in itself, but they are sometimes so closely intertwined as to be indistinguishable: Is Macbeth a "strong" character—stalwart and courageous—or is he "weak"—cowardly, overly-sensitive, even neurotic? Looking at the antithetical possibilities another way, so that sensitivity and imagination become sympathetic qualities: Is Macbeth primarily a "soldier" or a "poet"? The other broad question cuts even more deeply: Is Macbeth's an essentially noble nature which is gradually corrupted, or is it thoroughly evil from the beginning?

The traditional interpretation inherited by Garrick left little doubt about the answer to either of these questions. Macbeth was basically strong and courageous; basically noble and sympathetic. He had a flaw—excessive ambition—but without the supernatural soliciting of the Weird Sisters and the pressure from his fiendlike wife he would probably not have fallen. His struggles with his conscience before Duncan's murder and his remorseful consciousness of his own evil as he sank deeper and deeper in crime were indications of his original nobility, and his fight to the end against hopeless odds was evidence of his lasting courage. GARRICK himself strongly supported this interpretation in both his acting and his critical remarks; but, as we shall see, the very effectiveness with which he portrayed one aspect of the character may have helped to obscure another.

Garrick was not tall enough to realize the heroic image of Macbeth the Soldier that some critics have envisioned, but he could produce the illusion of physical strength through the extraordinary force of his acting. His description of Macbeth as "the most violent part I have"[135] suggests the physical vigor as well as the mental turbulence that he saw in the character. It was the latter, however, that was more important to him. Macbeth's basic nobility and the consequent self-torture after he succumbs to evil were the key to Garrick's interpretation. This is clear, not only from other writers' critiques of his acting, but also from his own poetic description of Macbeth's suffering:

> Under the Load of guilty pomp to groan,
>   And feel in Ling'ring Death, *the Dagger of ye Mind*.

> What Anguish past belief,
> What Horror is that Wretch's Share,
> Whose change of Torment is his Sole relief,
> From Guilt to Madness, and Despair.[136]

135. Letter to Grey Cooper, Esq., dated simply December 17. MS in the Folger Library. The letter is published in *The Letters of David Garrick*, ed. David M. Little and George M. Kahrl (Cambridge, Mass., 1963), II, 837-38. The editors conjecture the year to have been 1772.

136. These two stanzas on Macbeth are in the MS version of Garrick's "Jubilee Ode" in the Folger Library. The second stanza is separated from the first (it is on the next page) but is linked to it by asterisks. Both stanzas were cancelled in Garrick's final revision of the Ode, presumably because he could not fit them into his scheme.

Although Garrick undoubtedly connected courage with nobility in his conception of the character, his powerful depiction of a man horror-struck by guilt produced in some spectators the feeling that he gave less "daring and intrepidity" to Macbeth than former actors had done.[137] The highest moments in his performance, those that his acting made unforgettable, exhibited Macbeth at his most tortured and defenseless. His guilty anguish in the scene following the murder moved his fellow-actors to rapturous admiration. "Whoever heard the low, but piercing notes of his voice when the *deed is done,*" writes FRANCIS GENTLEMAN, ". . . without feeling a vibration of the nerves?"[138] THOMAS DAVIES tells of the "terrifying whispers" of this scene as acted by Garrick and Mrs. Pritchard, the "distraction of mind and agonizing horrors" of Macbeth as contrasted with the seeming composure and confidence of his wife.[139] And ARTHUR MURPHY makes the scene even more graphic:

he was absolutely scared out of his senses; he looked like a ghastly spectacle, and his complexion grew whiter every moment, till at length, his conscience stung and pierced to the quick, he said in a tone of wild despair,
>   Will all great Neptune's ocean wash this blood
>   Clean from my hand?[140]

For the average spectator, perhaps, there was little difference between fear of the adversary within and fear of dangers without; in spite of Garrick's intentions, Macbeth's paralyzing horror of his own first crime, as he portrayed it, may have cast doubt upon the idea of a normally courageous character. Then, too, since Garrick had a spectacular talent for communicating dread and awe in the presence of the supernatural, he may sometimes have overplayed Macbeth's fear in the scene with Banquo's Ghost. An anonymous critic pointed out on one occasion that Macbeth, being no coward, should appear less frightened and subdued at the words "Avaunt and quit my sight!"[141] Garrick evidently agreed, and from that time had Macbeth "recollect a degree of resolution"

137. *See* Percy Fitzgerald, *Life of David Garrick* (London, 1899), II, 69.
138. *Dramatic Censor,* I, 108.
139. *Dramatic Miscellanies,* II, 148-49.
140. *Life of Garrick,* I, 82.
141. *The Private Correspondence of David Garrick with the Most Celebrated Persons of His Time,* ed. James Boaden (London, 1831), I, 19-20.

upon the second appearance of the Ghost. When another critic objected that he was too bold in that scene, the actor replied:

Should Macbeth sink into pusillanimity, I imagine that it would hurt the character, and be contrary to the intention of Shakespeare. . . . I make a great difference between a mind sunk by guilt into cowardice, and one rising with horror to acts of madness and desperation, which last I take to be the case of Macbeth.[142]

Here, at least, is unmistakable evidence of his own conception.

With only one exception, the actor-critics contemporary with Garrick interpreted Macbeth in much the same way. Davies, for example, accepted the idea of a valiant Macbeth but felt that "the sensibility of the murderer" was even more important than his courage; the latter trait, he pointed out, was shared by "Banquo and others," but the former contributed "in a great measure" to the "rational and severe delight" experienced by spectators of this play. Macbeth's "extreme reluctance" to commit murder, his "uncommon affliction of mind" after the crime, and "the perpetual revolt of his conscience" with each new atrocity made him an object of some pity "in spite of his ambition and cruelty."[143] But the most interesting and thoughtful comments of this sort are by Arthur Murphy, whose ideas were molded by personal experience in acting the role (at Covent Garden, 1755) as well as by repeated observations of Garrick's performance. Murphy was particularly aware of paradox in Macbeth's nature: of "Intrepidity and Superstition, Remorse and Cruelty . . . all blended together." On the one hand, he noticed that strong imagination subjects Macbeth to "visionary Fears"; on the other, that "natural courage supports him under all afflictions." In describing the character's basic moral nature ("full of the milk of human kindness") and in tracing its corruption (he "hesitates, and yet deliberates, grows by degrees familiar with the horror of the deed, and in the end is reconciled to it") Murphy had much the same idea as other critics—for example, CHARLES DIBDIN.[144] But in discussing the after-effects of murder he was more original: Macbeth's mind is "full of Scorpions, which incessantly goad him,"

142. *Ibid.*, I, 134-36. See also *Letters of Garrick*, ed. Little and Kahrl, I, 350-52. Garrick's correspondent, who signed his letter "H.H." is conjectured to have been Hall Hartson. Garrick's letter is dated January 24, [17] 62.

143. *Dramatic Miscellanies*, II, 148, 191.

144. *Complete History of the Stage*, III, 327-28.

yet "the more he is goaded . . . the more he hardens himself in Villainy." In his remorse Macbeth does not, like Shakespeare's King John, "abandon himself to despair"; he does not, like Claudius, "endeavour at Repentance"; nor does he follow Richard III in attempting to "subdue his Tendencies to Remorse." Rather, "he is at once resolute and timorous, determined to pursue the bloody Tract of Ambition, and at the same Time a Prey to all the Vulture-Cares of Wickedness." Because of this complexity, Macbeth is "a different Villain from any other on the Stage."[145]

The only actor-critic of Garrick's period—indeed the only critic of any kind—who held a completely unsympathetic view of Macbeth's character was Francis Gentleman. Although even he was moved to some pity by Garrick's dying scene, he believed that Shakespeare meant to present Macbeth from the beginning as a "detestable monster." Our first view of the character, he argued, dispels all ideas of nobility that have been built up in the previous scene by accounts of his courage. In the soliloquy "Two truths are told. . . ." which follows the Witches' prophetic greetings and the immediate confirmation of the "Thane of Cawdor" salutation, Macbeth contemplates murder as the means of fulfilling the prophecy of royalty for himself. Since there are "many circumstances . . . to bring about the most unthought of changes in human affairs," the man who thinks of "the worst means at first" evidently has "by nature a deep depravation of heart." Even the struggles with his conscience ("If it were done. . . .") cannot redeem him, for a crime committed precipitately is easier to forgive than one determined upon after scrupulous deliberation. Macbeth's later actions show him "more actuated by jealous apprehensions than sound policy; more influenced by rage and desperation, than any degree of resolution; credulous, impatient, vindictive, ambitious without a spark of honour; cruel without a gleam of pity." Instead of imitating humanity in this character, Shakespeare has, "like Prometheus . . . made a man of his own" but has "stoln his animation rather from Hell than Heaven."[146] Gentleman's totally dark view of the character (1770) remained unique in all Macbeth criticism, as far as I know, for nearly seven decades, and in actors' criticisms for more than a century.

145. *Life of Garrick,* I, 86-87; "The Theatre," *London Chronicle,* February 26–March 1, 1757. *See also* Murphy's characterization of Macbeth in the preceding number of "The Theatre," February 24-26.

146. *Dramatic Censor,* I, 82-83, 106-7.

Not only was there no interpretation like Gentleman's for many years to come, but among actor-critics there was even a strong resistance to such signs of change as *were* occurring in the literary criticism of Macbeth. For in the late years of the eighteenth century a new tendency emerged, somewhat like that in Hamlet criticism—to reduce the heroic element in the character. As we have mentioned, Garrick's acting may have caused some of his audience to question Macbeth's courage before any formal questions were raised by critics. But as the critical habits of close analysis and psychological emphasis became more pronounced, there was a greater possibility that Macbeth's sensitivity and remorse would be allowed to weaken the old belief in his essential courage. In a sense Arthur Murphy had heralded the new kind of criticism in his essay comparing Macbeth's remorse with that of other Shakespearean characters (1757); but, although he had recognized the tension of opposite qualities in Macbeth's character, he had left its traditional virtues unblurred and unqualified. In 1785, however, the nontheatrical critic Thomas Whately, in an interesting essay, *Remarks on Some of the Characters of Shakespeare,* made a more elaborate study, using Murphy's comparative method for a complete analysis of Macbeth and Richard III; and, in contrasting the kinds of courage shown by these two characters he called in question (or seemed to do so) one of the chief components of Macbeth's nobility. Actually Whately did not deny Macbeth's courage, but he considered it an artificial, not a natural quality, the product of resolution rather than true intrepidity (like Richard III's), and therefore subject to collapse after the accomplishment of the particular act that had required it. He supported this idea with various passages from the text, some of which he discussed with a certain amount of insight. George Steevens, the Shakespearean editor, was considerably impressed by Whately's essay: he was convinced that Richard III was much more courageous than Macbeth, that the latter (after his first appearance in the play) succeeded sometimes in screwing his courage to the sticking-place but never in rising to "constitutional heroism." In only one point he disagreed with Whately, and he discussed this in a long note in his last editions of Shakespeare: in his opinion Macbeth had been naturally courageous at the beginning but, having lost his courage with his virtue, he attempted to substitute a kind of desperate resolution.[147]

All of this subtlety and qualification, this seeming denigration of Macbeth's character, filled JOHN PHILIP KEMBLE with impatient thoughts. He was more of Dr. Johnson's mind than of Whately's or Steevens' (the older critic had remarked that Macbeth's courage enables us to retain a certain esteem for the character despite his crimes), and he set out to combat the dangerous new tendency. Kemble, in fact, replied to Whately's *Remarks* almost immediately (his spirited *Answer* appeared in 1786), before Steevens had expressed his qualified approval of the new interpretation. But some years later (1817) he revised his essay, increasing it to more than twice its original size, in order to reply to Steevens' note as well. The new pamphlet was published under the title of *Macbeth and King Richard the Third*.

Kemble's chief anxiety (a prophetic one) was that if Macbeth's courage were weakened or disallowed his original nobility would be discredited and he would seem an outright villain from the beginning; in this case, Kemble wrote, his strivings with conscience would be reduced to mere cowardice, his remorse to imbecility. Although theoretically Steevens had forestalled this argument by admitting that Macbeth had *once* been courageous, Kemble decided (not surprisingly) that his argument was not sufficiently different from Whately's to warrant separate replies. For Kemble was primarily concerned with the effect of an interpretation on the theatre audience; and if, in all his onstage scenes, Macbeth loses his "constitutional heroism," will the audience not doubt that he ever possessed it?

Despite his air of rescuing a beleaguered hero from the enemy, Kemble presents his case, for the most part, in a logical and rather persuasive manner—though he sometimes, very naturally, insists upon a particular interpretation of a passage that might well admit of more than one. He takes up, point by point, the major contentions of the two commentators and attempts, with considerable success in some passages, to show their origin in misunderstanding of the text or failure to visualize the dramatic ineffectiveness of a suggested interpretation. (For example: According to Whately, Macbeth is agitated by the meeting with the Witches but Banquo takes a light, contemptuous attitude toward them. Kemble re-

147. *The Plays of William Shakespeare* (London, 1793), VII, 584-87.

futes this assertion by closely comparing the speeches of the two men in the relevant scene and by reminding the reader of Banquo's later references to his dream of the Weird Sisters, II, i, 6-9, 20-21; he also points out that the Witches cannot be effectively presented on the stage unless both Macbeth and Banquo react with wonder and astonishment.) Kemble then compares Macbeth and Richard III in an attempt to show that every situation adduced by Whately to prove Macbeth's fear has a counterpart in the other character. Both men, he argues, are sometimes terror-struck by the recollection of their crimes, but both are as fearless as men may be: Shakespeare's characters are always "human creatures," liable to the passions of their kind. The real difference between the two is that Richard III has a "simple" character, Macbeth a "mixed" one: "Richard is only intrepid, Macbeth intrepid and feeling." The remorse of the more complex character distracts us awhile from his valor, but at the end, when the necessity for action drives out conscience, we see his natural courage assert itself with full vigor.

Kemble's interpretation of Macbeth is at all points the traditional one: He is a brave and virtuous man "driven into guilt by the instigations of others." Reacting against the remorse that "preys on his heart," his actions take on an "irregular fury"; yet he never loses his "original sense of right and justice," and his "original valour remains undiminished." In the theatre, writes Kemble, "rude and learned" spectators alike respond with admiration when they see the tyrant, "hated, abandoned, overwhelmed by calamity public and domestic—still persist, unshrinking, to brave his enemies." This fact alone is sufficient to "demonstrate" Shakespeare's intentions.[148]

Among the other actor-critics who reaffirmed the traditional view was Kemble's sister, the great SARAH SIDDONS. If anything, she outdid her predecessors in eulogizing Macbeth's original goodness: "though he is ambitious, he is yet amiable, conscientious, nay pious"; he was undoubtedly the first to suggest the murder, but on thinking it over, was so conscience-stricken that he would have relinquished his purpose if his "evil genius" had not appeared at that moment and "by the force of her revilings . . . chase[d] the

148. John Philip Kemble, *Macbeth and King Richard the Third: An Essay in Answer to Remarks on Some of the Characters of Shakespeare* (London, 1817), *passim. See* especially pp. 97-98, 161-62, 166-70.

gathering drops of humanity from his eyes." Mrs. Siddons plainly agreed with her brother, too, about Macbeth's courage, for she referred to the character as "a hero so dauntless" and she described Lady Macbeth's "aspersion of cowardice" as "opprobrious." It is true that her emphasis upon Macbeth's "irresolute and fluctuating temper" and upon his wife's "unbounded influence over him" may suggest lack of courage to some readers, but she evidently intended no such interpretation.[149] Earlier critics had mentioned Macbeth's irresolution before Duncan's murder as evidence of his humanity, not his weakness, and his wife's forcefulness simply as an extenuation of his guilt; Mrs. Siddons doubtless held the same opinion. She may have been concerned, however, lest on the stage her dominant Lady Macbeth detracted from the character of Macbeth as she conceived it. At any rate, her famous description of the ideal Lady Macbeth, so different in some ways from her own impersonation, grew out of her conviction that only feminine fascination, not force, could have subdued a hero of Macbeth's rectitude and valor. (Hannah Pritchard's Lady Macbeth had been just as domineering as Mrs. Siddons', apparently without reducing the stature of Macbeth. But Garrick was, of course, a greater actor than Kemble.) Ironically, but also logically (as we shall see later), the new conception of Lady Macbeth which developed from Mrs. Siddons' suggestion would be accompanied by a considerably debased conception of Macbeth.

The fact that a strong Lady Macbeth did not, in all minds, imply a weak Macbeth is illustrated by WILLIAM CHARLES MACREADY's criticism. For Macready admired Sarah Siddons tremendously and he also found Charlotte Cushman's interpretation congenial, yet he held a particularly exalted conception of Macbeth's nobility and courage. In describing "one of the most successful performances of Macbeth [he] ever saw" (his own, at Plymouth, April 26, 1841) he wrote:

The general tone of the character was lofty, manly, or indeed as it should be, heroic, that of one living to command. The whole view of the character was constantly in sight: the grief, the care, the doubt was not that of a weak person, but of a strong mind and of a strong man.

149. From Mrs. Siddons's essay on Lady Macbeth, published in Thomas Campbell's *Life of Mrs. Siddons* (London, 1839), p. 171. This book was first published in 1834, and Campbell remarked that he had first seen the essay about nineteen years earlier.

And on another occasion he recorded of his death scene: "My soul would have lived on from very force of will: death could not have been felt by a man so resolute to resist it."[150]

There were other actor-critics of the period, however, like FANNY KEMBLE[151] and SHERIDAN KNOWLES,[152] whose criticisms reflected the transition in the interpretation of Macbeth. Miss Kemble (niece of Sarah Siddons and John Philip Kemble) was perhaps the more radical in her concept of Macbeth's basic morality, Knowles in his concept of Macbeth's courage.

Both of these emphasized the traditional idea of progressive corruption. (Knowles even named four specific passages in the text that mark successive stages in the hero's degeneration.) Neither, however, described Macbeth as a moral paragon at the outset. Knowles hedged a bit: Macbeth's "nature," he said, "is not exactly attempered to the commission of crime. He can admit the thought [as a result of the prophecies] . . . but . . . [not] without shuddering." Shakespeare, therefore, provides "provocation" in Duncan's naming Malcolm as Prince of Cumberland. Miss Kemble put more stress upon the latent evil in Macbeth's nature which sprang to life in response to the evil Witches. She contrasted his reaction to the prophecies with that of his foil, Banquo: the latter, with the "moral sensibility of the true soul," recognized at once that the Witches were evil, but Macbeth went through a "troubled, perplexed, imperfect process, half mental, half moral" about whether the supernatural soliciting were good or ill. Fanny Kemble did not consider Macbeth a "destestable monster," as Francis Gentleman had done (indeed she credited him with a certain basic nobility), but she certainly would not have described him in her aunt's phrase, "conscientious, nay pious." Although she put great emphasis upon Lady Macbeth's influence, she also regarded Macbeth himself as an example of flawed humanity.

In discussing the question of physical courage, Miss Kemble combined, with some modifications of her own, the views of both of her illustrious relatives. The preservation of Macbeth's dignity and the audience's sympathy, she wrote, "in spite of the pre-

150. *Macready's Reminiscences and Selections from His Diaries*, ed. Sir Frederick Pollock (New York, 1875), pp. 481, 320 (diary entries for April 26, 1841, and November 10, 1834, respectively).
151. *Notes upon Some of Shakespeare's Plays*, pp. 21-22, 26, 29-34, 72-79.
152. *Lectures on Dramatic Literature: Macbeth*, pp. 43, 62.

ponderance of his wife's nature over his, depends on . . . his un-
doubted heroism . . . and his great tenderness for the woman whose
evil will is made powerful . . . partly by his affection for her."
She admitted that in the penultimate part of the play valiant
Macbeth is not himself: he is "like one drunk—maddened by the
poisonous inspiration of the hellish oracles," delirious with
"mingled doubt and dread" as he "clings, in spite of the gradual
revelation of its falsehood, to the juggling promise . . . of a charmed
life." But, she insisted, "no sooner is the mist of . . . delusion
swept from his mind . . . than the heroic nature of the man once
more proclaims itself." The charge that he lacked true courage
is "triumphantly refuted" in his final encounter with Macduff.
Physical hardihood, however, did not protect him from weakness
of character: the "bitter consciousness" of his own degradation,
though it spoke of his essential love of goodness, betokened also
(like the "morbid feeling of his own pulse") a kind of spiritual
hypochondria. Knowles, on the other hand, could not divorce
Macbeth's moral weakness from physical cowardice: indeed he
considered the latter a significant ingredient in the degeneration
of the character. Knowles's interpretation was much like George
Steevens', in fact, but more graphically expressed. The second
act of the play, he wrote, is

a luminous exposition of the revolting, hideous nature of guilt, and
of the agony and degradation which it entails. Contemplate Macbeth
in this act; and recall the image of the man who . . . [first] presented
himself to you, flushed with the honest pride of victory achieved in
a virtuous cause. What is he now? A livid, nerveless, quaking coward,
whose eyes are plucked out . . . by the sight of that with which the
havoc of a hundred fields has made them . . . perfectly at home.

Few later actors followed Knowles in the idea of physical
cowardice; either they took the traditional view of Macbeth's
courage championed by Kemble and Macready or they compromised on one similar to Fanny Kemble's. The difference in opinion was usually concerned, not with the fact of Macbeth's courage,
but with the amount of emphasis that it should receive on the
stage or the manner in which it should be projected. Must an
image of the hero be built up by a large, robust physique, a ring-
ing voice, and positive, straightforward action? Or do these
characteristics merely obscure an equally important side of Macbeth's character? The "sensibility" which Davies had considered

even more important than courage and the "creative Fancy" which Murphy had paired with superstition as the antithesis to that courage were now referred to as the "poetic" element in the character. And the question "Is Macbeth primarily a soldier or a poet?" became a commonplace of criticism. Where stage interpretation was concerned, no doubt, the decision to emphasize one aspect of his personality or the other depended to a great degree on the physical endowments of the individual actor.

This fact is well illustrated by two American Macbeths of the nineteenth century. Edwin Forrest, sturdy of figure and stentorian of voice, gave an excellent demonstration of Macbeth's strength but was utterly lacking in sensitivity. According to JAMES MURDOCH,

He looked at the air-drawn dagger with such an intense scrutiny that one would have supposed he deemed it a juggler's illusion, and in a certain sense he expressed a feeling of anger that he was not able to clutch it. His manner did not indicate that conscience, leagued with imagination, had conjured up the fearful agent to appall him. . . .[153]

On the other hand, the small and slender actor EDWIN BOOTH, conscious of his physical "inappropriateness . . . for the stalwart scot,"[154] depicted the character (as he himself said) "more as a weak man, 'full of the milk &c &c' than a strong brute."[155] Of Forrest's burly soldier he wrote to a friend, "I suppose it's envy, but it's d-d bad!"[156] Booth's portrayal of Macbeth was obviously suited to his physical resources, but it seems to have reflected as well his sincere preference for the gentler, more imaginative side of Shakespeare's tragic heroes. OTIS SKINNER described it, along with his Othello, as "infinitely poetic and lovely."[157] CHARLOTTE CUSHMAN, however, preferred a Macbeth of the Forrest school. When she acted Lady Macbeth with Booth she expressed interest in the latter's unusual interpretation but "good-naturedly dissented from it saying 'Macbeth is the great grandfather of all the Bowery ruffians.' "[158]

153. Lena Ashwell, *The Stage* (London, [1929]), pp. 324-25.

154. *See* Booth's letter to William Winter, dated April 2, 1880. MS in the Folger Library.

155. Letter to William Winter, June 2, [1878]. MS in the Folger Library.

156. Letter to Lt. Col. Adam Badeau, dated only October 14 [evidently the early 1860's]. MS in the Folger Library.

157. *Footlights and Spotlights* (Indianapolis, 1924), p. 99.

158. This anecdote is told by several writers. William Winter says that Booth

Meanwhile more serious onslaughts had been made on Macbeth's character by literary critics—this time on his basic morality. Francis Gentleman's wholesale condemnation had gone unheeded, apparently, for many years. But, as we have already mentioned, changes in the conception of Lady Macbeth were having their effect on the interpretation of her partner in greatness. Although actresses were among the early advocates of the new attitude toward the feminine role, it was nontheatrical writers who produced the correlative version of Macbeth's character. Thus William Maginn, who published a series of iconoclastic "Shakespeare Papers" in *Bentley's Miscellany* (1837-39), set out to write his fifth paper on Lady Macbeth, but in proving her humanity he spent an equal amount of time showing the evil nature of Macbeth. George Fletcher was another critic whose unsympathetic view of Macbeth can probably be traced to an interest in Lady Macbeth. His essay on the two characters, published first in the *Westminster Review* (1843) and again in his book *Studies of Shakespeare* (1847), is longer and more detailed than Maginn's but basically very similar. Both critics sought to depreciate the virtues that had been attributed to Macbeth: Maginn interpreted the descriptions of his warlike feats (in I, ii) as indications, not of nobility, but of a natural bloodthirstiness; and Fletcher discredited his poetic tendency by the argument that it proceeded, not from "a glowing or even a feeling heart," but "exclusively from a morbidly irritable fancy." In both interpretations Macbeth was the sole originator of the plot against Duncan's life. Lady Macbeth's description of her husband's nature was rejected in each case, on the ground that she was blinded by love or that she interpreted his character in terms of her own. Selfishness and callousness were considered Macbeth's dominant traits: his irresolution before the murder and his horror afterwards were attributed to fear of the consequences rather than compunction or remorse. Fletcher saw in the character "the greatest physical courage" but also "the most entire moral cowardice." He believed that Macbeth's morbid nervousness would have prevented his going through with the crime, despite his strong desire to do so, had he not been fortified by his wife's spirit. According to him, Shakespeare "has combined in Macbeth an eminently masculine person with a spirit in other

himself told the story to him (see *Shakespeare on the Stage*, First Series [New York, 1911], pp. 477-78).

respects eminently feminine, but utterly wanting the feminine generosity of affection."[159]

Although the "Shakespeare Papers" must have attracted some attention since they all flouted conventional interpretations (they tried to show, for example, that "Falstaff was in heart melancholy and Jaques gay"), it is uncertain how influential they were: Maginn himself complained that he had been accused of writing them, not to comment on Shakespeare, but to demonstrate his own powers of argument.[160] It is quite certain, however, that Fletcher's essay was influential—if not on the critics of his own day, then on the actors of thirty years later. For a copy of it belonged to the actress Helen Faucit, a Lady Macbeth after Fletcher's own heart; and when HENRY IRVING was preparing for his first London performance of Macbeth, Miss Faucit's husband sent the essay to him.[161] According to Irving's grandson, Laurence Irving, the great actor was "profoundly influenced" by Fletcher's analysis, and he modeled his controversial interpretation of Macbeth on it—both the one of 1875, with Kate Bateman as Lady Macbeth, and the one of 1888-89 with Ellen Terry.[162] (Since the latter did not open until December 29, 1888, it will be referred to hereafter as the 1889 production.)

In 1895 Irving gave an address at Owens College, Manchester, explaining his interpretation, and he repeated it in the same year at Columbia University in New York. In it he set forth one of the most extreme of all arguments for a basically evil Macbeth. Irving contended that a careful examination of the text refutes the traditional interpretation of Macbeth as a "good man gone wrong under the influence of a wicked and dominant wife" and shows him to be instead "one of the most bloody-minded, hypocritical villains in all [Shakespeare's] long gallery of portraits." The text

159. William Maginn, "Shakespeare Papers.—No. V. His Ladies.—I. Lady Macbeth," *Bentley's Miscellany*, II (1837), 550-67; George Fletcher, *Studies of Shakespeare* (London, 1847), pp. 109-98.

160. See his eighth paper, "Iago," *Bentley's Miscellany*, V (1839), 43.

161. Theodore Martin's letter to Irving, on the occasion of sending Fletcher's work, is in the Irving Archive of the British Theatre Museum. It was written at the Martins' summer home, Bryntysilio, near Llangollen, Wales, on July 15, 1875.

162. Laurence Irving, *Henry Irving: The Actor and His World, by His Grandson* (London, [1951]), pp. 260, 499. According to the author, Irving never changed the conception that he formed in 1875. Bram Stoker points out, however, that he added to it: for example, that after the production of 1875 he found out the significance of Malcolm's being made Prince of Cumberland (see his *Personal Reminiscences of Henry Irving* [New York, 1906,] I, 108).

makes clear, for example (I, vii, 47-54) , that "before the opening
of the play . . . Macbeth had not only thought of murdering
Duncan, but had even broached the subject to his wife, and that
this vague possibility became a resolute intention under stress of
unexpected developments." The prophecy of the Witches did not
in itself suggest murder: it was, in fact, rather natural, for Macbeth was the logical successor to the throne during Malcolm's
minority. (Irving pointed out, as others have done, that since
Scottish law debarred minors, Malcolm was not considered the
heir until Duncan appointed him Prince of Cumberland—a move
that gave Macbeth a legitimate grudge.) But, since Macbeth had
previously thought of murdering Duncan, the prophecy recalled
the idea to him with fresh force.

Like Fletcher, Irving considered Macbeth a physical hero but
a moral coward. His interpretation of these terms must have differed somewhat from Fletcher's, however. I suppose that the label
of "Coward" merely referred to Macbeth's underhanded treachery, for Irving did not consider his morbid fancies a deterrent to
action even for the most selfish of reasons.[163] Indeed he credited
Macbeth with "the true villain's nerve . . . when pressed to kill."
Again like Fletcher, Irving denied that the beautiful and sensitive
speeches are evidence of conscience or remorse with traces of his
original nobility. The actor's language was stronger than the literary critic's, however, and his description of Macbeth's psychology
was even more revolting. Macbeth, he said, was Shakespeare's
greatest poet—but only "with his brain." His apparent struggles
with conscience were really the deliberations of "an intellectual
voluptuary": he "played with the subject" of his proposed crime
and "cultivated assiduously a keen sense of [its] horrors"; "one can
imagine him even . . . weeping for the pain of the destined victim . . . so that action and reaction of poetic thought might send
emotional waves through the brain while the resolution was as
grimly fixed as steel and the heart as cold as ice." Thus in the

163. Mr. Laurence Irving tells us (in *Henry Irving*, p. 260): "On the margins of
the first pages of his own copy of the play Irving had scribbled—, "LIAR,
TRAITOR, COWARD—and this before Macbeth had met his wife." Irving, however, in his address on the character of Macbeth makes only one reference to
cowardice of any sort, and he puts a question mark after this: "a moral nature
with only sufficient weakness to quail (?) momentarily before superstitious terrors."
Since Irving stresses Macbeth's cold-blooded resoluteness, it is obvious that weakness of will had no part in his conception. His acting, however, apparently did not
make this point clear.

passage about "Pity like a naked new-born babe" Macbeth was indulging in the same kind of sentimentality as Lewis Carroll's Walrus, who when he joined the Carpenter in devouring the unsuspecting oysters, "With sobs and tears . . . sorted out those of the largest size." Such a determined villain obviously needed no persuasion to go through with the murder, but the hypocrite very likely "led his wife to believe that she was leading him on."[164]

All other considerations aside, Irving's interpretation had obvious flaws as far as the theatre was concerned. Why, for example, in his 1889 production did he pride himself upon the serious presentation of the Witches as dark and ominous representatives of supernatural evil? It would seem that if the Macbeth of Irving's conception were effectively brought to life on the stage, he would have little need of such Witches; this Macbeth, it is true, had a "poetic mind on which the presages and suggestions of supernatural things could work," but he did well enough in the satanic line without any suggestions from headquarters. It seems questionable, however, that Irving's conception of Macbeth is capable of complete realization in the theatre. For one thing, how would an actor make clear that when Macbeth appears to be horrorstricken he is merely throwing over his crime "the glamour of his own self-torturing thought"?[165]

If this conception, in all its subtlety, _could_ be communicated, it would seem that Irving, known for his psychological acting, was

164. Henry Irving, "The Character of Macbeth," in _Modern Eloquence_, ed. Thomas B. Reed (Philadelphia, 1901), VIII, 724-35.

165. Irving's friend Lady Pollock obviously did not understand the actor's intention here. Walter Herries Pollock, in his _Impressions of Henry Irving Gathered in Public and Private during a Friendship of Many Years_ (London, 1908), pp. 61-62, quotes from an unpublished criticism of Irving's first Macbeth which his mother wrote. She refers to Irving's lack of impressiveness after the murder, even though all the details were present: an attitude of terror, a hoarse whisper, bent knees, a dropped jaw; "it can only be said that he fails to excite general sympathy." She suggests that Irving lacked the "inward emotion sufficient to give truth to the effects intended," not realizing that the effect intended _was_ absence of "inward emotion." Lady Pollock could hardly have failed to misinterpret this scene, for both she and her son believed Irving's "idea throughout the tragedy" to be that of "an originally great, finely-strung nature dragged down by vaulting ambition to that very brutality by which alone it would have been possible to plunge into a sea of crime." It seems strange that Pollock should have held this idea, for he reports that he and Irving had a conversation in a cab prior to Irving's first performance in which the actor expressed his "general views" about the character. Apparently he misinterpreted what Irving said or superimposed the traditional concept upon some very "general" statements.

the one person capable of the achievement. In 1875, it is true, his intended effects may have been contradicted or obscured by Kate Bateman's strong, Siddons-like Lady Macbeth; but in 1889 the situation could hardly have been more favorable: not only did Ellen Terry's gentler Lady Macbeth allow more scope for his interpretation, but the production had all the advantages that could be given it at the height of Irving's Lyceum reign. Even so, his fellow players—including two members of his 1889 cast (ELLEN TERRY herself and JOHN MARTIN-HARVEY) — considered Irving less than successful in conveying his ideas on the stage. These were the same actors, too, who praised his understanding of Macbeth's character and described his lecture as "very convincing."[166] HENRY CHANCE NEWTON explained that "Irving lacked the physique, or physical intensity, to get his splendid psychological study of the Guilty Thane over the footlights."[167] But Irving's conception would not seem to demand a particularly robust frame, and nervous intensity was a valuable part of his histrionic equipment. Had John Philip Kemble been alive, he might have had something to say about interpretations that do not hold up in acting.

Despite some harsh reviews of the major characterizations, however, the *Macbeth* of Irving's maturity—a beautiful and impressive production—was a popular success: it ran for one hundred fifty-one nights in London and was later taken to America. And Irving's own performance, though it was not all that he intended, was a landmark in the stage interpretation of Macbeth. Even if his morbid sensitivity gave the effect of real rather than pretended irresolution, it did not quite cancel out the effect of cruelty: thus the performance was a genuine experiment in the possibility of a basically evil Macbeth. Its influence on later actors, however, was probably greater in other ways. For example, more than one of them, whatever his own conception of the character, has attempted to reproduce Irving's famous look of a "famished wolf" (as Ellen Terry described him) in the last act. And some of them, no doubt, have been encouraged to adopt the "poetic" rather than the "soldierly" interpretation; for Irving was more successful in suggesting the morbid sensitivity that he saw in Macbeth than the "physical heroism of those who are born to kill."

166. Ellen Terry, *The Story of My Life* (London, 1908), p. 303; John Martin-Harvey, *Autobiography* (London, [1933]), p. 107.
167. *Cues and Curtain Calls* (London, 1927), p. 34.

Naturally there were some actor-critics who objected, not simply to Irving's stage portrayal, but to his whole conception of the character. One was JOSEPH JEFFERSON of *Rip Van Winkle* fame. During one of Irving's visits to New York, Jefferson called on him, and the two had a brief debate on the subject. Jefferson "pointed out that for a villain [Macbeth] made some fine philosophical speeches," and, to Irving's explanation that these were "intended to be satirical," he rejoined that "Shakespeare always makes his characters reveal their true selves when they soliloquize." Since Irving could hardly accept that dictum, and since Jefferson felt presumptuous, as a comedian, in pressing his opinions about tragedy, the argument ended there. But the objectionable theory rankled in Jefferson's mind, and he later relieved his frustration by expounding to a younger, more attentive actor his own unshakable convictions about the character. "Macbeth is a good man at the beginning of the play," he insisted. "He is so wrapped about with integrity that all the efforts of the witches—not one, but three—are necessary to shake him. To hold [otherwise] . . . is to hold that the play is a melodrama." To support his argument he resorted to that favorite sport of critics, contrasting Macbeth with Richard of Gloucester (this time in *III Henry VI* instead of *Richard III*). The two men's attitudes toward bloodshed are well epitomized, Jefferson thought, in Richard's ironic soliloquy after his murder of Henry VI ("See how my sword weeps for the poor king's death. . . .") and Macbeth's speech urging Macduff to avoid an encounter at arms (". . . my soul is too much charged / With blood of thine already") .[168]

Another actor-critic who disagreed with Irving's interpretation was GEORGE R. FOSS. Irving himself, he pointed out, had found "a soul of beauty in things evil" when he acted the murderer Mathias in *The Bells*. If he could transform that "petty melodrama" as he did by revealing "something lovable" in the villain, surely he could have applied the same understanding to Macbeth![169] Since Foss's criticism really belongs to the next generation (he was just nineteen when Irving's 1889 *Macbeth* was produced), we shall return to him later for his own interpretation of the character.

168. Francis Wilson, *Joseph Jefferson: Reminiscences of a Fellow Player* (New York, 1906), pp. 69-73.
169. *What the Author Meant*, p. 56.

In 1890, when Irving's portrayal of an evil Macbeth was still news, a retired veteran of the American stage, James Murdoch, wrote an article not only reasserting the traditional view of Macbeth but doing so in such exaggerated fashion that the word "sympathetic" is too mild to describe it. Although Murdoch may have been partly inspired by a desire to refute the controversial new conception, his criticism of stage performances was not aimed specifically at Irving or solely at the morbidly cruel Macbeth. Rather, he expressed concern about the tendency of actors to overemphasize any single aspect of Macbeth's character and thus to distort the figure as a whole. Like Arthur Murphy in the preceding century, Murdoch pointed out the paradoxical traits in the character, each of them strongly developed. For example, he considered Macbeth's heroism consistent and undiminished throughout the play: he explained the momentary reluctance to fight with Macduff as the result of superstition, not cowardice—"a superstition that . . . gave way before the flood of fiery spirit started by Macduff's word 'Coward.'" At the same time, he insisted upon the "overtopping greatness of Macbeth's imagination": "he heard the shrieking and howling of the exultant furies, while his wife could not rise above the commonplace sounds of the owl and the cricket." Similarly he balanced Macbeth's usual intrepidity with his irresolution in the matter of Duncan's murder—an irresolution born of his natural tenderness and humanity. It was only to make clear the original goodness of the character, he argued, that Shakespeare depicted Macbeth as "wavering and undecided, and yielding at first but temporarily to the more daring spirit of his wife." But actors, mistaking this intention, have gone to extremes in one direction or the other, giving the effect of either ruthless determination or "shrinking cowardice."

In his attempt to reconcile the contradictions in Macbeth's character Murdoch appealed to his favorite principle of ideality. And it was here that he lost touch, not simply with realism, but with the reality of Shakespeare's text.

The ideal is the informing principle of all poetry magnifying man's greatness and concealing . . . his weaknesses, uniting in one person to a surpassing degree the most excellent qualities of both sexes and elevating mankind almost to godship. In the whole range of poetry perhaps no hero approaches the height of ideality upon which Macbeth is enthroned.

Because of this impossibly elevated notion of Macbeth's character, Murdoch could explain his fall only by a tremendous emphasis upon the malignant power of the Witches: "What a reader or spectator is asked to behold in Macbeth is the soul of a hero almost god-like . . . solicited, overmastered, and finally betrayed by the powers of darkness."[170] But we need not accept literally the old actor's Promethean vision of Macbeth in order to find a timely value in his synthetic approach to the character.

In the present century the Macbeths of the stage have differed, as they did in the preceding period, according to individual physique and histrionic style as much as personal interpretation. For example, Beerbohm Tree never succeeded in representing the "soldier," though, judging by his wife's comments, he recognized that the fifth act, at least, demanded such a character. But his soliloquies were memorable because of the "wistful distraught face, the wistful distraught voice," and in the witch scenes, the murder scene, and the scene with Banquo's Ghost his "wild tragic intensity" achieved what LADY TREE considered the "essential effect that a great Macbeth must make: to make the blood run cold!"[171] SIR MICHAEL REDGRAVE, on the other hand, has been described as "a strong and vigorous rather than an imaginative Macbeth"[172]—though he privately believed that Macbeth was neither a courageous soldier nor a great poet.[173]

Written criticisms by modern actors show more definite trends. In the first place, these criticisms reveal very little, if any, influence from Henry Irving's avowed interpretation. Nearly all of them represent Macbeth as a sympathetic character—in the beginning, at any rate. Most actor-critics would agree with SIR LEWIS CASSON, no doubt, that if the protagonists are regarded as "criminals from the first" the drama loses much of its "poignancy."[174] Both he and GEORGE SKILLAN stress the necessity for establishing at the outset a strong positive image of the hero—as the latter puts it, to make as graphic as possible "the mighty valour of MACBETH, his tremendous spirit as a fighter, his virtue

170. "A Short Study of 'Macbeth,'" pp. 74-76, 79-80.
171. "Herbert and I," in *Herbert Beerbohm Tree: Some Memories of Him and His Art*, ed. Max Beerbohm (New York, [1920]), p. 150.
172. Crosse, *Shakespearean Playgoing 1890-1952*, p. 150.
173. "Shakespeare and the Actors," pp. 138-40.
174. Introduction to the Folio Society edition of *Macbeth*, p. 6.

as a king's champion."[175] Except for Redgrave, none of the modern actor-critics deny either Macbeth's courage or his original nobility. They do see tragic flaws, or potential flaws, in his character, but even those who stress such characteristics speak of moral weakness rather than moral cowardice. There is considerable emphasis, in some cases, upon his poetic imagination, but on the whole there is even more emphasis upon his heroic qualities. Although none of the recent actors have apotheosized Macbeth as James Murdoch did, a number of them have seen a kind of grandeur in his character. HARLEY GRANVILLE-BARKER wrote, for example, "About him there must be something colossal. . . . Macbeth is a valiant man and, even before he becomes king, of an almost regal demeanor."[176]

The heroic tendency in modern criticism of Macbeth is partly due to the influence of the Shakespearean scholar and critic A. C. Bradley. Granville-Barker's criticism particularly shows his influence, both by direct reference and by obvious borrowing of some basic ideas. There are individual differences, of course: Granville-Barker's final view of Macbeth, for example, seems to be more austere—the modern word is "alienated"—than Bradley's. Even at points where the interpretation is exactly the same, as in that of the banquet scene, Granville-Barker's original details make his description of Macbeth's behavior worth reading as a separate piece of criticism. But Bradley's firm rejection of the idea that Macbeth is "a half-hearted, cowardly criminal," his insistence upon the grandeur and even sublimity of the character, and, most of all, his discussion of the "remarkable *development*" of Macbeth's character after his first murder[177]—all have left their mark not only upon Granville-Barker's interpretation but upon a number of interpretations by later actor-critics. To a great degree Redgrave is probably right in blaming Bradley for the "great terrifying" figure that actors of Macbeth strive to represent and that audiences have come to expect.

But obviously neither Bradley nor any other critic could have seized the imagination of actors if there had not been something in their own reading of the character—and particularly in their own understanding of the requirements and possibilities of the

175. *Macbeth. French's Acting Edition*, p. 60.
176. *The Players' Shakespeare: The Tragedie of Macbeth*, p. xl.
177. *Shakespearean Tragedy*, pp. 351-65.

stage—that responded to his suggestions. One important reason for the triumph of the heroic tendency in modern criticism rather than the cowardly, the innately villainous, or the merely poetic is the desire to restore Macbeth to a central and dominant position in the tragedy—a position that, according to WILLIAM POEL[178] and George R. Foss,[179] among others, was too long usurped by Lady Macbeth. As the latter expressed it, the idea of a "poor-spirited henpecked" Macbeth had to be overcome if the play was to make its proper effect on the stage.

Although both of these actor-critics found an element of greatness in Macbeth, their interpretations of the character differed widely. Poel argued that Macbeth is a greater criminal than Lady Macbeth—not because he is basically evil but because, despite his keener conscience and better judgment, he allows himself "to be influenced, out of connubial love, into an action of which he knows his wife to be incapable of foreseeing the consequences." Playing Adam to an inferior but appealing Eve did not strike Poel as a weak role. Indeed this Adam seemed to him a Faust-like figure who, knowing the stakes, made a "daring attempt to defeat the supernatural." Foss, however, felt the need for sympathy as well as stature in the portrayal of Macbeth. He interpreted the character as a "thoroughly good man" who falls to temptation and commits a great sin—but not an unforgivable sin, as the wretched murderer believes. The tragedy is that, thinking himself damned, Macbeth sets his teeth and sinks "deeper and deeper into the mire." "His struggles to save something out of the ruin of his soul, either a little peace for himself or a legacy for his children" are pathetic, and his "despair," if it were well acted, would be "heart-rending."

Although few actor-critics have been willing to subordinate Lady Macbeth to the extent that Poel did, a number of them have adopted interpretations which reduce the effect of her dominance: for example, that husband and wife are equal partners in responsibility or that during the course of the play there is an exchange of "roles," Macbeth's evil strength in the last three acts counterbalancing Lady Macbeth's in the first two. Both of these ideas are found in H. B. IRVING's discussion,[180] and in Sir Lewis Cas-

178. *Shakespeare in the Theatre*, pp. 68-69.
179. *What the Author Meant*, p. 56.
180. *A Book of Remarkable Criminals* (London, [1918]), pp. 14-17.

son's.[181] These critics agree that the thought of murdering Duncan occurred to each of the Macbeths independently. According to Irving, the temptation came to Macbeth upon hearing the prophecies of the Witches, to Lady Macbeth upon reading of them in the letter. Casson argues that murder did not enter Macbeth's mind until Duncan suddenly named "the boy Malcolm" as successor to the throne, an honor that Macbeth himself had, with good reason, expected; and he suggests that, although Lady Macbeth was tempted when she read the letter, she did not actually embrace the temptation until she received the news of Duncan's coming. Casson interprets the first scene between husband and wife as a "fencing match," each trying to make the other give words to the thought; he postulates a lost scene in which Macbeth finally broached the subject; but he also notes that Macbeth later repented of his plan and would not have gone through with it except for the "passionate taunts" of his wife. Irving points out that, although the "germ" of evil was latent in both Macbeths, neither was ruthless enough to carry out the crime alone. Lady Macbeth had the stronger will for the deed, but even she could not kill the sleeping Duncan with her own hands. Only after "a deal of boggling and at serious risk of untimely interruption" did the two manage to perform the murder and smear the grooms with blood. But, "like so many criminals," Macbeth could not stop with his first crime. His sensibilities became dulled, and his "moral repugnance," originally stronger than his wife's, was now diminished until he was the more ruthless of the two. Casson makes the same point about the hardening of Macbeth's conscience.

At least two modern actor-critics—DAME FLORA ROBSON[182] and George Skillan[183]—have expressed the traditional view that Lady Macbeth was the dominant influence in Duncan's murder. But in each case there are other elements in the interpretation that help to offset the idea of Macbeth as a dependent weakling. Although Skillan points out a specific weakness in Macbeth's temperament which gave Lady Macbeth her psychological leverage (a matter to which we shall return when we discuss the more

181. Introduction to the Folio Society edition of *Macbeth*, pp. 6-11, especially pp. 6-7.
182. Flora Robson, "Notes on Playing the Role of Lady Macbeth," *Macbeth. The Laurel Shakespeare* (New York, 1959), pp. 27-31.
183. *Macbeth. French's Acting Edition*, pp. 67-69.

vulnerable side of the character), he puts so much emphasis upon Macbeth's military prowess, his intellectual acumen, and his basic integrity that it is difficult not to think of the total conception as heroic. As for Dame Flora, she assumes that a headstrong Lady Macbeth initiated the murder plot and persuaded her husband to undertake it against his own conscience, but she insists even more emphatically than H. B. Irving on the reversal of the two characters' attitudes later in the play.

If one version of the heroic Macbeth is accepted, the very change from humanity to brutality contributes to the stature of the character. For, as several actor-critics have noticed, the degeneration of Macbeth's morality is accompanied by a positive development—frightful but impressive—in another part of his character. Granville-Barker,[184] for example, points out that in the latter part of the play Macbeth's courage and will power remain tremendous in spite of reverses that would dismay a normal person. "His nerves may give way, but he will not be the victim of his nerves." In the banquet scene, when the Ghost vanishes the first time, Macbeth "dares it to come again, he drinks again to Banquo, his voice rises to the toast, clear, hearty, defiant. He means to test himself. . . . And though he trembles still, it would seem that he wins. . . ." As he "loses humanity, he seems somehow to grow in physical strength. The power that went to make him man now goes to make him doubly brute, till, at the end, tied to a stake, he fights and dies like a wild beast. . . ." Casson's conception[185] is similar: By the last act the man who reacted with "wild hysteria" to his first crime has become the "incarnation of triumphant evil, inhuman, callous, and utterly defiant of the forces of retribution. . . ."

Neither Granville-Barker nor Casson permits this brutal and fiendlike Macbeth to win any sympathy, regardless of his original nobility. Casson warns that "slow or sentimental playing" destroys the effect of the "rapid alternating scenes, Macbeth within the castle and the nemesis approaching from without," which, "if played with passion, speed and energy build up to a tremendous climax in the final combat between Evil and Good." The crux is the "Tomorrow" speech, a "challenging devil's creed of nihilism and atheism," which actors too often convert into "the solemn

184. *The Players' Shakespeare: The Tragedie of Macbeth*, p. xlii.
185. Introduction to the Folio Society edition of *Macbeth*, p. 11.

hymn of a repentant sinner." "Life's but . . . a tale told by an idiot" is "the supreme blasphemy, and it is answered at once by the Jove's thunderbolt of the Birnam Wood messenger." Similarly, Granville-Barker insists upon the bombastic element in Macbeth's "last fling of words" before the mortal duel with Macduff: though it has offended some critics, it is Shakespeare's intentional effect. There must be a "mighty combat," since any easy vengeance for Macduff would be "unsatisfying" and an easy defeat for Macbeth would be "incredible." But if Macbeth were also given a "finely worded end," it "would seem to redeem him, if ever so little. This Shakespeare will not do. He allows him one gleam of incorrigible pride, he leaves him his animal courage. For the rest, he sends him shouting to hell." That last phrase is evidently metaphorical. For in Granville-Barker's interpretation, *Macbeth*, a "tragedy of the unchecked will," shows us the self-damnation, in this present world, of the man who is willing to "jump the life to come." What we witness is Macbeth's gradual killing of his own soul. This explains why, in the interpretations we have just discussed, Macbeth at the end of the play is a totally different character from what he was at the beginning. The change is horrifying, yet the character, in his progress from nobility to brutality, never ceases to possess magnitude and strength.

Needless to say, the more traditional version of the heroic Macbeth—particularly the "great soul" envisioned by Foss—is less grim and inhuman at the end of the play. Advocates of this interpretation would wring every drop of sympathy from the "To-morrow" speech, add humanizing touches to the character wherever they could, and, of course, make the fight with Macduff as valiant as possible. Foss himself makes several suggestions for staging the play in order to increase the audience's sympathy and admiration for the hero. For example, pathos could be won by means of the character Seyton if he were portrayed throughout the play as a devoted follower of Macbeth: Seyton could be Macbeth's armor-bearer and page in Act I, the messenger who brings the letter to Lady Macbeth; later he could weep when he reports the Queen's death. "The horror and hatred by which Macbeth is surrounded is emphasized if he has one blindly devoted admirer." Foss would handle Macbeth's final combat so as to emphasize his near-invincibility as a warrior:

When he sees that the castle is taken, Macbeth should undo some joints in his armour—or unlace his chain-mail—in order to kill himself, before he says:
> Why should I play the Roman fool and die
> On my own sword?
And through this opening in his armour Macduff is able to kill him.
I think that in the final combat Macbeth should nearly succeed, disarm Macduff and beat him to his knees. Then just as Macbeth fancies he is going to conquer fate, Macduff should find this unguarded part with his dirk.[186]

Although a heroic Macbeth of one kind or another dominates the criticisms by modern actors, there are also a few interpretations that present a somewhat weaker view of the character. These do not deny Macbeth's courage, but they put so much emphasis on his suggestibility that they seem to imply a certain weakness of the will. As in criticisms of an earlier day, this flaw is linked with Macbeth's sensitivity and imagination—the "poetic" side of the character.

George Skillan's interpretation, which emphasizes Lady Macbeth's influence, has already been referred to briefly. The Macbeth that it presents is heroic in many respects yet weak enough morally to be wrought to her purpose by his unscrupulous wife. Skillan traces the corruption of Macbeth's better nature to the instability of his temperament, which lends itself to the workings of a highly-charged imagination. Naturally inclined toward the career of a valiant and honorable soldier, Macbeth reacts with horror when his wife broaches the "strange and hostile" idea of murder. But Lady Macbeth, "with remorseless persistence, drives against this finer instinct." By representing the murder as a "great quell" and by making it seem cowardly to draw back from it, she distorts his sense of courage. Under her intoxicating influence, Macbeth's "volatile nature is now as exalted as it was dejected." It is as if his power of choice were drugged, and, keyed up with a false sense of mission, he goes through with the crime. Thus we feel in his situation "the pathos of a fundamentally brave man galvanized into a perverted enterprise."[187]

The other actor-critics who trace Macbeth's fall to his extreme suggestibility emphasize the influence of the supernatural. LENA ASHWELL, for example, describes Macbeth as not only "brilliantly

186. *What the Author Meant*, pp. 57-58.
187. *Macbeth, French's Acting Edition*, pp. 67-69.

imaginative, morbidly neurotic" but also "strongly clairvoyant and clairaudient." According to her, his basically admirable character, full of "fine manhood and rare tenderness," is flawed by a Lucifer-like ambition; and through this flaw "foul spirits" gain entrance to his passively receptive mind. He becomes "obsessed and guided" by them, "ghost-haunted, maddened," and finally driven to destruction.[188] MARGARET WEBSTER also emphasizes Macbeth's almost psychic responsiveness to "every vibration of the atmosphere around him." Although she affirms the "duality" of his nature—soldier as well as poet—she is clearly less interested in his "enormous physical courage" than in his "preternaturally sharp" senses which translate sights and sounds into "vivid surrealistic images of a dream." In her interpretation, Macbeth's sensitive imagination makes him vulnerable to the strong reproaches of conscience. Though reluctant at first to "yield to that suggestion," he becomes more and more committed to his evil course. He must now throw himself into a "doomed frenzy of murder" in an effort to blunt his sensitivity, "lest imagination should come alive again and significance should flood back over the ashen, relentless path he is traveling."[189]

Several actor-critics who emphasize the supernatural influence see in Macbeth's actions a kind of automatism. Margaret Webster, for example, describes the latter phase of his story as "the driven, haunted slavery of one who has indeed given 'his eternal jewel' to the 'common enemy of man.'" GORDON CRAIG describes another kind of supernatural bondage, one that begins earlier in the play and releases its hold on Macbeth before the end. His interpretation assumes the existence of spirits whose duty it is to "test the strength of men by playing with their force upon the weakness of women." Lady Macbeth is weak—Shakespeare's weakest character, perhaps—and therefore the spirits possess and control her. She becomes their medium, and Macbeth, in turn, is hers. Thus we see the latter in the first four acts as if in a hypnotic trance. In the last act the spell is broken, and Macbeth "almost seems to be a new role. He is not the man some actors show him to be, the trapped, cowardly villain; nor yet is he . . . the bold, courageous villain as other actors play him. He is as a doomed man who has been suddenly awakened on the morning

188. *Reflections from Shakespeare*, pp. 121-23.
189. *Shakespeare Without Tears*, pp. 223-25.

of execution."[190] ROBERT SPEAIGHT differs from the other actor-critics of this group because he attributes a stronger will to Macbeth at the beginning of the play. According to him, Macbeth makes a deliberate Faustian contract in deciding to murder Duncan, and after this his will is bound by its terms: knowing the worth of his soul, he is powerless to reclaim it; his "conscience . . . can feel to the limits of torture but remains numb to the healing of grace."[191]

The difficulties in the interpretation of Macbeth have come chiefly, I believe, from the great compression of the play. What we are meant to see is exactly what most actor-critics have thought: the downward plunge of a courageous and basically noble character. But since Macbeth stands on the very brink when we first see him, there is no opportunity to show him in the performance of noble or courageous actions. Indeed his fall is so precipitous that, if we confine ourselves to Macbeth's actions and the literal meaning of his speeches, we find it easy to understand Gentleman's belief, and Irving's, that the man was evil from the first. Shakespeare's techniques for overcoming this difficulty are, first, to establish Macbeth as a hero through the epic-like speeches by the Bleeding Sergeant and Ross; second, to lift the character out of the realm of common villainy by endowing him with sensitivity and imagination; and, third, to point up the greatness of the temptation that assails him by using the supernatural element, as well as the strong Lady Macbeth. But the second and third of these are subject to misinterpretation, and so they do not always perform their proper function. Let us briefly consider these two points.

In the first place, I believe that A. C. Bradley is correct in describing the function of Macbeth's imagination: it is not evidence of weakness or morbidity; it is the messenger of his moral nature, warning him from or punishing him for evil. It is thus, as Bradley says, the best part of him. To read the soliloquy "If it were done. . . ." with attention only to the literal meaning of the words would lead to the idea, held by Fletcher and Maginn and later by Irving, that Macbeth is concerned only with the possible consequences to himself, not with the horror of the contemplated murder. But this is not the impression that we receive when we

190. *On the Art of the Theatre*, pp. 269-77.
191. *Nature in Shakespearian Tragedy*, p. 67.

listen to the speech, effectively spoken, without trying to analyze it. The imagery, as Bradley pointed out, suggests a deeper concern that Macbeth does not express in so many words. (Coleridge held a similar interpretation.) All of this is simply to put in theoretical language the traditional interpretation of the stage in the time of Garrick and Kemble. But, as we saw earlier, Garrick's vivid display of fear and horror arising from Macbeth's imagination, linked with conscience, may have helped to put his courage in doubt. Certainly a less gifted actor, attempting to imitate Garrick's method, would have been likely to produce this effect. Except for the passage in the murder scene (where Macbeth must be really paralyzed by the horror of his deed), the most imaginative speeches should be spoken, I think, not with the trembling voice of a neurotic, but with the exalted tone of a seer—one who is "rapt" by visions that thrill even as they appall.

As for the supernatural element, we have already noted that an overemphasis on its deterministic force reduces Macbeth's significance, making him a mere puppet of fate. But it is as bad, or worse, to eliminate the supernatural in the manner advocated by Guthrie and Campbell. Devilish temptation is important in Shakespeare's play, and the Weird Sisters, who are the instruments of this temptation, help to enforce the awesome implications that *Macbeth* offers about man's capacity for evil and its frightening relationship with his capacity for greatness. Bradley argues that "temptation" is too strong a word, since the Witches utter no syllable about murder, and that Macbeth interprets the prophecies as "supernatural soliciting" only because he has already entertained the idea of murder. But it is not only Macbeth who so interprets them. Banquo warns Macbeth not to trust the Witches, whose prophecies might "kindle" him to the crown; he rightly suspects them to be "instruments of darkness" who "Win us with honest trifles to betray's / In deepest consequence." And later Banquo himself, though he suppresses the evil influence in his waking hours, is plagued by "cursed thoughts" when he dreams of the Weird Sisters. No, these Sisters are not neutral toward Macbeth; they have designs on him. They resort to charms on each occasion when they expect to see him; this means that they are calling on a power outside themselves for assistance in dealing with him. Their prophecies, innocuous in themselves, are thus clothed in a suggestive power which appeals to his imagination and stirs a response in his ambitious thoughts. We must know what kind of creatures the Weird Sisters are before Macbeth meets them, so that we will not be taken in by "things that do sound so fair" and so that we will realize the potency of the temptation against which Macbeth must fight. That is why the first scene is important, and also the "hocus-pocus" preliminary to Macbeth's appearance in scene iii. We must know that Banquo is right about these instruments of darkness, yet see in the very next speech that temptation is strongly at work in Macbeth: the evil in the Witches' influence has spoken directly to the evil in Macbeth's own nature and has presented murder to his consciousness so vividly that it is more real to him than his present surroundings.

When I speak of the evil in Macbeth's own nature I do not mean that he is a villain from the beginning—not at all. If he were, the temptation would be unnecessary. But, like other "good" men, he has the possibility of evil within him, and it is to this that the Witches speak. We are meant to receive the impression, I feel, that the temptation first enters Macbeth's mind, with terrifying force, as he is "rapt" by the prophecies. It is a new and startlingly sudden thought, not the reminder of a predetermined plot or the focusing of a previously vague temptation, which has the power to shake his "single state of man" to its foundations. When Lady Macbeth, after reading of the prophecies, fears that her husband is "too full of the milk of human kindness/ To catch the nearest way," she gives not the slightest hint that he has ever suggested murder to her, much less sworn to do it. It is only later, in the height of passion, that Lady Macbeth speaks the famous passage with the stumbling block in it: "What beast was it then? . . ." The speech sounds realistic at the moment, but I do not think it is deliberately designed to send our minds back to reëxamining Macbeth's character or wondering just when it was that he "broke the enterprise" to his wife. Its chief purpose is to lead up to Lady Macbeth's horrifying assertion that she would kill her own baby rather than fail in a sworn purpose, and thus to lend a compelling power to her persuasiveness.

In *Macbeth*, as in *Othello*, Shakespeare is giving us a highly concentrated, much contracted story of a man's fall from nobility. There are many differences between the two men and the two stories, but there is one likeness: the fall is much more precipitate than would be realistically probable, and outside agency is used as a kind of short cut. Not that, given enough time, Othello would have fallen anyway, without Iago—not within the bounds of Shakespeare's imagined circumstances. But the realistic fall of such a character, in *any* circumstances, is difficult to imagine in the time covered by Shakespeare's play. Iago, by visibly demonstrating the constantly applied pressure, makes the fall dramatically if not realistically convincing. The Witches, and of course Lady Macbeth, do something of the same thing for Macbeth. And if Macbeth is not *played* as a weakling, the very fact that forces of such strength must be brought to bear upon him should demonstrate that he is himself a strong character.

LADY MACBETH

There are two principal questions about Lady Macbeth that have polarized the opinions of actor-critics. First: Is she a "fiend"—a terrible though possibly magnificent incarnation of evil? Or is she a recognizable, perhaps even a sympathetic, human being? And second: Is she "masculine"—imposing of figure and domineering of manner? Or is she "feminine"—either a wily temptress or a devoted wife, but, in any case, graceful and charming? At some points the answers to these questions overlap; for, regardless of the truism about "the female of the species," the more feminine Lady Macbeth has been made on the stage, the less fiendlike she has usually seemed.

In Garrick's age the traditional "good" Macbeth was usually accompanied by a "fiendlike queen." And Hannah Pritchard, who played Lady Macbeth to Garrick himself, was a particularly striking example. According to THOMAS DAVIES, she revealed "a mind insensible to compunction and inflexibly bent to gain its purpose. When she snatched the daggers from the remorseful and irresolute Macbeth, despising the agitations of a mind unaccustomed to guilt, . . . she presented to the audience a picture of the most consummate intrepidity in mischief." Davies was full of admiration for Mrs. Pritchard's performance, for it fully accorded with his own understanding of the character. He considered Lady Macbeth the "chief agent" of Shakespeare's plot, "a woman of unbounded ambition, divested of all human feelings," who, "to gain a crown, urges her reluctant husband to the murder of the king." In his opinion, Lady Macbeth not only instigates murder but "enjoys the fact when it is done." Her "undaunted spirit and determinedly wicked resolution" can be matched only by Aeschylus' Clytemnestra, a character that she resembles, too, in haughtiness and artful cruelty.[192]

It is obvious that such a Lady Macbeth could help to lighten the guilt of her husband and thus create some sympathy for him. And it would seem that the opposite might be true as well: that the concept of an "evil" Macbeth would suggest a softened attitude toward the lady. This kind of reversal, in fact, was to occur in a later period. But, according to FRANCIS GENTLEMAN, sole detractor of Macbeth in Garrick's age, the villainous hero shares his "aggravated load of guilt" with a "matchless lady" who exerts "uncommon talents of temptation." Despite her "savage inhumanity," Lady Macbeth seemed to Gentleman a "possible picture of the fair sex." But surely, he thought, "such sympathetic barbarity" as exists between this husband and wife "was never in nature!"[193]

Even at that time, however, when the conception of "fiendlike queen" remained unchallenged, there was one potential source of sympathy for Lady Macbeth—the powerful sleepwalking scene. It was this scene that COLLEY CIBBER remembered from early in the century when Mrs. Betterton had acted the role with her famous husband: he particularly admired her ability to "throw out those quick and careless [i.e. spontaneous] Strokes of Terror, from the Disorder of a guilty Mind" with a naturalness "that render'd them at once tremendous, and delightful."[194] Hannah Pritchard, too, for all the inhuman ruthlessness that she gave the character in the earlier scenes, was memorable for her depiction of "the terrours of a guilty conscience" which "keep the mind broad awake while the body sleeps." Davies compared her acting of Lady Macbeth's remorse to "those sudden flashes of lightning which more accurately discover the horrours of surrounding darkness."[195] The contrast between Lady Macbeth's usual invulnerability of spirit and her suffering in the sleepwalking scene struck Gentleman as well as Davies: the revelation of "the tormenting effects of a thorny conscience galling that female fiend beyond

---

192. *Dramatic Miscellanies*, II, 129; *Memoirs of Garrick*, II, 135-36.

193. *Dramatic Censor*, I, 84-85, 90.

194. *An Apology for the Life of Mr. Colley Cibber*, ed. Robert W. Lowe (London, 1889), I, 161-62.

195. *Memoirs of Garrick*, II, 135-36.

all power of disguise or composure" is the more pleasing because "it approaches us unaware, and beautifully vindicates the justice of providence, *even here upon this bank and shoal of time.*"[196] For Gentleman, and perhaps for Davies, Lady Macbeth's remorse was a punishment for her crimes, not an indication of her humanity. But with Mrs. Siddons would come a fuller recognition of its possible implications for the character.

Lady Macbeth's fiendishness was lifted above the sordid level, even before Mrs. Siddons. After all, there is a Lucifer-like grandeur associated with the idea of indomitable evil, and the figure of Clytemnestra (to which Davies compared Lady Macbeth) is not simply wicked but awe-inspiring. Cibber used the word "tremendous" of Mrs. Betterton's Lady Macbeth (though it must be admitted that he said nothing about her fiendlike nature). And MARY ANNE YATES, a Lady Macbeth contemporary with Mrs. Pritchard, remarked that this character's "dreadful cruelty" is dignified by the glory of her object—a crown—and that the "excess of such a passion as ambition, gives an importance to the part which supports an actress in its representation."[197]

With SARAH SIDDONS, however, the latent sublimity of the character was realized as never before or since. In Hazlitt's well-known words, "It seemed almost as if a being of a superior order had dropped from a higher sphere to awe the world with the majesty of her appearance. Power was seated on her brow, passion emanated from her breast as from a shrine; she was tragedy personified."[198] G. J. Bell's notes on Mrs. Siddons' performance provide details: for example, the "exalted, prophetic tone" with which she read Macbeth's letter about the Weird Sisters and the "slow hollow whisper" with which she spoke the invocation to the spirits of evil, her "voice quite supernatural, as in a horrible dream."[199] But, although she transcended Mrs. Pritchard in

196. *Dramatic Censor,* I, 98-99.

197. MS letter of December 25, 1782, in the Folger Library. The recipient was an Edinburgh playwright who had sent a tragedy for Mrs. Yates's consideration. The actress expressed dislike for the character Agnes in the play (the part that she would be expected to act), saying that, unlike Lady Macbeth, she is not supported by "that dignity of sentiment which alone cou'd throw light on the dreadful gloom which surrounds her, and reconcile us to so unnatural an exhibition as *female* cruelty in excess."

198. *See* the essay on "Macbeth" in "Characters of Shakespeare's Plays," *Complete Works of Hazlitt,* ed. P. P. Howe (London and Toronto, 1930-34), IV, 188-90.

199. Fleeming Jenkin, "Mrs. Siddons as Lady Macbeth: From Contemporary

poetic power, Mrs. Siddons evidently adhered, in the first act and much of the second, to the basic conception held by the earlier actress. In his notes, particularly those on the early scenes, Bell makes vivid for us her "turbulent and inhuman strength of spirit." "Like Macbeth's evil genius she hurries him on in the mad career of ambition and cruelty from which his nature would have shrunk." Only in the murder scene, apparently, did Mrs. Siddons display a certain vulnerability to human emotions—to suspense and horror—which set her conception apart from that of her inflexible predecessor. Hannah Pritchard would not have allowed her fiendlike spirit to be "overcome," even for a moment, "by the contagion of [Macbeth's] remorse and terror"; she would never have stood with her "arms about her neck and bosom, shuddering." Even in this scene, however, Sarah Siddons' Lady Macbeth steeled herself to combat Macbeth's "derangement," and her returning of the daggers was accompanied with as much contempt for her unnerved husband as Mrs. Pritchard had given the passage.[200]

It is well known that, after her acting days were over, Mrs. Siddons wrote an essay in which she confessed that her personification of Lady Macbeth had not entirely accorded with her personal convictions about the character. On the stage, she had used to advantage her own imposing physique, her flashing dark eyes, her famous classical features. The character that she created was a strong, "masculine" personality, imperiously willful and completely dominant over her husband—at least in the first two acts. Thus in temperament, as in character, she followed, up to a point, the Pritchard tradition. In her essay, however, she described her ideal Lady Macbeth as the kind of woman "most captivating to the other sex,—fair, feminine, nay, perhaps even fragile."

Notes by George Joseph Bell," *The Nineteenth Century,* February, 1878, pp. 301, 302. Mrs. Jameson, who had heard Mrs. Siddons read the part of Lady Macbeth, though she may not have seen her act it, writes that Lady Macbeth's first greeting of Macbeth is "surely the rapture of ambition! And those who have heard Mrs. Siddons pronounce the word *hereafter,* cannot forget the look, the tone, which seemed to give her auditors a glimpse of that awful *future,* which she in her prophetic fury, beholds upon the instant" (see *Characteristics of Women* [Boston, 1853], p. 329). *See also* the interesting article by Joseph W. Donohue, Jr., "Kemble and Mrs. Siddons in *Macbeth:* The Romantic Approach to Tragic Character," *Theatre Notebook,* XXII (Winter, 1967-68), 65-86.

200. Jenkin, "Mrs. Siddons as Lady Macbeth," p. 300. See also Bell's notes reproduced on pp. 301-8.

Such a composition only, respectable in energy and strength of mind, and captivating in feminine loveliness, could have composed a charm of such potency as to fascinate the mind of a hero so dauntless, a character so amiable, so honourable as Macbeth . . . and we are constrained, even whilst we abhor his crimes, to pity the infatuated victim of such a thraldom.

Occasionally I have seen the statement that Sarah Siddons' real conception of Lady Macbeth, as revealed in her essay, was diametrically opposed to her stage interpretation. Actually, her interpretation of Lady Macbeth's *character,* as distinguished from her *physical features* (and, by implication, perhaps, her manner), did not differ much in the essay from what it was on the stage. Fragile of body but not of spirit, ambitious not only for her husband but for herself, Mrs. Siddons' ideal Lady Macbeth had the same tremendous will power and exerted the same evil influence that the actress had demonstrated in her impersonation. In fact, Mrs. Siddons described her as Macbeth's "evil genius"—the precise phrase that G. J. Bell used of the conception suggested by her own performance. "In this astonishing creature," she wrote, "one sees a woman in whose bosom the passion of ambition has almost obliterated all the characteristics of human nature," a woman who, "having . . . delivered herself up to the excitements of hell, . . . is abandoned to the guidance of the demons whom she has invoked." When we first see her with her husband she is "so entirely swallowed up by the horrible design" that she forgets everything else—the perils he has encountered in battle, the joy of his safe return—and offers "not one kind word of greeting or congratulation." Although Macbeth "is frequent in expressions of tenderness to his wife . . . she never betrays one symptom of affection towards him, till, in the fiery furnace of affliction, her iron heart is melted down to softness."

So far the conception is much like the fiendlike one associated with Mrs. Pritchard. But Mrs. Siddons did take care to show that Lady Macbeth's inhuman wickedness was not a permanent state, that it was the result of uncontrolled ambition combined with a supreme effort of the will. When Lady Macbeth asserts that, to keep an oath, she would be willing to dash her infant's brains out, she is "horrific" indeed, but "the very use of such a tender allusion in the midst of her dreadful language, persuades one unequivocally that she has really felt the . . . yearnings of a mother towards her babe, that she considered this action the most enormous that ever required the strength of human nerve for its perpetration." Further, Mrs. Siddons believed that Lady Macbeth's temporary obsession lost hold of her in Act III, that "the sad and new experience of affliction . . . subdued the insolence of her pride and the violence of her will." In the scene with Macbeth following the brief soliloquy, "Naught's had, all's spent,"

Far from her former habits of reproach and contemptuous taunting, . . . she now listens to his complaints with sympathising feelings; and so far from adding to the weight of his affliction the burthen of her own, she endeavours to conceal it from him with the most delicate and unremitting attention.

She encourages her husband in his plan to murder Banquo, but, no longer fiendlike, she must endure the tortures of a guilty conscience; and in the banquet scene the Ghost appears to her as well as to Macbeth.[201] In Sarah Siddons' interpretation, then, the sleepwalking scene is not a sudden and surprising revelation but the culmination of the mental suffering whose development we have followed since the beginning of the third act.

It was in her softening of the later scenes and her insistence upon Lady Macbeth's essential humanity despite her desperate assumption of a fiendlike nature that Mrs. Siddons took a step toward the later "sympathetic" interpretation of the character. (This was true in her acting as well as in her essay, but the effect was not quite the same; for even in the sleepwalking scene her majestic presence was more awe-inspiring than pathetic.) Perhaps she did not so much depart from the old conception as she attempted to rationalize it. Actor-critics like Gentleman and Davies had been content to admire both the "savage inhumanity" of the murder scene and the remorse of the sleepwalking scene without making any attempt to reconcile these seemingly incompatible characteristics. Sarah Siddons was not.

The influence that the great actress exerted upon her successors was thus rather complex. When the term "Siddons tradition" is used, it generally evokes the image of a strong, "masculine," sublimely fiendlike Lady Macbeth. Yet, as we have just seen, her essay and, to some extent, her acting pointed the way toward a more human view of the character. And her essay alone laid the

---

201. See Mrs. Siddons' essay on Lady Macbeth, published in Campbell's *Life of Mrs. Siddons*, pp. 170-73, 174, 177.

groundwork for the "feminine" conception that later actresses were to develop further. The actor-critics' responses to her performance and her written analyses were, accordingly, divergent.

The interpretation that I have called the "Siddons tradition" was, of course, the most important immediate legacy, as far as the stage was concerned. Among actor-critics, SHERIDAN KNOWLES was a particularly emphatic adherent to this conception, as well as an enthusiastic admirer of Mrs. Siddons. In creating Lady Macbeth, he asserted, Shakespeare had "realized the highest feat of the terrible in romance, by embodying the spirit of a fiend in a human form." He did not deny that the character possessed some human sympathies, but he considered them utterly subservient to "the presiding evil principle." Thus, although she loves her husband, she is willing to sacrifice his honor, virtue, and peace "to the gratification of her own ambition." She is "no stranger" to maternal instinct, yet she can support the idea of dashing her baby's brains out. And her feeling for her father awakes only "a momentary compunction from the effects of which no sooner does she recover, than she is if possible twice the demon that she was before."[202]

Sarah Siddons' idea of Lady Macbeth's physical appearance occasioned considerable interest among actors, but it was some time before it developed into anything more than a novel topic for discussion. WILLIAM CHARLES MACREADY was intrigued but not convinced by it (he took the opposing side in a debate on the subject but was "pleased" by the arguments in defense of a "delicate and fragile" Lady Macbeth).[203] FANNY KEMBLE in a youthful diary note described Mrs. Siddons' suggestion as "very beautiful":

the deep blue eyes, the fair hair and fair skin of the northern woman . . . the frail feminine form and delicate character of beauty, which, united to that undaunted mettle which her husband pays homage to in her, constituted a complex spell, at once soft and strong, sweet and powerful. . . .[204]

But if she continued to subscribe to this "very original idea," the femininity that she associated with Lady Macbeth was no more

202. *Lectures on Dramatic Literature: Macbeth*, pp. 14-15. Knowles's praise of Mrs. Siddons' Lady Macbeth is given on pp. 17, 19-22.

203. *The Diaries of William Charles Macready*, ed. William Toynbee (New York, 1912), I, 264.

204. *Records of a Girlhood* (2d ed.; New York, 1883), p. 518.

than skin-deep. For in maturity Miss Kemble wrote one of the most "masculine" of all the descriptions of Lady Macbeth:

she possessed the qualities which generally characterize men, and not women—energy, decision, daring, unscrupulousness; a deficiency of imagination, a great preponderance of the positive and practical mental elements; a powerful and rapid appreciation of what each exigency of circumstance demanded, and the coolness and resolution necessary for its immediate execution. Lady Macbeth's character has more of the essentially manly nature in it than that of Macbeth.[205]

As far as Fanny Kemble was concerned, Sarah Siddons was mistaken in her attempts to humanize Lady Macbeth in the last three acts. The character was never an inhuman monster, Miss Kemble believed, but she was "godless, and ruthless in the objects of her ambition"—and so she remained. Being less fearful than her husband, she was also less bloody: "she would not have hesitated a moment to commit any crime that she considered necessary for her purposes, but she would always have known what were and what were not necessary crimes." Her forbearing to reproach her husband toward the end of their career was perfectly consistent with her tauntings in earlier scenes; when she felt that reproaches would be effective, she used them, but when they could do no good she refrained. She could not have seen the Ghost in the banquet scene; for she was not given to visions, and, besides, even she could not have retained her composure under such circumstances. The grimness of Fanny Kemble's conception is particularly evident in her comments on the sleepwalking scene. She could not see any evidence of guilt-consciousness or repentance here—only the "*unrecognized* pressure of her great guilt."

I think her life was destroyed by sin as by a disease of which she was unconscious, and that she died of a broken heart, while the impenetrable resolution of her will remained unbowed. . . . Never, even in her dreams, does any gracious sorrow smite from her stony heart the blessed brine of tears . . . never, even in her dreams, do the avenging furies lash her through purgatorial flames . . . and the dreary but undismayed desolation in which her spirit abides for ever, is quite other than that darkness, however deep, which the soul acknowledges, and whence it may yet behold the breaking of a dawn shining far off from round the mercy-seat.

Indeed, Lady Macbeth's perturbed sleepwalking epitomized for Fanny Kemble the soullessness of the wicked queen in contrast to

205. *Notes upon Some of Shakespeare's Plays*, pp. 56-58.

Macbeth's morbid awareness of his own damnation. "He may be visited to the end by those noble pangs which bear witness to the preëminent nobility of the nature he has desecrated. . . . But *she* may none of this: she may but feel and see and smell blood."[206]

It was Miss Kemble's younger contemporary HELEN FAUCIT who first attempted to bring to the stage a feminine and relatively sympathetic Lady Macbeth. In the 1840's, a little over a decade after the other actress wrote her early diary note, Miss Faucit added Lady Macbeth to her repertory; and it soon became evident to critics that a new dimension had been given to the character. Although she herself was not small and fragile, as Mrs. Siddons had conceived Lady Macbeth to be, she was graceful in form, and the womanly charm idealized by the Victorians came easily to her. Her Lady Macbeth, however, was feminine in a rather different way from the lovely temptress of Mrs. Siddons' imagination. One way in which she demonstrated Lady Macbeth's humanity as well as her femininity was through her interpretation of the fainting fit in the scene when Duncan's murder is discovered. Miss Faucit was convinced that it was genuine, not mere playacting designed to take the pressure off Macbeth.

Think . . . of her agony of anxiety, on the early morning just after the murder, lest her husband in his wild ravings should betray himself; and of the torture she endured while, no less to her amazement than her horror, he recites . . . with fearful minuteness of detail, how he found Duncan lying gashed and gory in his chamber! She had faced that sight without blenching when it was essential to replace the daggers . . . but to have the whole scene thus vividly brought again before her was too great a strain upon her nerves. No wonder that she faints.

In her remarks on the character (published in the 1880's, not long after Fanny Kemble's definitive discussion of the "masculine" Lady Macbeth), Helen Faucit confessed that in her early days she had hated to act this role, that the first two acts had filled her with "shrinking horror." But, she added, in the end she did not dislike the character as a whole. "I could not but admire the stern grandeur of the indomitable will which could write itself with 'fate and metaphysical aid' to place the crown upon her husband's brow." Lady Macbeth had been brought up in an age of violence, when murder "often passed in common estimation for an

206. *Ibid.,* pp. 50-54, 56-58, 67-68.

act of valour." Because of her background, "one murder more seemed little to her. But she did not know what it was to be personally implicated in murder, nor foresee the Nemesis that would pursue her waking, and fill her dreams with visions of the old man's blood. . . ." If we can enter imaginatively into the life of that time, "we can understand the wife who would adventure so much for so great a prize, though we may not sympathize with her."[207]

The idea that Lady Macbeth's ambition was a wifely one became the basis for all the sympathetic interpretations of the character. Although Mrs. Jameson had suggested the same idea a few years earlier, her interpretation as a whole was less feminine than Helen Faucit's.[208] In any case, the actress helped to popularize the idea through her womanly portrayal on the stage. It is difficult to say how much influence her Lady Macbeth may have exerted upon other actresses. It did not become one of her great parts until after she left the London theatres. Glowing critiques of the performance followed her about, however, from one theatre to another in Scotland, Ireland, and the English provinces; and when she acted the part during a London engagement in 1851 there were equally enthusiastic reviews. These must have had their weight with other Lady Macbeths. It is not without interest, perhaps, that Helen Faucit's brief comments on the character were published only a few years before Ellen Terry's controversial "feminine" Lady Macbeth made her appearance on the Lyceum stage. But, as we shall see, Miss Faucit's influence on the younger actress also took another route.

Whatever its effect on later players, the Faucit interpretation was certainly influential on critics and men of letters. William Carleton, the Irish novelist, acknowledged that the actress had opened up a whole new conception of the character for him.[209]

207. On Some of Shakespeare's Female Characters, pp. 234-35.

208. See Anna Jameson's essay on Lady Macbeth, Characteristics of Women, pp. 319-40. Mrs. Jameson shows the apparent influence of Mrs. Siddons at several points, but the idea that Lady Macbeth is ambitious only for her husband is an original one. (She comments in a note, p. 322, that she has not seen Mrs. Siddons' essay but has heard Mrs. Siddons discuss the character.) William Maginn, whose essay on Lady Macbeth has already been referred to in connection with his revolutionary views on Macbeth's character (see n. 159 of the present chapter), also insisted upon the unselfishness of Lady Macbeth's ambition.

209. See his letter to Dr. William Stokes of Dublin, published in the appendix of Miss Faucit's book, On Some of Shakespeare's Female Characters, pp. 345-47.

"Christopher North" (John Wilson, professor at the University of Edinburgh), who had formerly considered Sarah Siddons the ideal representative of Lady Macbeth, exclaimed after seeing Helen Faucit's performance, "This is the real Lady Macbeth! Mrs. Siddons has misled us!" And not long afterwards Paper No. 5 of his "Dies Borealis" series in *Blackwood's Magazine* reflected his new conception of the character.[210] Another critic who probably received some inspiration from Helen Faucit in forming his unusual idea of Lady Macbeth was George Fletcher. This writer had been so struck by her innovations in the character of Constance (in Macready's production of *King John*, 1842-43) that he had written an enthusiastic essay for the *Athenaeum* favorably contrasting her interpretation with the traditional one. After this, according to Theodore Martin (Helen Faucit's husband), Fletcher became acquainted with the actress, and "in his [essays on] Macbeth and Lady Macbeth, Juliet and Beatrice, he owed much to what he learned from her conversation as well as from her acting."[211] If Martin is correct, the conversations rather than the stage impersonation must have influenced the essay on the Macbeths, first published in the *Westminster Review*, August 12, 1843; for, although Miss Faucit had acted Lady Macbeth once in London several months earlier, Fletcher's concluding note makes clear that he had not seen the performance. This same note, however, also suggests the possibility that Miss Faucit's representation of Constance helped to direct the critic's thinking toward the new Lady Macbeth. In it he remarks that Sarah Siddons made "strong-willed ambition . . . rather than maternal affection" the "ruling motive of Constance" but that Miss Faucit had "courageously . . . disregarded theatrical prescription . . . and shown . . . that feeling, not pride, is the mainspring of the

The letter includes a critique of Miss Faucit's performance, setting forth her unusual interpretation of the character.

210. Theodore Martin, *Helena Faucit (Lady Martin)* (2d ed., Edinburgh and London, 1900), pp. 158-60. Wilson's article may be found in *Blackwood's Magazine*, LXVI (November, 1849), 620-54. Like the other papers in the "Dies Borealis" series, it is in the form of a Platonic dialogue; Christopher North and three friends are discussing *Macbeth*. There are occasional clashes of ideas, but there is no mistaking the main tendency of the discussion: it is to decry the glorification of Macbeth by such critics as Payne Knight and to show that Lady Macbeth (a "bold, bad woman—not a fiend") has a character superior to her husband's.

211. Martin, *Helena Faucit*, p. 93. For Fletcher's essay on the Macbeths, see his *Studies of Shakespeare*, pp. 109-98.

character." Since Mrs. Siddons' interpretation of Constance was "strictly analogous" to that of Lady Macbeth, it would be "most interesting" to see the new actress "exercise her unbiased judgment and her flexible powers" upon the latter character. When the essay was reprinted in Fletcher's book *Studies of Shakespeare* (1847) a new note was added describing Helen Faucit's Lady Macbeth on the basis of reports in the journals: "Her performance . . . would seem to have exhibited . . . not the 'fiend' that Mrs. Siddons presented . . . but the far more interesting picture of a naturally generous woman, depraved by her very self-devotion to the ambitious purpose of a merely selfish man." This is much the same as Fletcher's own interpretation set forth in his essay. Fletcher's unsympathetic interpretation of Macbeth—as we have seen, he was among the earliest literary critics to argue for Macbeth's original wickedness—may be considered a logical corollary to his softened view of the lady. (Consider that in all his other essays Fletcher confined himself to women characters—always those in Miss Faucit's repertory.) What more likely than that a critic who substitutes wifely devotion for fiendish compulsion in Lady Macbeth's character should shift the burden of criminal blame to Macbeth's shoulders?

Whatever Miss Faucit's contribution to Fletcher's conception of the Macbeths, she agreed with it and was no doubt encouraged in her acting by its written expression. A bound reprint of the 1843 article, now in the British Theatre Museum, bears Helen Faucit's signature with the date 1844. (Miss Faucit's very successful performance of Lady Macbeth in Paris took place early in January, 1845.) There is another signature on the same page: that of Ellen Terry, with the date 1888. This copy of Fletcher's essay is no doubt the one that Helen Faucit's husband sent to Henry Irving in 1875.[212] And the significance of the gift is recorded on the reverse side of the flyleaf in the following pencilled note: "Given to me by Ellen Terry. She told me that this criticism on 'Macbeth' had influenced Irving's and her reading of the characters more than anything else. TH."

Before discussing Ellen Terry's famous (and controversial)

212. See n. 161 of the present chapter. Mr. Laurence Irving notes (in *Henry Irving*, p. 499) that Fletcher's work held much interest for Ellen Terry, to whom Irving later gave it. There is also a copy of Fletcher's book, *Studies of Shakespeare*, with Ellen Terry's signature and many marginal notes in her hand; this is in the Shakespeare Collection of the Birmingham Reference Library.

interpretation we must pause to consider two Lady Macbeths of the nineteenth century American stage and the critical reactions to these performances by other players. The first is CHARLOTTE CUSHMAN, who presented a decidedly masculine and fiendlike Lady Macbeth in the Pritchard-Siddons tradition. The other is CLARA MORRIS, an intensely feminine Lady Macbeth, though not a "womanly" one in the sense that Helen Faucit was. It is, perhaps, unnecessary to mention that, regardless of the actor-critics' opinions of Miss Cushman, she was the leading Lady Macbeth of the American theatre and that Miss Morris remained relatively unknown in this role.

Actually Charlotte Cushman was closer to Hannah Pritchard than to Sarah Siddons in her interpretation; for she had all the energy, power, and daring of both actresses, but she evidently lacked the sublimity of the latter. She maintained that throughout the most important scenes both Macbeth and Lady Macbeth were "under the influence of wine."

She supported her opinion from the text, and believed that Shakespeare supposed it to be apparent that they were drunk. This suits well with the manner which Miss Cushman had at some points in the play, a reckless, swinging way of doing everything and an apparent carelessness of what happened.[213]

Charlotte Cushman's interpretation was not only immensely successful with the public; it was also appreciated by at least a few actor-critics. William Charles Macready, for example, was impressed by it when he acted Macbeth with her.[214] And LAWRENCE BARRETT has left a largely favorable critique:

Her own indomitable purpose was well illustrated in the fine scorn of *Lady Macbeth* when her vacillating lord hints at failure. She knew not that beast word. Her physique assisted her greatly. . . . Her face was plain, but of a noble expression; her form tall and elastic, her gait majestic. . . . Of a nervous, active temperament, her acting was of the restless type. Repose she never attained to nor seemed to desire.[215]

Several other actor-critics, however, were either dissatisfied with the performance or actually repelled by it. The most vivid, but

213. Clara Erskine Clement, *Charlotte Cushman* (Boston, 1882), pp. 82-83.
214. *Macready's Reminiscences*, ed. Pollock, p. 512 (diary entry for October 23, 1843).
215. Lawrence Barrett, *Charlotte Cushman: A Lecture* (New York, 1889), p. 14.

also the most unfair, criticism was made by JOHN COLEMAN: he described Miss Cushman's Lady Macbeth as a "domineering, murderous harridan," who "strides up and down, and grunts and growls," who "brow-beats every one she comes across, her wretched husband most especially; and in the Murder Scene . . . literally drags him off by the scruff of his neck."[216] GEORGE VANDENHOFF was not so blunt, but he, too, found her conception more "animal" than "intellectual."[217] JAMES MURDOCH's extended critique, intermixed with his own ideas about the character of Lady Macbeth, does better justice than the others to Miss Cushman's acting. At the same time, however, this discussion—and also Murdoch's later essay on *Macbeth*—presents an impossibly idealized interpretation of the character which a single actress could hardly hope to realize. (Sarah Siddons would have come nearer the mark than anyone else.) As in his remarks on Macbeth, Murdoch demands a reconciliation of gigantic opposites in the character of Lady Macbeth: of "materialism" and sublimity, wifely devotion and "masculine spirit." He describes her as "a towering nature," "a minister of fate," "an archangel ruined." Yet he stresses the fact of her basic humanity (particularly as illustrated by her inability to kill Duncan herself), and he even has the audacity to warn against the stage tradition of magnifying Lady Macbeth's importance to the extent of dwarfing Macbeth's. Charlotte Cushman seemed to him ideally suited to portray some aspects of Lady Macbeth's character because of her remarkable force, her keen and penetrating intelligence, her "intensely prosaic, definitely practical nature." But, in his opinion, she fell short of Shakespeare's conception because she lacked imagination and she had but little of that "glow of feeling which springs from the centre of emotional elements."

The grandeur of a poetic idea elevates the deed of blood, without divesting it of its horrors. . . . The heroine of the poet invokes the pall of darkness to hide the wound made by the bloody knife, while the heroine of the stage by a violent and inartistic manner plucks away "the blanket of the night" to show the dreadful deed in all its hideous deformity.[218]

216. John Coleman, *Fifty Years of an Actor's Life* (London, 1904), I, 301.
217. *Leaves from an Actor's Note-book; with Reminiscences and Chit-chat of the Green-room and the Stage, in England and America* (New York, 1860), p. 196.
218. *The Stage*, pp. 240-42.

If Charlotte Cushman followed the "Siddons tradition" of acting, Clara Morris attempted to follow the suggestions made in the
Siddons essay. Perhaps she was trying to refashion Lady Macbeth
in her own image when she seized upon the idea of a fair and
fragile temptress. Small in build herself, she wore red hair for
Lady Macbeth and acted the part as a kind of neurotic Delilah.
In her autobiography she explained that the "traditional, martial-
stalking drum-major of a woman" made Lady Macbeth's "final
remorseful breaking-down of brain and heart a contradiction, almost an impossibility." Besides, she reasoned that Macbeth—"a
fine soldier, big and bluff and physically brave"—would most
likely have been attracted to his physical opposite. "Fair, soft,
tender in seeming, this 'dearest chuck,' whose soft body housed a
soul of fire. . . ." The "fair-faced hypocrite" of Miss Morris' conception was not moved by wifely concern, as Helen Faucit's Lady
Macbeth had been, but used her womanly wiles on her husband
to gratify her own "devouring ambition." On the other hand, she
was not, like the character envisioned by Fanny Kemble, contemptuous of the finer sensibilities or immune to supernatural influences.

Crafty and subtle as she was, clever as her reading of Macbeth's character proves her to have been, she only became terrible as a fate
through her absolute reliance upon the supernatural power of the
witches. There is something appalling in her ready faith and eager
summoning of the spirits of evil to her aid; and right in that invocation I find my proof that *Lady Macbeth* was naturally womanly,
pitiful, capable of repentance for wrong done, and had sufficient
belief in God, to at least fear Him. For in that moment of exaltation,
when the promise of the crown was tightening every thrilling nerve
to a mad determination, her first demand of the "murdering ministers" is that they shall unsex her. . . .

The cool self-possession that she shows in the following scenes is
due, not to natural callousness, but to the sustaining power of her
trust in the forces of evil that she has invoked. "And when at
last it is borne in upon her that they have played her husband
false; that all stained with crime they two are left to face an outraged God, how quickly the delicate woman becomes a physical
wreck."[219]

There is not much reference to Clara Morris' Lady Macbeth
in the writings of her colleagues. The actress herself asserts, how-

219. Clara Morris, *The Life of a Star* (New York, 1906), pp. 30-34.

ever, that her reading of the character actually gained the approval of the Amazonian Miss Cushman. According to her story, the older actress rebuffed a man who was trying to curry favor by condemning the unusual performance. "I have for years recognized the absolute womanliness of Lady Macbeth," Charlotte Cushman reportedly told him. ". . . I played the part in the traditional manner, the big, heavy style, and it was lucky for me that the public liked it . . . for though intellectually I am for the feminine *Lady Macbeth*, physically . . . I am not well fitted for the coaxing, purring, velvet-footed, subtle hypocrite."[220] We can be reasonably sure that the series of adjectives represents Miss Morris' own choice of words rather than Miss Cushman's, but perhaps the story is not wholly apocryphal. The American Siddons may have been simply following her great counterpart in theory here as she had followed her in practice, according to her lights, on the stage. Clara Morris' performance met with less favorable reaction from FREDERICK WARDE. Not that he objected to a feminine Lady Macbeth: he himself described the character as a "wife who . . . gloried in [her husband's] strength, knew his weakness," and "deliberately sacrificed her peace on earth and hope of the hereafter, for the man she loved"; and he preferred Mrs. D. P. Bowers' portrayal to Charlotte Cushman's because it was "less domineering, more womanly." But he considered Miss Morris "unfortunate" in her interpretation because she attempted to "charm her husband by feminine fascination."[221] Any form of selfish manipulation, apparently, whether bluntly "masculine" or deviously "feminine," met with his disapproval.

By the end of the 1880's, when ELLEN TERRY was preparing to portray Lady Macbeth, the idea of a feminine and quite human character had gained considerable support from literary critics and, as we have seen, a certain amount from actors. But the earlier conception still had a strong hold on stage tradition and public expectation. Thus Miss Terry's Lady Macbeth—which, apparently, was even more sympathetic in effect than she intended it to be—seemed an innovation. "They speak of my Lady Macbeth as 'gentle & dove-like'!!!" she wrote to a friend in America. "Lor' a mussy!!! I feel all the while as if I were 'going on' like a Billings-

220. *Ibid.*, pp. 39-40.
221. *Fifty Years of Make-Believe* (New York, 1920), p. 107.

gate lady."[222] Ellen Terry always denied that Lady Macbeth (either Shakespeare's or her own) was "gentle," but she also denied just as stoutly that "Mrs. McB" was a "fiend who urged her little husband against his will to be naughty."[223] Remarks of this sort, some playful, some earnest, made in letters and conversations, tell as much about her conviction of Lady Macbeth's humanity as her more formal discussion of the character. For example, she told Mrs. Clement Scott that Lady Macbeth was "not good, but not so much worse than many women you know." And she declared, in her sympathetic way, "I do believe that at the end of that banquet the poor wretched creature was brought through agony and sin to repentance, and was forgiven."[224] To William Winter she wrote of her "feminine" Lady Macbeth:

I can only see that she's a *Woman*—A Mistaken Woman—& *Weak*—Not a Dove—of course not—but *first of all a Wife* I don't think she's *at all clever.* . . . She seems shrewd, & thinks herself so, at first . . . about her husband's character but oh, dear me how quickly he gets steeped in wickedness beyond her comprehension. . . .[225]

It is significant of Ellen Terry's attitude toward Lady Macbeth that in her Shakespeare lectures she discussed her under the heading of "The Pathetic Women." Here she described the character as she imagined her: "a small, slight woman of acute nervous sensibility" who, in the lines beginning "I have given suck . . ." is near hysteria.

This frenzied appeal is surely the expression of the desperation Lady Macbeth feels at the sudden paralysis of Macbeth's faculties in the hour of action. He must be roused, he must be roused. . . . She is beside herself. We really ought not to take her wild words as a proof of abnormal ferocity.

Miss Terry emphasized the partnership of Macbeth and Lady Macbeth and the latter's determination not to fail her husband. When the "dreamer finds [the burden of action] intolerably heavy," his wife must take it up.

222. MS letter to Mrs. William Winter, dated April 20, 1889. In the Folger Library.

223. MS letter to William Winter, in the Folger Library. It is undated, but it bears Winter's notation: "Rec'd October 29, 1895."

224. Mrs. Clement Scott, *Old Days in Bohemian London* (New York, n.d.), p. 137.

225. See n. 223, above. Miss Terry had just arrived, with Irving's company, in New York, where they were to give five performances of *Macbeth*. The letter shows her sensitivity to the criticism of her Lady Macbeth. *See also* her *Story of My Life*, p. 306.

Lady Macbeth's nervous force sustains her until Duncan's murder is accomplished. Then she collapses, and faints! I suppose I can say: "That's womanly"!

Henceforth she is "troubled with thick-coming fancies." In plain prose she has a nervous break-down. She is haunted by the horror of the murder. It preys upon her mind, and saps her physical strength. She dies of remorse. Surely this is good evidence that she is not of the tigress type, mentally or physically.[226]

According to Lena Ashwell, Ellen Terry "felt that her personality prevented her from fully representing the character [of Lady Macbeth] as she conceived it." This was probably true: the famous Terry charm caused critics to see sweetness and gentleness where these qualities were not intended. But Miss Ashwell seems to have misunderstood Miss Terry's remarks about Geneviève Ward's "womanly" performance: "she was bitterly disappointed . . . because Miss Ward, with her virile and hard personality, should have been able to convey all the attributes of cruelty, ruthlessness, and domineering energy."[227] (GENEVIÈVE WARD interpreted Lady Macbeth, instead, as a woman who has lost her children and therefore concentrates all her love and loyalty in her husband.[228]) Certainly Ellen Terry herself did not strive unsuccessfully to portray ruthlessness and cruelty, nor did she ascribe these characteristics to Lady Macbeth. But, despite her own "feminine" view of the character, she may well have considered the "masculine" interpretation the only intelligent one for the other actress. This attitude would conform to her general belief that Shakespeare's characters were flexible enough to permit of several interpretations. Particularly, it would be in line with her remarks about Sarah Siddons' stage interpretation as opposed to the one expressed in her essay. Miss Terry's own convictions corresponded with the latter, yet she had a tremendous admiration for the former as it had been described by those who saw it: "as a single, forceful dramatic figure," she believed, it was "far the most *effective*," even though the other was better "as part of a *whole*." The great actress had had three choices: she could make an effort, with the aid of makeup, to create the illusion of a feminine Lady Macbeth; she could create an inimitable (though not, in Miss Terry's

226. *Four Lectures on Shakespeare*, pp. 160-62.

227. *Reflections from Shakespeare*, pp. 135-36.

228. Geneviève Ward and Richard Whiteing, *Both Sides of the Curtain* (London, 1918), p. 150.

opinion, a Shakespearean) piece of drama by exploiting her own physique and personality; or she could refuse to act the part at all. Ellen Terry could never be sorry that she had chosen the second course.[229]

The idea of Lady Macbeth's femininity has been accepted by several actor-critics of the modern period—by WILLIAM POEL and GEORGE R. FOSS, HARLEY GRANVILLE-BARKER and SIR TYRONE GUTHRIE—specifically for dramatic reasons. Most of them have argued, for example, that a small, delicate Lady Macbeth is a better foil to Macbeth than a large, imposing one and is less likely to detract from his importance as the hero of the tragedy. Guthrie reasons that Lady Macbeth "*does* dominate" Macbeth spiritually in the first part of the play and that if she is allowed to be physically dominant as well he is in danger of seeming "a contemptible, rather than a tragic figure."[230] In this opinion he is less extreme than was either Poel or Foss, both of whom tried to subordinate Lady Macbeth to her husband in personality as well as appearance. Poel even reduced her ambition to the level of feminine frivolity, and he interpreted the most terrible of her speeches as a pettish protest against the "cruelty" of being denied a pretty gold crown.

Macbeth knew of her weakness for finery when he sought her approval of the deed; it was his bribe for her help. And women of Lady Macbeth's temperament do not care to be disappointed of their pleasures. To break promise in these matters, she tells her husband, is as cruel as it would be for her to kill her own child, that being a crime of which she is incapable, for she is a devoted mother.[231]

Foss pictured her as a "little thin, eager woman, blindly keen to get on in the world and utterly unscrupulous of the means that she employed."

She had no power of looking ahead or foreseeing consequences. What she desired she wanted at once. . . . An energetic, somewhat shallow woman, weary at the beginning of her quiet, lonely life as the mistress of Inverness Castle and longing to get out into the world. . . .

229. Ellen Terry's comments, written on the blank pages bound with Fletcher's essay, in the British Theatre Museum, include her meditations about Mrs. Siddons's two conceptions of Lady Macbeth—the written one and the acted one. Most of these comments are reproduced by Laurence Irving in *Henry Irving*, pp. 499-500.

230. *Shakespeare: Ten Great Plays*, p. 407.

231. *Shakespeare in the Theatre* (London and Toronto, 1913), pp. 65-66.

According to him, she is "all energetic excitement" until the murder of Duncan is accomplished; then she "collapses and is no further use to her husband and very little to the play."[232] Granville-Barker's approach was more moderate. Unlike Poel, who had cited passages from the text in support of Lady Macbeth's femininity (for example, Duncan's tribute to her charm as a hostess, Macduff's distress in having to tell her of the King's murder, her own partiality to the perfumes of Arabia), Granville-Barker admitted that there is no textual evidence concerning her physical appearance. He did find dramatic evidence of a subtler kind, however: the part had been written for a boy of seventeen, not a woman of forty, and this fact, he believed, was reflected in the characterization and structure of the play. The text demands "swiftness of method" and "lightness of touch": at the beginning "Macbeth . . . is the hanger-back, his wife is the speeder on. She is the gadfly stinging him to action." Such effects are gained best by a slight rather than a heavy character. Dramatic contrasts are heightened as well: not only contrast with the "colossal" figure of Macbeth but with her own "undaunted spirit," whose effect is "doubled if we marvel that so frail a body can contain it. There will be an appropriate beauty in her fainting. . . . And the thin-drawn tragedy of her end will be deepened."[233]

The stronger, more dominant conception of the character has continued to win some support, however. LENA ASHWELL considered Lady Macbeth a ruthless, inflexibly determined person who remained throughout the play the "centre of the tragedy."[234] Other actor-critics described the character in less "masculine" terms, yet emphasized the qualities of majesty, forcefulness, and imperious pride. ELEANOR CALHOUN, for example, envisioned a Lady Macbeth "as tall as Clytemnestra, and more impressive—akin to Prometheus rather."[235] And an ANONYMOUS ACTRESS (the one whom we encountered earlier in discussing Hamlet) described her as proud, aloof, and intellectual, yet capable of fierce intensity —a "fire and marble woman." She even provided specific details of Lady Macbeth's appearance:

232. *What the Author Meant*, p. 54. Foss attributes the description of Lady Macbeth as a "little thin, eager woman" to Mrs. Siddons, but it is not exactly what Mrs. Siddons said.

233. *The Players' Shakespeare: The Tragedie of Macbeth*, pp. xxxviii-xl.

234. *Reflections from Shakespeare*, pp. 140-42.

235. *Pleasures and Palaces*, p. 299.

Her face is the colour of ivory; her nose proudly cut, with somewhat wide and flexible nostrils; her lips are reserved and fine, and of vivid vermilion. Her hair falls over either shoulder in a thick, long plait of sheeny, sandy yellow. . . . From beneath tawny lashes her eyes, as grey as smoky steel, gaze out straight before her, their sombre glance plunged to the hilt in sinister memories. . . . She looks like a dreaming panther. . . .[236]

Here, obviously, is the female of the species, but she is hardly the "fragile" charmer of Sarah Siddons' dreams.

Most of the modern actor-critics have recognized Lady Macbeth's basic humanity, but some of them have described the character in terms that suggest a fiendlike nature, if only a temporary one. There are several who account for it by the idea that Lady Macbeth is "possessed" by the spirits of evil that she has invoked. In Eleanor Calhoun's words, she "asks and obtains a temporary extension of the faculties, by which in that intoxication of the imagination, she overleaps and overrides everything in her path."

Only when the deed is done . . . does that fire begin to fall back out of her veins and the cold reality come down like snow. . . . Then, because she was in verity great, a proud and royal soul, the glorious palaced realms of the self-intoxicated mind utterly vanish . . . and simple human truth remains, and takes her by all its bitter stony way down to the tomb.[237]

MARGARET WEBSTER and ROBERT SPEAIGHT also hold the "possession" theory, but their descriptions suggest less grandeur than Eleanor Calhoun's does (Speaight's Lady Macbeth is compared to Faust, but she is also compared to Iago); particularly, when the supernatural support is withdrawn, they see in her behavior human weakness rather than stoical suffering. Miss Webster remarks that, once the murder of Duncan is accomplished, Lady Macbeth is "exhausted, used up, the vitality and spring of life drained out of her." She still summons the remnant of her power to help Macbeth in the banquet scene, but "he has gone beyond her, obsessed, blinded, bound to the treadmill on which she had first set his feet."[238] Speaight points out that Lady Macbeth's fainting fit is the first sign of the "revenge" to be exacted by "offended nature." This revenge is completed in the sleepwalking scene,

236. The True Ophelia: and Other Studies of Shakespeare's Women. By an Actress (New York, 1914), pp. 163-65.
237. Pleasures and Palaces, pp. 301-2.
238. Shakespeare Without Tears, pp. 225, 227-28.

when we see her dying of a guilty conscience: here Shakespeare needs but a "single adjective"—"little"—"to depict the fragility of this woman, who, not so long ago, had thought herself turned to steel."[239]

There are some who impute Lady Macbeth's fiendish actions, not to borrowed supernatural power, but to certain qualities in her natural disposition combined with the influences of her family background. Lena Ashwell, though second to none in emphasizing the supernatural influence on Macbeth, traces Lady Macbeth's ruthlessness to a rooted singleness of purpose, a trait shared by many great leaders and reformers in real life. Such people are "so hypnotized by the object to be achieved that they see nothing and feel nothing concerning the people who have to be removed for the execution of their purpose." In Lady Macbeth's case, the blood feud between her family and Duncan's (mentioned in the Scottish chronicles, though not in Shakespeare's play) also helps to dull her sensitivity to murder.[240] The Anonymous Actress endows the character with bitter recollections of past turmoil, in which she was deprived—reportedly through Duncan's agency— of her first husband and her child. Lady Macbeth, as the Actress imagines, had been a vivid and ambitious girl; now she was married to a "stalwart lord" who was more often in the field than at home, and her life, far from city and court, was dull and lonely. Macbeth's letter about the prophecies changes everything: she is "wrapt in thrilled anticipation" as the fulfillment of her "lifelong hungry dream" seems to be at hand. Later, when Macbeth recoils from the treachery that she proposes, the threat to her newly aroused hopes brings a furious reaction: she springs toward him "with such a fierce snarl of interrogation that he shrinks back. . . . She has the temper of a fiend, though rarely roused, and both know it." Her speech "I have given suck. . . ." ends "on a low hiss. Her eyes are plunged into his, her lips are white with controlled passion"; he stares at her, half hypnotized[241]—and who can blame the poor man? Both Lena Ashwell and the Anonymous Actress, however, note some evidences of Lady Macbeth's human weakness: for example, the necessity of "drugging" herself with wine on the murder night. (The former remarks that she thereby heightens

239. *Nature in Shakespearian Tragedy*, pp. 50-51, 58, 66-67.
240. *Reflections from Shakespeare*, p. 139.
241. *The True Ophelia*, pp. 165-67, 178, 180-82.

the susceptibility of her imagination at the time when Macbeth talks of having murdered sleep; this suggestion works upon her subconsciously and culminates in the sleepwalking scene.) And both actresses write of the later scenes in distinctly human and sympathetic terms.

Several modern actor-critics have traced Lady Macbeth's unscrupulousness not to a hard or cruel personality but to a lack of imagination and understanding. Two are William Poel and DAME FLORA ROBSON. (SIR LEWIS CASSON is another, but his comments on the subject are briefer.) Of these Poel is the more insistent upon her limitations. It is wrong, he argues, to speak of the enormity of Lady Macbeth's sin since she herself is not conscious of guilt. A shallow little woman, with none of "the higher powers of reflection," she finds "her husband's talk about conscience and retribution . . . unintelligible."

Even the "spirits," to which her husband has alluded; those which she mockingly invokes to her feminine aid, have no reality to her. . . . With her limited outlook, the beginning and end of everything necessary to her husband's success in life is that he should be practical, inventive, and never appear embarrassed.

Her optimism fails her when Macbeth, in spite of being king, seems no nearer "mastery" than before. And her breakdown occurs, not because of remorse, but because of the tragic realization that, in terms of her personal happiness, the murder of Duncan was a mistake—"a blunder for which her husband deposes her authority."

Never again can she say, "From this time such I account thy love," but merely ejaculates, "Did you send to him, sir?" . . . It is the shock of her failure which paralyzes her power for further action . . . and to the last she is at a loss to understand why murdering an old man in his bed has divorced her husband's affection from her and turned him into a bloodthirsty tyrant.[242]

Flora Robson credits Lady Macbeth both with more strength of mind at the outset and more eventual sensitivity to remorse than Poel does. She puts particular stress on Lady Macbeth's experience in returning the daggers to the murder chamber, since it brought home to her the implications of murder that her mundane imagination had failed to envision. Lady Macbeth *"seems* unaffected" at the time, writes the actress, but we know from the sleepwalking

242. *Shakespeare in the Theatre*, pp. 64-65, 67.

scene later in the play what her real reaction was to the sight of the murdered Duncan. Apparently "she suffers a delayed shock"; perhaps the "drink that made her bold" carried her through the experience itself, and "the necessary haste to hide the crime" dulled her reactions. But when she faints in the following scene, the "full horror of the blood has finally overwhelmed her, and from that moment she wants *no more killing*." Since Macbeth, on the other hand, has become hardened to murder, the two are henceforth at cross purposes. In Act III, when Macbeth complains of the threat to security posed by Banquo and Fleance, his wife "wishes to dissuade him from these murders" at which he is hinting. (Sarah Siddons gave the line "But in them nature's copy's not eterne" as "the prompting of another murder," but Flora Robson, when she acted Lady Macbeth, gave it "a horrified question mark.") In the banquet scene, Macbeth seats his wife alone on the dais while he mingles with the guests because he fears that she will give away their secret. But when he himself breaks down at sight of the Ghost, she "has her Indian summer of courage."

She loves her husband dearly, and forces herself to take magnificent charge of the situation. . . . It is her last flare-up. When they are alone, the fire dies down very low. Her lines are short and dispirited. She is finished.[243]

Regardless of "masculine" or "feminine" interpretations of Lady Macbeth's personality, and regardless of the particular explanations given to reconcile her cruelty with her humanity, most modern criticisms by actors portray the character sympathetically in her later scenes. The quality of the pathos differs somewhat, however, in their various descriptions.

In the banquet scene, for example, Granville-Barker imagined his feminine Lady Macbeth "even physically weighed down with the crown and robes that she struck for . . . it should seem as if the lonely, wan figure upon the throne has no strength left to move."[244] Lena Ashwell, however, described the ordeal of this scene in terms that suggest the acceptance of the Siddons interpretation: Macbeth "reacts against [his wife's] growing horror" and at "the moment of supremest horror . . . the ghost of Banquo appears, passing between the woman and the disordered King. She drops the cup with a crash." (Apparently Lady Macbeth is meant

243. "Notes on Playing the Role of Lady Macbeth," pp. 27-31.
244. *The Players' Shakespeare: The Tragedie of Macbeth*, p. xxxix.

to see the Ghost herself.) She particularly mentions Adelaide Ristori's acting at the end of the banquet scene: "taking off the too-heavy crown and throwing it on the table, [she] sought some ease in mental and physical exhaustion, for she took up a goblet and drank, and drank, and drank."[245] And the Anonymous Actress, with her usual flair for romantic exaggeration, imagined Lady Macbeth, after the guests have left, sitting in stony-faced horror as her husband madly determines on further atrocities; shuddering as her gaze falls on the blood-red light from a ruby she is wearing; rising, trancelike, and sweeping "superbly down the slight steps," only to crash to the floor, unconscious, "looking, as she lies there amidst her sombre draperies, like a lost soul, drowned in blood. . . ."[246]

The sleepwalking scene has naturally drawn more sympathetic responses than any other passage. Granville-Barker and Lena Ashwell, for all their differences in interpreting Lady Macbeth's character, agree on her pathetic weakness in this scene. For the former, the appropriateness of her fragility is illustrated here: "we should hardly be sure . . . whether this wraith that sighs and mutters and drifts away is still a living creature or no."[247] For the latter, the scene is all the more affecting because of the contrast with the early forceful scenes: "There is nothing greater in Drama than the sight of this proud, unfettered spirit pitifully repeating the murder in this helpless fashion. . . ."[248] Even Poel, who saw no evidence of remorse in the sleepwalking scene, found its pathos heart-wringing:

The dim consciousness that somehow she was mistaken begins to prove too great a strain for her energetic little brain. It was also her misfortune, because not her fault, that she was without imagination. She was a devoted wife, and possessed sweet and gracious manners; and Shakespeare, in this last scene, in which she appears before the spectators, asks them to pity her now because of all that she is now suffering.[249]

LILLAH MCCARTHY, who acted Lady Macbeth in one of Poel's productions, gives us an interesting glimpse into his method of evoking pathos in this scene. He had the actress begin by seating

245. *Reflections from Shakespeare*, pp. 142-43.
246. *The True Ophelia*, pp. 209-11.
247. *The Players' Shakespeare: The Tragedie of Macbeth*, p. xxxix.
248. *Reflections from Shakespeare*, p. 144.
249. *Shakespeare in the Theatre*, pp. 226-27.

herself at her dressing table, taking off her rings and loosening her hair, like Desdemona in the willow scene.

The actress, who must presently reach such a dreadful climax of despair, can only rise to it if she begins on the lowest note in the scale of emotions. The tension of apprehension which the silence evokes will moreover have pity blended with it; pity for the poor distraught woman doing with hesitating fingers these trivial things of her daily life.[250]

One source of pathos for both of the Macbeths is the heavy modern emphasis on the relationship between husband and wife in this play. For if Lady Macbeth is a "partner" rather than a tyrant, it is possible to see the marriage as an ideal one. Actors, like other critics, have described the deterioration of this ideal union, the alienation of the partners caused by their common guilt, as an important part of the tragedy. Several of them—Casson, Granville-Barker, Eleanor Calhoun, CONSTANCE BENSON—have suggested methods (or described their own) of making clear to the audience the rift that develops between husband and wife: usually by keeping the two characters far apart on the stage in key scenes, their eyes averted from each other.[251] Flora Robson goes beyond the other actor-critics and finds not only alienation and indifference but actual hatred in Macbeth's final attitude toward his wife: "She should have died hereafter. . . ." "There is tragedy here," she writes, "in the destruction of what could have been a great man. But there is tragedy too in the destruction of a great love."[252] It is ironic that GEORGE SKILLAN, least sympathetic of Lady Macbeth's modern interpreters, is the one to insist most staunchly upon the deathless quality of the love shared by husband and wife: "Direness and horrors may have numbed his fears but this deepest of human feelings remains constant. How he would desire a time properly to lament his loss! He loved his wife, and she him. . . ."[253]

The length to which some modern actor-critics will go in order to rescue the once-detestable Lady Macbeth from obloquy is best illustrated by a suggestion made by Sir Lewis Casson. Like

250. Lillah McCarthy, *Myself and My Friends* (London, 1933), pp. 30-31.
251. Casson, Introduction to *Macbeth*, Folio Society edition, p. 9; Granville-Barker, *The Players' Shakespeare: The Tragedie of Macbeth*; Calhoun, *Pleasures and Palaces*, p. 300; Benson, *Mainly Players*, pp. 269-70.
252. "Notes on Playing the Role of Lady Macbeth," p. 31.
253. *Macbeth. French's Acting Edition*, p. 105.

Poel, he noticed that the only character in the play who con-
demns Lady Macbeth is Malcolm. Very well, then, the traducer
must be discredited. In the scene with Macduff in England (IV,
iii), let Malcolm be acted as the "Caesar Augustus ruling type"
who "callously uses Macduff's personal grief for his own, and
Scotland's, purposes." If this attitude is made clear by the actors,
it "tends to make us discount his description . . . of Lady Macbeth
as 'fiendlike,' and so may even produce a reaction of sympathy
for that wretched woman."[254]

It is obvious, then, that contemporary actors' criticisms are
heavily weighted on the side of the understandably human Lady
Macbeth, sympathetic in the latter part of the play if not in the
early scenes. Yet there are still at least two actor-critics who adhere to the "fiendlike" interpretation of earlier tradition. These
are SIR MICHAEL REDGRAVE and George Skillan. Redgrave, who
disapproves of all attempts to soften Lady Macbeth's character,
correctly traces the "modern" Lady Macbeth to the influence of
Mrs. Siddons. Her predecessor, Mrs. Pritchard, was, in his opinion,
the correct representative of the part: pictures of her show "a
quite relentless face, marked by none of these traits of sensitivity and spirituality which you will find in any of the Siddons
portraits." Not that Mrs. Siddons' whole performance was
a "wilful one": she evidently played the murder scene "for
all it is worth and as it is written." But she made the mistake of
showing a premature breaking of Lady Macbeth's character, and
in this she has been followed by "nearly every actress ever since."
According to Redgrave, there should be no hints of an ultimate
breakdown before the sleepwalking scene; otherwise the pathos
of that scene is weakened. It is true that the couplet, "Nought's
had, all's spent / Where our desire is got without content" (III,
ii, 4-5), may be interpreted as a sign of Lady Macbeth's weakening, but it can "perfectly well" be read in the opposite manner,
as reflecting "the character of the greedy ambitious woman who is
never satisfied." Redgrave particularly deplores Mrs. Siddons'
"unforgivable, inartistic" pretense in the banquet scene that she,
as well as Macbeth, saw the Ghost, but that she overcame her fears
while he succumbed to his. Aside from the fact that Macbeth
should be the center of attention here, it is less effective dramati-

254. Introduction to *Macbeth,* Folio Society edition, p. 11.

cally for both characters to see the Ghost.[255] It is with Skillan's description, however, that we actually come full circle in the interpretation of Lady Macbeth, for his phraseology is reminiscent of that used by Francis Gentleman and Thomas Davies in Mrs. Pritchard's own era: "a woman of unquenchable ambition" and "callous, cruel, conscienceless nature"; remarkable for "the concentrated fixity of purpose, the commanding power of words, the inflexible soul of relentless persuasion to evil fulfillment . . . she is the fourth witch, deadlier than all the others put together."[256]

Is it possible to speak some final word about Lady Macbeth's femininity? About her humanity?

Her physical appearance, of course,—whether titaness or sylph—must always depend on the actress of the moment. We all have our private visions of her, however, and I confess that mine is much of the Siddons type. It is true that the part was "written for" a boy actress, since only boy actresses were available at that time. In some instances Shakespeare's depiction of character may have been partly determined by this fact. To cite the inevitable example, it is possible that Cleopatra's erotic charms would have been more fully portrayed if the character had been designed for a woman to play. Granville-Barker is right, at any rate, in cautioning the actress not to emphasize Cleopatra's voluptuousness at the expense of her wit, her mercurial moods, her final transmutation to "fire and air." Yet the earthiness is there, too, and in revealing it the modern actress need not impose upon herself the imagined restrictions of Cleopatra's original representative. In other cases, like that of Volumnia, it seems obvious that the potentialities of Shakespeare's characterization can be more fully realized now that mature actresses are available than when the parts were taken, perforce, by boys (fine actors though the latter probably were). Let us determine Lady Macbeth's character, then, by the contents of the play, not by the conditions of the Elizabethan theatre. A small, fragile woman *would* offer a better contrast to her warrior husband—but why is a contrast necessary? The Macbeths are well matched "partners in greatness." Each of them is ambitious, and each knows that the other is so: Macbeth dispatches a letter about the prophecies to his wife so that, as he says, "thou mightst not lose the dues of rejoicing by being ignorant

255. "Shakespeare and the Actors," pp. 135-37.
256. *Macbeth, French's Acting Edition*, pp. 66, 67, 69.

of what greatness is promised *thee*"; Lady Macbeth, immediately after reading the letter, declares, "Glamis thou art, and Cawdor, and shalt be / What *thou* art promised"; when they are together she speaks of the "night's great business . . ./ Which shall to all *our* nights and days to come/ Give solely sovereign sway, and masterdom" (italics mine). The ambition is plainly a shared one—neither totally selfish nor totally unselfish. Moreover, both Macbeths are attuned to supernatural influences, and this fact seems to give, on occasion, a larger-than-life effect to their characters. (Physical size is not necessarily implied. No doubt some small women can produce the effect of intensity and dilation of spirit, but they will hardly seem, at such moments, dainty and fragile.) Much has been said about Lady Macbeth's materialism. It is perfectly true that Macbeth has visions (the dagger, the Ghost) which his wife does not have; perfectly true that her words at moments of crisis are mundane compared to his—though if we wish we can say that she overemphasizes the commonplace in order to combat his growing hysteria. (Mrs. Siddons' Lady Macbeth revealed her own horror in the murder scene but resolutely suppressed it when safety demanded immediate action). But it is impossible to read her invocation to the spirits without a sense of evil exaltation, of commitment to whatever metaphysical forces are necessary to the accomplishment of her aims. To describe this speech, as Poel does, as a "mocking" prayer, made to spirits in which she does not believe, is simply incredible. If the "feminine" Lady Macbeth depends upon such perverse interpretations as this, then the sooner she glides or flutters from the scene, the better. Nor do I feel that the sleepwalking scene would gain in pathos if Lady Macbeth were a pretty little creature of limited intelligence and little sense of guilty responsibility. Mrs. Betterton was "tremendous" in her remorse; so was Mrs. Siddons. And even if helplessness and weakness are emphasized here, they can be—as Lena Ashwell pointed out—more poignant in a woman who has been strong-willed and self-assured in her earlier scenes. Lady Macbeth is a woman, unmistakably. But she is neither a feather-headed doll nor a self-sacrificing wife whose only aim in life is to help her adored husband achieve his ambition. She is the kind of woman who inspires Macbeth to exclaim: "Bring forth men children only; for thy undaunted mettle should compose/ Nothing but males."

As for the other major question, its answer must be that Lady Macbeth is both human and fiendlike. Mrs. Siddons was surely right (as were Helen Faucit, Ellen Terry, and others) that the invocation—a prayer to be *made* inhuman—is actually an acknowledgement of a certain womanly weakness that must be overcome. Yet, listening to the terrible words of that prayer, and to those of the later speech "I have given suck, . . ." does not the audience have the impression that a character who is capable of conceiving and uttering such thoughts is well on the way to the fiendhood that she craves? Shakespeare gives us, it is true, a tiny but significant reminder of Lady Macbeth's humanity, even on the night of the murder: "Had he not resembled my father as he slept. . . ." It gives us pause, it makes us revise our opinion of her a bit, but it does not cancel out the effect that has been built up by the stronger, crueler speeches in the early scenes. And Lady Macbeth's prayer for cruelty is certainly answered: those critics that speak of her "possession" are right, for she acts with superhuman strength and nerve until the deed is done—indeed, until the prize is obtained. There are good psychological arguments for the genuineness of the fainting fit, but Lady Macbeth's unconvincing attempt to express natural emotion at the news of Duncan's death ("Woe, alas! / What, in our house?") tends to prepare us for a mock collapse. As Sheridan Knowles remarked, however, even if the faint is not genuine, we can imagine a real revulsion of feeling behind it. With Act III Lady Macbeth's strength and initiative sharply decline, and we begin to realize that we have undervalued her basic humanity, even as she herself has done. She is disillusioned and dispirited when we first see her as queen ("Naught's had, all's spent. . . ."), and she makes little effort to influence her husband after this except in the emergency of the banquet scene. To repeat what many others have said, her husband has gone beyond her, and there is no place for her practical counsel in his present course of wanton violence. Whatever dominance she may have exercised earlier (and she must exercise some, for the pressure on Macbeth should be great) is gone now. For this reason, among others, I do not see that a Lady Macbeth of stature is necessarily a threat to the stature of Macbeth—that is, if the latter character is acted as it should be.

III. FROM CRITICISM TO THEATRE

The most interesting suggestions for translating meaning into action in *Macbeth*—those of a kind peculiarly associated with this play—are more generalized and intangible than usual: they call upon the actor to convey an interpretation, not through any particular action or vocal inflection, but through imaginatively felt and subtly communicated moods. And the actor-critics who have particularly stressed the necessity for using the power of suggestion are those most interested in maintaining the importance of the supernatural element despite a skeptical age. They are JAMES MURDOCH in the nineteenth century and GORDON CRAIG, LENA ASHWELL, and MARGARET WEBSTER in the twentieth.[257]

The challenge that the supernatural element presents in the theatre has been stated very well by Miss Webster and by Craig. As the former remarks, "the subtle power of darkness becomes all-pervading" in this play: it "poisons the air with fear, preys on bloated and diseased imaginings, turns feasting to terror and the innocent sleep to nightmare"—yet *Macbeth* "contains no villain, no Iago, no Edmund. Evil is alive of itself. . . ." The audience should be made conscious throughout of the presence of this third protagonist (as Miss Webster calls the "power that is behind Macbeth and Lady Macbeth"). But how can this effect be achieved when the evil force never becomes incarnate except in the Witches —and when even they are no longer the "potent symbol" that they once were? As Craig expresses it, how can the "overpowering force of . . . unseen agencies" be made "clear and yet not actual"?

The most important answer to this problem—and the one agreed upon by all the actor-critics with whom we are at present concerned—is highly imaginative acting on the part of Macbeth and Lady Macbeth. According to Lena Ashwell, these characters should conjure up

the weird atmosphere surrounding persons living under Suggestion, attuned to the Unseen, haunted by the Powers of the Air, with constant thought-transference between themselves, and between themselves and the controlling demons. The lowered voice, the pauses so carefully indicated in the text, the breathless waiting until the sug-

257. Murdoch, "A Short Study of 'Macbeth,'" p. 78; Craig, *On the Art of the Theatre*, pp. 269, 271-72, 275-76, 279; Ashwell, *Reflections from Shakespeare*, pp. 124-25; Webster, *Shakespeare Without Tears*, pp. 223, 226-30.

gestion comes out of the air, the very mannerisms of the clairvoyant and the neurotic will drive Shakespeare's lesson into the hearts of the spectators.

Gordon Craig emphasizes the effect of hypnotic trance which Macbeth should produce, "seldom moving, but, when he does so, moving as a sleep-walker" (Lady Macbeth's later sleepwalking "is like the grim, ironical echo of Macbeth's whole life"). He also describes the changes in the manner of Macbeth and Lady Macbeth as they respond to the unseen influences: alone, each glories in the false sense of power instilled by the spirits; but, together, each becomes "furtive, alert, fearful" from seeing in the other's face something strange and shocking but also oddly familiar—the mirror of the evil experience common to both.

The representation of the Witches is also important, of course. This matter has been discussed earlier in the present chapter, but Margaret Webster's suggestions are appropriate here since they emphasize the technique of suggestiveness rather than full representation:

I believe that we should see as little as possible of the Witches in the flesh. . . . The unseen voice of evil, its imminence, its very facelessness, these things have a chilling power; we can use shadows of twisting silhouettes, the glimpse of hands, the outline of a head, shifting, hovering, formless; their voices should echo from the hollow rocks and stream away against the wind. We should see them by reflection, through the human beings who come so terrifyingly close to the unknowable.

One other point, naturally stressed by Gordon Craig more than by the others, is the visual aspect of the production—scenery and costumes—which can sometimes help to create an atmosphere of supernatural awe.

The extent to which intuition and suggestiveness are emphasized by these actor-critics, rather than specific stage business, is illustrated by their comments on the acting of particular scenes: Murdoch's, for example, on the hallucination of the air-drawn dagger and Craig's on the apparition of Banquo's Ghost. Both of these scenes are described as breathlessly effective in reading but disappointing in the theatre.

According to Murdoch, when we read the scene preceding the murder we feel the dead and heavy effect of the low arched apartments, the thick gloom of midnight broken only by [a] passing torch . . . or the glimmer of the smoky lamps; we see the flitting of the bat across the murky light; we hear the muttering thunder, and, anon, the howls and shrieks of the gathering tempest as it sweeps over the ivy-wrapt battlements . . . we see Macbeth stealthily approaching the chamber of his sleeping victim, overawed by the terrors of his conscience, his excited imagination calling up a thousand fearful images. . . . With bristling hair and quaking knees he stands for a moment appalled by a phantom-like outline hanging before his overstrained and uncertain vision, till will at length overcomes terror, and utterance is forced from his parched and palsied lips.

The actor who would produce this same effect must be in imaginative communion with the scene.

Such passages . . . cannot be analyzed; they must be felt, brooded over, until the soul is completely filled with their force and vastness, until, indeed, at times, physical action is paralyzed and speech choked. Yet upon the public platform we too often hear the language . . . in which is bodied forth the destruction of worlds . . . lisped in the glib fashion of the most commonplace and unemphatic prose.

Craig puts even more emphasis on the scene with Banquo's Ghost; for, in his opinion, "The whole play leads up to, and down from this point." The effect is ruined in the theatre, he writes (the Ghost too often provokes uneasy merriment rather than awe), because the scene is not properly prepared for: "the figures must not walk about on the ground for the first two acts and suddenly appear on stilts in the third. . . . We must open this play high up in an atmosphere loftier than that in which we generally grope. . . ." The director who hopes to arouse the audience to imaginative response must extract "from each act, each scene, each thought, action, or sound" in the play "some spirit, the spirit which is there."

And on the faces of the actors, on their costumes, and on the scene, by light, by line, by colour, by movement, voice and every means at [his] disposal . . . repeatedly and repeatedly bring upon the stage some reminder of the presence of these spirits, so that on the arrival of Banquo's ghost . . . we . . . should be so keenly expectant, so attuned to the moment and its coming that we should be conscious of its presence even before we saw it there.

CHAPTER SIX · *Conclusions*

The time has come to give some sustained consideration to two questions that so far have been only touched on occasionally: What, in general, is the relationship between the actors and the other critics of Shakespeare? What are the most characteristic—and the most valuable—contributions of the actors to Shakespearean criticism? Since the answers to these questions are interrelated at some points, there will be no attempt to keep the subjects completely separated.

Before launching into the discussion of these major issues, however, I must deal briefly with a third question which has been left almost untouched in the preceding chapters but which may seem to demand, even more obviously, an answer: How should actor-critics be rated as critics of Shakespeare? My reasons for considering this question less important than the others will become apparent in my discussion.

Some of the actor-critics have published book-length works of criticism which are consistently valuable—or as consistently so as those of any other critic: Thomas Davies, for example, in the eighteenth century, Sheridan Knowles in the nineteenth, Harley Granville-Barker in the twentieth. These writers are regularly mindful of both theatrical and literary values; they are not narrowly restricted to any particular system of thought; they can be read with profit and pleasure in any period, with only minimum allowances for vocabulary and ideas no longer current. Several other actor-critics could be named who have a substantial body of criticism to their credit, marked by the same virtues. But perhaps a brief discussion of the three we have mentioned will reveal, better than a mere list, the different kinds of writers who stand out as major contributors to the actors' criticisms of Shakespeare.

Davies' *Dramatic Miscellanies* is less coherent than Knowles's lectures (in their edited form) and Granville-Barker's *Prefaces*, and less literary. Sturdy common sense and interesting nuggets of theatrical criticism are his strong points. (His comments on linguistic and historical matters are often, for the modern reader, more distracting than enlightening.) Davies is less imaginative, sometimes, than his contemporary Arthur Murphy; but if he has nothing as perceptive as the latter's discussions of *Macbeth*, he shows better judgment than Murphy about the plot of *Hamlet*, and he is evidently more trustworthy in conveying an idea of Garrick's acting in the latter play. He is not as enslaved by literary, moral, and theatrical conventions as Francis Gentleman usually is, though he rarely throws out—as Gentleman occasionally does—some sudden spark of originality to startle and perplex the reader.

Knowles's lectures contain some excellent discussions of Shakespeare's dramatic craftsmanship, with a detailed analysis of *Macbeth* and a number of worthwhile comments on other plays. His inclination to judge all drama by structural standards which he considered absolute led him into occasional absurdities, as in applying the criterion of suspense-building in the same way to the dramas of Sophocles, Shakespeare, and the writers of his own day. On the other hand, his self-assurance in such matters made possible some acute and valid observations that a more timid critic would not have made. And his horizon was not bounded by the more mechanical aspects of structure: subjects like irony and illusion occupied his attention too. On the whole Knowles wears well. If his criticism sounds a bit old-fashioned, it is because it reminds us, not of his romantic and Victorian contemporaries (except in an occasional character analysis), but of our own immediate predecessors—critics like George Pierce Baker, for example. Perhaps the time has come when we *need* to be reminded again of the dramatic qualities of Shakespeare's plays—those that we take for granted in a general kind of way but that we sometimes consider (wrongly) too elementary for careful attention.[1] When Knowles died, his lecture notes were left in disarray, but Sydney Wells Abbott of the British Museum "deciphered them and made a sequence of their contents." Twenty-five presentation copies of the results, revised and edited by Francis Harvey, were published in 1873; and in 1875 a selection of material relating to *Macbeth* was published for general distribution. Neither volume is readily accessible today. It seems to me that a new edition of the lectures would be well worth undertaking.

As for Granville-Barker's *Prefaces to Shakespeare*, their value has been so often recognized that praise no doubt is superfluous. I must add my tribute, nevertheless. Granville-Barker's structural analyses reflect an awareness of the Elizabethan theatre combined,

---

1. A recognition of the need for such studies is shown by the recent reprinting of Arthur Colby Sprague's *Shakespeare and the Audience: A Study in the Technique of Exposition*, first published in New York in 1935. *Note:* Footnote references will not be provided in the present chapter for passages that have been presented in earlier chapters.

nearly always, with a sensitivity to effects that are not merely theatrical but dramatic in a subtler sense. His character studies are firmly anchored in the data of the plays; they are imaginatively, but not fancifully, developed. Thus in discussing Hamlet's character Granville-Barker explains the problem that Shakespeare faced in constructing the role; he gives the dramatic rationale for a Hamlet who is "neither mad nor sane"; but he also describes the "person" Hamlet—that dramatic person whom Shakespeare revealed in the course of his play. He is particularly fine in developing the hints of character that can be found in unexpected silences or understatements, in characteristic turns of expression, in passages where the words seem to be at odds with the feeling (e.g. his discussion of Desdemona's habitual reticence in moments of emotion; of the feeling behind Hamlet's insults to Ophelia). Occasionally his imagination falters (in his comments on the first scene of *Macbeth,* for example, and the conclusion of *Othello*), but not often.

None of these three actor-critics can be claimed exclusively for the stage. Although all were actors at one time or another, Davies was also a bookseller, Knowles a dramatist and schoolmaster, Granville-Barker a dramatist and director. But a thorough acquaintance, from the inside, with the practical needs and potentialities of the theatre is apparent throughout the work of each and gives it much of its value.

For the most part, however, the actor-critics are more significant as a group than as individuals. To put the matter another way, the individual actor-critic is frequently valuable, not for a large body of Shakespearean criticism, but for one or two influential essays; for stimulating, but brief and scattered, comments in works of a noncritical sort; for a set of notes designed for other actors; or for an occasional illuminating passage in a book of very uneven quality. Some of these critical offerings are much more substantial than others, of course, and the difference is not always one of physical length: for example, Gielgud's notes on *Hamlet* will repay a careful reading ("notes" is really too modest a word for them); on the other hand, *The True Ophelia,* a book by an anonymous actress, though it contains a few interesting suggestions, is chiefly negative in value—it should serve as a warning against reading so much between the lines that the lines themselves are overlooked. Some comments or discussions by actors are excellent criticisms by any standards: Macready's intelligent, pointed, and well-phrased remarks in his diary and reminiscences make us wish that this actor had expressed his ideas more fully and more frequently. Others derive a part of their value from circumstances or characteristics that rigid judges might consider extraneous but that I feel must be taken into account. (We give some weight to historical importance, after all, in assessing the value of literary criticism.) The importance of Mrs. Siddons's essay on Lady Macbeth outweighs its intrinsic merit simply because it was written by the greatest of all Lady Macbeths and because it was influential on numerous other actresses and critics. Garrick's comments on Othello, Lear, and Macbeth, made in conversations and personal letters, are significant because they tell us something essential about his intentions in portraying these characters. Hackett's discussion of King Lear is important less for its own acuteness than for the evidence it presents of the continuing strength of the Garrick tradition. Helen Faucit's book on Shakespeare's heroines is interesting because it tells us the reasons behind the innovations in her stage interpretations; because it provides insights into her method of thinking herself into her characters; and because it occasionally expresses ideas about the other characters in the plays which—acceptable or not—were ahead of their time. As for the worth of the essays simply as criticism, it is very mixed: the one on Desdemona, for example, was not only novel for its day, it is absolutely right in its essentials; the one on Ophelia, however, contains as much Faucit as Shakespeare.

If the actor-critics cannot easily be evaluated as individuals, perhaps some general statement can be made concerning their relative worth as a group of critics. For my own part, I consider Granville-Barker at his best a Shakespearean critic unsurpassed by any other writer, literary or theatrical. But, then, as I have said, he belongs to both worlds. As for the other actor-critics, the best of them lack the intellectual comprehensiveness, the occasional high moments of our greatest critics; but they compare favorably, I think, with the great body of writers on Shakespeare. Davies, for example, was far from being a Samuel Johnson, but who does not find him more rewarding to read than Gildon or Mrs. Montagu or—unless the reader is a hopeless devotee of the early romantics—Richardson? Ellen Terry is not only more entertaining than Mrs. Jameson but her intuitions are more firmly backed by the concrete realities of life, both real and theatrical.

At the same time, I feel that it is more important to understand the relationships between the actor-critics and the other critics than to attempt an assessment of relative merits; more important to determine what kinds of actor-criticisms are characteristic and significant than to evaluate these criticisms in their entirety. And so I return to the questions that I posed at the beginning of this chapter.

The mutual influence of stage and study has been, of course, a major driving force in the development of critical thought about Shakespeare's plays and characters. Let us consider, first of all, the influence exerted by the actors; for they have frequently held a significant place in the history of formal Shakespearean criticism, either through stage interpretations or through interpretations verbally expressed. It will then be in order to look at the other side of the picture.

The influence of stage interpretations upon literary criticism is a subject too large to be explored here, particularly since our main concern is with the actors' own opinions. But a few examples will suggest its importance. It seems likely that the vivid impressions of Shakespeare's characters gained from the stage contributed, in the eighteenth century, to the development of character analysis as a form of Shakespearean criticism.[2] More spe-

2. D. Nichol Smith suggests (*Shakespeare in the Eighteenth Century* [Oxford, 1928], p. 82) that certain early papers of theatrical criticism "give colour to the view that the examination of Shakespeare's characters had its home, as indeed we might expect, in the theatre rather than in the study" but says that as the eighteenth century advances theatrical criticism loses its value as an aid in the interpretation of Shakespeare's characters compared with criticism written by those who might never have seen a play acted. I believe the influence of the stage persisted throughout the century, though less directly in the writings of some critics. Arthur Murphy provides a good "bridge" between theatre and study. His analysis of the different workings of remorse in four Shakespearean characters (1757) was written shortly after his two-year stage experience (1754-56), and it is the earliest of such comparative studies, although they are usually associated with writers like Whately and Richardson. The argument over whether Lear feels most as a king or as a father began with Foote's criticism of Garrick, though it was later taken up by the nontheatrical critic Warton and then by Murphy (who was obviously supporting Garrick's interpretation). It is true that some of the character interpretations written during the last two decades of the century are untheatrical in tone and emphasis, but even these may show the influence of questions raised earlier as a result of stage performances. For a discussion of Aaron Hill's criticism, inspired rather early in the century by stage performances but

cific influences can be named too. For example, Garrick's robust performance of Hamlet apparently delayed the development of the romantic conception of the character; his performance of King Lear originated the new, pathetic conception; and his powerful depiction of remorse and supernatural terror may have contributed, inadvertently, to the critics' disposition to question the courage of Macbeth. In the next century the influence of Edmund Kean's acting was reflected directly in Hazlitt's criticisms: for example, his interpretation of Shylock eventually effected a change in the critic's understanding of that character;[3] and, in acting Hamlet, his kissing Ophelia's hand in the nunnery scene (a piece of business that opened up many possibilities for actors as well as critics) was described by Hazlitt as the finest commentary ever made on Shakespeare. Helen Faucit's womanly interpretation of Lady Macbeth bore immediate results in "Christopher North's" critical about-face. And George Fletcher in his book *Studies of Shakespeare* (1847) acknowledges the significance that Miss Faucit's unusual interpretations of Shakespeare's heroines held for him as a critic:

To the study of her performances . . . [the writer] mainly owes his lively and profound conviction of the indispensability of adequate acting, to bring the full sense of Shakespeare home to the minds and feelings of mankind,—and of its yet more pressing necessity, to aid the efforts of the literary expositor in eradicating false conceptions which the stage itself has implanted or confirmed.[4]

More pertinent to our present study is the actor-critic's frequent position as forerunner (or, at any rate, marcher in the front ranks) of new developments in Shakespearean criticism. Samuel Foote, for example, was one of the earliest "defenders" of Shakespeare against Voltaire (1847), and his phrase "Unity of Character" was echoed by other writers.[5] Nontheatrical critic Dr. Kenrick has sometimes been credited with giving the earliest public lectures on Shakespeare (1774), but an actor, Charles Macklin, was even earlier in this field of activity (1754).[6] Actors pro-

---

also showing "transitional" tendencies, *see* W. O. S. Sutherland, "Polonius, Hamlet, and Lear in Aaron Hill's *Prompter*," *Shakespeare Quarterly*, XLIX (1952), 605-18.

3. *The Complete Works of William Hazlitt*, ed. Howe, IV, 323-24; XVIII, 376-77.

4. George Fletcher, *Studies of Shakespeare* (London, 1847), p. xxiii.

5. Thomas R. Lounsbury, *Shakespeare and Voltaire* (New York, 1902), pp. 148, 158.

6. For Dr. Kenrick *see* Smith, *Shakespeare in the Eighteenth Century*, pp. 90-91;

vided several early examples of character studies, unusually detailed for that period: Foote's discussion of Othello, for example (1747). Theophilus Cibber's enthusiastic description of Falstaff (1748) can even claim the distinction of an early-flowering "vice" usually associated with romantic criticism: the tendency to remove a character from the play and imagine him in the surroundings of everyday life.

> Were jolly Sir *John* now living, and invited to regale with a set of *Bons Vivans* of the first Rank and Figure, he'd not be placed at the bottom of the Table; nay, let him take his Seat where he would, that would become the Head: And when the Company broke up (which I presume might be at Day-break) I question if they would not part from the jovial Knight with more Regret than from one another . . . each reminding him not to forget the Day and Hour of their next appointed Revel.[7]

Cibber was not fully "romantic" in his attitude here, since he was well aware that he was only imagining an offstage life for Falstaff (unlike Macready, in the next century, who argued so earnestly about Bassanio and Antonio that he was laughed at for speaking as if the characters were really alive—"Who is alive if they are not?" he demanded). Even so, the passage quoted above is the earliest example, as far as I know, of written criticism indulging in this kind of fantasy. Actor-critics have sometimes been the first to propound new interpretations of Shakespeare's characters. Among extant discussions of Hamlet, for example, the earliest fully-developed "romantic" analysis of the character is Thomas Sheridan's (reported by Boswell in 1756). Francis Gentleman was the first—and for many years the only—critic to set forth a completely "black" interpretation of Macbeth (1770). Sarah Siddons' essay on Lady Macbeth, containing the revolutionary idea of a "fair, feminine, nay, perhaps even fragile" character (published posthumously in 1834 but written and shown to friends at least nineteen years earlier) has already been referred to in another connection.

But, if actors have been important in the history of Shakespearean criticism, it is equally true that they themselves have

---

for Macklin *see* William W. Appleton, *Charles Macklin: An Actor's Life* (Cambridge, Mass., 1960), p. 103.

7. *A Serio-Comic Apology for Part of the Life of Mr. Theophilus Cibber, Comedian* (Printed with *Romeo and Juliet, A Tragedy, Revis'd and Alter'd from Shakespeare* (London, 1748), p. 102. The sketch of Falstaff begins on p. 101.

frequently been influenced by the theories of nontheatrical critics. In some cases they have been violently opposed to these theories: for example, John Philip Kemble's essay in defense of Macbeth's courage was inspired by Thomas Whately's supposed imputations of cowardice; and Sir Michael Redgrave tells of overemphasizing Hamlet's love for his father because of his own opposition to Ernest Jones's theory of the Oedipus complex. In other cases the actors have accepted wholeheartedly the ideas advanced by other critics. Several have been particularly attracted to A. C. Bradley's criticism, for example: Lena Ashwell commends his insight into Hamlet's emotions; Granville-Barker, his conception of Macbeth's character; Margaret Webster even accepts his argument that *King Lear* is unactable—though it drew fire from Granville-Barker. One reason for Bradley's popularity among actor-critics is, no doubt, the subjective quality of his criticism, which—though some modern critics take exception to it—reveals a certain affinity for the actor's approach to Shakespeare. As he himself remarks:

[Scholarly studies of sources, texts, etc. are less indispensable than] that close familiarity with the plays, that native strength and justice of perception, and that habit of reading with an eager mind, which make many an unscholarly lover of Shakespeare a far better critic than many a Shakespeare scholar.

Such lovers read a play more or less as if they were actors who had to study all the parts . . . they want to realise fully and exactly the inner movements which produced these words and no other, these deeds and no other, at each particular moment. This . . . is the right way to read the dramatist Shakespeare. . . .[8]

In some instances the actors have been intrigued by a particular critical theory but have found it ultimately untenable. Thus Thomas Davies tells of Garrick's having Polonius acted according to Dr. Johnson's view of the character but finding this interpretation ineffective; and Sir John Gielgud reports his lack of success in using Dover Wilson's idea of having Hamlet overhear Polonius's eavesdropping plan. The testing of critical theories in the medium for which they were intended would seem to be a valuable service to criticism itself, despite the obvious fact that not all valid insights can be so tested and that the results of such testing on the part of one actor with one kind of audience are not infallible. But, no matter what the actor's reaction to the theories

8. A. C. Bradley, *Shakespearean Tragedy* (London, 1941), pp. 1-2.

of his literary and academic contemporaries—whether favorable, adverse, or purely pragmatic—his own interpretation has been affected in some way by the contact.

The influence of literary criticism on the actors' interpretations has been greatest, I believe, in connection with the character of Hamlet. A brief survey of this influence will suggest some of the ways in which actors' interpretations have absorbed the ideas of other critics. During much of the eighteenth century the influence of the stage tradition was dominant: Hamlet was interpreted as vigorous, passionate, obviously sane but "lively" in counterfeiting madness. Even the questioning of this traditional conception may have come first from actors rather than from literary critics (except for the suggestion of real madness): Francis Gentleman's insistence upon Hamlet's weaknesses and inconsistencies preceded George Steevens' similar discussion by three years; Thomas Sheridan's analysis of Hamlet as a scholarly, irresolute character was a forerunner of Coleridge's. During the nineteenth century, however, the literary critics took the initiative; and, despite occasional rebellions by independent-minded actors, they have kept it—at least, as far as the actors' written criticisms are concerned. This statement needs qualifying, however. For one thing, the literary influence has often been general rather than particular. During the period of romantic criticism, for example, the prevailing view of Hamlet was that of a gentle, moody youth, brilliant of mind but inactive; some actor-critics undoubtedly adopted this view because it was held by the general public, not because they were persuaded to it by reading Hazlitt or Lamb. For another thing, the literary influence, though great, was never all-pervasive. Even at the height of romanticism some stage interpretations were less "quiet" and refined than the literary critics deemed proper—and sometimes less so than the written remarks of a particular Hamlet would suggest (Charles Kean, for example, said that Hamlet required more mental than physical illustration, yet his own performance was sometimes described as melodramatic). Nor did the romantic ideal completely triumph even in the actors' written criticisms: Macready, though he was influenced by it, continued to insist upon Hamlet's "energy" and strong passions. Later actors like Wilson Barrett and William Poel even led the way for critics in one important particular: the idea of Hamlet's youthfulness—an idea that seems to me both convincing and vital. All things considered, however, my original statement stands: Hamlet criticism by actors of the nineteenth and twentieth centuries is exceptionally oriented toward the interpretations that originated with literary and academic people.

Actors' comments about specific writers will give us some hints concerning the kinds of criticism that have appealed to them and the extent to which the attraction has influenced their own thought. Henry Irving, for example, responded to Hazlitt's interpretation because it was a challenge: Hazlitt had considered the thoughtful, introspective Hamlet essentially unactable; well, Irving would prove that *he* could act it. (This is not to say that Irving did not "really" believe in such a Hamlet. I think he did— up to a point.) It is not often, however, that we can pinpoint so definitely the reason for an actor's response. Perhaps Goethe is the critic of *Hamlet* whom actors have most frequently mentioned by name: in the nineteenth century both W. C. Macready and James H. Hackett praised his analysis of Hamlet, though neither adopted all its details; and in the present century John Barrymore found it congenial. As I have suggested elsewhere, part of the attraction may have lain in the simple fact that Goethe put the interpretation into the mouth of an actor, Wilhelm Meister. If this explanation is unbearably superficial, let me suggest another possibility. When Kate Field was describing Charles Fechter's performance—the most vigorous and determined Hamlet of that time, and one with which Miss Field herself was in sympathy— she compared it to Goethe's conception in one respect: i.e. that both Fechter and Wilhelm Meister considered grief a new and "heavy obligation" for Hamlet, not a natural condition of his mind. Had she merely remarked, without explaining, that Fechter's Hamlet reminded her of Goethe's conception, we would have been astonished, for we would immediately have contrasted the robust avenger of one with the "delicate flower" of the other. Some of the actors who have expressed interest in Goethe's conception may well have been struck forcibly by one or two points in it without being convinced by the whole. Macready was undoubtedly attracted to the analysis because of the *method* used in it, and probably he agreed with some of its details. But even Goethe, he remarked in a moment of particular exaltation, fell short of his own understanding of Hamlet. According to Sir

Tyrone Guthrie, Goethe's influence came down from the nineteenth century through Henry Irving, thence to Sir John Gielgud, and thence to the latter's younger followers. Guthrie blames it for the "stereotype" of Hamlet as a melancholy, irresolute dreamer, an interpretation that he rejects. However, Gielgud's own description of Hamlet balances sensitivity with vigor, gentleness with macabre humor. Like Macready's, it attributes to Hamlet more energy and passion than Goethe allowed to his sweet prince. And, if Ellen Terry is right, Irving's Hamlet had "strength" as well as "sensitivity." If, as Guthrie says, these actors perpetuated a "Young Werther" tradition, it was (in their own intention, at least) Werther fortified with a strong dose of beef, iron, and wine. The most striking "outside" influence on recent actors of Hamlet has been Ernest Jones, with his Freudian theory—which, however, has not been accepted wholeheartedly or permanently as a practical basis for stage interpretation. Salvador de Madariaga has struck a spark from at least two contemporary actors—Sir Alec Guinness and Sir Tyrone Guthrie. Neither has accepted his complete interpretation, but each has taken something: Guinness the idea of a Spanish influence, Guthrie the idea that Hamlet does not fail to act so much as he postpones action.

The impression that comes from a study of the actors' Hamlet interpretations is that their borrowing from literary critics, though fairly extensive, has been carried out in a cavalier, not a slavish, way. And this impression would hold true, no doubt, for their responses to the literary criticism of other Shakespearean characters. Actors have made incursions on the interpretations of other writers; they have taken what they wanted and discarded the rest without qualm. Or they have pounced upon an idea that interested them, taken it out of its context and developed it in their own way so that it sometimes emerged as something quite different from the original. This is as it should be, I think. As Paul Scofield has remarked, "it is not possible to interpret an interpreter." Then, too, the idea of another critic may be very helpful to an actor in working out his own interpretation, may enable him to give coherence and a sense of depth to his performance—as Gielgud has testified of Granville-Barker's comments on Hamlet in Act II—without actually carrying over to the audience in any direct, concrete fashion. The actors have not been respecters of persons, either. Their borrowing has not been confined to substantial, well-established critics. Something fresh, something vivid, something that provides a handle by which they can grasp a character—that is what they have looked for. Edwin Booth's interest in Vining, with his theory of a feminine Hamlet, is an extreme example. But Madariaga and Jones are also unorthodox and therefore stimulating. This is not to say that the actors have been irresponsible interpreters. They have been more open-mindedly receptive than most critics, more willing to take risks, quicker to experiment with new ideas—at least, some of them have (Sir Laurence Olivier is a good example)—but in the long run they have usually rejected supersubtle interpretations, since they cannot be effectively projected anyway, as well as interpretations that contradict some basic element traditionally associated with a character. When a really basic change has occurred and has been permanently maintained, it has usually originated with the actor himself, not with his attempt to embody the conception of another critic.

The interaction of stage and study is well illustrated by the Faucit-Fletcher-Irving chain reaction (as it seems to have been) in the interpretation of Macbeth. It is probable that the critic George Fletcher was influenced toward a darker view of Macbeth's character as a result of exchanging ideas with the actress Helen Faucit concerning a relatively sympathetic Lady Macbeth. Miss Faucit's copy of Fletcher's essay on *Macbeth* (1843) was presented to Henry Irving when the latter was preparing to undertake his first production of the play (1875). Irving adopted Fletcher's interpretation as a basis for his own; he continued to build upon it in his later performances (1889), and he defended his conception of a villainous Macbeth (still considered an innovation) in public lectures (1895). Irving's interpretation was never very successful, however, and it is doubtful that a Macbeth who resembles Iago from the first moment of the play will ever become a major tradition on the stage.

It is this possession of a "tradition" which, though it has bound the actor-critic in one way, has helped him to a certain measure of independence in another. For, although no human being can wholly escape the ties of thought and convention common to his period of history, often the actor's relationship to a living, continuous stage tradition has helped him to rise above—or see around—the critical fads of the moment. Even when a particular tradition—a "stereotyped" interpretation, as Guthrie would call it, or a style of acting, or a long-established theatrical system—gives way, a certain continuity remains: the pragmatic approach, the nothing-sacred attitude, the automatic assumption that any theory must stand a practical test. It is to this, as much as anything else, that the actors' criticisms owe their distinctive quality.

Take the matter of structure in Shakespeare's plays. All of the eighteenth century actor-critics were aware of the classical doctrine of the three "unities." They were also very much aware of the practical value of such structural ideals as lucid and painless exposition, dramatic progression, climactic suspense-building, effective denouement. Since it was obvious that adhering to the "unities" could make it easier to keep the story-line clear, these actors probably did not view the classical doctrine as a mere literary fetish. Even so, they knew from experience that some plays acted effectively despite broken rules. Although in their criticism they frequently mentioned Shakespeare's "irregularity" of structure, more often than not they also noted that in performance no feeling of improbability results, that the action is "pleasingly progressive," or that "strong situations" or "capital characters" compensate for structural lapses. (Thomas Davies even defended the much-attacked plot of *Hamlet,* and Charles Dibdin spoke out for the Shakespearean version of *King Lear,* Fool and all, despite the recognition that this character "retards the action.") On the other hand, in the romantic period, when most nontheatrical critics were no longer emphasizing formal structure, Sheridan Knowles was still giving lectures that read like a basic course in playwriting. Although he rejected the unities of time and place as hindrances rather than helps, he discussed such technical aspects of structure as progression and climax more fully than any of the preceding actor-critics had done.

The fact that dramatic concerns have encouraged a certain amount of continuity despite the swinging of the literary pendulum is illustrated by the similarity of Knowles's comments on *Hamlet* and those of Gentleman, Murphy, and Dibdin in the preceding period. And by the fact that Granville-Barker and Margaret Webster in the twentieth century have agreed with the eighteenth century critics that *King Lear* "suffers somewhat" under the double plot, even though these later actors had no thought of improving the structure of the play. Again, Granville-Barker is much like Knowles in discussing Shakespeare's brilliant solution to the problem of keeping up suspense in the last two acts of *Macbeth*. Both the romantic William Oxberry and the modern Granville-Barker have observed conflicts between an artistic ideal and theatrical necessity: Oxberry pointed out that some scenes in *Hamlet* are not strictly tied to plot progression but are rich in poetry and characterization; Granville-Barker made similar observations about the brothel scene in *Othello* and the encounter between mad Lear and blind Gloucester in *King Lear*. The difference between the two men (a difference born of different ages) is that Oxberry acquiesced in the omission of "superfluous" scenes on the stage whereas Granville-Barker thought that Shakespeare's design should be preserved intact, in the theatre as in the study.

The decline in the emphasis upon mechanical aspects of structure in recent actors' criticisms is, no doubt, a part of this same trend among critics in general. But practical theatrical concerns have probably united with the interests of the scholar-critics in bringing about the change. A knowledge of Elizabethan staging, and particularly a direct knowledge gained through attempts to apply Shakespeare's own methods to his plays, has been the major influence here. For a continuous method of staging tends, on the one hand, to obscure the impression of separate structural units and, on the other, to draw attention to such effects as echoes and juxtaposed contrasts.

Actually some of these "new" concerns are not completely new to actors. The interrelationship of structure and character, for example, a strong point in Granville-Barker's discussions of both *Hamlet* and *Othello,* was suggested during the first quarter of the nineteenth century in Oxberry's discussion of *Hamlet* and a little later in Knowles's discussion of *Macbeth*. Recent actors have had more to say about pattern (parallels, repetitions of image and theme, etc.) than about progression and denouement, just as other critics have done. But interesting examples of such discussions can be found, too, in criticism by eighteenth and nineteenth century actors. As early as 1770 Gentleman noticed the double plane of illusion achieved in the "Hecuba" scene and and the play scene of *Hamlet,* a point reiterated in modern times by Granville-Barker and Gielgud and by nontheatrical critics as well. In the nineteenth century Oxberry, in discussing the "willow" scene of *Othello,* and Knowles, in discussing the "temple-haunting martlet" passage in *Macbeth,* showed how a scene of calm repose can intensify rather than allay the tension of tragic anticipation; and Knowles pointed out the ironic preparation for tragedy in the Gravediggers' jests in *Hamlet.* Edwin Booth (in the late nineteenth century) noticed that in the last scene of *Othello* the words "For in my sense 'tis happiness to die" echo the "same sad refrain" heard earlier at the height of Othello's happiness, "If 'twere now to die, 'twere now to be most happy." (Granville-Barker was later to find a number of similar echoes in the same play.)

Nevertheless the two actor-critics who have contributed most significantly to this kind of criticism—Granville-Barker and Gielgud—have been inhabitants of an age in which irony is the lingua franca among critics. Their comments on the visual parallels in Shakespeare's plays—Lear's chair (not bed) in the reconciliation scene recalls, but ironically, his throne in the initial scene of the play; Claudius' "union" (which he may take from a ring and toss into the cup) ironically reminds the audience that Gertrude's death parallels that of her first husband—lend themselves to symbolic interpretations of a kind that is directly related to the theatre, not removed from it. Such criticism is particularly salutary, I think, in a day when imagery and symbolism are receiving great emphasis but of a sort, frequently, incompatible with the concept of the plays as drama.[9]

In the matter of character study, as in that of structural criticism, the actor-critics have shown the influence of the literary conventions of their respective periods, but they have also transcended this influence in many instances.

The eighteenth century actors were enough acquainted with literary criticism to know the principle of "decorum" in characterization. Furthermore, the stage tradition, inherited from Shakespeare's day, in which each actor in the company had his

9. But see Professor Clifford Lyons' significant essay, "Stage Imagery in Shakespeare's Plays," *Essays on Shakespeare and Elizabethan Drama in Honor of Hardin Craig* (Columbia, Missouri, 1962), pp. 261-74. Much of the allegorical significance that Maynard Mack sees in *King Lear* (*King Lear in Our Time,* pp. 45-80) is difficult to visualize in theatrical terms, but Mack does point out (p. 72) the possibilities of several symbolic stage pictures, including the one in the reconciliation scene noted earlier by Granville-Barker.

line of parts, supported the general idea embodied in this principle. Against this background Gentleman's concern about the sometimes unheroic actions of that "hero" Hamlet is understandable, and his annoyance with the ambivalent Gertrude. Yet, apparently without realizing the inconsistency of his position, Gentleman also admired Shakespeare's unusual ability to create individuals. The same set of conventions explains Macklin's disgust with Garrick for restoring the scene in which Othello, a general, falls in a trance at his ancient's feet and the one in which Lear, a king, falls asleep in a farmhouse as any laborer might do.

In their best moments, however, the actor-critics either went beyond the system or made it serve the purposes of imaginative criticism. Paradoxical as it may seem, some of the most original character interpretations in the eighteenth century were evolved by some of the most dogmatic devotees of the literary-cum-theatrical convention. Macklin's stage interpretations of Shakespeare's characters offer several good examples: his Shylock is the most striking,[10] but there are others; his Iago, with his "distant, obsequious manner," is praised by Davies as the first intelligent performance of that role (previous Iagos had made their villainy too obvious), and his Polonius ("oddity grafted upon the man of sense" rather than buffoon or sage) is described by Gentleman as the best interpretation of that part. It may be that Macklin simply transcended in performance his own announced principles; but it may also be that he found in character acting—his forte—a way to reconcile the eccentricities of Shylock with the character of a villain and those of Polonius with the character of a statesman.

10. The accuracy of the tradition that Macklin's Shylock was an innovation has recently been questioned by William S. E. Coleman (see "Post-Restoration Shylocks Prior to Macklin," *Theatre Survey*, VIII, No. 1 [May, 1967], 17-34). He takes the position that, since "almost a full generation passed before Macklin was described as the first serious post-Restoration Shylock," "it can be argued that the pre-Macklin comic Shylock was quite possibly a myth engendered and perpetuated by late eighteenth-century Macklin partisans"; and, after examining the evidence, he concludes that there is insufficient documentation to be certain what the true pre-Macklin Shylock was like. He corrects the too-frequent conception that Granville, in his adaptation, *The Jew of Venice*, remolded Shylock into a buffoon, and he points out that, although five of the six known Shylocks prior to Macklin were primarily comic actors, Macklin himself also frequently acted comic and character parts. The article is interesting, but, in my opinion, it is not sufficiently convincing to warrant setting aside the traditional assertion of Macklin's importance. To mention only one point, Coleman dismisses in a very cavalier manner two important pieces of evidence concerning Doggett's comic Shylock.

Among the written criticisms, the unusual interpretation of Macbeth by the dogmatic Gentleman has already been noted. Similarly Sheridan, conventional enough to censure Spranger Barry for making a "lover" out of the "warrior" Othello, was in advance of his own time in his interpretation of Hamlet.

Sheridan offered his interpretation as a way of proving that Hamlet, "notwithstanding of his seeming incongruities, is a perfectly consistent character." Was the desire to reconcile or explain away Hamlet's inconsistencies a specifically "eighteenth-century" characteristic, bred of the habit of determining a character's ruling passion and fitting his actions into place around it? Or was it a precocious "romantic" trait, associated with later attempts to find a real-life motivation for each action? It may have been either, both, or neither. But, whatever it was in Sheridan's background or his mental habits that compelled him to resolve Hamlet's inconsistencies and that dictated his method of doing so, his aim was the same as Macready's in the nineteenth century, when he sought to "make the mind of Hamlet apparent, to render his seeming inconsistencies reconcilable and intelligible," and as Gielgud's in the twentieth, when he said that it is the actor's duty to find and make manifest, amid Hamlet's complexity of traits, a "complete basic character in which the part may progress in a simple, convincing line." The aim of all these men, regardless of period, was to act Hamlet convincingly.

Many of the available discussions of character by eighteenth century actors are aimed outward at theatrical effect rather than inward at psychological motivation. But sometimes an actor who began with the former would go on to comment on the character in a way that suggests at least a tentative search into the "springs of motive." Thus, instead of explaining what in Macbeth's character justified the recovery of his courage in the banquet scene, Garrick simply averred that "pusillanimity" would "hurt the character" in the esteem of the audience. He did go on, however, to describe briefly Macbeth's state of mind in the last part of the play. Foote, after stating the actor's problem in undertaking Othello (to gain audience sympathy, if possible superior to what will naturally be granted to Desdemona), launched into a detailed discussion of the "tender-hearted" character that he conceived Othello to be, citing speeches and actions from the play just as any critic of a later period might have done. Once again, theatrical necessity was the mother—and the handmaid—of imaginative criticism.

In the nineteenth century the actors, who already had a head start in character criticism, took naturally to the romantic emphasis on character, with all its excesses: its probing for hidden motives, its construction of an offstage life for the dramatis personae, its "poetic" descriptions, difficult to paraphrase in plain prose. Yet the resulting character studies, since they were written by performers who would have to reduce their conceptions to concrete dimensions on a stage, took on a direction and an applicability that make many of them still worth reading today. Even Helen Faucit's reconstruction of Ophelia's childhood might very well retain a kind of usefulness for the newest actress of the part. It would at least provide for her consideration an alternative to the impure interpretation of Ophelia. (The improvisations or extemporaneous dialogues used by some modern actors as a means of getting inside their characters are something of the same sort.)

Actually, the imagining of offstage experiences for Shakespeare's characters has not been an exclusively romantic trait, as far as historical period is concerned. As early as 1773 George Swan had worked out in detail what Othello did, thought, and said between the time when he heard the noise of the street fight and the time when he entered Desdemona's bedchamber to commit the murder. And as late as 1955 Robert Speaight was imagining Hamlet's attempted visit to Ophelia on the day after the ghostly interview. There have even been speculations, by Granville-Barker and Speaight respectively, about the sex lives of Gertrude and Othello. A character must be, for the actor, not simply a figure in a series of isolated scenes. There must be a wholeness about him. And the extrapolation of offstage experiences from something in the play is one way of achieving that wholeness. Some actors, I feel sure, have no need of a conscious process of this kind. They trust to intuition and a sense of the theatre, to what Sir Michael Redgrave has called the "impressionistic" approach. But even Sarah Siddons, as Constance in *King John*, felt the need of listening from the wings to the decision to drop her son's claim to the throne (acting out, literally, an offstage experience) in order to express the grief and rage demanded of her on her next appearance.

Occasionally an actor has indulged in a character description that cannot be wholly reduced to rational terms. As James Murdoch said, in attempting to "conjure" with words his conception of the "air-drawn dagger" scene in *Macbeth,* some of Shakespeare's passages "cannot be analyzed; they must be felt, brooded over, until the soul is completely filled with their force and vastness. . . ." The attempt to suggest in words an impression that cannot be completely conveyed by words seems to have inspired such writings as Fanny Kemble's discussion of Lady Macbeth in the sleepwalking scene. Though it does not make complete sense as a realistic statement, it does evoke a *picture* of the character that the imagination accepts and, moreover, retains long after the memory has released its hold on the ideas contained in many a carefully reasoned study. (Actually the passage in question has some "realistic" basis, if modern ideas of the subconscious mind are invoked, but much of its effect comes from the overall impression rather than from literal meaning.) Even Miss Kemble's tendency toward "fine" writing can serve a purpose for the reader who can willingly suspend his belief in the principles of Freshman Composition. For those attuned to it, this swelling, adjective-laden, pseudo-Biblical style creates a spell which would be denied to straightforward exposition. Such writing obviously has its limitations, but it should not all be dismissed as sentimental gush. Since a "feeling" for a character or scene may be just as important as objective analysis in bringing the play convincingly to life, this can be, I think, a legitimate form of criticism if it is purposeful and well done. (It goes without saying that it should not be allowed to substitute for other forms of criticism or to masquerade as something it is not.)

The subjective element in actors' criticisms comes not only from simple imaginative vision, or dreamlike communion with the play, but also from the use of personal experience as a bridge to interpretation. The latter tendency occasionally produces results that are worthwhile as well as interesting: for example, Macready's diary notes on his own performances of Hamlet and Iago; Edwin Booth's account of his brush with death which confirmed his interpretation of Hamlet's grim flippancy. Even peculiarities of personal interest and belief that would be fatal to objective criticism can become grist for the actor's imaginative mill. The result may be three-fourths chaff, but what remains is sometimes both tasty and nourishing. For example, Lena Ashwell's belief in spiritualism is responsible for the compelling earnestness with which she urges the actor of Macbeth to make the audience feel his receptiveness to supernatural suggestion. She was convinced that the sense of spiritual presence could be powerfully evoked—and no wonder! She herself in acting the mother in *The Monkey's Paw* had once "seen" the apparition of the dead son so clearly that (according to her account) she had communicated the visual picture to some members of the audience. I think she is right, however, that Macbeth's temptation by supernatural agency is important to character and story. (We can simply ignore the "technical" talk of "malignant astrals.") Another example: It is amusing to find analyses of Iago, Claudius, and the Macbeths side by side with those of real-life murderers in H. B. Irving's *Book of Remarkable Criminals*. Yet there is an engaging liveliness that comes of this approach. Is there anyone whose day is not brightened when, in reading of Claudius' cleverness as the perfect murderer, he chances upon the remark that "a supernatural intervention" was "a contingency against which no murderer could be expected to have provided"? I must add that, oddly enough, much of what Irving says might have come from the most scrupulously detached Shakespearean critic of his period rather than from an amateur criminologist.

Actually the highly subjective elements that I have been discussing are only occasional flourishes upon the very substantial body of character criticisms by actors. For example, Fanny Kemble's impressionistic description to which we have referred is only a kind of mystical climax to her essentially rationalistic analysis of Lady Macbeth's character as a whole. In general, the actors' interpretations have been characterized by common sense as well as imagination, and, usually, by a consciousness of theatrical possibilities and limitations that acts as a check on the most wayward fantasy.

Although actors have worthwhile things to say on a number of subjects connected with Shakespeare, the character interpretations are—as we would expect—their most characteristic contribution to Shakespearean criticism, the one that springs most naturally from their own exuberant interest. Some of these are of value mainly to other actors; some are of interest because they epitomize a particular period or point of view, or even because they offer glimpses of what Shakespeare has meant to an interesting personality. But many of them raise valid questions, offer new insights, or give to scholar and general reader alike a sense of shared pleasure in Shakespeare's creations.

I have seen the statement—by actors themselves sometimes—that an actor's gift is not analytical, that what he has to impart about a character cannot be put into words. Surely the last part of this is true: his most significant "statement" is incapable of being so reduced and captured. An actor is faced with the task of bringing an ideal into the realm of reality, of giving concrete form to the abstract. In doing so he cannot *merely represent* the ideal, or there will be a grand display without any real audience contact. A certain humanness in his characterization must draw to itself that same quality from the audience. (We in the audience furnish the ectoplasm for the materialization of his conception.) The ideal becomes the breath of life animating a concrete body. That fusion, a kind of creative miracle even in good amateur performances, cannot be communicated in any form other than itself. Like a poem, it "should not mean, but be." But an actor's character analysis, when he composes one, is like the poet's rough draft or the artist's sketch, and as such it has a value of its own.

I am speaking here, and in the following paragraphs, from an admittedly "modern" point of view, for I am concerned with Shakespearean criticism that has relevance for a modern reader, playgoer, or actor. But even in periods when performances were more stylized than ours (if, indeed, they really were), there must have been in the representation of Shakespeare's plays some common human meeting ground for actor and spectator. Perhaps Burbage was expected to *represent* "grief" in a particular scene, or "Hamlet grieving," rather than to *become* the grief-stricken man named Hamlet; yet many in his audience must have felt, as a contemporary writer did, that "what we see him personate we think truly done before us."[11] I am not thinking of simple dramatic illusion—it is never simple or complete, even in a theatre with realistic scenery and acting—nor am I thinking of "realism" in a restricted sense, but rather of a feeling of abounding vitality communicated by some of Shakespeare's characters, even in the

11. "An Excellent Actor," *The Overburian Characters*, ed. W. J. Paylor (Oxford, 1936), p. 77. See Paylor's introductory essay for attributions of the various "Overbury" character sketches. John Webster, the dramatist, is the probable author of the one cited above.

reading, as if they were ready to burst into autonomous existence. If we try to explain this sense of reality, we reach a point at which we must give up; but we always find that it is *partly* due to elements that we can call realistic: e.g. convincingly human responses to particular situations by particular personalities; noticeable (if not consistent) differentiation of characters by the diction and cadence of their speech; implications of motives and feelings beyond those openly expressed. We must not reject the insights to be gained by an intelligent study of these characteristics simply because the characteristics themselves have been over-emphasized by some critics of the "psychological" type. We have seen develop in our own period a school of drama that is more emblematic than realistic, and we may discern in Shakespeare some scenes, characters, moments that will gain by the use of theatrical techniques associated with this type of drama. But there are many characters which, although they demand something broader than what is generally described as realistic acting, also proclaim their humanity and their reality with every word. As several of the actor-critics have remarked, Shakespeare's characters combine idealization and particularity, just as his language combines rhetorical splendor and colloquial simplicity. When Shakespeare had Hamlet describe the actor's duty "to hold, as 'twere, the mirror up to nature," he probably had a rather different conception of a mirror's function than the average modern playgoer gets when he hears the phrase, yet he was not (I am convinced) speaking a language that is completely foreign to us.

Character criticism, once highly rated, is frequently looked upon with suspicion at present, except in such combinations as "character and symbol," "character and structure," "character and society." I should like to speak a word—my final one here—for character criticism per se, especially that which the actors have to offer.

I am well aware of the perils. I realize that if every actor tried to "develop" his role into a complex human individual the play as a whole would suffer. I am also aware that a new and attractive interpretation of one major role may be devastating to other important characters in the play. And, as I pointed out in discussing Granville-Barker's interpretation of Othello, an over-emphasis upon minute analysis, particularly a literal adherence to such an analysis, may be destructive of larger values. (Both

Sir John Gielgud and Sir Michael Redgrave warn their fellow actors against the dangers of psychological dissection,[12] and Sir Donald Wolfit states flatly that it can result in reversing the positions of hero and villain.) Mistakes of all these kinds can be found in character analysis by one actor or another. Yet the old argument against puritanical opponents of the drama applies here as well: the abuses should not blind us to the value of the thing when it is properly used.

A Shakespearean play may be many things to many people: a poem, a fable, a philosophical discourse—but the one thing that it should be to everyone is a drama. The potentialities for stage performance should be one consideration, I think, in any critical work on Shakespeare. Not that the plays should be confined to the stage, even if excellent performances could somehow be conjured up at any moment and in any place. Seeing them in the mind's eye, analyzing them with the mind's tools can be satisfying and profitable, but not (I would say) if the results of these activities are in conflict with or totally irrelevant to possible stage interpretation or effect. It would be foolish to claim that all valid "meanings" will be immediately apparent, even in the best performances, but the suggestions for them should be implicit there. (It goes without saying that, not being Elizabethans, we may need special reading to appreciate some of these implications; and, one of us being less perceptive than another, we are bound to lose some of them anyway, just as the Elizabethans did themselves.)

Assuming that this is true, take all the qualities of Shakespearean drama that are being emphasized in scholarly or critical works today—its rhetoric, its imagery, its versification, its use of Elizabethan "science," its possible symbolic, allegorical, or mythical patterns—how do all these things "come across" (if they do) when the play is performed? Partly through visual effects, of course, through music and other such details of the performance. But primarily through actors in their representation of characters.

There are occasions when sight and sound can speak to us more directly than could the meaning of words or the impact of personality. Some of the Gloucester scenes in Peter Brook's production of *King Lear* are good examples. But such moments are,

12. Gielgud, "A Shakespearean Speaks His Mind," *Theatre Arts*, XLIII (January, 1959), 71; Redgrave, "Shakespeare and the Actors," in *Talking of Shakespeare*, ed. John Garrett (London, 1954), 144-46.

in my opinion, greatly outnumbered by the others—those in which the sound of the language may be melodious or cacophonous within itself, but the effect is terrible or moving or witty or revolting largely because of the feeling that has been built up for the speaker or the attitude that has been established toward him. Thus King Lear's storm speech ("Blow winds and crack your cheeks!") has the same harsh and dissonant sounds, the same turbulent imagery masking the same careful rhetorical structure, no matter what our concept of the character who utters it. But our responses to these qualities may vary widely, according to the concrete image we have of the man who is speaking—whether strong or feeble, responsible or irresponsible, wickedly proud or "more sinned against than sinning." If the character of King Lear has not come alive for us as a person by the time he is required to speak these words, the speech may strike the average member of the audience as merely a grand aria, very resounding and impressive but, as the voice of humanity in this age of understatement, more embarrassing than significant. But what if we are fortunate enough to be present at a performance like Paul Scofield's (in the same production of which we spoke a moment ago), when King Lear is from the first moment a fully-realized human being (not simply a "magnificent portent," in Granville-Barker's phrase, or a Promethean figure hurling "thunder and lightning," as Speaight would have him)? By the time we have reached the storm scenes with this Lear, his gigantic apostrophe, "unrealistic" as it is, seems to us the agonized cry of a man whom we have come to know. The emotions expressed are larger and more intense than any we might recognize as "normal," but because we can accept the reality of the speaker, he is able to lift us above the level of realism itself. Paradoxically, the concreteness of this Lear enables us to respond more fervently than we could otherwise do to the universal elements in his situation and his words. In the end the austere white figure may remind us of Oedipus at Colonus or, more abstractly, of man's capacity to endure suffering. In the end we may become aware that we have witnessed a vast morality play. But, not discounting either the carefully arranged stage pictures on the one hand or our possible scholarly knowledge on the other (knowledge pushed to the back of our minds if we are to experience the play and not simply watch and judge), such symbolic value as may emerge for us has been dependent primarily on the actors and what they have made of their story. "Meaning" comes last.

Sir Philip Sidney long ago reminded us that poetry is superior to philosophy in its power over human beings, even though the same truth may be the end of each. The old men who are lured away from their chimney corner and the children who gladly suspend their play do so for the tale, not for the truth in the tale; yet the truth (Sidney thought) operates in a subtly efficacious manner on the eager listeners. When the tale becomes drama—an action rather than a narration—the interests and emotions stirred by it have visible beings around which to cluster. It is the business of criticism, no doubt, to point out the "truth" in Shakespeare's plays, but it is also its business to show what the characters —the vehicles of that truth—are like. If a written character analysis can give us, even in a small way, an intelligible foundation for such an experience of the role as a great actor can give in performance, then it seems to me worthy to take its place alongside the most learned exposition of Renaissance thought, the most sensitive appreciation of poetic qualities, the most profound discussion of symbolic significance.

APPENDIX · *Biographical Sketches of the Actor-Critics*

ANDERSON, MARY. (1859-1940). American. Debut 1875. Successful in both America and England. Retired early, married Antonio de Navarro and settled in England. Shakespearean roles: Juliet, Lady Macbeth, Desdemona, Hermione and Perdita (doubled).

ANONYMOUS ACTRESS. (fl. early 20th century). Author of a book entitled *The True Ophelia: and Other Studies of Shakespeare's Women. By an Actress* (New York and Toronto, 1914). The University of North Carolina at Chapel Hill has a copy of this book with Samuel Tannenbaum's signature in it and, in his hand, a note: "by Miss Jess Dorynne." I have seen no attribution of authorship anywhere else, and I have been unable to find out anything about Miss Dorynne's career.

ARCHER, FRANK. Real name: Arnold. (1845-1917). English. Debut 1868. Acted at Manchester, Edinburgh, etc., also several London theatres. Shakespearean roles: Polixines and a variety of others in early days; later Ghost and Claudius (doubled), Hamlet.

ASCHE, OSCAR. Real name: John Stanger Heiss. (1871-1936). Australian-born; debut in London, 1893. Acted with Benson, also Beerbohm Tree. Theatre manager. Produced Shakespeare plays at His Majesty's with his wife Lily Brayton. Shakespearean roles: Pistol, Shylock, Claudius, Bottom, Othello, Jaques, Sly.

ASHWELL, LENA. Real name: Pocock. (1872-1957). Became Lady Simson. English. Debut 1891. Best known in non-Shakespearean roles like Leah Kleschna in the play of that name. Memorable for her service in entertaining the troops in World War I, for which she received the O.B.E. Theatre manager. Shakespearean roles: Prince of Wales in *Richard III,* Portia in *Julius Caesar,* Emilia, Rosalind.

ASTON, ANTHONY, known as Tony. (fl. first half of the 18th century). An Irishman of mercurial disposition and shifting interests, he participated in many different activities. Acted at Drury Lane for awhile; went to America (he is credited with being the first professional actor to appear here); toured the English provinces with an entertainment called a "Medley."

BANCROFT, SIR SQUIRE. (1841-1926). English. Debut 1861. Married Marie Wilton, managed Prince of Wales's Theatre with her, featuring drawing-room comedy; elaborate production of *The Merchant of Venice* (1875) unsuccessful except for Ellen Terry's Portia. Knighted 1897.

BANDMANN, DANIEL. (1840-1905). German-American. Debut with amateur group, New York, 1860. Acted in German drama at the Stadt Theatre. In English-speaking drama acted Shylock 1867. Tour of Australia, New Zealand and the orient, acting mainly in Shakespeare: *Hamlet, The Merchant of Venice, Macbeth, Richard III, Romeo and Juliet.*

BARNES, J. H. (1850-1925). English. Debut 1871. Leading man with Adelaide Neilson on U.S. visit, 1874. Another American visit 1881, after which he acted frequently in the U.S. as well as England. Acted in a variety of non-Shakespearean farces, melodramas, etc. Shakespearean roles: Romeo, Macbeth, Benedick, Leontes, Polonius.

BARRETT, LAWRENCE. Real name: Brannigan. (1838-1891). American. Debut 1853. Joint manager in San Francisco with John McCullough. Long association with Edwin Booth. Shakespearean roles: 1) with Booth: Cassius, Bassanio, Edgar, Laertes, Macduff, Othello and Iago (alternating); 2) on starring tours: Hamlet, Lear, Macbeth, Shylock, Richard III, Wolsey, Benedick.

BARRETT, WILSON. (1847-1904). English. London debut 1879 (experience in the provinces before that). Theatre manager. Famous for plays like *The Silver King* and his own religious melodrama *The Sign of the Cross.* Successful in London and on American tours. Frequently attempted Shakespearean roles but with less success. Most admired: Mercutio. His Hamlet considered by many contemporaries too melodramatic.

BARRYMORE, ETHEL. (1879-1959). American. New York debut 1894. Most successful in non-Shakespearean roles like Camille, Nora in *A Doll's House,* and heroines of modern plays. Acted in films as well. Shakespearean roles: Ophelia, Juliet, Portia.

BARRYMORE, JOHN. (1882-1942). American. Brother of Ethel. Debut 1903. Successful in light comedy, also serious roles like Peter Ibbetson in the play of that name. Film as well as stage career. Shakespearean roles: Richard III; Hamlet, the latter being successful in London as well as the U.S.

BELASCO, DAVID. (1854-1931). American. Extensive youthful experience as actor, stage manager, adapter and writer of plays in San Francisco; similar work later in New York. Writer of popular dramas like *The Girl of the Golden West.* Successful manager and producer of elaborate productions: e.g. *The Merchant of Venice* (New York, 1922-23).

BENSON, LADY CONSTANCE, *née* Gertrude Constance Samwell. Stage name during early career: Constance Featherstonhaugh. (1860-1946). English. Debut 1883. Married Frank Benson, in whose company she acted. Shakespearean roles: Lady Macbeth, Ophelia, and other leading parts.

BENSON, SIR FRANK ROBERT. (1858-1939). English. Professional debut 1882. Took over an acting company that became a prime training ground for Shakespearean actors. Produced all of Shakespeare's plays except *Titus Andronicus* and *Troilus and Cressida*. Shake-spearean roles: Richard III, Richard II, Petruchio, Caliban, Hamlet, Coriolanus, King Lear. Knighted 1916.

BERNARD, JOHN. (1756-1828). Anglo-American. Acted in English provinces and in Ireland; London career began 1787. Came to America 1797 and remained; one of the earliest theatrical managers in this country. Particularly known as a comedian. Shakespearean roles: Shylock, the Bastard Faulconbridge, Hotspur.

BETTERTON, THOMAS. (?1635-1710). English. Began acting when the theatres were reopened at the Restoration, and had a long career in acting and management: a member of the Duke's Company, he became its head at Davenant's death (1671) and retained the management until the merger with the King's Company (1682); in 1695 he broke from the Theatre Royal and again formed his own company, first at Lincoln's Inn Fields and later at the new theatre in the Haymarket. Was the greatest actor of his time, especially in Shakespeare's leading tragic heroes (Hamlet was one of his finest roles) but also in comic parts like Sir Toby Belch. He remains a major figure in English theatrical history. His wife, *née* Mary Saunderson, was an outstanding Lady Macbeth.

BOOTH, EDWIN. (1833-1893). American. Probably the greatest Shake-spearean actor produced by the U.S. Son of Junius Brutus Booth. Debut 1849. Experience on tours, in New York, and abroad (England, Germany). Manager of theatres, including the Winter Garden and the Booth. Long association with Lawrence Barrett; acted with Helena Modjeska, Adelaide Ristori, Tommaso Salvini. Shake-spearean roles: Romeo, Hamlet, Othello, Iago, King Lear, Macbeth, Shylock, Richard III, Brutus.

BOOTH, JUNIUS BRUTUS. (1796-1852). Anglo-American. Debut 1817 in London. Challenged comparison with Edmund Kean, but Kean soon outshone him. Moved to America in 1821, where he became one of the foremost actors of his day. Intemperate habits and eccentric temperament. Shakespearean roles: Richard III, Shylock, Iago were outstanding; also acted King Lear and other tragic heroes.

BOUCICAULT, DION. Full name: Dionysius Lardner Boucicault. (1822-1890). Irish-American. Debut 1852, London, in his own melodrama *The Vampire*. Prolific writer of popular plays like *The Coleen Bawn* and *The Octoroon*. Successful actor, especially in Irish character parts.

BURTON, RICHARD. (1925-   ). Born in South Wales. Debut 1943. Acted for O.U.D.S., Old Vic, etc. Most recent stage performance of Shakespeare: in Sir John Gielgud's production of *Hamlet* (Canada and New York, 1964). Career in films. Recently completed film of

The Taming of the Shrew with his second wife Elizabeth Taylor. Most successful Shakespearean performance: Hamlet in 1953. Others: Sir Toby Belch, Coriolanus, the Bastard Faulconbridge, Angelo, Caliban.

BYRON, ARTHUR. (1872-1943). American. Debut 1890 in his father's acting company. Had a stage career of fifty-four years, in which he acted more than 300 characters on stage and screen. Not generally associated with Shakespeare, but acted Jaques and Polonius (the latter in Guthrie McClintic's production with Gielgud as Hamlet, New York, 1937).

CALHOUN, ELEANOR. Became Princess Lazarovich-Hrebelianovich. (1865-1957). American-born, but went to England in her girlhood. Trained in Paris with Coquelin; acted in London and at Stratford-on-Avon. Married a Serbian of royal family and left the stage. Shakespearean roles: Lady Macbeth, Cleopatra, Rosalind.

CALVERT, LOUIS. (1859-1923). English. Son of Mr. and Mrs. Charles Calvert, Theatre Royal, Manchester. Debut 1879. Toured abroad and in English stock company, later was with outstanding London managements such as Terry-Nielson and Vedrenne-Barker. Formed and managed his own companies. Versatile actor: Shakespeare, Shaw, modern comedy, etc. Shakespearean roles: Mercutio, Casca, Falstaff, Hamlet, Caliban.

CAMPBELL, DOUGLAS. (1922-   ). British, born in Glasgow. Debut 1941. Toured in England and Scotland, acted at the Old Vic. Has been associated with the Shakespeare Festival, Stratford, Ontario, since its first season (1953). Organized the Canadian Players 1954. Shakespearean roles: Parolles, Pompey Bum, Casca, Falstaff, Pistol, Sir Toby Belch, Claudius, Touchstone, Othello, Menenius, Macbeth.

CAMPBELL, MRS. PATRICK, *née* Beatrice Stella Tanner. (1865-1940). English. Professional debut 1888. Acted with Ben Greet and at various London theatres. Most outstanding in plays of Pinero, Shaw, Ibsen. Shakespearean roles: Rosalind, Viola, Helena, Juliet, Ophelia, Lady Macbeth.

CARNOVSKY, MORRIS. (1898-   ). American. First New York appearance 1922 (previously acted in Boston). Has worked with the Group Theatre and the Actor's Laboratory of California. Film as well as stage career. Acted Shylock at the American Festival Theatre, Stratford, Connecticut, 1957, and King Lear, also at Stratford, 1963, both very successful.

CASSON, SIR LEWIS. (1875-1969). English. Professional debut 1903. Acted with William Poel, later with Irving, Asche, Granville-Barker. Toured with his wife, Dame Sybil Thorndike. Shakespearean roles:

Macbeth, Coriolanus, Shylock, Petruchio, Benedick, and others. Has also directed many productions of Shakespeare. Knighted 1945.

CIBBER, COLLEY. (1671-1757). English. Debut 1690, member of Betterton's company at Drury Lane. Later was one of a triumvirate who managed this theatre. Excellent in comic parts but not in tragedy, which, however, he frequently attempted. Unequalled in Shallow (*II Henry IV*); also acted Iago, Richard III, Gloucester (in *Lear*), Wolsey, Pandulph (in his own version of *King John*). Famous for his long-lived adaptation of *Richard III*. Also wrote original comedies.

CIBBER, THEOPHILUS. (1703-1758). English. Son of Colley Cibber. Debut in 1721. Acted at several London theatres; was actor-manager of Drury Lane for some time. His second wife was the great singer and actress, Susannah Arne (the Mrs. Cibber who often acted with Garrick). Highly discreditable personal life, particularly his part in the infamous Sloper affair. Most famous Shakespearean role: Pistol. Others: Casca, Cassio, Glendower, Jaques, Osric, Parolles, Roderigo, Slender; occasionally essayed such parts as Macduff, Othello, Iago, Richard III.

COLEMAN, JOHN. (1832-1904). English. Began acting with Mrs. William Macready (mother of W. C. Macready), and had a very long career. Acted in the provinces (including Scottish towns) and in London. Managed Drury Lane. One of his Shakespearean roles: Richard III.

COLLIER, CONSTANCE. (1878-1955). English. Juvenile actress; later acted with Beerbohm Tree. First American visit 1908; after this acted with success in both London and the U.S. Outstanding in non-Shakespearean parts like Nancy in *Oliver Twist* and the Duchess of Towers in *Peter Ibbetson*. Shakespearean roles: Cleopatra, Juliet, Gertrude (with Barrymore, London, 1925).

CONDELL, HENRY. (?-1627). English. Actor and coeditor, or compiler, of the First Folio of Shakespeare's plays (1623). Shakespeare's fellow actor in the Lord Chamberlain's (later the King's) Men.

COOPER, THOMAS APTHORPE. (1776-1849). Anglo-American. Debut at Edinburgh, 1792; later at London. Came to the U.S. 1796, acted at the Chestnut St. Theatre, Philadelphia, and spent the rest of his life in America except for two visits to London. Became joint manager of the Park Theatre, New York. Shakespearean roles: Macbeth, Othello, Hamlet, Hotspur, Petruchio.

CRAIG, EDWARD GORDON. (1872-1966). English. Son of Ellen Terry. First adult appearance 1889. Acted minor roles at the Lyceum under Irving, major roles on tours. Acting confined to his earlier career. Became known chiefly for his innovations in stage design. Founded a school for the Art of the Theatre in Florence, Italy; was influential through his writings and through his own designs for stage productions.

CUSHMAN, CHARLOTTE SAUNDERS. (1816-1876). American. Attempted a career in opera (debut 1835), but when her singing voice failed turned to drama, acting Lady Macbeth in New Orleans the same year. Managed the Walnut St. Theatre, Philadelphia; toured the U.S. as a star and also as Macready's leading lady. Acted in England with success. Appeared with leading American actors: Forrest, Booth, etc. Shakespearean roles: Lady Macbeth, Queen Katharine, Rosalind; also some masculine roles: Romeo, Hamlet, Wolsey.

DAVENPORT, E. L. (EDWARD LOOMIS) (1815-1877). American. Debut 1837. Toured for several years, acted in Shakespearean and other revivals with Mrs. John Drew (New York, 1843), visited England in 1848 and remained there for some time. Engaged in management in the U.S., also toured as a star with his own company. Shakespearean roles: Hamlet, Othello, Richard III, and others.

DAVIES, THOMAS. (*c.* 1712-1785). British, born in Scotland. Debut at the Haymarket, London, 1736. Left the stage temporarily and tried bookselling but returned to acting. Performed as a strolling player, then was engaged (1752) at Drury Lane, where he and his wife performed minor parts with occasional chances at more important roles. Left the stage for bookselling again in 1762 (it was at his shop that Boswell met Johnson) but became bankrupt. Shakespearean roles: Adam (in *As You Like It*), Antonio (in *Merchant of Venice*), Bassanio, Buckingham (in *Richard III*), Cymbeline, Angelo, Ford, Gloucester (in *Lear*), Henry IV (in *I Henry IV*), Claudius.

DE CAMP, MARIE THÉRÈSE. (1773-1838). English. Wife of Charles Kemble and mother of Fanny Kemble. She was a leading dancer at the Royal Surrey, later an actress (her debut at Drury Lane was in 1787). She was known for non-Shakespearean roles, such as Lady Elizabeth Freelove in *The Day after the Wedding,* which she wrote herself.

DIBDIN, CHARLES. (1745-1814). English. Singer, composer, and actor (comedian); was at Covent Garden for awhile, and at Drury Lane for some years until a quarrel with Garrick ended the connection. Engaged in theatre management at minor theatres, gave monodramatic entertainments, became famous for his many sea songs. Also composed dramatic pieces. Garrick used his music for the Shakespeare Jubilee in 1769. His only Shakespearean role: Silence in *II Henry IV.*

DYER, ROBERT. (fl. 1822-1833). English. Professional debut 1822 (amateur acting before that). Traveled with a provincial company. Managed the theatre at Tavistock and was connected with several other groups. No London experience. Shakespearean roles: He mentions acting Othello, and no doubt he played a number of others.

ELTON, EDWARD WILLIAM. Real name: Elt. (1794-1843). English. Educated for the law but became a strolling actor; London debut 1823. After further experience in the provinces became a popular favorite at minor London theatres. Was in Macready's company at Covent Garden 1837-39 and at Drury Lane 1841-43 acting secondary roles. Shakespearean roles: Richard III, Othello, Romeo at the Strand and the Surrey; Brabantio, etc. with Macready.

EVANS, MAURICE. (1901-   ). Anglo-American. Professional debut 1926. Joined the Old Vic 1934; came to the U.S., acted Romeo with Katherine Cornell (1935), Richard II in Margaret Webster's production (1937), Hamlet in an uncut version (also directed by Miss Webster, 1938), Malvolio with Helen Hayes (1940-41). Acted Macbeth with Judith Anderson as Lady Macbeth, 1941. *See* Ch. 1 for account of his "G.I. *Hamlet*." Shakespeare productions for television.

FAUCIT, HELEN. Full name: Helena Saville Faucit. Became Lady Martin. (1817-1898). English. London debut 1836. Acted with Macready during his managements of Covent Garden and Drury Lane. Later went on tours of the provincial theatres; very successful in Dublin, Manchester, Edinburgh, etc. Particularly effective in poetic drama. Shakespearean roles: Juliet, Desdemona, Ophelia, Portia, Queen Katharine, Lady Macbeth, Imogen, Beatrice, Rosalind, Constance, Hermione, Miranda.

FIELD, KATE. Full name: Mary Katherine Keemle Field. (1838-1896). American. Studied art, music, drama. Wrote for magazines. Stage debut 1874. Appeared on the stage at intervals for several years, both in the U.S. and London (used the name Mary Keemle sometimes). Acted as foreign correspondent for several American newspapers, engaged in various reform movements. No Shakespearean roles.

FOOTE, SAMUEL. (1720-1777). English. Stage debut under Macklin's sponsorship (Haymarket, 1744) in Othello. Used his talent of mimicry with satirical wit in such stage entertainments as his *Diversions of a Morning* and other pieces of his own composition. Played in London, Scotland, Ireland. Was patentee of the Haymarket.

FORBES-ROBERTSON, SIR JOHNSTON. (1853-1937). English. Debut 1874. Acted with Mary Anderson, the Bancrofts, Irving. Toured the U.S. in 1885. Managed the Lyceum with Mrs. Patrick Campbell, beginning 1895. Shakespearean roles: Romeo, Hamlet, Macbeth, Othello, Shylock; his Hamlet won particular acclaim. Knighted 1913.

FOSS, GEORGE R. (1860-1938). English. Acted at the Princess's Theatre,

London, during the 1880's under Wilson Barrett's management, playing "small parts in long runs." Acted Laertes to Nutcombe Gould's Hamlet (the Olympic, 1897). Directed productions for the O.U.D.S. and, in the last year of World War I, for the Old Vic, where, with ten actors and three stagehands, he produced fifteen of Shakespeare's plays.

GARRICK, DAVID. (1717-1779). English. Debut 1741; his Richard III won him success, instant and tremendous. Became the greatest actor of his day, excellent in both tragedy and comedy. Began acting at Drury Lane 1742; in 1747 became co-manager of this theatre, with the responsibility of producing the plays; remained here until his retirement in 1776. Among his Shakespearean roles: Benedick, Hamlet, Hotspur, Iago, Othello, King John, King Lear, Macbeth, Romeo, Antony, the Bastard Faulconbridge, Leontes, Mercutio, Posthumus.

GENTLEMAN, FRANCIS. (1728-1784). British, son of an Irish army officer. Was in the army himself for awhile. Began his theatrical career under Thomas Sheridan at the Smock Alley Theatre, Dublin. Acted in Scotland, Ireland, the English provinces. Was a minor writer of some versatility. Shakespearean roles in London: Antonio in *The Merchant of Venice*, Gloucester in *King Lear*, Hubert in *King John*, Richard III. He undertook Othello at Edinburgh, and he probably acted other major roles in provincial theatres.

GIELGUD, SIR JOHN. (1904-   ). English. Grandson to Kate Terry (Ellen Terry's sister). Professional debut 1922. One of the finest actors of our time, in comedy of manners as well as in tragedy. Began at the Old Vic in 1929; has played numerous roles in England, Canada, and the U.S. Shakespearean: Romeo, Richard II, Macbeth, Hamlet, Hotspur, Antony, Malvolio, Benedick, King Lear, Othello, Shylock, Angelo, Leontes, Cassius. Knighted 1953.

GRANVILLE-BARKER, HARLEY. (1877-1946). English. London debut 1891. Continued acting until 1910, but beginning in 1904 combined acting with directing. Took Shakespearean roles in the companies of Ben Greet and William Poel. Was joint manager (with J. E. Vedrenne) of the Court Theatre, where he produced plays by modern dramatists like Shaw, Ibsen, and himself. In 1912 began a series of Shakespearean productions using a platform stage, simple, rather stylized decor, continuous acting, rapid enunciation: *The Winter's Tale, Twelfth Night, A Midsummer Night's Dream*; influential on the later staging of Shakespeare's plays. Later career mainly literary.

GRIBBLE, DOROTHY ROSE. (contemporary). English. One of the founders of a company called Plantagenet Players, which toured the schools in the eastern and western counties of England, 1954, with a production of *Macbeth*. Acted Lady Macbeth when the play was presented in London.

GRIFFITH, ELIZABETH (MRS.), *née* Griffith. Used the stage name "Miss Kennedy." (1727-1793). English. Second wife of the actor Richard Griffith. Acted at Covent Garden. Only Shakespearean role: Ophelia (1754). Wrote sentimental fiction and ephemeral dramas (e.g. *The Platonic Wife*).

GUINNESS, SIR ALEC. (1914-   ). English. Debut 1934. Joined the Old Vic 1936-37. Has also acted at Stratford-on-Avon and Stratford, Ontario, as well as various London theatres. Successful career in films. Shakespearean roles: Hamlet, Richard II, Richard III, Menenius, Macbeth. Has also acted a number of secondary roles like Sir Andrew Aguecheek and the Fool in *King Lear*. Knighted 1959.

GUTHRIE, SIR TYRONE. (1900-   ). British. Professional debut 1924. In 1926 began directing the Scottish National Players, and since then has been known as a director rather than an actor. Directed at the Old Vic 1933-34 and 1936; administrator of Old Vic 1939-45. Made significant contributions to the success of the Shakespeare Festival at Stratford, Ontario: gave advice for the design of the theatre, directed the early productions (beginning in the summer of 1953). In 1963 founded the Tyrone Guthrie Theatre in Minneapolis, where he has directed Shakespearean and other plays. Knighted 1961.

HACKETT, JAMES HENRY. (1800-1871). American. Debut 1826. First real success: one of the Dromios in *Comedy of Errors*; longest remembered as Falstaff, which he first acted in 1828 and which he continued to act successfully in both the U.S. and London. Also played in tragedy (Hamlet, King Lear) but never with great success. Managed at various times several New York theatres.

HARDWICKE, SIR CEDRIC WEBSTER. (1893-1964). English. Debut 1912. Acted with the Bensons, at the Old Vic, and with the Birmingham Repertory Company. Began directing at the Lyric Theatre, 1928. Lived in Hollywood, 1938-44, making films. Among his best Shakespearean roles: First Gravedigger and Sir Toby Belch; also acted Iago. Knighted 1934.

HEMINGE, JOHN. (c. 1556-1630). English. Acted with the Queen's Men and Strange's Men; was a charter member of the Lord Chamberlain's (later the King's) Men, Shakespeare's company. Principal importance: his joint editorship (with Henry Condell) of the First Folio of Shakespeare's plays.

HENDERSON, JOHN. (1747-1785). English. Debut at Bath 1772. Went to London 1777; acted at the Haymarket, later at Drury Lane and Covent Garden. Won success in a variety of Shakespearean roles:

Falstaff, Benedick, Iago, Richard III, King John, King Lear, Macbeth, Hamlet, Leontes, Jaques, Wolsey.

HICKS, SIR EDWARD SEYMOUR. (1871-1949). English. Debut 1887. Acted with the Kendals, both in England and America. Performed in music halls as well as on the legitimate stage. Entertained the troops during both World Wars. Also wrote plays: e.g. *Sleeping Partners*. Knighted 1935.

HILL, JOHN. (1716?-1775). English. Apothecary and botanist who turned actor for a brief period in 1744 under Macklin's sponsorship (at the Haymarket). Shakespearean roles: Lodovico and Friar Laurence. At the end of the season returned to the apothecary business; also engaged in hack-writing and the concoction of patent medicines. Engaged in feuds with several prominent contemporaries, including Garrick, but his book, *The Actor,* includes passages praising the great actor.

HOLCROFT, THOMAS. (1745-1809). English. Debut 1770. Was one of a company of actors that Macklin took to Dublin. Later became a strolling player, acting old men and principal low comedy parts. Acted small roles at Drury Lane 1777-79. Then devoted full time to writing: poems, novels, theatrical pieces; e.g. *The Road to Ruin.* Arrested for high treason in 1794 because of his liberal activities but was honorably acquitted. Shakespearean roles: Polonius was one of his best parts at provincial theatres; undertook Hamlet but without much success. In London acted Gadshill, Malvolio, Pistol (in *Merry Wives*).

INCHBALD, ELIZABETH (MRS.), *née* Simpson. (1753-1821). English. Debut 1772. Acted in the provinces with her husband, Joseph Inchbald, until his death. After this acted at Covent Garden, London (1780-1789). Wrote dramatic adaptations, also original comedies and farces: e.g. *I'll Tell You What*; still remembered for her romantic novels: e.g. *A Simple Story*. Shakespearean roles: Mariana, Gertrude, Nerissa, Mistress Page, Lady Percy, Celia, Hero; in the provinces she acted Cordelia and other leading roles.

IRVING, SIR HENRY. Real name: John Henry Brodribb. (1838-1905). English. Professional debut 1856. Acted at provincial theatres, then in London. First great success in the psychological melodrama *The Bells* (Lyceum, 1871); other triumphs included *Hamlet* (1874-75) with a 200-night run. Took over the Lyceum in 1878, engaged Ellen Terry as leading lady, and began a brilliant period as actor-manager. Staged a number of Shakespearean revivals; made eight American tours. Particularly successful in character parts, especially villains like Iago and Richard III; excellent as a sympathetic Shylock (though his private convictions were against this interpretation) and popular as an introverted Hamlet; controversial in Macbeth; comparatively unsuccessful in Othello and Lear. Knighted 1895 (the first actor to be so honored).

IRVING, H. B. (HENRY BRODRIBB). (1870-1919). English. Son of Sir Henry Irving. Left the profession of law for the stage but retained a lifelong interest in criminology. Professional debut 1891. Joined Ben Greet's company 1894. Gained success in London in several plays by modern writers: *The Admirable Crichton, Dr. Jekyll and Mr. Hyde,* etc. Managed the Savoy Theatre, beginning 1913, where he revived a number of his father's old plays. His Hamlet was of particular interest.

JEFFERSON, JOSEPH. (1829-1905). American. Began acting at the age of three; first outstanding success, 1858. His great roles: Bob Acres in *The Rivals* and Rip Van Winkle in a play based on Washington Irving's story. Performed the First Gravedigger in an all-star production of *Hamlet* with Edwin Booth as Hamlet.

KEAN, CHARLES. (1811-1868). English. Son of Edmund Kean. Debut 1827. Acted in Glasgow, Edinburgh, and elsewhere in the provinces as well as at various London theatres; also made visits abroad, including America. With his wife (the former Ellen Tree), produced at the Princess's Theatre a series of elaborate, archaeologically "correct" productions of Shakespeare's plays. Was a conscientious actor but not an inspired one like his father. Acted King John, Macbeth, Richard III, King Lear, Shylock, Henry V, and other Shakespearean roles; Hamlet was one of his favorite parts.

KEAN, EDMUND. (1787-1833). English. After a difficult youth and many hardships as a provincial actor, made his London debut in 1814 and was phenomenally successful in the role of Shylock. Acted a succession of great Shakespearean parts at Drury Lane, his brilliant, fiery acting contrasting with the deliberate, classical style of John Philip Kemble. Made two visits to America (1820-21 and 1825-26). Some of his Shakespearean roles: Richard III, Othello, Iago, Macbeth, Hamlet, King Lear.

KELLY, FANNY. Full name: Frances Maria Kelly. (1790-1882). English. Began acting as a child; in 1800 won high praise for portrayals of Arthur in *King John* and the Duke of York in *Richard III.* Her adult career as actress and singer was mainly connected with Drury Lane, with occasional appearances elsewhere; acted Ophelia to Edmund Kean's Hamlet.

KEMBLE, CHARLES. (1775-1854). English. Younger brother of John Philip Kemble and Sarah Kemble Siddons. Debut 1792. Became an excellent portrayer of roles in comedy of manners, Mercutio and Benedick being his best Shakespearean parts; also good in serious characters of second rank like Laertes and Macduff. Was joint proprietor of Covent Garden for awhile and had many financial difficulties in this connection. Later in life gave Shakespearean readings and held the post of Examiner of Plays.

KEMBLE, FANNY. Full name: Frances Anne Kemble. (1809-1893). English. Daughter of Charles Kemble. Debut as Juliet, 1829, to help her father recoup managerial losses at Covent Garden; very successful. Toured the U.S. with her father, 1832. Married an American plantation owner, Pierce Butler, but later left him because of her antislavery views. Returned to the English stage, acted with Macready. Later won renewed popularity with Shakespearean readings. Shakespearean roles: Portia, Constance, Desdemona, Lady Macbeth, Ophelia; especially identified with Juliet.

KEMBLE, JOHN PHILIP. (1757-1823). English. Son of the provincial actor-manager Roger Kemble. Educated at Douai with a view toward the priesthood, but had no vocation. Acted in the provinces; made his London debut as Hamlet at Drury Lane, 1783. Acted many parts with success, using a solemn, stately style which served him best in Coriolanus. Other Shakespearean parts: Richard III, Wolsey, Brutus, King John, Othello, King Lear, Macbeth. Was manager of Drury Lane, then of Covent Garden, and produced his own version of a number of Shakespearean plays.

KENDAL, MADGE (MRS.), *née* Margaret Robertson. (1848-1935). English. Daughter of actors; sister of T. W. Robertson, who wrote *Caste, School,* etc. Debut as Ophelia at the Haymarket, 1865. Acted in the provinces and at several London theatres; with her husband, W. H. Kendal, entered partnership with John Hare in the management of St. James's Theatre (1877-1888). Toured the U.S. and Canada. Most successful in modern plays.

KNOWLES, JAMES SHERIDAN. (1784-1862). Irish- born, related to Thomas Sheridan. Served in the militia, studied medicine, finally adopted the stage. Acted in the provinces; supplemented his income by teaching. Acted in London at Covent Garden and at the Coburg Theatre; paid a successful visit to the U.S. A capable actor but not an outstanding one, he is better remembered as a dramatist, *Virginius* and *The Hunchback* being examples of his plays. Macbeth was among the Shakespearean roles he attempted. Became a Baptist preacher in the latter part of his life.

LE GALLIENNE, EVA. (1899-   ). Anglo-American. Daughter of the writer Richard Le Gallienne. Debut 1915. Came to America the following year and has remained. Founded, with Margaret Webster and Cheryl Crawford, the Civic Repertory Theatre (New York, 1926); contributed to the work of this group with notable productions of Ibsen's plays; also appeared in Shakespearean productions as Viola and Juliet. Later Shakespearean roles: Hamlet (1937), Queen Katharine (1946).

MCCARTHY, LILLAH. (1875-1960). English. Became Lady Keeble by her second marriage. Played Lady Macbeth and Romeo with William Poel's company; acted Juliet on a tour with Ben Greet; acted with Wilson Barrett's company, touring England, America, and the Antipodes in *Hamlet, Othello,* and non-Shakespearean plays. Acted in Shaw's plays at the Court Theatre with her first husband, Harley Granville-Barker; was associated with him in his experimental productions of Shakespeare, playing Hermione, Viola, and Helena. Also acted in several English versions of Greek tragedy.

MACKLIN, CHARLES. Real name: McLoughlin. (c. 1700-1797). Irish-born. Long career on the stage in England, Scotland, and Ireland. His revolutionary portrayal of Shylock (as an implacable villain rather than a low-comedy character) was given at Drury Lane, 1741. Among his other Shakespearean roles: Iago, Fluellen, Polonius, Mercutio, Touchstone, Macbeth. His special forte: character parts. Wrote successful theatre pieces: e.g. *The Man of the World.* Important for innovations in acting and costuming.

MACREADY, WILLIAM CHARLES. (1793-1873). English. Son of a provincial actor-manager. Attended Rugby and planned to study law, but was forced to leave school because of his father's financial troubles. Acted Romeo at Birmingham (1810), then toured the provinces; was engaged at Covent Garden in 1816, and after this had a long career at the major London theatres and on starring tours. Managed Covent Garden 1837-39 and Drury Lane 1941-43. Successful American visit in 1826; his visit in 1849 was marred by the Astor Place riots in New York, stemming from his feud with Edwin Forrest. Among his Shakespearean roles: Othello, King Lear, Macbeth, Richard III, Hamlet, Richard II, Coriolanus, Jaques, Benedick, King John.

MARLOWE, JULIA. Real name: Sarah Frances Frost. (1866-1950). American. English-born but came to the U.S. in childhood; juvenile actress using the name Fanny Brough. Adult debut 1887. She and her second husband, E. H. Sothern (whom she married in 1911) became famous for their productions of Shakespeare. Her roles: Juliet, Beatrice, Ophelia, Katherine, Portia, Viola, Lady Macbeth, Cleopatra.

MARTIN-HARVEY, SIR JOHN. (1863-1944). English. Debut 1881. Acted in Irving's company at the Lyceum for fourteen years; took over the Lyceum in 1899. Shakespearean productions included a very successful *Hamlet* (with himself as Hamlet), *The Taming of the*

Shrew, Richard III, Henry V. Was very popular as Sidney Carton in *The Only Way* but showed real tragic ability in the title role of *Oedipus Rex.* Knighted 1921.

MAYO, FRANK. Real name: McGuire. (1839-1896). American. Debut in San Francisco 1856; later acted in his native Boston, in New York, and in starring engagements around the country. Shakespearean roles: Ferdinand, Jaques, Iago, Hamlet, Richard III. Won his greatest success as Davy Crockett in a play of that name by Frank Hitchcock.

MOLONY, KATE (or KITTY). Full name: Katherine Brigham Molony. American. Was brought on the stage by Lawrence Barrett, a friend of her family's. Traveled with Edwin Booth during the season 1886-87 (evidently her third on the stage) in such parts as Jessica in *The Merchant of Venice.* Acted Lady Macduff in McKee Rankin's production of *Macbeth* (the Brooklyn Theatre, New York, 1887). Had non-Shakespearean roles with A. M. Palmer's company and was in the cast of *Captain Swift* with Maurice Barrymore (1888-89). Married the drama critic George P. Goodale of the Detroit *Free Press.*

MORRIS, CLARA. Real name: Morrison. (1848?-1925). American. After early experience in a stock company, acted in New York under Augustin Daly, beginning 1870. Became the foremost emotional actress of her day, excelling in such parts as Camille and the heroines of plays by Sardou and Feuillet. Acted at many theatres in the U.S. After her retirement wrote fiction and autobiography. Significant Shakespearean role: her controversial Lady Macbeth.

MUNDEN, JOSEPH SHEPHERD. (1758-1832). English. Served a difficult apprenticeship in the provinces; went to Covent Garden in 1790 and won success as Old Dornton in *The Road to Ruin.* Remained here for twenty years, then acted at Drury Lane. His forte: broad comedy. Shakespearean roles: Autolycus, Dogberry, Dromio of Syracuse, Grumio, Launcelot Gobbo, Polonius, a Witch in *Macbeth.*

MURDOCH, JAMES EDWARD. (1811-1893). American. Debut 1829 at the Chestnut St. Theatre in his native Philadelphia; acted in many theatres in the U.S. and was well received in London in 1856. One of the finest light comedians of his time; among his best Shakespearean roles: Benedick, Orlando, Mercutio, the Bastard Faulconbridge. Considered too pedantic an elocutionist to be really moving in Hamlet, Othello, and Macbeth, but frequently acted these roles. After his retirement gave readings and lectures.

MURPHY, ARTHUR. (1727-1805). Irish-born, educated at the English college, St.-Omer, France, a Jesuit school. Stage debut 1754 at Covent Garden as Othello; also played Hamlet, Richard III, and

Macbeth, replacing Spranger Barry, who had gone to Dublin for the season. Replaced Mossop at Drury Lane, 1755-56, acting Richard III and non-Shakespearean roles. Dissatisfied with his parts. Left the stage and resumed journalistic writing begun prior to his theatrical career; also wrote and adapted many plays.

NEWTON, CHANCE. Full name: Henry Chance Newton. (1854-1931). English. First worked as a carver of ivory; also practiced journalism and tried his luck on the stage. One of his most ambitious parts: Richard III. Gave up his theatrical ambitions because of throat trouble and turned seriously to journalism. Became known as a dramatic critic under the name "Carados" in the *Referee* and was the London correspondent for the *New York Dramatic Mirror,* using the name "Gawain." Also wrote many farces for the theatre.

OLIVIER, SIR LAURENCE. (1907-). English. Debut 1922. Acted in the Birmingham Repertory Company; alternated Romeo and Mercutio with Gielgud in the latter's company, 1935; joined the Old Vic in 1937, where he acted (among other roles) Hamlet, Sir Toby Belch, Hotspur, Henry V, Macbeth, Iago, Richard III, Antony, and Coriolanus. His Titus Andronicus (Stratford-on-Avon, 1955) was astonishingly effective, and his Othello (London, 1964) was one of the stage triumphs of our time. A successful film career includes his own productions of *Henry V, Hamlet,* and *Richard III.* Knighted 1947.

OXBERRY, WILLIAM. (1784-1824). English. Professional debut 1802. Acted in the provinces; failed in his first attempt at London (1807) but, after further provincial experience, succeeded in establishing himself on the London stage. Acted for some time at the Lyceum and at Drury Lane. Successful in comic parts in contemporary plays, also fine as Master Stephen in Jonson's *Every Man in His Humour* and as Slender in *The Merry Wives of Windsor.* Unsuited to such parts as Macbeth, Richard III, and Shylock, which he acted on occasion in the provinces.

PILON, FREDERICK. (1750-1788). Irish-born. Received a university education and was intended for a career in medicine but gave it up for the stage. Engaged in amateur theatricals in his native Cork; appeared professionally at the Cork Theatre Royal in 1770 as Oroonoko but without applause. Also acted in Edinburgh and with a minor strolling company. Failed in a second appearance at Cork, 1772, and soon gave up acting for dramatic writing, at which he was more successful. Went to London, where a number of his comedies and farces were produced at Covent Garden.

POEL, WILLIAM. Original spelling: Pole. (1852-1934). English. Debut 1876 with Charles Mathews' company on a provincial tour. Acted a variety of parts in several companies in the provinces. In 1879 formed a small company, "The Elizabethans," who toured giving costume recitals from plays. Produced the First Quarto *Hamlet* in 1881 on a bare platform at St. George's Hall, London. In 1894 organized the Elizabethan Stage Society, and the following year produced *Twelfth Night,* first in a series of productions using a platform stage, continuous acting, and other Elizabethan methods. Influenced Granville-Barker and others. Among his own Shakespearean roles: Angelo, Malvolio, Shylock.

REDGRAVE, SIR MICHAEL. (1908-   ). English. Taught at Cranleigh School, where he staged productions of *Hamlet, Lear,* etc. Professional debut 1934. Successful actor on stage and screen. Has played at the Old Vic, at Stratford-on-Avon, and at various other theatres in England; also in New York and a number of European cities. Has written plays, novels, discussions of dramatic subjects. Some Shakespearean roles: Hamlet, Macbeth, King Lear, Antony, Shylock, Benedick, Hotspur. Knighted 1959.

ROBINS, ELIZABETH. (1865-1952). American-born, but most of her professional life was spent in England. Debut 1885; remained with the Boston Museum stock company for some time, later toured with Booth and Barrett. London debut 1889. Much interested in Ibsen, and introduced some of his plays on the English stage. Published novels and theatrical reminiscences. Most important in non-Shakespearean roles.

ROBSON, DAME FLORA. (1902-   ). English. Debut 1921. Played in repertory with Ben Greet; acted at a number of theatres (including the Old Vic) in England and the U.S. Has also acted in films. Variety of roles (e.g. Abbie in *Desire under the Elms,* Alicia, in *Black Chiffon*) ; her special forte: parts demanding controlled nervous tension. Shakespearean roles: Lady Macbeth, Isabella, Queen Katharine, Paulina. Created D.B.E. in 1960.

SCOFIELD, PAUL. (1922-   ). English. Professional debut 1940. Acted with the Birmingham Repertory Theatre; later acted at Stratford-on-Avon; also in London, in Moscow, in the U.S. and elsewhere. Portrayed Sir Thomas More in *A Man for All Seasons* (both on stage and screen) ; has acted in plays by Shaw, Eliot, Fry, and other modern dramatists. Early Shakespearean roles: Autolycus, the Bastard Faulconbridge, Henry V, Don Armado, Sir Andrew Aguecheek, Cloten, Pericles. Greatest roles: Hamlet, King Lear (in Peter Brook's production—see Ch. 5). Received the C.B.E. in 1956.

SHERIDAN, THOMAS. (1719-1788). Irish-born. Debut at Smock Alley, Dublin; later managed the Theatre Royal in that city. Also acted in London, where his Shakespearean roles were Brutus, Coriolanus,

Hamlet, King John, Macbeth, Othello, Richard III, Romeo, Shylock. Taught elocution. Knew Boswell, Johnson, etc. Father of Richard Brinsley Sheridan, who wrote *School for Scandal.*

SIDDONS, SARAH (MRS.), *née* Kemble. (1755-1831). English. Daughter of provincial actor-manager, traveled with the company throughout her childhood. Married William Siddons, an actor. London debut (in Portia) with Garrick, 1775, unsuccessful; after further acting in the provinces made a tremendous success in London, 1882. Often acted with her brother John Philip Kemble. One of the greatest actresses of all time, especially in Lady Macbeth. Other Shakespearean roles: Juliet, Constance, Isabella, Queen Katharine, Volumnia, Desdemona, Ophelia. Less effective in Rosalind and other comic heroines.

SKILLAN, GEORGE. (1893-   ). English. Debut 1910. Acted with Oscar Asche, Matheson Lang, the Old Vic company. Has played a variety of Shakespearean roles at a number of different theatres: at Stratford-on-Avon, for example, he acted in 1926 Coriolanus, Brutus, Bolingbroke, Gratiano, Prospero; in 1927, Henry V, Enobarbus, Macduff, Orlando, Orsino, Laertes, Claudio; was also at Stratford for the 1940, 1942, 1945 seasons, during the last of which he acted Othello, Wolsey, Dogberry. Toured with ENSA as Malvolio during World War II. Frequent radio and television appearances. Edits Shakespeare's plays for French's Acting Editions.

SKINNER, OTIS. (1858-1942). American. Debut 1877. Was associated with the leading companies and performers of his day: with Booth and Barrett, Mme. Modjeska, Ada Rehan, Maude Adams, and others. Acted in at least fifteen Shakespearean plays, performing more than one role in some, but his most popular role was non-Shakespearean: Hajj in *Kismet.* Some Shakespearean parts: Hamlet, Laertes, Henry VIII, Macduff, Shylock, Bassanio, Petruchio, Claudio, Benedick, Orlando, Leonatus, Falstaff (in both *I Henry IV* and *Merry Wives*), Thersites.

SMITH, WILLIAM ("GENTLEMAN"). (1730-1819). English. Gained his nickname from his elegant figure and fine manners. Debut 1753 at Covent Garden, where he remained until 1774, when he went to Drury Lane. Created the part of Charles Surface in *The School for Scandal.* Acted major tragic roles as well as comedy of manners parts. Some Shakespearean parts: the Bastard Faulconbridge, Antony (in *Julius Caesar*), Cassius, Coriolanus, Edgar, Edmund, Hotspur, Henry V, Hamlet, Iago, Iachimo, Leontes, Macbeth, Richard III, Romeo. Retired in 1788.

SOTHERN, E. H. (EDWARD HUGH). (1859-1933). American. Son of the actor A. E. Sothern. Debut with his father in New York, 1879;

London debut 1881. Toured the U.S. with John McCullough; was the leading man in Frohman's Lyceum company. In 1904 began acting with Julia Marlowe, who later became his second wife. His roles in their Shakespearean productions: Petruchio, Shylock, Malvolio, Romeo, Hamlet, Antony, Macbeth.

SPEAIGHT, ROBERT. (1904-   ). English. Acted Falstaff in the O.U.D.S. First professional appearance, 1926. Acted Fluellen, Cassius, and Hamlet at the Old Vic, 1931-32; played Ulysses in a modern-dress *Troilus and Cressida,* Westminster Theatre, 1938. Has produced Shakespeare abroad: e.g. *Antony and Cleopatra* in Geneva, a French version of *Romeo and Juliet* in Montreal. Has lectured and worked with educational theatre in the U.S. Impressive literary career: novels, biographies, Shakespearean criticism, theatrical reviews (e.g. in the *Shakespeare Quarterly*). Shakespearean roles not listed above: Edmund, King John, Demetrius, Roderigo, Malvolio.

SULLIVAN, BARRY. (1821-1891). Irish. Began acting in the 1830's; was a member of various touring companies in Ireland, Scotland, and the English provinces. London debut, 1852, as Hamlet at the Haymarket. Acted for a season in Phelps' company at Sadler's Wells; toured the U.S. and Australia (1858); acted Benedick at the opening of the Shakespeare Memorial Theatre, Stratford-on-Avon, 1879. After this returned to the provincial theatres. Had a tremendous Shakespearean repertory: 50 to 60 parts; was particularly popular in Hamlet and Richard III.

SWAN, GEORGE. (fl. 1733-1773). English. A gentleman of good family, born in England. Became manager of the Aungier-St. Theatre, Dublin, about 1733. Acted Tamerlane with applause, and went on to other roles like Othello. Apparently left the stage when he left Dublin for England and (gossip said) an advantageous marriage. Renewed his theatrical interests while living at York, but in the capacity of adviser rather than performer.

TAYLOR, LARK. American. Acted in Shakespearean productions by E. H. Sothern and Julia Marlowe: at various times he acted Polonius, Claudius, and Guildenstern in *Hamlet;* Ross, the Bleeding Sergeant, and Seyton in *Macbeth.* Was with Barrymore in *Hamlet,* 1922-23, 1924.

TERRY, DAME ELLEN. (1847-1928). English. Came from a large family of actors. Juvenile debut as Mamillius in *The Winter's Tale,* 1856. Other early roles: Puck, Arthur, Fleance. Won recognition for her portrayal of Portia in the Bancrofts' production of *The Merchant of Venice,* 1875. Joined Irving at the Lyceum in 1878 and acted with him until 1902, playing the feminine leads in his productions and accompanying him on his American tours. Shakespearean roles: Ophelia, Juliet, Desdemona, Beatrice, Viola, Lady Macbeth, Queen Katharine, Cordelia, Imogen, Volumnia, Mistress Page (the last in Tree's production). Created D.B.E. in 1925.

TREE, SIR HERBERT BEERBOHM. Real name: Herbert Draper Beerbohm. (1853-1917). English. Half brother of Max Beerbohm. Professional debut 1878 after several years of amateur acting. Managed several London theatres; especially remembered for his lavish productions at Her (later His) Majesty's Theatre: e.g. *The Merry Wives, Hamlet, Richard II, Henry IV, Julius Caesar, King John, Twelfth Night, The Tempest, The Merchant of Venice, Henry VIII, Macbeth, Othello.* Shakespearean roles: Falstaff, Othello, Iago, Hamlet, Macbeth, Shylock, Richard II, and other major parts in his productions. Knighted 1909.

TREE, LADY MAUD, *née* Helen Maud Holt. (1863-1937). English. Married Beerbohm Tree and began a distinguished career of her own, acting leading roles in Tree's productions. Excelled in high comedy, particularly in Lady Teazle and Mrs. Malaprop, but also performed creditably in Shakespeare's comedies, histories, and tragedies. Performed Ophelia both in Poel's First Quarto *Hamlet* (1881) and in Tree's production of *Hamlet.*

VANDENHOFF, GEORGE. (1813?-1885?). Anglo-American. Son of the English tragedian John Vandenhoff. Left his law practice for nearly two decades on the stage. Debut at Covent Garden, 1839. Came to the U.S. in 1842: acted starring roles; also supported Macready, the elder Booth, Charlotte Cushman, etc. Returned to England in 1853 but settled in the U.S. about three years later, having married the American actress Mary Makeah. Left the stage for law again but gave public readings of Shakespeare.

WALLACK, LESTER. Real name: John Johnstone Wallack. (1820-1888). Anglo-American. Son of James William Wallack and nephew of Henry John Wallack. Acted in the English provinces, Dublin, etc. Came to New York, where he acted at several theatres, including Brougham's Lyceum, which was taken over by his father and renamed Wallack's. Later became manager of the new Wallack's theatre opened by his father in 1861. Acted a wide variety of roles, comic and romantic. Some Shakespearean parts: Sir Andrew Aguecheek, Benedick, Prince Hal.

WARD, GENEVIÈVE. Full name: Lucy Geneviève Teresa Ward. (1838-1922). American. As a singer used the name "Mme. Guerrabella," deriving from her unfortunate marriage to a Russian count, Constantine de Guerbel, with whom she never lived. Made her operatic debut in Paris, 1859; later in England and the U.S. When her singing voice failed, studied dramatics. Appeared at Manchester as

Lady Macbeth, 1873, and, after studying at the Comedie-Française, acted the same role in French, 1877. Dramatic debut in the U.S. 1877; acted in New York and throughout the country. Active for the next twenty years in England, America, Australia; after this in England. Joined Irving at the Lyceum 1893; acted, among other roles, Margaret in *Richard III.*

WARDE, FREDERICK BARKHAM. (1851-1935). American. Debut 1867 in a small touring company. Acted in stock companies; was at Booth's Theatre, New York, for several years; acted with McCullough, Booth, Charlotte Cushman; also toured with Mme. Janauschek and the Lingards. In 1881 began starring in his own company. In 1907 began lecturing. Shakespearean roles: Iago, Edgar, Petruchio, Richmond, Richard III, Othello, Macbeth, Shylock, King Lear.

WEBSTER, BENJAMIN NOTTINGHAM. (1797-1882). English. Descended from theatrical and musical family. Began as a dancer, then acted broad comedy; developed into an excellent character actor. Acted with Mme. Vestris at the Olympic and in 1837 became the lessee of the Haymarket, which he managed for sixteen years; in 1844 took over the Adelphi as well. Shakespearean roles: Old Gobbo, Roderigo, Oswald, Bardolph, Verges, Feste, Gratiano, Petruchio.

WEBSTER, MARGARET. (1905-   ). American. Granddaughter of the Webster noted above; daughter of Ben Webster and Dame May Whitty. Adult debut in London, 1924. Toured with Ben Greet. Was at the Old Vic, 1929-30 (acted Lady Capulet, Nerissa, Lady Macduff) and 1932 (acted Lady Macbeth). Came to New York in 1936 and has lived in the U.S. since then, with occasional visits abroad, as when she directed *The Merchant of Venice* at Stratford-on-Avon, 1956, and *Measure for Measure* at the Old Vic, 1957. Has continued to act but is best known as a director, her first triumph in this line being *Richard II* with Maurice Evans in the title role (1937). Has directed over a dozen other productions of Shakespearean plays, notably the uncut *Hamlet* (also with Evans, 1938) and Paul Robeson's *Othello,* in which she played Emilia (1943). Toured forty-four states with her Shakespeare Company, 1948-50. Has also directed Shakespearean operas and has given many lectures and recitals.

WILKINSON, TATE. (1739-1803). English. A clergyman's son, educated at Harrow; embraced the stage because of family difficulties and personal talent (the gift of mimicry). Acted for Garrick at Drury Lane in 1757 and again after a visit to Dublin with Foote; later acted at Bath and at Covent Garden. In 1766 began a thirty-year career as a successful provincial manager, taking over the York circuit with Hull and Leeds included. Some Shakespearean roles: Othello, Romeo, Hotspur, Richard III, Horatio, Hamlet, Lear, Petruchio.

WOLFIT, SIR DONALD. (1902-1968). English. First appearance 1920; London debut 1924. Much experience in repertory work: with Charles Doran, Fred Terry, the Arts League of Service, the Sheffield Repertory Company. Toured Canada with Sir Barry Jackson. Acted at the Old Vic and Stratford-on-Avon. Toured with his own Shakespeare Company in the fall of 1937 and again in 1938; opened his first London Season of Shakespeare in February, 1940. For his wartime Shakespeare at home and abroad, see Ch. 1. First appearance in the U.S. was in New York, 1947, as King Lear (perhaps his greatest role). In 1960 took a company on a Shakespeare recital tour which covered much of the world. Acted for radio and films. Was knighted in 1957. Some major Shakespearean roles: Hamlet, Othello, Lear, Macbeth, Shylock, Iago, Malvolio, Benedick, Petruchio; a variety of others, ranging from Cassius to Autolycus.

WOOD, WILLIAM BURKE. (1779-1861). American. First native-born actor to hold a high place in the American theatre. Began his career under Thomas Wignell, manager of the Chestnut St. Theatre, Philadelphia, whose company also performed in Baltimore and Washington. After Wignell's death, became co-manager, with William Warren, of the Chestnut St. Theatre. Particularly good in polished comedy, but also handled the lighter parts of tragedy well.

YATES, MARY ANNE (MRS.), *née* Graham. (1728-1787). English. Second wife of the comedian Richard Yates. Debut 1754 at Drury Lane. First Shakespearean role: Cleopatra to Garrick's Antony, 1759. After Susannah Cibber's death in 1766, was considered the chief representative of classical heroines. Acted at both major London theatres. Shakespearean roles: Lady Macbeth, Constance, Cordelia, Desdemona, Imogen, Isabella, Portia, Perdita, Gertrude, Rosalind, Viola.

INDEX